Yale Studies in English, 182

The
Parisiana Poetria
of
John of Garland

Edited with Introduction, Translation, and Notes by

Traugott Lawler

New Haven and London, Yale University Press, 1974

Publication of this book has been aided by a grant from the
Hyder Edward Rollins Fund of the English Department, Harvard
University.

Library of Congress catalog card number: 73-77156
International standard book number: 0-300-01572-0

Designed by Sally Sullivan
and set in IBM Baskerville type.
Printed in the United States of America by The
Murray Printing Company, Forge Village, Mass.

Published in Great Britain, Europe, and Africa by
Yale University Press, Ltd., London.
Distributed in Latin America by Kaiman & Polon,
Inc., New York City; in Australasia and Southeast
Asia by John Wiley & Sons Australasia Pty. Ltd.,
Sydney; in India by UBS Publishers' Distributors Pvt.,
Ltd., Delhi; in Japan by John Weatherhill, Inc., Tokyo.

For Peggy

Contents

AP. Horace, *Ars poetica.*

Baldwin. Charles Sears Baldwin, *Medieval Rhetoric and Poetic.* New York, 1928. Reprint. Gloucester, Mass., 1959.

Buc. Virgil, *Bucolica.*

CL. Classical Latin.

Cloetta. Wilhelm Cloetta, *Komödie und Tragödie im Mittelalter.* Halle, 1890.

Curtius. Ernst Robert Curtius, *European Literature and the Latin Middle Ages.* Trans. Willard R. Trask. New York, 1953.

Daniel, *TH.* H. A. Daniel, ed., *Thesaurus hymnologicus.* 5 vols. Leipzig, 1841-56.

de Bruyne. Edgar de Bruyne, *Études d'esthetique médiévale.* 3 vols. Bruges, 1946.

Denholm-Young. Noel Denholm-Young, "The Cursus in England," *Collected Papers of N. Denholm-Young.* Cardiff, 1969. Pp. 42-73.

DI. Cicero, *De inventione.*

Documentum. Geoffrey of Vinsauf, *Documentum de modo et arte dictandi et versificandi,* in Faral, pp. 263-320.

Du Cange. Charles Du Fresne Du Cange, ed., *Glossarium mediae et infimae latinitatis.* Paris, 1678. Rev. G. A. H. Henschel; Paris, 1840. Further rev. Leopold Favre; Niort, 1887.

EBV. John of Garland, *Epithalamium Beatae Virginis.*

Ep. Horace, *Epistulae.*

Faral. Edmond Faral, *Les Arts poétiques du XIIe et du XIIIe siècle.* Paris, 1924. Reprint. Paris, 1962.

Gräbener. Hans-Jürgen Gräbener, ed., *Gervais von Melkley: "Ars poetica."* Münster, 1965.

Hauréau. Barthélemy Hauréau, "Notices sur les oeuvres authentiques ou supposées de Jean de Garlande." *Notices et Extraits des Manuscrits de la Bibliothèque Nationale et Autres Bibliothèques* 27, part 2 (1879): 1-86.

Keil. Heinrich Keil, ed., *Grammatici latini.* 7 vols. Leipzig, 1855-80.

Manitius. Max Manitius, *Geschichte der lateinischen Literatur des Mittelalters.* 3 vols. Munich, 1911-31.

Met. Ovid, *Metamorphoses.*

ML. Medieval Latin.

NED. *A New English Dictionary on Historical Principles,* ed. Sir James A. H. Murray and others. 11 vols. Oxford, 1888-1933.

Paetow. Louis J. Paetow, ed. and trans., *Two Medieval Satires on the*

University of Paris: "La Bataille des VII ars" of Henri d'Andeli and the "Morale scolarium" of John of Garland. Memoirs of the University of California, vol. 4, nos. 1 and 2. Berkeley, 1927.

Papias. Papias Grammaticus, *Elementarium doctrinae rudimentum (Vocabulista).* Venice, 1496.

PL. J-P. Migne, ed., *Patrilogiae cursus completus.* Series latina. 221 vols. Paris, 1844-68.

Raby, *CLP.* F. J. E. Raby, *A History of Christian-Latin Poetry from the Beginnings to the Close of the Middle Ages.* 2d ed. Oxford, 1953.

Raby, *SLP.* F. J. E. Raby, *A History of Secular Latin Poetry in the Middle Ages.* 2 vols. 2d ed. Oxford, 1957.

RAH. Rhetorica ad Herennium.

Rashdall. Hastings Rashdall, *The Universities of Europe in the Middle Ages,* ed. F. M. Powicke and A. B. Emden. 3 vols. Oxford, 1936.

Rockinger. Ludwig Rockinger, ed., *Briefsteller und Formelbücher des eilften bis vierzehnten Jahrhunderts.* Quellen und Erörterungen zur bayerischen und deutschen Geschichte 9. 2 vols. Munich, 1863. Reprint. New York, 1961.

Servius. *Marii Servii Honorati in Virgilii carmina commentarii,* ed. G. Thilo and H. Hagen. 3 vols. Leipzig, 1902.

Walther, *Lateinische Sprichwörter.* Hans Walther, *Proverbia sententiaeque latinitatis medii aevi: lateinische Sprichwörter und Sentenzen des Mittelalters in alphabetischer Anordnung.* Carmina medii aevi posterioris latina 2. 5 vols. Göttingen, 1963-67.

Walther, *Versanfänge.* Hans Walther, *Initia carminum ac versuum medii aevi posterioris latinorum: alphabetisches Verzeichnis der Versanfänge mittellateinischer Dichtungen.* Carmina medii aevi posterioris latina 1. Göttingen, 1959.

Wilson, *Stella maris.* Evelyn Faye Wilson, ed., *The "Stella maris" of John of Garland.* Cambridge, Mass., 1946.

Introduction

1. THE AUTHOR

John of Garland was an Englishman who taught grammar and literature at the University of Paris during the first half of the thirteenth century. He was born ca. 1195, and studied at Oxford under John of London around the years 1210-13.[1] He must have gone to Paris after studying at Oxford; Paetow (p. 86) suggests that he went shortly after the Treaty of Lambeth between Louis of France and King John of England on September 11, 1217. A letter in the present text indicates that he was friendly with Simon Langton, who accompanied Louis to France after the treaty and remained at the French court until 1227 (see below, *1,* 93 ff. and note). Of course John may have made his acquaintance in England earlier.

At all events, he took up residence in Paris, and stayed there for most of the rest of his life, taking his surname from the *clos de Garlande* where he lived (Paetow, pp. 86-88; see below, *6,* 184-87). In 1229 he was chosen to be Master of Grammar at the new University of Toulouse. He stayed there for three years, returning to Paris in 1231, where he spent the remainder of his days teaching and writing, though he made at least one trip to England. He lived until at least 1258, the date of his *Exempla honestae vitae,* and was perhaps still alive in 1272, when a reference to him by Roger Bacon "distinctly gives one the impression" that he was still alive (Paetow, pp. 95-96). Though Paetow states in his foreword that "he never rose to prominence in his day," the favorable mention by Bacon, the selection of him for the chair at Toulouse, and the number of fifteenth- and early sixteenth-century printed editions of various of his works, as well as extensive manuscript remains, and the large number of spurious works to which his name became attached, all rather support Hauréau's claim that he "a joui de son temps d'un grand

---

1. Paetow, p. 83. (For bibliographical details here and elsewhere, see the preliminary table of Abbreviations and Short Titles.) Paetow introduces his edition of John's *Morale scholarium* with a complete account of his life and works, reviewing the history of early erroneous accounts and the gradual revelation of what facts are now known, and including all the relevant documentary evidence, mostly statements by John himself in his own works. I have relied heavily on Paetow's researches for my own brief outline of John's life; for further information, references, and sources, the reader is referred to that book.

crédit."[2] (See also Paetow's own testimony to John's contemporary fame on pp. 98-99.)

John of Garland was a tireless writer. Paetow discusses nine long poems, eight grammatical and rhetorical works, nine wordbooks, eight moral works, a work on medicine, four works on computus, four on music, and seventeen "miscellaneous" works which are known to be by, or have been attributed to, him. When doubtful attributions and lost works are put aside, we still have five major poems (*De triumphis ecclesiae, De mysteriis ecclesiae, Epithalamium Beatae Virginis, Stella maris,* and *Integumenta Ovidii*); five works on grammar and rhetoric (*Compendium grammaticae, Clavis compendii, Ars lectoria ecclesiae, Parisiana poetria,* and *Exempla honestae vitae*); two wordbooks (*Dictionarius, Commentarius*) and possibly six others; and a brief *Summa poenitentiae* in verse.[3]

2. THE AUTHORSHIP AND DATE OF THE *PARISIANA POETRIA*

The authorship of the *Parisiana poetria* has never been questioned. It is said to be John's in the introductory summary which precedes it in three of the five manuscripts, and in the title at the head of the text in one of the others; John's *Epithalamium Beatae Virginis* is referred to five times; the author of the letter at *1,* 93 is given as Johannes de Garlandia; the quatrain at *6,* 184-87 gives details of his life; and the work is mentioned

2. Hauréau, p. 1. For the printed editions, chiefly of his wordbooks, see *The British Museum General Catalogue of Printed Books,* s.v. Garlandia (Johannes de). Many works listed there are, however, false attributions. For lists of manuscripts, separation of genuine from spurious works, as far as has been possible, and further indications of printed editions, see Paetow's discussion of each of John's works on pp. 110-45.

3. Since Paetow's work appeared, the *Stella maris* has been edited by Evelyn Faye Wilson (Cambridge, Mass., 1946); the *Integumenta Ovidii* by Fausto Ghisalberti (Messina and Milan, 1933) and by Lester K. Born (University of Chicago thesis, 1929, which is described in *University of Chicago Abstracts of Theses,* Humanistic Series 7 [1930], pp. 429-32). Born has also studied the three grammatical works; see his "The Manuscripts of the Major Grammatical Works of John of Garland: *Compendium Grammatice, Clavis Compendii, Ars Lectoria Ecclesie,*" *Transactions and Proceedings of the American Philological Association* 69 (1938): 259-73 and "An Analysis of the Quotations and Citations in the *Compendium Grammatice* of John of Garland," *Classical, Mediaeval, and Renaissance Studies in Honor of Berthold Louis Ullman,* ed. Charles Henderson (2 vols., Rome, 1964), 2: 51-83. This extremely interesting essay provides convincing evidence of John's wide knowledge of classical and medieval authors.

in the *Ars lectoria ecclesiae* in a list by John of his own writings (cf. Paetow, p. 107).

Less certainty surrounds the date. Ludwig Rockinger, who first printed portions of the *Poetria* from the Munich manuscript, puts it in the seventh decade of the thirteenth century, purely on the basis of the letter at 7, 316, identifying its R., bishop of Paris, with Reginald III (1250-68) and G., abbot of Saint-Germain-des-Prés, with Gerhard (1255-79).[4] But Rockinger himself admits that the initial for the bishop of Paris fluctuates between M. and R., and there is even further variation when the other manuscripts are adduced. It is clear to me from the great variation of all such initial letters, for these as well as other personages in other sample letters and documents, that no certain arguments can be drawn from them. As Paetow points out (p. 127), Rockinger was too concerned to match John Bale's date of 1270 for a shadowy "Johannes Grammaticus," who was not known to Bale as John of Garland. Hauréau (p. 82) assigned the date "environ l'année 1260" from "quelques-uns des exemples"; but he does not say which ones. Paetow (p. 127) argues that the *Poetria* must postdate the *Epithalamium,* which it quotes, and which he asserts was written while John was at Toulouse. Thus he assigns it to the period between 1231, when John returned from Toulouse to Paris, and 1249, the latest possible date for the *Ars lectoria ecclesiae* with its list mentioning it; and he tentatively places it, with no further evidence, in 1234 (p. 109). But Evelyn Faye Wilson has shown that Paetow's placing the *Epithalamium* in John's Toulouse period is erroneous, the result of an emendation by Hauréau in a passage in the *De triumphis ecclesiae;* she places it in 1220-21.[5]

In 1933 Wilson published an article entitled "The *Georgica Spiritualia* of John of Garland," in which she presented important new evidence and significant argument on a number of points relating to John of Garland. She reasserts here her reasons for dating the *Epithalamium* in "1220-1223, probably as early as the first months of 1221," and she argues that the *Poetria* was written before that poem, not, as Paetow assumed on the basis of the quotations within the *Poetria,* after it.[6] She concludes

4. Rockinger, 1: 489-90.

5. "A Study of the Epithalamium in the Middle Ages: An Introduction to the *Epithalamium Beate Marie Virginis* of John of Garland" (University of California at Berkeley thesis, 1931), p. 252. Cf. Hauréau, p. 9. He substitutes *Biterris* (Beziers) for *Bituris* (Bourges).

6. The article is in *Speculum* 8 (1933): 358-77. The evidence she gives that the *Poetria* antedates the *Epithalamium* is not entirely convincing. (1) (pp. 360-361) A gloss in a Weimar manuscript of the *Epithalamium* states that John "sharpened his skill" for that poem by writing several other works in praise of the Virgin, including "carmen pastorale contra scismaticos et hereticos." Wilson (p. 361, n. 2)

(p. 371, n. 8) that "the date given in the example of the papal *privi-legium* [see Figure Seven, p. 154], the fourth year of the pontificate of Honorius III, or 1220, begins to have some significance as a possible date of composition. If 1220 is the date, then the examples in the *Poetria* which cite the *Epithalamium* might mean only that the two works were being composed simultaneously. Or they might be the result of a later revision." (Honorius took office in 1216; thus the fourth year of his reign actually began in 1219. Another letter from Honorius [7, 218 ff.] is dated "VII Kalendas Octobris, Pontificatus Nostri Anno Tertio" or October 25, 1218.)

Thus the range of time in which the work could have been composed is extended to 1218-49. Further arguments can be added to Wilson's to suggest an earlier date than Paetow's: there are two other references to Honorius (who died in 1227) (7, 156, 239) and the letter from him to Frederick II, the Holy Roman emperor (7, 156 ff.), clearly concerns the Fifth Crusade (1218-21). (Since Frederick reigned 1220-50, he is of little help.) More generally, it seems likely that the work is not very far removed in time from either the *Epithalamium* or Geoffrey of Vinsauf's *Documentum* (see Appendix Two); and the several letters (4, 321, 350) that concern the attainment of the mastership may also hint that John had only recently attained it himself.

---

identifies this with the poem "Cvm citharizat auis" in the *Poetria* (1, 407 ff.), saying "The glosses of Ms. Munich 6911, fol. 3, make clear what would otherwise never be guessed: that the poem is concerned with the struggle between the faithful and the heretics." This is an overstatement: only one gloss touches on the question; it says that *gregem* in l. 416 means "hereticos et alios malos homines." That is, when the girl Phyllis in the poem sings a song about Daphnis drawing together his flock, the real meaning is that Christ gathered into his fold heretics and other bad men. This does not make the poem concern "the struggle between the faithful and the heretics," nor does it explain how it praises the Virgin. All that can be said is that a part of it praises Christ. Yet no other pastoral poem by John has survived, and John may well have thought of this poem in these terms, given his devotion to Mary and his general inability to match his conceptions with his poetical performance. Furthermore, even if this is the poem the Weimar glossator meant, it does not follow that the whole *Poetria* preceded the *Epithalamium:* John wanted to give an example of a pastoral poem at this point, and he might well have used one he had already written separately.

(2) The second piece of evidence is the fact that in the list of John's works in the *Ars lectoria ecclesiae* the *Poetria* is mentioned second, and Wilson refers (p. 361, n. 2) to a gloss in Ms. Brit. Mus. Add. 15832, fol. 27ᵛ which claims that the order of the list is the order of their composition. This would be important evidence, but neither she nor Paetow, who mentions the same gloss on p. 109, actually quotes it. Yet there is no reason to think that either misinterpreted it, and on the whole it seems probable to me.

Though the many letters in the text make reference to various other historical persons, most of them are of little value for dating it. As I have said, the initials are wholly untrustworthy. In the companion letters at *2,* 52 and 129, for example, one person is called R. and G. in the manuscripts in one letter, M., I., C., and P. in the other; the other person is called R. in all the manuscripts in one letter, but G. in all the manuscripts in the other letter. The bishop of Paris has a total of eight different initials through the work (cf. *2,* 52, 129; *5,* 439; *7,* 263, 329, 355, 414, 435, and textual notes); the abbots of Saint-Victor and Sainte-Geneviève have also several initials, none of which corresponds with the name of any actual abbot of either place for the period involved. One person identified only by his initial, however, may be more certain. That is Simon, archdeacon of Canterbury 1228-48 (see above, p. xi and note to *1,* 93-94). In this case all the manuscripts agree on the initial S. If it is indeed Simon, we have some evidence for a later date of composition, or at least completion.

There is, furthermore, one name that is spelled out in all the manuscripts and that supports Paetow's later dating. The letter at *1,* 34 is from Mauritius, archbishop of Rouen; Mauritius held that office from July, 1231 to January, 1235 (see note to *1,* 34). Clearly then the book could not have been finished before 1231. Perhaps the best explanation is Wilson's suggestion of "later revision." She has also spoken (p. 361, n. 2) of "John of Garland's habit of taking up works already composed from time to time, expanding, rededicating, and 'publishing' them in a formal manner." One clear hint of such expansion here is the *ars rhythmica* (see note to *7,* 467). All the facts and probabilities taken together suggest that the work was originally composed about 1220, and revised, at least to the extent of the inclusion of the letter from Archbishop Mauritius, somewhere between 1231 and 1235. No firmer date can be established.

3. SOURCES AND TRADITION

To unravel all the sources of this complicated work would mean to write the whole history of rhetoric and literary criticism in the Middle Ages. As many sources as I have been able to discover for individual passages are pointed out in the notes. What should be said here is that its chief debt is to three works: the *Rhetorica ad Herennium,* Horace's *Ars poetica,* and Geoffrey of Vinsauf's *Documentum de modo et arte dictandi et versificandi* (a short version of which is printed in Faral, pp. 263-320). The frequent dependence on the last work suggests that John was working within a tradition of literary criticism that owed much to Bernard Silvestris and the school of Chartres, and was in actual use at the schools and the University of Paris—a tradition he himself helped to develop both in his teaching and in writing this work.[7] That literary criticism evidently induced many of its principles from poems themselves, and not only the poems of the ancients, but also those of more recent masters such as Bernard Silvestris, John of Hanville, and Alain de Lille. There are a good many things in this work whose peculiar form is best explained as the result of John's practical experience as a teacher. The precepts on *dictamen* and *rhythmus* are certainly derivative, but no single work is obviously their source. For *rhythmus,* see especially the note to 7, 467; for Geoffrey's *Documentum,* see Appendix Two as well as the notes to Chapters 2-5.

The work offers few individual precepts that are new. Its originality lies rather in its totality: it is the only thorough attempt we have to gather three distinct areas of the medieval arts of discourse (*ars poetica, ars rhythmica,* and *ars dictaminis*) under a single series of rules.[8] The fact is that John often fails at this attempt; his general rules seldom apply to more than one form, and most of the time he is obliged to discuss each form separately. Still his concept is valid, even though he neglects to make some important general distinctions, to point out which aspects of the three forms are common, and which peculiar to each.

7. The title of the work stresses its connection with Paris. Knowing the contemporary practice of calling a book by its *incipit,* John began it with the word *Parisiana* purposely; the title *Parisiana poetria* means not only "The Art of Poetry that begins '*Parisiana* . . .'" but also "The Art of Poetry as it is taught at Paris." Horace's *Ars poetica* was commonly called *Poetria;* Geoffrey of Vinsauf invited comparison with it by calling his book *Poetria nova;* John's title alludes to both, and indicates that his work both complements and departs from Geoffrey's.

On Bernard Silvestris and his relation to the later Parisian school, see Edmond Faral, "Le Manuscrit 511 du 'Hunterian Museum' de Glasgow," *Studi medievali,* n.s. 9 (1936): 18-119, esp. 69 ff., and Winthrop Wetherbee, "The School of Chartres and Medieval Poetry" (University of California at Berkeley thesis, 1967), esp. pp. 74 ff., 235; some of the material of this valuable thesis is incorporated in the author's article, "The Function of Poetry in the 'De Planctu Naturae' of Alain de Lille," *Traditio* 25 (1969): 87-125. I have not yet seen Wetherbee's book, *Platonism and Poetry in the Twelfth Century* (Princeton, 1972).

8. On this point, as well as for a good general introduction to the subject, see James J. Murphy, "The Arts of Discourse, 1050-1400," *Medieval Studies* 23 (1961): 194-205; see also his *Medieval Rhetoric: A Select Bibliography* (Toronto, 1971). An earlier work which touches on both rhymed and quantitative verse in the course of a treatment of prose *dictamen* is Alberic of Monte Cassino's *Breviarium de dictamine,* edited in part by Rockinger, 1: 29-46; see also below, note to 7, 467. But Alberic's intent cannot be called synthetic, as John's can.

John also separates himself from his fellow writers of both *artes
dictaminis* and *poetriae* by organizing his discussion according to the
classical division of the parts of rhetoric. Thus, although his treatment
of Invention is incomplete and his concept of it mechanical, he does
treat it, while others do not. John seems to have sought originality; he
never mentions Geoffrey's *Documentum,* for example, and usually
changes what he takes from it for no apparent reason other than to
avoid the charge of plagiarism. Still, it may be said with safety, even
though many particular sources may be irrecoverable, that the work is
on the whole clearly derivative. It is a summary for students of contemporary thinking on how to learn to write, not a new departure,
though something of a new synthesis, in literary criticism.

4. THE WORK ITSELF

Though every reader must make his own assessment of this book, and
though I have used the notes to say what I have to say about it, let me
speak briefly here of its general character and value. John makes a number of very important contributions to our understanding of medieval
literature. These include especially the discussions of the four prose
styles (*5,* 402 ff.); the levels of style (*5,* 45 ff.; *1,* 383 ff.; *2,* 116 ff.; *4,*
416 ff.); genres (*5,* 303 ff.; *4,* 462 ff.; and briefly in various other places);
the *ars rhythmica.* A number of other discussions are less striking, yet
important because they differ greatly in substance or emphasis from the
teachings of the writers Faral has edited: the sources of invention, especially proverbs (*1*); the art of selection (*2*); memory (*2,* 87 ff.); the
Horatian meters (*7,* 1478 ff.). In addition, there are scattered throughout the book various statements, some rather difficult to understand
precisely, which can give us new points of view on literary matters both
large and small. Of course there is much that is commonplace; Chapter
Three, for example, on how to begin, and Chapter Six, on figures and
tropes, are standard fare, although the two lengthy poems that the
couplets illustrating individual figures of speech go to make up are interesting tours de force. On the whole, however, the particular colloca-
tions and emphases with which John marshals his material, and his many
homemade examples, make the work consistently interesting and original, even though, as I have said above and as I have tried to show in the
notes, most of its substance has a source elsewhere. The examples are
particularly noteworthy. They are the chief ingredient in a certain appealing literary quality which the book exhibits, and which others like
it, the shorter version of Geoffrey's *Documentum* for example, seem to
me to lack. John had to read, and had to write, a lot of poetry to complete it. That poetry, and the general sense of personal conviction and

experience of reading, writing, and teaching that show through the doctrine, enable John to create a personal voice, a very pedantic voice, to be sure, yet a vital, enthusiastic voice too, that unifies the work and gives it distinction. Though it is, and will be used as, a tool, one might do worse than to read it through for its own sake: as a kind of literary manifesto accompanying a collection of the author's poems, it is not altogether unlike, at least in intention, Pope's *Pastorals, with a Discourse on Pastoral,* or *Lyrical Ballads* with its preface.

The book has shortcomings, some very great. The prose style is rather graceless, though of course John was writing what he calls "technigraphic" prose, which does not call for grace. Much of his doctrine is superficial and mechanical, his approach overly grammatical. Some of his definitions are unclear or off the point, and he has a tendency to lose sight of his announced organization, a fault that is intensified by the straightforward format of medieval books. He had an associative rather than an analytical mind, but had not the devices like parentheses, footnotes, and appendixes that we are accustomed to use in order to keep digressions in their place. (One should keep in mind through all the digressions that the basic principle of organization of the book is the classical division of the parts of rhetoric: Invention, Arrangement, Embellishment, Delivery, and Memory. Chapters One and Two treat Invention, Chapters Three and Four Arrangement, Chapter Six Embellishment. Chapter Five interrupts the scheme to deal with style, which is perhaps thought of as an aspect of Embellishment. Chapter Seven is a collection of examples, plus the *ars rhythmica.* Delivery and Memory receive some brief treatment along the way. I have attempted to make the organization of Chapters Two through Five clearer by beginning the notes to each with a general survey of its contents; similarly, the note to 7, 467 surveys the organization of the *ars rhythmica,* and the note to 1, 75 the treatment of Invention.)

Some of these shortcomings are to be referred, I think, to the audience. Whom did John expect to read his work? There are many indications that it was intended for students, not mature writers—and for students at a very elementary stage.[9] Thus the opening poem gives a picture of the masters tending their flocks of students, and the students are called *teneri agniculi,* absorbing the food of *primae doctrinae.* Several passages tacked on to the end of theoretical discussion (1, 514 ff.; 4, 30 ff., 74 ff.)

---

9. Cf. Gervase of Melkley (Gräbener, p. 2): "Opusculum hoc rudium est," and Gräbener's comment, p. xxxi. Douglas Kelly, in "The Scope of the Treatment of Composition in the Twelfth- and Thirteenth-Century Arts of Poetry," *Speculum* 41 (1966): 262, 268-69 has shown that Matthew of Vendôme and Eberhard the German were also writing for elementary students.

bring the work back down, as it were, to the level of the classroom—and
in them the students are called not *scholares* but *pueri*. Many of the
sample letters deal with student problems. The paragraph on memory
(*2*, 87) is largely on how to take notes in class.

[margin note: X importance of the intended audience]

The age at which the average medieval student entered the university
is unknown, but there is evidence that some of them were very young
indeed.[10] Nor is it clear how much preparation a student had in the
lower schools; but it is certain that at least some of the universities had
to teach grammar,[11] on a higher level perhaps than that of the schools,
but grammar nonetheless. Thus the grammatical emphasis of John's
treatise and the rudimentary nature of some of its precepts are certainly
to be referred at least in part to the fact that it was intended for a young
and not very literate audience. Furthermore, it was probably intended
to be used in the classroom, not read in private. That means that, even
if the students had copies, the teacher was to comment and expand on
it in his lectures, and may help to explain the sketchiness it occasionally
exhibits. A student who owned a copy might later use it in private, but
then he would have the master's glosses to supplement it. The glosses in
the Bruges manuscript may have arisen in just this way. My difficulty in
distinguishing families of manuscripts (see below, p. xxiii) may also be
due to the fact that several copies were circulating simultaneously among
students in Paris. John was aware that his treatise only touched the surface (*1*, 73-74); he blamed it on a modern craze for what is brief and
immediately useful, but I think also he was aiming primarily to provide
a set of notes as a starting point for teaching.

[margin note: glosses]

5. THE MANUSCRIPTS

This edition is a collation of the following six manuscripts, which to my
knowledge are the only extant copies of the work.[12]

10. Louis J. Paetow, *The Arts Course at Medieval Universities* (Urbana-Champaign,
Ill., 1910), p. 55.

11. Cf. Lynn Thorndike, "Elementary and Secondary Education in the Middle
Ages," *Speculum* 15 (1940): 403; Rashdall, 3: 351-52.

12. Paetow (p. 126) lists six manuscripts, which, as he says, he copied from Edwin
Habel, "Johannes de Garlandia, ein Schulmann des 13. Jahrhunderts," *Mitteilungen
der Gesellschaft für deutsche Erziehungs- und Schulgeschichte* 19 (1909): 25. Their
total of six is arrived at erroneously, however. The two manuscripts listed by both as
"Cambridge, Ms. More 121; LI 1. 14" are actually a single manuscript under two
different designations. The latter is the more modern ("LI" should be "Ll"). They
did not know of the Paris manuscript.

B. Bibliothèque Publique de Bruges, Ms. 546, ff. 148ᵛ-174ᵛ, 145ᵛ.[13] This manuscript contains only works by John of Garland; the *Poetria* is the closing piece. It ends incomplete on f. 174ᵛ after 7, 1829, but f. 145ᵛ contains the missing portion. It is a vellum quarto, French, of the second half of the thirteenth century, extensively glossed throughout. The *Poetria* is written in double columns in two reasonably clear hands (the change occurs at f. 170ᵛ), and contains many corrections as well as ⊥ glosses, both interlinear and marginal. There are paragraph titles and large initial letters in faded red ink through f. 162ᵛ (*6, 1* in the present text); thereafter the spaces for them are blank. For the glosses, see Appendix One; for the corrections, see textual notes.

C. University Library, Cambridge, Ms. Ll. 1. 14, ff. 55ʳ-69ʳ. Quarto, vellum, double columns, rare spaces for initial capitals, none filled in, late thirteenth or early fourteenth century. The codex also contains the Virgilian cento of Proba, a grammatical treatise, St. Benedict's *Rule,* and some miscellaneous Benedictine material. See *A Catalogue of the Manuscripts Preserved in the Library of the University of Cambridge,* vol. 4 (Cambridge, 1861), p. 8. The text of the *Poetria* is incomplete, ending with the word *terminatur,* 7, 26.

M. Bayerische Staatsbibliothek, Munich, Ms. Lat. 6911, ff. 1ʳ-22ᵛ. Quarto, vellum, double columns, paragraph titles and initials in red, late thirteenth or early fourteenth century. The codex contains three other works on *dictamen,* a grammatical treatise, an anthology of miscellaneous

---

There are three other corrections to be made in Paetow's notice of the manuscripts. The Abbey of Admont in Austria sold many of its holdings in the late 1930s, and Admont 637 became in 1936 Oxford, Bodleian Library Ms. Lat. misc. d. 66; cf. *The Bodleian Quarterly Record* 8 (1936): 255, and E. P. Goldschmidt and Co., Ltd., "Catalogue One Hundred" (London, 1953), p. 11. The relevant folios of this manuscript are 1ʳ-40ᵛ. Finally, Paetow says that "Tanner and Cloetta state that there is a manuscript at Oxford." But Cloetta (p. 15) merely says that Tanner says there is one; and he misread Tanner, who only refers to the Cambridge manuscript (Thomas Tanner, *Bibliotheca Britannico-Hibernica* [London, 1748], p. 434).

13. The best description is by A. DePoorter, "Catalogue des manuscrits de grammaire latine médiévale de la bibliothèque de Bruges," *Revue des bibliothèques* 36 (1926): 119-33. Other descriptions: P. J. Laude, *Catalogue des manuscrits de la bibliothèque publique de Bruges* (Bruges, 1859), pp. 478-85; A. Scheler, "Trois traités de lexicographie latine du XIIᵉ et du XIIIᵉ siècle," *Jahrbuch für Romanische und Englische Literatur* 6 (1865): 43-59; Paetow, p. 149; Wilson, *Stella maris,* pp. 80-81. None of these writers reports the fact that f. 145ᵛ contains part of the *Poetria.* Paetow, who gives the folios for the *Compendium grammaticae* as 89ʳ-145ᵛ (p. 120, n. 1), notes that it is "here entitled *Ars Versificatoria* in the *explicit* which is inserted by another hand." The real explanation is that the *Compendium grammaticae* ends on f. 145ʳ; Paetow was reading the *explicit* to the *Poetria.*

verse, and a series of excerpts from classical poets. See Carolus Halm et Georgius Laubmann, *Catalogus codicum latinorum bibliothecae regiae Monacensis* (Munich, 1868), vol. 1, part 1, p. 127. Rockinger (1: 97) describes the codex, and puts it contemporaneous with John's work, i.e. 1260. This manuscript has some scattered glosses, for which see Appendix One.

O. Bodleian Library, Oxford, Ms. Lat. misc. d. 66, ff. 1ʳ-40ᵛ (formerly Admont 637; see above, note 12). Quarto, paper, single column, spaces for initial capitals, filled in only on f. 1ʳ, written in Germany in a cursive script of the late fourteenth or early fifteenth century. The codex contains five other *artes dictaminis* and three formularies of letters in Latin and German. See E. P. Goldschmidt, Ltd. (cf. above, n. 12) and Mari's edition (described below, p. xxii), pp. 883-85.

P. Bibliothèque Nationale, Paris, Ms. Lat. 11867, ff. 46ʳ-57ᵛ. Quarto, vellum, double column, initial capitals in red, French, late thirteenth century. The codex also contains the *Summa dictaminis* of Thomas of Capua, another *summa dictaminis,* and various poems and letters. John's treatise is not identified as his; instead a late hand in the margin of f. 46ʳ has identified it as "tertia pars dictaminis magistri thomae campani." Delisle's summary description (*Bibliothèque de L'École des Chartres,* ser. 6, 1: 204) did not uncover this error. K. Hampe (*Sitzungsberichte der Heidelberger Akademie der Wissenschaften, philosophisch-historische Klasse* [1910], Abhandlung 8, p. 6) was the first to discover that it is actually a text of John's *Poetria.* Paetow does not list this manuscript. For further description and references, see Peter Dronke, *Medieval Latin and the Rise of European Love-Lyric,* 2d ed. (Oxford, 1968), 2: 573-74. Various portions of the *Poetria* are missing; it begins at *Qvi 1,* 26 and ends incomplete on f. 57ᵛ with the words *prodeunt, etc. 7,* 1473.

V. Osterreichische Nationalbibliothek, Vienna, Ms. Lat. 3121, ff. 154ᵛ-158ᵛ. Folio, paper, single columns, spaces for initial capitals, none filled in, written in a very clear and beautiful fifteenth-century hand. For a list of its extensive miscellaneous contents, cf. *Tabulae codicum manu scriptorum praeter graecos et orientales in bibliotheca palatina Vindobonensi asservatorum* (Vienna, 1868), 2: 201. This is a brief summary of the *ars rhythmica* only, with many omissions; it starts with the words *Rithimica ars est species* (*sic;* see *7,* 469) and ends with the words *ab Odis Oratii* (*7,* 1478). John of Garland is not named as the author.

6. PREVIOUS EDITIONS

Portions of this work were first published by Rockinger (1: 485-512). Rockinger used the Munich manuscript only, and printed only brief passages with summaries in German in between; he did, however, print all the sample letters and documents in Chapter Seven.

F. Zarncke, "Zwei mittelalterliche Abhandlungen über den Bau rhythmischer Verse," *Berichte über die Verhandlungen der königlich sächsischen Gesellschaft der Wissenschaften zu Leipzig, philologisch-historische Klasse* 23 (1871): 34-95, printed the section on *ars rhythmica* (7, 468-end), in the truncated version of Vienna Ms. Lat. 3121, on pp. 48-81. Neither Rockinger nor Zarncke identified the work as John of Garland's; nor did Zarncke's manuscript give him any indication that the *ars rhythmica* was part of a larger work.

Giovanni Mari published the complete *Poetria* in two parts, and was the first to present it under John of Garland's name. The section on *ars rhythmica* is in his *I trattati medievali di ritmica latina* (Milan, 1899), pp. 35-80. The main part of the treatise is in *Romanische Forschungen* 13 (1902): 883-965. Mari used the Oxford (Admont) and Munich manuscripts; he includes variant readings, but does not identify references nor offer any critical comment or annotation, except for the *ars rhythmica*.

When Faral published his ground-breaking collection of texts in 1924, he did not reprint this text, but he discusses John on pp. 40-46 and gives an outline (excluding the *ars rhythmica*) on pp. 378-80. As Faral points out on p. 46, Mari's edition is frequently in error, partly because he did not have enough manuscript evidence (he especially needed Bruges 546), partly because he misread in places the manuscripts he had, or chose poorly between alternative readings. My original aim was merely to provide a translation of Mari's text; but it turned out to be so unreliable that I was forced to make a new edition of my own to translate. Mari's text is reported in the textual notes wherever he chooses a reading I reject; I have not, however, reported the many places where he misreads the manuscripts altogether. It is an act of piety to state that, despite its faults, Mari's text has made my work easier, and I have used it regularly, though with caution, in interpreting the manuscripts.[14]

14. Some of the poems are collected in *Analecta hymnica*, 50: 545-57. Paetow's notice of previous editions of fragments of this work (p. 126) needs correction. The publications he lists by Wright and Halliwell, Thurot, and Fierville are unrelated to this work; each prints from a different manuscript a brief *ars rhythmica* which has some points in common with John's treatment of that subject, but is in reality a wholly separate work. These mistakes are repeated in J. H. Baxter, C. Johnson, and J. F. Willard, "An Index of British and Irish Latin Writers, 400-1520," *Archivum latinitatis medii aevi (Bulletin Du Cange)* 7 (1932): 151; and B. A. Park and Elizabeth S. Dallas, "A *Sequentia Cum Prosa* by John of Garland," *Medievalia et humanistica* 15 (1963): 54n.

7. THE PRESENT TEXT AND TRANSLATION

I have not been able to construct a reliable stemma for the manuscripts. There is a general connection between the Bruges (*B*) and Oxford (*O*) manuscripts on the one hand and among the Munich (*M*), Cambridge (*C*), and Paris (*P*) manuscripts on the other; and yet many errors common to *B* and *M* as against *O* and *P*, and *B* and *P* as against *O* and *M*, as well as many cases where three agree against one, have rendered the family relationship utterly obscure. *C* is hard to place in any consistent grouping. Clearly there has been a good deal of scribal collation of several manuscripts, and copying of corrected manuscripts, as well as much contamination and scribal independence.[15] *B*, because of its age and its many corrections, is clearly the best manuscript. It has more errors than *O*, though fewer major errors. *O* is the most carefully written, yet contains a good many clearly untenable readings. *M*, though it omits much and displays many idiosyncrasies, is on the whole rather good; *C* has many small errors and little independent value; *P* omits so much and has so many stupid errors that it is virtually of no value; so too *V* for its short span.

My text, then, is the text of *B*, emended frequently for sense or meter and occasionally for the sake of a majority reading from the other manuscripts.[16] Spelling is that of *B*. The spelling of emended words is that of *O* whenever possible, otherwise *M*. The textual notes present all variations from *B*, or from *B* as emended, in all the other manuscripts in word order and rubrication and, of course, in actual wording. Variations in spelling only are not recorded. I have listed separately in the textual notes all corrections in *B* not obviously made by the original scribe. Capitalization and punctuation in the text are mine. Emendations to *B* are marked by

---

15. Cf. George Kane's well-known demonstration of the variety of ways in which manuscripts become contaminated in his *Piers Plowman: The A Version* (London, 1960), pp. 115-72. The persuasive case for editorial judgment made in that book has supported me in my choice of editorial method. For another telling demonstration of why editors should keep meaning in mind, see E. T. Donaldson, "Chaucer, *Canterbury Tales*, D117: A Critical Edition," *Speculum* 40 (1965): 626-33.

16. Aside from several changes in the lists at the end which are contained in *M* only, I have made the following eight emendations without manuscript authority: *1*, 459-60 a quantitate, a qualitate (*order reversed*); *2*, 151 Si sit proprium: plura (proprium et plura *BCMOP*); *3*, 43-44 a prouerbio sumpto iuxta principium materie (iuxta principium materie sumptum a principio *BCMOP*); *4*, 143 De Arte Uestiendi Nudam Materiam (*rubric taken from l. 157*); *5*, 107 Ut si diceret (Ac si diceret *BCMOP*); *6*, 298 ueritatem (uirtutem *BCMOP*); *6*, 388-89 Demonstratio est quando res exprimitur ut ante oculos videatur (*combined from M rubric and text*); *7*, 276 Initial R. (B. *BMOP*).

an asterisk in the text, except that omissions are not marked; additions or changes of more than one word are marked by an asterisk after the first word of the phrase.

In reporting the spelling of *B,* I have adopted the following special principles:

1. *u/v* obscured by abbreviation is reported as *u* (e.g. *uel, adiectiua*).

2. *ti/ci* before a vowel is reported:

a. when spelled out, as whichever it looks more like, often without conviction (thus *1,* 46 *Discretioni* but *1,* 47 *presencium*).

b. when abbreviated, as *ti* after *a, e, c* (*probatio, pretium, lectio*) and as *ci* after *i, o, n, r* (*uicium, negocium, intencio, tercius*), this being, as far as I can tell, the normal (though not perfectly consistent) practice in instances where these combinations are spelled out.

3. All other abbreviations are expanded to normal modern spelling (e.g. *nihil, sed* even though these are occasionally spelled out as *nichil, set* in the manuscript).

Readers unaccustomed to medieval Latin spelling should bear in mind not only the ubiquitous *e* for *ae/oe, i* for *j, y* for *i* and *i* for *y, u* for *v* and *v* for *u,* but also the free omission or insertion of initial *h* before a vowel (*Oratius, Hennius*) or in combination with *c, t,* or *r* (*scolaris, rethorica*), gemination and simplification (*occulus, oportunitas*), intrusive *p* (*columpna*), and especially variation between *s/c/sc/sch* before front vowels (the word *schema,* for example, apparently pronounced *sema,* can be written as *sema, cema, scema,* or *schema;* and since *c* and *t* vary before *i* plus a vowel, a form such as *promoscio* [7, 175] for *promotio* is also possible).

The translation is not meant to replace the Latin text, but rather to provide both an interpretation of it and a means of gaining rapid acquaintance with its contents. I have assumed that my reader knows some Latin, and thus have not, for example, translated Latin phrases or sentences quoted in the notes. The translation should stand for itself without a lengthy introduction. My aim has been to produce a readable modern English version without straying too far from John's syntactical patterns. Occasionally the former aim has had to submit to the latter. It is not a translator's responsibility to put bad Latin into bad English, yet at times to improve John's style would have meant to "improve" the meaning, and I have rejected any such falsification. Thus many sentences are cast in a form that is not modern, and yet I hope not too grating to the modern ear. The "embellished" letters are translated quite literally, since to leave them in Latinate form and diction seemed the best way to reproduce their very mannered effect. The poems are also translated reasonably literally in order to make their obscure Latin syntax apparent.

At times I have strayed from precision in order to reproduce a pun or a rhythmic pattern.

In the notes I have been more willing to be too full than too sketchy. Medievalists will find many of them unnecessary; I have tried to keep in mind the needs of graduate students. I have assumed, in fact, that the average reader of this text will be puzzled by the same things that puzzled me; the notes are simply the best solutions I could find or work out for the puzzles.[17]

This book originated as a Harvard Ph.D. thesis. Morton Bloomfield and B. J. Whiting, who directed it, deserve my special gratitude both for that direction and for much else, as does Madeleine Doran, who first introduced me to the study of rhetoric. Neil Ker, James J. Murphy, John Pope, and Richard Sylvester gave me particular advice and encouragement. I also owe thanks to Jeremy Adams, Herbert Bloch, William Bond, Christopher Brookhouse, George Brown, Raymond Cormier, A. Bartlett Giamatti, Richard Hunt, Jean Krochalis, Leon Plantinga, Richard Schoeck, Louis Solano, William Waite, and Evelyn F. Wilson. A Dexter Fellowship from the English Department of Harvard University enabled me to go to Europe in the summer of 1966 to examine manuscripts. I received aid while I was there from many helpful people at the British Museum, the Bodleian Library, the Cambridge University Library, the Bibliothèque Nationale, and the Bruges Public Library. To the authorities of the last four, and of the Bayerische Staatsbibliothek and the Österreichische Nationalbibliothek, I am grateful for photographic reproductions of the manuscripts, and for permission to print their contents. A Morse Fellowship from Yale in 1969 gave me time to make extensive revisions. Linda Clifford, Stephanie Hadley, Elaine Heumann, Grace Michele, Doris Pfuderer, Gale Pollen, and Susan Winston of the Yale English Department worked on the typescript at various stages cheerfully and well, and Barbara Rader and Patricia Woodruff of the Yale University Press made it far fitter than it was to print.

17. Ernest Gallo, The "Poetria nova" and Its Sources in Early Rhetorical Doctrine (The Hague and Paris, 1971) came to my attention too late to enable me to add references to it in my notes. Readers who desire further discussion of the sources of any particular doctrine should consult the appropriate place in Gallo's excellent essay on Geoffrey's sources, pp. 133-223.

Parisiana Poetria de Arte Prosaica, Metrica, et Rithmica

Qvinque sunt inquirenda in principio huius opusculi: scilicet
materia, intentio auctoris, vtilitas audientis, cui parti philosophie
supponatur, quis sit modus agendi. Materia est[ars dictandi,]metri-
candi, rithmicandi; sed ad has tres recedunt alie* quinque, que
5   sunt ars inueniendi, eligendi, memorandi, ordinandi, et ars ornandi. Intentio auctoris est tradere artem eloquentie. Vtilitas est scire
tractare quamcumque materiam prosayce, metrice, et rithmice.
Liber iste tribus speciebus philosophie supponitur: Gramatice,
quia docet congrue loqui; Rethorice, quia docet ornate dicere;
10   Ethice, quia docet siue persuadet ad honestum, quod est genus
omnium uirtutum secundum Tullium. Is est modus agendi: auctor docet inuenire uocabula secundum species inuentionis, scilicet substantiua et adiectiua et uerba proprie et transumptiue*
posita, in quolibet genere dictandi, siue sint littere curiales siue
15   scolastice,* siue elegiacum carmen tradatur, uel comedia, uel
tragedia, uel satyra, uel hystoria. Agitur autem aliquando de
arte prosayca, aliquando de uersificatoria, mutua* vicissitudine;
aliquando de rythmica, sed hoc uersus finem, et in fine specia-
liter de metrica,* ubi formantur x et ix metra* diuersa secundum
20   Oratium, qui tot metra composuit diuersa in odis suis, ad aliquod
unum quorum reducuntur alia metra et ymni. Hac autem ratione
modo tractatur de hac materia, modo de illa, partim et uicissim;
quia sunt et aliqui qui exserperent a libro artem prosaycam per
se, et* aliqui qui excerperent artem metricam uel rythmicam uel
25   uersificariam pro uoluntate sua, et ita libellus per panniculos
distraheretur. Vnde qui partem uult habere, necesse est ipsum
habere totum.

   In versibus positis in principio continentur tria: occasio operis,
vtilitas, et prelibatio. Occasio quidem est—non dico causa—quod
30   studium adaugetur Parisius, cuius instrumenta debent* consequenter adaugeri, scilicet libri. Vnde hac occasione dicitur libellus iste componi vbi dicitur "Parisiana iubar"; exprimitur utilitas
ubi dicitur "Prime doctrine"; operis prelibatio et modus agendi
innuitur ubi dicitur "Quorundam longi tractatus." Si de titulo
35   queratur, is est: "Incipit *Parisiana Poetria* Magistri Iohannis
Anglici de Garlandia de Arte Prosaica, Metrica et Rithmica"; et
sumitur titulus a prima fronte libri.

Introductory Summary

Five things about this short work should be examined at the start: the subject matter, the author's purpose, its usefulness for its audience, what field of knowledge it belongs to, the method. The subject matter is the art of writing letters, of quantitative verse, and of rhymed syllabic verse; but behind these three lie five others, which are: the art of invention, of selection, of memory, of arrangement, and of embellishment. The author's purpose is to publish a manual of style. Its usefulness is that it imparts a technique for treating any subject whatever in prose, quantitative verse, or rhymed syllabic verse. This book belongs to three particular fields of knowledge: Grammar, since it teaches how to speak properly; Rhetoric, since it teaches how to speak elegantly; and Ethics, since it teaches or instills a sense of what is right, and from this according to Cicero every virtue springs. This is the approach: the author teaches how to invent, according to the categories of invention, words, that is, substantives, adjectives, and verbs used both literally and metaphorically, in any kind of composition, whether it be a legal or academic letter, or an elegiac poem, or a comedy, or a tragedy, or a satire, or a history. For he deals sometimes with the art of prose, sometimes with that of poetry, back and forth from one to the other; sometimes with rhymed syllabic verse, but this toward the end; and at the very end he deals in a special way with quantitative verse, where nineteen poems, each in a different meter, are created in imitation of Horace, who assembled nineteen different meters in his odes, to one or another of which any other metrical poem or hymn is reducible. Thus he treats now of this matter, now of that, in part and by turns; for there are some who might cut the art of prose out of the book for its own sake, and others who might cut out the art of quantitative verse, or of rhymed syllabic verse, or of poetry in general, as they wish, and thus the poor book would be torn up into rags. As it is, you must take all or nothing.

The verses placed at the beginning contain three things: the motive of the work, its usefulness, and a foretaste of it. The motive, as distinct from the cause, is to increase study at Paris, whose instruments ought consequently to be increased, namely books. This book is said to be composed from this motive, in the lines beginning "The glory of Paris"; its usefulness is explained in the lines beginning "Let the tender lambs"; a foretaste of the work and its method are suggested in the lines beginning "Some people's long treatises." The final question is the title; here it is: "Here begins the *'Parisiana Poetria'* of Master John of Garland, the Englishman, on the Art of Prose, Quantitative Verse, and Rhymed Syllabic Verse." The title is taken from the first word of the book.

3

Incipit* Poetria Magistri Iohannis Anglici de Arte Prosayca, Metrica, et Rithmica

Prologus

Parisiana iubar diffundit gloria, clerus
  Crescit, Apolineas fons iaculatur aquas.
Pascua, grex, pastor, vernat, crescit, studet; vsu
  Pascua, grex studio, pastor amore gregis.
5 Prime doctrine teneri noua pabula carpant
  Agniculi; pastor spectet, ouile terat.
Quid dedignaris, tu qui maiora requiris?
  Vidimus in plano sepe labare pedem.
Ne pes ignoret ubi sistere debeat, artis
10 Regula dat pontem; ponte repone pedem.
Quorundam longi tractatus equora fundunt;
  Hic ars dictandi stringitur ampne breui.
Metrica prosaice, metrice subiungitur arti
  Ridmica: tres unus iste libellus habet.

15 *Capitula Principalia.* Presentis tractatus septem suberunt particule. Primo tradetur doctrina inueniendi; deinde docebitur* de modo eligendi materiam; postea de dispositione et de modo ordinandi materiam; deinde de partibus dictaminis; postea de uiciis uitandis in quolibet genere dictandi. Consequenter constituitur
20 tractatus de rethorico ornatu, necessario tam in metro quam in prosa, utpote de coloribus materiam abbreuiantibus et ampliantibus ad scribentis electionem. Septimo et ultimo subiciuntur exempla litterarum curialium et dictaminum scolasticorum, et uersuum et rithmorum ornate compositorum, et diuersorum
25 metrorum.
Diffinicio et Diuisio Prose. Qvi tradit artem debet diffinire quod dicitur, et diuidere, et exempla subicere. Dicatur quid sit prosa. Prosa est sermo sentenciosus ornate sine metro compositus, distinctus clausularum debitis interuallis. Et dicitur a "pros" quod est
30 "ad," quasi "sermo ad alios"; uel a "prosopa" quod est "persona," quasi "personalis," id est "uulgaris"; uel a "prosum," quod est "productum," secundum Ysidorum, quasi "sermo productus."

Exemplum prosayci dictaminis.

Mauricius, Dei gratia Rotomagensis Archiepiscopus; venerabili
35 viro Magistro G., dilecto filio in Christo* Remensi, Parisius ad

4

Here begins the Treatise on Poetry of Master John the Englishman on the Art of Prose, Quantitative Verse, and Rhymed Syllabic Verse

Prologue

The glory of Paris diffuses splendor, the body of scholars grows, the fountain gushes forth Apollonian waters. The pasture is flourishing, the flock grows, the shepherd is busy; the pasture because it is in constant use, the flock through study, the shepherd because he loves the flock. Let the tender lambs snatch up the new food of the elementary course; let the shepherd watch over them, let him tread the sheepfold. Why are you scornful, you who are seeking greater things? We have often seen the foot stumble in the plain. Lest the foot find no foothold, art's straight-edge provides a bridge; put your foot back on that bridge. Some people's long treatises pour forth seas; the art of composition is here channeled in a short stream. The art of quantitative verse is joined to that of prose, the art of rhymed syllabic verse to that of quantitative verse: this one little book contains three.

The Principal Chapters. This treatise will have seven sections. First to be given will be the theory of invention; then a lesson on the method of selecting material; after that on arrangement, how to put the material in order; then on the parts of a letter; after that, on avoiding vices in any kind of writing. Then comes a careful treatise on rhetorical embellishment, covering both quantitative verse and prose, and including figures to shorten or lengthen material, as the writer chooses. In the seventh and last part are appended examples of legal and academic letters, of elegant compositions in both quantitative and rhymed verse, and of various meters.

Definition and Division of Prose. Anyone who presents an art ought to define his terms, make distinctions, and include examples. What then is prose? Prose is pithy and elegant discourse, not in meter but divided by regular rhythms of *clausulae*. It comes from *pros,* which is "to," as it were "a discourse to others"; or from *prosopa,* which is "person," as it were "personal," that is, "popular"; or as Isidore says from *prosum* (*prorsum*), which is "led forward," as it were "a discourse led forward."

Example of a Letter in Prose.

Maurice, by the grace of God Archbishop of Rouen; to the venerable Master G., his beloved son in Christ from Reims, diligent in the pulpits

5

pulpita Theologie studioso; salutem, et vitam consequi beatam
quam per studium inuestigat.

    Laudabilia sunt premia que uiris prudentibus pro fructuosis
et longis laboribus conferuntur, et que tandem in senectute
40   florida possidentur. Vestram recolimus prudenciam et laudabi-
lem fidelitatem in Dei seruicio promissum a nobis beneficium
expectasse. Sed nondum se nobis optulit oportunitas qua uobis
competens beneficium conferremus,* et qua uos a pulpitis
scolasticis ad sedem canonicam uocaremus. In ecclesia tamen
45   nostra vacat prebenda que valet sexaginta libras Parisienses in
ecclesia residenti. Quare Discretioni Vestre mandamus quatinus
cum latore presencium nostram uideatis ecclesiam, si tantillum
beneficium Uestra suscipere Discretio condignetur.

    Item prosa alia tegnigrapha, a *"tegni"* quod est "ars" et
50   *"graphos"* quod est "scriptum," qua utitur Aristotiles et alii
tradentes artem; alia ystorialis, qua utitur ecclesia, et tragedi et
comedi aliquando, et alii nonnulli philosophi; alia dictamen,]quo
utitur curia et scola, cuius species inferius apparebunt; alia ⌡
rithmus, quo utimur* in prosis ecclesiasticis. Sed notandum
55   quod rithmica species est musice, ut ait Boetius in Arte Musica:
"Tria genera sunt que circa artem musicam uersantur: vnum
genus quod instrumentis agitur; aliud quod fingit carmina;
tercium quod instrumentorum opus carmenque diiudicat, scilicet theorica . . . Isque est musicus cui adest facultas, secundum
60   rationem et speculationem propositam ac musice conuenientem,
de metris, rithmis, de generibus cantilenarum . . . ac poetarum
carminibus iudicandi"; de quibus dicetur in fine.
Diffinicio et diuisio metri. Post* hoc diffiniatur quid sit metrum.
Metrum est certa pedum commensuratio suis uersibus distincta,
65   et dicitur a "metros" quod est "mensura." Pes est certa dimensio
sillabarum et temporum. Versus est ipsorum pedum comprehensio
regularis. Item metrum* aliud spondaicum, aliud dactilicum, aliu
iambicum, aliud trochaicum, aliud coriiambicum; et sunt alie
species que sunt in odis Oratii, quibus utitur* Oratius, Boetius,
70   et Marcianus, que aliquando dicuntur ab inuentore, aliquando a
pedibus: ab inuentore ut asclepiadeum ab Asclepio* inuentore, a
pedibus ut dictum est iambicum. Albinouanus* uero* composuit
Librum Centimetrum, sed quia* breuibus et utilibus gaudent
moderni, quod est nobis necessarium prosequamur.
75   *De Inventione.* * Sicut dicit Oratius in Poetria de inuencione materie et electione, prius debemus inuenire quam inuenta eligere,
et prius eligere quam electa* disponere. Dicit ergo:

of Theology at Paris: greeting, and may he achieve the eternal life which he is investigating in his studies.

Laudable are the rewards which are bestowed on prudent men for long and fruitful labors, and which at length are possessed in flourishing old age. We recall that your prudence and praiseworthy faithfulness in the service of God had expected a benefice promised by us. But the opportunity has not yet offered itself to us by which we might confer on you a suitable benefice and so call you from school pulpits to a canon's chair. Still, there is vacant in our church a living worth sixty Parisian pounds to someone residing in the church. And so we beg Your Discretion to come and see our church with the bearer of this letter, if Your Discretion should condescend to accept so small a benefice.

Furthermore, one type of prose is technigraphic (from *techne,* "art," and *graphos,* "writing"), which Aristotle and others who publish manuals use. Another is narrative, used by the Church and by writers of tragedies and comedies sometimes, and by various other learned men. Another is *dictamen,* which is employed by universities and courts, and whose various species will appear later on. Another is *rhythmus,* which we use in the "proses" or sequences of the liturgy. But note that the rhythmic is a species of music, as Boethius says in his *Art of Music:* "The art of music embraces three general areas: one such area deals with instruments, a second area with making songs; the third is theory, which assesses those instrumental works and songs . . . And a musician is a man who has the skill to assess, by his systematic knowledge and by careful thought coupled with a 'feel' for music, meters, rhythms, and all varieties of songs . . . and lyric poetry." *Rhythmus* will be dealt with at the end of this treatise.
Definition and Division of Meter. The next step is to define meter. Meter is a certain series of uniform feet, divided into verses, and so called from *metros,* which is "measure." A foot is a certain length of syllables and quantities. A verse is a regular grouping of these feet. And so one meter is spondaic, another dactylic, another iambic, another trochaic, another choriambic; and there are other kinds, found in the odes of Horace, and which Boethius and Martianus use as well as Horace. These sometimes take their names from the inventor, sometimes from the feet: from the inventor, as the Asclepiad, from Asclepius its inventor; from the feet, as the iambic. Albinovanus even put together a "Book of a Hundred Meters," but since people today take pleasure in what is brief and practical, let us stick to what is necessary for us.
On Invention. As Horace says of invention and selection of material in his *Art of Poetry,* we must first invent before selecting from what is invented, and first select before arranging what is selected. Here are his words:

Sumite materiam uestris, qui scribitis, equam
Viribus, et uersate diu quid ferre recusent,
80   Quid ualeant humeri; cui lecta potenter erit res,
Nec facundia deseret* hunc, nec lucidus ordo.

Exposicio istorum uersuum patebit inferius. Prius igitur tracte-
mus de arte inueniendi quam de aliis partibus premissis.
De Arte Inueniendi et Quid Sit Inuencio. <u>Inuenire est in ignote</u>
85   <u>rei noticiam ductu</u> [proprie rationis] <u>uenire.</u> Et sicut dicit Tullius
in Secunda Rethorica: "Inuencio est rerum uerarum et veri simi-
lium excogitatio que causam probabilem reddant."
De Speciebus. Sub inuencione species sunt quinque: vbi, quid,
quale, qualiter, ad quid.
90   *Prima Species: Ubi Inuenitur.* Per "ubi" tria notantur, videlicet
persona, exempla, ethimologia dictionum et earundem exposi-
ciones, ut in hoc exemplo de exaudicione precum.

Viro uenerabili virtutibus vernanti Magistro S., Archidiacono
Cantuariensi; Magister Iohannes de Garlandia: salutem, et sin-
95   cere dilectionis obsequium intimo* cum affectu.

Ad honestatis limitem directum spectat amicos honestis in
peticionibus exaudire. Cum Deus, summe misericors* et Amator uerus hominum, omnem filium quem recepit flagellet,
dulcia sunt flagella tam pii Patris, Cuius manus tetigit A., la-
100   torem presencium, quem infirmum efficit ut ille Secum sanus
discumbat, quem in corpore deformat ut eum in anima Sibi
reformet, quem deicit in terris, sicut pium est credere, ut possit in celis locum celsitudinis uendicare. Sic igitur in uiri predicti debilitate speculum terroris et castigationis manus Ex-
105   celsi proposuit, in quo patet quod cito iuuentutis lilium deli-
liatur, quod in breui probitatis flosculus defloratur, quod
caduca sunt que solent firmitudinem iactitare, et nullescit
gloria qua mundus prestigiat intuentes. Quod etiam ego considerans, porrigere preces Discretioni Uestre dignum duxi, vt,
110   divine pietatis intuitu, et precum mearum interuentu, ei locum
inter consimiles in aliquo misochomio uestris intercessionibus
inpetretis. Fuit enim honeste conuersacionis clericus; "nec,"
ut dicit Seneca, "quisquam prudens sapienciam paupertate

You who write, take material equal to your talents, and consider at length what your shoulders can bear and what they will refuse; neither facility nor lucid order will desert the man who chooses a subject within his power. (38-41)

The explanation of these lines will appear later (cf. *2*, passim). First, therefore, let us treat of the art of invention, before the other parts I mentioned.

On the Art of Inventing and What Invention Means. To invent is to come into knowledge of an unknown thing through the agency of one's own reason. Here is what Cicero says in the *Second Rhetoric:* "Invention is thinking up things that are true or at least realistic to make your case plausible" (*RAH* 1.2.3.).

On Its Species. Under invention there are five species: where, what, what kind, how, and why.

The First Species: Where to Invent. "Where" has three sources: character, examples, and etymologies of words and the explanations that go with them. Here is an example, on the subject of hearing requests favorably.

> To that venerable man, blooming with virtues, Master S., Archdeacon of Canterbury; Master John of Garland: greeting, and submission of sincere love and the deepest affection.

> It belongs to the straight path of righteousness for friends to listen to righteous petitions. Since God, merciful in the highest degree and the true Lover of men, "scourges every son whom He receives" (Heb. 12:6), sweet are the scourges of so devoted a Father, Whose hand has touched A., the bearer of this letter, whom He makes infirm in order that he might rest in health with Him, whom He deforms in body in order to reform him for Himself in soul, whom He humbles on earth, as we piously believe, that he might lay claim to an exalted place in heaven. For in the weakness of the aforesaid man the hand of the Most High has displayed a mirror of terror and castigation—a mirror in which it is plain that the lily of youth is soon unlilied, that in a short time the little flower of worth is deflowered, that things whose constant boast is firmness are tottering, and that the glory by which the world deceives its spectators turns to nothing. And so, turning all this over in my mind, I have resolved to extend prayers to Your Discretion, hoping that, in consideration of the divine goodness and by the intervention of my prayers, you might obtain a place for him among his fellows in some leper hospital by your intercession. For he has been a cleric of honest dealings; and, as Seneca says, "no prudent man will ever condemn wisdom on account of poverty, for the lover

dampnabit, sed amplas opes philosophus possidebit." Qua-
115   propter preces meas clemencie uestre dulcedo ducat ad effectum quam cito poteritis, ut lator presençium illud dictum
Senece collaudet: "Vita beata est securitas et perpetua tranquilitas," Vos etiam, si uobis placuerit, illud Tullianum in libro De
Amicicia mecum attendatis: "Hec prima lex amicicie sanxitur,
120   ut ab amicis honesta petamus, amicorum causa honesta facia-
mus, nec ad rogationes exaudiendas nimium expectemus."

In hoc iam dicto dictamine inuenitur materia et qualitas carminis
a persona infirmi et a personis amicorum.
Tria Genera Personarum et Tria Genera Hominum. Tria genera
125   personarum hic debent considerari secundum tria genera hominum, que sunt curiales, ciuiles, rurales. Curiales sunt qui curiam
tenent ac celebrant, ut Dominus Papa, cardinales, legati, archiepiscopi, episcopi, et eorum suffraganei, sicut archidiaconi, decani, officiales, magistri, scolares. Item, imperatores, reges,
130   marchiones, et duces. Ciuiles persone sunt consul, prepositus, et
cetere persone in ciuitate habitantes. Rurales sunt rura colentes,
sicut uenatores, agricole, uinitores, aucupes. Secundum ista tria
genera hominum inuenit Uirgilius stilum triplicem de* quo
postea docebitur.
135   *Secunda Species: Quid inuenitur.* Per hoc quod dicitur* "quid"
notatur quid sit inueniendum; in litteris precipue et in negotiis
secularibus, ista scilicet: seditiones, homicidia, bella, furta,
rapine; simonie, donationes, amicicie, peticiones, et gesta ec-
clesiasticarum personarum.
140   *Subdiuisio: Quid Inueniatur* in* Personis.* Contingit quid
inuenire in personis, in exemplis, in ethimologiis. In personis
duo, ut in regibus: bene regnum regere, vel regnum tirannide
dilacerare; in prelatis: diuine contemplationi insistere, uel negociis secularibus ociari; in ciuilibus: urbis negocia tractare, rem
145   publicam augere uel dissipare; in ruralibus, contingit circa ruralia
desudare uel cessare.
In Exemplis Quid Inueniatur.* Qvid inueniatur in exemplis
consideremus. Exemplum est dictum uel factum alicuius
autentice persone imitatione dignum. Vnde ibi inueniuntur dicta
150   et facta, auctoritates, et prouerbia. Sed si non habeamus prouerbium, vtendum est hoc artificio.
Ars Inueniendi Prouerbia. Consideremus laudem uel uituperium in persona mittentis, et in persona recipientis, in ipso

of wisdom has riches enough" (cf. *De Vita Beata* 13.1). And so, may
the sweetness of your clemency bring my prayers to fruition as soon as
you can, that the bearer of this letter may do homage to that saying
of Seneca's, "A blessed life is security and perpetual tranquillity."
And please consider with me also that saying of Cicero's in the book
On Friendship (cf. 44); "the first and sacred law of friendship is that
from our friends we ask only for what is right, for the sake of friends
we do what is right ourselves, and we do not expect too much in the
way of getting requests granted."

In this letter the subject matter and style are invented from the character
of a sick man and from the characters of friends.

Three Kinds of Characters and the Three Types of Men. Three kinds of
characters ought to be considered here, according to the three types of
men, which are courtiers, city dwellers, and peasants. Courtiers are those
who dwell in or frequent courts, such as the Holy Father, cardinals,
legates, archbishops, bishops, and their subordinates, such as archdeacons, deans, officials, masters, scholars; also emperors, kings, marquises,
and dukes. City dwellers are count, provost, and the whole range of
people who live in the city. Peasants are those who live in the country,
such as hunters, farmers, vine dressers, fowlers. According to these three
types of men, Virgil invented a triple style, which will be dealt with
later.

The Second Species: What Is Invented. By the word "what" is meant
what is to be invented; in practical affairs, and letters in particular, it
means such things as seditions, murders, wars, thefts, plunderings,
simonies, presentations, friendships, petitions, and the activities of ecclesiastical personages.

Subdivision: What may be Invented as to Persons. What to invent pertains to persons, examples, and etymologies. With persons there is always a pair of alternatives; as with kings: to rule the kingdom well, or
to tear the kingdom to pieces like a tyrant; with prelates: to pursue
divine contemplation, or to idle about in secular affairs; with city
dwellers: to carry on the business of the city, to strengthen the republic,
or to squander it; with peasants, it means sweating over rural duties, or
giving up.

What Is Invented in Examples. Let us consider what is invented in examples. An example is a saying or deed of some authoritative person
that is worthy of imitation. Here, then, are invented sayings and deeds,
authorities, and proverbs. But if no proverb is available to us, we should
employ the following device.

On the Art of Inventing Proverbs. We should consider whether we wish
to praise or blame, the character of the sender, the character of the

negocio, et ita ex tribus duplici ratione, scilicet laudis uel uitu-
155   perii, honesti uel inhonesti, poterimus prouerbia comparare
ponendo similitudines et comparationes, quod dilucidabitur in
sequenti.
Descriptio Prouerbii. Prouerbium est sententia breuis ad instructionem dicta, comodum uel incomodum grandis materie
160   manifestans.
Incipiunt Prouerbia. Prouerbia quedam* sumuntur* a naturali-
bus rebus, vt quando assumuntur similitudines ab herbis, a lapidi-
bus, ab animatis, ab inanimatis rebus. Quedam prouerbia sumuntur
a moralibus, quando uersus et auctorum sententie proponuntur,
165   ut "Imperat aut seruit collecta pecunia cuique." A rationali
philosophia sumitur raro* prouerbium, sed thema frequenter, ut
"Omne quod est rotundum est uolubile"; "Quodlibet totum est
maius sua parte." Possunt prouerbia inueniri a laude, a uituperio,
a similitudine, a negocio rei, a personis ipsis, ut patebit hic.
170   *A Persona Mittentis. Quando petitur consilium.* In rebus ambiguis
consilium solet a prudentibus emanare.
A* Persona Cui Mittitur. Quando reprehenditur sacerdos. Fermenti modicum in sacerdote per exemplum defluit in subiectos.
A* Negotio. De inpedimento. Qvi uotum impedit honestum
175   reus efficitur et contrarius honestati.
A* Laude vel a Uituperio. De communi dampno. Commune
dampnum tangere debet amicos qui mutuo se tenentur sub
aduersitatis honere* supportare.
A* Similitudine. De corruptione mentis. Radix uiciosa contagium
180   transcribit in surculum, et* mentis uicium multociens contagiat
superficiem corporalem.
Ad amicos separatos. Frequens nunciorum* legatio reconsiliat
absentes, qui per interuenientes nuncios colloquuntur.
Principale nomen et uerbum ipsius prouerbii ponatur in narra-
185   tione. Et notandum quod per hanc particulam "cum" prouerbium erit de substantia narrationis cum huiusmodi mediis: "non
est admirandum," "sequitur," "patet," "iustum est," et similia,
verbi gratia: "Cum legacio uestra me uobis reconsiliet, patet
quod uestris absencia mea colloquiis confortatur."
190   *Ad artificem alicuius operis.* Est apud Deum et hominem
lucrosum quociens probatus artifex conatur fideliter operari.
Quando petitur auxilium* contra inimicos. Ab infortunio vix
aut numquam sibi poterit precauere qui multis circumuallatur
latentibus inimicis.

recipient, and the matter at issue; then, by applying to each of these
three the double criterion, that is, praise or blame, right or wrong, we
should be able to furnish ourselves with proverbs by putting in similitudes and comparisons. What follows will make this clearer.

Definition of a Proverb. A proverb is a brief statement, moral in purpose,
setting forth what is good or what is bad in an important matter.

Proverbs. Some proverbs are taken from natural things, as when similitudes are drawn from plants, stones, animate or inanimate things. Other
proverbs are taken from moral truths, when verses or aphorisms are cited
from classical authors, as, "A man is either the slave or the master of his
money" (Horace *Ep.* 1.10.47). Proverbs are seldom taken from rational
philosophy, but axioms often, as "Everything that is round can spin";
"Any whole is greater than its part." Proverbs can be invented from
praise, from blame, from similitude, from the nature of the subject at
issue, and from the character of the persons involved, as will be plain in
the following.

From the Character of the Sender. When counsel is sought. In doubtful
matters good advice usually emanates from the prudent.

From the Character of the Recipient. When a priest is being reprimanded.
The slightest agitation on the part of a priest finds its way to his people,
who follow his example.

From the Nature of the Subject. On obstruction. He who blocks a righteous vow incurs guilt, and takes sides against righteousness.

From Praise or Blame. On sharing adversity. Friends who commit themselves to mutual support in adversity should share it when it comes.

From Similitude. On mental corruption. A defective root transfers
disease to the sprout, and vice in the mind frequently infects the body
without.

For separated friends. Frequent sending of messengers unites those who
are away from each other, for they converse through the messengers going between them.

The principal noun and verb of the proverb are put in the narration;
and note that the proverb may be incorporated in the narration by using
the particle "since" in conjunction with phrases of this sort: "no wonder," "it follows," "it is plain," "it is right," and the like, for example:
"Since your sending unites me to you, it is plain that my absence is
comforted by your conversation."

For the artificer of any work. Both God and man are the gainers whenever a master craftsman sets faithfully to work.

When aid is sought against enemies. The man who is surrounded by
many hidden enemies will rarely or never be able to guard himself in advance against misfortunes.

195   *Ad redarguendum aliquem.* Compaciuntur membra capiti quo-
       cienscumque passio caput satagit molestare.
       De conuiuio. Leti uultus et festiuitas mense fecunde solent
       conuiuas* in leticiam suscitare.
       De pastore qui reprehenditur. De pastor criminis irretit uinculo,
200   se spontaneus inescat oprobrio, qui deuiantem ouem ad uiam
       ab inuio non reducit.
       Ad scolares. Qvi gloriam et amicorum delectabilem copiam
       desiderat, artis regulis et ratione prudencium muniatur.
       De amonicione. Qvi nouit* uires suas metiri nihil agreditur quod
205   eum cogat pudenter a proposito uestigia reuocare.
       Ad persuadendum. Qvando plantula caret radicibus et irriguo,
       marcorem induit et inutilis extirpatur.
       De paciencia. Qvicumque potest tolerare aduersa, uirtus illum
       paciencie coronabit.
210   *Ad parentes.** Columpnis subtractis tota moles corruit machina-
       lis.
       Ad matrem.* Cvm materna dilectio dilectioni cuiuslibet prefera-
       tur, materne dilectionis operacio preferri debet operibus aliorum.
       Ad petendum aliquid. Qvanto quis propinquior est naturali gradu
215   sanguinis, tanto magis consanguineo conferre beneficium obliga-
       tur.
       Ad recte iudicandum.* Cvm leges ad hoc inuente fuerint ut secun-
       dum illas recte iudicetur, prelati maxime debent in legibus premi-
       nere.
220   *Ad discordes.* Sicut est frigidum saniei repressiuum et calidum
       dissolutiuum, sic odium et amor contrarium operantur.
       Infimus petens auxilium a superiori.* Ouina simplicitas metuens
       lupum balando petit opem supliciter pastoralem.
       De aliquo qui intendit legere. Quo quisquam sapiencie salsamenta
225   studiosius optat condire, degustata magis illum alliciunt condi-
       menta.
       De castigacione. Meretricis labia fauum distillant, sed absinthium
       eius nouissima subministrant.
       Ad auxilium maternum. Pater adamantem gerit in pectore qui
230   nati sui precibus aures possidet induratas.
       Dominus seruo. Seruilis naufragatur sedulitas ubi languens* in
       torporem dormitat mentis oculus et cessat circumspectio uigilare.
       De vsuris. Vix repperitur maior captiuitas uel carcer angustior
       quam Iudeorum grauedine uel feneratorum pro reddenda
235   pecunia choartari.
       Ad castigationem. Cham pudenda patris deridendo meruit male-
       dici.

For refuting someone. When suffering is busy molesting the head, the members suffer along with it.

Of a banquet. Happy faces and the festivity of an abundant table have a way of rousing guests to cheerfulness.

Reprimanding a pastor. When a shepherd does not lead back a wandering sheep from the wilderness to the straight path, he entangles himself in the chains of crime, and involves himself voluntarily in opprobrium.

To students. He who desires glory and delights in many friends should fortify himself with the rules of art and the teachings of prudent men.

Admonition. The man who knows the limits of his ability will enter on nothing that may force him to draw back his footsteps in shame from what he set out to do.

For persuading. When a young plant lacks roots and moisture, it begins to wither and, useless, is pulled up.

On patience. The virtue of patience will crown the man who can tolerate adversity.

To parents. Remove the uprights and the entire structure collapses.

To a mother. Since a mother's love is preferred to the love of anyone else, the deeds that stem from a mother's love ought to be preferred to the deeds of others.

For a petition. The nearer a man is in blood, the more he is obliged to do his relative a favor.

For judging rightly. Since laws were invented as a standard for right judgment, prelates have a special obligation to excel in the laws.

For discordants. As cold tends to coagulate discharged blood and heat to dissolve it, so hate and love work contrary effects.

A man of low estate seeking help from a superior. The simplicity of the sheep, fearing the wolf, humbly seeks the shepherd's aid by bleating.

Of anyone who intends to take a scholastic course. The more eagerly anyone wishes to spice the sauces of wisdom, the more will the spices, once tasted, entice him.

Chastisement. The lips of a whore drop honey, but her depths give wormwood (cf. Prov. 5:2-4).

For maternal aid. The father who has hardened ears for his son's prayers is turning his heart to stone.

A master to his servant. A servant's zeal is shipwrecked when his mind's eye slips into drowsiness and dozes, and his circumspection can stay awake no longer.

Of usury. A greater captivity, or a tighter prison, than the pressure of Jews and usurers to return money is scarcely to be found.

For chastisement. Ham deserved to be cursed for making fun of his father's private parts (cf. Gen. 9:18-27).

Ad memoriam. Cvm quisquam ab oculis corporis submouetur, a*
mentis frequenter oculis elongatur.

240 *De dilectione.* Licet localis distantia amicum submouerit ab
amico, dilectio tamen mentis occulo presentatur.
Ad separandum hereticos a fidelibus. Separari debet triticum ab
inani palea, et* infideles digni sunt a communione fidelium separari.

245 *De infidelibus.* Si basis edificii uacillet, nutanti machine quam
cicius erit necessarium subuenire.
Ad religiosos. Cvm in materiali milicia diligatur corona, pocius
in agone spirituali desideratur laurea triumphalis.
De parcitate contra magistrum. Discipulorum parcitas meretur

250 inuenire magistralis scientie parcitatem.
De luxuria. Qvi luxuriam amplectitur veneno dulcedinis in-
quinatur.
De consilio. Viri prudentes nihil aggrediuntur quod non ad
metam felici termino deducatur.

255 *Ad perseuerenciam.* Qvi fessus heret in operis primo limine non
solum incurrit populi cachinnum, sed famam obfuscat et perdit
premia meritorum.
*De improuidorum derisione.** Inprudentes et idiote despiciunt
cum derisione uiros de futuro* pronostica speculantes.

260 *De misericordia.* Qvam diu Stella Maris prerogatiuam decoris
super omnia post Deum optinebit, rigori iusticie dulcedo miseri-
cordie preminebit.
De iudicibus. Svb ambiguitatis perpendiculo iudex discretus
determinare dubitabilia non presumit.

265 *De illo qui multa promittit et pauca dat.* Crebrescit in eius
oprobrium infamia* qui magnificus in uerbis, in* factis pusil-
lanimis reperitur.
De obliuione. Qvem sera porte clause longe remouet a domo,
constat quod frequenter ab amicorum oculis mentalibus

270 absentatur.
De iniquo possessore. Iuri derogat qui presumit aliena contra
iuris debitum possidere.
Ad castigandum illos qui sustinent suos in clericos seuire.*
Diadematis honorem conculcat, legibus contradicit, nature

275 derogat priuilegio, qui laicalem permittit manum in personas
ecclesie deseuire.*
De rusticitate. Rvsticitatis nodi inamabiles insiti naturaliter
nequeunt amputari.

For memory. When someone is removed from the eyes of the body, he is often withdrawn from the eyes of the mind.

Of love. Although distance removes friend from friend, love is still present to the mind's eye.

For the separation of heretics from the faithful. Wheat should be separated from empty chaff, and infidels deserve to be separated from communion with the faithful.

Of infidels. If the foundation of a building shifts, it will be necessary to repair the shaky structure as soon as possible.

To religious. Since in worldly warfare a crown is prized, all the more in the spiritual battle is the laurel of victory to be desired.

On stinginess toward a teacher. Stinginess on the part of students deserves to meet with a stinginess of the teacher's knowledge.

On lechery. He who embraces lechery is corrupted by the deadly drug of sweetness.

On counsel. Prudent men undertake nothing that may not be brought to the goal in a happy ending.

For perseverance. The man who tires and hangs back at the starting line of his task not only draws the hoots of the crowd, but darkens his good name and forfeits the prizes that go to those who excel.

On the laughter of the improvident. Fools and idiots look down with laughter on men who keep an eye to signs of the future.

On mercy. As long as the Star of the Sea retains her prerogative of being honored above all things except God, the sweetness of mercy will surpass the rigor of justice.

Of judges. The discreet judge does not presume to make an exact determination in dubious matters by dropping a perpendicular that may itself be ambiguous.

Of one who promises much and gives little. Infamy is piled onto opprobrium for the man who is found to be magnificent in words and puny in deeds.

On oblivion. It happens frequently that a man whom the bar of a closed door drives far from his home is dismissed from the mental eye of his friends.

Of a wrongful possessor. A man who presumes to possess others' things, against what he owes in justice, disrupts justice itself.

For chastising those who allow their subjects to rage against the clergy. A ruler who permits the lay arm to rage against persons of the Church tramples on the honor of his crown, flouts the laws, and dishonors nature in favor of privilege.

On country manners. Naturally implanted knots of country manners, though they may be unlovely, cannot be cut off.

De eodem. Item quod insitum est* a natura potest mitigari, non
280   tamen penitus exstirpari.
De papelardis. Frontis nulla fides cum de mente laruata facies
menciatur.
De religiosis. Frequens auri decoctio contagium auri comprobat,
et uitam iusti separat tribulatio frequens a scoria uiciorum.
285   *De exaltatione rustici.* Si rusticus extollatur, claros genere conculcat et moribus perspicuos aspernatur.
De magistro qui insufficiens cathedram magistralem tenet. *
Dignus est Cheruli derisione qui presumit artis regulas edocere,
quas in docendo cernitur ignorare.
290   *De duricia materna.* Mater Medeam induit, proprios occidentem
filios, que filium in honestis permittit studiis indigere.
De castigacione. Facilis est ad uicia descensus, et ascensus difficilis ad uirtutes.
De auxilio. Patrocinium inplorat ecclesie quem inimicus expugnat
295   qui iura presumit ecclesiastica conculcare.
Ad cyrographum. Scripti testimonio committitur humanum
negocium, ne mordaci lima temporis corrodatur.
De amore. Sensibile peremptum perimit sensum, sed non conuertitur;* sic ego te subsequens et a te dependens sine te uiuere
300   non ualebo.
De cismaticis. Virtus se diligit et aspernatur contraria; secundum
hoc non habet iustus conuenienciam cum iniusto.
De iuditio per simile. Oportet Catelinam homicidam necari, cum
ei similis Graccus fuerit interemptus.
305   *Inuitatio ad uirtutem.* Firmamenti motus, soli contrarius, regirat
secum eundem; sic sensualitas debet subcumbere rationi.
Ad reuocandum aliquem a facultate in qua diu studuit. Si vita
breuis et ars longa, tempus acutum et experimentum fallax,
oportunum est quod est sanum anime sicut corpori iudicare.
310   *Quid Inuenitur in Ethimologiis.* In ethimologiis locum habemus
inueniendi, ut, si aliquis intendat laudare Dominum Papam,
dicat: "Vere dominus papa piissimus pater; dicitur 'pater patrum,'
quod ipsius nominis ethimologica exposicio manifestat, et dicitur
a 'pape' grece quod est 'admirabile' latine. Vnde 'papa' 'sacerdos
315   admirabilis,' quod in eo ex prerogatiua uite et scientie declaratur."
"Quale" * est Tertia Species. "Qvale" ponit qualitatem

On the same. Or, what is implanted by nature can be cut short, but cannot be utterly uprooted.

On hypocrites. There is no trusting appearances when masked faces encourage false recognition.

On religious. Frequent boiling down of gold isolates the impurities in the gold, and frequent tribulation separates the life of the just man from the slag of his vices.

On the rise of a peasant. A peasant who has made good steps on the toes of the nobly born and despises people whose good breeding is evident.

On an unqualified teacher who holds a teacher's chair. Anyone who presumes to teach the rules of art, when it is clear by his teaching that he knows nothing about them, deserves to be laughed at like Choerilus.

On a mother's cruelty. The mother who lets her son carry on his honest studies in penury is taking the part of Medea, who killed her own children.

For chastising. The downward path to vice is easy, the ascent to virtue hard.

On assistance. The man who presumes to trample on ecclesiastical rights is imploring the protection of a church which he has assaulted as an enemy.

For an Indenture. Human transactions are committed to the testimony of writing, lest they be worn away by the gnawing file of time.

Of love. Cutting off the object of one's feeling hinders the feeling, but it is not altered; thus I tag after you, and hang on you, and cannot live without you.

Of schismatics. Virtue loves itself and spurns its opposites; accordingly, the just man has no traffic with the unjust man.

On sentencing from precedent. Catiline the murderer must be put to death, since Gracchus was executed for the same crime (cf. Cicero *I Catiline* 1.3).

Invitation to virtue. The motion of the firmament carries the sun with it in its revolution, even though the sun's own movement is in the opposite direction; so should sensuality submit to reason.

For recalling someone from a faculty in which he has long studied. If life is short and art long, time acute and experiment fallacious, it is time to decide what is healthy for the soul as well as for the body.

What Is Invented in Etymologies. In etymologies we have a topic of invention; for example, if someone means to praise my lord the Pope, he may say, "Truly my lord the Pope is the most holy father: the word means 'father of fathers,' as its etymology shows, for it comes from *pape* in Greek, which is *admirabilis* in Latin. Whence 'Pope' means 'admirable priest,' which his preeminence in life and knowledge declares."

"What Kind" Is the Third Species. "What kind" raises the question of

materie inueniende; quia, sicut dicit Tullius, "Est genus cause
honestum et turpe"; sic est materia honesta et materia turpis.
In materia honesta utendum* est sentenciis planis et uerbis
320   materiam declarantibus. In turpi materia, si velimus latere,
vtendum est insinuacione, sicut dicit Tullius, qua* propositum
quibusdam tangimus circumlocutionibus quibus manifestari non
poterit turpitudo. Ut, si sacerdos accuset uel uituperet adulte-
ram, dicat: "Mulier mollis alienum subintrat cubiculum et
325   cotidianis nupciis delectatur." Si laudet aliquem, dicat: "Castitate uoluntaria Sabinas rigidas imitatur."
       *Ad Quid Inuenitur.** Qvia dicitur in premissis "ad quid," at-
tendendum est quod per hoc denotatur finis inuentoris, scilicet
[vtilitas et honestas;] et licet intendat accusare vel dampnare,
330   secundum se finis bonus* est.
       Quinta Species. Que Diuiditur in vij Species et Partes. Ad hoc
quod dicitur "qualiter" notandi sunt vij colores quibus adorna-
tur et* ampliatur materia, qui sunt: Annominatio, Traductio,
Repeticio, Gradatio, Interpretatio, Diffinicio, Sermocinatio.
335   Annominatio ponit litteras et sillabas consimiles in principio
et in medio, ut Virgilius in Georgicis:

> A̅uia tunc resonant* ăuibus uirgulta canoris.

Si consideretur Correpcio, erit in hoc exemplo alia species
Annominationis, que habet speciem vnam in Correptione et
340   Productione.
       Traductio dicetur quando uidelicet vna dictio traducitur de
casu in casum cum frequencia, ut in Stacio Tebaydos;

> vmbone repellitur* umbo,
> Ense minax ensis, pede pes, et cuspide cuspis.

345   De speciebus Traductionis* postea dicetur.
       Repeticio est in principio dictionis, ut in Ouidio Fastorum:

> Sic sedit, sic culta fuit, sic stamina neuit,
> Iniecte collo sic iacuere come.

       Gradatio repetit eandem dictionem, si est nomen, mediate uel
350   inmediate, uel uerbum conuersum in participium. Mediate repetitur eadem dictio, ut hic:

the quality of the subject matter invented; for, as Cicero says, "There are two kinds of causes, honorable and disreputable" (cf. *RAH* 1.3.5); thus there is honorable subject matter and disreputable subject matter. In honorable subject matter use plain sentences and words that put the case in the open. Disguising disreputable subject matter calls for subtlety, as Cicero says (cf. *RAH* 1.4.6). That means touching on the issue with various circumlocutions, which will keep the disreputable subject from showing through. For example, if a priest should accuse or blame an adulteress, he might say, "This tender woman enters a strange bed and has the pleasure of daily nuptials" (cf. *RAH* 4.34.45). But in praise of a woman, he might say, "In voluntary chastity she imitates the rigid Sabines" (cf. Juvenal 10.299).

To What End One Invents. Since "to what end" is mentioned above, let us notice in passing that this denotes the inventor's purpose, which is of course to promote what is both useful and right, and even though he intends to accuse or condemn, that purpose is still good in itself.

The Fifth Species, Which Is Divided into Seven Subspecies and Parts. In considering the meaning of "how," we should note seven figures by which the subject matter is embellished and amplified. They are: Paronomasia, Transplacement, Repetition, Climax, Synonymy, Definition, and Dialogue.

Paronomasia is the use of words with similar letters and syllables, both in the beginning and in the middle, as in Virgil's *Georgics:*

Then the burred groves resound with singing birds. (2.328)

If we take into account the Shortening of Quantity, this example also displays another species of Paronomasia; for Shortening and Lengthening of Quantity is a subspecies of that figure.

Transplacement is the name for the figure in which a word is transferred from one case to another repeatedly, as in Statius's *Thebaid:*

Shield is driven back by shield, threatening sword by sword, foot by foot, and spear by spear. (8.398-99)

The various species of Transplacement will be discussed later on (cf. 6, 83 ff.; 7, 878 ff.).

Repetition takes place in the beginning of a phrase, as in Ovid's *Fasti:*

Thus she sat, thus she was dressed, thus she spun the yarn, thus her curls lay thrown about her neck. (2.771-72)

Climax is the repetition, with or without something intervening, of the same word, if it is a noun, or if it is a verb, of its participial form. Here the same word is repeated with something intervening:

Tres tribus urgentur: uir, serpens, femina; uictu
Vir, serpens aluo, femina prole sua.

(Hoc exemplum sumptum est ab Epytalamico Beate Uirginis.)
355 Participium repetitur immediate, ut in Ouidio Methamorfosios:

viscera traxit,
Tractaque calcauit, calcataque rupit, et illis
Crura quoque impediit.

Interpretatio est in isto epithafio:

360   Petrus eram, quem petra tegit; dictusque Comestor
Nunc* comedor, etc.

Interpretatio aliter sumitur inferius quando idem per aliud
uerbum dicitur; sic* accipitur hic.
Diffinicionis exemplum est in Lucano:

365   neque enim ista uocari
Prelia iure decet, patrie sed uindicis iram.

Sermocinacio ponit status et dignitates et officia et proprietates
personarum, ut in libro Methamorphosios:

"Aspice," ait, "Perseu, nostre primordia gentis," etc.

370   (Notandum igitur quod qui mittit litteras debet dignitates suas
et nomen officii sui proprio nomini supponere, sine prescripcione.
Sed cum aliquis scripserit alii, preponenda est prescriptio, ut:
"Illustrissimo Regi," "Sanctissimo Patri ac Domino," "Venerabili Sacerdoti," "Piissimo Pastori." Et notandum est quod epi-
375   scopi et archiepiscopi uocant se "Fratres"; Dominus uero Papa
vnicam habet formam scribendi fere omnibus, et eos quibus mittit vocat "Dilectos Filios." Speciale nomen tamen attribuit* Regi
Francorum, dicens: "Dilecto Filio, Uiro Catholico." Notarius
Domini Imperatoris dicit: "Fredericus, Dei Gratia Romanorum
380   Imperator et Semper Augustus, etc.")
De Arte Inueniendi Nomina Sustantiua. Sequitur de arte inueniendi nomina substantiua et adiectiua et uerba, habita et excogitata materia. Excogitanda sunt omnia nomina illa que pertinent
ad talem materiam; ut, si materia sit de pastore, excogitanda* sunt
385   huiusmodi nomina: pascua, grex, ouis, aries, lupus; que possumus
facere exemplo Uurgilii, dicentis de epytaphio Iulii Cesaris:

Daphnis ego in siluis, hinc usque ad sidera notus,
Formosi pecoris custos, formosior ipse.

The three are burdened by three things: the man, the serpent, the woman; the man by his bread, the serpent by its belly, woman by her children.

(This example was taken from the *Epithalamium of the Blessed Virgin.*) In the following example from Ovid's *Metamorphoses,* a participle is repeated with nothing intervening:

He dragged his entrails, what he was dragging he trod on, what he was treading on he burst, and tangled his legs in them. (12.390-92)

Synonymy occurs in this epitaph:

Peter I was, now I am petrifying; and called Eater, now I am eaten.

Other forms of Synonymy, in which the same thing is expressed by a different word, are taken up later on (cf. *4,* 410 ff.; *6,* 244 ff.); this form will serve for now.

An example of Definition occurs in Lucan:

For it is not enough to call these righteous battles, but the wrath of the avenger of the fatherland. (2.539-40)

Dialogue dramatizes the social position, rank, office, and personal characteristics of people, as in the *Metamorphoses:*

"See, Perseus," he said, "the origins of my family," etc. (5.190)

(Note, in this regard, that the sender of a letter ought to write his rank and the title of his office after his own name, without any honorific adjectives. But the writer should always precede the recipient's name with an honorific, as "To the Most Illustrious King," "To the Most Holy Father and Lord," "To the Venerable Priest," "To the Most Pious Pastor." And it should be noted further that bishops and archbishops call each other "Brother"; but the Holy Father has a single form of writing for almost everybody, calling his correspondents "Beloved Sons." However, he grants a special title to the king of France saying, "Beloved Son and Catholic Man." My Lord the emperor's secretary writes: "Frederick, by the Grace of God emperor of the Romans and ever Augustus, etc.")

On the Art of Inventing Nouns. The next subject is the art of inventing nouns and adjectives and verbs, after the subject matter is firmly in mind. A list should be made up of all the nouns that pertain to that subject; for example, if the subject is a shepherd, make up a list of nouns like these: pasture, flock, sheep, ram, wolf. We can do this by following the example of Virgil, when he speaks an epitaph for Julius Caesar:

I am Daphnis the woodsman, known from here to the stars; the guardian of a lovely herd, myself more lovely than they. (*Buc.* 5.43-44)

Quia Uirgilius posuit hic nomen pastoris, scilicet Daphnis, dicit
390   "formosi pecoris" et cetera. Eodem modo contingit inuenire de
Saluatore Incarnato:

> Ex oue procedit pastor, procedit ab agna
> Dux aries, agnum mistica lana p m it.

Sic patet que sunt cognata uerba et propria materie. Verba
395   cognata materie sumuntur in exemplo subsequenti, quod est
carmen elegiacum, amabeum, bucolicum. Elegiacum quia de
miseria contexitur amoris; amabeum quia representat proprietates amantum; bucolicum *apo toy bucolou,* idest ab hoc nomine *bucolon* quod est "custodia boum." Vnde, secundum ordi-
400   nem quem seruat Uirgilius, hoc carmen debet esse primum, quia
in eo obseruatur humilis stilus, quem sequitur mediocris et
grauis. Est autem materia uersuum quomodo iuuenis oppressit
nimpham, cuius amicus erat Coridon. Per nimpham significatur
caro; per iuuenem corruptorem, mundus uel diabolus; per
405   proprium amicum, ratio. Dicitur ergo sub persona mundi sic:

Carmen Elegiacum, Amabeum, Bucolicum, Ethicum. *

Cvm citharizat auis siluis dulcedine quauis,
     Que requiem donant organa uerna sonant;
Vestem pingit humus, renouat sua tegmina dumus;
410   Ponit utrumque genus sub pede blanda Uenus;
Laxat humum Phebus radiis, Nestor fit ephebus;
     Flos rupto leuiter cortice querit iter.
Phillis oues pauit, sub fago se recreauit,
     Ducens fila colo sola uirente solo,
415   Et breuiter tacta decantat Daphnidis* acta:
     Quam bene sub legem traxerit ipse gregem;
Daphnin* predones canit illa fugasse leones.
     Sim licet in laqueo, liber amator eo.

"Daphmidis est* natus uicto gregis hoste probatus
420   Dignus laudari, dignus amore pari:
Hic implet mundum uiuaci laude rotundum.
     Par facie matri, parque uigore patri,
In corpus, mentem, sortitur utrumque* parentem,
     Flos presens iuuenum, gemma futura senum."
425   Dum sic gratatur pastoria, sicque iocatur,
     Candoris niuei mulceo pectus ei;
Spondeo dum dona, sibi carum fert Coridona.
     Illam sum* reprimens, nil Coridona timens;
Emulus ecce uenit, Coridon, quem fistula lenit:
430   Sim licet in laqueo, liber amator eo.

Occurritque uidens nos nexos denteque stridens,
     Hanc trahit ad foueam, sed cadit hic in eam.

Since Virgil here has used a shepherd's name, that is, Daphnis, he says "lovely herd" and so on. It is possible to invent similarly of the Incarnate Savior:

> From the sheep proceeds the shepherd, proceeds the leader ram from the young ewe; the mystical fleece brings forth the lamb. (*EBV* 7.261-62)

Thus it is plain what "cognate words" and "words appropriate to the subject" are. Words cognate to the subject are drawn on for the following example, which is an elegiac, amoebaean, bucolic poem. Elegiac because it is woven of the tragedy of love; amoebaean because it represents the characteristics of lovers; bucolic, *apo tou boucolou,* that is, from the noun *boucolon,* which is "cowherding." Whence, according to the order that Virgil holds to, this poem is rightly the first poem in the book, because it keeps to the low style, which comes before the middle and high styles. The subject matter of the verses is how a youth ruined a nymph whose beloved had been Corydon. The nymph signifies the Flesh, the young seducer the World or the Devil, the beloved Reason. The speaker of the poem is the World, who says:

An Elegiac, Amoebaean, Bucolic, Moral Poem.

> When the bird in the woods strikes his lute in his sweet way, Spring's whole rest-giving orchestra takes up the sound; the earth embellishes its clothing, the thornbush renews its vesture; Venus brings both sexes under her charming foot; Phoebus loosens the earth with his rays, an old man become a young one; the flower gently bursts its shell and bends toward the road. Phyllis drives her sheep, and is now relaxing beneath a beech, alone on the lush ground spinning threads from her distaff, and she sings a short song about Daphnis's exploits, how well he drew his flock under the law. She sings that Daphnis used to put to flight robbers and lions. Though I be in the trap, I go about a free lover.
>
> "The enemy of Daphnis's flock is conquered, and the son is proven worthy of praise, and just as worthy of love; he fills the round world with praise that will never die. His mother's equal in beauty, his father's in inner vigor, he draws on each parent for his body and mind, the present flower of youths, the future gem of the old." While thus the shepherdess enjoys herself, thus she takes her pleasure, I am stroking her snow-white breast. While I am promising gifts, she still holds her Corydon dear. I am pressing her, never fearing Corydon at all, when, behold, my rival comes—Corydon, soothing himself with his pipe. Though I be in the trap, I go about a free lover.
>
> And he runs up, seeing us embracing, and, gnashing his teeth, he drags her to a pit—but he falls in himself. She pushed him in an

Hunc rea detrusit, sic clamans libera lusit:
"Hic, Coridon, iaceas; hinc nec abire queas.
435 Non te mundabo, non te de sorde levabo.*
Ludere nos iuuenes ne* prohibete, senes!
Istos per colles cum mecum ludere nolles,
Lusorem tenui rusticitate tui."
Sic ait: "O Philli, colludas, depprecor, illi;
440 Dos ualet ascribi pellis ouina tibi;
Non solam pellem sed oues tibi tradere uellem."
Sim licet in laqueo, liber amator eo.

Phillis ait clare: "Sequar hunc qui nouit amare,
Nec solet in ludis dulcibus esse rudis.
445 Est iuuenis letus, saliens, probus, et requietus;
Est Coridon uilis tegmine, pelle, pilis.
Huius amor floris nectar distillat amoris;
Hic rudis ignauus, dulcis at ille fauus."
Tu mecum, Phillis, solita es lucisse lapillis;
450 Frondoso thalamo Phillida tectus amo.
Sic uir amo quod amor, ergo non hamo nec hamor;
Hamo sic hamor quem mihi tendit amor.
Dum spirat uita me, Phillis, linquere uita.
Sim licet in laqueo, liber amator eo.

455 Sic Caro mechatur, Ratio dum subpeditatur;
Est Mundus mechus, Carnis inane decus.

De Arte Inueniendi Adiectiua. Sequitur de adiectiuis inueniendis, de quibus alia datur cautela. Inueniuntur enim adiectiua ab istis, videlicet: ab effectu, ab euentu, ab habitu, a loco, a genere, a
460 quantitate,* a qualitate—et hoc dupliciter, a qualitate exteriori et interiori. Ab effectu, ut "hasta mortifera," "anguilla infirma." Ab euentu, ut "mutilatus," "mancus," "loripes," "cecus," et si qua sint similia. Ab habitu exteriori, ut "miles galeatus," "pedes* hastatus," "monacus cucullatus." A loco, ut "Callidonius heros,"
465 "Ytalicus furor," "Ytalicum bellum." A genere, ut "Peleya* uirgo," "Priameius heros." A quantitate, ut "homo giganteus," "puella nana." A qualitate exteriori, ut "pallidus," "luridus," "niger," "candidus." A qualitate interiori, ut "ferus," "benignus," "iracundus," "magnanimus," "luxoriosus." Hunc modum ob-
470 seruat Lucanus, dicens:

Fraterno primi maduerunt sanguine muri.

Adiectiua Arte Ordinantur. Artificiosa posicio adiectiuorum cum vnico uerbo hic patet:

Pax agnina, salus hylaris, via tuta, uoluntas
475 Libera Iusticie mansitat ante pedes.

De Arte Inueniendi Uerba. In uerbis inueniendis debemus esse cauti, quia raro licet noua uerba inuenire, quod tamen licet per

accused woman; now free again, she made fun of him, shouting: "Here
may you lie, Corydon; you can't get away. I shan't clean you, nor lift
you out of the filth. Don't try to stop us young people from playing,
old men! Since you didn't want to sport with me through these hills,
I got someone else to play with—blame it on your own backwardness!"
He said, "Go ahead and play with him, Phyllis; you're even worth a
dowry of a sheepskin—I'd like to give you not just a skin but all my
sheep." Though I be in the trap, I go about a free lover.

Phyllis said loudly, "I like a man who knows how to love, who has
learned not to be crude in sweet games. This fellow is cheerful, lively,
decent, and easygoing; Corydon is gross in his clothing, skin, and hair.
The love of this flower drips the nectar of love; that one is crude and
lazy, but this one is my sweet honeycomb." Phyllis, you have always
played at pebbles with me; secretly, in a leafy marriage bed, Phyllis
has become my love. Thus, like a man, I love because I am loved, and
therefore I neither fish nor get hooked: I am caught by the hook which
Love tends me. For as long as you live and breathe, Phyllis, don't
leave me. Though I be in the trap, I go about a free lover.

Thus the Flesh commits adultery, while Reason is trampled on; the
World is an adulterer, the beauty of the Flesh is vanity.

On the Art of Inventing Adjectives. The next subject is the inventing of
adjectives; the rule for them is different from that for nouns. Invent adjectives from the following categories: effect, outcome, dress, place,
family, size, and quality. (This last is twofold: exterior and interior
quality.) From effect, as "a death-dealing spear," "a withering whip."
From outcome, as "mutilated," "maimed," "clubfooted," "blind," and
the like. From outer dress, as "a helmeted soldier," "a spear-carrying
infantryman," "a hooded monk." From place, as "a Scottish hero,"
"Italian rage," "Italian war." From family, as "the Pelean virgin," "the
Priamean hero." From size, as "a gigantic man," "a dwarf girl." From
exterior quality, as "pale," "sallow," "black," "white." From interior
quality, as "fierce," "benign," "wrathful," "magnanimous," "wanton."
Lucan observes the adjectival mode when he says:

The original walls dripped with fraternal blood. (1.95)

Art Applied to the Order of Adjectives. The artificial position of adjectives with a single verb is evident from this example:

At the feet of Justice dwell peace lamblike, health jovial, the way
safe, the Will Free. (*EBV* 1.67-68)

The Art of Inventing Verbs. In inventing verbs we must be careful because it is rarely permissible to invent new verbs; and yet the permission

Aristotilem dicentem: "Oportet assignare conuenienter ad id
quod dicitur; et si forte nomen sit positum, facilis erit assigna-
480   tio; si non positum sit, necessarium est nomen fingere." Hoc
dicit Oratius in Poetria:

> In uerbis esto tenuis cautusque serendis;*
> Dixeris egregie, si notum callida uerbum
> Reddiderit iunctura nouum.

485   Excogitanda est igitur dictio nota* in ueteri significatione, ut
hec dictio "ympnus," quod est "laus Dei in cantico"; inde fingitur "hymnizo, -nizas," quod est "cantare," ut in Epitalamico
Beate Uirginis:

> Organa si cordis hymnizent consona uoci,
490   > Concordi corda musica dulcis erit.*

De Arte Transumendi Uerba. Item quedam uerba pertinent ad
animam, ut "discerno," "doceo"; quedam ad corpus, ut "seco,"
"lauo"; quedam ad utrumque, ut "langueo," "doleo." Congrua
fiet transumpcio uerborum, duram excludens transumpcionem,
495   si uerbum quod pertinet ad corpus transferatur ad animam, et e
contrario, ut "pungere mentem contricione," "lauare sordes
anime," "elementa docent," "prata rident."
De Circumlocutione. Item quandoque circumloquimur rem
uerbi, quandoque nominis, ut rem huius uerbi "doceo": "doc-
500   trina magistri discipulum informat"; rem* nominis ut si* dicerem: "Roma urbs caput est mundi."
Argumentum vitandi usitatum loquendi modum. Item si locutio
est nimis usitata, uerbum in nomen conuertatur, ut "ego sedeo":
"me capit hec sedes"; "me reficit membris cessio grata meis."
505   *Quot Modis Dicatur Materia.* Non est pretermittendum quod
quelibet materia vi modis potest dici, secundum vi casus nominis;
ut, si aliquis dicat "noscat Dilectio Uestra," sic dicitur uno modo,
per nominatiuum; sed per genitiuum alio modo: "Dilectionis
Uestre noticie manifestum fiat"; per datiuum eiusdem dictionis:
510   "Dilectioni Uestre reseretur"; per acusatiuum: "Dilectionem
Uestram preterire nolo"; per uocatiuum: "tibi, dilecte, mea notum facit humilitas (uel, sedulitas)"; per ablatiuum: "a Dilectione
Uestra sciri desidero."
De Arte Inueniendi Materiam. Hoc artificio vtendum est in aliis
515   orationibus, quod pueri uolentes ampliare et uariare materiam
obseruent, non pretermittentes causas principales quattuor,

is implicit in Aristotle's saying, "A correlative term must be precisely designated; if a noun already exists, the designation will be simple; if there is no noun, it will be necessary to coin one." This is what Horace says in his *Art of Poetry:*

> In diction be sparing and cautious of innovation; you will have spoken exceptionally if a skillful combination has given a familiar word new currency. (46-48)

So you should take an old word whose meaning is perfectly familiar, like "hymn," which means "a song in praise of God"; from it comes the coinage "hymnize," "to sing," as in the *Epithalamium of the Blessed Virgin:*

> If the organs of the heart hymnize in tune with the voice, the music from that harmonious string will be sweet. (10.547-48)

On the Metaphorical Use of Verbs. Furthermore, certain verbs pertain to the mind, such as "discern," "teach"; others to the body, such as "cut," "wash"; and some to both, such as "languish," "suffer." A verb which pertains to the body may be transferred to the mind, or vice versa, but in either case the metaphor should be appropriate: eschew harsh metaphors. Here are some examples: "to sting the mind with contrition"; "to wash the filth of the soul"; "rudiments teach"; "meadows laugh."

On Circumlocution. Furthermore, we occasionally paraphrase the simple meaning of a verb or noun, as for the verb "teach": "The master's teaching informs the students"; for a noun, as in the phrase, "The city of Rome is the head of the world."

A Way to Avoid a Trite and Banal Mode of Speech. Again, if a phrase is *variation* overused, a verb may be turned into a noun, as: "I sit"; "This seat receives me"; "Sitting, pleasing to my limbs, refreshes me."

In How Many Ways One Thing May Be Said. I should not overlook the fact that any statement may be made in six ways according to the six cases of a noun. For example, if someone were to say, "Let Your Honor know . . . ," that is just one way to say it, with the nominative. It may be said otherwise; with the genitive: "let it be exposed to the notice of Your Honor . . ."; with the dative of the same word: "let it be unlocked to Your Honor . . ."; with the accusative: "I do not wish Your Honor to overlook . . ."; with the vocative, "To you, honored one, my humility (or zeal) makes known . . ."; with the ablative: "I desire it should be known by Your Honor . . ."

A Way of Inventing Subject Matter. Here is a device that is useful in certain kinds of writing; students particularly who aim to amplify and vary their subject matter may observe it. I mean they should not overlook

scilicet causam efficientem, cuiuslibet rei sibi proposite. Ut, si
tractet de libro suo, commendet eum uel uituperet per causam
efficientem, idest per scriptorem; per causam materialem, idest
520   per pargamenum et incaustum; per causam formalem, ut per
libri disposicionem et litterarum protractionem; per causam
finalem, considerando ad quid factus est liber, ad hoc uidelicet
ut in eo et per eum nescientes scientes reddantur.

the four principal causes—the efficient cause, and so on—of any subject proposed to them. Thus, suppose one of them is treating of his book. He might praise it or criticize it through the efficient cause, that is, through the writer; through the material cause, that is, through the parchment or the ink; through the formal cause, as through the layout of the book or the size of the letters; or through the final cause, by considering for what purpose the book was made, namely, that in it and through it the ignorant may be made more knowledgeable.

Secundum* Capitulum· de ·lı·te Eligendi. Post inuencionem materie sequitur de electione materie. Tullius post inuencionem ordi-
nat disposicionem, inde elocutionem,* inde artem memorandi,
et ultimo pronunciationem; sed poetice scribentibus et dictanti-
5   bus post inuencionem utilis est* ars* eligendi.
De Causa Eligendi. Notandum ergo quod eligere debemus materiam triplici de causa, uel quia pretendit nobis iocundum, uel
delectabile, uel proficuum: iocundum in mente, quadam ameni-
tate; delectabile in uisu, pulcritudine; proficuum ex rei utilitate.
10   *Item Que Sunt Eligenda.* Item eligendum est breue, prolixum,
leue, planum. Breue, in curialibus negociis; prolixum, in poetarum
tractatibus; leue, ad scribendum;* planum,* ad intelligendum.
Sed si contingerit materiam esse difficilem, debemus eligere ea
que materiam leuem reddunt et enodem, que postea ponentur.

15   *Theologus Sic Scribat Episcopo pro Clerico Suo.*

      Reuerendo Patri in Christo ac Domino N., Dei gratia
Carnotensi Episcopo; Magister I., in Teologia Parisius Celestis
Magistri seruulus: salutem, et Sanctitati Sue debitam obedi-
enciam et deuotam.

20   Opera karitatis explentur quociens exaudiuntur honeste
preces humilium a maiore. Pro latore morigerato presencium,
in scolis Teologie erudito, preces Sanctitati Vestre porrigere
dignum duxi pro beneficio quodam, a Sanctitate Uestra sibi
concesso, sed ex parte talis abbatis adhuc uacillante, qui de
25   beneficio concedendo latori presencium spem infudit, qui
speratum* facillime concedet* beneficium,* si Caritatis Uestre
precibus stimuletur. Quare, pater ac domine sanctissime,
diuine dilectionis intuitu predictum abbatem precibus uestris
ad predicti concessionem beneficii moueatis. Et quod a uobis
30   in hoc fiet articulo, mihi fieri reputabo, uobisque gratiarum
actiones in tempore cumulabo.

      Viro uenerabili B., Abbati de loco sic dicto; Magister G.,
Theologie Facultatis humilis Lector Parisius: salutem, et

The Art of Selection. The next subject after Invention of subject matter is the Selection of subject matter. Cicero (cf. *RAH* 1.2.3, *DI* 1.7.9) puts Arrangement after Invention, then Style, then the Art of Memory, and last Delivery; but poets and writers of *dictamen* will find it useful to have the Art of Selection after Invention.

On the Principle of Selection. Note then that we should select subject matter from a threefold principle; because it offers to us what is either entertaining, or attractive, or profitable: the entertaining appeals to the mind, by reason of a certain pleasantness; the attractive appeals to the eye, by reason of its beauty; the profitable appeals by reason of its utility.

What Should Be Selected. Again, we should select both the brief and the prolix, what is light, and what is plain. The brief, for official business; the prolix, for treatises of poets; the light, for ease in writing; the plain, for ease in understanding. But should difficult matter be unavoidable, we select things that will make it smooth, not knotty, as in the following letters.

How a Professor of Theology Might Write on Behalf of His Student.

> To the Reverend Father and Lord in Christ N., by the grace of God Bishop of Chartres; J., Master of Theology at Paris, humble servant of the Heavenly Master: greeting and the obedience due and vowed to His Holiness.
>
> The works of charity are discharged whenever the righteous prayers of the humble are heard by one of the great. On behalf of the bearer of this letter, an obedient man and one learned in the schools of Theology, I have resolved to extend prayers to Your Holiness in regard to a certain benefice, promised him by Your Holiness, but up to now vacillating in the hands of Abbot So-and-So, who has infused hope in the bearer of this letter concerning the granting of the benefice, and who will readily grant the hoped-for benefice, if he is stimulated by the entreaties of Your Charity. Wherefore, Father and most Holy Lord, in consideration of divine love, I beg you to rouse the said abbot by your entreaties to the granting of the said benefice. And what is done by you in this matter, I shall consider to be done for me, and I shall pile up acts of gratitude to you in this world.
>
> To the venerable man B., Abbot of such-and-such a place; Master G., humble Lecturer in the Faculty of Theology at Paris: greeting, and

post claustri miliciam in celesti curia coronari.

35   Ad altare sanctum non vrtice mordaces sed amena lilia collo-
cantur. R., lator presentium, conformis lilio castitatis albedine,
doctrinamque* Theologie redolens, pridem promcrult ad altaris
ministeria promoucil. Vnde, cum a Sanctitatis Uestre gratia
spem susceperit de beneficio concedendo, vestre concessionis*
40   gratiam prestolatur. Quapropter, sub eterne remunerationis
prestolatione, et interuentu* precum mearum, R.,* latori
presencium, scolari meo, speratum beneficium concedatis, ut
uobis in tempore possim occurrere graciosus.

Ars de Difficili Ornatu. Set si materia fuerit leuis, possumus eam
45   reddere grauem et autenticam hiis nouem, que sunt: proprietas
pro subiecto; materia pro materiato; consequens pro antecedente;
pars pro toto; totum pro parte; causa pro causato; continens pro
contento; genus pro specie, et e contrario. Quorum exempla in
hoc dictamine reperientur, aliquo magistro conquerente episcopo
50   de violenta* manuum iniectione.

Exemplum de Difficili Ornatu.

Sanctissimo Patri ac Domino G., Dei gratia Parisiensi Episcopo;
Magister* R., humilis inter magistros Parisienses sicut inter
lauros mirica: salutem, et Reuerendi Patris pedibus caput pro-
55   cliue.

Ad Sanctitatis Uestre vestigia, Pater piissime, confugio, conquerendo quod R., miles de loco sic dicto, ferrum tenens uulni-
ficum, et quod satellites domino consimiles, non mediocres
habentes baculos sed quercus aereas, multo sudore procurrerunt
60   in me, nudum et pacientem et vtramque maxillam percussionibus offerentem. Tandem miles predictus, cum tota domo sua,
sanguine meo saciauit mentem suam sceleribus imputam, et in
me pro mortuo dimisso liuentis inuidie uestigia dereliquit.
Quapropter, secundum clemenciam uestram mihi grabatum
65   obseruanti salutaris calicem propinetis, uocis mee suspiriosos
gemitus exaudiendo. Et predicti militis ita sentinam scelerum
expietis ut per penam unius presumptuosa multorum insolencia
terreatur.

Proprietas ponitur* pro subiecto vbi dicitur "Sanctitatis*
70   Uestre uestigia," etc. Materia pro materiato vbi dicitur "ferrum,"

after his militant service in the cloister may he be crowned in the heavenly court.

On the holy altar we set, not biting nettles, but pleasant lilies. R., the bearer of this letter, like to the lily in the whiteness of his chastity, and redolent of the teaching of Theology, has long since merited to be promoted to the ministry of the altar. In view of that, and since he has taken hope from the kindness of Your Holiness that he will be given a benefice, he is now expecting the kindness of the actual grant from you. Wherefore, with the expectation of eternal remuneration, and by the intervention of my prayers, I beg you to grant to R., the bearer of this letter and my student, the benefice he is hoping for so that I can meet you in this world with gratitude.

Complex Embellishment. But if the subject matter is slight, we can make it grave and authoritative by these nine devices: property for the subject; the material for the thing made with the material; consequence for the antecedent; part for whole; whole for part; cause for effect; container for thing contained; genus for species, and vice versa. Examples of these will be found in this letter, in which a master complains to his bishop of a violent assault.

Example of Complex Embellishment.

To the Most Holy Father and Lord G., by the grace of God Bishop of Paris; Master R., a humble man among the masters of Paris, like a tamarisk among laurels: greeting, and a head bowed before the foot of the Reverend Father.

I flee to Your Holiness's footsteps, most pious Father, to complain that R., knight of such-and-such a place, brandishing the wound-making steel, and his satellites, like their master carrying no mere sticks but "towering oaks" (cf. *Aeneid* 3.680), assaulted me with a good deal of sweat, while I, naked and compliant, turned the other cheek to their blows (cf. Matt. 5:39). In the end the aforesaid knight, with all his house, fed his crime-infected mind to satiety on my blood, and leaving the marks of his livid hatred on me, dismissed me for dead. Wherefore, in accordance with your clemency, I beg you to offer "the chalice of salvation" (Ps. 115:13) to me as I keep my couch, by listening to the gasping groans of my voice. And I beg you so to purge the bilge water of crime in that knight that through the punishment of one the presumptuous insolence of many may cringe in terror.

A property is put for the subject in the phrase "Your Holiness's footsteps." The material for the thing made with the material in the word

quod est materia gladii. Consequens pro antecedente ubi dicitur
"multo sudore." Pars pro toto ubi dicitur "maxillam." Totum
pro parte vbi dicitur "tota domus." Causa pro causato ubi dicitur "liuentis inuidie," quia inuidia est causa efficiens uulneris.
75   Continens pro contento ponitur ubi dicitur "salutaris calicem
propinetis." Vnde quociens dicitur, "Noscat Dilectionis Uestre
gratia," uel "Filiatio," uel "Maiestas," uel aliquid tale, proprietas pro subiecto ponitur. Si dicat scolaris poscens denarios,
"Crumena mea totum euomuit argentum, mihi non relinquitur
80   nec aurum quod non abierit pro pane," materia pro materiato
ponitur. Si dixerit, "Ad cathedram anelo," "In elenchis desudo,"
"Pro denariis suspiro," consequens ponitur pro antecedente.
Alia exempla satis per se patent. Sed genus ponitur pro specie
si dixero, "Arma gero bona," idest "gladium" uel "cultellum";
85   species pro genere si dixero, "Hoc nephas gladius* expiabit,"
idest, "quecumque arma."
*De Arte Memorandi.** Set quia dicitur Electio, quasi extra multa
aliquorum lectio, debemus eligere dicenda adminiculo artis
memorandi, que poetis materiam ordinantibus est necessaria.
90   Vnde secundum Tullium debemus in mente quamdam aream
disponere, nec in loco nimis obscuro nec nimis claro, quia hec
nouercantur memorie et electioni. Illa area debet intelligi distingui per tres partes principales et columpnas. In prima parte uel
columpna triparciantur curiales, ciuiles, rurales, cum armis suis
95   et instrumentis propriis, causis et officiis. Si ab ore magistri
proferatur aliqua dictio significans aliquid quod pertinet ad aliquam trium personarum predictarum, ibi erit inuenienda et
eligenda. In secunda parte uel columpna debent intelligi distingui exempla et dicta et facta autentica, et magistri a quibus
100   audiuimus, et libri quos legimus. Si aliquid deciderit nobis a
memoria, debemus recolere tempus clarum uel obscurum in
quo didicimus,* locum in quo, magistrum a quo, in quo* habitu,
in quo gestu, libros in quibus studuimus, paginam candidam uel
nigram, disposiciones et colores litterarum; quia hec omnia
105   introductiua erunt rerum memorandarum et nobis eligendarum.
In tercia columpna intelligamus scribi omnia genera linguarum,
sonorum, et uocum diuersorum animancium, et ethimologias,
interpretationes, differentias, secundum ordinem alphabeti; et
leta mente consideret unusquisque que uox conueniat cum
110   lingua sua. Sed quia nescimus omnes linguas, nec omnes

"steel," which is the material of a sword. Consequence for antecedent in the phrase "with a good deal of sweat." A part for the whole in the word "cheek." The whole for a part in the phrase "all his house." Cause for effect in the phrase "livid hatred," because hatred is the efficient cause of the wound. The container is put for the thing contained in the phrase "offer the chalice of salvation." And any phrase like "Let Your Honor's kindness know," or "Your Sonship," or "Your Majesty," makes use of a property for the subject. If a student asking for money should say, "My purse has vomited all its silver, there is not left me any gold that has not gone for bread," the material is put for the thing made with the material. If he says, "I pant for a chair on the faculty"; "I am sweating over refutations"; "I gasp for money"; the consequence is put for the antecedent. There are plenty of other examples which speak for themselves. The genus is put for the species in the sentence, "I bear good arms," that is, "sword" or "knife"; the species for the genus in the sentence, "The sword shall avenge this crime," that is, "some weapon or other."

On the Art of Remembering. But since it is called Selection, as it were a drawing aside of a few things from a large number, we should select what we are going to say with the support of the Art of Remembering, which is essential for poets organizing their material. So, following Cicero, we should put aside in our minds some vacant spot, in a place which is neither too hazy nor too bright, because these qualities are inimical to memory and selection. This vacant spot is to be imagined as separated into three main sections and columns. The first section or column is subdivided into three parts, for courtiers, city dwellers, and peasants, with their arms and their respective implements, their concerns and their duties. If any word falls from the mouth of the teacher which means anything which pertains to any one of the three kinds of persons mentioned, there it will be, for later inventing and selecting. The second part or column should be imagined as containing, in separate compartments, examples and sayings and facts from the authors, and the teachers from whom we heard them, and the books in which we have read them. If memory should fail us on some point, we must then call to mind the time, be it vivid or hazy, when we learned it, the place in which, the teacher from whom, his dress, his gestures, the books in which we studied it, the page—was it white or dark?—the position on the page and the colors of the letters; because all these will lead to the things that we want to remember and select. In the third column let us imagine to be written all kinds of languages, sounds, and voices of the various living creatures, etymologies, explanations of words, distinctions between words, all in alphabetical order; and with a ready mind let each consider what word fits his own language. But since we do not know every

[margin note: memory and the system of "places"]

dictiones audiuimus, recurrimus ad illas quas audiuimus; et cum
magister aliquid dixerit litteratorie uel ethimologice exponendo,
in tercia illa columpna collocemus cum aliqua re naturali que
illud quod profertur significet;* et per suum signum poterimus
115   illud memorare et ad proferendum eligere.

Curiales cum litteris suis	Magistri cum libris suis	Animalia terrestria
Ciuiles	In loco	volatilia
Rurales cum instrumentis suis	In tempore	Voces ethimologice

Figure One*

Item notandum quod in rota Uurgilii, quam pre manibus
habemus, ordinantur tres columpne et in circuitu per multas
circumferencias ordinantur tres stili. In prima columpna comparationes continentur, similitudines, et nomina rerum ad humilem
120   stilum pertinencium; in secunda ad mediocrem; in tercia ad
grauem. Et si proferatur aliqua* sentencia in vno stilo, que reperitur in proximo, patet quod est* egressus a stilo illo; et ideo
eligenda sunt uerba inuenta ad quemlibet stilum in suo stilo.
Ad Difficilem Materiam Alleuiandam. Materiam difficilem pos-
125   sumus reddere leuem et planam uitando ix predicta, que sunt
proprietas pro subiecto, materia pro materiato, etc.; ut patet in
hoc dictamine.

Littere Citatorie.

I., Dei gratia Pastor uel Minister humilis Ecclesie Parisius; G.,
130   Militi de loco sic dicto: offensionem Sancte Matris Ecclesie
corrigere filiali timore.

(Et nota quod non dicitur "salutem," cum miles habeatur pro
excommunicato. Inde sequitur prouerbium:)

Qui matrem offendere non expauescit, minus fratres, multo
135   minus alienos ledere formidabit. Magister R., cuius nobili
sciencia, cuius fecunda doctrina, cuius moribus et fama floret

language, nor have heard every word, we resort to those which we have heard; and when the teacher makes a philological or etymological explanation of any word, let us gather it into that third column, along with some natural phenomenon that may symbolize the word in question; and by means of its symbol we shall be able to memorize it and later select it for our own use.

Courtiers with their letters	Teachers with their books	Creatures of the earth
City dwellers	Place	of the sky
Peasants with their implements	Time	Etymologies of words

Figure Two

It should be noted that Virgil's Wheel, which we have in front of us (see Figure Four, p. 41), also contains an arrangement of three columns; here the three styles are arranged inside a circle along a series of concentric circumferences. The first column contains comparisons, similitudes, and names of things appropriate to the low style; the second to the middle; the third to the high. To express in one style a sentiment which is only to be found in the next is clearly a departure from the proper style; we should select for any given style only words invented in that style. *Simplifying Difficult Subject Matter.* We can make difficult subject matter light and plain by avoiding the nine devices I spoke of before, namely property for subject, material for thing made with the material, etc.; as this letter shows.

A Letter of Summons.

J., by the grace of God Pastor or humble Minister of the Church in Paris; to G., Knight of such-and-such a place: may he correct his offense by filial fear of Holy Mother Church.

(And note that "greeting" is not said, since the knight is treated as an excommunicate. Then follows a proverb:)

The man who does not tremble at the thought of offending his mother will be less afraid to injure his brothers, much less strangers. Master R., whose noble learning, whose fruitful teaching, whose

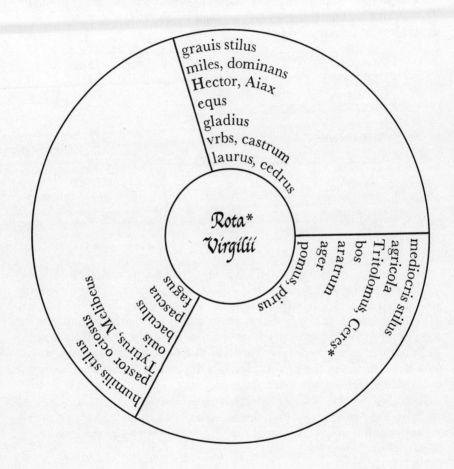

grauis stilus
miles, dominans
Hector, Aiax
equs
gladius
vrbs, castrum
laurus, cedrus

Rota*
Virgilii

pomus, pirus
ager
aratrum
bos
Tritolomus, Ceres*
agricola
mediocris stilus

fagus
pascua
baculus
ouis
Tytirus, Melibeus
pastor ociosus
humilis stilus

Figure Three (*cf.* l. 116)

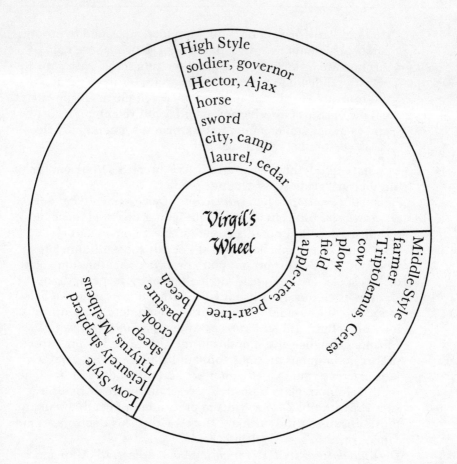

High Style
soldier, governor
Hector, Ajax
horse
sword
city, camp
laurel, cedar

Virgil's Wheel

Middle Style
farmer
Triptolemus, Ceres
cow
plow
field
apple-tree, pear-tree

Low Style
leisurely shepherd
Tityrus, Meliboeus
sheep
crook
pasture
beech

Figure Four

studium Parisiense, nobis edidit conquerendo quod in propria
persona, gladium exsertans fulmineum, longo labore dolosas
machinante insidias, in eum furialiter cum seruis coarmatis
140   irruisti; tandemque, cruore suo fuso, satiatus in eo uulnerato,
pro mortuo dimisso tue uirus nequicie reliquisti. Quapropter,
tali die Parisius nobis faciem tuam facias presentem, ut uel
purges uiolentam manuum iniectionem in clericum, uel Deo
et leso de predicta satisfacias lesione.

145   Et notate quod ubi dicebatur in litteris premissis "ferrum," in
hiis dicitur "gladius," et vitantur predicta.
*De Facili Ornatu per Determinaciones Uerborum, Adiectiuorum,
et Substantiuorum.* Item, si velimus leuiter dicere et plane, determinare debemus nomina et uerba. Si est nomen, aut est
150   proprium aut est appellatiuum; et hoc aut substantiuum aut
adiectiuum. Si sit proprium: plura propria ponantur cum ablati-
uis, ut, si clericus commendauerit aliquem episcopum, dicat,
"Paulus es eloquio, Petrusque fide, Symeonque spe, sensu Salomon, et pietate Dauid." Item, plura propria determinantur pluri-
155   bus* adiectiuis, ut hic: "Mitis es Andreas animo, castusque
Iohannes, Iob paciens, mundus Loth, niueusque Ioseph." Item,
propriis nominibus pluribus apponuntur plura verba, vt, si scolaris diceret ei qui exibet eum in scolis, hoc modo scribit: "Que
sciuit Salomon, Plato monstrauit, reserauit pectus Aristotilis,
160   sunt reserata tibi." Item, vnicum proprium nomen determinatur
pluribus substantiuis, ut hic: "Hic est Gregorius doctrina, famine,
fama, consilio, gestis, religione, fide."
De Appellatiuorum Determinatione per Adiectiua. Aliquando
plura adiectiua unico substantiuo adiunguntur; aliquando plura
165   uerba unico substantiuo apponuntur; aliquando plura uerba obliquis pluribus determinantur; quod in hoc dictamine poterit
apparere.

Littere Petitorie Continentes Exempla Determinacionis.

Reuerendo Patri ac Domino W., Dei gratia Archiepiscopo
170   Remensi; R., Scolaris Parisiensis in cliuum arduitatis Aristotilice nitens: salutem, et ad eterni Veris pascua peruenire.

Si Dedalus alis caruisset, numquam pelagus transuolando de-
siderate portum patrie tetigisset. Cum per pelagus profundum
rationis Aristotilice sit ausa paruitatis mee fragilis nauicula

character and renown have caused the intellectual life of Paris to flourish, has registered a complaint with us: that you, personally, unsheathing a murderous sword, and after long toil devising a cunning ambush, assaulted him furiously, with your servants who were also armed; and at length, after spilling his blood, and glutting yourself with the sight of his wounds, you dismissed him for dead, leaving behind the stench of your wickedness. Wherefore, you are commanded to appear in person before us in Paris on such-and-such a day, that you may either clear yourself of the accusation of violent assault against a cleric, or make satisfaction to God and to the injured man for the aforesaid injury.

And note that for the previous letter's "steel," this letter has "sword"; and the devices I spoke of before are avoided.

On Simple Embellishment by Means of Modification of Verbs, Adjectives, and Substantives. Another way to achieve lightness and plainness is to modify nouns and verbs. Nouns are either proper or common; common nouns either substantives or adjectives. In the case of proper nouns: several proper nouns may be put with ablatives; for example, if someone in minor orders is praising a bishop, he might say, "You are a Paul in eloquence, a Peter in faith, a Simeon in hope, a Solomon in wisdom, and a David in piety." Similarly, several proper nouns are modified by several adjectives, as here: "You are mild Andrew in spirit and chaste John, patient Job, pure Lot, and snow-white Joseph." Again, several verbs are attached to several proper nouns; for example, a scholar addressing the man who is putting him through school may write in this way: "What Plato demonstrated, what Solomon knew, what Aristotle's breast unlocked, have been unlocked for you." Again, a single proper noun is modified by several substantives, as here: "This man is a Gregory in teaching, in discourse, in fame, in counsel, in deeds, in religion, in faith." *On Modifying Common Nouns with Adjectives.* Sometimes several adjectives are joined to one substantive; sometimes several verbs are attached to one substantive; sometimes several verbs are modified by several oblique cases; all this can be seen in this letter.

A Letter of Request Containing Examples of Modification.

To the Reverend Father and Lord W., by the grace of God Archbishop of Reims; R., Scholar at Paris, struggling up the hill of Aristotelian difficulty: greeting, and may he arrive at the pastures of eternal Spring.

Had Dedalus lacked wings he would never have touched the port of the land he sought by flying across the sea. The fragile bark of my insignificance has dared to run a course through the deep sea of

175   decurrere, mihi paupertatis abyssum hyare prospicio, nisi
        dextera uestra prudens, iusta, fortis, moderata, uela studii mei*
        quam cicius sumat et dirigat et deducat. Hinc enim uilla
        sumptuosa me spoliat; hinc domus onerat; hinc turba uisitat;
        hinc magister respicit* ut eius longus labor largo munere com-
180   pensetur. Quapropter, illa generalis apud omnes munificencia
        uestra michi maturet dona compluere, denarios cumulare, ut
        hospitii mei granarium habundet Cerere, penus fluat Bacho,
        familia ueste iuuenescat, magister competenti munere uel bene-
        ficio gratuletur.

185 Plura adiectiua unico substantiuo adiunguntur ubi dicitur "dexte-
    ra uestra* prudens, etc." Plura uerba vnico substantiuo adiungun-
    tur* ubi dicitur "sumat et dirigat, etc." Plura verba pluribus sub-
    stantiuis adiunguntur ubi dicitur "villa sumptuosa me spoliat,
    etc." Item plura uerba pluribus obliquis determinantur vbi dici-
190 tur "granarium habundet Cerere, penus fluat Bacho, etc." Item
    vnum uerbum pluribus obliquis determinatur, ut hic: "rumpuntur
    digitis crines, cutis ungue,* furore uestis, singultu uerba, domusque
    sono."
        Verbum aliquando pluribus substantiuis et adiectiuis simul
195 determinatur, ut in hoc rithmo de quodam clerico absoluto a
    Domino Papa. Si sub retrogradatione legatur rithmus, versus
    dupliciter erunt leonini; vt hic:

        Patribus hec omnibus, genibus curuatis,
        Levatisque manibus, pedibus nudatis   scribo.

200   Canibus a uilibus grauibus saluatus,
        Iocatusque paribus, gradibus firmatus   ibo.

        Creticus est rusticus liricus blanditor,
        Sititorque tetricus, Geticus largitor   mortis.

        Patria me Iulia uenia ditauit,
205   Leuauitque Furia, muria mundauit   sortis.

    In hoc rithmo fiat retrogradatio sic, ut fiant uersus dupliciter
    leonini:

        Scribo, nudatis pedibus, manibusque leuatis,
        Curuatis genibus, omnibus hec patribus.

210 Hoc modo legantur alii secundum retrogradationem.
    De Sustantiuorum Determinatione. Item adiectiua plura eligun-
    tur ad determinandum vnicum substantiuum, ut si dicerem:
    "pestis pessundans, perniciosa, potens." Item genitiui determi-
    nant* substantiua, ut hic: "Serpentis uirus, feritatem tigridis,

Aristotelian reasoning; and now I see the abyss of poverty opening before me, unless your right hand, prudent, just, strong, moderate, should as quickly as possible raise and trim and spread full the sails of my study. For here this expensive town is ruining me; here my household is a burden to me; here the crowd is forever visiting me; here the teacher is looking to me for a large reward as compensation for his long labor. Wherefore, may that munificence of yours, known to all, hasten to rain gifts on me, to heap up coins, in order that the pantry of my lodgings might abound in Ceres, the cellar flow with Bacchus, the servants be rejuvenated with new livery, and the teacher thank me for a suitable reward or benefice.

Several adjectives are joined to a single substantive in the phrase "your right hand, prudent, etc." Several verbs are joined to a single substantive in the phrase "raise and trim, etc." Several verbs are joined to several substantives in the clauses "this expensive town is ruining me, etc." Similarly, several verbs are modified by several oblique cases in the clauses "that the pantry might abound in Ceres, the cellar flow with Bacchus, etc." One verb may also be modified by several oblique cases, as here: "Hair is torn by fingers, the skin by a fingernail, clothing by rage, words by sobbing, and a home by noise."

Sometimes a verb is modified by several substantives and adjectives at once, as in this rhymed poem about a certain cleric absolved by the Holy Father. If each rhymed couplet is read backward, it will form a leonine.

I write these to all fathers, with knees bent, hands raised, feet bare.

I shall go about saved from vile and oppressive dogs, and laughing to my friends, my rank as a cleric reaffirmed.

The judge is a rustic, melodious flatterer, a cruel thirster, a Gothic dispenser of death.

The land of Caesar has enriched me by its kindness, freed me from the Fury, cleansed me from the dregs of my lot.

Here is how to read the rhyming couplets backward to make them leonines:

> Scribo, nudatis pedibus, manibusque levatis,
> Curvatis genibus, omnibus hec patribus.

The others may be read backward in the same way.

On Modifying Substantives. Likewise, several adjectives are selected to modify one substantive; for example: "a crushing, ruinous, overpowering plague." Genitives similarly modify substantives, as here: "You have within you the snake's venom, the tiger's ferocity, the boar's wrath,

215   iram apri, seuiciam fulminis intus habes." Item egregie dicitur
quando plura adiectiua eliguntur ad determinandum plura substantiua sine copulatiua coniunctione; ut, si mater castiget filiam,
dicat: "Sit tibi lingua modesta, oculus pudicus, gestus compositus."
Item in facilitate ornata uarientur* composiciones dictionum et

220   exitus earundem, ut hic: "Proficit vnum* bonus; tabescit liuidus,
eius profectum tollit, defectum querit honoris, impedit effectum,
confectus tabe ueneni, sordibus infectus, peruersus ad omnia
factus."

De Adiectiuorum Electione. Sequitur de electione et adiectiuorum
225   determinatione. Adiectiua igitur eligenda sunt aut proprie posita
aut inproprie. Si proprie velimus illa eligere, recurrendum est ad
illum tropum qui dicitur *epiteton,* quando ponitur proprie
proprium, ut: "Aquilo frigidus," "Auster calidus," "nix alba,"
"Ethiops niger." Sed raro ponuntur talia nisi causa maioris expres-

230   sionis. Adiectiuum improprie positum secundum tropum, methaphorice, eligitur; de quo postea dicetur. Aduerbium uero dicitur
adiectiuum uerbi. Vnde causa ornatus ad plura uerba determinandum, debent apponi plura huiusmodi adiectiua, ut si dicerem:
"Questa fuit mulier meste, sedit lacrimose, ingemuit iuste, condo-

235   luitque pie." (Adiectiuum quod est participium eligitur causa
breuiloquii, ut: "lego et proficio"; "legens proficio.")

    Si repetatur coniunctio copulatiua, erit *polisinteton,* idest,
"plurium copulatiuarum coniunctionum positio"; et dicitur
"membrum orationis" a Tullio. Vt hic:

240   Et contristatur tempus, lacrimatur et aer
               Nubilus, et plangit funera mesta dies.

Interiectiones eliguntur causa leticie exprimende, uel metus, uel
doloris, uel admirationis. Prepositiones repetuntur causa pietatis
uel indignacionis inducende,* ut: "Pauper affluit* in lacrimas,

245   in singultus, in suspiria"; "Mulier mechatur propter carnis illece-
bras, propter lucri dulcedinem, propter gulam adimplendam."
Item contingit aliquando dictionem per se poni uiciose, que si
frequenter ponatur causa maioris expressionis uicium excusat,
vt hic:

250   Sic seruire Deo, sic semper uiuere semper,
               Dat regnare Deo, semper amare Deum.

    Si* adiectiuum reddat orationem obscuram quia pluribus
potest adaptari, debet ablatiuo determinari, ut si dicerem

lightning's savageness." Another exceptional literary device is to select
several adjectives to modify several substantives without a conjunction
to join them; for example, a mother reprimanding her daughter may say,
"Keep a modest tongue, a bashful eye, a quiet manner." Also within
the bounds of embellished simplicity is the variation of compounds of
words, and their endings, as here: "A good man does something profitable; a spiteful man grows corrupt, takes away his profit, seeks a defect
in his honor, impedes his effectiveness; a confection of corruption and
poison, infected with filth, in fact perverse toward everything."
On Selection of Adjectives. The next subject is the selection and modification of adjectives. Adjectives are to be selected either as strictly appropriate to their nouns, or in a transferred sense. If we wish to select
what is strictly appropriate, we resort to the trope known as Epitheton,
in which a regular property of some noun is explicitly mentioned, as:
"the cold North wind," "the warm South wind," "white snow," "the
black Ethiopian." But such properties are rarely specified except for the
sake of greater expressiveness. An adjective used in a transferred sense
is selected tropically, that is, metaphorically; I will speak of this later
(l. 255). "Adverb" simply means "the adjective of a verb"; and so putting several adjectives of this type together to modify several verbs is another method of embellishing; for example: "The woman lamented sor-
rowfully, she sat tearfully, she mourned justly, and condoled piously."
(A participial adjective is selected for brevity, as: "I read and I profit";
"Reading, I profit.")

The repetition of a copulative conjunction is Polysyndeton, that is,
"the placing of many copulative conjunctions"; Cicero calls this *membrum orationis.* Here is an example:

And the time is sad, and the cloudy sky sheds tears, and the gloomy
day laments the death.

Interjections are selected to express joy, or fear, or sorrow, or wonder.
Prepositions are repeated in order to induce pity or indignation, as "The
poor man is rich in tears, in sobs, in sighs"; "A woman commits adultery
on account of the allurements of the flesh, on account of the sweetness
of money, on account of the urge to satisfy gluttony." Likewise, it sometimes happens that a word is used faultily by itself, whereas frequent use
of it for the sake of greater expressiveness excuses the fault, as here:

To serve God in such a way, always to live in such a way—always!—
always to love God: that is what it means to acknowledge God's king-
ship.

If an adjective is likely to make a phrase obscure because it can be inter-
preted in several ways, it should be modified by an ablative, as in this

de obitu alicuius uiri: "Aspectu simplex, uerbo mansuetus,
255   honorus gestu, sincerus corde, magister obit." Si adiectiuum
transumptiue teneatur, exigit determinari per obliqum, vt si
dicerem, "uirgo candida," causa specificandi:

    Candida carne placet et candida mente pudica.

Et notandum quod aliquando transfertur unica dictio, sicut sub-
260   stantiuum uel adiectiuum uel uerbum, aliquando tota oratio. Si
substantiuum, debet determinari per adiectiuum, ut si dicerem
"rosa uirgo," possum dicere "rosa uirgo pudica," (uel, "rosa
uirgo pudoris"). Si est adiectiuum, determinetur ut patet in hoc
uersu:

265   Florida carne placet et florida mente pudica.

Ars Iudicandi Propriam Transumptionem Verbi. Item de trans-
umptione uerbi talis erit ars assignanda. Eligenda sunt duo uerba,
vnum magis commune et aliud minus commune, que se habent
aliquo modo secundum similem statum; ut hoc uerbum "mouere"
270   commune est ad animata et ad inanimata, quantum ad hominem
et ad aquam et ad tempus. Hoc uerbum "currere" est commune
ad pedes habencia, et est sub hoc uerbo "mouere," et proprie
potest transumi pro illo, excludendo duram transumptionem, ut
hic:
275   Dum uersus uerto transcurrit mobilis hora,
   Dum metrice scribo piscosus Secana currit.

Si oratio tota methaphorice dicatur, exponi debet in subse-
quentibus, ut in hoc dictamine quod magister pauper scribit
abbati.

280   *Exemplum Transuncionis in Litteris Scolasticis.*

  Venerabili Uiro R.,* Abbati de tali loco; Magister I., de loco
sic dicto: salutem.

  Cum flores primeuos inceperit arbor parturire, si Borealis
incubuerit flatus, caduca marcescunt folia, floresque de fructu
285   menciuntur, cum promissos fructus non persoluant, sed a
Semele rosa mutatur in Beroen, et a uirgineo statu degenerans
pallorem induit senectutis.

Ecce hac posita similitudine, debet exponi per litteram subse-
quentem, sic:

290   Non longe discrepat status meus ab arbore florescente, quia
discipline longo labore cathedram occupaui magistralem dum,

eulogy for a dead man: "Master So-and-So—simple in appearance, mild
in speech, honorable in his dealings, ingenuous in affection—is dead." If
an adjective is conceived metaphorically, it requires modification by an
oblique case; for example, the phrase "a white virgin" is clarified thus:

[handwritten margin note: metaphorical conception of adjective → oblique modification]

> White in complexion, and white in her pure mind, she is altogether
> agreeable.

And it should be noted that sometimes a single word is used metaphorically, such as a substantive or an adjective or a verb; sometimes a whole
sentence. If a substantive, it ought to be modified by an adjective; for
example, if I want to say "that virgin is a rose," I can say "that virgin is
a blushing rose," (or "that virgin is a rose of blushes"). If it is an adjective, it may be modified in the way suggested in this line:

> Rosy in complexion, and rosy in her blushing mind, she is altogether
> agreeable.

How to Judge a Proper Verbal Metaphor. Here is the way to compose a
verbal metaphor. Select two verbs, one more general and the other less
general, but which have some area of common meaning. For example,
the verb "move" is applied in general to both animate and inanimate
things, to man and water and time. The verb "run" is restricted to things
with feet, and comes under the verb "move," and so can properly be
substituted for it in a metaphor that is not too harsh, as here:

[handwritten margin note: verbal metaphor]

> While I turn verses the mobile hour runs on, while I write in meter the
> fish-crowded Seine is running.

If a whole sentence is spoken metaphorically, it should be explained in
the next sentence, as in this letter which a poor teacher writes to an abbot.

Example of Metaphor in a Scholar's Letter.

> To the Venerable Man R., Abbot of such-and-such a place; Master
> J., of so-and-so: greeting.

> If a northern blast bears down on a tree which has just begun to
> bring forth blossoms in springtime, the leaves droop and wither and
> cheat the blossoms of their fruit, for they do not deliver the fruits they
> contracted for; instead the rose is changed from Semele into Beroe and
> degenerates from its virgin state to take on the pallor of old age.

Once this similitude is posed, it should be explained in the rest of the letter, thus:

> My situation is not unlike that blossoming tree. For I have been carry-
> ing out a master's duties in the long task of teaching; I had laid down

in gramatica radicatus, induebam uirorem in logica, flores
rethoricos incipiens proferre, fructum in quadruuialibus
promittentes. Sed ecce paupertatis Aquilo surrepens michi
295   radices concutit, virorem exurit, flores impellit, fructus auertit;
quia non est aliquis—usque ad unum   qui michil supponat stipi-
tem curruenti, qui michi ministret* irriguum arescenti,* qui
iumento suo uulneratum imponat, qui stabulario saltem unum
denarium administret.
300   Vnde sicut possum turbini Fortune resisto, nunc cursum
legendo, nunc in tedio discipulos instruendo, cum uestram
gratiam quasi tabulam naufragii, uel quasi serenitatis beneficium, in tenebris expectem, non semel circumspiciens, non
oculo sompnolento considerans, si* mihi pietatis dextera
305   porrigatur. Maturet igitur prudencie uestre circumspectio, non
secundum meritorum meorum exigenciam, sed secundum
pietatis uestre columbinum intuitum, mihi porrigere piam*
dexteram in naufrago regimine magistratus; ut a Deo contem-
placionem uite eterne recipiatis, et ut ego, si me Dei fauor
310   exaltauerit, grates uobis possim temporales congerere copiose.

roots in grammar, I was taking on a green coat in logic, and just beginning to bring forth rhetorical blossoms, which held out promise of
fruit in the quadrivium. Then, suddenly, the north wind of poverty
creeps up on me, shakes my roots, dries up my greenness, routs my
blossoms, turns away my fruit; for there is no one—except one—to
place a prop under me as I fall, to apply irrigation to me as I dry up,
to set a wounded man on his beast, to give even one penny to the host
(cf. Luke 10:34).

And so I resist the whirlwind of Fortune as I can, now by giving a
course of lectures, now in tedious private instruction, while I wait in
the darkness for your kindness as for a plank in a shipwreck, or as for
the favor of calm weather, glancing around time and again, peering
with an eye that does not sleep, to see whether the right hand of compassion will be stretched out to me. May, therefore, your prudence,
with its watchful eye, hasten, not according to what is due to my
merits but according to the dovelike glance of your compassion, to
stretch forth a compassionate right hand to me now that the rudder
of my magistracy is wrecked; so that you may receive from God the
Vision of eternal life, and so that I, if God's favor shall raise me up,
may be able to pile up acts of gratitude to you in this world in
abundance.

De Arte Inchoandi. Post inuentionem et electionem materie
sequitur de inchoatione et disposicione ipsius. In qualibet materia considerantur tria: principium, medium, et finis; (vel,
principium, progressus, et operis conclusio, etc.). Preordinande
5 sunt iste partes in mente, quia prius debet esse uerbum in mente
quam sit in ore. Si materia continet plura negocia, maius negocium
est preordinandum, et alia negocia continuanda sunt huiusmodi*
dictionibus: "preter* cetera," "preterea," "predictis adicimus,"
"subiungimus." Si continget* forsitan materiam esse poeticam,
10 tunc possumus ordiri materiam aut secundum principium naturale
aut secundum principium artificiale. Principium naturale est
quando res narratur eo ordine quo geritur.
De Principio Artificiali et viij Speciebus Eius. Principium artificiale est quando inchoamus a medio materie vel a fine, et hoc
15 possumus facere viij modis; vnde hoc principium viij habet ramos.
Primus ramus uel prima species est quando sumitur principium
artificiale uel a medio materie uel a fine, sine prouerbio et sine
exemplo. Principium aliquando sumitur a prouerbio sumpto
iuxta caput materie, uel iuxta medium, uel iuxta finem. Iterum
20 aliquando sumitur ab exemplo sumpto iuxta principium materie,
uel iuxta medium, uel iuxta finem; et ita erunt viij species. Subiun-
gamus exempla a uita et hystoria Beati Dyonisi. Principium materie est quod ipse studuit Athenis; medium quod predicauit in
Gallia; finis quod decapitatus fuit pro Domino.
25 *Principium Naturale.*

Vir magnus fama, vir in actu maior, Athenis
Floruit; effectus maximus inde fide.

Primus Modus.* Principium artificiale sumptum est a medio
materie, sine prouerbio et exemplo, ut hic:

30 Gallorum tenebras, Dionisi, luce fugasti
Dum Uere Lucis pandis adesse iubar.

Recurrendum* est ad principium materie huiusmodi dictionibus:
"qui," "que," "quod," "qualis," "quantus," vt hic:

Qui radios olim fudisti solis Athenis,
35 Inter Piereos lux radiosa choros.

On the Art of Beginning. The next subject after Invention and Selection of subject matter is how to begin and arrange it. Any subject has three aspects: beginning, middle, and end (or commencement, development, and conclusion of the work, and similar labels). These parts should be put straight first of all in the mind, because a word must be in the mind before it may be in the mouth. If the subject embraces several issues, arrange the greater issue first: then turn to other issues with phrases such as "besides all that," "furthermore," "we add to the aforesaid," "we subjoin." In poetry, we can launch the subject with either the natural or the artificial beginning. The natural beginning is when a story is told in the order in which it takes place.

On the Artificial Beginning and Its Eight Types. The artificial beginning is when we start in the middle of the subject or at the end: we can do it in eight ways, and so this beginning has eight branches. The first branch or first type is when the artificial beginning is drawn either from the middle of the subject or from the end, without a proverb and without an example. The beginning is sometimes made with a proverb, which may concern the head of the subject, or the middle, or the end. Again, it is sometimes made with an example, which may concern the beginning of the subject, or the middle, or the end; and there you have the eight types. Let us subjoin models from the life story of St. Denis. The beginning of the subject is his study in Athens; the middle is his preaching in Gaul; the end is his beheading for the Lord.

The Natural Beginning.

A man great in fame, a man greater in deed, flourished in Athens; then he was made greatest in faith.

The First Type. The artificial beginning is drawn from the middle of the subject, without a proverb or example, as here:

You put to flight the darkness of the Gauls with light, Denis, as you made it known that the splendor of the True Light was among them.

The transition to the beginning of the subject should be made with words of this kind: "who," "which," "that," "what sort," "how great"; as here:

You, who once before extended the sun's rays in Athens, a radiant light among the Pierian choirs.

Secundus Modus. Principium sumitur artificiale a fine sine prouerbio et exemplo, sic:

> Portator capitis Dionisius innuit intus
> Se portasse Deum, se placuisse Deo.

40   Recurrendum* est ad principium materie sic:

> Qui fuit Acthee caput urbis philosophie,
> Fons* triuii, certa quadruuiique via.

Tercius Modus. Principium artificiale sumitur a* prouerbio
sumpto iuxta principium materie, ut hic:

45
> Qui scit quique potest et qui facit, ille preesse
> Debet, et indoctos arte docere sua.

Propter prouerbium, quod sumitur a principio materie, continuandum est aliis dictionibus quam premissis, hiis scilicet:
"docet," "indicat," "attestatur"; continuetur ergo sic:

50
> Hoc docet Actheus* Dionisius: ille preesse
> Et prodesse suis gaudet in urbe sua.

Quartus Modus. Principium artificiale sumitur a prouerbio
sumpto iuxta medium materie, vt hic:

> Seruus in aduersis domino parere fidelis
55   > Audet, et in casu se probat esse probum.

Hoc posito principio, sic continuandum est:

> Hoc attestatur Dionisius: extera regna
> Aggreditur, Domini semina iussa serit.

Quintus Modus. Item artificiale principium sumitur a prouerbio
60   sumpto a fine materie, vt hic:

> Se nullus poterit melius monstrare fidelem
> Quam qui pro Domino dat sua colla neci.

Hoc posito principio, continuetur* sic:

> Indicat hoc tua mors, Dionisi, dum tua portant
65   > Mortua uitali membra uigore caput.

Sextus Modus. Item si principium sumatur ab exemplo, premittitur quedam similitudo que debet corpori materie* adaptari, vt hic:

> Qui scit uenari uenatur; mittit in hostem
> Qui nouit ualida mittere tela manu.

The Second Type. The artificial beginning is drawn from the end, without a proverb or example, as here:

Though he carried his head, Denis nodded within that he had carried God, that he had been pleasing to God.

The transition to the beginning of the subject should be made thus:

He who was head of philosophy in the Attic city, fountain of the trivium and sure road of the quadrivium.

The Third Type. The artificial beginning is made with a proverb which concerns the beginning of the subject, as here:

The man who knows how and who can and who does—such a man should be a leader, and instruct the ignorant in his art.

Since we are now dealing with a proverb, here taken from the beginning of the subject, the continuation should be made with other words than the ones I gave before; for example: "teaches," "shows," "is witness to." Thus it may be continued:

Denis the Athenian teaches this; he is glad to be a leader and to profit his own people in his own city.

The Fourth Type. The artificial beginning is made with a proverb which concerns the middle of the subject, as here:

The faithful servant has the courage to attend his lord in adversity, and in misfortune he proves himself worthy.

Continue this beginning thus:

Denis is witness to this; he travels to foreign realms, sows the Lord's seed as he is bidden.

The Fifth Type. Likewise, the artificial beginning is made with a proverb which concerns the end of the subject, as here:

No one can better show himself faithful than the man who gives his neck to be cut for the sake of the Lord.

Continue this beginning thus:

Your death shows this, Denis, while your dead limbs carry your head with living strength.

The Sixth Type. To make the artificial beginning with an example, put some similitude first, then adapt it to the body of the material, as here:

The man who knows how to hunt, hunts; the man who knows how to

70   Tali posito principio, propter similitudinem continuandum est
      aliis dictionibus quam premissis. Hec enim erunt media: "a
      simili," "a pari," "non aliter," "eodem modo," "eo pacto,"
      "pari ratione"; continuetur ergo sic:

              A simili prudens Dionisius ex Elycone
75   Haustas quas nouit fundere fundit aquas.

      Septimus Modus. Item artificiale principium sumitur ab exemplo
      sumpto iuxta medium materie, vt hic:

              Nescit sub modio lumen latitare, sub alga
                Gemma, sub urtice cespite verna rosa.

80   Hoc posito principio, sic debet continuari predicte materie:

              Affectu simili sancti latitare lucerna
                Nescit, scintillans nostra per arua fide.

      Octauus Modus. Item artificiale principium sumitur ab exemplo
      sumpto a fine, vt hic:

85   Dum pastor conseruat oues, dispendia sepe
                Incurrit, multas seruet ut vnus oues.

      Hoc posito principio, sic erit continuandum:

              Consimili ratione, cadit ferientis in ictu
                Vir sanctus; sancto pro grege pastor obit.

90   *Nonus Modus.* Sicut predictum est exhordiri debemus in poema-
      tibus aput modernos; quidam tamen antiquorum, sicut Uirgilius
      et Lucanus, artificiale principium obseruaucrunt narrationi pre-
      ponentes proposicionem, inuocationem, et causam hystorie.*
      Dicit enim Uirgilius in libro Eneydos:

95   Musa, mihi causas memora, quo numine leso, etc.

      Eum sequens Lucanus dicit:*

              Fert animus causas tantarum promere rerum.

send forth powerful missiles with his hand, sends them against the enemy.

Since now we are dealing with a similitude, a beginning such as this must be continued in other words than those I gave before. Here are some ways: "similarly," "equally," "otherwise," "in the same manner," "in that way," "with equal truth"; thus it may be continued:

Similarly, prudent Denis pours waters drawn from Helicon which he knows how to pour.

The Seventh Type. The artificial beginning is also made with an example which concerns the middle of the subject, as here:

The light does not know how to hide under a bushel (cf. Matt. 5:15), nor the pearl under seaweed, nor the rose of spring under a clump of nettle.

This beginning may be connected to our subject thus:

In a similar spirit, the lamp of the saint does not know how to hide, shining with faith throughout our lands.

The Eighth Type. The artificial beginning is also made with an example which concerns the end, as here:

A shepherd keeping his sheep often runs risks in the attempt to guard many sheep single-handed.

Continue this beginning thus:

In much the same way, the holy man falls beneath the blow of the executioner; the shepherd dies for the holy flock.

A Ninth Type. We moderns are supposed to begin, in poems, in the ways I have just prescribed; nevertheless, certain of the ancients, Virgil and Lucan for instance, observed the artificial beginning by putting before the narration the proposition, the invocation, and the motivation of the plot.

observation of modern departures

For Virgil says in the *Aeneid:*

Muse, tell me why, for what infraction of her majesty, etc. (1.8)

Following him, Lucan says:

The mind strains to bring to light the causes of such great events. (1.67)

De Partibus Dictaminis. In dictaminibus aliter erit exordiendum. Si dictamen aliquod componimus quod salutationem contineat, aut scribimus maiori, aut minori, aut equali, aut mixtim. Si maiori, aut maiori* scientia—et*tunc subtilius et hornacius dice-
5 mus;* si maiori dignitate uel etate, vsus erit obseruandus, et ponentur nomina honorem et reuerenciam exibencia. Si minori, pro voluntate nostra et secundum materiam scribemus. Si equali-bus, eodem modo; sed causa reuerencie et humilitatis aliquando equales, aliquando minores preponuntur.
10 Notandum igitur quod aliquando plures, aliquando pauciores partes litteris attribuuntur; quedam enim continent exordium, narrationem, conclusionem; quedam narrationem et conclu-sionem; quedam alias partes cum istis, de quibus postea dicetur. In exordio debent esse tria: beneuolencia (ubi utilitas aperietur);
15 docilitas (ubi apperietur modus agendi); attentio (ubi aperietur difficultas).
De Speciebus Exordii in Litteris. Exordium faciemus in litteris viij modis. Primus modus exordiendi est a prouerbio: secundus ab exemplo; tercius a comparatione; quartus a similitudine;
20 quintus a condicione, que fit per hanc coniunctionem "si"; sex-tus fit per hanc particulam "cum"; septimus per hoc aduerbium "dum"; octauus modus* incipiendi est per ablatiuum absolute positum. Subiungantur exempla.
Primus Modus Exordiendi: a Proverbio. * Si exordiamur a pro-
25 uerbio—et sit* autenticum—consideremus si sint ibi duo uerba; ex re uerbi primo positi constituemus narrationem nostram repe-tendo post prouerbium ipsum uerbum uel rem uerbi; et tracte-mus materiam usque ad conclusionem. In conclusione ponetur ultimum uerbum uel res significata per uerbum.
30 *Ars Inueniendi Litteras sine Salutatione.* Si puer stupefactus de materia inuenienda habuerit hoc prouerbium, "Quod noua testa capit, inueterata sapit," repetat primum* uerbum in narratione uel rem ipsius uerbi, hoc modo:

Laciui pectoris mei thalamus pridem ocia cepit; ociorum et
35 ludorum capcione decipitur, et sic in caput meum sagitta reuertitur deceptionis, que mentem meam mortificatam facit

On the Parts of a Letter. Letters are begun differently. Any letter we may write with a salutation is addressed either to a superior, or to a subordinate, or to an equal, or to a combination of these. If it be to a superior, he is either superior in learning—and in that case we will speak both more subtly and more elegantly; or superior in rank or age, in which case custom should be observed by using nouns and adjectives which show honor and reverence. If to a subordinate, we may write as we like, taking our cue from the subject matter. The same holds for equals; but occasionally, to show reverence and humility, both equals and subordinates are named first.

It should be noted, by the way, that the number of parts to a letter varies with the letter; for some contain exordium, narration, conclusion; some, narration and conclusion; some, other parts in addition to these, which I shall bring up later on. Three elements are necessary in the exordium: benevolence (achieved by revealing usefulness); docility (achieved by announcing your approach); attention (achieved by introducing a difficulty).

On the Types of Exordium in Letters. There are eight ways to make an exordium in a letter. The first way to begin is with a proverb; the second, with an example; the third, with a comparison; the fourth, with a similitude; the fifth, with a condition, using the conjunction "if"; the sixth is made with the particle "since"; the seventh with the adverb "while"; the eighth way to begin is with the ablative absolute. Examples follow.

The First Way of Beginning: with a Proverb. If you begin with a proverb—and it ought to be genuine, not made up—suppose it has two verbs; build your narration around the connotations of the first verb by repeating after the proverb that same verb, or its general sense. Then develop your subject to a conclusion, and in the conclusion put the last verb, or the general sense of that verb.

A Way of Inventing a Letter (without a Salutation). Suppose a student has been given the proverb, "What the young head takes in, the old one is wise about," but is stuck over inventing subject matter to go with it. He might repeat the first verb, or the general sense of that verb, in the narration in this way:

The inner chamber of my fun-loving breast has long since taken up idleness; it is taken in by the captivation of idle games, and thus the arrow of deception flies back on my own head and deadens my mind,

40   laciuie uulneribus interire. Sed quia doctrina magistralis nititur
          mentem meam morbidam suscitare, si potero resurgam ut, qui
          prius fatuus inueniebar, sapere de cetero possim,* et locum in-
          ter sapientes per sapienciam inuenire.

          Ecce consideretur duo uerba ipsius prouerbii resumpta: primum
          in principio ipsius narrationis, scilicet "cepit"; ultimum in con-
          clusione, scilicet "sapere."
          Ab Exemplo: Secundus Modus. Si sumamus exordium ab exemplo
45   in litteris, continuandum est ut* in premissis, ut hic: "Ius exigit
          sagittam fraudis redire celeriter in dolosum uerticem sagittantis."
          Hoc principio posito, cum prouerbium pertineat ad dolum, con-
          tinuandum est hiis uerbis: "a simili," "a pari"; et inde proce-
          dendum est secundum narrationem.
50   *Tercius: a Comparacione.* Item in litteris inchoare possumus a
          comparatione, per quam dilucidabitur narratio; ut si rex diceret
          alicui militi:

          Sicut in fornace flammarum apex inestuat, sic ire feruor et
          indignationis caminus flammescit in pectore nostro, donec G.
55   Miles pro uoluntate nostra propter illatas nobis* iniurias*
          puniatur.

          Quartus: a Similitudine. Si ponatur similitudo loco principii, si
          sit aliqua parabola uel fabula proposito conuenienter adaptata,
          sit* quod recreat auditores, sicut dicit Tullius; vt hic: "Coruus
60   cadauere delectatur, sono tamen accusat seipsum et cadauere
          quod possederat spoliatur." Poterit alia parabola sumi a uulpe
          et a lupo, et ab Appologis Auiani. Appologus est sermo fictus, a
          brutis animalibus sumptus, ad instructionem humane uite intro-
          ductus.
65   *Quintus: a* Condicione.* Inchoabimus a conditione ut hic: "Si
          leges sopite teneant silencium, nihil tutum apud homines relin-
          quitur";* et inde procedendum est secundum tenorem materie.
          Sextus: per Aduerbium Cum. Item, si littere fuerint sine pro-
          uerbio, inchoandum erit* per hoc aduerbium "cum," quod
70   fecit Priscianus: "Cum omnis eloquencie doctrinam* et omne
          studiorum* genus,* etc.," et Porfirius: "Cum sit necessarium,
          etc."
          Septimus per Dum, vel per Ablatiuum Absolute Positum.*
          Exordium frequenter fit aput pueros per hoc aduerbium "dum,"
75   uel per ablatiuum absolute positum.
          Ars Inueniendi Materiam. Qvi, si velint sufficienter materiam
          inuenire, artem istam sequantur. Primo ponant ablatiuum absolute

causing it to perish by the wounds of frivolity. But because the teaching of the master strives to revive my deadened mind, if I can I shall
rise again, so that I who first seemed so empty-headed can be wise
about things in the future, and through wisdom find a place among
the wise.

The two verbs of the proverb, you see, are, in effect, repeated: the first
in the beginning of the narration, by "takes"; the last in the conclusion,
by "be wise about."

The Second Way: with an Example. If you use an example for the exordium of a letter, continue it as I described before. For instance:
"Justice demands that the arrow of fraud return with celerity on the
wily head of the archer." Since the saying is only one special instance
of deceit, continue this beginning with words like "similarly" or "equally"; then go on with the narration.

The Third Way: with a Comparison. You can also begin a letter with a
comparison that will shed light on the narration. For example, a king
may say to some knight:

As the tips of flame rage in a furnace, so the heat of wrath and the
forge of indignation shall flame out in our breast until the Knight G.
be punished as we desire for the affronts he has committed against us.

The Fourth Way: with a Similitude. If you put a similitude in first position, some parable or tale that you can bend to your aim, make it something that will amuse your audience, as Cicero says (cf. *RAH* 1.6.10). For
instance: "The raven enjoys a carcass, but tattles on itself with its croak-
ing, and is robbed of the carcass which had been all its own." Other possible sources of parables are the fox and the wolf, and the *Fables* of
Avianus. A fable is a fictitious story from the animal world with a moral
application to human life.

The Fifth Way: with a Conditional. Begin with a conditional in this
manner: "If the laws of the wise man keep silence, nothing is left safe
among men"; and go on from there in whatever direction the subject
matter demands.

The Sixth Way: with the Adverb "Since." Should a letter not lend itself
to a general statement, begin it with the adverb "since," as Priscian does:
"Since the teaching of all eloquence, and every field of study, etc."; and
Porphyry: "Since it is necessary, etc."

The Seventh: with "While," or with the Ablative Absolute. Students
commonly make an exordium with the adverb "while," or with the ablative absolute.

A Way of Inventing Material. Such students, if they want a reliable way
of inventing material, may use this trick. Put an ablative absolute first,

positum, inde causam rei, postea effectum ipsius cause; et si
uoluerint ampliare materiam, ponant* exclamationem, et in
80   exclamatione tangant comodum uel incomodum rei, hoc modo:
"In aurora garritu volucrum a lecto me celeriter excitante, mihi
materne dilectionis sedulitas libellum et tabulas afferebat." Hoc
dicto, subiungat causam: "ut librum aperirem, apertum legerem,
lectum memorie commendarem." Subiungatur huius rei effectus:
85   "quia lecta memorie commendata discipulum perficiunt, et perfectus ad magistratus cathedram exaltatur." Si puer voluerit*
ampliare materiam, exclamet* hoc modo: "Pape! quam delecta-
bilis est philosophia, quam fructuosus est amor sciencie, qua*
thesaurus indeficiens possidetur!" Hoc dicto, poterit ipse multa
90   per exclamationem supponere et comodum uel incomodum in-
cludere.
    De Principiis Litterarum. Item notandum quod "exordium" ali-
quando large sumitur, scilicet illud totum quod antecedit narrationem; aliquando stricte, scilicet prouerbium (uel illud quod
95   est in* loco prouerbii). Est autem Exordium rethoricum principium ad persuadendum. Proemium est preordinacio libri ad in-
struendum. Prologus est inductiuus sermo subsequentis operis,
siue contineat talia* prohemialia siue non. Epigrama est principium
continens causam et similitudinem, et modum agendi demonstrans.
100   Thema est principium diuine predicationis. Prefacio est principium
in diuinis cantibus et ministeriis, vt hic: "Exultat iam angelica
turba celorum, etc."
    Item cum in principiis literalibus multa attendantur, notandum
quod in litteris numquam debet dici "Dei gratia," nisi in litteris
105   Domini Pape et archiepiscopi et episcopi et cardinalis, uel aliud*
loco eius positum, ut "Dei miseracione." Item in litteris imperatoris et regis dicitur "Dei gratia," sed adulacionis causa. Notarii
ducis et comitis ita dicunt, sed non bene.
    Item imperatori et regi dicimus "illustrissimo," "potentissimo,"
110   "iustissimo," "nobilissimo."* Comiti uel duci dicimus "strenuis-
simo," "generosissimo." Episcopis dicimus "sanctissimo Patri ac
Domino," "reuerendo," "reuerentissimo." Decanis, archidiaconis,
officialibus, magistris: "venerabilibus viris," "viro discreto,"
"viro prudenti," "viro uirtutibus uirenti." Si scribimus abbati, sic:
115   "deuoto ac deuotissimo Patri ac Domino," "viro religioso," "viro
venerabili." Si presbiteris: "venerabili viro." Si scolari: "studioso
viro" (uel "socio"). Si ciuibus: "discreto preposito," uel "dilecto
mercatori," etc. Si subditus scribat* domino, dicat "karissimo."
Si rusticis mittantur* littere, simpliciter nominentur, vel dicatur

then the (cause of the matter,) then the [effect] of that cause; to amplify
the material, add an exclamation, and in the exclamation touch on what
is good or bad in the matter. Thus: "The chatter of birds rousing me
quickly from my bed at dawn, the zeal of motherly love would bring in
my little book and writing tablets." To this he adds the cause: "for me
to open the book, to read what I opened to, to commit what I read to
memory." Then the effect of these actions: "because committing his
reading to memory perfects a student, and the perfected man is promoted to a master's chair." Then, if the student wants to amplify his
material, he may exclaim in this manner: "Indeed! how delightful is
philosophy, how fruitful is the love of knowledge, in which is possessed
a 'treasure that faileth not'" (cf. Luke 12:33). After this he can bring
in many more things by way of exclamation and discuss what is good or
bad about them.

Beginnings for Letters. Note also that "exordium" is sometimes defined
broadly, as everything that precedes the narration; sometimes strictly, as
the proverb (or whatever is in the place of the proverb). An Exordium,
then, is a rhetorical beginning whose purpose is persuasion. A Proem is
an advance outline of a book's contents, whose purpose is instruction. A
Prologue is an introductory discussion to the work which follows it; it
may or may not contain such "proemial" matter. An Epigram is a beginning that states a cause and a similitude, and that explains the approach. A Theme is the beginning of a sacred sermon. A Preface is the
beginning to sacred songs and services, for example, "Now the angelic
host of heaven rejoices, etc."

Furthermore, although epistolary beginnings cover many matters, it
should be noted that letters never contain the expression "by the grace
of God," or some substitute for it such as "by the mercy of God," except letters from the Holy Father, an archbishop, a bishop, or a cardinal.
"By the grace of God" is also used in letters from the emperor or a king,
but merely for flattery. The secretaries of a duke or a count also use it,
but they should not.

In addressing the emperor or a king, we say "most illustrious," "most
powerful," "most just," "most noble." To a count or duke we say "most
diligent," "most generous." To bishops we say "most holy Father and
Lord," "reverend," "most reverent." To deans, archdeacons, other
church officials, masters: "venerable men," "discreet man," "prudent
man," "man blooming with virtues." If we are writing to an abbot, thus:
"devoted and most devout Father and Lord," "religious man," "venerable man." To priests: "venerable man." To a scholar: "studious man"
(or "colleague"). To those in civil life: "discreet governor," "beloved
merchant," etc. If a subordinate should write to his lord, he might say
"dearest." If letters are sent to peasants they may be simply named, or

120   "laborioso colone,"* "lacertoso," "forti," "valido." Si scribimus
        mulieribus, dicatur "karissime," "dulcissime," "piissime," "pu-
        dice," "generose." Si meretricibus, "curiali," "formose," "facete,"
        "urbane."
        De Supersalutatione. Salutationem sequitur Supersalutacio, uel
125   additio salutis, quam hoc artificio debemus inuenire: ab officio,
        ab etate, a dignitate, a meteria ipsa, a summa rei, vel a negocio
        rei, ut: "regnum iuste gubernare"; "Regi regum complacere,"
        "Deo militare," "non seculo sed Deo studere," "bonis operibus
        Deo complacere," "ad portum salutis eterne applicare"; "disci-
130   pulos fideliter instruere"; "gregem sibi commissum salubriter
        custodire"; "candore pudicicie uernare," "virginitatem illibatam
        custodire," "Sabinas rigidas imitari"; "oues ad viam ab inuio
        reuocare"; "paternis pedibus caput procliue," "sancte caniciei
        reuerenciam," "deuotam in omnibus obedienciam," "iuuenum
135   contuberniis nullatenus consentire"; "Deo placite contemplari,"
        "in claustro mentis claustrum Domino dedicare"; "infirmitatem
        suam celeriter uisitare," "miserie iugum mitigare"; "contra
        Crucis hostes hostiliter dimicare"; "Sue Sanctitatis uestigia
        osculari." In litteris Domini Pape semper continetur "salutem et
140   apostolicam benedictionem." Item archiepiscopi et episcopi
        vocant se fratres ad inuicem; a negociis suis ponunt addicionem
        salutis, ut patet ante.
        De Arte Uestiendi Nudam Materiam. Sequitur de materia nuda
        uestienda. "Materiam nudam" uoco illam que non est rethorice
145   ampliata neque ornata, ut contingit in simplici dictamine, quod
        habet tamen tres partes post salutationem, que sunt narratio,
        mandatum, et conclusio; vt hic:

        Littere Curiales et Ciuiles.

        Generoso viro Comiti Campanie; R., humilis abbas, et
150   Conuentus Sancti Germani de Pratis: salutem.

        Cum pars terre nostre iaceat contermina terre G.,* militis de
        loco* sic dicto, ut utrique terre dominetur sibi presumit quan-
        dam terre nostre particulam vendicare. Quare Nobilitatem
        Vestram suppliciter exoramus, quatinus predictum militem
155   instanter amoneatis, vt nos permittat terram nostram integram
        more solito possidere.

        Iste littere uulgares et nude possunt uestiri si sex narrationi
        preponantur et sequatur exclamatio, rei comoda uel incomoda

one may say: "hard-working farmer," "muscular," "strong," "stout." If we are writing to women, we may say: "dearest," "sweetest," "most pious," "modest," "generous." To courtesans: "courtly," "beautiful," "clever," "urbane."

On the Supersalutation. The supersalutation, or addition to the greeting, follows the salutation. We should invent it by means of the device of referring to office, age, rank, or the subject matter itself, its chief point or main business, as: "may he govern his kingdom justly," "may he be pleasing to the King of Kings," "may he do battle for God," "may he be zealous not for the world but for God," "may he please God with good works," "may he arrive at the harbor of eternal salvation"; "may he instruct his students faithfully"; "may he watch over the flock entrusted to him to their advantage"; "may she blossom with the whiteness of modesty," "may she keep her virginity unimpaired," "may she imitate the rigid Sabine women"; "may he call his sheep back to the road from the wilderness"; "a head bent before paternal feet," "reverence to sacred gray hair," "vowed obedience in all things," "may he by no means stoop to fraternizing with the young"; "may his contemplation be pleasing to God," "within his cloister may he dedicate the cloister of his mind to the Lord"; "may he visit the writer's sickness quickly," "may he soften the yoke of misery"; "may he fight the enemies of the Crusade as their enemy"; "may he kiss the footprints of his Holiness." The Holy Father's letters always have "greeting and the apostolic benediction." Also, archbishops and bishops call themselves each other's brothers; they draw the addition to the greeting from the main business of their letter, as is clear above.

On the Art of Dressing Up Naked Matter. The next subject is dressing up naked matter. I call "naked matter" whatever is not rhetorically amplified or embellished. Such is the case with a simple letter, which still has three parts after the salutation: narration, request, and conclusion. For example:

A Letter Concerning Civil Law.

    To that generous man, the Count of Champagne; R., humble abbot, and the community of St. Germain des Prés, greeting.

    Since part of our land borders on the land of G., Knight of such-and-such a place, he has presumed, in order to be master of both plots, to claim a certain small portion of our land as his. We humbly pray Your Nobility to warn the said Knight immediately that he should allow us to keep our land in one piece as we always have.

This vulgar and naked letter can be dressed up by putting six things before the narration, and following it with an exclamation to lay bare what

manifestans. Salutationem debet sequi additio salutationis; inde
160   sequitur prouerbium, uel propositio, quod idem est; item probatio propositionis, uel declaratio prouerbii, quod idem est; post
erit assumpcio et eius probatio; et inde conclusio premissorum*—
non dico litterarum—hoc modo:
"Generoso uiro Comiti etc., salutem, et per presentis uite
165   miliciam in celesti curia triumphare. Potentes principes terrenis
honoribus preficiuntur ut per eos fraudes et iniurie relidantur."
Hoc posito prouerbio, eius sequitur declaratio, hec scilicet:
"Quia nihil esset tutum aput inferiores nisi metus pene retunderet
effrenem maliciam iniquorum." Hoc dicto, sequitur assumpcio:
170   "Sed sunt* nonnulli qui non abhorrent abuti sua potestate."
Hoc* dicto, sequitur probatio, sic: "quia degrassantur in subditos
et sua per rapinam faciunt aliena." Hoc dicto, ecce premissorum
conclusio: "Est igitur necesse uel spoliatos* conqueri, uel spolia-
tionem in paciencia sustinere." Hoc dicto, sequitur uinculum
175   siue medium inter prouerbium et narrationem, quod fit huiusmodi dictionibus: "hoc declaratur," "non multum discrepat,"
"a simili." Continuetur ergo narratio premissa, hoc modo: "Hoc
per G. Militis maliciam declaratur, quia cum pars terre nostre
iaceat contermina" etc., usque ad finem narrationis. Inde ad
180   ornatum et ampliacionem narrationis sequatur exclamatio, sic:
"O, quanta redundat in potentibus malicia qui sibi potenciam
ignorant a Deo collatam ut, propriis metis contenti, puniant
delinquencium* errores, et minus peritos instruant per exemplum!
O, quid faceret* insaciata predicti militis auaricia si fieret po-
185   testate Iulius Cesar, cum, hereditatis ample possessor, posses-
sionis nostre parue conetur particulam per hyantcm auariciam
obsorbere!" Sic ampliata narratione, sequitur mandatum et
conclusio, sicut patet in premissis; sed addatur quedam sentencia
generalis, sic: "Valet enim quam plurimum superioris exortatio;*
190   vox enim domini plus ualet in iubendo quam serui gladius in
pugnando."
De Vi Partibus Orationis. * Sequitur de sex partibus orationis,*
que sunt: Exordium, Narratio, Partitio, Confirmatio, Confutatio,
Conclusio. Hiis vi partibus debemus uti si uelimus ornate dicere
195   ad persuadendum uel dissuadendum. Exordium est principium
orationis rethorice, continens beniuolenciam, docilitatem, attentionem. Narracio est rerum gestarum uel sicut gestarum expositio. ("Sicut gestarum" dicitur propter fabulosas narrationes.)

is good or bad about the matter. An addition to the greeting should follow the salutation; after that comes the proverb, or major premise, which
is the same thing; then the proof of the major, or the explanation of the
proverb, which is the same thing; after that come the minor premise and
its proof; and then the conclusion of these premises (not to be confused
with the conclusion of the letter); in this way:

"To that generous man, Count etc., greeting, and may militancy in this
present life lead him to triumph in the celestial court. Powerful princes
are set up with earthly honors so that through them crimes and abuses
may be avenged." The proverb down, its explanation follows, to wit:
"for nothing would be safe among the small if the fear of punishment
did not check the unbridled malice of the wicked." Next comes the
minor premise: "But there are not a few who do not shrink from abus-
ing their power." Then its proof: "for they set upon their subjects and
make others' things their own by plunder." Then the conclusion of
these premises: "The plundered are therefore forced either to complain
or to suffer plunder in silence." Next comes the link or medium between
the proverb and the narration, in some such phrase as: "this is exemplified," or "not much different is," or "similarly." The narration I have
already given is then continued, in this manner: "This is exemplified by
the malice of the Knight G., for, since part of our land borders on"—and
so on through the end of the narration. Then, for embellishment and
amplification of the narration, an exclamation may follow, thus: "Oh,
how much malice redounds on the powerful who ignore the fact that
their power is conferred on them by God in order that, free from fear
for themselves, they might punish the offenses of wrongdoers and instruct the less-educated by their example! Oh, what might the insatiable
avarice of the Knight do if he had the power of a Julius Caesar, when,
already possessing an ample inheritance of his own, he tries in his yawn-
ing avarice to swallow up a portion of our small possessions!" The narration thus amplified, the request and conclusion come next, as may be
seen in the letter I have given above; but some general sentiment may be
added, like "For the urging of a superior works better than anything
else; for the voice of the master commanding is mightier than the sword
of the slave fighting."

On the Six Parts of an Oration. The next subject is the six parts of an
oration, which are: the Exordium, the Narration, the Division, the Confirmation, the Refutation, the Conclusion. We should make use of these
six parts if we wish to speak eloquently for the purpose of persuasion or
dissuasion. The Exordium is the beginning of a rhetorical oration, containing devices to secure benevolence, docility, attention. The Narration
is an account of events which have taken place, or seem to have taken
place. (I say "seem to have taken place" to allow for fictional narrations.)

200 Partitio est diuisio nostre cause a causa aduersarii nostri, ostendens
in quibus conueniamus* cum aduersario, in quibus autem non.
Confirmatio est nostre partis cum quadam asseuerancia* frequens
assertio, quando scilicet affirmamus causam nostram uirorum uel
deorum testimonio. Confutatio dicitur infirmatio uel reprehensio
205 argumentationum partis aduerse. Conclusio est artificiosus terminus orationis. Quorum exempla in hiis uersibus subiciuntur, in
quibus est persuasio ad Crucem accipiendam.

	Exordium	Si graue delires, surgendi collige uires; Succedet tibi res quando uigore uires.
	Narracio	Ierusalem meret quia uiribus hostis inheret; Hanc Cruce qui queret premia digna feret.
210		Planctus Ierusalem planctum generat generalem; Plangit ruralem templa tenere Palem.
	Persuasio* vel*	Summi signa Ducis ducas, qui gaudia ducis Luceat ut lucis Lux tibi, tyro Crucis.
215	Ampliacio	Sic colleteris cum mundo, ne lacrimeris, Si bene tristeris et bene letus eris.
		Agmen uirtutum duc* Christi castra secutum, Cum non sit tutum carnis amare lutum.
220		Marte mori morum facias aciem uiciorum; Vi Crucis illorum rex cadet* ante chorum.
		Principe prostrato, virtute Crucis superato, Castra solo fato cetera queque dato.
		Vi superare Dei si uires uis aciey, In fundo fidei stes et in arce spei.
225	Partitio	Deuictus raro uoto ruit hostis auaro: Se Mundo caro iungit amica Caro.*
		Sanguine quos emit Rex, immo morte redemit, Mundi pompa premit dum Caro blanda fremit;
230		Insidias Sathane formida* vespere mane; Ne certes uane fine, canenda cane.
	Confirmatio	Valle sedens humilis animus decertat* herilis. Si desit bilis, qua nichil est nisi lis,
		Fastus sublimis cadet; arx sta uallibus imis: Floreat illimis mens redimita thimis.
235		Bellum disponat Fronesis que Marte coronat, Consilium donat qua tuba iussa tonat.

The Division is the separation of our case from the case of our opponent, showing where we agree with our opponent and where we do not. The Confirmation is the thorough presentation of our side with a certain earnestness, that is, when we strengthen our case with the testimony of men or gods. Refutation means weakening or finding flaws in the argument of the other side. The Conclusion is an artful ending to the oration.

To exemplify these, I have included the following verses, which are a persuasion to join the Crusade.

Exordium   If you be seriously awry, gather together your strength
                  to rise; things will go your way when you grow in vigor.

Narration   Jerusalem is grieving because she is stuck in the power
                  of the enemy. Whoever seeks her in the Crusade will bring
                  back worthy rewards. Jerusalem's lament generates a
                  general lament; she laments that rustic Pales has posses-
                  sion of her temples.

Persuasion or   You may lead the standards of the highest leader, O
Amplification   recruit of the Cross, you who produce joys that the Light
                  of light may shine upon you. Thus you may rejoice to-
                  gether with the world, not cry, if you grieve well and will
                  be joyful well. Lead the army of virtues which has fol-
                  lowed the camp of Christ, since it is not safe to love the
                  clay of flesh. You may bring the battle line of vices to
                  their death by the military power of virtues; by the power
                  of the Cross their king will fall before his host. Once their
                  prince is down, conquered by the virtue of the Cross,
                  give what remains of their camp to the soil they were
                  destined for. If you wish by the power of God to conquer
                  the power of that battle line, stand in the depth of faith
                  and on the high fortress of hope.

Division   The enemy rarely falls prey to the vow of a man who
                  remains covetous: the amiable Flesh joins herself to her
                  beloved World. Those whom the King bought with His
                  blood, indeed, redeemed with His death, the pomp of
                  the World presses while enticing Flesh murmurs; fear the
                  ambushes of Satan morning and evening; lest you strug-
                  gle in vain in the end, sing the things that should be sung.

Confirmation   Soul, humble but heroic, sitting in the valley, fights on.
                  If bitterness is absent, which only serves to intensify strife,
                  haughty contempt will fall; stand a high fortress in the
                  depths of valleys, let the pure mind blossom, surrounded
                  with thyme. Let Prudence, who crowns with Mars, settle
                  the battle; let her give counsel at whose bidding the horn

Iusque modumque tene, pietate fluant tibi uene:
　　Lene cor in iuuene sit, sapiensque sene.
Gratia diuina tibi morbi sit* medicina.

240　　　　　　　Vires ingemina, cum Cruce uise Sina,
Sterne Machometum,* da leto, destrue letum
　　Riuus in fletum uerte, repende metum.
Victrici uita soluentur menia trita;
　　Tu uicium uita; victor abibis ita.

245　Confirmatio　Nil dextre poterunt ubi mentis prelia deerunt:
　　　Ampliandi　　　Spicula uota serunt, menia firma terunt.
　　　Causa*　　　Pergama Phebeya non subuertet Cytharea
　　　　　　　Pomum Dircea si capit alma dea.
Tu bene bellaris si castus amator amaris;
250　　　　　　　Gaudes antiparis* nescius esse Paris.
Hector saluatur, mentis uigor, urbsque iocatur
　　Cordis.* Letatur cur? Quia palma datur.
Virtus Pellide torpet, uirtus et Atride:
　　Quam pugnet tepide* uulgus inherme uide.

255　Exposicio　Est furor Eacides ire, Sathanas et Atrides;
　　　Mistica　　　Hiis frenum nisi des, Pergama capta uides.
Surrepens motus sit Ulixes, non bene notus,
　　Fraude latens totus, naufragiique nothus:
Blanditur praue detensa* flamine naue;
260　　　　　　　Per tempus suaue turbinis arma caue.
Frangitur Aiacis septemplex vmbo minacis
　　Si septem pacis tyro trophea facis,
Crimina septena si vincis funere plena,
　　Si mundas pena te, lacrimante gena.
265　Da sponse lorum, Ratio, Carnique decorum:
　　Diuerso morum tegmine sterne thorum.
Vir regat uxorem, doceat seruare pudorem;
　　Ne preter morem lusitet, obde forem.
Rex dominans, Ecube pugnandi federe nube,
270　　　　　　　Hanc tibi uoce tube subdere colla iube.
　　　Confutatio　Vult Caro mechari, Mundoque cupit sociari:
　　　　　　　Mecha maritari nititur illa Pari,
Vult Helene fieri, nescit peccare uereri,
　　Festinatque feri demonis arte teri.
275　Cedit Cesareus feruor, cedit Capaneus,
　　Cedit ei Tydeus cui fouet* arma Deus.
Magnus Hic est, uere magnus ui castra tenere;
　　Magno cessere menia, claustra, sere.

roars. Observe right and moderation; let goodness flow
in your veins; let the young heart be gentle and the old
wise. May divine grace heal your sickness. Redouble your
strength; see Sinai with the Crusade; overthrow Mahomet,
give him to death, destroy death, turn his laughter into
tears, requite fear. The walls will be worn down and destroyed by conquering life. You shun vice; thus will you
emerge the victor.

Confirmation   Right hands will be powerless where mental fortitude
for   is lacking; vows are the seed of spears, and wear away
Amplification   firm walls. Phoebean Cytharea will not overturn Troy if
the kindly Dircean goddess takes the fruit. You will fight
well if you are loved as a chaste lover; you rejoice to be
Paris, ignorant of shields. Hector, vigor of mind, is saved,
and the city of the heart laughs. Why does it rejoice? Because it is given the palm. The courage of Achilles grows
sluggish, and the courage of the son of Atreus; see how
slackly that mob fights without its weapons.

Mystical   Achilles is the fury of wrath, the son of Atreus is Satan;
Exposition   unless you apply the rein to these, you see Troy captured.
Let Ulysses be a creeping motive, not well noted, completely hidden by deceit, a bastard bringing shipwreck; he
flatters wickedly with a breeze while the ship is calm; in
smooth weather beware the attack of the whirlwind. The
sevenfold shield of menacing Ajax is broken if seven times
you, the recruit, make the sign of peace, if you overcome
the seven sins with full destruction, if you cleanse yourself by penance with tearful cheek. Apply the rein to your
bride, O Reason, decorum to the Flesh; spread the marriage bed with a many-colored coverlet of virtues. Let the
husband rule the wife, teach her to observe modesty; lest
she keep up her immoral playing, shut the door. You have
dominion, O King: marry Hecuba by treaty of war, sound
the horn and command her to submit her neck to you.

Refutation   The Flesh wants to commit adultery, desires to consort
with the World: that adulteress strives to be married to
Paris, wants to become Helen, knows no fear of sinning,
hastens to be destroyed by the art of the wild demon.
Caesar's fervor yields, Capaneus yields, Tydeus yields to
him whose arms God cherishes. He is great, great indeed
in His power to hold the camp; walls, locks, and bars have
yielded to the Great One.

Conclusio   Esto Dei tyro; dabis hosti uincula diro,
280   Cernes in giro cedere mille uiro.
                          Mortem ne timeas: inuade manus Cananeas;
                          Perdens* ne pereas: percute, sterne reas.
                          Sit pax uictori, Dominus, requiesque labori;
                          Viuentisque chori m▪▪▪▪ ▪▪▪▪▪▪ ▪▪▪▪.

285   *De Arte Abbreuiandi Materiam.* Sequitur de abbreuiatione et
        ampliatione materie. Que abbreuiant materiam v sunt: Emphasis,
        Disiunctum, uerbum conuersum in participium, ablatiui absolute
        positi, dictionum materiam exprimencium electio. Emphasis est*
        vehemens laudis vel vituperii expressio Emphasis igitur est ut:
290   "Virgo uirginum est ipsa castitas." Disiunctum est color rethori-
        cus quo copulatiue coniunctiones subtrahuntur, ut in Eneyde:

                              Ite,
                Ferte citi flammas, date tela, impellite remos.

        Item in Epitalamico:

295   Mars furit, exundat cruor, impetus imperat, ardet
                   Ambitus, excrescit preda, rapina metit.

        Verbum conuersum in participium abbreuiat materiam sic: "Veni
        ut legerem et proficerem"; "Veni ut legens proficerem." Ablatiui
        absolute positi breuitatis causa ponuntur, ut: "Ego surrexi hodie
300   mane. . ."; "Me surgente mane. . ." Item eligere debemus uerba
        illa in quibus consistit uis materie, quod maxime considerandum
        est in prohemiis, in quibus tractatus subsequens declaratur; ut in
        Epitalomico Beate Uirginis, in quo describitur domus regia in
        qua virtutes triumphant, per quam intelligitur Beata Uirgo,
305   sponsa et mater Saluatoris. Hoc totum notatur in duobus uersibus
        primis, scilicet hiis:

                Aula triumphalis *uirtutum,* florida *uirgo,*
                Florida *sponsa* Dei, florida *mater,* aue!

        De Arte Ampliandi Materiam. Qvinque sunt que* ampliant ma-
310   teriam,* hec* scilicet: Digressio, Descriptio, Circumlocutio, Pro-
        sopopeya, Apostrophatio; et sub hac ultima intelliguntur v
        colores rethorici, qui sunt: Conduplicatio, Exclamacio, Subiectio,
        Dubitatio, Interpretatio.
        Primus Modus Ampliandi. Digressio fit aliquando ad id quod est
315   de materia, ut quando fit aliqua descriptio uel comparatio. Item
        digressio fit aliquando ad id quod non est de materia, sed materie
        conuenienter adiungitur, ut quando interseritur fabula, vel* apo-
        logus adaptatur. Digressionis exemplum in hoc dictamine apparet,

Conclusion   Be a recruit of God; you will put the fearful enemy in
chains; you will see a thousand yield to one man in a
circle about you. Do not fear death: invade the Canaanite
bands. Do not lose and perish; strike, overthrow the guilty.
May the victor have peace, and rest from toil; may the
Lord be with him; merit to die the death of the host that
lives on!

On the Art of Shortening Material. The next subject is the shortening and
amplifying of material. There are five ways to shorten material, namely:
Emphasis, Asyndeton, the participle, ablative absolutes, and choosing
words that express the essence of the subject matter. Emphasis is the
strong expression of praise or blame; thus this is Emphasis: "The Virgin
of virgins is chastity itself." Asyndeton is a rhetorical figure in which
copulative conjunctions are left out, as in the *Aeneid:*

Go, bring fire quickly, hurl weapons, drive the oars! (4.593-94)

Likewise in the *Epithalamium:*

Mars rages, blood flows, violence reigns, the walls burn, plunder in-
creases, rapine gathers in. (1.59-60)

A participle shortens material, thus: "I have come that I might read and
that I might profit"; "I have come that, reading, I might profit." Ablative
absolutes are used for the sake of brevity, as: "I rose early this morning. . ."; "Me rising early. . ." Finally, we should choose words that go
to the heart of the matter. Pay particular attention to this in proems, in
which the treatise to follow is summarized; as in the *Epithalamium of
the Blessed Virgin,* in which is described a royal dwelling where the
virtues go in triumph, which stands for the Blessed Virgin, spouse and
mother of the Savior. All this is noted in the first two verses:

Triumphal palace of the virtues, flowerlike virgin, flowerlike spouse
and flowerlike mother of God, hail!

On the Art of Amplifying Material. There are five ways to amplify material, namely: Digression, Vivid Description, Periphrasis, Prosopopoeia,
and Apostrophe; and under this last are included five more rhetorical
figures, which are: Reduplication, Exclamation, Hypophora, Indecision,
and Synonymy.
The First Way. A digression is sometimes made to what is itself part of *(digression to*
the subject matter; for example, a description or comparison. A digres- *part of the
subject matter*
sion is also made sometimes to what is not part of the subject matter
but is aptly connected to it, as when a story is inserted or a fable adapted.
An example of a digression appears in this letter, which a student sends

320   quod scolaris mittit alicui amicorum suorum de nouo principio
       magistrali quod intendit facere. Dicit ergo sic:

       Littere Magistrales Ampliande.*

           A. B. Salutem.

           Largitatis est gratia signumque dilectionis alios exhortari
       quorum opitulamine suorum indigencia fulciatur. Cum Pari-
325   siane scientie militia laboriosa me longo tempore fatigauerit,*
       tandem laboris* longi brauium compendere decertaui: ma-
       gistralem cathedram—non sine frequenti disputationis con-
       flictu—conscendendi* licenciam accepi. Set penuria rerum
       iniciales michi distulit apparatus. Mos enim est Parisius non
330   solum disputationum frequencia sed festiuarum apparatibus
       epularum honorem suscipere cathedralem.

       Hoc dicto, sic ampliatur* materia per comparationem:

           Sicut enim magnanimi Neptholomi mos est non solummodo
       suam corporali conflictu gloriam ampliare, sed mensa solempni
335   sibi gratiam amicorum extendere, sic qui sapiencie commilitat
       hec considerat et adimplet, uel inter homines homo degeneran-
       tis nature uelut symia derideatur.
           Dignetur igitur Generositatis Uestre dilectio commendabilis
       patri meo persuasiones efficaces proponere, quatinus manum*
340   dignetur* ad magistratus mei principium ampliare. Cumque
       talia laycalis ignoret simplicitas, illi* diligenter ostendatis quot
       et quanta magistrale petat inicium, et quantus honor et fructus
       magistris oriatur, qui per scienciam tandem secularibus honori-
       bus prouehuntur.

345   *Secundus Modus Ampliandi Materiam.** Item ampliatur materia
       per Discripcionem quod est quandoque necessarium tam in
       poematibus quam in dictaminibus, ut in presenti patet dictamine
       quod nouus inceptor fratri uel alii amicorum poterit delegare
       sic:

350   *Littere Ampliande.*

           A. B. Salutem.

           Labor fructuosus in studio non solum studenti parit hono-
       rem sed studentis amicos prouehit multotiens ad honores.
       Frequenti dieta* longoque sudore sciencie margaritas Parisius
355   collegi, et, tandem sudoris terminum adeptus optatum, inter
       magistros magister sederem, si parentum et amicorum sentirem
       dexteram largiorem.

to one of his friends on the inception which he is about to undergo as a new master.

A Master's Letter, for Amplifying.

A. to B., greeting.

It is simple gratitude for past generosity and a sign of love to exhort others to support the pennilessness of the people they love by their aid. Although the laborious campaign of Parisian knowledge has fatigued me by its length, I have won the right at last to weigh in the balance the prize of that long labor: I have received a licentiate to mount a master's chair—not without the repeated battle of disputation. But penury has delayed the initiating ceremonies for me. For the custom at Paris is to receive the honor of a chair not only with a multitude of disputations, but with the ceremonies of festive banquets.

At this point the material is amplified by means of a comparison, thus:

For just as it is the custom of a great-hearted Neoptolemus not only to extend his glory in physical combat, but to increase the gratitude of his friends toward him by giving a formal dinner, so the man who fights in the army of wisdom remembers these requirements and carries them out, or among men that man of base nature is laughed at like an ape.

May, then, the praiseworthy love of Your Generosity deign to bring effective arguments to bear on my father, that he may deign to extend a hand toward the inception of my mastership. Although lay simplicity is ignorant of such matters, I beg you diligently to show him how many and how great things a master's initiation demands, and what great honor and reward arise for teachers, whose knowledge eventually raises them to worldly honors.

The Second Way of Amplifying Material. Material is also amplified by Vivid Description, which is sometimes necessary in letters as well as in poems, as is clear in the present letter, which the new inceptor might send to his brother or another of his relatives, thus:

vivid description

A Letter for Amplifying.

A. to B., greeting.

Fruitful labor in study not only gives birth to honor for the student, but often exalts that student's relatives to honors as well. By dint of frequent fasting and long sweating, I have been gathering the pearls of knowledge at Paris, and, having attained at long last the desired end of that sweat, would now be sitting a master among the masters, if I felt in my parents and relatives a more liberal right hand.

Hoc dicto, amplietur materia per Descripcionem sic:

360

Sed frigescit in parentibus meis feruor dilectionis, subcumbit
natura, torpet affectus, expirat gratia, dum scolaris pallescit
studio, macrescit* esurie, vilescit panniculis, qui faciunt
Homerum cum Hennio residere.

Cum igitur dilectio carnalis in uobis ex affinitate sanguinis
post patrem meum magis ad hoc moueri debeat et ad hoc

365

mecum aspirare, vos diligenter hortor et exhortor quatinus in
hoc casu uestrum senciam subleuamen, quia futurum est,
annuente Deo, ut per magistralem honorem et scientiam amicos meos eleuare uidear ad culmina dignitatum.

Tercius Modus. Item Circumlocutio materiam extendit, quod

370

erit necessarium quando laudare uel uituperare intendimus,
tangendo uirtutes et probitates uel enormitates et vicia in
personis ipsis.

Quartus Modus. Prosopopeya est introductio noue persone,
quando res inanimata introducitur loqui, ut in Ouidio Metha-

375

morphosios tellus conqueritur Ioui de incendio Phitontis.

Quintus Modus. Apostrophatio est subita conuersio sermonis
ad aliquem virum absentem causa laudandi uel uituperandi, ut
dictum est ante.

Sextus Modus. Conduplicatio materiam elongat. Conduplicatio

380

est color rethoricus quando sub Interrogatione una dictio uel
due repetuntur in fine orationis que ponebatur in principio, ut
in Iuuenale:

Tune duos vna, seuissima uipera, sena?
Tune duos?

385

Septimus Modus. Auctores vtuntur Exclamatione ad ampliatio-
nem sue materie, sicut Lucanus dicens:

O male discordes nimiaque cupidine ceci,
Quid miscere* iuuat vires* orbemque tenere?

Octauus Modus. De Subiectione non habemus exemplum in

390

metricis auctoribus, preterquam in Noua Poetria, et in Epitalamico, in cuius decimo libro in laudem Beate Uirginis colores
rethorici ponuntur; ubi ponitur persuasio ne uirgines* assensum
prebeant petitoribus qui multa promittunt ut decipiant; quibus*
potest responderi per Subiectionem, que est crebra et frequens

395

ostensio rei quam proponimus, aliquando cum interrogacione,
aliquando cum affirmatione, aliquando cum negatione, ut in
uersibus istis:

Qvisquam promittit fallax patrimonia, quero
Cuius erant patris. Fur pater eius erat;

At this point the material may be amplified by means of a Vivid Description, thus:

> But the warmth of love is growing cool in my parents, nature is sinking, affection is numb, kindness is dying, while study is making the scholar pale, hunger is making him thin, rags are making him filthy—which can put Homer in a class with Ennius.
>
> And so, since the kindred love that is in you from your being closest to me in blood after my father ought to be moved the more to this and to pant for it with me, I diligently urge and exhort you that I might feel your support in this case, because, God willing, it will not be long before, by reason of the honor and knowledge that are a master's, I shall be seen to elevate my relatives to the heights of prestige.

The Third Way. Periphrasis also extends material, and it will be necessary when we intend to praise or blame by pointing out the virtues and good qualities or enormities and vices in people's characters.

The Fourth Way. Prosopopoeia is the introduction of a new character by bringing on an inanimate thing to speak, as when in Ovid's *Metamorphoses* (2.272-300) the earth complains to Jove of Phaeton's fire.

The Fifth Way. Apostrophe is suddenly turning to address some absent person, to praise or blame him, as mentioned earlier.

The Sixth Way. Reduplication stretches the material out. Reduplication is a rhetorical figure in which, as part of an interrogation, a word or phrase which appeared at the beginning of a sentence is repeated at the end, as in Juvenal:

> You (poisoned) two at one meal, O cruellest of vipers? You poisoned two? (6.641-42)

The Seventh Way. The classical authors use Exclamation to amplify their material, as when Lucan says:

> O you disastrously at odds, and blinded by too much greed, why does it please you to join your forces and rule the world? (1.87-88)

The Eighth Way. Of Hypophora we have no example in the metrical authors except in the *Nova Poetria* and in the *Epithalamium,* in whose tenth book rhetorical figures are employed to praise the Blessed Virgin; it includes an attempt to persuade virgins not to give in to suitors who promise everything in order to seduce them. They can be answered by *(hypophora* means of a Hypophora, which is an intensive and many-sided exposition of the facts of a case, achieved through a combination of questioning, assertion, and denial, as in these verses:

> Whenever some liar promises his patrimony, I ask what father it came from. This man's father was a thief; his grandfather never had a penny

400   Vixit auus, uixit proauus, sine re, sine tecto:*
            Nec* valet hic heres ullius esse uagus.
          Quis scurre, mecho profugo sua det bona? Nemo.
            Sed dices, "Lucrum colligit arte sua."
          Ne dicas; ars talus ei, ciphus, alea, furtum;
405   Hystrio cui uilis denegat esse pater.

Nonus Modus. Dubitatio est color rethoricus quando cum hoc uerbo "nescio" plura ponuntur quibus res debeat nominari, vt hic: "Nescio si 'medicum' dicam, pociusue 'salutem,' 'ipsam uel uitam,' quo mihi uita datur."

410 *Decimus Modus.* Interpretatio, secundum Tullium, idem repetit aliis uerbis, vt hic: "Qui lepram mentis exterminat, ulcera curat peccati, cuius munere morbus obit." Hec tria nomina, "lepra," "ulcera," "morbus," pro "peccato" ponuntur; vel, ydemptitas est in ipsa re, diuersitas in uoce—quantum ad uerba, que sunt

415 "exterminat," "curat," "obit."

Undecimus Modus. Item tenor ipsius stili ampliat materiam quando ad grauem stilum graues eliguntur sentencie, ad mediocrem, mediocres, ad humilem, humiles—si tamen ne in humili materia nimis deiecti simus et sine coloribus, ipsius* stili

420 elingues.* Quod in comediis est obseruandum, ut in quadam comedia hic posita, cuius est hec materia.

    Spiritus malignus* in partibus Gallie cuidam se immisit sisterne, et transeuntibus et euntibus dabat responsa.* Ad quem quadam die rusticus quidam forum petens venit dicens, "Quis

425 uocaris?"* Cui diabolus respondit Gallica* uoce, "Guinehochet vocor." Et dixit rusticus, "Quot pueros habeo?" Cui Guinehochet, "Duos." Rusticus cum cachynno subiecit, "Mentiris, quia quattuor habeo pueros." Cui Guinehochet, "Immo tu,* rustice pessime, mentiris, quia duo pueri sunt presbiteri uille tue." Cui

430 rusticus, "Quinam sunt illi?" Cui Guinehochet, "Vade, rustice, pasce et illos et illos."

    Hanc comediam ornacius possumus describere hoc modo:

          Est ex Plutonis fouea prolata colonis
          Gallica uox, leta, iocunda, nouella, faceta:
435   "Hac in cisterna lateo, terreque cauerna
          Hospitor et ludo; uentura latencia nudo.
          Ginnehocher Baratri me uulgus nominat Atri;
          Gvinehocher Pluto—cuius nutu cado, nuto—
          Me baptizauit, Flegetontis flumine lauit.
440   Vaticinans dico nostro que poscit amico."
          Rusticus ergo uenit repetens fora, res ubi uenit;

in his life, his great-grandfather never a roof. Nor is this loafer worthy
to be anyone's heir. Who would leave his possessions to a dandy, to a
roving fornicator? Nobody. You may say, "He has made his fortune
by his own skill." Don't say it; skill to him means dice, liquor glasses,
games of chance, theft; he is an actor to whom a tramp disclaims pa-
ternity. (*EBV* 10.231-38)

The Ninth Way. Indecision is a rhetorical figure wherein several possible
names for something are listed, with the phrase "I don't know," as here:
"I don't know whether I should call him 'doctor,' or rather 'health,' or
'life itself'—he grants me life."
The Tenth Way. Synonymy, according to Cicero (*RAH* 4.28.38), repeats
the same thing in other words, as here: "He wipes out the leprosy of
the mind, cures the sores of sin; by his aid disease dies." These three
nouns, "leprosy," "sores," "disease," all mean "sin"; in other words,
there is identity in meaning, but variety of terms—and in the verbs as
well: "wipes out," "cures," "dies."
An Eleventh Way. Furthermore, the level of style itself amplifies the
material, when high sentiments are chosen for the high style, middling
ones for the middle style, low ones for the low style—provided that in
treating a low subject we be not too lackluster and unfigurative, confusing that style with inarticulateness. This caution is to be observed in
comedies, as in the comedy I am including here, whose subject matter is
this.

An evil spirit settled in a certain well in a part of France, and used to
give answers to those who went by the well, or came to it. One day a
certain peasant on his way to market came up to him and said, "What
is your name?" The devil replied, in French, "My name is Guinehochet."
And the peasant said, "How many sons do I have?" Guinehochet answered, "Two." The peasant guffawed, and said, "You're a liar; I have
four sons." Guinehochet said, "No, you are the liar, you naughty peasant—two of your boys are the village priest's." "Which ones?" the peasant asked. And Guinehochet answered, "Go, peasant, feed both his and
yours."
We can describe this comic incident more eloquently, this way:

From Pluto's pit to the farmers comes a French voice, fun-loving,
full of jokes, novel, witty: "I hide in this well, I sojourn in this hole in
the earth, and I play; I lay bare the hidden future. The mob calls me
Guinehochet of Black Hell; Guinehochet Pluto—at whose nod I tremble
and fall—baptized me, washing me in the river Phlegeton. I'll give our
friend here the oracle he seeks."
A peasant comes along then, on his way to market to sell his produce.

Guinehocher uisit obiter, quem mente reuisit.
"Guinehocher leta, per Gallica* rura propheta!"
Colloquio facto, uox est hoc edita pacto:
445   R.* Maxime fatorum reserator, quot puerorum,
Dic mihi, uiuo pater, quos seruat adhuc sua mater?
G. Esse tuos ego dico duos quos pascis in ede.
R. Mentiris fabricasque uiris hac friuola sede!
G. Non ego mencior aut uagus ocior hoc referendo.
450   R. Sunt mihi quatuor, hos* ego contuor era merendo.
G. Presbiteri gemini pueri sunt, rustice nequam!
R. Ede duos capiatque suos; rem non facit equam.
G. Nolo.
            R. Cur?
455   G. Pueris teneris malus efficieris.
Binis uocalis pater es, binisque realis;
Victricus esto pater, hostis pius, albus et ater.
Nomina dum celo, fuge, rustice, rumpere zelo!

Expositio nominis dicti fit metrice in Gallica* lingua hoc modo:

460   Guinehocher locher fait vilayn, sailer, et hocher,
Guiner, rechinier, par curteysie chapinier.*

Qvia in premissis positum est exemplum de proprietatibus in
comedia obseruandis, notandum quod comedia perfecta debet
habere quinque partes, secundum quinque personas introductas,
465   teste Horacio:

Neue minor nec sit* quinto productior actu
Fabula, que posci uult et spectata reponi.

Introducitur in comedia perfecta maritus et eius uxor, et adulter
et minister adulteri—uel eius castigator—et nutrix adultere uel
470   seruus mariti. Non tamen semper* introducuntur quinque persone
in qualibet comedia, quia quandoque materia iocose recitata comedia nuncupatur. Comedia dicitur a "comos," quod est "uilla,"
et "odos," quod est "cantus," quasi "uillanus cantus," quia de
materia uili et iocosa contexitur.
475   Notandum autem quod partes[hystorie] non sunt certe et determinate, quia per uoluntatem[hystoriographi]et secundum ipsa
gesta distinguitur* hystoria. Idem* dicitur de tragedia, sed est
differencia inter tragediam et comediam; quia comedia est car-
Donaties   men iocosum incipiens a tristicia et terminans in gaudium; tragedia
480   est carmen graui stilo compositum, incipiens a gaudio et terminans

Guinehochet sees him on the road, and he sees Guinehochet, too, in his mind:

"Fun-loving Guinehochet, send an oracle through the French countryside!"

They exchange words, and the voice comes forth, thus:

P. O greatest unlocker of destinies, tell me: of how many sons, still in their mother's keeping, live I the father?

G. I say there are two of yours whom you feed and house.

P. You lie and fabricate to men in this frivolous seat.

G. I do not lie, nor do I idly stray in giving this answer.

P. I have four; I take care of them with the money I earn.

G. Two boys are the priest's, you worthless peasant!

P. Name the two and let him take his; he is acting unjustly.

G. No.

P. Why?

G. You'll be mean to the poor boys. You are twice a father in name, twice in deed; be stepfather and father, a good enemy, white and black. I'll conceal the names; flee, peasant, be broken up with jealousy.

Here is an explanation in French verse of the above name:

Guinehochet (scowl-squirm) makes the peasant shake, leap, and squirm, scowl, grimace, and, to speak politely, cut up.

The foregoing presents an example of the proprieties to be observed in a comedy; it should also be noted that a correct comedy should have five parts, matching the five characters introduced into it, as Horace says:

A play that expects to be in demand for a long run should have neither more nor less than five acts. (*AP* 189-90)

A correct comedy has the following cast: a husband and wife, an adulterer and the adulterer's accomplice—or his critic—and the adulteress's nurse, or the husband's servant. Yet there are not always five characters in every kind of comedy, since sometimes any humorous treatment of a subject is called a comedy. Comedy comes from *comos*, "village," and *odos*, "song"—a "peasant song" as it were, since it is composed of low and humorous matter.

It should be noted, however, that there are no definite, fixed parts for a narrative, since a narrative takes its shape from the narrator's intention and from the events themselves. A tragedy has five parts, too, but there is a difference between tragedy and comedy; for a comedy is a humorous poem beginning in sadness and ending in joy; a tragedy is a poem composed in the high style, beginning in joy and ending in grief, and is so

in luctum, et dicitur a "trages," quod est "hyrcus," et "odos,"
quod est "cantus," quasi "hyrcinus cantus," idest "fetidus," uel
quia tragedi remunerabantur hyrco.

Post partes ornati dictaminis et poematis, notande sunt cir-
485   cumstancie pro partibus in cartis, in cyrographis, in querelis, in
citationibus, in transactionibus, et in quibusdam aliis, quorum
exempla in presentibus subiciuntur versibus:

> Carta tenet quid, cur, quando, testesque, sigillum,
> Quantum, quale, locum, "legitimeque datum."
490 Cedunt in geminas partes cyrographa secta,
> Et prefinito tempore pacta tenent.
> Ledentem lesum causam querimonia profert;
> Actio sacrilega uult reserare locum.
> Prefigit tempus causamque citatio dicit,
495 Iudice sub certo terminat illa locum.
> Terretur primo qui contumet; hinc anathema est;
> Subsequitur pena, lege iubente sua.
> Federa testatur facta transactio lite,
> Sub certa pene condicione sue.
500 Qvod pars aduersa non uenit, littera testis
> Signatur; memorat iudicis ora sui;
> Attendat quisquis, examinat acta; reatum,
> Causam, personas, tempora, signa, locum.

Item notandum quod emergunt casus noui cotidie ex quibus
505   componuntur littere; sed quia sic possemus procedere in infinitum, tradetur doctrina de quibusdam generalibus casibus ex
quibus littere componuntur, ut in uersibus presentibus est
exemplum.

to what extent are these examples seen as hypotheses?

> Emergunt casus; homicidia, furta, rapine,
> Verbera, litigium, prelia, dampna, lucrum,
510 Luxus, symonia, uis, fraus, iniuria, morbus,
> Mors, dos, ius, heres, ordo, capella, preces.

Exempla istorum uersuum ponentur in fine huius tractatus, sicut
promissum fuit ab inicio.

called from *trages,* "goat," and *odos,* "song"—a "goatish song" as it were, that is, "unpleasant," or because tragedians used to receive a goat as a prize.

Now that we have discussed the parts of an embellished letter and a poem, the next thing to note is the criteria for parts in deeds, indentures, suits, summonses, compromises, and other such documents, models for which are subjoined in these verses:

A deed contains what, why, when, witnesses, seal, how much, what kind, the place, and "lawfully given."

Indentures are cut to form two matching parts, and contain agreements for a predetermined time.

A suit brings to light a cause that is harming an injured party; an action for sacrilege will reveal the place.

A summons sets a time in advance and states a cause; it fixes a place, under a certain judge.

He who is in contempt is first warned; then he is anathema; the penalty follows, for the law demands what is owed it.

A compromise witnesses agreements made in a disputed matter, and contains a definite sanction of penalty.

A letter attesting the absence of either party to a suit is sealed; it serves as a record of the judge's statements. But should someone be present, he examines the proceedings; the charge, cause, parties, times, seals, place.

It should be noted, of course, that new cases emerge daily for which documents are drawn up; but since we could thus go on forever, I offer a guide for just a few general cases for which documents are drawn up— as exemplified in these verses:

Cases emerge: homicides, thefts, ransackings, beatings, litigation, disputes, losses, illegal gain, debauchery, simony, force, fraud, injury, illness, death, endowment, rights, heir, order, benefice, petitions.

Models for the actions touched on in these verses will be included at the end of this treatise, as I promised at the beginning.

De Uiciis in Metro VI Specialibus. Post partes sufficienter assignatas tam in poemate quam in dictamine, sequitur* de viciis uitandis tam in metro quam in prosa; sed prius dicendum est de uiciis uitandis in metro. Sunt ergo uicia sex uitanda in poemate.

5 Primum est incongrua parcium disposicio; secundum, incongrua materie disgressio; tercium, obscura breuitas; quartum,* incongrua stilorum uariatio; quintum, incongrua materie uariatio; sextum, finis infelix.

De Primo Uicio in Metro Uitando. Species recti est congrua

10 parcium disposicio, a qua deuiat aliquis quando assumit sibi membra et partes alterius materie, ut si aliquis describeret comediam in qua partes debent obseruari ad laciuiam pertinentes, transfert* se ad partes tragedie, que sunt de grauibus personis et de earum sentenciis contexte.* Et hoc uitatur per obseruationem

15 parcium similium; de quo uicio dicit Oracius in Poetria:

Serpentes auibus geminantur, tigribus agni.

Per serpentes intelligimus humiles, per aues elatos; per tigrides homines feros, per agnos homines mansuetos, quorum non erit conueniencia.

20 *De Secundo Uitio.* Incongrua materie digressio deuiat a specie recti. Est enim species recti a materia digredi duplici de causa, scilicet* causa difficultatis explanande, et causa mouendi animos auditorum et instruendi in difficilibus. Sed fit digressio incongrua quando ponitur aliqua descriptio uel comparacio uel

25 similitudo causa mouendi, cum non deberet fieri; de quo uicio dicit Oracius:

Purpureus, late qui splendeat, vnus et alter
Assuitur pannus.

Hoc uicium uitatur quandoque duplici de causa—quia ut predic-

30 tum est—fit digressio uel ad id quod est de materia, ut* quando describitur locus uel castrum uel aliquid tale, uel ad id quod non est de materia, sed materie competenter adaptatur, ut contingit in posicione similitudinis.

De Tercio Uicio Uitando. Item species recti est breuiter dicere pro

35 loco et pro tempore; sed fit aliquando declinatio in vicium, quando propter breuitatem obscuri sumus in dicendo; ad quod uicium excludendum, eligenda sunt uerba manifestancia materiam. Verbi gratia: Iubiter hospitatur in domo Lycaonis, qui obsidem interfecit

Chapter Five

On the Six Vices Peculiar to Verse. I have charted out the parts for both a poem and a letter fully enough; the next subject is the vices to avoid both in verse and in prose. Let me speak first of the vices to avoid in verse.

There are, then, six vices to avoid in a poem. The first is incongruous arrangement of parts; the second, incongruous digression from the subject; the third, obscure brevity; the fourth, incongruous variation of styles; the fifth, incongruous variation of subject matter; the sixth, an awkward ending.

The First Vice to Avoid in Verse. The ideal is a consistent arrangement of parts, from which a writer deviates when he appropriates bits and pieces from another subject, as when someone writing a comedy, all of whose elements should be suited to light entertainment, shifts to elements of tragedy, which are made up of serious characters and sentiments suited to them. Avoid this by holding strictly to similar elements; Horace says of this vice in his *Art of Poetry:*

Serpents are paired with birds, lambs with tigers. (13)

Serpents mean lowly men, birds lofty men; tigers fierce men, lambs gentle men, between whom there will never be any fitness.

The Second Vice. An incongruous digression from the subject deviates from the ideal. For ideally there are only two excuses to digress from the subject, namely, to explain a difficulty, and to move the minds of one's audience and to instruct them in hard matters. But it becomes an incongruous digression when a description or comparison or similitude is put forward, for the sake of moving, when it should not be done, of which vice Horace says:

A purple patch or two is sewn on, and sticks out all over. (*AP* 15-16)

This vice is avoided whenever, for either of two reasons—the reasons given above—a digression is made either to what is itself part of the subject matter, as when a place or a castle or the like is described, or to what is not part of the subject matter, but is aptly fitted to it, such as a comparison.

The Third Vice to Avoid. Here the ideal is to speak as briefly as circumstances permit; but this sometimes declines into a vice, when brevity leads to obscurity. To do away with that vice, choose words that make the matter plain. For example: Jupiter is a guest in the home of Lycaon, who has killed a hostage in order that he might place human flesh on

40 ut carnes* humanas mensis Iouis apponeret; quod Iupiter com-
periens mutauit Licaonem in lupum et tecta sua succendit. Eli-
gantur huiusmodi uerba: "Iupiter," "hospes," "obses," "Archas,"
"lupus," "mutatur," "crematur." Istis collectis, fiant versus, sic:

> Iupiter est hospes; cibus ut sit ei cadit obses;
> Archas mutatur: lupus est, tectumque crematur.

45 *De Quarto, et Tribus Stilis.* Item sunt* tres stili secundum tres
status hominum. Pastorali uite conuenit stilus humilis, agricolis
mediocris, grauis grauibus personis, que presunt pastoribus et
agricolis. Pastores diuicias inueniunt in animalibus, agricole illas
adaugent* terram excolendo, principes uero possident eas in-
50 ferioribus donando. Secundum has tres personas Virgilius tria
composuit opera: Bucolica, Georgica, Eneyda. Potest grauis
materia humiliari exemplo Virgilii, qui uocat Cesarem Titirum—
uel seipsum, Romam fagum; potest et humilis materia exaltari,
ut in graui materia coli muliebres uocantur "inbelles haste."
55 Exemplum grauis stili est hic:

> Karolus, ecclesie clipeus pacisque columpna,
> Armis arma domat et feritate feros.

In hoc stilo eligenda sunt nomina significancia instrumenta posita
in superiori ordine; in mediocri, instrumenta posita in mediocri
60 ordine; in humili, instrumenta posita in humili ordine.
De Viciis Vitandis que sunt Collateralia Stilis. Grauis stilus habet
duo uicia collateralia, scilicet turgidum et inflatum: turgidum ex
parte uerborum, inflatum ex parte sentenciarum; vt hic:

> Excelsus collis bellorum, belligeratrix
65 > Rolandina, manus clauaque pacis erat.

Mediocris stilus habet sub se duo uicia collateralia, scilicet fluctuans et dissolutum:* fluctuans ex parte uerbi uel uocis; dissolutum ex parte sentenciarum; quia cum mediocris stilus capiat ab
extremis, scilicet a* gravi et ab humili, aliquando poeta fluctuat
70 uoce, in sententia dissolutus. Exemplum mediocris stili secundum
speciem recti est hic:

> Karolus ecclesie custos, protectio plebis
> Iusticie cultor, pacis amator erat.

Exemplum uicii sub hoc stilo subsequitur in uersibus istis:

75 > Milicie baculus rex est et blandus amator
> Vxoris; fortes precipit esse suos.

Species recti in humili stilo est in hiis uersibus que subsequuntur:*

Jove's table; when Jupiter found out, he changed Lycaon into a wolf and set fire to his house. Choose words of this sort: "Jupiter," "guest," "hostage," "the Arcadian," "wolf," "is changed," "is burnt." When the list is complete, turn it into poetry, thus:

> Jupiter is a guest; as food for him, a hostage falls; the Arcadian is changed; he is a wolf, and his house is burnt.

The Fourth Vice, and the Three Styles. There are, again, three styles, corresponding to the three estates of men. The low style suits the pastoral life; the middle style, farmers; the high style, eminent personages, who are set over shepherds and farmers. Shepherds find riches in animals; farmers accumulate them by cultivating the earth; but princes possess them by giving them away to inferiors. Virgil composed three works to correspond to these three types, the *Eclogues,* the *Georgics,* and the *Aeneid.* High matter can be lowered, in imitation of Virgil, who calls Caesar—or himself—Tityrus and Rome a beech; and low matter can be exalted, as when in a treatment of a high subject women's distaffs are called "the spears of peace." Here is an example of the high style:

> Charles, the shield of the Church and the column of peace, tames arms with arms and the fierce with ferocity.

In this style, nouns should be chosen which signify things placed in the top row; in the middle style, things placed in the middle row; in the low style, things placed in the bottom row. *[memory scheme]*

On Avoiding the Vices Associated with the Several Styles. The high style has two vices associated with it, bombast and inflation: bombast is a function of words, inflation of ideas. Here is an example:

> That most supernal peak of wars, the warrioress Rolandina, was the hand and club of peace.

The middle style has two vices associated with it, fluctuation and looseness: fluctuation is a function of words or diction, looseness of ideas. For since the middle style is a compromise between extremes, that is, between the high and the low, sometimes a poet fluctuates in diction and is loose in ideas. Here is an ideal example of the middle style:

> Charles was the guardian of the Church, the protection of the people, a cultivator of justice, a lover of peace.

The following lines exemplify the vices to which this style is liable:

> The king is the staff of the army and a smooth lover to his wife; he bids his men be brave.

The following lines are an ideal example of the low style:

> In tergo clauam pastor portat; ferit inde
> Presbiterum cum quo ludere sponsa solet.

80   Svb hoc stilo sunt duo uicia collateralia, scilicet arridum et* exsangue: arridum quantum ad sentencias que non sunt succose et*
sapide, exsangue quantum ad uoces quarum superficies non est
purpurata; ut hic:

> Rusticus a tergo clauam trahit et ter tonse
85   > Testiculos aufert; prandia leta facit.

   Item notandum quod "stilus" dicitur transumptiue.* Est enim
stilus medietas columpne, cui supponitur epistilium, cuius inferior pars dicitur basis. Est ergo "stilus" in hoc loco "qualitas
carminis" uel "rectitudo" seruata per corpus materie. Stilus dici-
90   tur aliquando[carmen ipsum.] Stilus dicitur officium poete, ut in
Anticlaudiano:

> Autoris mendico stilum phalerasque poete.

Stilus etiam* dicitur graphium quo scribimus.
De Quinto Vicio. Qvintum vicium poematis, ut dictum est, dici-
95   tur incongrua materie uariatio. Est enim species recti uariare materiam causa fastidii tollendi et idemptitatis uitande. Est enim
mater ydemptitas sacietatis, que ducit auditores in tedium, ad
quod tollendum debet uariari materia. In iocoso tractatu pro-
ponenda sunt iocosa, quod facit Horacius in satyra, introdu-
100   cendo murem urbanum et rusticanum ad collacionem uite
urbane et uite ruralis. In graui materia introducenda sunt grauia,
quod facit Lucanus narrando luctam Anthei gigantis et Herculis.
Sed incidit poeta in uicium narrando grauem materiam per iocosa
et comica, iocosam materiam per grauia, de quo dicit Horacius:

105   > Qui uariare cupit rem prodigialiter vnam,
> Delphinum siluis appingit, fluctibus aprum.

Ut* si diceret, "proprietates aquarum attribuit siluis, et proprietates siluarum attribuit aquis." Et nota quod digressio fit causa
materiam ampliandi, materie uariatio causa ydemptitatis uitande.
110   De Sexto Vicio et Quot Sunt Genera Conclusionum. Finis infelix
est sextum vicium, quod dicitur inconueniens operis conclusio,
ad quod uitandum finis siue conclusio aliquando sumi debet a
corpore materie per recapitulationem precedencium, quod pertinet ad oratores et predicatores, aliquando a licencia, vt aput
115   Virgilium in Bucolicis:

The shepherd carries his club over his shoulder; he uses it to beat the priest his wife has been playing with.

The two vices associated with this style are aridity and bloodlessness: aridity refers to ideas that are not juicy and tasty; bloodlessness refers to words whose surface is not purpled, as here:

The peasant draws the club from his shoulder, and in three strokes removes that shorn sheep's testicles; he has a happy supper.

Notice, by the way, that "style" is used metaphorically. For a style is the middle section of a column, on which rests the epistyle, and whose lower section is called the base. "Style," then, in this sense is "the poetic quality," or an "uprightness" preserved throughout the body of the matter. Sometimes style means the poem itself. Style means the office of a poet, as in the *Anticlaudianus:*

I beg the style of an author and the trappings of a poet. (Prol. 1)

Finally, style means the pen we write with.

The Fifth Vice. The fifth vice of a poem, as I said above, is called incongruous variation of the subject matter. The ideal here is to vary the subject matter in order to forestall revulsion and avoid monotony; for monotony is the mother of satiety, which in turn produces boredom in the audience. To forestall that, vary the subject matter. In an amusing piece, bring in amusing things, as Horace did in one of his satires (2.6.79-117) by introducing a city mouse and a country mouse for a comparison of city life and country life. In a grave subject, bring in grave things, as Lucan did (4.609-55) by telling the story of the wrestling match between the giant Antaeus and Hercules. But a poet falls into vice if he tries to describe a grave subject by means of amusing and comic details, or an amusing subject by means of grave details, of which Horace says:

The man who has an urge to vary one thing a thousand ways paints dolphins in the woods, boars on the waves. (*AP* 29-30)

That is to say, "he attributes the properties of the sea to woods, and the properties of woods to the sea." And note that a digression is made in order to amplify the subject matter; variation of subject matter in order to avoid monotony.

The Sixth Vice, and the Various Kinds of Endings. The sixth vice is an awkward ending, which means a conclusion inappropriate to its work; to avoid it, the ending or conclusion should be derived sometimes from the body of the matter, by way of recapitulation of what has gone before, which is appropriate for orators and preachers; sometimes purely from the poet's pleasure, as Virgil does in the *Eclogues:*

Ite domum, sature, uenit Hesperus, ite capelle.

Et apud Stacium:

> O mihi bissenos multum uigilata per annos
> Tebays, etc.

120 Aliquando accidit per exemplum quod continet similitudinem,
ut in fine Poetrie:

> Quem* uero arripuit, tenet occiditque legendo,
> Non missura cutem, nisi plena cruoris, yrudo.

Aliquando a prouerbio ut in Epistolis Horacii:

125
> Lusisti satis, edisti satis atque bibisti;
> Tempus abire tibi, ne potum largius equo
> Rideat et pulset* laciua decensius etas.

Item curiales littere concluduntur ut frequencius per has dictiones: "ut," "ne," "quia." Per "ut" subiungitur comodum;
130 per "ne" dissuadetur incomodum; per "quia" subiungitur ratio
premissorum. Exemplum variationis* materie et conclusionis
per exemplum est in litteris istis* quas mittere potest scolaris
amico, reddendo ei gratias pro beneficiis ei collatis, hoc modo:

Littere Scolastice.

135   Vnico et speciali amico suo G. de illo* loco; suus inte-
graliter per omnia B., tyrunculus sapiencie Parisiensis: salutem,
et veri salutaris permanens salutare.

Veritas non querit angulos, nec amor uerus immo simulatus
adulationis uelamine picturatur. Quid pro tot et tantis bene-
140 ficiis a uobis mihi collatis Liberalitati Vestre debeam exoptare,
nescit penitus animus meus inuenire, nec nouit lingua mea
balbuciens reserare.

> Dos uite, uirtutis amor, constancia pacis,
>   Orbis honor, celi sit tibi leta quies.
145
> Carta rudis, stilus incomptus, deiecta Camena,
>   Quis sim quidque uelim nuncia certa uenit.
> Verborum faleris et claro cemate pingi
>   Nescit amor uerus; pingere nescit humum,
> Non querit paleam sine grano, non sine fructu
150
>   Subridet foliis, non tegit atra niue.
> Olim nudus amor pictus fuit; omnia nuda,
>   Omnia que sua sunt monstrat aperta suis.

Go home fully fed, Hesperus comes, go home, she-goats. (10.77)

And Statius:

O Thebaid, the object of my waking hours for twice six years, etc. (*Theb.* 12.811-12)

Sometimes it takes place by means of an example which contains a similitude, as in the end of the *Art of Poetry:*

But anyone he has got hold of, he clings to and reads to death—a leech who won't let go of the skin till he has had his fill of blood. (475-76)

Sometimes it is taken from a proverb, as in the epistles of Horace:

You have played enough, eaten and drunk enough; it is time for you to pass on, lest playful youth—whose behavior would be more becoming than yours—mock you and beat you for having drunk more than you should. (*Ep.* 2.2.214-16)

Letters on legal matters are brought to a conclusion as often as possible with these words: "so that," "lest," "since." "So that" introduces a good; "lest" dissuades from an evil; "since" introduces the reason for what has preceded. Variation of subject matter and conclusion by means of example are exemplified in this letter, which a student can send to his friend to thank him for favors received.

A Student's Letter.

To his unique and special friend, G., of such-and-such a place; B., completely his in everything, a recruit in the wisdom of Paris: greeting, and the permanent salve of true salvation.

Truth doesn't seek out corners, nor indeed is true love depicted in art as disguised by a veil of flattery. What I ought to wish to Your Liberality for so many and so great favors done by you for me, my mind is utterly unable to discover, nor can my stammering tongue reveal.

May the gift of life, the love of virtue, continual peace, honor in the world, and the joyful quiet of heaven be yours. My rude paper, artless pen, and humble Muse all come announcing plainly both who I am and what I want. True love knows not how to be painted in the ornaments of words and brilliant figures, knows not how to spread paint over plain soil, does not seek the chaff without the grain, does not smile at leaves without fruit, does not cover blackness with snow. Formerly Love was painted naked; he shows everything naked, everything that is his open to his own.

Hoc igitur attendens, vsus sum nudo stilo uobis, ne uulpinam
palliare uidear arguciam dum statum meum et fortune mee
155   mutatoria perstringo coloribus. Nudam ueritatem propono,*
nuditate culpam simulationis amoueo, nec in plano quero
fraudis offendiculum inuenire. O mihi dilecte, O vere dilecte,
O ueratius preelecte, in huius opinionis tramite procedo, vobis
scribens magis in ueritatis propatulo* quam in vanitatis obum-
160   braculo, nequaquam sub lingue Tulliane larua uenator fictitii,
sed integritatis Christiane sine simulationis scrupulis amplexator.
Sed quid confert amorem iactari* sermone, tociens in medium
statuere, et aura leui serenitatem crastinam promittere, cum
aduersitatis forsitan suborta rixans procella contradiceret, et
165   ruborem incuteret* falcidice faciei?
Decencius est igitur mihi de amicicia modicum uoce tenus
disserere, et multum in die temtationis opere complere, quam
si in contrarium res accidat, nec forsitan mihi credideritis* quantum in pectoris archano uos defixi. Sed cum a procella scolastice
170   paupertatis emerserim, et Deus uoluntatem meam a latebris
euoluerit, quod uobis de amicicie constancia disserui perfectius*
operis comprobabitur argumento, quia dicitur in uulgari, "Non
a serenitate matutina sed serotina dies preconia promeretur."

Variatio* materie in prosa fit per uersus, ut in presenti dictamine,
175   aut uariatur materia per nuditatem Cupidinis, que materie adaptatur. Item conclusio fit per exemplum ubi dicitur "non a serenitate matutina, etc."
Item de Aliis Viciis. A predictis uiciis sunt multa alia uicia uitanda
et in metro et in prosa, scilicet species Soloecismi et Barbarismi,
180   quibus ad presens supersedemus. Sed quia licet modernis perfectis
uti Sinalimpha—sed raro—notandum quod semper vna sillaba
superhabundans eliditur per Sinalimpham, scilicet antecedens si
ex pura uocali constituatur. Quia, cum prior uocalis primo proferatur, in ipsa prolatione deperit, et subsequens prodit* in esse,
185   que potestatem habet illam elidendi que perit a prolatione. Hec
littera *m* aput modernos eliditur, et quare elidatur hec est ratio:
m est liquida et formatur in extremitate labiorum clausorum
quando profertur, et* parum habet soni. (Id enim quod ore aperto
profertur cum hyatu profertur, sed secundum maius et minus.)
190   Vnde propter originem quam habet debilem hec littera *m* eliditur
a uocali subsequente.
De Viciis Metri. Item uitanda est frequens concursio uocalium
in prosa sicut in metro, causa hyatus uitandi; frequens etiam

Attending then to this, I have used a naked style to you, lest I seem
to cloak a foxy slyness by cursing my state and my changes in fortune
in fancy language. I put forth the naked truth, by nakedness I cast off
the charge of dissimulation, nor, in my plainness, do I seek to invent
an obstacle of deceit. O my beloved, O truly beloved, O so truly chosen,
I go along on the path of this decision, writing to you rather in the
open air of truth than in the shade of vanity, by no means under the
mask of a Ciceronian tongue a hunter after artifice, but an embracer of
Christian integrity, free of the subtleties of dissimulation. For what
good does it do for love to be vaunted in speech, to set up so often in
public, and gaily to promise serenity for tomorrow, when perhaps a
quarrelsome storm of adversity may spring up to contradict it, and
bring a blush to the lying face?

disavowal of artifice

And so, it is more becoming for me to rant on of friendship but little
in words and to accomplish much in deeds in the day of trial, than that
the thing should come out the other way around, and you perhaps not
believe how firmly I have fixed you in the secret folds of my breast.
But when I have emerged from the storm of scholastic poverty, and
God has rolled out my will from its hiding place, my rantings to you
on the constancy of friendship will be affirmed more perfectly by the
argument of deeds; for, as the popular saying goes, "Not by morning
but by evening calm does the day earn public acclaim."

Variation of subject matter in prose is accomplished by verse, as in this
letter; the subject matter is further varied by introducing the nakedness
of Cupid, which fits this particular subject. And the conclusion is made
with an example, in the words "Not by morning calm, etc."

Other Vices. Besides the vices I have mentioned, there are many other
vices to avoid both in meter and in prose, namely the various kinds of
solecism and barbarism, which I pass over for now. But since correct
modern poets are permitted to use Synaloepha, though rarely, I should
point out that Synaloepha simply means the elision of one extra syllable,
namely a pure vowel followed by another vowel. For although the prior
vowel is uttered first, it vanishes at the moment of utterance, and the
second springs into being, which has the power of eliding the one which
is lost from utterance. Modern poets elide the letter *m,* and here is the
reason why it may be elided: *m* is a liquid, and is formed at the tip of
the closed lips when it is uttered, and has little sound. (Thus, what is
uttered with the mouth open is uttered with more or less of a pause.)
Whence on account of the feeble origin it has, the letter *m* is elided by a
following vowel.

On Vices in Meter. On the other hand, avoid frequent running together
of vowels, in prose and meter both, and you will avoid awkward pauses;

concursio consonancium uitanda est, ut si dicerem hoc modo:

195   Te gemmam mundi virgo commendo Maria.

Hec dictio "gemmam" finitur a littera qua subsequens dictio
incipit, quod vicium est, Debet ergo transponi sic: "Te mundi
gemmam etc." Sed si frequenter sillabe concurrunt* immediate,
uicium erit, ut hic: "Uultur turpis auis"; nisi fiat cum frequencia
200   per totum uersum causa delectationis* et ioci, ut in uersu quem
scolaris fecit de carcerario carceris Parysiane:

          Vi vito, Thoma, male ledi, dire retortor.*

(Obiciebatur carcerario quod solebat percutere incarceratos, qui
uocabatur Thomas. Dixit ergo scolaris hoc modo: "O tu, Thoma,
205   dire retortor"—idest crudelis flagellator—"vito male ledi ui tua.")
      Item dictio non debet repeti immediate nisi causa pietatis
mouende, ut: "Deus, Deus meus"; vel causa admiracionis, ut:
"Penitus, penitusque iacentes despexit* terras"; uel causa af-
firmationis, ut "Ita, ita." Si oratio repetatur, erit per Ysologia,
210   nisi repetatur aliis uerbis, et tunc erit color,* scilicet Interpretatio.
Sed notandum quod aliquando uicio utimur pro uirtute causa ioci
et derisionis, ut si dicerem, "Tua disputatio est mihi dis-putatio";
"Iste clericulus est mihi cleri culus."
      Item notandum quod littere uel sillabe adduntur et subtrahun-
215   tur, mutantur, transmutantur. Aliquando causa ornatus additur
littera, ut hic:

          Spiritus exsiccat nostre mare carnis amare.

Subtrahitur littera ut hic:

          Virus Adam mortis Paradisi fudit in ortis;
220   Vi Martis necnon artis nos luserat anguis.

Additur sillaba, ut hic:

          Hvius mens amens male debaccatur amantis.

Subtrahitur sillaba, ut hic:

          Non uis humorum dat nobis munera morum,
225   Sed qui condonat errata piacula donat.

Item littera mutatur, ut hic:

          Hic chorus est carus Domino, qui crimina uitat,
          Et peccare uetat hunc qui deformiter errat.

even frequent running together of consonants is to be avoided. For example, suppose I wrote,

Virgin, world's gem, Mary, I commend you.

The word "gem" ends with the letter with which the next word starts, and that is a vice. So shift it, thus: "Virgin, gem of the world, etc." And running together two similar syllables consecutively is also a vice, for example, "Vulture, churlish bird"; unless it is done consistently throughout a line as a pleasant diversion, as in the line a student made up about the jailer of the Paris jail:

Tommy, my back begs off of cur's curs'd whip—hips too.

(There had been a hue and cry that the jailer, whose name was Thomas, made a practice of beating the inmates; and so the student said, "O Thomas, severe torturer"—that is, cruel whipper—"I dislike being wickedly injured by your brutality.")

Also, a word should not be repeated immediately, except to excite piety, as "O God, my God" (cf. Matt. 27:46); or for shock, as "He looked down on the lands lying far, far below" (cf. Ovid, *Met.* 2.178-79); or for affirmation, as "Yes, yes." The name for exact repetition of a phrase is Isologia; repetition of the same idea in different words is a figure, namely Synonymy. And note that sometimes we use vice as a virtue for joking or mockery, as to say, "Your disputation is dis-putation to me"; "If you ask me, that rector's cleric is the clergy's rectum."

Another device is to add, remove, change, or transpose letters and syllables. This line is embellished by adding a letter:

The spirit dries up the sea of our carnal drives.

Here a letter is removed:

The poisonous bane laid Adam under ban in the early days in Paradise; the serpent had mocked us by a power both martial and artful.

Here a syllable is added:

The lover's distraught sense raves over nonsense.

Here a syllable is removed:

The humors that comprise us give no prize for virtue, but he who forgives sins gives penances.

Here a letter is changed:

This choir will cheer the Lord, who despises evil, and, despite man's desires, forbids him to sin.

Item Sillaba mutatur vt hic:

230
>Hostes infirmat intacta puerpera nostros,
>Robur et affirmat, et pectora nostra reformat.

Transmutatio littere et sillabe est in hiis duobus uersibus:

>O malum, mala quanta sapis, quod prebuit aspis!
>Quo bona frangit Eua, fracta resarcit Aue.

235
Item contingit uiciosa posicio in uersibus, quia, si uersus est
exameter, non debet grandis dictio locari in fine, sed in principio
uel in medio; ut si dicerem, "ledit dolor interiora," ponatur sic
in principio: "interiora dolor ledit"; vel in medio, sic: "dolor
interiora cruentat."* Item dictio trissillaba uel quadrisillaba non
240
debet poni in fine uersus pentametri sic:

>Ne mea sit* puppis naufraga pertimeo.

Amoueatur hec dictio "pertimeo" sic:

>Ne sit pertimeo naufraga nostra ratis.

Item finis dictionis semper debet esse in principio tercii pedis ut
245
uersus bene cadat, vt hic: "Arma uirumque cano"; vel* si non
finiatur ibi dictio, ponantur ibi dactili, et egregie procedet uersus,
ut in Bucolicis:

>Formosam resonare doces Amarillida siluam.

Item copulatiua coniunctio numquam debet copulare uerbum
250
presentis et preteriti, nisi forte copulet totam sentenciam ante-
cedentem, ut in Lucano:

>Iamque ire patuere deum, etc.

Item ne sentencia sit dissuta in uersibus non debent frequenter
uariari tempora, ut si modo ponatur uerbum presentis temporis,
255
et modo uerbum preteriti, nisi forsitan istud exquirat sententia.
Item dictio que intelligitur per uerbum non debet poni in uersu,
nec etiam in prosa, ut sic: "ore locuta est"; nisi determinetur
per aliquod adiunctum quod sit causa illius dicti, ut si dicerem,
"prudenti ore locuta est."
260
De Viciis in Litteris et de Partibus Earum* Viciosis. Consequenter
dicendum est de uiciis uitandis in salutatione et supersalutatione

Here a syllable is changed:

The virgin in labor makes our enemies infirm, confirms our strength, and reforms our breasts.

These two lines contain transposal of both letter and syllable:

O apple from the asp, how evil your sap! Though Eva shattered good, the Ave repairs the break.

Word order is subject to vice in poetry. In a hexameter line, a long word should not be put at the end, but at the beginning or in the middle; for example, if you want to say *ledit dolor interiora* ("grief hurts the heart"), put the long word at the beginning: *interiora dolor ledit;* or in the middle: *dolor interiora cruentat* ("grief wounds the heart"). Similarly, a three-syllable or four-syllable word should not be put at the end of a pentameter line, thus:

Ne mea sit puppis naufraga pertimeo.
("I fear shipwrecks lest the ship be mine.")

Put *pertimeo* somewhere else, like this:

Ne sit pertimeo naufraga nostra ratis.
("I fear shipwrecks lest the boat be ours.")

Again, to give the line the proper cadence, the arsis of the third foot should coincide with the end of a word, as here: *Arma virumque cano;* or, if a word does not end there, the line will still go along nicely if you make the second and third feet dactyls, as in the *Eclogues:*

Formosam resonare doces Amarillida silvam.
(You teach the wood to echo fair Amaryllis' name.) (1.5)

A copulative conjunction should never join a verb in the present tense with one in the past, except when it joins the whole preceding idea, as in Lucan:

And now the anger of the gods was manifested, etc. (2.1)

Likewise, to keep the sense from coming unstitched, in poetry tenses should not be constantly changed, one verb appearing in the present tense, the next in the past, except when the sense demands it. And a word which is implied in the verb should not be expressed, in poetry or even in prose, like this: "She spoke with her mouth"; unless it is modified by some further word which is the occasion of using that word, for example: "She spoke with a prudent mouth."

On Vices in Letters and in Parts of Letters. The next subject is the faults to avoid in the salutation, the supersalutation, and the proverb, in the

et prouerbio, in narratione, in mandato, in conclusione. Si salutatio sit nimis prolixa uiciosa est, uel nimis deiecta, uel si salutatio fiat ubi non debet* fieri.

265   *Diffinitio Dictaminis.* Est enim <u>dictamen litteralis edicio,</u>
<u>clausulis* distincta,</u> uerborum et sentenciarum coloribus ad-
ornata. Epistola sic describitur: epistola est libellus certe desti-
natus persone, mittentis animum declarans, quandoque salutationem continens, quandoque non.

270   *Quare Non Dicatur Salutem.* Qvare non contineat salutationem
tria sunt, scilicet infidelitas, hostilitas, reuerencia. Dominus Papa
non dicit "salutem" Saladino cum sit infidelis, sed loco "salutis"
ponitur: "humani generis cognoscere Saluatorem." Inimicus
inimico dicit "salutis antifrasim," uel "illud quod meruit," vel

275   "in laqueos incidere quos tetendit." Aliquis prelatus dicit Summo Pontifici propter reuerenciam loco salutis, "Talis Episcopus
licet indignus (uel 'humilis minister') tam debitam quam deuotam
obedienciam," vel "deuotissima pedum oscula beatorum," vel
"Sanctitatis Sue pedibus se prostratum." Ipse scribens archi-

280   episcopis et episcopis uocat eos "Fratres Venerabiles." Si
episcopus scribat archiepiscopo uel cardinali uel legato, dicit:
"Reuerendo Patri ac Domino." Item notandum quod usus curie
obseruandus est cuiuslibet, quia quidam se aliquando anteponunt,
aliquando postponunt. Sed Imperator nulli cedit nisi Domino

285   Pape, cui scribit in hunc modum: "Sanctissimo Patri ac Domino,
etc.;* F., Romanorum Imperator, semper Augustus, Sue Sanctitatis Filius: salutem, et deuote fidelitatis obsequium." De aliis
personis dictum est superius sufficienter.
        Quomodo Plures Scribunt Pluribus. Si plures mittant simul,

290   digniores preponendi sunt, et si eis mittatur in executione,* secundum ordinem loquantur hoc modo: "Ego Magister Iohannes
Dilectioni Uestre mitto libellum. Ego W. Subdiaconus Uestre
significo Prudencie quod denarios omnes quos postulastis, mittere non possum donec tempus preterierit autumpnale." Sic dicant*

295   alii si plures fuerint; si pluribus scribatur, secundum priorem ordinem sua negocia proponantur.
        De *Uiciosa Supersalutatione.* Svpersalutatio uiciosa erit si fuerit
nimis prolixa, uel si due supersalutationes* simul fuerint, uel si
non pertinet ad personam cui mittitur, de quo superius dictum est.

300   Item prouerbium nimis longum uel obscurum vel inpertinens
uiciosum est. Multa reddunt narrationem uiciosam, sicut incon-
tinuatio, prolixitas, obscuritas, mendacium.
        De Speciebus Narrationum. <u>Qvia uero narratio communis est</u>
<u>prose et metro, dicendum est quot sunt genera narrationum,</u> et

305   quot genera carminum. Notandum igitur quod est triplex genus
sermonis. Primum est *dragmaticon* uel *dicticon,* idest imitatiuum

narration, in the request, in the conclusion. A salutation is at fault if it is too wordy, or too abject, or if a salutation is used where there should be none.

Definition of Dictamen. Dictamen is a letter marked off by *clausulae* and embellished by figures of words and sentences. An epistle is defined as follows: an epistle is a letter directed to a certain person, laying bare the mind of the sender, sometimes containing a salutation, sometimes not.

Reasons for Not Saying "Greeting." There are three reasons to omit the salutation: unbelief, enmity, and reverence. The Holy Father doesn't say "greeting" to Saladin, because he is an unbeliever, but in place of the greeting puts "may he come to know the Savior of Mankind." An enemy says to an enemy, "the opposite of greeting," or "just what he has deserved," or "may he fall into the traps he has laid." Instead of "greeting" a prelate says to the Holy Father out of reverence, "Bishop So-and-So, although unworthy (or 'a humble servant'), obedience both owed and vowed," or "most devout kisses of the holy feet," or "himself prostrate at the feet of his Holiness." And when the Pope writes to archbishops or bishops, he calls them "Venerable Brothers." If a bishop writes to an archbishop or cardinal or papal legate, he says "to the Reverend Father and Lord." Note also that the usage of the particular court is to be observed, for sometimes certain people name themselves first, and sometimes last. But the emperor bows to no one except the Holy Father, to whom he writes in this way: "To the most Holy Father and Lord, etc., F., Emperor of the Romans, ever Augustus, his Holiness's Son: greeting, and the obedience of vowed fidelity." Other persons have been dealt with sufficiently earlier (*1,* 370 ff., *4,* 103 ff.).

How Several Write to Several. If several people send a letter together, the higher in rank should appear first in the salutation, and if they are writing one by one they should speak in order of rank, in this way: "I, Master John, enclose a booklet for Your Belovedness. I, Subdeacon W., make known to Your Prudence that I cannot send all the money you asked for until after autumn." And so on, if there are more. If there are several recipients, each one's business should be dealt with by priority of rank.

Faulty Supersalutations. A supersalutation is faulty if it is too wordy, or if there are two supersalutations at once, or if it does not suit the recipient, which was treated above (*4,* 124 ff.). Similarly, a proverb that is too long, or too obscure, or not to the point, is at fault. There are many pitfalls for the narration, such as discontinuity, wordiness, obscurity, and falsehood.

On the Kinds of Narration. But since the narration is common to both prose and poetry, I should mention the various kinds of narration and the various poetic genres. Note, then, that the genus "discourse" is threefold. The first kind is dramatic or deictic, that is, imitative or interrogative;

uel interrogatiuum. Secundum est *exagematicon* uel *apageticon,*
idest enarratiuum, quod a quibusdam dicitur *ermeneticon,* idest
interpretatiuum. Tercium est *micticon* uel *chelion,* idest mixtum
310   uel commune, et dicitur *didascalicon,** idest doctrinale. Aliquo
istorum trium utitur quicumque loquitur. Sub secundo cadit narratio, que diuiditur secundum Tullium sic. Est genus narrationis
alienum et remotum a causis ciuilibus, et illud duplex.* Vnum
est quod in negociis positum est, aliud quod in personis. Sed quod
315   positum est in negociis tres habet species siue partes, scilicet
Fabulam, Hystoriam, Argumentum.
De Fabula.* Fabula est que nec res ueras nec uerisimiles continet;
vnde si contingit narrationem esse fabulosam, ne sit uiciosa,
mentiri debemus probabiliter, ut dicitur in Poetria:

320   Aut famam sequere aut sibi conueniencia finge.*

De Hystoria. Hystoria est res gesta ab* etatis nostre memoria remota; hanc si quis tractauerit, ut uitet vicium, premittat propositionem, inuocationem, narrationem; et utatur illo colore rethorico qui dicitur Transicio, et est color per quem animus auditoris
325   per premissam narrationem percipit* futura. (Alio modo dicitur
Epilogus, vnde "epilogare," idest dictis* dicenda continuare.)
De Argumento.* Argumentum est res ficta que tamen fieri potuit,
ut contingit* in comediis. Item in comedia non debet fieri inuo-
cacio, nisi fuerit difficultas in materia, sicut dicit Horacius:

330   Nec deus intersit, nisi dignus uindice nodus
Inciderit.

Idest non fiat inuocatio diuina nisi difficultas inciderit.
*Item Subdividitur.** Item hystoricum aliud Epytalamicum, idest
carmen nupciale. Aliud Epichedion, idest nudum sine sepultura
335   carmen, scilicet quod fit de insepultis, vnde Virgilius de Cesare:

Extinctum nimphe crudeli funere Dafnim
Flebant, uos corili testes et flumina nimphis.

Aliud Epithafium, idest carmen supra mortuum, vt ibi:

Dapnis ego* in siluis, hinc usque ad sidera nothus,
340   Formosi pecoris custos, formosior ipse.

Et hic:

the second is exegetical or apangeltic, that is, expository, which some
call hermeneutic, that is, interpretative; the third is mictic or koinon,
that is, mixed or common, also called didactic, that is, instructive. Whoever speaks uses one or another of these three. Under the second falls
the narration that Cicero (*RAH* 1.8.12) divides as follows: there is a
kind of narration that is alien to, and remote from, legal causes, and it
is twofold. One kind is rooted in plot, the other in character. That
rooted in plot has three species, or parts, namely Fable, History, and
Realistic Fiction.
On Fable. A Fable contains events that are untrue, and do not pretend
to be true; it follows that avoiding vice in fabulous narratives means
lying with probability, as it says in the *Art of Poetry:*

  Either follow tradition or make up a consistent story. (119)

On History. A History reports an event which has taken place long before the memory of our age; whoever deals in it, to escape vice, should
include, in order, proposition, invocation, and narration; then he should
use the rhetorical figure called Transition, a figure whereby the mind of
the listener, with the aid of the preceding narration, understands what
is to come. (It is otherwise called the Epilogue, whence "to epilogue,"
which means to join what is still to be said to what has been said.)
On Realistic Fiction. A Realistic Fiction is a fictitious event which nevertheless could have happened, as is the case in comedies. And no invocation should be made in a comedy, except for an insoluble complication
in the plot, as Horace says:

  Let no god intervene, unless a knot develop that deserves such a
  deliverer. (*AP* 191-92)

That is, a god should not be called on unless an insoluble complication
develops.
A Further Subdivision. Furthermore, one kind of historical narrative is
an Epithalamium, which is a wedding poem. Another is an Epicedium,
which is a plain song apart from a burial, that is, one that is composed
for someone not yet buried; whence Virgil of Caesar:

  The nymphs shed tears for Daphnis, extinguished by a cruel murder;
  you, hazels and rivers, were witnesses to the nymphs. (*Buc.* 5.20-21)

Another is an Epitaph, which is a poem inscribed over a dead body, as
here:

  I am Daphnis the woodsman, known from here to the stars; the
  guardian of a lovely herd, myself more lovely than they. (Ibid., 43-44)

And here:

> In cinerem uersus, solitus componere uersus,
> Dormit in hoc strato, saxo pro syndone strato.
> Eternis annis illustres, Uirgo, Iohannis,
345 Sancta parens, animam ponens sublimius imam.

Aliud est Apoteosis, idest carmen de leticia deificationis uel
glorificacionis. Aliud Bucolicum, idest de custodia boum. Aliud
Georgicum quod est de* agricultura. Aliud Liricum, quod est de
potatione et comestione* vel commessatione et amore deorum.
350 Aliud Epodon, idest clausulare, quod fit de certamine* equestri.
Aliud Carmen Seculare (uel hymnus, quod est laus Dei cum
cantico), et dicebatur "seculare" quia in centesimo decimo anno
aput Romanos erat annus iubileus, idest annus* relaxationis
seruitutis, et tunc cantabatur ab Horatio, cum contigisset in
355 tempore suo, scilicet ultimum metrum Odarum, hoc scilicet:

> Phebe, siluarumque potens Diana.

Cuiusmodi carmen est hoc:

> Vt queant laxis resonare fibris, etc.

Item Subdiuiditur. Item hystoricum aliud Inuectiuum, in quo
360 dicuntur turpiloquia causa malignandi; aliud Reprehensio siue
Satyra, in qua recitantur malefacta causa correctionis, cuiusmodi*
satyre proprietates hiis versibus retinentur:

> Indignans satyra deridet, nudat operta,
> Voce salit, viciis fetet, agreste sapit.

365 Item hystoricum aliud Tragedicon, scilicet carmen quod incipit
a gaudio et terminatur in luctum. Aliud Elegiacum, idest miserabile carmen quod continet uel recitat dolores amancium. Elegie
species est Amabeum, quod aliquando est in altercatione personarum et in certamine amancium, ut in Teodolo et* in Bucolicis
370 aliquando. Item notandum quod illa species narrationis que dicitur Argumentum est Comedia, et omnis Comedia est elegia, sed
non conuertitur.
De Personarum Introductione.* Illa species narracionis que consistit in posicione personarum, ne sit uiciosa, vi exquirit proprie-
375 tates a sex rebus sumptis, que sunt: fortune condicio, etas, sexus,
officium, natio, ydioma; quod notatur* hiis* uersibus in Poetria:

> Intererit multum Dauusne loquatur an heros,
> Maturusne senex an adhuc etate iuuente
> Feruidus, an matrona potens, an sedula nutrix,
380 Mercatorne uagus, cultorne uirentis agelli,
> Colcus an Assirius, Thebis nutritus* an Argis.

Turned now to ashes, he used to turn verses. He sleeps in this bed on
a pillow of bedrock. Virgin, holy mother, may you shine forever,
and raise John's soul from the depths to the heights.

Another is an Apotheosis, which is a poem that celebrates deification
or the coming of a soul to glory. Another is a Bucolic, which is about
cowherding. Another is a Georgic, which is about agriculture. Another
is a Lyric, which is about drinking and eating or feasting and love of the
gods. Another is an Epode, that is, "a line resembling a *clausula*," which
celebrates horse racing. Another is the Secular Song (or hymn, which is
praise of God with singing); it was called "secular" because for the
Romans every one-hundred-tenth year was a jubilee year, that is, a year
of relaxation of slavery; one was sung on one such occasion by Horace,
since it occurred in his lifetime. I refer to the last poem of the *Odes,* the
one beginning:

Phoebus, and Diana, ruler of the woods.

Another poem of this kind is this:

That (your servants) may loose their fibers and resound. . .

Another Subdivision. Again, one kind of historical narrative is Invective,
in which slanderous things are said with full intent to malign. Another is
Reprimand or Satire, in which evils are recited with the hope of correct-
ing them. The following lines contain the chief features of this kind of
Satire:

Indignant satire mocks, lays bare secrets, skips around, stinks of vices,
smacks of coarseness.

Again, one kind of narrative is Tragedy, that is, a poem which begins in
joy and is brought to an end in grief. Another is Elegiac, which is a song
of misery that contains or recites the sorrows of lovers. A species of Elegy
is Amoebaean, which usually consists of a contest between two characters,
or a lovers' spat, as in Theodolus and in various places in the *Eclogues.*
And note that the type of narration called "Realistic Fiction" is comedy,
and every Comedy is an Elegy, but not vice versa.
On Depicting Character. The type of narration that consists in depiction
of character, if it is to escape vice, requires propriety in each of these six
aspects: social position, age, sex, calling, nationality, and dialect, as these
lines from the *Art of Poetry* note:

It will matter very much whether the speaker is John Doe or a hero, a
man in his ripe old age or a boy still in his hot youth, an important
matron or a busy nurse, a well-traveled merchant or the tender of a
sprouting half-acre, Colchian or Assyrian, from Thebes or Argos. (114-18)

De U.* Rebus Que Dampnant Carminem.* Item quinque sunt
que reddunt carmen dampnabile, scilicet nimia quantitas,
nimia festinancia, scribentis negligencia, artis ignorancia, iudicis
385   malicia.
De Arrogancia Vitanda in Principio. Item si hystorica narracio
precesserit, sic debet sumi principium ut possit* fieri per materiam
assensus, ad quod persuadet Horatius, dicens:

> Dic mihi, Musa, uirum, capte post menia Troie, etc.

390   *Quomodo Dilucidanda est Materia.* Si in narratione contingit
aliquid obscure dici, dilucidetur per figuram que dicitur Efflexegesis, idest exposicio littere precedentis. Si narratio fuerit
obscura, per fabulam appositam uel per appologum clarificetur,
per Integumentum quod est ueritas in specie fabule palliata. Et
395   notandum quod omnis appologus est fabula, sed non conuertitur.
Est enim apologus sermo brutorum animalium ad nostram instructionem, ut in Auiano et in Esopo. Si aliquis scripserit istud
genus carminis quod supra dicitur Appoteosis, idest carmen de
leticia et glorificatione, ut in legendis et premiis sanctorum,
400   interseri debent hystorie et exponentur per allegoriam. Dicitur
autem Allegoria ueritas in uerbis hystorie palliata.
*De 4 Stilis Curialibus Preter Stilos 3 Poeticos et de Pedibus
Seruandis in Dictamine.* Item preter tres* stilos poeticos sunt et
alii stili 4 quibus vtuntur moderni, scilicet Gregorianus, Tullianus,
405   Hyllarianus, Hysydorianus. Stilo Gregoriano utuntur notarii
Domini Pape, cardinalium, archiepiscoporum, episcoporum, et
quedam alie curie. In hoc stilo considerantur pedes sponday et*
dactili,* idest dictiones cadentes ad modum spondeorum et
dactilorum.*
410   *De Stilo Gregoriano.* Dactilus dicitur dictio trissillaba cuius
penultima corripitur, licet alie sillabe* producantur. Spondeus
dicitur in dictamine dictio dissillaba, uel partes polisillabe
dictionis cadentis ad modum spondeorum. Et notandum quod
dictio quadrisillaba cuius penultima producitur,* uel due dic-
415   tiones dissillabe, semper ponuntur in fine clausule, dictio uero
posita in penultimo loco semper corripit penultimam, vt hic:
"humilitati nostre se uestra dignetur gratia conformare." Et
notandum quod uiciosa est oratio si duo* dactili vel plures simul
cadant, uel multi spondei sine dactilo. Item, si contingat dictionem
420   finalem esse trissillabam, penultima dictio producat penultimam
sillabam, et* dictio que est ante penultimam dictionem corripiat
penultimam sillabam, ut hic: "humilitati nostre* dignetur se
uestra per omnia conformare gratia."
De Stilo Tulliano siue* Scolastico. Item in stilo Tulliano non est

On the Five Things That Doom a Poem. There are five things that make a poem liable to censure, namely: overlength, too much haste, carelessness in the writer, or ignorance of his art, and malice in the critic.

On Avoiding Arrogance in the Beginning. Also, if a narrative poem is to excel, its beginning should be such as will allow for a rising course through the matter. Horace is urging this on us when he quotes:

Tell me, Muse, of the man, beyond the walls of captured Troy, etc. (*AP* 141)

How to Elucidate a Subject. Should an obscure phrase occur in a narrative, it may be elucidated by means of a figure called Epexegesis, or explanation of the preceding word. If a whole narrative is obscure, it may be made plain by means of a suitable story or fable, through the device known as Integument, which is truth cloaked in the outward form of a story. And notice that every fable is a story, but not vice versa. For in a fable dumb animals are made to speak for our edification, as in Avianus and Aesop. Anyone who writes the kind of poem which above is called an Apotheosis, that is, a poem that celebrates the coming of a soul to glory, as in legends of saints and their heavenly rewards, should set down factual accounts and explain them allegorically. Allegory means truth cloaked in the words of history.

On the Four Curial Styles, Which Are Separate from the Three Poetic Styles, and on the Use of the Metrical Foot in Prose. In addition to the three poetic styles, modern authors also employ four other styles, namely the Gregorian, Ciceronian, Hilarian, and Isidorean. Secretaries of the Holy Father, of cardinals, archbishops, and bishops, and certain other courts employ the Gregorian style. In this style, spondees and dactyls, that is, words whose rhythm approximates that of spondees and dactyls, are treated as metrical feet.

The Gregorian Style. A dactyl is any three-syllable word whose penult is short, although the other syllables may be long. A spondee, in prose, is any two-syllable word, or two-syllable portion of a polysyllabic word, whose rhythm approximates that of spondees. And it should be noted that a *clausula* always ends with a four-syllable word whose penult is long, or with two two-syllable words, while the word before that word or pair of words is always short in the penult, as here: "to our humility may Your Grace deign to be condescending." It should also be noted that two or more consecutive dactyls will vitiate a passage, or too many spondees without a dactyl. Furthermore, if it should happen that the last word has three syllables, the next-to-last word must be long in the penult, and the word before that must be short in the penult, as here: "may Your Grace condescend our humbleness to consult in everything."

The Ciceronian or Academic Style. In the Ciceronian style attention is

425   obseruanda pedum cadencia, sed dictionum et sententiarum
coloracio; quo stilo utuntur uates prosayce scribentes et magistri
in scolasticis dictaminibus. Huius non est assignandum exemplum
quia quasi* curreret in infinitum.

De Stilo Hyllariano. Item in stilo Hyllariano ponuntur* duo
100   spondey et dimidius spondeus, idest vna sillaba, et dactilus;
cuiusmodi dictamen est hic:

> Primo dierum omnium
> Quo mundus exstat conditus.

(Et notandum quod hic intelliguntur pedes ut ante.) Quoniam
435   uero stilus iste propter sui nobilitatem aput multos est in vsu,
subicitur domesticum exemplum, vt hic, archidiacono sese
excusante* per infirmitatem quod non potest esse in synodo.

Littere Excusatorie sub Stilo Hyllariano.

    Reuerendo* Patri ac Domino G., Dei gratia Episcopo Parisius;
440   R. Archidiaconus talis: salutem, et patri deuotam obedienciam.

    Sepe furtiuis gressibus surrepit infortunium, quod ad felicem
exitum opus humanum inuidet peruenire. Cum essem in itinere
sacram tendens ad synodum, caput meum infirmitas oppressit
ita subito quod despero resurgere portumque uite tangere, nisi
445   Dei clemencia me uisitare marcidum condignetur.
    Quare, pater piissime, Uestra dignetur Sanctitas* infirmo
mihi compati, meque languentem habeat excusatum. Nam nihil
est incertius quam mors et salus hominis, quia dum leti ludimus
uenit hora mortalibus lacrimosa.

450   *De Stilo Ysydoriano.* In stilo Ysydoriano, quo utitur Augustinus
in libro Soliloquiorum, distinguntur clausule similem habentes
finem secundum leoninitatem et consonanciam; et uidentur esse
clausule pares in sillabis quamuis non sint. Item iste stilus ualde
motiuus est ad pietatem uel ad leticiam.

455   Pre pudore genus humanum obstupeat, de communi dampno
quilibet abhorreat, admirentur serui, stupescant* liberi, dum
uocantur ad cathedram elingues pueri, conformantur magistris
leues discipuli, dum causa studii fauor est populi. Prius legunt
quam sillabicent; prius uolant quam humi curcitent; antequam
460   sciant partes connectere, versus iactant miros componere.

paid not to the rhythm of feet but to rhetorical figures of words and sentences. This style is employed by poets when they write in prose, and by masters in academic compositions. I must not give an example of this because it would be liable to go on forever.

The Hilarian Style. The Hilarian style is a succession of two spondees, then a half-spondee, that is, one syllable, then a dactyl. Here is a piece in that style:

> That first of all awakenings,
> That day the world was founded on. . .

(Note that feet are understood here in the same sense as before.) Since this style, on account of its nobility, has many practitioners, I am appending an example of my own, in which an archdeacon offers the excuse of illness for his absence from a synod.

A Letter of Excuse in the Hilarian Style.

To his Reverend Father and Lord, G., by the grace of God Bishop of Paris; Archdeacon So-and-So: greeting, and the obedience he has vowed.

Bad luck is forever creeping up with stealthy steps, for it hates to see any work of man come to a happy end. I was on my way to the holy synod when a sickness attacked my head with such suddenness that I have lost all hope of rising again to lay hold of the door of life, unless the kindness of God should condescend to visit my wasted body.

And so, best of fathers, may Your Sanctity stoop to have compassion on me in my illness, and hold me excused since I am languishing. For nothing is more uncertain than a man's death and salvation, since while we mortals play happily our tearful hour comes.

The Isidorean Style. The Isidorean style, which Augustine employs in the *Soliloquies,* consists of balances of *clausulae* with similar endings— that is, rhyming in the manner of leonines; and the *clausulae* seem to be equal in syllables, though in fact they may not be. This style has great power to stir piety or joy.

Let the human race be struck dumb at the shame, let every man shiver at the general blame, let slaves be shocked, free men appalled, when stuttering children are called to professorships, irresponsible schoolboys turned into masters, when the cause of scholarship is the plaything of the mob. They read lectures before they can sound out syllables, they fly before they can hop along the ground, before they know how to connect nouns with verbs they brag they compose

Quidam prius transcendunt Logicam quam per preuiam cerpant
Gramaticam; prius montes scandunt Quadruuii quam per ualles
incedant Triuii. Volant ad astra nec pennas possident, implumes
adhuc casum non preuident. In pilleo Mineruam sacram qui
465   iactitat, in anulo claro Galienum predicat. Ergo de die luna
reluceat et Phebus de nocte cursum faciat, dum stulti rationis
obuiant nature qui presumunt absentem sapienciam predicare.

De* Mandato. Item circa mandatum notanda sunt ista. Dominus
Papa mandatum suum uariat, quia si scribat dilecto et pacifico
470   dicit, "Quare, Discretioni Vestre per apostolica scripta mandantes,
precipimus, etc."; si scribat rebelli et cismatico, "Quare per
apostolica scripta tibi* mandamus et precipimus, etc." Aliarum
curiarum notarii secundum uoluntatem suam dicunt hiis dictionibus: "quare,"* "quapropter," "quam ob rem," "hinc est," "inde
475   est," "qua de causa." Sed uiciosum ponunt mandatum nisi trahat
ortum a narratione. Sed sunt nonnulli qui simul ponunt mandatum et narrationem sine conclusione, dicentes, "Salutem. Mandamus uobis quatinus statim, uisis litteris, etc." Et huiusmodi mandatum, licet uiciosum sit, tamen tollerabile est propter ignorantes.
480   Item conclusio uitiosa est que maior* est narratione, ut si pes
humanus esset maior corpore humano.

marvels of verse. Some of them pass beyond Logic before they can crawl through basic Grammar; they scale the mountains of the Quadrivium before they can walk through the valleys of the Trivium. They fly to the stars, yet have no wings; still without feathers, they foresee no fall. The man who vaunts his holy wisdom in a Master's cap preaches Galen in a Doctor's glittering ring. The moon may as well shine by day and Phoebus run his course at night, when fools pervert the very nature of reason by presuming to preach a wisdom they lack.

On the Request. A few things should be noted about the request. My Lord the Pope varies the form of the request: if he is writing to a beloved and docile subject, he says, "Wherefore, commanding Your Discretion by the authority vested in us in Scripture, we order, etc."; if he is writing to a rebel and schismatic, he says, "Wherefore, by the authority vested in us in Scripture, we order and command you, etc." Secretaries of other courts use any of these expressions, as they choose: "wherefore," "on account of which," "in view of which," "hence," "whence," "for which reason." But they make the request badly unless it rises naturally from the narration. There are many who put the request and narration together without a conclusion, saying, "Greeting. We command you, as soon as you read this letter, etc." A request of this sort, though it is bad, is nonetheless tolerable if people do not know any better. And a conclusion is bad if it is longer than the narration, as if the human foot were bigger than the torso.

Sextum Capitulum: de Ornatu Metri. De Arte Ordinandi Partes
Orationis in Dictamine.* Sequitur sextum capitulum, secundum
quod promissum est a principio, de ornatu metri et prose. Sed
quia ordinatio parcium orationis congrua et uenusta reddit ora-
5   tionem congruam et uenustam, prius dicendum est de ordine
uenusto partium orationis.

    Nomen secundum naturam et rationem constructionis precedit
uerbum. Sed nominum aliud proprium, aliud apellatiuum, aliud
diminutiuum. Si est proprium, semper preponitur nomini signifi-
10   canti officium et dignitatem, vt "Donatus Gramaticus," "Tullius
Rethoricus," "Vulcanus Faber," "Hector Miles"; et sic de aliis
nominibus preterquam de istis nominibus "dominus," "magister."
Dicimus enim "Dominus Willelmus," "Magister Ricardus," et non
e contrario, et hec est ratio. Hoc nomen "magister" commune est
15   ad omnia artificum nomina, quod semper excellencia dicitur, et
hoc nomen "dominus" propter excellenciam preponitur nominibus officiorum. Item substantiuum petit sibi apponi adiectiuum,
quod naturaliter sequitur, per* artem tamen anteponitur cum
aliqua determinatione facta per genitiuum uel per ablatiuum, ut
20   "summa Dei clemencia," "strenua Regis familia," "serena uultu
puella," "egregia cultu* familia." (Eodem modo possunt determinari nomina diminutiua causa uituperii uel laudis, et nomina pleni-
tudinem significantia similiter, ut "uultu uirgo rubicunda," "ore
niueo formosa.")

25   Pronomina quedam causa discretionis et maioris expressionis
propriis nominibus apponuntur, ut* "Ille ego qui quondam, etc."
Possessiua semper postponuntur, ut "Dominus illuminatio mea et
salus mea, etc." Anteponuntur* tamen eggregie cum aliquo inter-
medio, ut "Uestra noscat Dilectio," "mea subcumbit imbecillitas."
30   Item si uerbum sit trissillabum uel quadrisillabum egregie poni-
tur* in fine orationis, dictione casuali antecedente que regitur a
uerbo, vt: "Cognicio Deum omnia gubernare," "Vestre proposui
Dilectioni mee pondus miserie propallare." Sicque etiam debet
ordinari participium, ut: "Cognicio Deum omnia gubernantem."
35   "Me uestra uideat misericordia mendicantem."

    Item uerbum absolutum ponitur* cum determinatione aduer-
biali uel nominali anteposita, quia quod secundum naturam debet
postponi, anteponitur eggregie per artem, ut: "Aristotilis vtiliter
in philosophia studuit, prudenter in logica disseruit." Inculcatio
40   aduerbiorum post uerba positorum leporatam facit* orationem, ut:

Chapter Six

On Embellishment of Poetry. Word Order in Prose. Chapter Six, as I announced at the beginning, deals with embellishment of poetry and prose. But since the fitting and elegant arrangement of the parts of speech makes sentences fitting and elegant, let me speak first of elegant word order.

A noun precedes a verb, both by nature and by art. Nouns are classified as proper, common, and diminutive. A proper noun always precedes a noun that denotes office or rank, as "Donatus the Grammarian," "Cicero the Rhetorician," "Vulcan the Smith," "Hector the Warrior"; and so with all such nouns, except the nouns "lord" and "master." For we say "Lord William" and "Master Richard," and not the other way around, and here is why. The title "master" may be added to the name of any skilled man: it simply implies excellence; and the title "lord" implies excellence before the name of any official. A substantive is normally accompanied by an adjective, which naturally follows it; but the adjective is put first by art when it is accompanied by a modifying genitive or ablative, as: "God's preeminent mercy," "the king's vigorous family," "a placid-of-face girl," "an exceptional-in-culture family." (Diminutive nouns can be modified in the same way, whether for blame or for praise; the use of pleonastic nouns is similar, as "a virgin blushing in the face," "beautiful in her snow-white countenance.")

Certain pronouns are added to proper nouns, to make a distinction or for greater expressiveness, as "I am he who once, etc." Possessives always follow, as *Dominus illuminatio mea et salus mea, etc.* ("The Lord is my light and my salvation, etc." Ps. 26:1). But when there is something to come between them and their noun, it is a nice touch to put them in front, as *Vestra noscat Dilectio* ("Your Love should know"), *mea succumbit imbecillitas* ("my foolishness defers").

If a verb has three or four syllables it goes very well at the end of the sentence, preceded by a word in an oblique case which it governs, as "I know that God all things dominates." "I have proposed to Your Honor the burden of my misery to indicate." The same rule applies to participles: "I know that God in all things is dominating." "May your mercy look on me supplicating."

A verb without an object may follow an adverb or noun phrase which modifies it, because what should follow by nature may very well precede by art, as: "Aristotle in philosophy usefully studied, in logic prudently discoursed." Insistent repetition of adverbs following verbs makes for a pleasing sentence, as "He studies usefully, he disputes strenuously, he

111

"Studet utiliter, disputat nerualiter, incedit honeste, se gerit eggregie." In quibus tres sunt partes quas habet totalis* connexio,
scilicet suspensiua, constans, finitiua, ut: "Sencio magistrum dis-
putare sapienter, legere uero curialiter, respondere discipulis
45   patienter."*

Item de ordinatione coniunctionis talis reddenda est ratio: que
sunt communes indifferenter preponuntur et postponuntur. Sed
hec coniunctio "igitur" causa ornatus anteponitur, ut ibi: "Igitur,
Beatus Martinus." Item trina positio copulatiue coniunctionis
50   colorat orationem, ut ibi: "Et me ledebas, et nil tibi proficiebas,
et nostros super hiis inimicos letificabas." Que sunt prepositiue et
que postpositiue dictatoris est per se considerare.

Circa preposiciones* talis cautela est danda. Dictator consideret
quam circumstanciam notet preposicio; et si nolit suo casuali
55   preposicionem preponere, circumstantiam preposicionis ponat
loco illius, ut: "Uado ad scolas"; hec preposicio "ad" notat lo-
calem circumstanciam, dicat ergo sic:

> Est mihi causa uie studii locus, est mihi meta. ⟩ *figuratiue*

Et sic de aliis preposicionibus intelligendum est. Sed ipsa prepo-
60   sicio in oratione posita egregie ponitur inter duo casualia, ut:
"dilectum ad patrem," "copiosam aput uillam," "excelsas ante
domos"; et sic de aliis.

Interiectiones semper preponuntur, aliquando in oratione inperfecta, aliquando perfecta, et hoc quando exprimitur affectus
65   doloris, uel gaudii, uel metus,* uel admirationis. Sed magis exprimitur affectus per orationem inperfectam quam per orationem
perfectam, quia inperfectio inexpressibilem exprimit affectum,
ut in Lucano:

> O faciles dare* summa deos, eademque tueri
70   > Difficiles!

De Coloribus Uerborum et Sententiarum. Repetitio. Repetitio
est cum ab vno eodemque uerbo in* rebus dissimilibus et diuersis
eadem* principia sumuntur.

> Te mens affatur presens, te lingua salutat,
75   > Te uidet ista palam, te petit illa procul.

Repetitio a fine, uel Conuersio, est quando ad postremum
conuenienter reuertitur ad idem uerbum.

> "Salue!" mens inquit; sed vox, "Cur me fugis?" inquit,
> "Dic ubi dormit amor, dic ubi regnat amor."

goes his way honestly, he conducts himself unusually well." In statements such as these, the complete rhythmical unit is composed of three
parts: a suspensive, a constant, and a complement, as: "I think the master disputes wisely, reads elegantly, answers his students patiently."

As for the position of conjunctions, the rule is this: common conjunctions go first or second in their clause indifferently. But putting the conjunction *igitur* first is a device of ornament, as here: *Igitur, Beatus Martinus* ("Therefore, Blessed Martin"). Triple repetition of a copulative conjunction makes a sentence figurative, as here: "When you did that, you
both injured me, and did yourself no good, and made our enemies happy."
Each writer must decide for himself which conjunctions go first and
which go second.

A word of advice about prepositions: a writer should consider the
circumstance a preposition denotes, and then if he does not want to put
the preposition before its object he may describe the circumstance of
the preposition instead, as: "I am going to school"; the preposition "to"
denotes place; he may say then:

The place of study is the aim of my journey, it is my goal.

The same process can be applied to any other preposition. But if you do
use the preposition when its object has a modifier, it is a nice touch to
put it between the modifier and the object, as: *dilectum ad patrem* ("to
his beloved father"), *copiosam apud villam* ("in the rich town"), *excelsas
ante domos* ("before the high dwellings"), and so on.

Interjections always go first, whether in an incomplete sentence or in
a complete one. They are used to express a feeling of sorrow or joy or
fear or wonder. But feeling is expressed better in an incomplete sentence
than in a complete sentence, for incompleteness expresses inexpressible
feeling, as in Lucan:

O gods, so quick to grant supremacy, so slow to uphold it! (1.510-11)

On Figures of Words and Sentences. Repetition. Repetition is the use of
the same word to begin successive phrases which treat of several different
things.

You my mind addresses as if it were by you, you my tongue greets,
you the one sees clearly, you the other calls from afar.

End-repetition, or Antistrophe, is the fluent use of the same word to end
successive phrases.

"Hail!" my mind says; but "Why do you avoid me?" my voice says,
"Show me the hiding place of love, show me the throne of love."

80   *Complexio.* *

> Qui duo sunt vnum? Duo nos. Qui corpore distant
> Non animo? Duo nos. Qui cor idem? Duo nos.

Traductio. * Traductio est distinguens equineea, cum idem uerbum
crebrius ponitur ut conclimior reddatur oratio.

85
> O uirtus Parche, tu nos disiungere parce,
> Corpus enim solum constat inire solum.

> Inter nos loca sunt; nos interualla locorum
> Non poterunt uariis dissociare locis.

> Sum de Plasseto; placido* mihi corde placeto.
90
> Si tu me places, cordis amore places.

Contencio. * Contentio est cum ex contrariis rebus oratio conficitur.*

> Sum passus casum uarium; qui ludit in atro,
> Fulgurat in claro, prelia pace mouet,
95
> In luctu ridet, risu luget, sacieque
> Esurit, esurie se cibat, ampne sitit.

Exclamacio. * Exclamatio est ex dolore uel letitia.

> O fallax Fortuna! Nimis Fortuna proterua!
> Cur mihi Parisius esse nouerca studes?

100   *Interrogacio.* * Interrogacio est quando confirmat orationem
superiorem.

> Dic, Fortuna, mihi, si tu me pellis ab urbe
> Pyeridum, merces que tua, quodue lucrum?

Raciocinacio. * Ratiosinatio est cum a nobis petimus vniuscuiusque
105   explanationem rei uel rationem.

> Nubila mesticie mihi veri gratia Solis
> Depulerat subito. Cur? Quia uelle fuit.

Sentencia. * Sententia est oratio significatiua quid sit in uita
utile.*

110
> Vix aliquis poterit uirtutum scandere culmen
> Quem Fortuna sinu blanda fouere solet.
> Summe uirtuti uia non est inuia. Demon,
> Victus abis; cedis, O Caro; Munde, fugis!

Interlacement:

Who are two, yet one? We two. Who are apart in body, not mind? We two. Who are one heart? We two.

Transplacement. Transplacement distinguishes between homonyms; it is also the frequent reuse of the same word in different cases to make a sentence more elegant.

O spirit of death, don't spirit him away; for it is a grave truth that a man enters his grave alone.

Places come between us; but disparity of place shall have no power to separate us, in whatever place.

I am from Plassetum; please me with your placid heart. If you free me from care, you will please me by your heart's care for me.

Antithesis. Antithesis is the construction of a sentence out of a series of paradoxes.

I have been the victim of a fickle fortune, which fools in cloudy times, fulminates in bright, starts battles in peace, laughs at grief, grieves at laughter, hungers in satiety, is gorged amidst hunger, thirsts even as it drinks.

Apostrophe. Apostrophe arises from sorrow or joy:

O false Fortune! Fortune too wanton! Why are you so eager to be my stepmother in Paris?

Interrogation. Interrogation reinforces the previous sentence.

Tell me, Fortune, if you do drive me from the city of the Muses, what will be your prize, what will you gain by it?

Reasoning by Question and Answer. Reasoning by Question and Answer is the figure in which we seek the explanation or the reason for each statement from within ourselves.

The grace of the True Sun had suddenly driven the clouds of sadness from me. Why? Because He wanted to.

Maxim. A Maxim is a practical statement about life.

Rare is the man who can scale the heights of virtue while flattering Fortune has him in her lap.

The road to high virtue is not impassable. Devil, you will lose, and leave me; Flesh, you are letting up; you flee, World!

*Contrarium.** Contrarium est cum ex duabus diuersis rebus altera*
115   breuiter conficitur.

> Nec mirum, quia quos in plano uicit, ab alto
> Non uincet; carne non deytate domat.

*Membrum.** Membrum est res breuiter absoluta, que alio membro
orationis exoritur cum copulatiua coniunctione.

120   Et per uos ruimus,* et nil mercedis habetis,
> Hostis et exultat. Que tamen inde seges?

*Articulus.** Articulus est cum singula uerba interuallis distinguntur
cesa oratione.

> Ad uos uertetur lapis quem uuoluitis; in uos
125   Strage, labore, metu, clade, dolore cadet.

Compar in Numero Sillabarum.* Compar in numero sillabarum:

> Me fortem cepit in mollibus edita uilla,
> Florida deliciis, imperiosa* uiris.

Similiter Cadens in Casibus Similibus.* Similiter cadens in casibus
130   similibus est quando plura uerba isdem* casibus efferuntur.

> Hic tuus est; carus sit Christo, gratia sanus,
> Discipulus fultus, prosperitate probus.

Similiter Desinens.* Similiter desinens est sub quo uersus leonini
et rithmi inuenti sunt.

135   Huc dudum ueni, tetigi loca litore* leni.
> Si Christus faueat, prospera puppis eat;
> Assit per maria mihi preuia stella Maria,
> Dux pia, spes, uenia, gloria, meta, uia.

Annominatio cum Suis Speciebus. Annominatio est quando ad
140   idem uerbum acceditur* cum mutatione vel additione vnius
littere aut litterarum, aut cum ad res dissimiles similia uerba
acomodantur.

*In Additione Littere Annominacio:**

> Quod sic uersiculos condo, talique sapore
145   Condio, sunt de me cognita signa tibi.

Annominacio in Subtractione Littere:*

> Non quod me nostis bene fari, sed quia notis
> Formam namque mei te puto nosse stili.

Reasoning by Contraries. Reasoning by Contraries is a kind of quick proof of a statement by contrasting it to its opposite.

No wonder, for those he conquered in the open plain he will not conquer on the heights; his weapon is flesh, not godliness.

Colon. A Colon is a brief and self-contained idea which is linked to another colon in the same sentence by a copulative conjunction.

You are ruining us both, and getting nothing for it, and our enemy is overjoyed. So what good is it?

Comma. Comma is a series of single words separated by pauses in clipped speech.

That stone you're rolling is going to roll back on top of you; panic, suffering, fear, disaster, pain will accompany its fall.

Equality of Syllables. Here is an example of equality of syllables:

That soft and lofty city has undermined my resistance: a flower bed of pleasures, imperial in its power.

Case-Rhyme. Case-Rhyme is achieved by employing several words in the same case:

He is yours; make him Christ's beloved, religion's boast, learning's prop, prosperity's child.

Rhyme. Rhyme is what prompted the invention of leonines and syllabic verse:

I came here long before, touched down on this gentle shore. If Christ will please, my ship will sail on with ease. May Mary be along with me in every sea, a guide by my side, my hope, my way, my goal, my stay.

Paronomasia and Its Various Species. Paronomasia is a figure in which the change or addition of a letter or letters produces a new word nearly like the first word; that is, in which similar words are made to fit dissimilar things.
Paronomasia by Adding a Letter:

You should recognize a favor from me to you in the little poems I make up and flavor with spices.

Paronomasia by Subtracting a Letter:

Not because you know that I write well, but because by now you should recognize the familiar devices of my style.

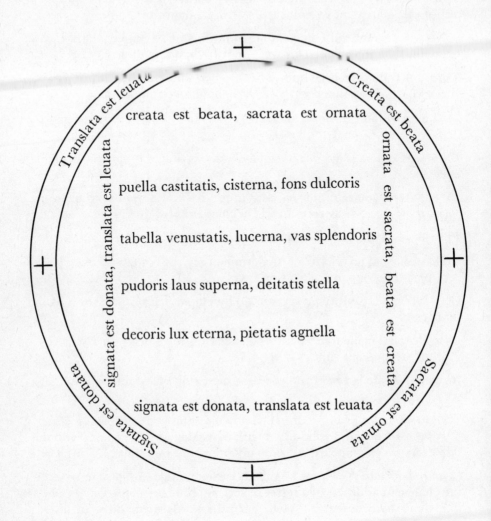

creata est beata, sacrata est ornata

puella castitatis, cisterna, fons dulcoris

tabella venustatis, lucerna, vas splendoris

pudoris laus superna, deitatis stella

decoris lux eterna, pietatis agnella

signata est donata, translata est leuata

Creata est beata

ornata est sacrata, beata est creata

Sacrata est ornata

Signata est donata

signata est donata, translata est leuata

Translata est leuata

Figure Five (follows 1. 138, apparently to illustrate rhyme)

(*Margins*)
She is a creature, yet blessed,
Sanctified, beautified,
Marked out and presented,
Transported, assumed.

(*Center*)
Girl of chastity, well and fount of sweetness
Picture of beauty, lamp and vessel of brightness,
Highest glory of demureness, star of deity,
Eternal light of gracefulness, lamb of piety.

Figure Six

Annominacio* in Additione Sillabe:

150   Hyblam rethorice scis quod colo, quod prius acta
     Inter nos recolo; pendo, rependo uices.

Annominacio* in Subtractione Sillabe:

     Hec tibi consortis legatur epistola, sese
     Dedidit ille tibi, cui sua seque* dedit.

155 *Annominacio* in Litteris Mutandis:*

     O dilecte mihi, verum delecte Iohanni,
     Pre reliquis aliquis hec tibi forte feret.

In* Litteris Transmutandis:

     Presumit metra pingens, monstrataque matre
160   Ecclesia spernit publica* uerba sequi.

In Similitudine Principii:

     Quid me sic mordet, quare sic cogitat, et quo
     Felle nocet? Feci que* mala, quemue cidi?

Species* Annominationis in Retrogradatione. Versus retrogradi
165 reducuntur ad istum colorem ratione transmutationis et* cor-
reptionis et productionis.

     Pātronum laudō, fecti qui cuntă, sŭpremum,
     Sūpremum, cuntă qui fecit, laudō pătronum.

     Rĕtrouersa dabō que mĕtro notificabo,
170   Notificabo mĕtro que dabŏ uersa rĕtro.

In Coreptione et Productione:

     Hoc multum decōris docto, sapit immo decōris
     Quod decōro socii gesta decōre metri.

In Litteris Inicialibus:

175   Donari debent socio dignissima dona
     Cui dare dignetur premia digna Deus.

In Mutatione Vnius Dictionis:

     Nos Christus ditet, nostri consortia seruet,
     Nobis aspiret, nos super astra leuet.

Paronomasia by Adding a Syllable:

You know that I gather the flowers of rhetoric, as we have done together before; I consider and reconsider every turn of phrase.

Paronomasia by Subtracting a Syllable:

This is a letter from your friend to you; he has surrendered himself to you, rendered up to you himself and all he has.

Paronomasia by Changing Letters:

I love you, and would not lose you. If only my letter can reach you before others!

By Shuffling Letters:

His verse is presumption; he spurns the teachings of Mother Church to serve up cant.

By Starting Words Similarly:

Why does he bite me so? Where does he get such notions? What is behind his poisonous slanders? When have I done wrong? Whom have I injured?

Palindromes a Type of Paronomasia. Palindromes come under this figure because they involve shuffling and shortening and lengthening.

I praise the supreme patron who made all things.

I shall produce things turned backward, which I shall make known in meter; I shall make known in meter things which I shall produce turned backward.

By Lengthening and Shortening:

Since he is very learned in decoration, surely he knows, with his sense of decorum, that I decorate the deeds of my friend decorously in poetry.

By Alliteration:

Most gracious gifts should be given to a friend whom God graces with the gift of grace.

By Declining a Single Word:

May we be enriched by Christ, may He preserve our fellowship, may He be favorable to us, may He raise us above the stars.

180   *In Mutatione Diuersarum Dictionum:*

Castor ero, teneas mentem Pollucis, Horesti
Sta similis, Piladem presto, Iohanne mane.

In Uaria Composicione Dictionum:

185   Anglia, processi de te, cui cesserat orbis
Angulus; accessi Parisiusque fui.
Parisius vici cum sit Garlandia nomen,
Agnomen florens contulit illa mihi.

Conduplicacio. * Conduplicatio est iteratio eiusdem causa ampliationis aut admirationis.

190   Numquid sepe leges uersus a me tibi uersos,
Numquid? Nonne petis quod peto, nonne petis?

Subiectio. * Svbiectio est quando querimus quid debeat dici, et illud subicimus.

An uiuent illi sicut nos uiuimus,* alter
195   Quorum de socio perfidus ista* refert?
Perfidus esse sibi dicet patrimonia. Quero,
Cuius erant patris? An patris eius erant?
Vixit auus, uixit proauus, sine re, sine tecto;
Non hiis terra, pecus, non domus ulla fuit.
200   Se feret heredem peregrini. Quis peregrino,
Quis forti furi det sua? Nemo quidem.

Gradacio. * Gradacio est quando prius* non ad consequens* uerbum descenditur quam ad superius.

Sed non uersutum furem noui; neque noui,
205   Nec mea seruaui, sed mala multa tuli.
Et mala multa tuli, mihi nec caui; neque caui,
Nec mihi profeci, mente nec Argus eram.

Alia Species Gradacionis.*

Simplicitas iuuit gestum, gestusque tegebat
210   Mentem, mens struxit famina, famen opus.
Si uirtus socii potuisset* scisse quid esset,
Non socium fraudis falleret arte suum.

Diffinicio:

Consortis uirtus est ueri restis amoris,
215   Sorte duos* vna, menteque, reque ligans.

Transicio. * Transitio post ostensum proponit breuiter quod consequitur.

Quid uirtus fuerit socii clarescit in istis;
Huius sed fuerit noscite qualis amor.

By Declining Several Words:

I shall be Castor, may you keep the attitudes of Pollux; stay like to Orestes, I'll play Pylades; stay by John.

By Varying Compound Forms of Words:

England, I proceeded from you, to whom a corner of the world ceded; I succeeded in reaching Paris. The name of my section of Paris is Garland, which bestowed on me a flowery nickname.

Reduplication. Reduplication is the repetition of the same word for amplification, or to express wonder.

Do you often read over the lines I turn out for you? Do you? Aren't my aims your aims? Aren't they?

Hypophora. Hypophora is the figure in which we ask what ought to be said, then say it ourselves.

Can their life be compared to ours, when one of them so treacherously tells these tales about his friend? Now that betrayer will insist the money is his patrimony. My question is, from what father? His? His grandfather never had a penny in his life, his great-grandfather never had a roof; they had no land, no livestock, no home. Then he'll say he's the heir of "a stranger." Who would give all he owned to a stranger, a burly thief? No one, I assure you.

Climax. In Climax one proceeds to the next verb only after repeating the previous verb.

But he was so cunning I didn't realize he was a thief; I didn't realize it, and I didn't keep my money, and I suffered for it. Yes, I suffered for it, I didn't watch myself; I didn't watch myself, and I didn't help myself—I was no Argus.

Another Kind of Climax.

His sympathy aided his manner, his manner masked his mind, his mind devised his "line," his line did the job. If he could have known the value of a friend, he would not have practiced his skill at fraud on his friend.

Definition:

The value of a friend is that he is a rope of true love that binds two people together in one fate, one purpose, one task.

Transition. Transition is a brief summary, and a brief statement of what is to follow.

The value of a friend, then, is plain; now you will find out what this man's love was like.

220   *Correctio:*

> Iste mihi consors, sed* discors rupit amoris
> Fedus. Uir fidus? Perfidus immo nimis!

Occupacio. * Occupatio est quando dicimus nos preterire* quod non preterimus.

225
> Quid referam consanguineum suspendia passum?
> Huic cesum ciuem preteriisse sinam.
> Preterio mimas, mimos, quibus heserat ille,
> A quibus hunc rapui, moribus inde dedi.

Disiunctio. * Disiunctio est cum* eorum de quibus dicimus aut
230   vtrumque aut vnumquodque certo concluditur uerbo.

> Quo lucror officio rogat, ad bona singula mancum
> Estimat, officium dedidicisse putat.

Coniunctio. * Coniunctio est quando ponitur uerbum in oratione media.*

235
> Per tenebras noctis uadit nebulasque diei,
> Vel dampno gaudet siue cruore uiri.

Adiunctio. * Adiunctio fit verbo posito in principio uel in fine.

Adiunctio * Verbo Posito in Principio:*

> Fecerat heredem precelse me pater aule;
240   > Prebuit huic genitor sarcula, rastra, lutum.

Adiunctio * Verbo Posito in Fine:*

> Talia consortes consortia non imitamur;
> Perpetuo stabiles nos in amore sumus.

Interpretacio. * Interpretatio est que idem aliter* dicit secundum
245   aliud uerbum.

> Tempore duret amor longo; dilectio longa
> Regnet; nos talis firma cathena liget.

Commutacio. * Commutatio est cum sentencie discrepant ut a
priore posterior contraria proficiscatur.*

250
> Quem retinere uolo nequeo retinere sodalem;
> Quem uero teneo, non tenuisse uolo.

Permissio. * Permissio est qua* nos concedimus uoluntati alicuius.

Correction:

> He was my friend, but he grew factious, and burst the bond of love. A man whose word was his bond? No, an utter bounder.

Praeteritio. Praeteritio is saying we are passing over something when we really are not.

> Why should I bring up his brother who was hanged? I do him a kindness, and pass over a certain murdered citizen; I pass over the actors and actresses he resorted to until I snatched him from them and put him on the path of righteousness.

Disjunction. In Disjunction, each of two or more statements ends with a synonymous verb.

> He wonders by whose patronage I advance, he considers himself cut off from every kind of favor, he thinks patronage has passed him by.

Conjunction. In Conjunction, the verb is put in the middle of its clause.

> In the darkness of night he goes about, in the mists of day; harm-doing delights him, and human blood.

Adjunction. In Adjunction, all the verbs are placed at the beginning, or all at the end.

Adjunction with the Verbs at the Beginning:

> My father made me heir to a noble castle; his sire left him hoes, rakes, mud.

Adjunction with the Verb at the End:

> We are comrades, but such camaraderie we do not copy; in perpetual love firmly we stand.

Synonymy. Synonymy repeats the same thing in a different way, in other words.

> Long may our love endure; may lasting friendship prevail; may so firm a chain bind us.

Reciprocal Change. Reciprocal Change occurs when two ideas are discrepant in such a way that the second proceeds from the first and is contrary to it.

> The friend I want to keep I can't keep; the one I have I wish I hadn't kept.

Surrender. Surrender is the figure by which we yield to someone else's will.

> Me tibi concedo; fac uelle per omnia de me,
> Sum quoniam totus corpore mente tuus.

255   *Dubitacio.** Dvbitatio est cum dubitamus quid de pluribus potissimum dicatur.

> M̶ ̶n̶c̶ ̶d̶e̶c̶e̶t̶ dici fatuum quo nomine dicam
> Affectus tales sic quibus ipse trahor.

*Expedicio.** Expedicio est quando plura proposita tolluntur et
260   necessarium relinquitur.

> Alas uel currum vel equum deposco, sed ista
> Deficiunt. Per quos* inspiciare mihi?

*Dissolucio.** Dissolutio est quando separatis partibus aliqua proferuntur sine copulatiua coniunctione.

265
> Visere querit amor dilectos,* stringere caros
> Amplexus, mentem promere, grata loqui.

*Precisio.** Precisio est quando uerbum necessarium subticetur.

> Quid, Fortuna, noces? Numquid tua facta renarrem?
> Tu ne rotam facilem—sed reticere uolo.

270   *Nominacio.** Nominatio, imitationis causa et rei designande, est quando ponitur appellatiuum pro appellatiuo, ut "fragor" pro "sono."

> In nostros actus rudis. O, cur rudis, asella?
> Bos uelut altisona fauce minante tonas.

275   *Pronominacio.** Pronominatio est* que satyrice fit quando extraneo nomine appellatur quod sic non potest appellari, ut: "Uidete* quomodo asinus iste loquitur, sic quod cognomen eius sit Asinus."

> Hec est Instabilis Ales, Lupa Perfida, Monstrum
280   > Letiferum, Fallax Risio, Fictus Amor.

*Denominacio.** Denominatio que fit sine discripcione est quando instrumentum ponitur pro actu uel pro domino, uel materia pro materiato, vel inuentor pro inuento.

> Hanc aquilis superet Romanus, Gallia frenis
285   > Conculcet, libris Grecia docta terat.

Denominatio que fit cum descripcione est cum a rebus finitimis trahit orationem, qua* possit intelligi res* que non suo uocabulo fuit apellata.

I yield myself up to you; do what you want with me in everything; for I am yours completely, mind and body.

Indecision. Indecision is hesitation over which of several ways of speaking is best.

I am not the one to say what name of names I can give to feelings whose pull I feel myself.

Elimination. In Elimination, several suggestions are discarded and the right one retained.

I need wings, or a coach, or a horse, but these I lack. How can I keep you in my sight?

Asyndeton. Asyndeton presents a series of separate phrases without a copulative conjunction.

Love seeks to see the beloved, to wrest precious embraces, to pour out its thoughts, to say sweet things.

Aposiopesis: Aposiopesis occurs when an essential word is left unsaid.

Fortune, why do you hurt me? Shall I list your sins? You no easy wheel—but I will be silent.

Onomatopoeia. Onomatopoeia aims at precise imitation, at letting a thing stand for itself, by substituting an alternate word for the usual one, as "crash" for "sound."

You bray against our action. O why do you bray, little ass? You thunder like a cow in your loud, menacing throat.

Antonomasia. Antonomasia is a satirical device in which something whose real name cannot be named is referred to by a kind of nickname, as: "See how that ass talks? Ass could be his middle name!"

The Lady I speak of is the Fickle Bird, the Treacherous Wolf, the Beast that Brings Death, the False Laugh, Sham Love.

Metonymy. Metonymy without description occurs when the instrument is put for the act or for the wielder, or the material for the thing made of the material, or the inventor for the invention.

May the Roman eagle conquer her, may France trample her with its bridles, may learned Greece wear her down with books.

Metonymy by description draws from closely related things an expression by which the thing meant can be understood without calling it by its own name.

290
>　　　Est populosa polis Francorum, quam studiosa
>　　　Turba colit uatum, qua mea Clio studet.

Circuicio. * Circuitio* est quando rem simplicem circumloquimur,
vt hic:
>　　　Parisius uiuo; me Parisiana chohercent
>　　　Viuentem studia: me men uitu luuat.

295　*Transgressio.* * Transgressio est quedam dictionum transpositio.

>　　　Continuum propter studium mea defluit etas,
>　　　Florida primeui labitur hora boni.

Superlacio. * Superlatio est oratio superans ueritatem* alicuius
augendi minuendiue causa.

300
>　　　Sidera Parisius famoso nomine tangit,
>　　　Humanumque genus ambitus urbis habet.

Intellectio a Parte ad Totum:

>　　　Crux exaltatur illic; campana renarrat
>　　　Ecclesie laudes et capit ara preces.

305　*Translacio.* * Translatio est quando ipsum uerbum transfertur,
aliquando ipsa oratio, aliquando nomen.

>　　　Hic in cismaticos mittit sentencia fulmen,
>　　　Hic ambigea manus canonis ense perit.

Abusio. * Abusio est quando abutimur propria significatione
310　dictionis alicuius.

>　　　Consilium longum datur hic, oratio magna,
>　　　Visque breuis, paucus sermo, Minerua nitens.

Permutacio. * Permutatio est ut si parcus diceretur prodigus, et e
contrario.

315
>　　　Hic canis, immo lupus grassatur, pastor ouilis
>　　　Qui fertur; tendit dilacerare gregem.

Conclusio:

>　　　Hic ego si maneo, socium nec uiso fidelem,
>　　　Pectora languescent* saucia iure mihi.

320　*DE COLORIBUS SENTENCIARUM.*

>　　　Picta colorari poterit sentencia tali
>　　　Scemate si sapiat clausa medulla fauum.

Distribucio. * Distributio attribuit vnicuique quod suum est.

There is a populous city of the French, where the studious poet-crowd
gathers, and in which my own Clio finds inspiration.

Periphrasis. Periphrasis is a roundabout description of a simple idea, as
here:

I live in Paris; Parisian studies hem in my life; living here pleases me.

Hyperbaton. Hyperbaton is transposed word order.

In constant study away my life is flowing; the blooming hour is
slipping past of youthful talent.

Hyperbole. Hyperbole is an expression that goes beyond the truth, either
to heighten or to belittle.

The famous name of Paris reaches to the stars, and its borders contain
the human race.

Synecdoche of Part for the Whole:

There the cross is raised high, the bell announces over and over the
praises of the Church, and the altar receives prayers.

Metaphor. Metaphor is the use of a verb, or sometimes a noun, or sometimes a whole phrase, in a transferred sense.

Here the sentence sends a thunderbolt against schismatics, here the
Albigensian's hand is cut off by the sword of Canon Law.

Catachresis. Catachresis is intentionally misapplying a word to an unusual context.

Here you will find long advice, and huge speech, as well as short sense
and tiny chatter, and glittering wisdom.

Allegory. By Allegory a miser is called a philanthropist, or vice versa.

Here a dog—no, a wolf—goes about, passing for a shepherd; he is bent
on tearing apart the flock.

Conclusion:

If I remain here without a faithful friend to visit, my wounded breast
will pine away in me, and with justice.

FIGURES OF THOUGHT.

Any idea you portray can be ornamented by one of these figures, if
the enclosed kernel should taste the honeycomb.

Distribution. Distribution assigns to each what is his own.

Discipulis doctoris erit monstrare sophiam;
325   Discipuli uoces est retinere suas.

Licentia cum Reprehensione:

Discipulis inerit et risus uanus et error
Stultus dum licitum ludere uoctor habet.

Diminutio.* Diminucio est cum aliquis se humiliat.

330   Hanc tenuem cartam videat calamumque pusillum,
Si quis uersiculos uult reperire nouos.

Descriptio.* Descripcio fit* cum quadam similitudine ueritatis sumpta.

Discipulus segnis it cum testudine lenta,
335   Turgescens epulis, ebrietate cadens.

Diuisio. Diuisio remouet vnam rem ab alia et vtramque absoluit.

Erige te, doctor, probitas si te comitatur.
Ne piger esse uelis; es piger, ergo malum.

Frequentacio.* Frequentatio est quando multa ad unum col-
340   liguntur.

Es piger, elinguis, indoctus, perfidus, effrons;
Hosti munificus, Hostis es ipse tuis.*

Expolicio.* Expolicio* est quando idem dicimus aliis uerbis causa ornatus.

345   Indoctus doctor pueros necat, amputat illis
Guttura, diffundit uicera, corda rapit.

Commoracio.* Commoratio est quando nos dicimus uelle com-
morari.

Vos hac parte morans doctores corrigo doctos.
350   Amoneo; validi sitis, amate probos.

Contencio.* Contentio est quando orationes contendunt et con-
trarie sunt.

Si pigri sitis, letabitur Hostis; at ille
Tristis erit si uos uiderit esse probos.

355   *Similitudo:*

Nauem nauta regit et fluctibus imperat arte;
Arte sua doctor corrigit, arte regit.

It is up to the teacher to display wisdom before the students; it is up to the students to retain what he says.

Frankness of Speech, with Reprimand:

But silly smiles and stupid mistakes mark students whose teacher condones fooling.

Understatement. Understatement is authorial modesty.

A person with an urge to invent novel verses might consider this frail page and insignificant pen.

Vivid Description. Vivid Description is made by assuming a certain lifelike tone.

The slack student proceeds at a turtle's pace, puffy with overeating, stumbling with too much drink.

Division. Division separates one idea from another and resolves them.

Rouse yourself, teacher, if you have a conscience. Granted you don't want to be lazy; you are lazy, and that is wrong.

Accumulation. Accumulation gathers many ideas into a single outburst.

You are lazy, tongue-tied, unprepared, untrustworthy, arrogant; you play into the hands of Satan; you are yourself Satan to your own students.

Refining. Refining is saying the same thing in other words as a stylistic frill.

An unprepared teacher destroys boys, cuts their throats, scatters their guts, tears out their hearts.

Dwelling on the Point. Dwelling on the Point is when we say we wish to linger.

I dwell on this matter to keep you teachers who are well prepared on the straight path; I admonish you: maintain your strength, love conscientiousness.

Antithesis. Antithesis places contrary statements in opposition/with each other.

If you are lazy, Satan will rejoice; but he will be sad if he sees you are conscientious.

Similitude:

By his skill the sailor controls his ship and governs the waves; by his skill the teacher guides, by his skill he controls.

*Exemplum.** Exemplum est quando nos proponimus dicta uel facta autentica.

360
> Arte docens exempla Plato donabit, et eius
> Testis Aristotiles qui sua dicta sapit.

*Ymago.** Ymago est collatio* forme ad formam,

> In facinus quidam serpunt ut lubricus anguis
> Vt noceant aliis, ut sua lucra legant.

365 *Effictio cum Qualitate Corporis Cuiusdam.** Effictio* se habet ad signa exteriora.

> Hos ut cognoscas, macilenti sunt, sapiuntque
> Lucrum, pallenti virus in ore gerunt.

*Notacio.** Cum Natura Certis Describitur Signis.* Notacio est
370 quando nos notamus aliquem per aliena signa.

> Hii sunt quos pascit aliena pecunia; sese
> Iactant eggregios magnificosque viros.

*Sermocinacio.** Sermocinatio est quando alicui persone sermo attribuitur et idem exponitur ratione dignitatis:

375
> Iactator dicit, "Perfecte gramata noui;
> Gramatice, logice disputo; vera sequor.
> Fallaces alii, quia decepere minores.
> Condoleo; liceat dicere vera michi."

*Conformacio.** Conformatio est quando res inanimata intro-
380 ducitur loqui, et est similis Prosopopeye.

> Se magnus paruo conformat, talia dicens:
> "De cumulo modico paucula grana sero;
> Fonticulum gustate meum, uos sumite parua
> De paruo; paruum me dare parua decet."

385 *Significatio Fit* Cum Quadam Suspicatione:*

> Tu qui sub ferula luges, quem uirga frequenter
> Castigat, repetas lecta: relecta placent.

*Demonstratio.** Demonstratio est* quando res exprimitur ut ante oculos videatur.

390
> Magnus Aristotiles magno studuisse labore
> Dicitur, et studio se macerasse graui.
> In cathedra digne positus sua Topica scripsit;
> Soluit ad extremum quicquid Elenchus habet.

Exemplum. An Exemplum is quotation of authorities, or an account of their actions.

Plato is a good example of skillful teaching: Aristotle, too, shows himself to be a man who knows what he is talking about.

Simile. Simile is comparison of one object to another.

There are people who crawl into crime like a slippery snake, to harm others, to snatch their money.

Portrayal by Means of Bodily Characteristics. Portrayal deals with external details.

Here is how you may recognize them: they are thin, and they smell of money, and they carry poison in their yellow mouths.

Character Delineation, or Describing Inner Nature by Outer Signs. In Character Delineation, we designate someone by his idiosyncrasies.

They are the kind who get their meals on other people's money; they boast that they are special and splendid men.

Dialogue. Dialogue is the assignment to characters of speeches, which must be in accordance with their station.

The braggart says, "I know grammar perfectly; my arguments are absolutely grammatical and logical; I am a follower of truth. Others are liars, for they have tricked children. I feel for them, but may it be allowed me to speak the truth."

Personification. Personification is the figure by which an inanimate thing is presented as speaking; it is like Prosopopoeia.

The truly great man belittles himself, and speaks in this manner: "From my modest store I sow a very few seeds. Taste my little fountain, take the simple offerings of a simple man. I am simple; I can only give simple things."

Implication is Done by Suggestion:

You who grieve beneath the whip, whom the rod frequently chastens, repeat what you have read; second readings are pleasant.

Ocular Demonstration. Ocular Demonstration uses language to put an object before our very eyes.

They say great Aristotle toiled greatly at his studies, and tortured himself with his weighty investigations. Imagine him, raised to the magisterial chair he deserved, writing the *Topics;* analyzing to the last little detail the whole subject of the *Elenchus.*

De XI* Attributis Persone ex Quibus Loci Rethorici Eliciuntur.
395   Svfficienter* propositis coloribus uerborum et sentenciarum, qui
tractat materiam aliquem sibi pro uoluntate partem eligat; aut
colores ampliantes in amplianda materia, aut colores abbreuiantes
in abbreuianda materia (de quibus supra dictum est, scilicet de
abbreuiacione et ampliacione materie). Sed ad utrumque neces-
400   saria sunt xi attributa persone ex quibus eliciuntur loci rethorici:
nomen, natura, conuictus, fortuna, habitus, consilium, affectus,
studium, casus, factum, oratio. Nomen, ut, "Est Uerres, ergo est
latro." Natura, ut, "Est barbarus, ergo crudelis." Conuictus, ut,
"Uixit in curia, ergo est* amator nobilium." Fortuna, ut* diues
405   vel pauper. Habitus, ut, "Est sapiens" (uel stultus, furiosus).
Concilium: "Precessit deliberatio." Factum: "collocutio." Affectus, ut, "Est amans" (auarus). Studium, ut, "Est* geometer"
(gramaticus*). Casus, ut exul, felix, dampnatus. Et notandum
quod hec tria⌊attributa,⌋ casus, factum, et oratio, considerantur
410   ex tribus temporibus, scilicet: quid aduersarius fecerit, quid illi
acciderit, et quid dixerit; quid faciat, uel quid illi* accidat, uel
quid* dicat; quid facturus sit, quid illi casurum sit, qua oratione
usurus* sit.
    Et sciendum quod illa que dicta sunt, nisi iuuerint ad exemplum
415   uenerabilium virorum, venerabilis gestus et modus pronunciationis
nichilii uidebuntur.

On the Eleven Personal Characteristics Which Furnish the Rhetorical Commonplaces. So much for figures of words and sentences; each author is free to choose for himself the part that suits him—whether it be figures of amplification for filling out his subject, or figures of abbreviation for cutting his material down. (I have treated both above, that is, abbreviation and amplification.) But in either case he will find essential the eleven personal characteristics which furnish the rhetorical commonplaces: name, nature, social position, wealth, character, motives, disposition, occupation, circumstances, actions, and words. Name, as "He is Verres, and so is a thief." Nature, as "He is a barbarian, and so cruel." Social position, as "He has lived at court, and so is a lover of the nobility." Wealth, as rich or poor. Character, as "He is wise" (or stupid, wrathful). Motives, as "He thought it over first." Actions: "He spoke to others about it." Disposition, as "He is kindly" (miserly). Occupation, as "He is a geometrician" (grammarian). Circumstances, as exiled, happy, damned. Note that the last three characteristics, that is, circumstances, actions, and words, are considered under three tenses, namely: what one's opponent did, what happened to him, and what he said; what he is doing, what is happening to him, what he is saying; what he will do, what will happen to him, what words he will use.

    And let me make it clear that unless what I have said here is useful, as an example of admirable men, admirable gesticulation and mode of delivery will be worthless.

De* Proprietatibus Tragedie. Expletis con capitulis tractatus
superius promissi, sequitur septimum capitulum et ultimum,
quod diuiditur in plures partes. In principio huius principalis
capituli ponitur exemplum tragedie versifice composite. Vnica

5 uero tragedia scripta fuit quondam ab Ouidio apud Latinos, que
sepulta sub silencio non venit in vsum. Hec est secunda tragedia,
cuius proprietates diligenter debent notari. Post tragediam
sequntur dictamina; et* post dictamina, breuiter et procincte
data, sequitur ars rithmificandi et exempla rithmorum, quibus

10 positis presens opusculum terminatur.

Summa tragedie est hec. Sexaginta milites obcessi fuerunt in
castello quodam, inter quos due erant lotrices. Vna supleuit
vices lauandi et coeundi xxx militibus, alia aliis xxx. Sed vna
dilexit quemdam militem qui fuit de parte alterius lotricis; quod

15 ut ei notum erat, suborta fuit contencio inter lotrices, que sese
ad inuicem uerberabant. Contingit quod vna nocte ille miles
dilectus lotrici* inuentus est dormiens cum illa lotrice ab alia
superueniente lotrice, quos ut uidit dormientes, ambos accepto
gladio interfecit. Et ne facinus eius de die pateret, castellum

20 apperuit occulte et intromisit hostes, qui cuntos milites castelli*
interfecerunt; inter quos interfectus est* frater ipsius lotricis,
que etiam proprio fratri non pepercit ut interfectos a se cum
militibus interfectis ab hostibus occultaret.

Huius tragedie proprietates sunt tales:* graui stilo describitur;

25 pudibunda proferuntur et celerata; incipit a gaudio et in lacrimas
terminatur.

Incipit* Tragedia.

　　　Qvasdam turma ducum firmas obsederat arces,
　　　Infra quas pauci fuerant; sed marcia uirtus
30　　Compensat numerum, que sese sola fatetur
　　　Prelia posse pati, uacuareque menia firma:
　　　Pugnat posse famem tolerare sitimque potentes:
　　　Ad iuga mittentem, sed non ad talia, turmam
　　　Que munita fuit fallax detrusit egestas.
35　　Se numerosa choors tutas diffuderat extra
　　　Arces, insidians inclusis; maxima torsit
　　　Ad muros saxa non dampna ferencia muris.
　　　Bellatrice sue frustra subrepere firmo

On the Characteristics of Tragedy. Now six chapters of the treatise I promised at the start have been completed; here is the seventh and last chapter, which is divided into several parts. At the beginning of this, the longest chapter, I present an example of a tragedy composed in verse. Among the Roman writers, a single tragedy was written once by Ovid, which is buried in silence and no longer extant. This is the second tragedy; take careful note of its characteristics. After the tragedy come some letters; and after the letters, which are given in a brief and handy form, comes a treatise on rhymed syllabic verse, with examples of rhymed poems. When that is done, this little work is at an end.

Here is a summary of the tragedy. Sixty soldiers were besieged in a certain castle. With them were two washerwomen; one furnished the services of laundry and copulation for thirty soldiers, the other for the other thirty. But one was in love with one of the soldiers in the other washerwoman's group. She found out; a squabble developed between the washerwomen, and they came to blows. It fell out one night that the injured washerwoman found her rival sleeping with the soldier she loved; and seeing them asleep, she took a sword and killed them both. Then, lest her crime be revealed in the morning, she secretly opened the castle and let in the enemy, who killed all the soldiers in the castle. Among the slain was that washerwoman's brother; she did not even spare her own brother, so anxious was she to hide her victims among the soldiers killed by the enemy.

These are the characteristics of this tragedy: it is written in the high style; it deals with shameful and criminal actions; it begins in joy and ends in tears.

A Tragedy.

An army and its leaders were besieging a certain sturdy castle. The band inside was small, but courage in war makes up for numbers: courage, whose boast it is that it can endure battles by itself, by itself clear out strong fortifications. It contends that it can stand hunger and thirst, powerful though they are; for deceitful hunger has been known to compel an entrenched army to submit to yokes—but not to such yokes as these. A numerous force had deployed outside the secured castle, lying in wait for those within, and hurling huge rocks at the walls, which did the walls no damage. Using as cover the constant threat of arrows from their lady of war, the crossbow, they tried to

         Temptauit uallo balista tela minanti:
40   Percuciunt; rident insultus menia cassos.
            Que dum clausa choors retinet,* uigilantque cohortes
         Excluse, res disposuit prudencia caute
         Militis inclusi, et uiuendi copia cuique,
         Vt peciit procerum reuerencia, digna dabatur.
45   Bis xxx scias inclusos menibus illis
         Esse, due quorum lotrices corpora cultu
         Pulcre curarunt, debentes esse parate
         Ad cohitus equitum; quia marcet forma uirilis
         Ad caros cultus hominum si femina desit,
50   Cuius dulcedo uirus, concordia bellum.
         Assignata fuit vni* pars vna choortis,
         Altera pars alii: tot sustinet ista quot illa;
         Suppleuere uices Veneris cultusque ministre.
            Vnius partis optauit partis alius
55   Vir quidam famulam; famule non parua secunde
         Gloria, namque suus fuerat prius; altera partes
         Eius surripuit precibus preciisque subacta.
         Altera liuore torquetur pelice pulsa;
         Iras accendit uerbis congressa pudendis
60   Dum stetit* ad stagnum mundans cum pellice uestes.
         "Dic," ait, "O lati pelex infamia mundi,
         Fedus ut hyrcus olens, meretrix, rabiesque canina,
         Ad coitus nuncquid pauci triginta fuere,
         Qui tua prerapido pruritu membra fricarent?
65   Cur alienasti iuuenem mihi? Cur minuisti
         Turbe praua mee numerum? Cur surripuisti*
         Qui meus exstiterat? Est lucrum dedecus orbis!
         Infames fient per te que nil meruere.
         Vt bubo est uolucrum latitans eiectio, sic sis
70   Contemptu gentis erratica; nec requiescas,
         Sed tibi terra neget sedem, tibi deneget unda!"
            Hec, et feda magis, que non decet ora pudica
         Dicere, dicebat. Sed sauccia tela remittit
         Pectoris illa sui, iacit illita tela ueneno.
75   In fornace sui cordis fabricantia tela
         Hec sua sunt: ira, liuor, mentis tumor ortus,
         orta fuit quando dolus; iste tela sorores
         Tabe sua maculant, grauius que ledere possint.
         Ferre silenda palam letalis precipit ira;
80   Humanam carnem facit illam rodere liuor;
         Hanc tumor instigat mentis non posse minori
         Cedere dum sufflat quasi bufo pectore pleno;
         Illius* est operum dolus, ignis inignit in illa
         Tela mali; quippe dedit hec natura iacenti
85   In cunis, cuius donum discedere nescit.
         Verborum rabiem probrorum* lesa procellam
         Emittit rapidam. Stes hic modo muta pudore,
         Melpomone; pudeat, pudeat tot probra referre!

steal up the sturdy rampart, but in vain. They strike; the walls mock
their futile thrusts.

The force within holds on, the forces outside wait for their chance.
Meanwhile, the comfort of the soldier inside has been arranged for,
with prudence and caution; their solicitous officers have taken care
that each man is provided with a satisfactory fullness of living. There
were sixty of them, to be exact, inside those walls, plus two pretty
washerwomen, who tended their bodies with devotion. It was their
duty to be available for copulation with those knights; for the male
frame withers if it lacks the female of the species for its fond caresses,
though her sweetness is poison, her peace, war. One half of the force
was assigned to one woman, the other half to the other; this one serves
as many as that one; the maidservants supplied the offices and devotion of Venus.

But one of the men in one group conceived a desire for the other
group's girl; no small glory for the second girl, since he had been the
other's sweetheart before; but she was brought under by his entreaties
and bribes, and stole her role. The first girl, pushed aside for the paramour, is tortured with envy; she confronts the paramour as they
stand at the sink washing clothes, and kindles her anger with shame-
less words. "Tell me," she says, "kept-mistress, disgrace of the whole
wide world, filthy, stinking goat, whore, dog-froth, were thirty too
few for your pleasure, thirty to rub your member with eager lust? Why
have you made my man a stranger to me? Why have you reduced the
number of my crowd, you traitor? Why have you stolen one who was
mine? Money is the shame of the world! Because of you, infamy will
be the lot of the most deserving of women! As the owl is the skulking
pariah among birds, so may you wander, despised by your race; may
you never rest, but may land and sea alike deny you repose!"

This and fouler things, which a modest tongue should never utter,
she uttered. But the other, wounded to the quick though she is, returns weapons of her own, hurls back weapons dipped in poison. What
are the things that mold weapons in the furnace of her heart? Anger,
envy, swelling pride; one by one they rose, and guile rose with them;
these sisters stain her weapons with venom to make them hurt all the
more. Deadly anger urges her to bring into the open things that should
remain silent; envy causes her to gnaw human flesh; swelling pride
urges her never to yield to her inferior; she puffs like a toad with swol-
len lungs. Guile is another of her tools: fire ignites in her weapons of
evil; indeed, nature gave her them as she lay in her cradle, a gift she
does not know how to lay aside. Hurt, she thrust forth a madness of
words, a quick storm of insults. Stand here now, speechless from
modesty, Melpomene; shame on her, shame to return so many insults!

Si ter prima decem, centum furiosa secunda
90   Aggerat, exponens quasi certo nomine quemque.
Expuit et nasum rugis uelut aere leso
Contrahit, ut feriat occurrens alite gressu.
        Vtraque luctatur digitis euellere crines
Alterius; caput huc illucque* rotant, lacerantque
95   Tolonos montes. Quam uerbis leserat ante,
Dente suo ledit, faciemque cruentat ab ungue.
Discedunt, iterum choeunt, ferulasque lauando
Que feriunt uestes sumunt, seseque fatigant
Ictibus innumeris, iuuenes ut cestibus apti.
100   De raptu cari prior appellauit amici,
Altera defendit, et se decernere iurant
Presidio Martis utrius uir debeat esse.
        Hiis gestis, tegimen secreti, sista tegendi,
Larua doli, celerum thalamus, nox implicat orbem.
105   Que supplantarat aliam, que pinguius uber
Inuida uicine subduxit, pomaque carpsit
Vberiora, sibi meruisse fatetur ephebum
Litigio, probris, inpulsu, uerbere, plagis,
Iussu vindicte. Lateri maturat ephebi,
110   Collaterare latus quod amat; circumligat ulnis.
        Altera baccatur furiali concita motu;
Inflammata tumet ira, celerique parata,
Cladibus accincta, fas commixtura nephasque.
Induit immitem Medeam, plus potuisse
115   Progne, plus Cilla, plus Fedra, plus* Clitemestra.
Seua suum stimulat parente* furore furorem,
Quodlibet ausa nephas, describi digna tragedo.
        Omnia nocte silent media, uigilesque sopori
Inuitat labor insompnis; nigriore lacerna
120   Nox celeris fautrix caput altum palliat orbis.
Hec pauonino sublato poplite passu
Peruenit ad lectum, quam ducit Herinis, amantum.
Insolita reperit sua lumina clusa quiete,
Et nexos firmis placidisque Cupidinis alis.
125   Aggreditur ferro. Dextram regit Heumenis atra
Femineam, uiteque diem caligine mortis
Implicat et pacem sompni rigat imbre* cruoris.
Que solet amplecti manibus, perplectitur ense
Colla; quibus pacis dedit oscula, decutit ora.
130   Dum fumat calidus utriusque cruor, manus ardet
Ad scelus ulterius, sitit insatiata cruorem.
Vt lea cum primum suscepit sanguinis haustum,
Nil preter cedem sitit irriguumque cruoris.
        Legis decretum timet iudiciumque diei,
135   Et ne morte piet mortem, uitamque rependat*
Pro uita, laxat portarum claustra, retrusis

If the first made thirty, the furious second hurls a hundred, exposing
almost everything with unsparing clarity. She spits, and contracts her
nostrils, wrinkling them up and cutting off the air in order to run up
and strike her with an attack of breath.

Each struggles to clutch the other's hair and tear it out; they wheel
their heads this way and that, and rip their long dresses. Each turns
from wounding with words to wounding with teeth, and bloodies her
rival's face with her nails. They part, clash again, and take up the sticks
they use to pound clothes in the wash, and wear themselves out with
innumerable blows, like boys handy with boxing gloves. One preferred
charges about the rape of her sweetheart, the other made her defense,
and they swear to decide at the tribunal of Mars whose the man should
be.

By now night, the mantle of secrecy, the covering lid, the mask of
deceit, the bedchamber of crimes, embraces the world. And she who
had replaced the other, who, envying her neighbor, had stolen the more
fertile pap, and plucked the riper fruits, claims she has won the youth
for herself by argument, abuse, beating, flogging, blows, by the force
of her self-defense. She hurries to the side of the youth, to join the
side she loves, and entwines it in her arms.

The other flies into a rage, impelled by a Fury-like passion; she
swells and flames with anger, ready for crime, girt for destruction, in-
tending mingled justice and wrong. She takes the part of ruthless
Medea, thinks herself more destructive than Procne, than Scylla, than
Phaedra, than Clytemnestra. In her rage, she whets her own fury with
a parent fury, bold for any crime, worthy a tragedian's pen.

Everything is silent in the middle of the night, and hard work without sleep lures the sentries into drowsiness. Night, the patroness of
crime, covers the high head of the world with a still blacker cloak.
With peacock strut and haughty knee, she arrives at the lovers' bed; a
Fury leads her on. She finds them with their eyes closed in unaccustomed rest, clasped tight in the firm and placid wings of Cupid.
She makes for them with the sword. A black Fury rules that lady's
right hand; she wraps their life's day in death's darkness, and floods
the peace of sleep with a shower of blood. Necks she once would
stroke in love she strikes now with the sword, and cuts up the faces
she planted tender kisses on. Their hot blood steams, and her hand
burns for further crime, thirsts unsatisfied for more blood. Like a
lioness after her first gory swallow, she thirsts for nothing but slaughter
and streaming blood.

She fears the sentence of the law, the judgment day will cast; she
knows she must atone for death with death, and pay back life for life.
So she thrusts back the bolts and opens the locks on the doors, and

Vectibus, et castro* furtiuis clauibus hostes
Admittit, nec eam frater commouet* in alta
Arce uigil. Vigilum sompnos perterruit ensis
140   Primus: eos primo iussit prosternere ferro,
Primoque ostendit—nec fratrem luget ademptum.
Hinc generosa thoris equitum diffusa supremis
Corpora demonstrat, duplicato dedita sompno
Noctis et illate mortis. Cruor altus inundat
145   Stratis, et, quamuis aliqui stridore gementum
Euigilent, strati subita formidine bello
Degenerant—superant hostes numeroque modoque.
     Et facinus muliebre uiris ascribitur, alta
Strages cesorum tegit execrabile factum:
150   Femina quos strauit proceres strauisse putantur.
Femina deuicit quos non insultus et arma
Vicerunt; risere alacres hostilia bella,
Lacrima sed finit risus; est femina causa.

Littere. *

155   *Summus* * *Pontifex Imperatori.*

Honorius Episcopus, Seruus Seruorum Dei; F., dilecto filio,
Romanorum Imperatori, semper Augusto: salutem et apostolicam benedictionem.

Imputabitur negligencie sopnolenti pastoris si lupina laceran-
160   tur* ouicule feritate. Licet Summi Regis infallibilis Prouidencia
predecessorem nostram, quem hominibus in terra prefecit, iam
triumphatorem in celo cum sanctis, ut dignum est credere, col-
locauerit, non tamen idcirco* successit iniquis* qui Matris Ecclesie preceptis* obuiare, filiali timore deposito, presumpserunt.
165   Cum enim diuina misericordia nos honori tanto succedere uoluerit, in nobis animus esset degener, et rationi contrarius, si, uel
timore secularis potencie uel honeris impositi grauedine, miliciam Crucis huc usque celestem ad patriam ardenter festinantem
permitteremus in cinerem elanguere. Flores enim rosarum iam
170   apparuerunt in terra nostra per sanctos predicatores, et ortus
Syon fructus promisit germinando, cum pene tota Militans Ecclesia Saluatoris ad honorem et ad salutem propriam subire
martyrium non expauit.
     Sed iam surgit gens contra gentem, et euigilant seditiones per
175   loca diuersa, quibus promoscio Terre Promissionis ad repro-
borum leticiam impeditur. Sed excommunicatos et anatemati-
zatos tenemus omnes qui tempestate persecutionis perflant
Ecclesie floriditatem et austrum Sancti Spiritus, pace perturbata.

with stolen keys admits the enemy to the castle; though the castle guard is her own brother, it moves her not. The first sword rudely shook the dozing sentries. The first steel laid them out, and she ordered it. The very first, and she shows them how. Her brother carried off, and she doesn't cry. On she goes, pointing out noble bodies of knights, stretched out on their last beds, sent off to a double sleep, of night, and death too. Deep blood floods the beds, and even those who wake up at the cries of men in pain freeze with sudden fear and lose their courage; the enemy has the edge in men and means.

And the woman's crime is laid to the men, the vast heap of the slain hides her accursed deed: her very victims are thought to have overthrown their officers. Armed assaults could not bring them low, but a woman could and did. They were quick to laugh at the enemy's efforts; but tears are the wages of their laughter, and it is a woman's doing.

Letters.

The Pope to the Emperor.

Honorius, Bishop, Servant of the Servants of God; to F., his beloved son, Emperor of the Romans, ever Augustus: greeting, and his apostolic blessing.

If lambs are torn apart by lupine ferocity, the blame will fall on the shepherd for carelessly dozing. Although the unerring Providence of the Highest King has gathered in our predecessor, whom He placed in authority over men on earth, and who, it is fitting to suppose, is now in glory in heaven with the saints, it has not necessarily come out well for those wicked men who have presumed to lay aside filial fear and oppose the commands of Mother Church. For since the divine mercy has willed that we succeed to so great an honor, our soul would be unnatural, and an enemy to reason, if, either from fear of the secular power or from the weight of the burden put on us, we should permit the army of the Crusade, now ardently hastening from here to our spiritual fatherland, to fade into ashes. For the rosebuds have already appeared in our land through the efforts of our holy preachers, and the garden of Sion has begun to sprout and promise fruition, and almost the whole Church Militant has not been afraid to suffer martyrdom for the honor of their Savior and their own salvation.

But now nation rises up against nation, and seditions wake on every side, impeding the advance to the Promised Land, to the joy of the reprobate. But we hold excommunicate and anathema all those who raise storms of persecution and blow down the blossoms of the Church and the south wind of the Holy Spirit by disturbing the peace. They

180   Nullatenus promerentur inducentes discordie sue nequicie
      flatibus aquilonem.

      Quocirca Crucis miliciam in paciencia pro deliciis amplectaris,
      confidentie tabulis cohereas,* anchoram spei defigas in miseri-
      cordia* Crucifixi. Stabit enim Ecclesia constanter: dimicatrix
      tam pro regno necnon et honore militis sui, quam pro Crucis
185   agone fideliter dimicabit. Non enim redditur a matre filio
      dampnum et maledictio qui pro matris honore paratur fundere
      cruorem et animam* exalare.

      De Cruce Recipienda.*

      F., Dei gratia Romanorum Imperator, semper Augustus;
190   vniuersis principibus et potentibus per* Imperii sui fines consti-
      tutis* ad quos presencia peruenerint: salutem et omne bonum.

      Studet nautica prouidencia uitare superbi maris contumelias
      et insultus aeris ventorum litigio comminantis. Cum potentes
      vniuersi debeant ceruicem humilem Ecclesie imperiis inclinare,
195   que mundanis impellitur procellis, mandatis venerabilis Patris
      nostri Summi Pontificis uerticem porrigimus* inclinatum, cum
      instanter persuaserit* ut Sancte Terre Ierosolimitane maturum
      presidium conferamus. Vos autem nostris tenemini mandatis
      aures obediencie fauorabiles exibere, cum nostrum sit proposi-
200   tum infirmare Crucis hostes salutifere, qui polluunt Sacram Ter-
      ram, roseo Christi sanguine purpuratam. Commouemur autem,
      et multum condolemus, de libera Sarracenorum rebellione;
      profundiore uero uulnere doloris* ledimur pro bellis nobis
      domesticis et Christianorum enormi presumpcione, qui Sum-
205   mum in Patrem et in uenerabilem Eiusdem sponsam, videlicet
      sacrosanctam Ecclesiam, inpudenter presumunt cotidie* rebel-
      lari, dum filius matrem iniqus impetit furiali conflictu, matris
      permittens inimicum habenis liberis euagari.

      Quare uestre mandamus vniuersitati, precipientes quatenus,
210   maiestatem imperialem offendere pertimentes,* in die Purifi-
      cacionis Beate Uirginis in nostra Colonie compereatis presencia,
      quia tunc ibi nostram proponimus curiam celebrare, et quod ad
      oportunitatem rei publice pertineat et honorem Ecclesie, uestris
      sicut expediet consiliis adimplere. Offendit enim naturam et
215   obuiat rationi qui matri clamose non succurrit cuius castum
      gremium a pollutis hostibus inquinatur.

      Papa Iudicibus Delegatis.

      Honorius Episcopus, Seruus Seruorum Dei; dilectis filiis,

have deserved no less, for bringing on the north wind of discord with the breezes of their wickedness.

Wherefore, we urge you to submit to us and embrace the army of the Crusade as your delight, to hold on to the planks of faith, to fix the anchor of your hope in the mercy of the Crucified. For the Church will stand firm, a champion who will fight faithfully, not just for the aims of the Crusade, but for the empire and for the honor of its knight as well. For when a son is ready to shed his blood and breathe out his soul for the honor of his mother, will his reward from her be pain and curses?

On Undertaking a Crusade.

F., by the grace of God Emperor of the Romans, ever Augustus; to all the princes and appointed overlords throughout his empire who see this document: greeting, and every good.

The foresighted sailor takes care to avoid the affronts of a proud sea and the insults of a threatening sky and striving winds. Since all earthly powers ought to bow their necks in humility before the authority of the Church, which is buffeted by the storms of the world, we offer our bowed head to the commands of our venerable Father the Pope, who has been pressingly urging us to bring speedy assistance to the Holy Land of Jerusalem. And you in turn are bound to turn favorable ears of obedience to our commands, now that we have determined to bring low the enemies of the Cross that brought us salvation, who are defiling that sacred land dyed with the crimson blood of Christ. For we are moved, and much pained, by the unchecked rebellion of the Saracens; but we are rent by a deeper wound of sorrow over wars within our own borders, and over the outrageous gall of Christians who every day impudently presume to rebel against the Almighty Father and against His venerable spouse, the all-holy Church, like a depraved son who makes furious war on his mother while he gives her enemy free rein to go where he will.

Wherefore we command all of you, under pain of serious offense to our imperial majesty, to appear in our presence at Cologne on the feast of the Purification of the Blessed Virgin; for we intend to convene our court then and there, and to implement, with your advice, and as well as we can, a plan of action that will work to the advantage of the state and the honor of the Church. For nature is affronted, and reason mocked, by a son who does not rush to the aid of his screaming mother whose chaste bosom is being defiled by her impious enemies.

The Pope to His Delegated Judges.

Honorius, Bishop, Servant of the Servants of God; to his beloved sons

220   Sancti Victoris et Sancte Genouefe Abbatibus, et Priori Sancte
      Genouefe Parisius: salutem et apostolicam benedictionem.

      R. clerici de Sancto N. accepimus questionem quod W. de
      Sancto Dyonisio, et G. presbiter, et quidam alii clerici et laici
      Carnotensis et Parisiensis dyocesium, super debitis et rebus
      aliis iniuriantur eidem. Ideoque Discretioni Vestre per aposto-
225   lica scripta mandamus quatinus partibus conuocatis audiatis
      causam; et apellatione remota, vsuris cessantibus, fine debito
      terminetis, facientes quod statueritis per censuram ecclesiasti-
      cam firmiter obseruari. Testes autem qui nominati fuerint, si
      se gratia* vel odio vel amore subtraxerint, per censuram
230   eandem,* appellatione cessante, cogatis veritati testimonium
      perhibere. Quod si non omnes hiis exequendis potueritis
      interesse, duo uestrum nihilominus ea exequantur.

      Datum Laterani VIJ Kalendas Octobris, Pontificatus* Nostri
      Anno Tertio.

235   *Citatio* Facta a Iudicibus Delegatis.*

      C. Sancti Victoris Parisius et F. Sancte Genouefe, Abbates,
      et F. Prior Sancte Genouefe Parisius; B. et C., de locis sic dictis
      Sacerdotibus: salutem.

      Mandatum Domini Pape suscepimus in hec uerba: "Honorius
240   Episcopus, Seruus Seruorum Dei, etc." usque ad istum locum,
      "Ideoque Discretioni, etc." Quapropter auctoritate* Domini
      Pape, qua fungimur in hac parte, vobis mandamus quatenus G.
      et R., et alios clericos et laicos Parisiensis et Carnotensis dio-
      cesium, citetis ut in Octaua Purificationis Beate Marie Parisius
245   in nostra compareant presencia, R.* clerico de loco sic dicto
      responsuri.

      Generalis Doctrina.* Vt secundum artem pauca sufficiant ex-
      empla generalia, tradenda sunt documenta circa composicionem
      scriptorum in quibus secularia continentur negocia. Omnis igitur
250   carta continet donationem. Donatio aliquando* est gratuita,
      aliquando ex meritis proueniens. Donationum alia dos, alia ele-
      mosina, alia libertas uel manumissio. Quecumque fuerit istarum,*
      semper debet assignari causa. Item tria debet notarius considerare
      in scriptis curialibus, quecumque fuerint, que sunt: causa, con-
255   suetudo, uoluntas. Causa duplex, precipue efficiens et finalis;
      consuetudo, quia diuerse curie diuersas habent consuetudines;
      voluntas, quia pro voluntate domini sepius mutat stilum consue-
      tum notarius. Et hec dicta sufficiant, ne nimis prolixum fiat opus,

the abbots of Saint Victor and Saint Genevieve, and the Prior of Saint Genevieve, in Paris: greeting and his apostolic blessing.

We have received a complaint from R., cleric of Saint N., that W. of Saint Denis, and G., a priest, and certain other clerics and laymen of the dioceses of Paris and Chartres are doing injury to him over debts and other matters. Wherefore, by the authority vested in us in Scripture, we command Your Discretion to summon the parties and hear the case; withhold the right of appeal, stop the usury, and bring the matter to an end with a due fine, ensuring strict concurrence with your decision by means of ecclesiastical censure. But if any of the parties to the case named herein should withdraw themselves as a favor to either side, you will force them, by means of the same censure, to testify with no appeal. And if you cannot all be present at the proceedings, at least two of you must be there.

Given at the Lateran, the 25th of September in the third year of our Pontificate (1218).

Summons Made by the Delegated Judges.

C., Abbot of Saint Victor of Paris, and F., Abbot of Saint Genevieve, and F., Prior of Saint Genevieve of Paris; to B. and C., priests of such-and-such places: greeting.

We have received an injunction from the Holy Father, as follows: "Honorius, Bishop, Servant of the Servants of God, etc." through the sentence "Wherefore by the authority, etc." Wherefore by the authority of the Holy Father, which we are discharging in this matter, we command you to summon G. and R., and other clerics and laymen of the dioceses of Paris and Chartres, to appear in our presence in Paris on the Octave of the Purification of the Blessed Virgin Mary, to answer the charges of R., cleric of such-and-such a place.

Some General Rules. Here I shall give, as models for those who must write them, some documents relating to secular transactions, in the hope that a few general examples will be a sufficient guide. Every deed, then, involves a grant, which is either gratuitous or merited. Some examples of grants are: endowments, alms, and liberty or manumission. Whatever the grant, the reason for it should always be expressed in the deed. A court secretary should keep three things in mind for any official document, of whatever type: cause, custom, and preference. He should keep in mind the two chief causes: efficient and final. He should keep custom in mind, since various courts have various customs; and preference, since frequently enough a secretary must abandon his accustomed style if his master prefers another. Let that suffice for rules, before this work gets

260 quia magistri diem* detinent scolaribus diuersimode* dictando.
Item aliquando premittitur prouerbium carte, cum maiores
scribunt persone ecclesiastice; in cartis plebis nequaquam.

Carta. *

H., Dei gratia minister humilis Ecclesie Parisius; vniversis ad
quos presencia peruenerint: salutem in Vero Salutari.

265 Cum temporis mobilitas omnia secum temporalia precipitet,
a memoria labentur humana facta nisi litterali testimonio
perhennentur. Notum igitur sit vniuersitati vestre quod R.,*
Burgensis Parisiensis, dedit et concessit B., de loco sic dicto,
xxx arpenta terre iuxta Secanam, extra uitreatum, inter duos
270 muros in orientali parte, hereditario iure possidenda; et xv
arpenta uinearum iuxta uillam eandem, ex parte Regie Strate,
iuxta vineam monachorum Sancti Martini, similiter iure hereditario possidenda predicto B. de Sancto Dyonisio et heredibus suis, a predicto R. Burgensi Parisius et heredibus suis,
275 libere et quiete, plenarie et integre, absque omni seculari seruitio, excepto hoc: quod dabit predicto R.* et heredibus suis
annuatim, de recognitione, vnam libram piperis ad festum
Sancti Remigii, item vnam libram cymini ad Natale, item dimi-
diam libram thuris ad Pascha, quam sacerdos eiusdem uille
280 recipiet.
Sed ne possit in posterum aput heredes suboriri* calumnia,
C. et D. heredes predicti R., iam infra annos discretionis con-
stituti, istam donationem, mediante sacramento, in nostra
presentia concesserunt, astantibus ibidem B. et C. et D. et
285 multis aliis. Et ut hec apud posteros habeant firmitudinem,
fecimus presentem paginam sigilli nostri munimine roborari.*
Anno Domini etc.

Item notandum quod aliis modis incipiunt carte, ut: "Sciant
presentes et futuri," "Notum sit vniuersis," etc.

290 *Cyrographum.* *

Sciant presentes et futuri quod hec conuentio* facta est inter
G., Militem Crucesignatum, et A., Militem de loco sic dicto,
quod G. Miles de illo loco commisit uillam suam, cum omnibus
pertinenciis suis, A. Militi predicto usque in vij annos, cum dua-
295 bus carucatis terre, et c ouibus, et duobus pratis, et vno nemore,
hac condicione: quod ipse A.* Miles predictus dedit quingentas
libras predicto* G. peregre Ierosolimam proficiscenti. Quod si

too wordy; for teachers prolong the day by making precepts of all sorts for their students. Let me just add that sometimes a proverb is prefixed to a deed, but only if the writer is a cleric of rank; never in civil deeds.

Deed.

H., by the grace of God humble minister of the Church in Paris; to all who see this document: greeting in our True Salvation.

Since the onward march of time drives all temporal things headlong before it, the actions of men will slip from memory unless they are perpetuated by the testimony of the written word. Be it known, therefore, to all and some, that R., a citizen of Paris, has granted and conceded to B., of such-and-such a place, thirty arpents of land along the Seine, beyond the glass works, between the two walls in the eastern sector, to be held by hereditary right; and fifteen arpents of vineyards adjoining that same estate, on the side of the King's Highway, and bordering on the vineyards of the monks of Saint Martin's, to be similarly held by hereditary right by the said B. of Saint Denis and his heirs, from the said R., citizen of Paris, and his heirs, freely and peacefully, wholly and completely, without any tenant service due; except that he shall give to the said R. and his heirs annually, as an acknowledgment, one pound of pepper on the feast of Saint Remigius, and one pound of cumin at Christmas, and half a pound of incense at Easter, to be placed in the hands of the priest of that same estate.

And to prevent false claims from arising in the future from his heirs, C. and D., heirs of the said R., having now reached the age of discretion, have sworn to concede this grant, in our presence, and in the presence of B. and C. and D. and many others. And that this may bear weight with posterity, we cause the present document to be strengthened by the fortification of our seal.

In the Year of Our Lord, etc.

Note that deeds also begin in other ways, such as: "Let all present and future men know," "Be it known to all," etc.

Indenture.

Let all present and future men know that this agreement has been made between G., Knight and Crusader, and A., Knight, of such-and-such a place, that the Knight G. of that place has leased his estate and everything connected with it to the said Knight A. for seven years, including two carucates of land, one hundred sheep, two meadows, and one wood; in consideration whereof he, A., the said Knight, has given five hundred pounds to the said G., at his going abroad for Jerusalem.

300
contigerit ipsum viam uniuerse carnis ingredi, siue nondum in
Dei moratur seruitio, predictus A. tenebit interim predictam
uillam donec preterierit terminus assignatus; et tunc predictus
G., siue heres eius, recipiet uillam predictam ita munitam et
restauratam, et in quali statu dimiserat eam Ierosolimam profli-
ciscens. Anno Domini, etc.

305
Hoc facto, scribatur "Cyrographum," et scindatur per medium,
et tradatur* vna pars vni et altera pars alii. Vel possunt sigilla
autenticorum virorum apendi, vel si habeant sigilla, vnus ap-
pendat sigillum suum in cyrographo alterius.

De Examinatione. Svperius* dictum est de querela et de cita-
tione, et quid in eis exigatur. De examinatione diuerse regiones

310
diuersas habent consuetudines. Quidam examinantur* secrete,
quidam publice; tunc autem scribatur sic: "R., requisitus de
loco, de tempore, de numero personarum, de modo facti, de
causa, per omnia concordat, uel idem dicit, cum B. et C. Sed
dicit se vnius nomen ignorare." (Et hoc si forte ignorauerit, et

315
sic de aliis, scilicet loco et tempore.)

De Transactionibus. *

Notum sit presentibus et futuris quod ego G., Miles de loco
sic dicto, controuersiam habui pro uilla sic dicta contra abbatem et monachos* Sancti Germani de Pratis, qui terciam

320
partem uille predicte dixerunt ad ecclesiam suam ab antiquo
tempore pertinere. Sed ex concensu G. abbatis et monachorum,
ita conuenit inter nos quod ego* G. Miles et heredes mei tenebi-
mus totam uillam predictam a Domino Rege sicut prius tenu-
eram, sed hoc addito: quod de recognitione sopite controuersie

325
ego et heredes mei dabimus in singulis annis xl solidos in Quadra-
gesima ad monachorum pitanciam predictorum.

Quod ut ratum habeatur aput posteros, presens pagina sigil-
lis* G. predicti abbatis et capituli confirmatur, hiis testibus:
Episcopo Parisiensi R., et* B. et C. et multis aliis.

330
Et notandum quod compositio et transactio in hoc differunt,
quod compositio demonstrat et recitat statum preteritum, facta
concordia sine pena et mutatione; transactio demonstrat nouam
institutionem preter consuetudines. Transactio est de re dubia

But if it should happen that he goes the way of all flesh, or if he remains in the service of God for less than that time, the said A. shall
continue to hold the estate until the designated term is passed; and
then the said G., or his heir, will receive the said estate thus preserved
and kept in repair, and in the same state as he delivered it on his departure for Jerusalem.

In the Year of Our Lord, etc.

When this is done, the word "Indenture" should be written in, and the
page torn down the middle of that word, and one part should be given
to one party and the other part to the other. Or the seals of officials can
be affixed, or, if the parties themselves have seals, let each affix his seal
to the other's copy.

Examination of Witnesses. Complaints and summonses have been treated
above, and what is required in them. As for examination of witnesses,
various regions have various customs. Some witnesses are examined secretly, some in public; in the latter case, the report should follow this outline: "R., questioned about the place, the time, the number of persons,
the nature of the act, its cause, agrees with B. and C. on every point, or
speaks to the same effect as they, but he says he does not know the name
of one party." (That is how to report ignorance of this point or others,
such as place and time.)

Compromises.

Be it known to all, present and future, that I, G., Knight of such-and-
such a place, have had a dispute over such-and-such an estate with the
abbot and monks of Saint-Germain-des-Prés, who claimed that a third
of the said estate had belonged to their church from ancient times. But
with the consent of Abbot G. and the monks, it was agreed between us
that I, G., Knight, and my heirs will continue to hold the entire said
estate from my Lord the King as I held it before, but with this new
condition: that, in recognition of the settlement of the dispute, I and
my heirs shall give forty *sous* every year in Lent toward the said monks'
pittance.

And in order that this may be considered binding among my descen-
dants, the present document is confirmed by the seals of G., the said
abbot, and of his chapter, with R., Bishop of Paris, and B. and many
others as witnesses.

Note also that a settlement and a compromise differ in this respect,
that a settlement merely sets forth in writing an already existing state of
things, when an agreement has been made without concession or change;
a compromise sets forth a new arrangement, an alteration of a customary

335   uel lite incerta, aliquo dato uel mutato uel retento, non gratuita
       pactio. (Exactio est quod sacerdos extorquet iniuste.)

Littere* Memoriales.

       Officialis Curie Parisiensis, etc.

       M., latrix presencium, in die Lune post festum Beati Martini
       sufficienter expectauit in curia nostra R.,* aduersarium suum,
340   qui nec uenit nec pro se misit responsalem aliquem. Ob cuius
       rei memoriam, ad petitionem predicte mulieris M., nostro
       sigillo presentes littere sigillantur.

Cytatio.*

       Officialis Curie Parisiensis; R., Archipresbitero Sancti Seuerini:
345   salutem in Domino.

       Mandamus vobis quatinus, si citastis ad diem Ueneris post
       octabas Trinitatis R. Anglicum, quia nec ad illam diem venit nec
       pro se misit responsalem,* magistro R. eodem die prout debuit
       contra eum expectante, ipsum ter vocatum excommunicetis nisi
350   vobis fidem dederit de comparendo.*

Priuilegium.* "Priuilegium" a "priuatione legum" dicitur, quia
       illum cui traditur auctoritate tradentis defendit. Scribitur litteris
       longis hoc modo in principio: "Honorius Episcopus, Seruus
       Seruorum Dei; venerabili fratri G., Senoniensi Archiepiscopo
355   (uel 'M. Parisiensi Episcopo,' uel 'dilectis filiis abbatibus B. et
       C.') . . . in perpetuum." Hoc erit pro salutatione. Post generalis
       sentencia ponetur, sic: "Ex iniuncto* nobis apostolatus officio
       preces humilium exaudire debemus, et eorum iustis petitionibus
       assensum prebere." Deinde sub persona Domini Pape tota pro-
360   cedat subsequens oratio, que quandoque confirmat* habita,
       quandoque non habita sed habenda. Ea tamen solummodo con-
       firmabit que licite sunt habita uel debent haberi. Post confirma-
       tionem anathema terribile sequatur, hoc modo: "Quecumque
       igitur ecclesiastica persona vel secularis presentem paginam in-
365   firmare presumpserit, in extremo die districti* iudicii (uel,
       'examinis') cum iniquis recipiat portionem." Post hoc, benedic-
       tionem proferet super illos qui priuilegium seruant tali modo:
       "Omnibus autem hec uerba seruantibus, pax sit in Domino,
       quatenus et in presenti uita bonorum omnium retribucionem
370   recipiant, et eterne* premia beatitudinis consequantur."

state. A compromise concerns a contested matter or a disputed suit, resulting in a concession or change or reversion, not a gratuitous arrangement. (Compromise or transaction is not to be confused with an exaction, which is what a priest wrongfully extorts.)

Letter of Record.

Official of the Court of Paris, etc.

M., the bearer of this letter, on the Monday after the feast of Saint Martin, waited a reasonable time in our court for her opponent R., who neither appeared himself nor sent a representative. As a record of this fact, at the request of the said woman M., this letter is sealed with our seal.

Summons.

Official of the Court of Paris; to R., Archpriest of Saint Severinus: greeting in the Lord.

We command you that, if you have issued a summons to R., the Englishman, for the Friday after the Octave of the feast of the Trinity, since he neither appeared on that day himself nor sent a representative, though Master R. was duly waiting for him on that day, you should excommunicate him, now thrice summoned, unless he has given you surety that he will appear.

Privilege. Etymologically, "privilege" means "removal of law"; it grants legal protection to the recipient by the authority of the giver. It opens with a phrase like this, written in tall letters: "Honorius, Bishop, Servant of the Servants of God; to his venerable brother G., Archbishop of Senones (or, 'M., Bishop of Paris'; or 'to his beloved sons, the abbots B. and C.') . . . forever." Thus the salutation. Next comes a general statement, such as this: "It is a duty of the papal office, imposed on us, to hear the prayers of the humble and give our assent to their just petitions." All the rest of this paragraph should be written in the first person by the Holy Father; sometimes it confirms privileges already in existence, sometimes it establishes new privileges—but it will only confirm those which are lawfully held, and it will only establish new ones in accordance with the law. After the confirmation should follow a terrible anathema, such as this: "And if any person, ecclesiastical or secular, presumes to invalidate this document, may he, on the last day of severe judgment—or 'examination'—receive his portion with the damned." After this he will confer his blessing on those who honor the privilege, in words such as these: "But may all who honor these words find peace in the Lord, and may they receive their share of all good things in this life, and achieve the rewards of eternal blessedness."

Hoc modo finitur priuilegium. In fine tamen ponitur quandoque
figura, quandoque* non. Si ponatur, in dextera parte cartule
priuilegii sint* duo circuli,* quorum unus includat alterum; et
inter duos circulos fiat crux parua in superiori parte, et post oru
375   cem scribatur vnus uersus de Salterlo. Dominus illuminatio, etc.,"
ud^m circumferentiam circuli, uel alius versus secundum uoluntatem
Domini Pape. In medio circuli fiat crux longa, attingens ad circum-
ferenciam circuli; super medium brachium scribatur nomen
Domini Pape, et inferius quotus sit in illo anno. Et in sinistra parte
380   sit quedam figura continens "ualete." In dextra parte in circuitu
scribantur* nomina cardinalium et subscriptiones eorum, sic: "B.
Presbiter Titulus Beate Marie," "N. Subdiaconus Cardinalis," et
sic de aliis.

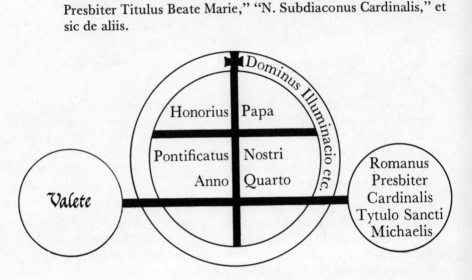

Figure Seven*

Petitio de Scola Habenda.*

385   A. B. salutem.

Trahit in periculum ouiculas pastoris ignorancia cuius exemplo, quo deberent instrui, corrumpuntur. Non aliter inducit
anime corruptelam magistri uel pastoris tutela cuius mentem
sepelit ignorancia, cuius corpus corrumpit centina libidinis
390   cenolente. Sicut ex consciencie uestre didici nuper archano,
proponitis quandam remouere beluam, cuius uestigia secuuntur
discipuli bestiales. Vnde uirum conscientie uestre morsum
auferre peritum inueni, videlicet latorem presencium, qui*
sciencie splendore fulgidus, sed honestate morum* fulgidior,

That concludes the privilege, though a device may or may not be included at the end. If it is included, two circles should be drawn on the right side of the charter granting the privilege, one inside the other; a small cross should be put at the top, between the two circles, and after the cross should be written a verse from the Psalter: "The Lord is my light, etc." (Ps. 26:1), around the circumference of the circle, or some other verse, as the Holy Father wishes. In the middle of the circle should be put a long cross, extending to the circumference of the circle. Above the middle of the arm should be written the Pope's name, and beneath it the year of his reign. On the left side there should be some figure containing the word "farewell." On the right side should be written in a circle the names of the cardinals and their titles, as: "B., Cardinal Priest, Title of Saint Mary," "N., Cardinal Subdeacon," and so of others.

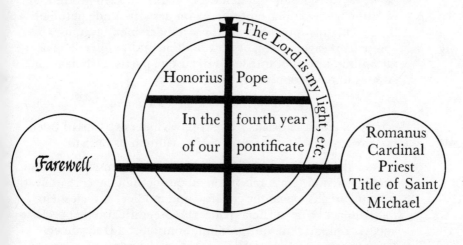

Figure Eight

Request for a Teaching Position.

A. to B., greeting.

Ignorance in a shepherd puts the sheep in danger: his supervision destroys when it should guide. A teacher's or a pastor's guidance promotes mental decay in exactly the same way, if his mind is buried in ignorance, and his body corrupted by the bilge water of filthy lust. As you have recently disclosed the workings of your conscience to me in private, you plan to rid yourself of a certain brute whose footsteps the students are following like sheep. Well, I have found an experienced man to take away the gnawing of your conscience; I refer to the bearer of this letter, who shines in the splendor of knowledge, but shines still

395   totam faciet de se patriam refulgere.

          Quapropter uirum uobis mitto uirtuosum et sciencia
uirentem, cum summo petens affectu quatenus ei regimen
scolarum tallis uille per biennium concedere uelitis, ut simplices
per eius compositam uitam regantur et per instructionem salu-
400   berrimam corrigantur.

Item Petitio Facta Summo Pontifici.

          Ego Iohannes, talis ecclesie sacerdos Parisiensis diocesis,
Sanctitati Uestre significo quod, cum talis sacerdos locum soli-
tarium, secus ecclesiam nostram situm, ex permissione* Ponti-
405   ficis intrare uellet, ego, dampnis ecclesie mee uolens obuiare,
dignum duxi ad sedem apostolicam apellare. Sed memoratus
sacerdos, apellationi non deferens, locum eundem intrauit, et
oblationes meas mihi subtrahere non desistit. Vnde peto iudices
B., C., D., qui, apostolica auctoritate fulti, memoratum exire
410   compellant sacerdotem, et postmodum, audita querela mea et
rationibus auditis et intellectis utriusque partis, iusticiam nullatenus impendere pretermittant.

Littere Episcopi de Elemosina Ecclesie Facienda.*

          H., Dei gratia Parisiensis Episcopus; vniuersis* Christi fideli-
415   bus presentem paginam inspecturis: salutem in Christo.

          Transitoria sunt temporalia, sed eternum premium consequi-
tur beneficium temporale. Cum ad perfectionem ecclesie Beati
Iuliani Parisius exigantur expense non modice, nec eiusdem
loci monachorum sufficiat paupertas ad edificationem ecclesie
420   sue, ei compati tenentur proximi, bonisque* a Deo sibi collatis ministrorum Domini paupertatem et inperfectam ecclesiam ad perfectionis terminum subleuare. Quare caritatem
uestram diligenter exortamur in Domino, quatenus ad ecclesie
predicte fabricationem, secundum facultatum uestrarum exi-
425   genciam, auxiliarem dexteram extendatis, vt bonorum
omnium que fient in ecclesia predicta participes efficiamini.

          Et nos, auctoritate Dei et Domini Pape, et Gloriose Uirginis
Dei Genetricis Marie et Beati Petri et Pauli et aliorum apostolorum et sanctorum meritis confidentes, viginti dies impendi-
430   mus in ueniam et in relaxacionem* peccaminum illis omnibus
qui sub vera uiuunt uel decedunt penitentia, suarum elemosinarum ad predicte perfectionem ecclesie beneficia conferenti-
bus.

more in the uprightness of his character, and will make the whole country reflect his brilliance.

And so I send him to you—a virtuous man, a man blooming with knowledge; and I beg most feelingly that you will see fit to grant him the charge of the students of so-and-so town for two years, that those impressionable boys may find a model in his well-ordered life, and be set right by his very salubrious instruction.

Another Petition, Made to the Pope.

I, John, priest of such-and-such a church in the diocese of Paris, make known to Your Holiness that, when such-and-such a priest wished to enter a hermitage situated right next to our church, with the permission of the Bishop, I, wishing to prevent losses to my church, thought fit to appeal to the apostolic seat. But the aforementioned priest, ignoring my appeal, has entered that place, and has not ceased to draw away my offerings from me. Wherefore, I request the judges B., C., and D., by the power of their apostolic authority, to force the said priest to leave, and then, after hearing my complaint, and hearing and understanding the arguments on both sides, to see that justice is done in every particular.

Letter of a Bishop, on Giving Alms to a Church.

H., by the grace of God Bishop of Paris; to all the faithful of Christ who will see this document: greeting in Christ.

Temporal things are transitory, but temporal generosity obtains an eternal reward. Since no small expense is required to complete the church of Saint Julian in Paris, and since the slight means of the monks of that place will not be enough to build their church, those who live near it are obliged to share its difficulties, and, from the goods conferred on them by God, both to alleviate the poverty of the ministers of the Lord and to raise the unfinished church to a perfect conclusion. Wherefore, we diligently exhort your charity, in the name of the Lord, to extend a helping hand, within the limits of your ability, toward the building of the church, that you may be made participators in all the benefits that shall come from the church.

And we, by the authority of God and the Holy Father, and trusting in the merits of the Glorious Virgin Mary, Mother of God, of Saints Peter and Paul, and of the other apostles and saints, apply twenty days toward the pardon and remission of their sins to all those who live or die in true penitence, and who contribute to the completion of the said church.

Littere* Conuersi ad Fidem Katholicam.

435   H., Dei gratia Parisiensis Episcopus: vniuersis Christi fidelibus
ad quos presencia peruenerint:* salutem, et Deo bonis operibus
complacere.

Misericorditer tenetur Ecclesia agere cum illis precipue qui
sacram ad fidem nouiter conuertuntur. Cum ab errore Iudaice
440   secte discedens B., lator presencium, data de celo gratia sacro
fonte primum parentem purgauerit et nudus recognouerit
Verum hominum* Amatorem, dignum est ut elemosinis Christi
fidelium sustentetur. Quare cum de baptismo predicti B., latoris
presencium, simul et de paupertate sua testimonium perhibe-
445   amus, uestram exortamur in Domino dilectionem quatinus
consilium et auxilium predicto B.* misericorditer impendatis,
ne uelut canis ad uomitum cogatur ad errorem Iudaicum
resilire.

Littere* de Indulgencia. In talibus litteris potest dici, "Indulge-
450   mus in ueniam terciam partem penitenciarum de criminali et
medietatem de uenialibus iniunctarum." Item: "Peccata oblita,
vota fracta, si ad eadem redierint, et offensam patris et matris
nisi manus iniecerint violentas."* Item: "Indulgemus xx dies in
relaxationem penitenciarum sibi iniunctarum."

455   *Littere* de Indulgencia Ordinationis.*

A. B. salutem.

Non defertur ad altare pungens urtica, sed candens lilium,
quod tam odore grato veneratur altaria quam candore. Cum
odore suaui bone* fame nomen nepotis nostri G. late redoleat,
460   castitate candeat et scientie melle* sapiat, meretur ad altaris
misteria promoueri. Qua de causa uite sue caste lilium ad altaris
sacrificium erigatis, sic tamen ut ipse beneficio subleuetur, et
per eum eius beneficium honoretur. Post gradum subdiaconatus
stolam accipiat diaconalem et inde, sacerdotali decoratus infula,
465   mereatur* ad mensam Domini suscipere de sacro calice Saluatorem.

Explicit* de Arte Prosaica et Versificatoria. Incipit Ars Rithmica.
Postquam sufficienter tractatum est de arte prosayca et metrica,
consequenter tractandum est de rithmica. Rithmica est species
470   artis musice. Musica enim diuiditur in mundanam, que constat
in* proporcione qualitatum elementorum, et in humanam, que

Letter for a Convert to the Catholic Faith.

H., by the grace of God Bishop of Paris; to all the faithful of Christ who see this document: greeting, and may you please God by your good works.

The Church has an obligation to treat with particular kindness those who are newly converted to the holy faith. Since B., the bearer of this letter, has forsaken the error of the Jewish religion, and with heavenly grace has purged his first parent in the sacred font, and in his naked-ness has acknowledged the True Lover of men, it is fitting that he be supported by the alms of Christ's faithful. Wherefore, since we bear witness both to the baptism of the said B., the bearer of this letter, and also to his poverty, we exhort your love in the name of the Lord mercifully to extend counsel and aid to the said B., lest "like the dog to its vomit" (cf. Prov. 26:11) he spring back to the error of Judaism.

Letters Granting Indulgences. Such letters may be worded: "We remit a third of the penances enjoined for mortal sin, and a half of those for venial sins." Or: "(We remit) forgotten sins and broken vows, if the vows have been resumed, and the offense of father and mother, except in the case of murderers." Or: "We grant twenty days toward the remis-sion of the penances enjoined on him."

Letter on the Granting of Ordination.

A. to B., greeting.

The stinging nettle is not brought to the altar, but the white lily, which does honor to altars by its pleasing fragrance as well as by its whiteness. Since the name of our nephew G. is redolent far and wide with the sweet odor of good repute, since he is lily-white in chastity and savors of the honey of knowledge, he deserves to be promoted to the mysteries of the altar. And so I beg you to exalt the lily of his chaste life to the sacrifice of the altar, and in such a way that he may be elevated to a benefice, and his benefice may be done honor to by him. After the rank of the Subdiaconate may he receive the Deacon's stole, and from there, decked in the sacerdotal chasuble, may he earn the right to receive the Savior from the sacred cup at the table of the Lord.

End of the Art of Prose and Quantitative Verse: Here Begins the Art of Rhymed Poetry. Enough has been said of the art of prose and quantita- ~rhymed poetry~ tive verse; now we must turn to the art of rhymed poetry. Rhymed, ~part of~ poetry is a branch of the art of music. For music is divided into the cos- ~music~ mic, which embraces the internal harmony of the elements, the humane,

constat in proportione et concordia humorum, et in* instru-
mentalem, que constat in concordia instrumentali. Hec diuiditur
in mellicam, metricam, et rithmicam. De aliis speciebus nihil ad
475   presens; de rithmica uero ad presens dicetur.
Quid* sit Rithmus. Rithmica est ars que docet rithmum facere.
Rithmus sic describitur: rithmus est consonancia dictionum in
fine similium, sub certo numero sine metricis pedibus ordinata.
"Consonancia" ponitur pro genere; est enim musica rerum et
480   uocum consonancia, uel "concordia discors"* vel "discordia
concors." "Dictionum in fine similium" ponitur ad differenciam
mellice. "Sub certo numero"* ponitur quia rithmi ex pluribus et
paucioribus constant sillabis. "Sine metricis pedibus" ponitur ad
differenciam artis metrice. "Ordinata" dicitur quia ordinate
485   debent cadere dictiones in rithmo. Rithmus sumpsit originem,
secundum quosdam, a colore rethorico qui dicitur "Similiter
Desinens." Quidam uero rithmus cadit quasi metrum iambicum,
quidam quasi metrum spondaicum. "Iambus" in hoc loco intel-
ligatur* "dictio cuius* penultima* corripitur"; iambus enim
490   constat ex breui et longa. "Spondeus" hic dicitur "dictio stans
ad modum spondei."
Quis* Rithmus sit Simplicior. A* simpliciori igitur erit incho-
andum, scilicet a rithmo qui constat ex duabus percussionibus,
quia, cum rithmus imitetur metrum in aliquo, illud metrum
495   quod est breuius constat ex duabus percussionibus, sicut iambicum dimetrum, quod* constat ex duobus metris, et metrum ex
duabus percussionibus, ut illud: "Iam lucis orto sydere."
*Diuisio Rithmi: Quis sit Simplex; quis Monomicus, quis Spon-
daicus, quis Dispondaicus, quis Trispondaicus, quis Tetra-
500   spondaicus.* Item rithmorum alius simplex, alius compositus.
Simplex est ille qui constat ex partibus vel membris consimilibus
et eiusdem generis; compositus est ille rithmus qui constat ex
dissimilibus partibus uel membris que* sunt alterius generis. Item
rithmus simplex alius dispondeius siue dispondaycus, alius
505   trispondeus, alius tetraspondeus, et iste triplex: quia tetraspondeus alius bimembris, alius trimembris, alius quadrimembris. Quare enim precedentes non sunt trimembres uel quadrimembres dicetur in sequentibus—quamuis possint esse secundum
artem. Item rithmus iambicus alius bimembris, alius trimembris,
510   alius quadrimembris. Ex uocibus spondaicis et iambicis fiunt
compositi. Rithmus dispondaicus continet quattuor percussiones,
que sunt ex quattuor dictionibus uel partibus earundem* dictionum.
Rithmus* Monomicus. Rithmus uero non fit ex singulis dictioni-
515   bus, licet egregie possint stare hoc modo:

which embraces the harmony and concord of the humors, and the in- *tripartite division*
strumental, which embraces the concord evoked by instruments. This *of music*
includes melody, quantitative verse, and rhymed verse. There is nothing
here about the other branches; my present subject is rhymed poetry only.
Rhymed Poetry Defined. The art of rhymed poetry is that which teaches
how to compose a rhymed poem, which is in turn defined as follows. A
rhymed poem is a harmonious arrangement of words with like endings,
regulated not by quantity but by number of syllables. "Harmonious ar- *genus—*
rangement" serves as the genus; for music is a harmonious arrangement *harmonious*
of disparate elements and tones—"discordant concord" or "concordant *arrangement*
discord." "Words with like endings" distinguishes it from melody. "By
number of syllables" refers to the fact that a rhymed poem consists of
some precise number of syllables, be it many or few. "Not by quantity"
distinguishes it from the art of quantitative verse. "Regulated" indicates
that the words in a rhymed poem should fall in a regular cadence.
Rhymed poetry owes its origin, some say, to the rhetorical figure called
"Similiter Desinens." Rhymed poems may be likened to quantitative
meters: they are either quasi-iambic or quasi-spondaic. "Iamb" in this
context should be understood as "a word whose penult is short," for an
iamb must contain both short and long. "Spondee" here means "a word
that functions like a spondee."
The Simplest Rhymed Poem. We should begin with what is simplest,
namely with a rhymed poem whose line consists of two stresses, for
rhymed poetry imitates quantitative poetry in various ways, and the
shortest quantitative measure consists of two stresses; iambic dimeter,
for instance, has two measures, and each measure has two stresses, like
this: "Iam lucis orto sidere" (Daniel, *TH* 1:56, 4:42).
*Division of Rhymed Poems: the Simple; the One-Foot Line; the Spon-
daic: Dispondaic, Trispondaic, Tetraspondaic.*
Rhymed poems are either simple or composite. Simple poems are those
whose parts or lines are regular and of the same basic meter; composite *simple*
poems have irregular parts, that is, lines of different basic meters. A *and com-*
simple rhymed poem may be dispondaic, trispondaic, or tetraspondaic; *posite*
and this last kind is threefold: a tetraspondaic poem may have two,
three, or four lines to one rhyming sound. Why the first two cannot
have three or four such lines will be explained later (539)—though it is
possible as a special technique. An iambic poem can have two, three, or
four lines to one rhyming sound. Composite poems are mixtures of spondaic and iambic rhythms. A dispondaic couplet has four stresses, whether
in four separate words or as parts of the same words.
Lines of One Foot. A rhymed poem is not made purely of rhyming
words, though it can be done as a kind of *tour de force,* thus:

520   Deo/Meo/Raro/Paro/Titulum:
             Astra,/Castra/Regit,/Egit/Seculum.

        De* Rithmis Dispondaicis. Exemplum rithmi dispondaici fit hic:

             O Maria,/Uite uia,
530   Per hoc mare,/Singulare
             Lumen, aue,/Ceptis faue.

        De* Trispondaicis. Rithmus qui habet tres percussiones clarescit
        in hoc exemplo sequenti:

535   Rosa sine nota,/Gemma pulcra tota,
             Lutum peccatorum/Ablue nostrorum.

        Non bene sedent tria membra uel quatuor in talibus rithmis sine
540   differentia, de quibus postea plenius dicetur.
        De* Quadrispondaicis. Rithmus* constans ex quattuor percus-
        sionibus est in hoc exemplo subsequente:

             Hodierne lux diei
             Celebris in Matris Dei
545   Agitur memoria. . . .

        et in hoc domestico exemplo:

             Eua mundum deformauit,/Aue mundum reformauit.

        Addatur tercium membrum et erit tale quale illud:

550   Verbum bonum et suaue,

        et hoc:

             Eua mundum deformauit,/Aue mundum reformauit,*
             Munda mundum emundauit.

555   Si addatur quartum membrum, dicetur rithmus quadrimembris;
        addatur sic:

             Eua mundum deformauit,/Aue mundum reformauit,
560   Munda mundum emundauit,/Pia nephas expiauit.

        De* Rithmis Iambicis. Item rithmus iambicus aliquando constat
        ex viij sillabis, aliquando ex vij. Ex viij vt ibi:

             Ve, ve, mundo a scandalis,
             Ve nobis ut acephalis.

565   Ex vii vt si dicerem:

             Aue, plena gratia,
             Aue, culpe uenia.

        Bimembris rithmus constat in hoc exemplo:

For my God who is unique I carve out a motto: He rules stars and castles, He makes the world go round.

Dispondaic Rhymed Poems. Here is an example of a dispondaic rhymed poem:

O Mary, way of life, singular light, hail, guide those who have embarked on this sea.

Trispondaics. Here is a clear example of a rhymed poem of three stresses per line:

Rose without blemish, Gem all beautiful, wipe away the mud of our sins.

In such measures it would not sit well to extend the same rhyming sound through three or four consecutive lines. I will explain them more fully later (722-40; 1018-64; 1281-1341).

On Quadrispondaics. Here is an example of a rhymed poem of four stresses per line:

Today the light of day does its duty in honor of the illustrious Mother of God (Daniel, *TH* 2:216; 5:138).

Another, homely example:

Eve deformed the world, "Ave" reformed the world.

A third line with the same rhyming sound may be added, as in the hymn "Verbum bonum et suave" (Daniel, *TH* 2:93; 5:254), and this:

Eve deformed the world, "Ave" reformed the world, a pure one purified the world.

If a fourth rhyming line is added, the poem is called four-membered; thus:

Eve deformed the world, "Ave" reformed the world, a pure one purified the world, a good woman made good the sin.

On Iambic Rhymed Poems. An iambic rhymed poem consists of either eight or seven syllables per line. Of eight, as here:

Woe, woe to the world because of scandals, woe to us as men without heads.

Of seven, as should I say:

Hail, Full of grace, Hail, Pardon of guilt.

An example of a two-membered iambic poem:

570   Maria, perge preuia,/Nos transfer* ad celestia.

Addatur* tercium membrum sic:

> Maria, perge preuia,/Nos transfer ad celestia,
> Prius emundans uitia.

575   Quartum membrum addatur et erit quadrimembris rithmus
iambicus, sic:

> Maria, perge preuia,/Nos transfer ad celestia,*
580   Prius emundans uitia,/Fons uite, culpe venia.

De Rithmis Compositis.*Ex iam dictis patet quod v sunt species
rithmorum qui sunt spondaici et simplices, et tres qui sunt*
iambici et simplices; ex permixtione eorum octo ad inuicem
resultant compositi. Simplices uero non ita sapiunt sicut compositi,
585   vnde, cum ydemptitas sit mater sacietatis, uariari debent rithmi
per composicionem. Iambici enim recipiunt spondaicos et spondaici iambicos secundum illud Oracii: "Spondeos stabiles in iura
paterna recepit."
De Consonanciis et Proporcionibus Rithmorum.* Consonancie
590   rithmales habent se ad proportionem sexqualteram et sexquiterciam, cuiusmodi proportiones contingunt in musica: in secundo ut in duplo, sicut inter vnum et duo, ubi est dupla proportio; in tercio, sicut inter duo et iij, vbi est sexqualtera proportio; in quarto, sicut inter tria et quatuor, ubi est sexquitercia
595   proportio. Contingit etiam* consonanciam esse in secundo et
tercio, in quarto et in quinto, in discantu et organo; et hoc ad
modum dyapente, que consistit in v vocibus, uel ad similitudinem
dyatessaron, que consistit in 4 uocibus, uel ad similitudinem
dyapason, que est consonancia consistens in pluribus; compre-
600   hendit enim dyapente et dyatassaron.

Commisceantur ergo spondaici et iambici sic quod prima linea
copule respondens sit tercie,* et secunda quarte, que est tercia a
secunda, ita quod spondaycus precedat et sequatur iambicus, et
e converso; et erunt due species rithmorum compositorum, hoc
605   modo:

> Pulcra casta Katerina,
> Flos et gemma Grecie,
> Sub scolari disciplina
> Donum sumpsit gratie.

610   Vel potest iambicus precedere, ut dictum est, et sequi spondaicus,
duabus sillabis subtractis, ut cicius veniat ad aures, hoc modo:

> Flos et gemma Grecie,
> Casta Katerina
> Donum sumpsit gratie,
615   Tendens ad diuina.

Keep leading us, Mary, carry us across to the heavenly regions.

A third member may be added thus:

Keep leading us, Mary, carry us across to the heavenly regions, first washing away vices.

A fourth line with the same rhyming sound will make it a four-membered iambic, thus:

Keep leading us, Mary, carry us across to the heavenly regions, first washing away vices, Fountain of life, Pardon of guilt.

On Composite Rhymed Poems. From all this it is clear that there are five types of simple spondaic rhymed poems and three of simple iambics; composite poems are the result of combining these eight with each other. And since simple poems have a different taste from composite poems, identity being the mother of satiety, rhymed poems ought to be varied by combination. For iambics welcome spondaics, and spondaics iambics, as Horace says: "It welcomed stable spondees to share its patrimony" (*AP* 256).

On Consonances and Proportions in Rhymed Poems. The rhymes in rhymed poems conform to the proportions of 2:3 and 3:4. Proportions of this kind occur in music: in the number two, or double one, as between one and two, where the proportion is 1:2; in the number three, as between two and three, where the proportion is 2:3; in the number four, as between three and four, where the proportion is 3:4. *Discantus* and *organum* also happen to employ consonances at intervals of a second, third, fourth, or fifth; and there is a likeness, too, to a diapente, which is made up of five tones, or a diatessaron, which is made up of four tones; or it can be like a diapason, which is a consonance consisting of several consonances, for it comprises a diapente and a diatessaron.

proportions akin to those in music

Spondaics and iambics, then, are mixed together, so that the first line of a composite stanza corresponds to the third, and the second to the fourth, which is the third line from the second, so that a spondaic line precedes and an iambic follows, and vice versa. That makes two types of composite rhymed poems, thus:

Beautiful, chaste Catherine, flower and gem of Greece, under scholarly discipline received the gift of grace.

Or the iambic can precede, as has been said, and the spondaic follow, less two syllables so that it comes more swiftly to the ear, thus:

Flower and gem of Greece, chaste Catherine received the gift of grace, for her mind was on the things of God.

Huiusmodi rithmus est ille antiquissimus:

620
>   Taurum sol intrauerat*/Et ver, parens florum,
>   Caput exeruerat/Floribus decorum.

Exemplum Domesticum de Principio Magistrali.

>   Ad insultus equoris   nutat parua ratis
>   Que non rata pertimet   minas tempestatis:
>   Vos faselum dubiam   mee paruitatis
625
>   Ad portum, beniuoli   naute, dirigatis.
>
>   Intro cum formidine   magna magnum mare.
>   Non est mirum militem   nouum formidare;
>   Sed uos mihi speculum   letor radiare,
>   Per quos viam speculer   timens oberrare.

630
>   Faciem in speculo   virgo speculatur,
>   Prospicit in facie   si quid deformatur.
>   Emundata facies   ampne reformatur
>   Et formosa speciem   niuis* emulatur.

635
>   Speculo sic ratio,   more puellari,
>   Nature primordia   fertur speculari.
>   Triplex sed est speculum: triplex contemplari
>   Triplici se radio   studet consolari.

neo-Platonism

640
>   Primum lucet uitreum   in quo perscrutatur
>   In subiecto qualiter   forma maritatur,
>   Quid miscet concrecio   et quid immutatur,
>   Quid perit, quid generat,   et quid generatur.

>   Ex argento speculum   aliud candescit:
>   Hic subiectum prospicit   quomodo quiescit,
645
>   Vt res formis uidua   fluctuare nescit;
>   Forma cum abstraitur   pura iuuenescit.

>   Tercium hinc speculum   auro depuratur;
>   Meliori specie   res hic* figuratur.
>   Hic ydea nobilis   Deo decoratur,
>   Mundi flens exilio,   longe deriuatur.

650
>   Fontis sui specie   caret obfuscata,
>   Orbata principio,   patre uiduata,
>   Res terrestris subiacet   ceno deturpata,
>   Huc illuc in fluctibus   orbis agitata.

>   Sic fit ut in tempore   ueris palliatur
655
>   Tellus, palla uiridi   tota picturatur;
>   In parentis gremio   dum flos educatur,
>   Carpi nondum rustica   manu lamentatur.

>   Cum rixatur Aquilo   tempore brumali
>   Et aquas incarcerat   claustro claciali,
660
>   Iam expirant lilia   flatu boreali,
>   Rosa pallens moritur   frigore letali.

A rhymed poem of this type is that very old one:

The sun was entering Taurus and Spring, mother of flowers, was
bringing forth her head, adorned with flowers.

A Homely Example on Beginning as a Teacher.

The small boat wobbles under the blows of the sea; in its weakness,
it greatly fears the threats of the storm. O friendly sailors, guide the
uncertain vessel of my smallness into port.

I enter the great sea with great fear. It is not unusual for a recruit
to be afraid; but I am glad that you shine like a mirror on me, for
through you I may see my way when I fear I am losing it.

The maiden sees her face in the mirror, peers in her face for
blemishes; cleansed with water, her face is renewed, and her beauty
rivals the splendor of snow.

Thus by a mirror, in the manner of a girl, the reason is led to con-
template the first principles of nature. But the mirror is threefold:
threefold reason studies to console itself with a threefold ray of
contemplation.

The first shines like glass in which reason examines how the form
is wedded to the subject; what concreteness dilutes, what is unchanged;
what dies, and what generates, and what is generated.

The second mirror glitters of silver; here reason examines the subject
at rest, as an essence widowed of forms withdraws from flux; when the
form is abstracted, the essence recovers its original purity.

The third mirror has the purity of gold; here the essence is reflected
with a finer splendor, here a noble idea takes its beauty from God; it
bewails its exile in the world, for it comes from a distant shore.

It misses the obscured beauty of its fountainhead; bereft of its beginning, deprived of its father, disfigured by filth, a mere thing of
earth, it lurks here and there, wherever it is driven in the waves of the
world.

Thus in springtime the earth is cloaked, fully adorned in a mantle of
green: while the blossom is being nurtured in its mother's lap, it has no
inkling of the sorrow of being plucked by a peasant's hand.

When the North Wind wrangles in the wintertime and imprisons the
waters in an icy cloister, then the lilies perish in the northern blast, the
rose fades and dies in the lethal cold.

Ver eternum possidet   Causa Primitiua;
In hoc Sancti speculo   cunta uident uiua,
Que subiecta tempori   nutant defectiua,
665   Per peccatum Stigie   mortis incursiua.

Hic esse fantasticum   nostrum lamentamur;
Illic Deo similes,   hic adnihilamur;
Illic esse uerius   longe contemplamur,
Sed hic esse perdimus,   culpa deformamur.

670   Ergo si nos uolumus*   Deo reformari,
Exules uirtutibus   decet renouari.
Culpa sapienciam   dedit ignorari;
Virtute sciencia   petit restaurari.

Prout est sciencia   donum, uirtus erit.
675   Ex uirtute defluit   viciumque terit;
Habitu disposita   extra si se gerit,
Virtutis originem   nullam sibi querit.

Suscitata studio,   surgit rediuiua
Et crescit sciencia,   uirens* ut oliua:
680   Seritur in pueris   hora sementiua,
Floret in iuuenibus   fructus redditiua.

Viri fructum colligunt   cum maturitate,
Auctori consimiles   mentis honestate;
Planta sapit arborem   vite uenustate,
685   Et radicem surculus   morum nouitate.

Quia status optimus   uirtus floret mentis
Speciali gratia   cunta largientis,
Rore suo compluat   os insipientis
Vt uirtutum uireat   nouis incrementis.

690   Si ferar Platonicam   per opinionem,
Euagatur animus   per digressionem;
Sed sic philosophicam   tangam rationem,
Licet usus arguat   hanc assertionem.

In nobis sciencia   ceca sepelitur,
695   Corporis ex carcere   languens inanitur;
Vt sintilla flamine   paulum* enutritur,
Et adulta dogmate   longo reperitur.

Descendit ut pluuia   mentis irrigatrix,
Quemque suo modulo   uisit amplexatrix;
700   Hic ut, mentis nubilo   pulso, sit uiatrix,
Attulit huc Logica   me sermocinatrix.

Via patet Logices   ueri directiua
Et ad certitudinem   rerum deductiua;
Huius comes Mathesis   est demonstratiua,
705   Vera tantum* eligens   ex hiis processiua.

ᴛᴇ First Cause possesses eternal spring; on this mirror of the Holy
One all living things gaze, things which tremble in the grip of time,
defective, liable through sin to death and hell.

Here we lament that our existence is imaginary; there like to God,
here we are brought to nothing; we look from afar on truer existence
there, but here we lose existence, we are deformed by sin.

Therefore, if we wish to be formed again in God, exiles that we are,
we must be renewed in virtue. Sin turned wisdom to ignorance; knowledge looks to restoration through virtue.

Knowledge is a gift, and so will virtue be. Knowledge flows from
virtue and wears down vice; though habit may dispose it to hold itself
aloof, it never claims to be the source of virtue.

Stirred by study, knowledge bursts into new life, grows and flourishes
like the olive; it is sown in boys at the proper time for sowing, it blooms
in adolescence and returns fruit.

Men gather the fruit with maturity, like to the Sower in integrity of
mind; the sprout savors of the tree in grace of life, the twig of the root
in moral purity.

The virtue of a mind that gives of all it has with a special grace is the
best and most fully alive state of man; it rains its dew on the mouth of
the ignorant man, that he too may flourish with new offshoots of
virtue.

If I have been led into Platonic thinking, I have allowed my mind to
digress; but thus I shall touch philosophical truth—though custom may
censure that assertion.

knowledge imprisoned

In us knowledge is blind and buried; pining in the prison of the body,
it fades into nothingness; but like a spark it is nourished a little by
every puff of wind and, brought to maturity by long teaching, it finds
its place once more.

The irrigatrix of the mind descends like rain, the embracer visits each
man with her little measure; and so that she may remain a pilgrim here
after the cloud of the mind has been driven away, Logic the discourser
has brought me here.

The way of Logic is an open path that guides to truth, leads by
deduction to certain knowledge of things; her companion Mathematics
is demonstrative, choosing only truths that proceed from these deduc-
tions.

> Rationis speculum   uestre porrigatis
> Speculer ut vicium   mee ruditatis,
> Vt limetur ruditas   lima nouitatis
> Et illimis pateat   uia veritatis.

710   *De Membris Rithmorum.* * Item dicitur rithmus discolos, triscolos, tetrascolos, pentascolos, et poliscolos. Discolos dicitur ille
qui compositus est ex duabus speciebus diuersis, triscolos ex
tribus, tetrascolos ex quattuor, pentascolos ex v, poliscolos ex
pluribus: *polis* enim Grece* "pluralitas" Latine,* *colon* "mem
715   brum." Habent enim huiusmodi rithmi membra diuersarum
specierum, ut contingit* aliquando in prosis que cantantur in
Ecclesia.
De Nominibus et Consonantia Rithmorum. * Item dicitur distrophos rithmus, tristrophos, tetrastrophos, pentastrophos. Distro
720   phos est quando diuersa consonancia contingit in secunda linea
copule,* tristrophos est quando in tercia, tetrastrophos quando
in quarta, pentastrophos quando in quinta. Et non procedit
ulterius rithmus compositus nisi multi* fiant ex eadem consonancia.
Quod ut manifestum fiat coniungamus predicta exempla, ita quod
725   dispondaicus rithmus habeat iambicam differenciam in tercio, hoc
modo:
Spondaica et Iambica Coniunguntur.

> O Maria,/Uite uia,
730   Nobis perge preuia;
> Stella maris/Singularis,
> Duc nos ad celestia.

Trispondaicus accipit iambicam differenciam in tercio, hoc modo:

735   Rosa sine nota,/Gemma pulcra tota,
> Nostra dele uicia.
> Lutum peccatorum/Ablue nostrorum,
740   Vita, uia, uenia.

De illis dicetur plenius in sequentibus. Tetraspondaico bimembri
addatur in tercio hoc modo:

> Eua mundum deformauit,/Aue mundum reformauit,
745   Stella maris preuia.

In* quarto addatur sic:

> Eua mundum deformauit,/Aue mundum reformauit,
750   Munda mundum emundauit,/Nostra mundans uicia.

Addatur in quinto ad similitudinem diapente sic:

> Eua mundum deformauit,/Aue mundum reformauit,
755   Munda mundum emundauit,/Pia* nephas expiauit,
> Via uiris inuia.

Iste v differencie cum v spondaicis simplicibus constituunt

Hold up the mirror of your reason, that I may see the flaws in my roughness; that my roughness may be smoothed by the file that renews and the clear path to truth may lie open.

On the Lines of Rhymed Poems. Rhymed poems are also said to be discolic, triscolic, tetrascolic, pentascolic, and polyscolic. A discolic is a poem that combines two different kinds of line, a triscolic three, a tetrascolic four, a pentascolic five, a polyscolic more than five: for *polis* in Greek means "plurality," and *colon* "member." Rhymed poems of this sort, then, have members or lines of different kinds, as is sometimes the case in the sequences sung by the Church.

On Harmony and Its Terminology. Rhymed poems are also said to be distrophic, tristrophic, tetrastrophic, and pentastrophic. A distrophe has a harmonic variation in the second line of a couplet, a tristrophe in the third line of a three-line stanza, a tetrastrophe in the fourth line, a pentastrophe in the fifth. Composite rhymed poems do not exceed this limit, except that the harmonic variation itself may extend to several lines. To make all this clear we add here the examples given above, arranged so that a dispondaic poem has an iambic variation in the third line, like this:

Spondaics and Iambics Joined.

O Mary, way of life, keep leading us: singular star of the sea, lead us to the heavenly regions.

A trispondaic takes an iambic variation in the third line, like this:

Rose without blemish, gem all beautiful, wash away our vices. Wipe away the mud of our sins, Life, Way, Pardon.

I will speak more fully of these later (1281-1341). An iambic third line may be added to a tetraspondaic couplet like this:

Eve deformed the world, "Ave" reformed the world, Star of the sea, our guide.

As a fourth line to a triplet:

Eve deformed the world, "Ave" reformed the world, a pure one purified the world, washing away our sins.

As a fifth line to a quatrain, like a diapente:

Eve deformed the world, "Ave" reformed the world, a pure one purified the world, a good woman made good the sin, a path for men, yet unapproachable.

These five variations along with the five types of simple spondaic

x species; cum predictis duabus speciebus ex proportione sequaltera, et sic erunt xij species. Tres uero simplices* iambici recipiunt
760   spondaicam differenciam in tercio, in quarto, in quinto. In tercio
hoc modo:

O virgo, perge pruuia,
Nos transfer ad celestia,
Que mundum emundasti.

765   In quarto sic:

O uirgo, perge preuia,
Nos transfer ad celestia,
Prius emundans vicia,
Que nephas expiasti.

770   In quinto:

O uirgo, perge preuia,
Nos transfer ad celestia,
Prius emundans uicia,
Fons uite, culpe venia,
775   Que culpam conculcasti.

Et nota quod spondaica differencia in iambico rithmo incipit ab
imo et tendit in altum in scansione, et addicione vnius sillabe ut
sit similis iambico. In spondaico rithmo iambica differencia incipit ab alto et tendit in imum scandendo, subtracta vna sillaba
780   ut sit similis spondayco.
Subiciantur exempla copiosa de Beata Katerina.

Vita nobis exemplaris,   In tristi leticia
Vita tota militaris   Amica seuicia
Katerine floruit: Iocundari negligit,   800
785   Virgo, gemma virginalis,   Sed dulce naufragium,
Norma uite triumphalis   Mellitum absinthium,
Nos pugnare docuit.   Dedignanter abigit.

Flos est soli Pelopei   Nam ut fuit morti parens
Katerina, sponsa Dei,   Virginis uterque parens,   805
790   Costi regis filia;   Celi creuit pluuia.
Flos in bruma plus vernauit,   Cum in patris tectis manet,
Ydolatras dum perflauit   In tyranno bruma* canet;
Congelans malicia.   Surgit flos audacia.

Nescit pudicicie   Flos pruinam reprehendit: 810
795   Sigillum confringere,   Argumentis ad hoc tendit,
Nescit immundicie   Vernet ut iusticia.
Blandimenti* cedere.   Quinquaginta uiri docti
                                        Sunt conuersi, flamma cocti
                                        Pro uitali gloria.   815

make ten types; add the two aforementioned types in 2:3 proportion and there are twelve spondaic types altogether. The three simple iambics take a spondaic variation in the third, fourth, and fifth lines respectively. In the third:

O virgin, keep leading us, carry us across to the heavenly regions, you who purified the world.

In the fourth:

O virgin, keep leading us, carry us across to the heavenly regions, first washing away our vices, you who made good the sin.

In the fifth:

O virgin, keep leading us, carry us across to the heavenly regions, first washing away our vices, fountain of life, pardon of guilt, who trampled out guilt.

And note that the spondaic variation in an iambic poem begins with an unstressed syllable and so has an upward movement in scansion, yet has an extra unstressed syllable at the end to make it more like an iambic. In a spondaic poem the iambic variation begins with a stressed syllable and scans with a downward movement; dropping the usual unstressed syllable before the first stress makes it more like a spondaic.
These are fully exemplified in these verses on Saint Catherine.

The life of Saint Catherine is an example for us of a totally militant life: that virgin, that jewel of virgins, by the model of her triumphant life, has taught us how to fight.

The flower of the Peloponnesian soil is Catherine, the bride of God, the daughter of King Costus; the flower blossomed more fully in wintry weather, when frosty malice blew through the idolaters.

She knows not how to break the seal of modesty, she knows not how to yield to the filth of flattery.

In her sober joy she can find no pleasure in loose living, for all its friendly air, but thrusts aside scornfully that sweet shipwreck, that honey-coated wormwood.

For when both parents of that virgin had submitted to death, a shower of heavenly grace came upon her; while she remains in her father's house, winter whitens in the tyrant, the flower springs up amidst audacity.

The flower rebukes the snow, and by her arguments causes justice to blossom: fifty learned men are converted, and cooked in flame for the sake of immortal glory.

Est illesa coma, uestis;
Rosam grauis artat restis,*
Et est flecti nescia:
Rosa, heus, incarceratur.
820   Hanc regina consolatur,
Porfirii socia

Nutrit rosam sol de celo
Et illustrat sacro zelo,
Tormentorum ut in prelo
825   Rideat uictoria.
Angelus hanc consolatur:
Vir, regina roseatur
Cum ducentis, et ornatur
Morum per crinalia.

830   Rosa flagris flagellatur,
Et plus trita decoratur
Rotis, clauis media.
Has Cursates* rotas fecit;
Angelus rotas deiecit,
835   Quater sternens milia.

Rosa* uernat inoffensa;
Sed regina, laude pensa,
Trans mamillas est suspensa,
Fixa per hastilia.
Christi miles gladiatur,   840
Cum ducentis laureatur,
Est eductus ut cedatur
Flos ab Alexandria.

Vox oranti fauet Dei,
Quod qui laude seruit Ei   845
Que uult sumat* premia.
Lac est fusum pro cruore,
Et celorum flos odore
Spirat in sublimia.

Hec in montem nouo more   850
Est delata cum canore
A* celesti curia.
Oleum de tumba manat,
Morbos omnes fide sanat:
Flos nos sanet venia.   855

Predictis differenciis assignatis et adhuc aliis assignandis, considerandum est quod ipsa consonantia ad* differenciam facit in rithmo simplici, vt hic de Beata Uirgine:

860   Hec regina ueniens
Ab* haustrinis finibus
Astupescit* rediens
Salomonis dotibus.

De Coloribus Rethoricis.* Item colores rethorici necessarii sunt in rithmo* sicut in metro, et isti precipue: Similiter* Desinens, 865   Compar* in Numero Sillabarum, Annominatio et eius species, Traductio, Exclamatio, Repetitio. Similiter Desinens est color rethoricus continens rectas consonancias in fine dictionum, que dicuntur "leoninitates" a Leone inuentore. Compar in* Numero Sillabarum ponit pares sillabas in numero, in Latino sermone 870   precipue, quia qui componunt cenographa Romana componunt rithmos ita ut paritas uideatur esse in sillabis licet non sit. Annominatio ponit similia principia, et correptionem et productionem attendit, ut hic:

875   Nos trans mundi maria
Ducas, O Maria;
Deuiis per auia
Nobis esto uia.

Her hair and clothing are unscathed, but heavy rope constrains the rose so that she cannot move: the rose, alas, is imprisoned. The empress comforts her, along with Porphyry.

The sun nourishes the rose from heaven, illuminates her with holy zeal so that victory smiles even under the pressure of the rack. An angel comforts her; officer and empress are made more roselike with two hundred others, and adorned with the crown of righteousness.

The rose is scourged with whips, and what is more, when worn down by them, gets wheels and nails for jewelry. Cursates made these wheels; the angel unmade them, smashing them into four thousand pieces.

The unoffending rose still blooms, but the empress, after a hymn of praise, falls across her breast, transfixed with spears. The soldier of Christ is put to the sword, receives his crown with the two hundred; the flower is led from Alexandria to be cut down.

The voice of God is favorable to the suppliant, for whoever serves him with praise receives the reward he desires. Milk flows instead of blood, and the flower breathes skyward a heavenly fragrance.

She is taken up onto the mountain in her new form amidst singing from the heavenly court. The fragrance flows from the tomb, and heals all those failing in faith; may the flower heal us with her favor.

Now that the aforementioned variations have been explained, and before I explain any more, I should notice here that the rhyme itself makes for variation in a simple rhymed poem, as here, from a poem on the Blessed Virgin:

She is the queen who comes from southern parts and returns amazed at Solomon's gifts (cf. below, 980-83).

On Rhetorical Figures. Rhetorical figures are just as essential in rhymed poetry as in quantitative poetry, particularly these: Rhyme, Equality of Syllables, Paronomasia and its species, Transplacement, Apostrophe, Repetition. Rhyme is a rhetorical figure in which sounds match at the ends of words, which are called Leonines from their inventor Leo. Equality of Syllables features phrases of the same number of syllables, especially in Latin; for those who compose "coenographa" or vernacular writings in French write rhymed poetry in such a way that there seems to be equality of syllables when in fact there is not. Paronomasia plays on words with similar stems, and extends also to shortening and lengthening, as here:

Lead us across the seas of this world, O Mary; through pathless ways be a way to wayward us.

Traductio trahit dictionem de casu in casum, et distinguit equi-
uoca, ut si dicerem: "Cur illum curas, qui multas dat tibi curas?",
880   et in hoc rithmo:

> O maris tranquillitas,
> Aura procellarum,
> Mare motum mitiges,
> Dulcorans amarum,
885   > Cum sis mare sapidum,
> Mater et aquarum,
> Ad quam cuncta commeant
> Dona gratiarum.

Cum dico "mare . . . amarum" et "mater aquarum" et "maris
890   tranquilitas," est Traductio, secundum quod dictio inflectitur
per diuersos casus; secundum similia principia ibi est Annominatio. Exclamacio uero est ibi vbi dicitur "O maris tranquilitas, etc."
(Et notandum quod talis rithmus compositus qui constat ex xiij
sillabis aliquando consonanciam habet dupplicem, aliquando
895   vnicam; dupplicem in medio et in fine, vnicam in fine tantum.)
Item Repetitio est color obseruandus in rithmis, sed est Repetitio mediata et inmediata; mediata uirtutem inportat, inmediata uicium, nisi fiat arte. Mediata Repetitio est hic:

900   > O Maria,/Mater pia,
> Mater Saluatoris:
> Tu nos audi,/Tue laudi
> Grata sit laus oris.

905   (Et notandum quod in tali rithmo dispondaico est consonantia
spondaica* faciens differenciam sine uicio; in maioribus rithmis
spondaicis spondaica differencia est uiciosa, sicut patebit inferius.) Repetitio inmediata aliquando cadit in uicium, nisi fiat
causa admirationis uel indignationis uel doloris uel leticie; sed
910   quidam gaudent tali rithmo qui suum ingenium uolunt experiri,
ut hic:

> Pallentis Aurore
> Rore uultus defluit;
> Fluit ex amore,
915   > More qui mox corruit.

Item similitudo in dictionibus obseruanda est, ut hic:

De Beata Virgine Rithmus Diuersimode Coloratus.

> Virgo, Mater Salvatoris,   In hoc mari sis solamen
> Stella maris, stilla roris,   Nobis, cimba, dux, tutamen,   925
920   > Et cella dulcedinis: Remex, aura, statio.
> Da spiramen ueri floris,   Aura perfles in hoc mari,
> Florem fructus et odoris,   Que prefulges singulari
> Fructum fortitudinis.   Semper igne preuio.

Transplacement takes one word from case to case, and also distinguishes between homonyms, as should I say, "Why do you care for him, who gives you so much care?", and in this rhymed poem:

O calm of the sea, gentle breeze for tempests, soothe the turbulent sea and sweeten the bitter; for you are a saltless sea, and the mother of waters, to whom all gifts of grace habitually come.

When I say *mare . . . amarum* and *mater aquarum* and *maris tranquillitas,* it is Transplacement in that a word is inflected through several cases, and Paronomasia on the score of the similar stems. And there is Apostrophe in the phrase *O maris tranquillitas, etc.* (Note also that a composite rhymed poem such as this, alternating lines of seven and six syllables, sometimes has double rhyme, sometimes single: in double, both odd and even lines rhyme, in single the even lines only.) Repetition is a figure that should be made use of in rhymed poetry; but Repetition is both interrupted and immediate. Interrupted repetition is fine, but immediate repetition makes for bad verse, except as a special technique. This is interrupted repetition:

O Mary, Mother so kind, Mother of the Savior; do you hear us, let the praise in our mouth be welcome to your Praiseworthiness.

(Note that in a dispondaic rhymed poem such as this a spondaic rhyme can constitute a proper variation; in some longer spondaic poems a spondaic variation is improper, as will be made clear later [1081 ff.].) Immediate repetition sometimes results in bad verse, unless it is done to excite wonder or indignation or sorrow or joy. There are, however, those who exult in such poetry because their chief desire is to test their own ingenuity, as here:

The face of pale Dawn flows with dew; it flows from love, which is soon destroyed by habit.

These various repetitive devices, then, are to be observed, as they are here:

A Rhymed Poem on the Blessed Virgin, Displaying Various Rhetorical Figures.

Virgin, Mother of the Savior, star of the sea, drop of dew and chamber of sweetness: give a breath of the true flower, the fruitful fragrant flower, the fruit of fortitude.

Be our comfort in this sea, our boat, leader, protection, oarsman, breeze, anchorage. Be a breeze that blows through us on this sea, you who shine before us with a unique and constant guiding flame.

930 Hec est archa Noe viua,
Hec columba cum* oliua,
Hec est pacis nuncia.
Hec est Sarra nobis ridens,
Sibi risum dari uidens
935 Ysaac ex gratia.

Dat Rebecca luctatorem,
Rachel Iosep prouisorem
In Egipti finibus.
Hec est uia Rubro Mari,
940 Per quam uiam naufragari
Nequis mundi fluctibus.

Hec post mare timpanizat,
Hec Sauli citharizat;
Dauid mundo pariens,
945 Hec est Dauid Sunamitis,
Casto thoro casta, mitis,
Thorum uiri nesciens.

Ruth in agro spicas legit,
Booz sponsam hanc elegit,
950 Salutaris nuntius.
Hec Susanna quam accusat
Nunc Iudeus et incusat,
Fraudis ficte conscius.

Raguelis hec est nata,
955 O Tobia, tibi data
Seruato coniugio.
Ester* uxor hec Assueri,
Per quam Aman contorqueri
Meruit suspendio.

Holofernem Iudith strauit;   960
Iahel clauo perforauit
Te fugacem, Cisara.
Hec est palme numptiatrix,
Hec sub palma Iudicatrix,*
Manu forti Delbora.   965

Semper lucens est lucerna,
Extra Bethleem cisterna
Quam Rex Dauid sitiit;
Manna gomor adimpletur
Quo plebs Christi sacietur   970
Diu quod esuriit.

Parturit ex Elcana
Tandem Anna filium;
Spes Saulis orphana
Quo ius perdit regium.   975

Samuelem parturit
Quo pastor inungitur;
Rex austerus deperit
Et puer extollitur.

Hec regina ueniens   980
Ab austrinis finibus,
Astupendo rediens
Salomonis dotibus.

Terra plaudit fontibus
Helim duodenis   985
Et palmis uirentibus*
Decies septenis.

Isti sunt apostoli
Fontes duodeni,
990 Et palme discipuli
Decies septeni.

Quid intrico tot scripturas
Et extrico tot figuras?
Hec est nobis omnia:
995 Hec est decus uirginale,
Et exemplum speciale,
Mulierum gloria.

She is the living ark of Noah, she is the dove with the olive branch (Gen. 8:11), she is the herald of peace. She is Sarah laughing because of us, watching the laugh returned to her by the kindness of Isaac (Gen. 21:6).

As Rebecca she brings forth the wrestler (Gen. 32:24-32), as Rachel she brings forth Joseph, the provider in the land of Egypt. She is the path through the Red Sea, a path through which you cannot be ship-wrecked in the waves of this world.

She sings after the crossing (Exod. 15:1), she plays the harp for Saul (1 Sam. 16:17-23); she brings David into the world, she is the Shunammite for David (1 Kings 1:3, 15): in a chaste bed chaste and gentle, innocent of the bed of a man.

As Ruth she gathers ears of corn in the field; Boaz, the herald of salvation, chooses her to wife (Ruth 2; 4). She is Susannah whom the Jew accuses over and over, aware of his wicked lie (Dan. 13).

She is the daughter of Raguel, given you, O Tobias, in a long-preserved marriage (Tob. 14:15). She is Esther the wife of Assuerus, through whom Haman deserved to writhe on the gibbet (Esther 8:10).

As Judith she overthrew Holofernes (Jth. 13); as Jahel she drove the tent peg into you, Sisara, as you fled (Judg. 4:21). She is the herald of victory, the prophetess beneath the palm, Deborah of the strong hand (Judg. 4:5).

She is a light that always shines, the well outside Bethlehem for which King David thirsted (2 Sam. 23:15); she is the manna, filling the omer, by which the people of Christ are fed after long hunger (Exod. 16:16).

As Hannah she at long last bears a son by Elkanah (1 Sam. 1:20); Saul's hope is lost, and so he loses the royal power.

She brings forth Samuel, by whom the shepherd boy is anointed (1 Sam. 16:13); the harsh king perishes and the boy is raised up.

She is the queen coming from southern parts and returning amazed at Solomon's gifts (1 Kings 10:5-13; Matt. 12:42).

The land rejoices at the twelve springs of Elim and its seventy flourishing palms (Exod. 15:27; Num. 33:9).

The twelve springs are the apostles, and the palms the seventy disciples.

Why do I entangle so many scriptures, and draw out so many

De* Nono et Decimo Modo. Preter predictos* x et octo modos
rithmorum, est nonus decimus, rithmus decasillabus iambicus,
1000   quo utebatur Statius, ut dicitur, sicut habetur in rithmo "De
Querela Edippi," sic:

> Diri patris infausta pignora,
> Ante ortus dampnati tempora,
> Quia* vestra sic iacent corpora
1005   > Mea dolent introrsus pectora.

Iste modus rithmi auctenticus est ab antiquo tempore. Sed posset queri quare dicatur iambicus et non dactilicus. Soluatur hoc
modo: in fine uidetur cadere dactilus* cum semper corripitur
penultima; sed ultima aliquando corripitur, aliquando produci-
1010   tur. Rithmus uero iambicus dicitur ideo et non dactilicus quia
Sancta Ecclesia utitur frequentius metro iambico in quibusdam
hymnis,* et quia precipue cadunt in scandendo ad modum
metrorum iambicorum.
De Spondaicis Differrentibus Spondaica Differencia et de
1015   *Iambicis Differentibus* Iambica Differencia.* Item sunt sex-
decim species rithmorum sibi differentes, sed duodecim sunt
spondei differentes spondaica differencia, quatuor uero iambici
differentes iambica differencia. Circa rithmum dispondeum sunt
iiij differencie, item quatuor circa trispondeum, item quatuor
1020   circa tetraspondeum; potest enim esse differencia uel in tercio,
uel in quarto, uel in quinto, uel una differentia in una linea et
alia differencia in alia linea. Ponantur exempla hoc modo.
Primo de rithmo dispondeo:

1025   > O Maria,/Mater pia,
> Mater Saluatoris.

Hic ponitur differencia, idest cauda ipsius rithmi, in tertio loco;
sed in quarto sic:

1030   > O Maria,/Mater pia,/Uite uia,
> Mater Saluatoris.

In quinto sic:

1035   > O Maria,/Mater pia,/Uite uia,/Mente dia,
> Mater Saluatoris.

Quarta species sic dicatur:

1040   > O Maria,/Mater Dei,/Uite via,/Salus rei.

Et sic patent hec quattuor differencie et quattuor species.
1045   Item quaternarius attenditur in rithmo trispondaico, sic:

> Rosa sine nota,/Gemma pulcra tota,
> Mater Saluatoris.

emblematic meanings? She is everything to us: the ornament of virgins, a unique model, the glory of women.

A Nineteenth Type. In addition to the eighteen types of rhymed poems I have described, there is a nineteenth, the ten-syllable iambic, which some say Statius employed, and which is illustrated in the poem called "The Lament of Oedipus":

O unfortunate children of an ill-omened father, damned before you were even born, my breast groans within me because your bodies are lying so.

This type of rhymed poem has the authority of antiquity. One may ask why it is called iambic and not dactylic. The reason is this: a dactyl seems to have a falling movement, since the next-to-last syllable is always short; but the last syllable may be long or short. This meter is thus called iambic and not dactylic, both because Holy Church uses the iambic quantitative meter more frequently for certain hymns, and more particularly because it has the falling movement characteristic of iambic quantitative poems.

On Spondaics with Spondaic Variation and Iambics with Iambic Variation. There are sixteen types of rhymed poems whose variation has the same basic meter as the body of the poem: twelve are spondaics with spondaic variation, four are iambics with iambic variation. A dispondaic poem can take four kinds of variation, a trispondaic four, and a tetraspondaic four; for the variation can come in either the third, fourth, or fifth line, or there can be one rhyme in one line and another in the next. Here are examples; first of a dispondaic poem:

O Mary, mother so kind, mother of the Savior.

Here the variation or "tail" occurs in the third line; it may also be in the fourth:

O Mary, mother so kind, way of life, mother of the Savior.

Or in the fifth:

O Mary, mother so kind, way of life, godlike in mind, mother of the Savior.

The fourth type may go like this:

O Mary, mother of God, way of life, refuge of the accused man.

Thus these four different modes of variation make four types.
The possibilities for a trispondaic are also fourfold, thus:

Rose without blemish, gem all beautiful, mother of the Savior.

Sic ponetur caudula in quarto:

1050   Rosa sine nota,/Gemma* pulcra tota,/Domino deuota,
           Mater Saluatoris.

Item in quinto, sic:

1055   Rosa sine nota,/Gemma pulcra tota,
           Domino deuota,/Nullo luxu mota,/Mater Saluatoris.

1060   Item alterna differencia in* eodem ponitur sic:

           Rosa sine nota,/Mater Saluatoris,
           Gemma pulcra tota,/Uasculum honoris.

1065   Item modo predicto assignentur quattuor differencie in rithmo
       tetraspondeo: in tercio, in quarto, in quinto, cum alternatione
       rithmi per singulos uersus, que facit quartam differenciam, sic:

1070   Eua mundum deformauit,/Aue mundum reformauit/Christum pariendo.

Item sic:

           Eua mundum deformauit,/Aue mundum reformauit,
1075   Munda mundum emundauit/Christum pariendo.*

Item sic:

           Eua mundum deformauit,/Aue mundum reformauit,
1080   Munda mundum emundauit,/Pia nephas expiauit/Christum pariendo.

       Item notandum quod spondaica differencia in tali rithmo in
       quinto loco posita uiciosa est et* impropria, non quia non possit
       sic bene esse secundum consonantiam musicam, que fit in dia-
1085   pente, sed quia non est in usu. Quarta species demulcet aures
       magis quam consonantie propinque, sic:

           Munda mundum emundauit/Christum pariendo,
1090   Pia nephas expiauit/Uirgo permanendo.

       Item notandum quod huiusmodi rithmi non ita sunt secundum
       artem conpositi sicut illi in quorum composicione aduenit dif-
       ferencia alterius speciei rithmorum.
           Item quattuor differencie, ut superius dictum est, notantur in
1095   rithmo iambico, sic:

           Qui solus cunta condidit,/Maria Christum edidit,
           Intacto uernans gremio.

Item* sic:

1100   Qui solus cuncta condidit,/Maria Christum edidit
           Et vitam nobis reddidit,/Intacto vernans gremio.

Item sic datur alia differencia:

The tail may also appear in the fourth line:

Rose without blemish, gem all beautiful, devoted to the Lord, mother of the Savior.

Or in the fifth:

Rose without blemish, gem all beautiful, devoted to the Lord, unmoved by any vice, mother of the Savior.

Or the variation may appear in every other line, just as before, thus:

Rose without blemish, mother of the Savior, gem all beautiful, vessel of honor.

In the same way four different types of variation may be given a tetraspondaic: in the third, fourth, or fifth line, or by alternating the rhyme in every other line, which makes the fourth type of variation. Thus:

Eve deformed the world, "Ave" reformed the world by bearing Christ.

Eve deformed the world, "Ave" reformed the world, a pure one purified the world by bearing Christ.

Eve deformed the world, "Ave" reformed the world, a pure one purified the world, a good woman made good the sin by bearing Christ.

But it should be remarked that a spondaic variation in the fifth line in such a poem is faulty and improper, not because it is against the laws of musical harmony, for it is done in a diapente, but simply because it is not the practice. The fourth type pleases the ear more than consecutive rhymes, thus:

A pure one purified the world by bearing Christ, a good woman made good the sin, yet remained a virgin.

Note also that rhymed poems of this kind are not defined as composite, unlike those whose structure includes a variation of the other basic meter.

There are also, as I said above, four ways of introducing an iambic variation into an iambic poem, thus:

Mary brought forth Christ, the sole Creator of all things, her bosom blooming undefiled.

Or:

Mary brought forth Christ, the sole Creator of all things, and gave back life to us, her bosom blooming undefiled.

Here is another variation:

1105   Qui solus cuncta condidit,/Maria Christum edidit;
             Virago mundum perdidit,/Maria uitam reddidit,
             Intacto uernans gremio.

1110   Uel sic quod unus uersus sit vnius consonantie et alter alterius,
       primus cum tercio, secundus cum quarto, sicut sepe dictum est:

             Maria Christum edidit,/Intacto uernans gremio;
1115   Maria uitam reddidit/In Summi Patris Filio.

       Ecce iam habemus xvi differencias rithmorum non composi-
       torum, qui tamen uidentur esse compositi propter differenciam
       siue consonantiam siue caudulam positam in diuerso loco.
       Iungantur iste xvi species cum xix speciebus superius enumeratis
1120   et erunt xxxv; xxx uero sex si ponatur in numero talis species
       rithmi quando singule dictiones faciunt consonanciam, ut hic:*

             Deo/Meo/Raro/Paro/Titulum:
1130   Astra,/Castra/Regit,/Egit/Seculum.

       Huiusmodi rithmus in iambicis magis cadit egregie, ut:

1135   Ne sedeas/Ad aleas,/Sed transeas/Ad laureas, etc.

       Item sunt quidam rithmi in quibus sunt gemine differencie con-
       sonantes siue caude consimiles; sed non constituitur diuersa
       species propter* hoc, cum accidens non uariet esse rei; ut in illo
1140   cantu qui sic incipit:

             Vita iusti gloriosa/Mors ut esset preciosa*
             Apud Deum meruit;/ Et qui sibi uiluit*
1145   A Datore gratiarum/Cum fine miseriarum
             Gloriam optinuit,/Et decorem induit.

       Enumeracio Predictorum Rithmorum.* Superius dictum est v
1150   esse species spondaicorum rithmorum simplicium, quorum
       quilibet sumit iambicam differenciam et constituuntur iterum
       quinque species, que sunt* x. Item sunt tres species iambicorum
       rithmorum que* sunt simplices: bimembres, trimembres, quadri-
       membres; si adueniat* spondaica differencia, vel* in tercio, uel
1155   in quarto, uel in quinto, erunt tres species, que coniuncte tribus
       antecedentibus iambicis erunt sex species, que sex coniuncte x
       precedentibus spondaicis erunt xvi species. Item sunt due* species
       rithmi, uel quando antecedit* uersiculus spondaicus et sequitur
       iambicus, uel e converso cum* antecedit iambicus et sequitur
1160   spondaicus; que due species coniuncte cum aliis faciunt x et octo.
       Item rithmus Statii, scilicet "Diri patris infausta pignora, etc.,"
       facit decimam nonam speciem. Iste species sunt magis auctentice,
       sed illa que minor est que facit consonantiam est vicesima in
       singulis dictionibus, de qua specie superius dictum est. Iste xx
1165   species coniuncte cum xvi speciebus premissis spondaicis faciunt

Mary brought forth Christ, the sole Creator of all things; the
Woman lost the world, Mary gave back life, her bosom blooming
undefiled.

Or so that one verse has one rhyme, the other the other, the first rhyming with the third, the second with the fourth, as I have said so often:

Mary brought forth Christ, her bosom blooming undefiled; Mary gave
back life in the Son of the High Father.

Thus we now have sixteen variations of rhymed poems that are not
composite but seem so because of the variation or "new rhyme" or
"tail" placed in various positions. Add these sixteen types of rhymed
poems to the nineteen types listed above and you have thirty-five, or
thirty-six if we count the type of rhymed poem in which each word
makes a rhyme, as:

> For my God who is unique I carve out a motto:
> He rules stars and castles, He makes the world go round.

A rhymed poem of this kind is even more noteworthy in iambics, as:

Don't sit dicing but move on to laurels, etc. (cf. Walther 11668).

There are also certain rhymed poems that feature twin variations or like
tails, rhyming with each other; but that doesn't make a separate type
since accidents do not change the essences of things. An example is the
hymn that begins:

The glorious life of the just man has earned from God that death
should be precious; and he who has humbled himself has obtained
from the Giver of graces glory and an end to misery, and has put on
beauty.

A Review of All the Types. I said above that there are five types of simple spondaic rhymed poems, each of which may take an iambic variation,
making five more types, or ten in all. There are three types of simple iambic rhymed poems, two-membered, three-membered, and four-membered;
introducing a spondaic variation, in either the third, fourth, or fifth line,
makes three types; these with the three iambics already mentioned make
six types, and those six added to the ten types of spondaics make sixteen
types. There are also those two types of rhymed poems, one in which a
spondaic line precedes an iambic line and the other in which an iambic
precedes a spondaic; these added to the others make eighteen types. The
poem of Statius, namely, "Diri patris infausta pignora, etc." makes a
nineteenth type. These are the more genuine types; but a minor one,
where each word makes a rhyme, a type I have mentioned just above, is
a twentieth. These twenty types along with the sixteen spondaic types

xxxvi species, et non est aliquis rithmus* qui non reducatur ad
aliquam predictarum specierum. Sed posset queri, si xx uersiculi
uel xxx simul consonent,* ad quam speciem reducuntur tales
rithmi? Dicendum est quod reducuntur ad rithmum quadri-
1170 membrem spondaicum (uel iambicum), quia quaternarii plures
ibi coniunguntur in eadem consonantia.
De Rithmis Qui Uidentur Rithmice Componi et Non Computan-
tur Pro Specie Quia Sunt Metra Leonina. Item nonulli sunt qui
uersibus gaudent metricis qui rithmice componuntur. In talibus
1175 rithmis tres copule tres habent caudulas, scilicet tres fines uersuum, que caudule si simul proferantur constituunt uersum
sentenciosum. Ponamus exemplum de Iulio Cesare, sic:

> Pollens imperium mundum subiecerat; orbi
> Excidium Cesar incusserat ense cruento;
1180 > Ensi* Cesareo subcumbit Gallia bello
> Sanguineo;* subdunt* se menia, ciue retento.
> Contra Cesarios insultus, Grecia, contra
> Tot cuneos densos, Pharsalia,* stare memento.

In istis vi versibus* est duplex rithmus, quorum fines dicunt
1185 sentenciam totius si iungantur hoc modo:

> Ense cruento, ciue* retento, stare memento.

Sed non est species rithmi nisi per accidens, quia pertinet ad
metricam et non ad rithmicam artem.
    (Item contingit fieri uersum retrogradum,* qui si directe lega-
1190 tur laudat, si retro uituperat, ut hic:

> Esse decus de te, presul, gens prouida dicit.

Retrouertatur* sic:

> Dicit prouida* gens, presul, te dedecus esse.

Item potest fieri uersus lioninus directe et retrograde, ut hic:

1195 > Vrbe petit parte regnum turbe Nero Marte.

Retrouertatur:*

> Marte Nero turbe regnum parte petit urbe.

Item uidetur aliquando oratio esse prosaica et tamen metrica
reperitur, ut ibi:

1200 > Misit rex et soluit Eum princeps populorum
> Et dimisit Eum, etc.

Item contingit aliquando* orationem esse prosaicam sed* in
retrogradatione esse metricam, ut "Hic est Iesus Nazarenus, Rex
Iudeorum." Retrouertatur sic:

just treated make thirty-six types in all, and there is no rhymed poem which is not reducible to one or another of those types. One may ask, suppose twenty or thirty consecutive lines all rhyme together, what type does that go under? The answer is, a four-membered spondaic (or iambic), since all you would have in such a case is a series of quatrains united by the same rhyming sound.

On Rhymed Poems That Seem to Be Syllabic, but Are Not Counted as a Rhymed Type Because They are Leonines, Which Are Quantitative. There are a lot of people who are fond of rhymed quantitative verses. In rhymed poems of this kind, three couplets have three rhyming tails, that is, three line-endings, which, if put together, make up a single line of moral instruction. Let us use an example of Julius Caesar:

> A powerful empire had conquered the world; Caesar had inflicted ruin on the globe with his bloody sword; Gaul gives way to Caesar's sword in bloody war; walls yield themselves, citizens are captured. Against Caesar's attacks, O Greece, against so many thick phalanxes, Pharsalia, remember to stand firm.

In these six lines is buried a twofold rhymed poem; the endings of the couplets speak the moral of the whole if they are joined together, thus:

> Remember to stand firm before the bloody sword, the capture of citizens.

But it is not a type of rhymed poem, except by accident, because it belongs to the art of quantitative, and not of rhymed syllabic, poetry.

(Another odd type is the palindrome, which praises when read forward and condemns when read backward, like this:

> Thoughtful people say, bishop, that grace springs from you.

Backward, it goes like this:

> Thoughtful people say, bishop, that you are a disgrace.

A leonine verse can also be read either backward or forward:

> Nero greedily seeks power over the mob in the city by force of arms.

Sometimes also a passage seems to be in prose and yet is found to be metrical, as here:

> The king sent Him, and the governor of the people absolved Him and dismissed Him.

It also happens sometimes that a passage of prose is metrical if reversed, as: "Hic est Iesus Nazarenus, Rex Iudeorum." Backward, it goes:

1205   Iudeorum Rex Nazarenus Iesus est hic.

Item uidetur esse prosa licet sit metrum quia non distinguitur
consonantia que est in mediis sillabis, ut hic: "Qui me prostra-
uerunt cum baculis habitauerunt imis carceribus et sum uictor
in arce." Punctetur ucisus hoc modo:

1210   Qui me prostraue-
                              runt cum baculis habitaue-
                              runt imis carce-
                              ribus et sum uictor in arce.

Preter hos magistratus sunt et alii multi* in uersibus retrogradis,
1215   rithmis, et prosis, quibus ociosi suum gaudent ingenium experiri.)
        Posset* queri vtrum plures sint rithmi species quam predicte 36.
Contingit aliquando versum autenticum adiungi rithmo, de quo
superius nihil dictum est. Ad hoc dicendum quod versus appositus
non facit diuersam speciem, quia versus apponitur illi rithmo, in
1220   quarto loco, qui constat ex 13 sillabis; qualis est ille rithmus
"Taurum sol intrauerat/et ver, parens florum, etc." Exemplum
domesticum de licencia contra Natale.
Exemplum Domesticum de Rithmis quibus Versus Auctorum
Adiungitur; de Licencia Puerorum.

1225   Ludo preter solitum   et ludendo salto;
                              Applico qui fueram   fluctuans in alto:
                              Regis natalicia   celestis exalto:
                              "Iam noua progenies celo dimittitur alto."

                              Carceris excutio   cathenas a collo,
1230   Cum plausu repatrians   quod est meum tollo;
                              Per quem iugum tollitur,   Dominum extollo:
                              "Casta faue Lucina, tuus iam regnat Apollo."

                              Doctorem laudabimus,   eum describentes
                              Quem benignum sensimus,   sepe delinquentes.
1235   Sepe nos adduxerat   secum colludentes:*
                              "Sepe refert animus lusus grauitate carentes."

                              Sua pulcritudine   superat affines;
                              Gallicanos vndique   perscruteris fines:
                              Eum ferre lauream,   uelis aut non, sines
1240   "Ob digitos Baco dignos et Apolline crines."

                              Nature ditauerat   largitas doctorem,
                              Dans illi dulcedinis   mellite canorem;
                              Singularem contulit   florentis honorem
                              "Oris et in niueo mixtum* candore ruborem."

> Iudeorum Rex Nazarenus Iesus est hic.
> This is Jesus of Nazareth, King of the Jews.

And something can seem to be prose even though it is metrical, because a rhyme in the middle of a word is not made distinct, as here: "Qui me prostraverunt cum baculis, habitaverunt imis carceribus et sum victor in arce." It may be punctuated as verse this way:

> Those who beat me to the ground with their clubs have taken up their abode in the deepest bondage, while I stand victorious on the heights.

Besides these pedantic little matters there is much more in the way of palindromes, rhymes, and sequences at which people like to test their skill in their spare time.)

One may ask whether there are more types of rhymed poems than the thirty-six I have mentioned. It does happen sometimes that a line from a classical author is added on to a rhymed poem, a device of which I have said nothing above. But I would say that an attached line does not make a separate type; for such a line may be attached, as the fourth line of a quatrain, to the rhymed poem of thirteen syllables, such as the poem "Taurum sol intraverat/et ver, parens florum, etc." Here is a homely example on excessive Christmas merrymaking.

A Homely Example of Rhymed Stanzas to Which Are Attached Lines from the Classical Authors, on the Licentiousness of Boys.

> I abandon my sober habits to dance and enjoy myself; I was tossing on the sea but now I come to land: I honor the birthday of the King of Heaven: "Today a new offspring is sent down from high heaven." (Virgil, *Buc.* 4.7)

> I shake the chains of prison from my neck; joyfully returning to my native land, I claim what is mine, I praise the Lord through whom the yoke is lifted: "Be favorable, chaste Lucina, your Apollo now reigns." (Ibid., 10)

> We write to praise a certain doctor, a man we think benign though our conduct rarely shows it; he has often urged us to join him in recreation: "My mind often recalls his playful moments, when he had laid aside his gravity." (Ovid., *Epis. ex Ponto* 1.9.9)

> He surpasses all around him in beauty. Search the length and breadth of France: whether you like it or not, you will let him wear the laurel "On account of his fingers worthy of Bacchus and his hair worthy of Apollo." (Cf. Ovid., *Met.* 3.421)

> Nature in her bounty enriched that doctor, giving him a voice as sweet as honey; she bestowed on him the rare honor of a healthy "Complexion, a blush mixed with a snowy whiteness." (Ibid., 423)

1245   Sapit linguam Tullii   uox oris facundi,
        Fontem pigmentarium   pectoris profundi,
        Doctrinale balsamum   sermonis iocundi
        "Dictaque mirantum magni primordia mundi."

        Ratione logica   destruit errores,
1250   In arte sintaseos   superat maiores,
        Dirigit erraticos,   instruit minores,
        "Hic canit errantem lunam solisque labores."

        Cur ergo nequissimus   Uerres paret uerri?
        Optet ut in Socratem   Anetus deferri?
1255   Aut ut Nero Senecam   faciat* efferri?
        "Quis furor, o ciues, que tanta licentia ferri?"

        Cicius auertite   scuticarum lora,
        Aut de uestro scelere   personabunt fora;
        Nascetur confusio,   cessabunt priora,
1260   "Secula ceu mundi suprema coegerit hora."

        O doctor liberrime,   dissolue cathenas,
        Et disiungas compedes,   et laxes habenas,
        Que nostras ex studio   minuere genas:
        "Parte leua minima nostras et contrahe penas."

1265   Magister de cetero   ludet cum magistra,
        Dicens, "Crura candida   nobis subministra!",
        Ostendendo mentule   turgide registra
        "Ceu gerat in dextra baculum clauamque sinistra."

        A modo refugium   inuenire spero:
1270   Ludam cum puellulis   —illud est quod quero.
        Petrus noster socius   bacatur ex mero
        "Et clauam ostendens, 'Hec,' ait, 'arma gero.'"

        Noster doctor, doctior   inter doctiores,
        Est inter discipulos   mitis mitiores,
1275   Comis comes omnibus   siue sint algores,
        "Ceu mulcent Zephiri natos sine semine flores."

        Ergo qualis fuerit   doctor si quis querat,
        Ex predictis animum   certiorem gerat;
        Hic doctorem audiat,   et audita serat;
1280   "Inscribat foliis, 'Naso magister erat.'"

Suppletio* Eorum Que Superius Dicta Sunt. Item sunt alie
species de quibus nichil dictum est,* quia, si rithmus est dispondaicus uel trispondaicus, potest esse iambica differencia in tercio

His voice when he speaks in public smacks of the tongue of Cicero, when he tells his deepest thoughts it seems a fountain of spices, even in his casual talk one senses an educational balm, "And the origins of this great world explained to the wondering crowds." (Ibid., 15.67)

He crushes errors with logical argument, he outsmarts his superiors in literature, he guides the erring, he instructs the young, "He sings of the wandering moon and the labors of the sun." (Virgil, *Aen.* 1.742)

Why then does that most worthless Verres allow himself to get carried away? So that Anytus might wish to be denounced before Socrates? Or that Nero might have Seneca carried off? "Why this madness, citizens, why such freedom with the sword?" (Lucan 1.8)

Put away quickly your thongs and whips, or the public squares will resound with your crime; chaos will come again, things will never again be as they were, "As if the world's last hour were bringing all its ages to a close." (Cf. ibid., 73)

O most liberal doctor, loosen the chains and unlock the shackles and free the reins that have thinned our cheeks with study; "Raise us up from this trivial role and reduce our pains." (Ovid, *Epis. ex Ponto* 2.8.35)

Then the master will play with the mistress, crying, "Supply us with white legs," expounding the annals of the swelling penis, "As if he wielded a club in his right hand and a stick in his left." (Cf. Ovid, *Fasti* 1.99)

From now on my hope is to find relief: I'll play with the girls—that's my ambition. Our servant Peter is drunk with wine, "And showing his stick he shouts, "Here's my weapon!" (Cf. ibid., 254)

Our doctor, most learned even among the learned, is gentle among his more gentle students, a good friend to all, whether they be ice cold or whether "As if the zephyrs caress the flowers that spring up without having been planted." (Cf. Ovid, *Met.* 1.108)

Thus, should anyone ask what sort of doctor he was, let him make up his mind from these lines: here let him hear the doctor, and let him sow what he has heard, "Let him inscribe his pages, 'Ovid was my master.'" (Cf. Ovid, *De Arte Amatoria* 3.812)

Supplementary Remarks. There are also some other types I have not mentioned. Any dispondaic or trispondaic rhymed poem can take an

1285
uel in quarto uel in quinto; in primo rithmo dispondaico uel in
secundo trispondaico, et erunt vi species. Verbi gratia:

> O Maria,/Mater pia,/Hiis succurre miseris.

1290
Hec species ante ponitur; non computetur hic. Differencia iambica
cadit hic* in tertio loco; sed in quarto in exemplo subsequenti:

> O Maria,/Mater pia,/Vite uia,
> Hiis succurre miseris.

1295
In quinto, ut hic:

1300
> O Maria,/Mater pia,
> Uite uia,/Mente dia (*siue* Rachel, Lia*)
> Hiis succurre miseris.

Iste due species non ponuntur superius. In trispondaico sic:

> Rosa sine nota,/Gemma pulcra tota,
> Hiis* succurre miseris.

1305
Hec species ante ponitur; non computetur hic. Vel sic:

> Rosa sine nota,/Gemma pulchra tota,/Domino deuota,
> Hiis succurre miseris.

1310
Uel sic:

1315
> Rosa sine nota,/Gemma pulcra tota,
> Domino deuota,/Labis carens nota,
> Hiis succurre miseris.

Iste due species non ponuntur ante.

Item posset queri quare, sicut contingit in aliis rithmis spondaicam differenciam precedere et iambicam subsequi, ita posset
contingere in istis paruis rithmis. Ad quod dicendum quod bene
1320
posset contingere secundum artem, sed inusitatum est:

> O Maria,/Cerne miseros;/Uite uia,/Redde liberos.

1325
Uel sic:

> Cerne miseros,/O Maria;/Redde liberos,/Uite uia.

1330
Et erunt* iste due species diuerse a predictis quattuor, et erunt*
sex. Item in rithmo trispondaico secundum artem poterit idem
contingere, sic:

1335
> Rosa sine nota,/Nobis succurre miseris;
> Domino deuota,/Aspira seruis liberis.

Et* e conuerso sic:

iambic variation in the third, fourth, or fifth line: since all three possibilities apply both to the dispondaic and the trispondaic, that makes six types. For example:

O Mary, mother so kind, come to the aid of these in their misery.

This type appears above (728), so do not count it here. Here the iambic variation comes in the third line; in the following example it comes in the fourth:

O Mary, mother so kind, way of life, come to the aid of these in their misery.

Here, in the fifth:

O Mary, mother so kind, way of life, godlike in mind—*or,* Rachel, Leah,—come to the aid of these in their misery.

These last two types have not appeared before. Trispondaic:

Rose without blemish, gem all beautiful, come to the aid of these in their misery.

This type appears above (735), so do not count it here. Or:

Rose without blemish, gem all beautiful, devoted to the Lord, come to the aid of these in their misery.

Or:

Rose without blemish, gem all beautiful, devoted to the Lord, lacking any slightest mark of sin, come to the aid of these in their misery.

These last two types have not appeared before.

One may ask whether, in poems with such short lines, spondaic and iambic lines can alternate as they do in other rhymed poems. I would answer that they certainly can as a special technique, but it is not usually done:

O Mary, look on us in our misery; way of life, make us free.

Or:

Look on us in our misery, O Mary; make us free, way of life.

These two types are distinct from the four just described, and make six in all. A trispondaic may alternate with an iambic as a special technique, thus:

Rose without blemish, come to our aid in our misery; O devoted to the Lord, look with favor on your servants and children.

And the other way around, thus:

Nobis succurre miseris,/ Domino deuota;
1340   Aspira seruis liberis,/Labis carens nota.

Notandum quod talis rithmus qui modo vltimo ponitur frequenter contingit in Gallicis consonantiis; sed hec ultima species
ante dicta est,* ubi fit mentio de tali rithmo "Taurum sol
1345   intrauerat, etc.," sed in hoc rithmo vna superhabundat sillaba.
Vnde patet quod sine illis duabus differenciis iam habemus sex
differencias nouas siue species a predictis speciebus que sunt xxxvi
Et erunt ita xl et due, uel quattuor duabus* aliis premissis com-
putatis, et ut estimo non poterunt plures inueniri; nisi aliquis
1350   uelit rithmum facere sicut layci qui non considerant artem sed
tantummodo similes exitus, ita uidelicet ut subsequens uersiculus in pari quantitate respondeat uersiculo precedenti, sic:

> "Beatus vir qui non abiit in consilio impiorum,"
> Et qui sibi caute cauit* ab enormitate uiciorum.

1355   Si quis diligenter considerat in tali rithmo reperietur paritas sillabarum, sed artifex extra predictas artis regulas euagatur.
Ars* De Hymnis Vsitatis. Post* predicta dicendum est de metris
aliquid, que necessaria sunt hymnis; ad quod notandum quod
quidam hymni rithmice componuntur sine metro, quidam sine
1360   rithmo et sine metro, quidam tantum metrice componuntur sine
rithmo. Sed in toto hymnario quo nos utimur non sunt nisi tres
diuersitates metri autentici. Vnum est* Asclepiadeum, ab Esclepia
deo inuentore dictum, quod consistit ex pedibus istis: primo est
spondeus; inde est coriiambus, constans ex trocheo et iambo; et
1365   in fine pirrichius, ex duabus breuibus, uel est ibi iambus; ut* in
hoc hymno quem composui de conceptione Beate Uirginis Marie,
que conceptio intelligitur sanctificacio in utero.

Metrum Asclepeadeum Coriiambicum.*

> Rerum* frena tenens, conditor omnium,
> 1370   Portus naufragii, dextra natantium,
> De stella rutilans sol sine motibus,
> Nobis surge cadentibus.

> Uirtus omnipotens, uera sciencia,
> Perdurans bonitas, omnibus omnia,
> 1375   Stellam mitte tuam nocte uiantibus
> Que sit dux, uia gressibus.

Come to our aid in our misery, O devoted to the Lord; look with favor
on your servants and children, O you who lack any slightest mark of
sin.

This last form is common in French lyrics. I have also spoken of it before where I mentioned the poem "Taurum sol intraverat," except that
in this instance the iambic has an extra syllable. It is clear then that aside
from these two variations we now have six new varieties or types in addition to the thirty-six previously described. That makes forty-two, or
forty-four if we count the two I have just excepted, and as far as I can
see there are no more to be found, unless you want to write like the
dabblers who do not care about rules as long as the last words rhyme,
that is, as long as one verse matches the one before it with the same
number of syllables, like this:

"Blessed is the man that walketh not in the counsel of the ungodly"
(Ps. 1:1), and who has carefully guarded himself from the outrages
of sin (cf. Walther 2107).

If you dutifully count the syllables in this poem you will find they answer, but the artist has wandered from the principles of his art as I have
explained them.

Quantitative Meters Used in Hymns. So much for rhymed poems; now
let me speak briefly about the quantitative meters one needs to know to
write hymns. (Note, by the way, that some hymns are composed in
rhymed syllabic verse with no quantitative meter, some with regard
neither to rhyme and syllables nor to quantity, and some are composed
purely by quantity, without regard to rhyme or syllables.) but in the entire hymnal now in use there are only three varieties of genuine quantitative meter. One is the Asclepiad, named for its inventor Asclepiades,
which consists of the following feet: first comes a spondee, then a
choriambus, which is a trochee plus an iamb, and at the end a pyrrhic
or two shorts, or else an iamb; as in this hymn of my own composition,
on the conception of the Blessed Virgin Mary, the conception being
here understood as a sanctification in the womb.

The Asclepiadean Choriambic Meter.

Holder of the world's reins, creator of all things, port after shipwreck, right hand to swimmers, motionless sun, glowing redder from
a star, raise us up, for we are falling.

All-powerful virtue, true knowledge, everlasting goodness, all things
to all men, send your star to us as we travel by night, to be our guide,
the path for our steps.

Floris* principio prata uirentia
Dant risum, genito flore recentia;
Gaudet mater humus, gaudet et incola
1380   Concepta sibi uernula.

Matris,* Christe, tue festa colentibus
Purgatis tribuas ethera* sordibus;
Letum redde diem quo rosa gignitur,*
Flos florum tibi pingitur.

1385   Promissam canimus laude prophetica,
Que lux est miseris stellaque nautica;
Lucis principium nox* colit infima
Ne nox luce sit ultima.

Udam* fons hodie dulcis humum facit,
1390   Granum leticie cultor humi iacit;
Fenix concipitur, iaspis et vnica,
Lampas scalaque celica.

Mundi,* Christe, salus ueraque phisica,
Falli uulneribus nescia practica,
1395   Concepte* meritis, pectoris ulcera
Mundes, qui regis ethera. Amen.

Cantus huius hymni est idem cum cantu illius hymni qui sic
incipit, "Sanctorum meritis inclita gaudia, etc."
    Item est alius hymnus compositus de conceptione Beate
1400 Uirginis. Metrum est constans Saphicum Adonicum—Saphicum
a Sapho, que mulier fuit inuentrix huius metri; Adonicum ab
Adone inuentore, metrum scilicet quod perficiunt duo ultimi
pedes. Primus pes Saphici metri est trocheus, secundus spondeus,
tercius dactilus, quartus trocheus, quintus similiter trocheus uel
1405 spondeus, quia ultima non refert. Tres lince similes sunt sibi;
vltimum est Adonicum, hic scilicet "Florida salue." Cantus idem
est cum illo hymno "Ut queant laxis."

Metrum Saphicum Adonicum.*

O parens uirgo pariens parentem,
1410   Splendor estiuus sine carnis estu,
Dumus incensus, sine rore uirga/Florida, salue.

Germinat radix, humus irrigatur,
Planta pubescit, rosa purpuratur;
1415   Ortus alludit, uiole resultant,/Incola plaudit.

Lucis allatrix, medicina morbi,
Sordium lotrix, lauacrum reorum,
1420   Gratie mater, genitiua pacis/Surgit oliua.

Virgo lactatrix, genitrix pudica,
Leta spes, uernans uia, sol obumbrans,
Umbra perlucens, inarrata tellus,/Perdita reddis.

At the birth of the flower the green meadows smile, the meadows fresh with the newborn flower; mother earth rejoices, the farmer rejoices, at the child they have conceived.

As we keep the feast of your mother, O Christ, purify our uncleanness, grant us heavenly glory; make the day joyful on which the rose is born, and the flower of flowers takes on her colors for you.

We sing of her who was promised in prophetic song, the light of the wretched, the star of the sea; deepest night cherishes the beginning of light, lest night remain, too far from light.

Today the sweet fountain moistens the earth, the cultivator of the earth scatters the seeds of joy; the phoenix is conceived, the rare jasper, the lamp and stair to heaven.

Christ, health of the world, and its true medicine, healer who knows every wound, by the merits of her conceived today cleanse the sores from our breasts, O you who rule the skies. Amen.

This hymn is sung to the tune of "Sanctorum meritis inclita gaudia" (Daniel, *TH* 1:203; 4:139).

Here is a second hymn of mine on the conception of the Blessed Virgin. Its meter is Sapphic Adonic (Sapphic from Sappho, the woman who invented it; Adonic from Adonis its inventor); the Adonic makes up the last two feet of the stanza. The first foot of the Sapphic line is a trochee, the second a spondee, the third a dactyl, the fourth a trochee, and the fifth either another trochee or a spondee, since the last foot need not be precise. Three identical Sapphic lines are followed by an Adonic, here "Florida salve." It is sung to the tune of "Ut queant laxis" (Daniel, *TH* 1, 209; 4, 163, 370; Raby, *CLP* 166).

The Sapphic Adonic Meter.

O virgin parent who bore your own parent, summer brilliance with no summer heat of the flesh, burning bush (cf. Exod. 3:2), sprouting staff without benefit of dew (cf. Num. 17:23), hail.

The root springs up, the earth is moistened, the plant ripens, the rose takes on color; the garden rejoices, fiddles resound, the farmer claps his hands.

The bringer of light, the cure of the sick, washer of the defiled, bath of the guilt-stained, mother of grace, the olive branch that brings peace shoots up.

Virgin nurse, maidenly mother, glad hope, grassy road, shade-giving sun, shining shade, unplowed earth, you reclaim what is lost.

1425   Dirigas* lapsus, tenebras serena,
               Uise desertos fragilesque firma,
               Pauperes* dita, moderare motum,/Pectora munda.

               Vasculum fusum Ioachim decorum
1430   Nectar includit, saciem* uirorum,
               Manna de celo, medicum reorum,/Cuncta regentem.

               Summe Rex clemens, tribuas colenti
               Festa concepte genitricis alme
1435   Posse celestem patriam uidere,/Te duce, Christe. Amen.*

Notandum quod ista caudula, "Te duce, Christe," est uersus Adonicus, ab Adone inuentore dictus, constans ex dactilo et trocheo.

    Item est metrum iambicum dimetrum, quale est illud, "Iam
1440   lucis orto sidere," constans ex iambis positis indifferenter cum
interposicione spondeorum, qui ponuntur semper in impari loco,
ut hic:

Iambicum Dimetrum.*

               Solis superni regia,   Semen solo committitur
1445   Te summa fulsit gratia   Quo uita mundo redditur;
               Septem columpnis aureis   Suo colonus semine
               Et clausulis eburneis.   Loto reuiuit crimine.

               Piropus illic emicat   Serena uirgo uirginum,   1460
               Opusque fabrum predicat;   Noctem serena flencium;
1450   Materie preiudicat,   In hoc mari uolubili
               Hanc Christus edem uendicat. Tu risus esto flebili.

               Huius domus inceptio   Pedes* regas per lubricum
               Est uirginis conceptio;   Pedem* regendo metricum,   1465
               Case colunt hanc corporum   Ne uox opusque iambicent
1455   Ut tecta mundet pectorum.   Statumque mentis inplicent.

                        Oliua, pacis uirgula,
                        Nos expiet uirguncula,
1470   Reisque rumpens uincula
                        Saluet suos* per secula. Amen.*

Cantus huius hymni idem est cum cantu illius hymni qui sic incipit, "Uexilla regis prodeunt,* etc." Est quoddam metrum
Asclepiadeum Adonicum, compositum ex premissis, sumptum
1475   a diuersis auctoribus, ut de Assumptione Beate Uirginis, hoc*
scilicet, "O quam* glorifica luce choruscas, etc." Constat ex
medietate uersus exametri et fine suo.

    Huiusmodi metra sumuntur ab Odis Oratii que sunt x et ix, ad
que uel ad membra quorum alia metra reperta reducuntur.
1480   Qualia sunt hec x et ix metra, que composui ad castigationem

Make right our falls, clear up our darkness, visit the forsaken and strengthen the weak, enrich the poor, calm frenzy, cleanse breasts.

The beautiful vessel cast by Joachim contains the nectar that fills men to the full, manna from heaven, the physician of the guilty, the ruler of everything.

O highest King, grant in your clemency that I who keep the feast of the mother who nourished you, conceived today, may be able to see the heavenly fatherland, by your guidance, O Christ. Amen.

Note again that this tail, "Te duce, Christe," is an Adonic verse, named for Adonis its inventor, consisting of a dactyl and a trochee.

The third quantitative meter for hymns is iambic dimeter, the meter of "Iam lucis orto sidere" (Daniel, *TH* 1:56; 4:42; cf. above 497). It consists of iambs, which may be varied at any point by spondees; the spondees do not form any regular pattern, as here:

Iambic Dimeter.

Court of the highest sun, highest grace sustains you with seven columns of gold and ivory walls.

Gold mixed with bronze shines forth here, the work reveals the artificer: Christ chooses the material and claims the building as his.

The first stone of this building is the conception of the virgin; the cottages of (her parents') bodies cultivate this building in order that it might cleanse the roofs of their own breasts.

Seed is buried in the soil that life may be returned to the world; the sower takes new life from his own seed, and his guilt is washed away.

O bright virgin of virgins, brighten the night of us who weep; in this tossing sea be a smile to the weeper.

Direct my feet through slippery ways by directing the feet of my meter, lest voice and work falter and entangle the upright mind.

May that maiden, the olive branch, the staff of peace, atone for us, and by breaking the chains of the guilty save her dear ones forever. Amen.

This hymn is sung to the tune of "Vexilla regis prodeunt" (Daniel, *TH* 1:60; 4:70). There is also a meter called the Adonic Asclepiad, a combination of the two meters I have described above, in imitation of various classical authors. An example is the hymn on the Assumption of the Blessed Virgin, "O quam glorifica luce coruscas" (Daniel, *TH* 1:245; 4:188). It consists of the middle and the end of a hexameter verse.

cuiusdam formosi iuuenis post lapsum uiriliter resurgentis.

Carminibus depelle tuo, Pari, corde uenenum,
    Que canit arte x Flaccus et arte nouem.
Cantu* proponam primum, gemineque sorores
1485   Ordine decantent* cetera metra suo.
Metri cognitio, ⸻ ⸻ in aure,
    Et Pariden saluans gratia fructus erit.

Incipiunt XIX Ode Que sunt Diuerse in Oratio. Metrum Primum:
Oda de Laude Dauid Qui Cito Penituit post Factum.*

1490   Metra cano pedibus Asclepei: bis coriiambus
    Spondeum sequitur, pirrichiusque semel;
Trocheus et iambus coniunctus erit coriambus
    Et pes pirricheus est geminata breuis.

    Carmen te decet hoc, non Ueneris canor:
1495   Cantent* celicole cantica celica.
    Orati, modulis metra canam tuis,
    Que fundant Paridi dulcia pocula.
    Paucis psalterium dic mihi militis,
    Lapsus egregii dic releuamina,*
1500   Dic et iusticiam dicque fidem Dauid
    Qui miles fuerat, rex, famulans Deo.

    Patris paruulus hic pauperis in domo
    Patris pauit oues, cui Samuel dedit,
    Precepto Domini, ceptriferum decus.
1505   Qui clarus cithara psalterio simul
    Laxat uincula Saul, demonium* domat:
    Hostem cum potuit perdere noluit,
    Ceptrum iusticie, milicie rosa,
    Dulcor, spes, pietas, dextera pauperum.
1510   Vriam perimit coniuge pro sua,
    Sed se punit, in hoc concilians Deo.
    Lapsus continuo surgit, et eruit
    Peccati laqueis dedita brachia:
    Suspirans, lacrimans, rex ueniam petit;
1515   Culpe seruicio subdere se negat.

    Seruat iussa x que statuit Deus:
    Spernit sacra deum, sacra Dei colit.
    Periurus fieri ueridicus timet.
    Custodit reuerens septima Sabbata.
1520   Matri subicitur pronus, amat patrem.
    Furum perfidiam, legis amans, cauet.
    Mechari metuit candidus et placens.
    Si quando rubuit sanguine dextera,
    Ipsum penituit nequicie sue.
1525   Nullos decipiens testis erat malus,
    Vicinique thorum resque cauens suas.
    Purgauit lacrimis singula turpia.

Meters like these are taken from the *Odes* of Horace, which comprise nineteen different meters. To these meters, or elements of them, any other meter you can find is reducible. They are exemplified in the following nineteen quantitative poems which I composed to chasten a certain handsome youth who recovered manfully from a serious lapse.

Expel the poison from your heart, Paris, with the nineteen songs that Flaccus sang so artfully. I shall sing the first meter, then let my twin sisters sing the rest in their turn. Their fruit will be knowledge of meter, melody sweet in the ear, and saving grace for Paris.

Here Begin the Nineteen Types of Horace's Odes. The First Meter: Ode in Praise of David Who Atoned Swiftly for His Sins.

I sing meters in the feet of Asclepius: a double choriambus follows a spondee, then a single pyrrhic. A choriambus is a trochee and an iamb joined together; the pyrrhic foot is a twin short.

This song befits you, not the sweet tones of Venus: let those who seek heavenly things sing heavenly songs. Horace, I shall sing meters in your measures; let them pour sweet draughts on Paris. Tell me in brief of a soldier's harp, tell me the falls and the rises of a great man, tell me the justice, and tell me the faith of David, who was soldier, king, servant of God.

As a child in the home of his poor father he tended his father's sheep until, at the Lord's command, Samuel gave him the honor of bearing the scepter. Brilliant on both harp and lute, he frees Saul's chains by silencing his evil spirit: he refused to ruin his enemy when he could have, the scepter of justice, rose of the army, sweetness, hope, goodness, right hand of the poor. He kills Uriah for his wife's sake, but punishes himself and this conciliates God. He keeps rising after falling, and plucks out limbs caught in the toils of sin; sighing, weeping, the king seeks forgiveness; he refuses to admit that he has given himself over to the service of evil.

He keeps the ten commandments that God established. He spurns what is sacred to the gods to venerate what is sacred to God. He tells the truth, dreading perjury. He reverently keeps the seventh day as the Sabbath. He kneels to his mother and loves his father. Loving the law, he avoids the treachery of thieves. He keeps pure and acceptable, fearing adultery. Though his right hand has at times been stained with blood, he has done penance for his crime. He never deceived anyone with false witness. He kept away from his neighbor's bed and goods. He cleansed his vices one by one with tears.

Exemplis imitans surge celer paris
Illum quem Dominus lumine uisitat.
1530   Actu propositum ne, Pari, compleas:
Ledit uelle malum, peius obest opus.

Descriptio* Vrania Que Preest Stellis.

Sic hoc Tersicore: medicamen* ad intima cordis
Discendit Paridis et prope sanat eum.
1535   Sic* leuis Uranie* procedit, cuius in ore
Flamma rubet rutulo, que solet esse polo.
Stellarum fulgor uestem depingit in illa:
Obnitens tardat quisque planeta polum.
Inferior Phebo Phebe meat; hic* Citharea
1540   Orbem Stilbontis implicat orbe suo;
Ense tonat Mauors; mansueto Iuppiter ore
Ridet; Saturni frigida barba riget.
Pingitur hic cur canet hyemps, cur estuat estas,
Terra sedet, uolitat ignis, et unda fluit,
1545   Aer uitalis spirat; quid uentus et ymber,
Quid nix, quid grando, quid boreale gelu;
Eclipsis solis fuerit quo climate mundi,
Quo lune, necnon causa uidetur ibi.
Hec est celestis re, nomine; dextera speram
1550   Sustinet ut cursus, tempora, signa notet.
Signifer oblicus quibus orbibus oscula donet
Spectat, qua nexus parte colurus eat;
Tardos maturos occasus spectat et ortus
Signorum; noctes ponderat atque dies.
1555   Non tamen ad presens ad speram lumina flectit,*
Sed sic celestem predocet illa uiam.

Metrum* Secundum: Oda de Diuersis Dignitatibus Clericorum.

Aure bibas metrum Saphicum, Pari: trocheus ante it,
Spondeusque sequi, dactilus inde petit;
1560   Trocheus hinc duplex, uel trocheus et sibi iunctus
Spondeus, cum sit ultima quantalibet.
Tres uersus similes sunt; quartus Adonicus, in quo
Dactilus exultat, trocheus inde comes.

Concinat letas lira mentis odas,
1565   Voxque sit lete comes equa menti:
Hiis opus firmo sociare cantor/Federe temptet.

Dic Deo factis* modulos placentes,
Lacrimis summo modulare duci,
1570   Per preces temptes penetrare celum/Tramite stricto.

Vt uiam discant, fugiant scolares
Deditos carni uiciique seruos;
1575   Semper insistant* operi uenusto,/Seria querant.

By means of these examples of a person in a like state, rise quickly, imitating him whom the Lord visits with his light. Do not turn temptations into deeds, Paris, for to desire evil is harmful, but the act is still more so.

A Description of Urania, Who Presides over the Stars.

Thus Terpsichore, descending with her soothing powers into the inmost heart of Paris and helping to cure him. Now gentle Urania, the heavenly one, in whose shining face a flame glows, continues. The splendor of the stars is pictured in her gown: each planet struggles to retard the motion of the heavens. Phoebe travels here beneath Phoebus, here Citharea enfolds the orbit of Stilbon in her own orbit; Mars thunders with his sword, Jupiter smiles his customary smile; Saturn's cold beard stands stiff. Here is pictured forth why winter is gray, why summer is hot, why the earth is still, why fire flits, why water flows, why air blows; what is wind and what is rain, what snow, what hail, what hoarfrost; where in the world the sun will be in eclipse, where the moon—nor is its cause here unseen. She is celestial in both fact and name: her right hand holds up a globe, that she may note courses, seasons, zodiacal signs. The sign bearer watches from an angle to what orbits she may give her kisses, in what region the colures travel joined. She watches early and late falls and rises of signs; she balances nights and days. Not yet at present does she bend the lights to her sphere; but thus she guides the heavenly ways in advance.

The Second Meter: Ode on the Various Ranks of the Clergy.

Drink into your ears the Sapphic meter, Paris: a trochee comes first, a spondee seeks to follow, then a dactyl; next a double trochee, or a trochee and a spondee, since the last foot is as you please. Three verses go like this; the fourth is an Adonic, in which a dactyl skips with his friend the trochee.

Let the lyre of the mind harmonize with merry odes, and let the voice be boon companion to the merry mind: let the singer try to join his work to these in a firm friendship.

Speak with your deeds measures pleasing to God, sing to the Supreme Leader with your tears, with your prayers try to reach heaven by the straight and narrow path.

If they want to learn the way, let scholars flee those devoted to the flesh and the servants of vice; let them always pursue lovely deeds, put their minds to serious things.

Me iuuat laudes studii leuare,
Fonte nos cuius dea sacra potat,
Que reseruatrix Eliconis affert/Nectaris haustum.

1580 Cuius exhausit Nicholaus undam,
Et bibit plene Katerina potum,
Et salutaris siciebat aque/Pocula Paulus.

Non honus fortes retrahit cateruas,
1585 Lucta sed dulcis reuehit quietem:
Hiis labor ludum sapit et uoluntas/Robur adauget.

Vita florescit speciosa cleri,
Pulcra si Pallas comitatur illum,
1590 Et fugit Cipris, fugit et gementis/Planctus auari.

Non dolo fallax aliena raptat:
Diues est quando nichil est in archa;
1595 Poculum dicit fluuiale Bachum,/Paruula laudans.

Vnus in dignam cathedram leuatur,
Claustra gratatur reliqus tenere,
Alter in densis heremita siluis/Pascitur herbis.

1600 Hic oues pascit dape spiritali,
Hiis facit uite scaturire fontem;
Hic studet turbam studii rigare/Fonte Minerue.

Oda* de Constantia Beate Katerine: Tertium Metrum.

1605 Tedia ne pariant* eadem, Gliconius unus
        Asclepeique sequens* ordine uersus erit.
    Primum spondeus coriiambus pirrichiusque
        Constituunt; supra cerne quis alter erit.

1610 Huc aduerte libens, Pari,/Mentem, mundicie uerbaque suscipe,

Que claudas animo tuo,/Que fructum pariant* dentque tibi cibum.

Sexus debilior uirum/Prudens induerat uirgo, Deo placens,

1615 Costi progenies pia—/Heu fortes pudeat magnanimos* uiros!

Hos dum femina preterit,/Et carnis stimulos milicia domat,

1620 Vincit supplicii minas:/Non horret tenebras, uincula, uerbera.

Scandit clauigeras rotas,/Pene nescit honus saluifica* fide,

Quam dat gingnasii labor/Et doctrina Dei, limes in ethera.

1625 Quartum Metrum: Oda* de Fuga Carminum Poeticorum.

Archilochi primum uersum nunc accipe: nomen
    Tetrametri* primus uersus herilis habet,
Trocheus est ter ei iunctus collofonius;* alter
    Quem pentimemeris iambica reddit erit—
1630 Illam constituit cum iambo sillaba bino—
    Trocheus in fine ter sociatur ei.

My pleasure is to raise up praises to study, whose holy goddess gives us to drink from her fountain: the guardian of Helicon, she brings us draughts of nectar.

Nicholas drank her water, and Catherine drank her drink to the full, and Paul thirsted for cups of that saving water.

Hardship doesn't hold back such brave soldiers; rather, the sweet struggle brings peace: for them toil smacks of game, and will adds strength.

The life of a cleric will blossom into beauty if lovely Pallas is his companion, and if the Cyprian flees him, and the petulant groan of the miser.

He does not take what belongs to others with tricks and lies: he is rich when there is nothing in his purse; he calls his cup of water "the river of Bacchus," for he praises little things.

One is raised to the honor of a See, another is happy to keep to the cloister, a third is a hermit, feeding on herbs in the thick of the woods.

One feeds the sheep with the food of the spirit, causing the fountain of life to gush out for them; another makes it his study to irrigate the studious crowd from the fountain of Minerva.

The Third Meter: Ode on the Perseverance of Saint Catherine.

Lest the same kind of thing get monotonous, here is one Glyconic verse followed by an Asclepiad. A spondee, a choriambus, and a pyrrhic make up the first; for the other, see above.

Turn your mind this way, if you please, Paris, and listen to a tale of purity; lock it firmly in your mind that it may bear fruit to nourish you. The weaker sex put on the man, that prudent virgin, so pleasing to God, the virtuous daughter of Costus; shame on the men, with their "bravery" and their "large spirit!" While this woman is outstripping them, and cooling the fleshly impulses of the soldiery, she also wins out over threats of torture: she fears neither darkness, chains, nor blows. She mounts the spiked wheel and scarcely feels the pain, so great is her faith in her Savior, the fruit of her hard study at divine lore, the pathway to heaven.

The Fourth Meter: Ode on Fleeing the Songs of the Poets.

Learn now the greater Archilochian: the first verse is a dactylic tetrameter with a triple trochee added as a colophon; the second has an iambic penthemimeris—two iambs plus a syllable—accompanied by a triple trochee at the end.

Lectio celestis placeat tibi, lectio salutis,
Medela mentis, lux iterque uite.

1635 Picta* poetarum fuge carmina, que uenena fundunt,
Luxus lutosi polluuntque puros.

Morales libros lege, perlege, corde lecta scribe;
Legas agendo quod facis legendo,

Ne culpet factum tua lectio, ne manus loquela,
Ne scandalizent facta uocis usum,

1640 Ne caput humanum prerideat, ater inde piscis,
Et excitetur risus intuenti.

Hec faciens recipit sua premia: uiuit hic misellus,
Minus beatus Tartaro sepultus.

Oda de Uiciis Prelatorum: Quintum Metrum.

1645 Tempero nunc aliter citharam, sint vt duo uersus
    Asclepei, cecini quo duce metrum prius;
Tercius est uersus Feregracius: aduehit illum
    Primo spondeus, dactilus inde comes,
Spondeus sequitur; quartus Gliconius aures
1650   Inbuit, explicui quo pede metrum prius.

Extra qui rutilat fulgure faminis	Albatus paries interius perit, 1655
Nec concors opus est uocibus aureis,	Cedit uermiculis optimus ignibus;
Extra cernitur aurum,	Flos hic est sine fructu*
Cuprum sublatitat tamen.	Quem sternit boreas ferus.

Multos hic laqueat morbus episcopus,
1660 Qui cordis penetrat letifer intima:
Mites sunt foris agni,
Intus sunt rapidi lupi.

Sextum* Metrum.

Versus Asclepei cano tres; Gliconius addit
1665   Uersiculus quarto consona metra loco.

Largi pollicitis munera differunt:
Apparent alique,* sunt nichili tamen.
Qui gratis capiunt nulla quidem* dabunt,
Duri debita reddere.

1670 Parui Parisius gingnasiis student
Magnos quos Dominus postea subleuat:
Prebende, redditus, aut cathedre uacant,
Et fit magniloquis locus.

Ascendunt cathedras, suscipiunt honus—
1675 Descendunt animo; mutat eos honor,
Ignorant socios antea cognitos;
Non sunt qui fuerant prius.

Let heavenly reading be your joy, reading that brings salvation, the mind's medicine, light and way of life. Flee the painted songs of the poets, which spout poisons and whose filthy debaucheries contaminate the pure. Read and reread moral books, learn them by heart. And read more morality by actually doing what you do in your imagination when you read—lest your reading find fault with your deeds, your words with your hands, lest your deeds scandalize your voice, lest a human face smile in front and a foul fish behind, arousing the mockery of all who see you. The man who does such things gets what he deserves: he lives here in misery, and he is still less happy when he is buried in hell.

The Fifth Meter: Ode on the Vices of Prelates.

Now I tune my lute differently, so that two verses are those of Asclepius, under whose guidance I sang an earlier poem; the third is a Pherecratic: a spondee leads it, then his friend the dactyl, and a spondee brings up the rear; a Glyconic fills the ears in the fourth verse, in whose feet I set forth an earlier poem.

He who shimmers on the surface in the lightning of his speech, but whose deeds do not harmonize with his golden words, seems like gold on the surface, but copper lies underneath.

A whitewashed wall decays within, even the best gives way to termites or fire; here is blossom without fruit, which the fierce north wind scatters.

A corrupt bishop is a trap for the multitude, bringing death to their deep hearts' core; outside they are gentle lambs, within they are wolves that will tear you apart.

The Sixth Meter.

I sing three Asclepiads; a short Glyconic makes for harmony in the fourth line.

People who are rich in promises spread their favors around; some actually emerge, but are worthless. Such people take freely but never give, and are painfully slow to pay their debts.

Those small-fry at their books in the schools of Paris are, by the grace of God, tomorrow's great men: livings, revenues, or Sees are vacant—and to be had by anyone who talks loud enough.

They step up to their Sees, take on the burden—and step down in soul: success spoils them; they snub their former friends; they are not the same people they were before.

Oda de Delectatione Peccandi: *Metrum Septimum.*

1680
Plectra sonora mouet heroicus integer;* alter
Exametri uersus ultimus illa mouet.

Curantes alios medici depellere morbum
Non proprii de corpore possunt.

Non sentire uolunt, non* cernere quod leuet egros,
Delectat sed eos sua febris.

1685
Culparunt alios sed nunc culpantur ab illis;
In dominos est uersa sagitta.

Simonis exosus erroribus errat in hiisdem,
Et reprehendit auarus auaros,

Dampnantesque gulam gula nexis strangulat illos
1690
In laqueis; Uenus inuenit hostes

Illos in uerbis, in factis laudat amicos—
A paucis deuicta gemiscit.

Oda *de Hiis Que Sacerdos Agere Tenetur: Metrum Octauum.*

Nunc coriiambus adest et bachius amphibracusue.*
1695
Hunc breuis et longe constituere due;
Heret in amphibraco breuibus succincta duabus
Longa; quibus pedibus metra priora meant.
Metrum quod sequitur epitritum cerne secundum
Ad finem tardo constituisse pede.
1700
Bis socium poscit coriiambum bachius ipse,
Amphibracusue suus exigit esse comes.

Si fueris sacerdos,/Tu modum uite uideas, prouideasque uitam.

1705
Presbiteri periti/Sint, bone fame, placidi, colloquio pudico,

Sollicitique libris./Que legunt promant aliis, uerba sequantur acta,

Ne pudeat doceri/De quibus mussant. Modico uiuere collaborent,*

1710
Pompa procul recedat./Compati discant miseris ueste, ciboque, tecto.

Sit mulier Caribdis,/Castitas portus. Presibus templa Dei frequentent.

Oda de Archidiaconis: Nonum Metrum.

1715
Alcaici primi duo sunt quos carmine promam:
Est pentimemeris iambicus iste canor,
Bis tamen huic iungi uult dactilus. Additur autem
Tercius hiis uersus in statione sua:
Iambicus est dimeter* ypercathalecticus. Inde
1720
Cerne lagoedicum passibus ire sonum:
Dactilus est primus pes eius, post coriiambus;
Bachius hiis socius amphibracusue subit.

Princeps statutus forte diaconus
Es, ut regendo pectora dirigas;
1725
Iudex sede plebi timenti,
Diuitis haut precio coactus.

The Seventh Meter: Ode on the Pleasures of Sinning.

A complete heroic verse moves the sounding plectrum; the second verse moves it with the last half of a hexameter.

Though they cure others, doctors cannot drive the sickness from their own bodies; they do not want to discover what will make them better, for their own fever delights them. They have diagnosed others' ills, now they are diagnosed themselves: the arrow is turned on the masters. The hater of Simony strays into that very failing; the miser chides misers; gluttony squeezes the condemners of gluttony in her nets; Venus finds her enemies in word are her friends in deed; these she applauds—her groans of defeat are rare.

The Eighth Meter: Ode on the Duties of a Priest.

Now the choriambus appears, and a bacchic or an amphibrach. A short and two longs make a bacchic; in an amphibrach a long is hemmed in by two shorts. Those are the feet of the first line. Notice that a second epitritus is next, moving to its goal on slow feet. Then a bacchic demands that its friend the choriambus appear twice, or else it is the amphibrach that wants it for its companion.

If you want to be a priest, see here what kind of life it is, and prepare for that life. Priests should be skillful, of good repute, gentle, modest in speech, and fond of books. They should use their reading for the good of others, and their deeds should match their words, lest one blush to learn what they are holding back. They should cooperate to live cheaply, shunning display. They should learn to share their clothing, food, and homes with the poor. Let woman be their Charybdis, chastity their harbor; and let them storm the temples of God with their prayers.

The Ninth Meter: Ode on Archdeacons.

Two Alcaics are the first things I set forth in this poem. This form has an iambic penthemim, to which a double dactyl is eager to be joined. A third verse is added to these in its turn, an iambic dimeter hypercatalectic. Then you will observe a logaoedic rhythm going its paces: its first foot is a dactyl, then a choriambus; and a bacchic or an amphibrach walks in company with them.

As a deacon you have been, as it were, made a prince, to rule and guide souls. Sit in judgment over the trembling populace—but don't be swayed by the little presents of the rich.

Decanus* idem despice munera,
Ne decanum sis agmine sordido.
Inter uiros canos probosque
1730   Consilium teneas disertus.

Minas relaxa, fulgura comprime,
Sit ira fracta, uerbaque suscipe,
Audi querelas, pronus esto
Cum tibi, diues, inops obedit.

1735   *Oda* de Subdiaconis: Decimum Metrum.*

En metra prorumpunt coriiambica! Ter coriiambus
Spondeum sequitur, pirichiusque semel.

Istis inferior si gradus est, sit sacer et ratus,
Sit factis radians, sit stabilis Christicola fide,
1740   Qui sumpsit galeam que prior est milicie decor.
Cultu mundicie mens tibi sit candidior niue:
Prudens acolitus fortis opus militis acolat.
Simplex clericus es,* milicie lectus es armiger:
Ne* sors displiceat quam Dominus prestiterat tibi.
1745   Hii qui despiciunt officium quod Domino placet
Labuntur miseri, spernit eos spiritus et caro.
Miles degenerans grata mouet prelia demoni:
Arbor floruerat sed uiridis* marcuit, aruit,*
Igni digna dari quam resecat ruricole manus.

1750   Cantibus Uranie Paridis sic debriat aures
Et uario mulcet pectora mota sono.
Sed iam Caliope properat complere sororum
Inceptum; summum uasis adimplet aqua,
Immo mero dulci, sed nectare; uisibus* escas
1755   Auribus et nectar corpore uoce pluit.
Callida Calliope testatur nomine uocis
Dulcorem, fundens nomine, uoce fauos.
Illius in cithara dulcedo musica dulci
Voci concordat pollicibusque suis.

1760   *Oda de Conflictu Carnis, Mundi, et Demonis, quam Decantavit*
Calliope.

Incipiam metrum, mea quod germana decora
Premisit; sumes* gracius inde nouum.

1765   Mundus, spiritus, et caro/Forti bella mouent tristia milite.

Incautos oculos foris/Mundus blandiciis mitibus allicit;

Paret prosiliens caro/Pulsu quam subito precipitat Sathan.

1770   Contra uiribus utere/Vires; esca Dei sermo dabit sacer

Vires. Belligerans* iocus/Furtim debilitat, frangit et ocium,

1775   Mentis menia diruit/Risus, uox cithare, trica,* merum, cibus.

As dean, too, ignore bribes, and you will distinguish yourself from most of that filthy crew; among venerable and upright men, keep your counsel eloquently.

Soften your threats, keep your lightning flashes under control, dissolve your anger; be available, hear out complaints, be eager to please, rich man, though the poor man obeys you.

The Tenth Meter: Ode on Subdeacons.

Lo, choriambic meters burst forth! a triple choriambus follows a spondee, then one pyrrhic.

Though his rank is beneath theirs, let him be dedicated and determined, shining in deeds, firm in the Christian faith, a man who dons his helmet, the chief ornament of the army. In its quest for purity let your mind be whiter than snow: let the strong and prudent acolyte attend to the duty of a soldier. You are a plain cleric, chosen to carry a weapon in the army: do not chafe at the lot the Lord has chosen for you. Those who despise a role that pleases the Lord sink into wretchedness—flesh and spirit alike reject them. The degenerate soldier invites the attacks of the devil: the tree once flourished but has withered and died in the height of its greenness, good now only to be cut by the woodsman and thrown into the fire.

Thus Urania intoxicates the ears of Paris with her songs, and soothes his turbulent breast with ever-varying sound. But now Calliope hastens to complete what her sisters have begun; she fills his cup to the brim with water, no, with sweet wine, no, with nectar; with her voice she rains food and nectar on his eyes, his ears, his body. Skillful Calliope gives witness by her name to the sweetness of her voice, pouring forth honeycombs with her name and her voice. The sweetness in her lyre harmonizes with the music in her sweet voice and her fingers.

Ode on the Conflict of the World, the Flesh, and the Devil, Sung by Calliope.

I shall initiate a new meter, which my beautiful sister taught me: you will accept the novelty more willingly because of that.

The world, the evil spirit, and the flesh wage painful wars on the strong soldier. The world entices careless eyes from without with smooth flatteries; the eager flesh leaps to comply: Satan may topple it with a sudden impulse. Use strength against strength: God's food, the sacred Word, will give strength. A joke is a sly weapon to weaken the walls of the mind, idleness breaks them, laughter ruins them, and so do the sound of a lute, a girl's hair, wine, food.

Oda Quod Omnis Sciencia In Se Bona Est. Metrum* Undecimum.*

Carmen habe fultum, Paris, amphimacro* pede primo
    Quo cingit duplex sillaba longa breuem.
Adde bis huic iambum; uersus catelecticus alter
1780   Iambicus est trimeter—sillaba fraudat eum.

Hinc ego uiros probos   Impero* uiro seni
Vocabo* scire phisicam, replendo   Periculosa frigidos docere.

Quicquid hec docet, iubet: Nunc puer sedet docens
Sciencias in se bonas fatebor.   Pares, parum pericior* pusillis   1790

1785 Sed iuuentus insolens   Quos docet, nichil timet
Libencius nociua scire querit.   Puer parem sibi statu iocoso.

Metrum* Duodecimum: Oda de Causidicis et Legistis.

Ionicus ecce minor tibi dat solatia: duplex
1795   Hunc breuis et duplex dat tibi longa pedem.
Ionicus est maior ex longa duplice primum,
    Post correpta duplex hunc properare facit.
Ionicus ergo minor tibi prodit in ordine uersus
    Legistas feriens causidicosque leues.

1800   Geme paucos bene leges dare iuri,   *legal satire*
Quia causas miserorum reprimendo
Meruerunt maledici baratrique
Lacrimoso cruciatu sepeliri.
Phaleratus sibi rethor placet uni;
1805   Nisi iudex sit honestus sit et equs;
Logicorum tumidum cor crepat intus
Sine rixa, sine bello, sine flamma.
Logici uix potuerunt logicari,
Tumuerunt sibi uates studiosi;
1810   Perit ommis labor illis,* etiam laus;
Nec habebunt studio quod meruere.

Tertium Decimum Metrum. Oda Quod Arismetici Ignorant Finem Vite Sue.

Vt leteris adhuc cantu, dilecte, pudico,
1815   Quem nunc proponam uersus herilis erit;
Alter uersus erit pars mutans ultima uersus
    Pentimetri: clauda rectius ire docet.

Mensurare modum nescit geometra, docendo
Rebus inesse modum.

1820   Nescit arismeticus lucem numerare supremam
Qua moriturus erit;

Et si prescierit, cur non uiuit quasi mortis
Presserit* hora caput?

Musicus iste melos sitit, in dulcedine nescit
1825   Cantica grata precum.

The Eleventh Meter: An Ode Arguing that Every Science Is Good in Itself.

Accept this poem, Paris, supported in the first line by the amphimacer, in which two long syllables surround a short; add to this a double iambic. The second line is iambic trimeter catalectic, or "short one syllable."

I call hither upright men to learn natural science by cramming themselves with whatever it teaches, whatever it demands: my thesis is that the sciences are good in themselves. But insolent youth has a better appetite for learning harmful things. So I order those recalcitrants to teach their dangerous things to an old man. Now a boy takes the chair, to teach his peers, a boy hardly smarter than the children he is teaching; but the boy no longer fears his teacher, who is now his equal in this game of pretend.

The Twelfth Meter: Ode on Barristers and Lawyers.

Here is the lesser Ionic to soothe you: a double short, then a double long gives you this foot. (The greater Ionic is a double long first, then a double short makes it hurry to its conclusion.) The straight lesser Ionic line comes forth for you, then, to strike out at lawyers and irresponsible barristers.

Deplore how few of them make laws for the common good! For suppressing the cases of the poor they have deserved to be cursed and buried in the howling torture-chamber of Hell. The orator in his fancy harness pleases himself alone; if a judge is not upright, let him at least be fair; the bloated hearts of those wordmongers rattle inside them though there is no battle, no war, no sign of flame. As logicians they could scarcely be reasoned with, as poets their only study was swelling their own egos: all effort, even praise, is thrown away on them, nor will they ever have anything they earned by studying hard.

The Thirteenth Meter: An Ode on the Theme that Mathematicians Ignore the True Purpose of Life.

Since you are pleased with my modest songs so far, beloved, I shall now present one heroic verse followed by the second, variable half of a pentameter verse: it teaches the lame to walk more normally.

The geometrician does not know how to measure the mean, for he teaches that the mean is to be found in things. The mathematician does not know how to figure out his last day, the day on which he is doomed to die. And if he has foretold it, why does he not live as if the hour of death were pressing down on his head? The musician thirsts for melodies,

Hic notat astrorum uires, quem regula uite
Visque superna latet.

Sic sapiunt ut desipiunt,* concludat ut illis
Optima Baucis anus.

1830   *Quartum Decimum Metrum: De* Sancta Cruce.*

Si fortasse iuuat te cantus amoris, amorem
    Christi decantes ecclesieque sue
Versiculos istos audi: trimeter* prior, alter
    Iambicus est dimeter subsidiumque tibi.

1835   Licet malis erroribus uelit caro   Morti crucis ludibriisque turpibus,
        Frequenter esse subdita,   Quem luce reddit tercia.

        Deus tamen labentibus refundere   Vobis tamen dilectio ligans duos
        Lucem sue uult gratie.*   Abest fugitque longius:

        Patebat hoc cum Summus Artifex Pater   Viuit vorax detractio, premit bonos
1840   Prolem suam morti dedit,   Et clericos et milites.   1846

*Quintum Decimum Metrum: Oda de Detractoribus et Superbienti-
bus de* Scientia Sua.*

Nunc aliter cordas mutato tempero* cantu.
1850   Uersiculus tremeter iambicus unus erit:
        Alter herilis erit uersus pars prima, comesque
            Iambicus est dimeter consociatus ei.

        Amor fidelis exulat,* fugit fides,
        Deserit et socios si spens* recedat premium.*

1855   Quandoque premium speratur et tamen
        Premia qui recipit secreta fert* obprobria,

        Et si careret premio, nichil quidem
        Cerneret in domino dignum reprendi* crimine.

        Istud scolasticos sodales polluit:
1860   Inuidet hic alii magister, illi detrahens.

        Hic* est asello uilior leo fremens,
        Inuidus est asinus licet leonem iactitet.

        Doctrina uilet pauperis, sed diuitis*
        Pallada* sermo sapit: diues ministrat dicia.

1865   *Sextum Decimum Metrum: Oda de Infamia Luxurie.*

Paulum mutabo cordas: heroicus unus,
    Alter erit* dimeter dimidiusque labans.

Cerne quis* exspectat pollutos Cipride finis:
Primo dolor fit* pectoris, corporis inde labor.

1870   Est Uenus infamis, et in hostes mutat amicos,
        Exaurit archam funditus, fetet ut hyrcus olens,

        Inflammat rixas, condensat prelia, fraudes
        Nouat, nouatis luditur crimine lusa suo.

but does not know the lovely tunes that lie in the sweetness of prayers. Another knows the power of stars, but the rules for good living and the power that is above all lie hidden from him. Thus they are witless in their very wisdom, as goodwife Baucis might conclude of them.

The Fourteenth Meter: On the Holy Cross.

Should you happen to like a love song, listen to these verses that sing the love of Christ and his Church. The first is iambic trimeter, the second iambic dimeter: both will help you.

Though the flesh is always hankering to give in to wickedness, God is still eager to pour the light of his grace on those who fall. The great Creator and Father made this clear when he surrendered his Son to death, the death of the Cross with all its foul mockeries, and returned him to us on the third morning. Yet the love that binds those Two to you is missing, has fled too far off: only hungry slander stays with us, pressing hard on the good cleric and soldier.

The Fifteenth Meter: Ode on Backbiters and Those Who Are Impressed with Their Own Knowledge.

Now I tune my strings in a new way, changing my song. One verse is iambic trimeter; the second is the first half of a hexameter joined by its friend the iambic dimeter.

Trusting love is exiled, trustworthiness between friends is lost if one party abandons the other to pursue a prize. Sometimes a prize is striven for and the person who wins the prize holds secret resentments; whereas if he missed the prize he would see nothing reprehensible or criminal in his master. This disease infects academic friendships: one teacher envies another and spreads slanders about him. Such a man is a roaring lion more lowly than the ass, for an envious person is an ass though he may play the lion. The teaching of a poor man is thought worthless, but every word of a rich man smacks of Pallas: a rich man has rich things to offer.

The Sixteenth Meter: Ode on the Heinousness of Lust.

I shall change my strings a little: one verse is a hexameter, the other a dimeter, plus "half a sinker," or a dactylic penthemim.

Look what end awaits those whom the Cyprian pollutes: first she brings sorrow to the breast, then torture to the body. Venus is notorious for changing friends into enemies, she turns your purse inside out, she smells like a stinking goat, she starts quarrels, instigates battle after battle, invents deceits, and is deluded by her own inventions, as well as

1875
Hos reddit fures, illos suspendit, ac istos
Detruncat, illos strangulat, flumine mergit eos:

In Baratri puteo tandem submergit amicos
Fetus* sueque curie; quos amat odit amans.

Talia militibus dat premia, talia op ut ut
Carnis sititor, quem premit mundus, agitque Sathan.

1880
Septimum Decimum Metrum: Oda de Simoniacis.

Lene tibi carmen uariat lira: uersus herilis
    Tardus hic est, demeter cursitat ille cito.

Clericus esse putat sapientior omnibus illis
Quos ars ei non copulat;

1885
Sed quandoque tamen capriorem monstrat in actu,
Hunc ut capre derideant.

Clericus et solum se clamitat esse facetum,
Facescie sed* derogat.

Conculcans uicium, te dicas esse facetum:
1890
Vrbanus esto moribus,

Simonis expellas uicium, cuius ruditate
Offenditur Rex etheris.

Huic uicio nullum splendorem spiritus affert,
Quo spiritus dos uenditur.

1895
Metrum Octauum Decimum: Oda de Fantastica Deceptione
Mulierum.*

Muto tibi cantum, uitam mutare memento
    In melius; primus uersus herilis erit—
Vt sis fortis herus heroica canto}-sed ille
1900
    Iambicus est trimeter,* federa firma tenens.

Quosdam Tirecie uel Mantos carmina uana
Stulte iuuant, qui poculum* mortis trahunt.

Hii fallunt alios, sed fallit eos sua norma:
Doctrina uana decipit duces suos.

1905
Demonis illectos laqueis Christi ferit ensis;
Illos suus rex suscipit uorans suos.

Decipiens aliquis mulieres demonis arte
Deceptus est, dans colla rethibus suis.

Eterno regno prefertur femina, cuius
1910
In ore nectar creditur, quo fel fluit

Quod corpus mentemque necat; mulier speciosa
Formosa queque* destruit libidine.

Metrum Decimum Nonum: Oda de* eo quod Clerici Debeant*
Ire Ultimo ad Theologiam.*

1915
Vnus adhuc cantus conformi uoce resultat:
    Se pede fert trimetri* iambicus iste tibi.

by her sin. She makes one man a thief, hangs another, beheads one, strangles another, sinks another into the bottom of the river: in the end she buries all her friends, all the products of her court, in the pit of Hell, for those she loves she hates by loving them. Those are the rewards she gives soldiers, those are the things the thirster after flesh may hope for, the man whom the world goads and Satan drives.

The Seventeenth Meter: Ode on Simoniacs.

Let my lyre throb a gentle song for you: one verse is the slow hexameter, the other a speedy dimeter.

The cleric thinks he is wiser than all those whose lack of education separates them from him; but sometimes he proves even more goatish than they in his actions, so that the very goats make fun of him. The cleric also claims that he alone is elegant, yet he dishonors true elegance. If you really want to say you are elegant, trample sin, be urbane in morals, rid yourself of Simon's vice, which is a piece of bad manners that offends the King of Heaven. Spirit lends no splendor to this vice, by which the dowry of the spirit is sold off.

The Eighteenth Meter: Ode on Deceiving Women with Phantasms.

I change my song for you; remember to change your life for the better. The first verse is a hexameter—I sing heroic verses so that you will become a brave hero—but the other is iambic trimeter, holding strictly to its contract.

Vain poems of Tiresias or Manto stupidly delight some people, who are pouring themselves a cup of death. They do it to fool others, but are fooling themselves with their own tricks, for vain teachings deceive only their own promoters. The sword of Christ smites all those whom the devil has lured into his traps; for Satan is a king who receives his subjects to devour them. Anyone who uses black magic to deceive women has been deceived himself; he has caught his head in his own nets. In death's eternal kingdom Woman is enthroned forever; from her mouth flows gall that is taken for nectar, and kills body and soul. Woman is lovely, beautiful—and destroys everything through lust.

The Nineteenth Meter: Ode on the Reason Why Clerics Must Ultimately Go to Theology.

One more song resounds to the harmonizing voice: the iambic comes before you in the foot of the trimeter.

Spes premii diuina sit sciencia;
Artes pedissece caput subdunt ei,
Noctes diesque militant honoribus,
1920   Summe sciencie nitore fulgurant,
Nam si qua nigra grauci lilt, lauit dea
Flue beata sanguinisque purpura
Quo crux rubebat, sustinens qui sustinet
Celum, fretum, terreque pondus infimum.
1925   Qua semita tendant docet pediscecas,
A qua recedens deuiat per aspera.
Ergo, Paris, dee uigore milites,
Vt sit tibi uite corona prestita.

Pirrichius est constans ex duabus breuibus, temporibus duobus,
1930   ut "fuga."
Spondeus est constans ex duabus longis, et quatuor temporum,
ut "estas."

Trocheus est constans ex longa et breui, et trium temporum, ut
"meta."
1935   Iambus est constans ex breui et longa, et trium temporum, ut
"parens."

Tribracus est pes constans ex tribus breuibus, et trium temporum, ut "macula."
Molosus est pes constans ex tribus longis, et temporum sex, ut
1940   "Mecenas."*

Anapestus est pes constans ex duabus breuibus et longa, et quatuor temporum, ut "dominus."
Dactilus est pes constans ex longa et duabus breuibus, et
quatuor temporum, ut "Menalus."

1945   Amphibracus est pes constans ex breui et longa et breui, et
quatuor* temporum, ut "arator."
Amphimacrus* est pes constans ex longa et breui et longa, et
quinque temporum, ut "insule."

Bachius est pes constans ex breui et duabus longis, et quinque
1950   temporum, ut "Achates."
Antibachius est pes constans ex duabus longis et breui, et
quinque temporum, ut "natura."

Proceleumaticus est pes constans ex quatuor temporibus et
breuibus, ut "auicula."
1955   Dispondeus est pes constans ex quatuor longis et octo temporibus, ut "oratores."

Diiambus est pes constans ex breui et longa et breui et longa,
et sex temporibus, ut "propinquitas."

   Let the study of divinity be your hope of reward; the ancillary arts
bow their heads to her, honor her with their service night and day, and
shine with the reflected light of the highest science. For if their works
be dark, the goddess theology washes them in holy faith and in the
crimson blood that reddened the cross; for He sustains her Who sustains
the sky, the sea, the full weight of the earth. She teaches her attendants
what path to take, then withdraws from it herself to strike new paths
through the wilds. Serve that goddess, then, Paris, with all your strength,
and you will be rewarded with the crown of life.

A Pyrrhic consists of two shorts and two beats, as *fuga*.
A Spondee consists of two longs and four beats, as *estas*.

A Trochee consists of a long and a short, and three beats, as *meta*.
An Iamb consists of a short and a long, and three beats, as *parens*.

A Tribrach is a foot that consists of three shorts, and three beats, as
macula.
A Molossus is a foot that consists of three longs, and six beats, as
Mecenas.

An Anapest is a foot that consists of two shorts and a long, and four
beats, as *dominus*.
A Dactyl is a foot that consists of a long and two shorts, and four
beats, as *Menalus*.

An Amphibrach is a foot that consists of a short, a long, and a short,
and four beats, as *arator*.
An Amphimacer is a foot that consists of a long, a short, and a long,
and five beats, as *insule*.

A Bacchic is a foot that consists of a short and two longs, and five
beats, as *Achates*.
An Antibacchic is a foot that consists of two longs and a short, and
five beats, as *natura*.

A Proceleusmatic is a foot that consists of four beats and four shorts,
as *avicula*.
A Dispondee is a foot that consists of four longs, and eight beats, as
oratores.

A Di-iamb is a foot that consists of a short and a long, a short and a
long, and six beats, as *propinquitas*.

Dithrocheus est pes constans ex longa et breui et longa et
1960   breui, et sex temporum, ut "Cathelina."

Antipestus est pes constans ex breui et longis duabus et breui,
et sex temporum, ut "reseruare."

Coriambus est pes constans ex longa et duabus breuibus et
longa, et sex temporum, ut "armipotens."

1965   Yonicus maior est pes constans ex duabus longis et duabus
breuibus, ut "Iunonius."*

Yonicus minor est constans ex duabus breuibus* et duabus
longis, et sex temporum, ut "Diomedes."*

Peon primus est pes constans ex una longa et tribus breuibus,
1970   et v temporum, ut "legitimus."

Epitritus primus est pes constans ex una breui et tribus longis,
et septem temporum, ut "sacerdotes."

Peon secundus est pes constans ex una breui et secunda longa
et duabus breuibus, et v temporum, ut "colonia."

1975   Epitritus secundus est pes constans ex prima longa et secunda
breui et duabus longis, et vij temporum, ut "conditores."

Peon* tercius est pes constans ex duabus breuibus et una longa
et breui, et v temporum, ut "maneamus."

Epitritus tercius est pes constans ex duabus longis et una
1980   breui et una longa, et vij temporum, ut "ludibriis."

Peon quartus est pes constans ex tribus breuibus et una longa,
ut "celeritas."

Epitritus quartus est pes constans ex tribus longis et quarta
breui, vt "exultare."

1985   Rithmus monomicus.
Dispondeus.
Trispondeus.
Tetraspondeus bimembris.
Tetraspondeus trimembris.
1990   Tetraspondeus quadrimembris.
Rithmus iambicus bimembris.
Iambicus trimembris.
Iambicus quadrimembris.

Dispondeus bimembris cum iambica differencia.
1995   Dispondeus trimembris cum iambica differencia.
Dispondeus quadrimembris cum iambica differencia.
Dispondeus antecedens, iambica differencia in secundo.
Iambica differencia antecedens, dispondaica differencia in secundo.

A Ditrochee is a foot that consists of a long and a short, a long and a short, and six beats, as *Catalina*.

An Antipest is a foot that consists of a short, two longs, and a short, and six beats, as *reservare*.

A Choriambus is a foot that consists of a long, two shorts, and a long, and six beats, as *armipotens*.

An Ionicus *a maiore* is a foot that consists of two longs and two shorts, as *Iunonius*.

An Ionicus *a minore* consists of two shorts and two longs, and six beats, as *Diomedes*.

The first Paeon is a foot that consists of one long and three shorts, and five beats, as *legitimus*.

The first Epitritus is a foot that consists of one short and three longs, and seven beats, as *sacerdotes*.

The second Paeon is a foot that consists of a short, a long, and two shorts, and five beats, as *colonia*.

The second Epitritus is a foot that consists of a long, a short, and two longs, and seven beats, as *conditores*.

The third Paeon is a foot that consists of two shorts, a long, and a short, and five beats, as *maneamus*.

The third Epitritus is a foot that consists of two longs, a short, and a long, and seven beats, as *ludibriis*.

The fourth Paeon is a foot that consists of three shorts and a long, as *celeritas*.

The fourth Epitritus is a foot that consists of three longs and a short, as *exultare*.

One-foot line.
Dispondaic.
Trispondaic.
Two-membered Tetraspondaic.
Three-membered Tetraspondaic.
Four-membered Tetraspondaic.
Two-membered Iambic.
Three-membered Iambic.
Four-membered Iambic.

Two-membered Dispondaic with Iambic Variation.
Three-membered Dispondaic with Iambic Variation.
Four-membered Dispondaic with Iambic Variation.
Dispondaics and iambics alternating, the dispondaic first.
Dispondaics and iambics alternating, the iambic first.

Trispondeus bimembris cum iambica differencia in tercio.
2000 Trispondeus trimembris cum iambica differencia in quarto.
Trispondeus quadrimembris cum iambica differencia in dyapente.
Trispondeus antecedens, iambica differencia subsequens.
Iambica differencia antecedens, trispondaica differencia subsequens.

Tetraspondaicus bimembris cum iambica differencia.
2005 Tetraspondaicus trimembris cum iambica differencia.
Tetraspondaicus quadrimembris cum iambica differencia.
Tetraspondaicus antecedens, iambica differencia subsequens.
Iambica differencia antecedens, tetraspondaica subsequens.

Rithmus iambicus bimembris cum spondaica differencia in tercio.
2010 Iambicus trimembris cum spondaica differencia in quarto.
Iambicus quadrimembris cum spondaica differencia in quinto uel
dyapente.
Iambicus antecedens, spondaicus subsequens.
Spondaicus antecedens, iambicus subsequens.

2015 Iambicus decasillabus qualis est ille rithmus.

Dispondaicus bimembris cum consonancia spondaica que facit
differenciam.
Dispondaicus trimembris cum consonancia spondaica que facit
differenciam.
2020 Dispondaicus quadrimembris cum consonancia spondaica.
Dispondaicus antecedens, consonancia spondaica subsequens.

Trispondaicus bimembris cum consonancia spondaica.
Trispondaicus trimembris cum consonancia spondaica.
Trispondaicus quadrimembris cum consonancia spondaica.
2025 Trispondaicus antecedens, consonancia spondaica subsequens.

Tetraspondaicus bimembris cum consonancia spondaica.
Tetraspondaicus trimembris cum consonancia spondaica.
Tetraspondaicus quadrimembris cum consonancia spondaica.
Tetraspondaicus antecedens, consonancia spondaica subsequens.

2030 Rithmus trispondaicus cum iambica differencia subsequente
facit duas species xiij sillabarum. Sic erunt quadraginta quatuor.
Perfecto libro sit laus et gloria Christo. Amen.

Two-membered Trispondaic with Iambic Variation in the third line.
Three-membered Trispondaic with Iambic Variation in the fourth line.
Four-membered Trispondaic with Iambic Variation in the diapente.
Trispondaics and iambics alternating, the trispondaic first.
Trispondaics and iambics alternating, the iambic first.

Two-membered Tetraspondaic with Iambic Variation.
Three-membered Tetraspondaic with Iambic Variation.
Four-membered Tetraspondaic with Iambic Variation.
Tetraspondaics and iambics alternating, the tetraspondaic first.
Tetraspondaics and iambics alternating, the iambic first.

Two-membered Iambic, with Spondaic Variation in the third line.
Three-membered Iambic with Spondaic Variation in the fourth line.
Four-membered Iambic with Spondaic Variation in the fifth line or
diapente.
Iambics and spondaics alternating, the iambic first.
Iambics and spondaics alternating, the spondaic first.

The Ten-syllable Iambic, as in "The Lament of Oedipus."

Two-membered Dispondaic with a new spondaic rhyme for a variation.
Three-membered Dispondaic with a new spondaic rhyme for a variation.
Four-membered Dispondaic with a new spondaic rhyme.
Dispondaics alternating with a new spondaic rhyme.

Two-membered Trispondaic with a new spondaic rhyme.
Three-membered Trispondaic with a new spondaic rhyme.
Four-membered Trispondaic with a new spondaic rhyme.
Trispondaics alternating with a new spondaic rhyme.

Two-membered Tetraspondaic with a new spondaic rhyme.
Three-membered Tetraspondaic with a new spondaic rhyme.
Four-membered Tetraspondaic with a new spondaic rhyme.
Tetraspondaics alternating with a new spondaic rhyme.

A Trispondaic with an iambic variation following makes two types of
thirteen syllables; that totals forty-four.

The book is finished; praise and glory to Christ. Amen.

Notes

INTRODUCTORY SUMMARY

The questions asked are standard; see Edwin A. Quain, "The Medieval *accessus ad auctores,*" *Traditio* 2 (1945): 215-64. Quain traces the practice back to the second-century Greek commentators on Aristotle; the chief vehicle for its transfer to the Latin Middle Ages seems to be Boethius's introduction to his commentary on Porphyry's *Isagoge* in Victorinus's translation. The number and nature of the points treated vary somewhat, but there is clearly a homogeneous tradition at work. Quain (p. 239) refers to a legal treatise, the *Summa Ambrosii* (ca. 1210-15), which lists the same five points as our work. To his references add Manitius, 3:196; Josef Frey, *Über das mittelalterliche Gedicht "Theoduli ecloga" und den Kommentar des Bernhardus Ultraiectensis* (Münster, 1904); Curtius, pp. 221-25, 466; R. B. C. Huygens, ed., *Conrad de Hirsau: Dialogus super auctores* (Brussels, 1955), and his augmented revision, *Accessus ad auctores, Bernard d'Utrecht, Conrad d'Hirsau: Dialogus super auctores, édition critique entièrement revue et augmentée* (Leiden, 1970); and Leslie G. Whitbread, "Conrad of Hirsau as Literary Critic," *Speculum* 47 (1972): 234-45.

John may well have written it, as Hauréau (p. 87) assumes; but its absence from *O* and the fact that it was added by a later hand in *C* suggest that if he did so he wrote it some time after completing the text.

The statement that the book belongs to Ethics may be compared with John's statement at the end of Chapter Six that what he has said is worthless if it does not contribute to virtue in his readers; but how it does that is not wholly clear. Two of the poems ("Si graue delires" [4, 207], and the series of couplets in Chapter Six) have a didactic purpose, and many of the letters display righteousness, generosity, honesty, etc., on the part of their writers, or suggest that virtue is rewarded and vice punished. The proverbs (1, 161-309), too, are a fund of moral instruction. But beyond all this there is also, I think, the old humanistic attitude that the proper end of all education is virtue. If the classical authors did not make their reader virtuous as well as literate, they were worthless; John's aim is to give his readers a better understanding of the art of poetry, which should make them, and their readers in turn, better men. See also *Anticlaudianus* 3.175-77, in a list of the functions of rhetoric:

> Quid cause genus efficiat, quo tendat et ad quem
> Deueniens finem deliberet utile, iustum
> Iudicet, affirmet rectum, demonstret honestum.

11 *secundum Tullium.* I cannot find any such statement in either *RAH* or the genuine works of Cicero. However, *honestum* is frequently called *solum bonum* and *summum bonum* in *De finibus bonorum et malorum, De officiis,* and *Tusculan disputations;* e.g.: "Necesse est, quod honestum sit, id esse aut solum aut summum bonum" (*De officiis* 3.34).

CHAPTER ONE

27 *Prosa.* This definition seems to be John's own, and rather a definition of *dictamen* in its broad sense of stylized prose than of prose itself. (Compare the definition of *dictamen* in its narrow sense of a letter in stylized prose, 5, 265).

It is too narrow to cover all the species of prose listed in ll. 49-54 below. *Prosopa* is properly πρόσωπον. *Prosos (prorsus)* is the correct etymology, although it is a contraction of *proversus,* not *productus.* Isidore says (*Etymologiae* 1:38): "Prosa est producta oratio et a lege metri soluta. Prosum enim antiqui productum dicebant et rectum."

34 *Mauricius.* Maurice was archbishop of Rouen from July 1231 to January 10, 1235. Cf. L. Fallue, *Histoire politique de l'église métropolitaine et du diocèse de Rouen* (Rouen, 1850), 2:59-70.

51 *Ystorialis* here evidently means "narrative," or even, to include *philosophi* in its strict meaning of "philosophers," "expository," in its broadest sense: as opposed to *tegnigrapha,* it embraces all nontechnical accounts of a subject, whether that subject be a series of facts or of ideas. *Philosophi* may also mean just "learned men," as I have translated it. Tragedians and comedians are merely narrative poets, writing about grave or low matter respectively. John himself provides us with examples of occasions when both write in prose: see the prose accounts that precede his comic poem (*4,* 433) and his tragedy (*7,* 28). Poets writing prose are referred to again in *5,* 426. Church use of historical prose perhaps refers to hagiography, for example in the breviary; or, as de Bruyne supposes (2:20), to "les récits bibliques." Martianus Capella and Boethius may be the sort of philosophers whose prose can be thought of as having a narrative quality, so that a relatively narrow definition of both *philosophi* and *ystorialis* is still possible. Later (*5,* 311 ff.), speaking of poetry, John divides *narratio* into *historia, fabula,* and *argumentum,* and puts tragedy under *historia,* comedy under *argumentum.*

"Ecclesiastical proses" are the sequences, as the gloss notes; see *NED,* s.v. prose, 2, and Curtius, p. 150. No dictionary I have consulted lists *technigraphus;* but its Greek form τεχνογραφος ("writer on rhetoric") is used in the prefatory letter to the pseudo-Aristotelian *Rhetorica ad Alexandrum,* which may be the *ars* of Aristotle John has in mind here.

56 Boethius, *De institutione musica,* ed. G. Friedlein (Leipzig, 1867), 1:34. John's telescoped quotation requires some explanation. The title of the chapter is "Quid sit musicus." Boethius says that in every art theory is more honorable and more important than practice, and music is no exception. He then lists three areas of the art of music: "Tria igitur genera sunt, quae circa artem musicam versantur. Unum genus est, quod instrumentis agitur, alius fingit carmina, tertium, quod instrumentorum opus carmenque diiudicat." There follow several sentences to the effect that the practitioners of the first two pay no attention to theory and are thus not real musicians. The third area, however, differs. "Quod scilicet quoniam totum in ratione ac speculatione positum est, hoc proprie musicae deputabitur, isque est musicus, cui adest facultas secundum speculationem rationemve propositam ac musice convenientem de modis ac rhythmis deque generibus cantilenarum ac de permixtionibus ac de omnibus, de quibus posterius explicandum est, ac de poetarum carminibus iudicandi." Boethius's emphasis is of course on *facultas diiudicandi;* John is only interested in his mention of *rhythmis* in the same sentence as *Isque est musicus.*

72 *Albinouanus.* The only known *Centimetrum* is that by Servius. The introduction

to Bernard of Utrecht's eleventh-century *Commentary on Theodolus* (see note to
Introductory Summary above), after discussing how meters are named, continues:
"Cetera de metris qui plenius nosse desiderat, librum Marii Servii grammatici ad Al-
binum de metrorum ratione conscriptum, vel eum qui Centrimetrum inscribitur,
legat." Bede, at the end of his *De arte metrica* (*PL* 90, col. 173) says, "Preterea
sunt metra alia perplura quae in libris Centimetrorum simplicibus monstrata exemplis quisque cupit, reperiet." Vagueness seems to have surrounded the subject early;
at least it is clear that it was something of a commonplace as a way of shutting off
a discussion of meters. A final parallel is a gloss on f. 139ʳ of ms. Bruges 546, to a
passage in John's *Compendium grammaticae* which deals with Horace and which is
written in the first Asclepiadic meter. The gloss speaks of various meters, then refers to Horace, "qui ponit x et ix metra diversa in odis et in epodis, ad que vel ad
quorum alique reducuntur cetera metra [cf. Introductory Summary, ll. 19-21 and
7, 1478-79], de quibus albinovanus composuit librum centimetrum, quod ipse reprehendit in epistolis hiis verbis, Albi nostrorum sermonum candide iudex. . . . Cetera
metra patent in summa quam composuit de metrica, rithmica, et prosaica, que sic
incipit. Parisiana iubar diffundit gloria, etc." The epistle quoted is 1.4.1, addressed
to Albius Tibullus, and in no way reprehending him for a *Centimetrum*. The previous epistle, however, 1.3, does reprehend a certain Celsus for his derivative poetry.
Most commentators identify him with the Celsus Albinovanus addressed by his full
name in *Ep.* 1.8. John may have known a tradition which assigned a *Centimetrum* to
this Albinovanus and perhaps saw a reference to it in *Ep.* 1.3; and the writer of this
gloss, his memory slipping with the help of the name Albius, wrongly quoted Epistle
4 instead of Epistle 3. (There is another Augustan poet named Albinovanus Pedo,
but he did not write a treatise on meter, nor is there a clue that anyone ever thought
he did.)

The gloss *magister Caroli* to the correction *Albinus* in *B* refers to Alcuin, who
called himself Quintus Albinus Flaccus. Since he wrote a rhetoric, the attribution
of the *Centimetrum* to him is easily made.

75 *De Inventione.* John's treatment of Invention is extremely sketchy, and arranged in a novel manner. It contains various dim recollections of the vast array of
topics of invention and devices for invention in Cicero's *De inventione* and *Topica;*
but the method of arrangement is peculiarly John's. The first part of the chapter
is based on the five questions Where, What, What Kind, How, Why. Under "Where,"
John lists three topics: persons, etymology, and examples. "Persons" appears as a
topic in *DI* 1.24, where the "attributes of persons" are named. John does not give
these here, but mentions them much later, as an appendage to the chapter on Figures (*6*, 394 ff.). Etymology is treated as a topic of invention in *Topica* 8.35. Examples are related to the argument from authority, mentioned in various places in
Topica (e.g. 4.24) but never carefully treated by Cicero.

These three topics are then subjected to the second question. Under "What is
invented in persons," there appears a brief version of Cicero's topic of contraries,
(cf. *Topica* 9.46-49), though it is not so named. "What is invented in examples"
brings John to what he clearly regarded as his principal contribution to the subject of Invention, his list of "Proverbs." "What is invented in Etymologies" merely
gives an example of an etymology.

With the third question, "What Kind," we leave the subject of topics of invention for a brief exposition of how to approach one's subject according as it is "honestum aut turpe." This subject really belongs under the Exordium, where it is put in *DI* and *RAH;* here we see John moving from consideration of matter, which is the proper realm of Invention, to form, which is his chief preoccupation throughout the treatise. The fourth question, "Why," has also little to do with Invention as such. The fifth question merely calls forth an apparently arbitrary list of seven figures of speech.

We may perhaps see behind this curious arrangement the common scholastic device of examining a subject through its various causes: questions one and two deal with the material cause of a work, and so are closest to the classical idea of Invention; questions three and five consider the formal cause, question four the final cause. This might at least explain why question four is included at all.

The second part of the chapter concerns the invention of words to body forth one's ideas; nouns, adjectives, and verbs are treated in order, with various considerations that pertain to them. This is even further removed from the classical conception of Invention, and shows John's grammatical bent.

Part of John's difficulty, of course, was that he was trying to fuse rhetoric, letter writing, and the art of poetry into one treatise; this may account for his choosing to consider the topic of "persons" (*1*, 126) according to the poetic tradition of three classes rather than the rhetorical tradition of the attributes of persons. The other late-medieval authors of *poetriae* do not treat Invention.

93-94 *S., Archidiacono Cantuariensi.* Simon Langton, brother of the illustrious Stephen Langton, archbishop of Canterbury, was archdeacon of Canterbury from 1227 to his death in 1248. The repeated expressions of friendship in the letter suggest that John may have known him. Before Simon was archdeacon he took part against King John with Louis the Dauphin, who made him his chancellor when both were expelled from England in 1217. Thus John may have met him in Paris as well as in England. Perhaps, however, he is merely being impressive.

111 *misochomio.* Apparently unrecorded elsewhere. But the gloss *maladerie* and the general sense of the passage leave no doubt that it means "leper house"; cf. also John's *Clavis compendii,* ms. Bruges 546, f. 41ʳ: "Pauper que capiat xenodochia sunt peregrinus,/ Et leprosorum misocomia sunt miserorum."

117 I cannot locate this quotation in either the authentic or spurious writings of Seneca. The closest thing to it is *De vita beata* 3.4: "Intelligis, etiam si non adiciam, sequi perpetuam tranquillitatem libertatem, depulsis eis quae aut irritant nos aut territant."

122 *qualitas carminis.* Cf. *5*, 88-89 and gloss to *1*, 133; it clearly means "style." *Qualitas carminis* is one of the questions in Servius's *accessus* to Virgil's *Aeneid,* where it means "the kind of poem"; since each kind of poem has its appropriate style, the development to this meaning is easy.

124 *Tria Genera Hominum.* Elsewhere John divides men into soldiers (or princes), farmers, shepherds (cf. Figure Three, p. 40; the levels of style, *5*, 45). This was in accord with normal medieval doctrine, based on Virgil's three poems, and drawn from Donatus's *Life of Virgil.* (Cf. Curtius, p. 201n., p. 232; Faral p. 87; for a full treatment of the whole subject and its connection with the levels of style, see Franz

Quadlbauer, *Die antike Theorie der genera dicendi im lateinischen Mittelalter* [Vienna, 1962]. Quadlbauer collects all of John's remarks on the subject and discusses them, chiefly in terms of their sources and relation to the tradition, on pp. 113-25.) But here, despite the statement connecting them with Virgil, we have obviously a different (and more realistic) triad. The two different triads are once again tacitly connected in *2*, 90-127, where, after discussing memory according to the courtiers-city-dwellers-peasants triad, John moves immediately to the wheel of Virgil and its soldier-farmer-shepherd triad.

Although it does not appear in any of the texts in Rockinger's collection (though something similar appears in the treatise of Ludolfus, Rockinger, 1: 360-61; see Quadlbauer, p. 274, who points out that John's and Ludolfus's works are related, though the priority is uncertain), John's new triad is clearly connected with the problems of letter writers, and it seems that what we have here is an original but not thoroughly thought-out attempt to fuse *dictamen* and *poetria* (cf. Quadlbauer, p. 116).

158 As the examples show, by "proverb" John does not mean a popular maxim but a brief general statement invented by the author of a letter to suit his purpose, by serving as a kind of major premise on which he can construct the argument of his letter. Even when the sentiment is proverbial, as is frequently enough true, the expression is always that of the *dictator,* never of the folk.

229 Cf. Ovid, *Metamorphoses* 9.614-15: "Nec rigidas silices solidumve in pectore ferrum/Aut adamanta gerit."

255 Cf. *Anticlaudianus* 1.169-70: "in primo limine fessus/Heret."

263 *De iudicibus.* That is, unknown angles are measured by dropping perpendiculars. If an error is made in drawing the perpendicular, the measurement of the angle will also be in error. Thus a judge does not "measure" a dubious case on the basis of some law or principle which is itself in doubt.

281 *Frontis nulla fides.* Cf. Juvenal 2.8: "fronti nulla fides."

288 *Cheruli.* Horace's type of a bad poet. Cf. *AP* 357; *Epistles* 2.1.233.

292 Cf. *Aen.* 6.126: "Facilis descensus Averno."

298 A difficult sentence. My translation attributes two different senses to *perimo,* which is unlikely; and yet *perimit sensum* cannot mean "cuts off the feeling itself." Possibly *sensum* is the past participle of *sentio,* "the thing felt," and equivalent to *sensibile:* "cuts off only the object of feeling; the feeling itself is unchanged." But it seems likely that in that case *sensibile* would have been repeated, and the subject of *conuertitur* expressed.

Another possibility is that *sed non conuertitur* means "but not vice versa," as it does at *5*, 372, 395. Then the proverb would mean, "If you send me away from you, your feeling for me will die; but if you kill your feeling for me—as you have done—it does not follow that I will go away; thus I tag after you, etc." If this is the meaning, the first phrase may be an epistemological axiom: if there is no sense-object, then the sense has only a potential, not an actual, existence: there can be no actual hearing without sound, though there can be sound without hearing. This is good Aristotelian doctrine, though I cannot find the phrase as such in the *De anima* or elsewhere.

305 According to the Ptolemaic astronomy, the sun has two movements. In the first place, it takes part in the daily revolution of the whole Heavens (*firmamentum*) from east to west about the earth, the fixed center. This accounts for day and night, and is the motion referred to in *regirat secum eundem*. But the sun also appears to move annually from west to east among the signs of the zodiac. See Mary A. Orr, *Dante and the Early Astronomers*, rev. ed. (London, 1956), pp. 22-24, and *The Comedy of Dante Alighieri; Cantica* I: *Hell*, trans. Dorothy L. Sayers (New York, Basic Books, n.d.), p. 292. Cf. *De planctu naturae*, Prose 3: "Et sicut contra ratam firmamenti volutionem motu contradictorio exercitus militat planetarum, sic in homine sensualitatis rationisque continua reperitur hostilitas."

307 *Ad reuocandum.* The faculty apparently is medicine (cf. gloss to *experimentum*), although according to Rashdall (1:428) the earliest statute of the faculty of medicine at Paris is ca. 1270-74.

314 There is no such Greek word meaning "admirable"; but Papias sheds light on the derivation: "Papa: παπα admirabilis, maior pater et custos, a pape." "Pape (papae): παπυ interiectio est admirantis; unde papa idest admirabilis." *Papa* is actually derived from πάππος, "grandfather."

333-34 *Annominatio . . . Sermocinatio.* All these figures are treated again in Chapter Six, several at greater length. There seems no reason for choosing these particular seven, as all the figures treated in Chapter Six serve both to "embellish and amplify." For *Annominatio*, see *5*, 214-34; *6*, 139-87; *Traductio*, *6*, 83-90; *Repetitio*, *6*, 71-79; *Gradatio*, *6*, 202-12; *Interpretatio*, *6*, 244-47; *Diffinitio*, *6*, 213-15; *Sermocinatio*, *6*, 373-78. A somewhat different list of devices for amplification is given at *4*, 309 ff.

337 Literally, "The pathless groves." The same pair of words is used in *RAH* to illustrate Paronomasia by Shortening a Letter: "Hinc avium dulcedo ducit ad avium" (4.21.29).

354 *Epytalamico Beate Uirginis.* An unedited poem of about 6600 lines by John of Garland. Cf. Paetow, pp. 113-14. This couplet is Book One, ll. 362-63 (British Museum Ms. Cotton Claudius A. x., f. 5^v, ll. 19-20). All subsequent quotations from this poem (*EBV*) are identified in the translation by book and line from this manuscript. Though Paetow and others use the classical form *Epithalamium,* John consistently writes *Epithalamicum,* evidently making a substantive out of the adjective in the phrase *epithalamicum carmen.* For a thorough study of its background and discussion of its encyclopedic contents, see Evelyn Faye Wilson, "A Study of the Epithalamium in the Middle Ages: An Introduction to the *Epithalamium Beate Marie Virginis* of John of Garland" (University of California at Berkeley Ph.D. thesis, 1931); on p. 172n. Wilson explains the form *epithalamicum.* Some of the material of this thesis is contained in Wilson's article, "Pastoral and Epithalamium in Latin Literature," *Speculum* 23 (1948):35-57; for John's poem see esp. pp. 43-52. Cf. also two articles in *Quadrivium* 1 (1956): Antonio Saiani, "L' 'Astrologia spiritualis' nell' *Epithalamium* e nella *Stella maris* di Giovanni di Garlandia," pp.

208-55, and Giuseppe Vecchi, "Modi d'arte poetica in Giovanni di Garlandia e il ritmo *Aula vernat virginalis,*" pp. 256-68.

360 Literally, "Peter I was, whom the rock covers." The full text of this famous epitaph, said to have been composed by Peter Comestor himself, is as follows:

> Petrus eram, quem petra tegit, dictusque Comestor
> Nunc comedor. Vivus docui, nec cesso docere
> Mortuus, ut dicat qui me videt incineratum:
> "Quod sumus, iste fuit; erimus quandoque quod hic est."
>   (*PL* 198, col. 1048)

It is quoted in full in one of the works on *Equivoca* attributed to John. See Hauréau, p. 62.

367 *Sermocinacio* is dialogue; one of its characteristics is that it must fit the speaker's rank and character. Cf. *RAH* 4.52.65, and below, 6, 373. But here John curiously defines it through its characteristic rather than through its essence; though the example is a piece of dialogue, he clearly chose it for the phrase *primordia gentis.* This emphasis on rank leads to the parenthetical discussion of proper salutations, a topic dealt with more fully in its proper place in 4, 103-42 and 5, 260-96; most of what is said here is repeated in one of those places.

379 *Fredericus.* Frederick II of Sicily was Holy Roman emperor 1220-50.

385 *pascua, grex, ouis.* Note that these three words occur in the "pastoral" poem that opens Chapter One.

392-93 As the glosses note, *oue, agna,* and *lana* are Mary, *pastor, dux aries,* and *agnum* Christ. For Gideon's fleece (gloss), cf. Judg. 6:36-40.

396 *amabeum.* CL *amoebaeus,* which means "responsive," "alternating," and was applied to a pastoral singing match in which the second competitor replies to the first in the same number of verses. Virgil's third and eighth eclogues exemplify this, as does Spenser's August eclogue. John's poem, then, is not truly amoebaean, although since it contains an altercation in dialogue it approaches being so, and conforms to John's more or less correct definition of the form at 5, 368. Yet both here and there he clearly derives the word from *amo;* it is uncertain whether the incorrect spelling (it should be *amebeum* in ML) is the cause or the effect of that mistaken etymology. The gloss *ab inuentore* introduces further confusion.

399-400 Cf. note to *1,* 124; see also *2,* 116-23 and *5,* 45-60.

407-56 John had a precedent for using the pastoral form for Christian allegory in the *Eclogue* of Theodolus, the Carolingian poem which was a common school-text for beginners, and which he mentions at 5, 369 as an example of an amoebaean poem. Indeed his opening situation (spring; a shepherd and shepherdess relaxing from sheep-herding to play instruments and sing) closely parallels that of Theodolus's poem.

Personifying the World or the Devil, the Flesh, and Reason was a favorite device of John's; he uses it again in the poem "Si graue delires" (*4,* 226, 265, 271) and also at 6, 113 and 7, 1760. Here a youth, the World or the Devil, lures Phyllis (Flesh) from her former lover Corydon (Reason).

Since it is not always immediately clear who is speaking, I append the following outline. The first stanza is spoken by the narrator, the youth (the World or the Devil). The first six lines of the second stanza are spoken by Phyllis; they comprise part of her song on Daphnis (Christ). The youth speaks again through the third line of the third stanza. There follows an exchange between Phyllis and Corydon; the last line of stanza three is spoken by the youth. Phyllis speaks the first six lines of stanza four, and the youth (not Corydon) the final six lines. The closing couplet is outside the poem proper, and is spoken by the poet.

The "low style" is to be found in the use of shepherds' names (especially Daphnis for Christ), the references to objects that pertain to sheepherding: *oues, fago, gregem, fistula;* and also perhaps in the natural imagery. The coarse activities of the youth and Phyllis, Corydon's falling into the ditch, and Phyllis's vituperation of Corydon are probably not of themselves features of the low style, since similar characteristics are present in the poem "Qvasdam turma" (7, 28), which is said to be written in the high style. Nor does the low style prevent John from using precious words like *citharizat, Nestor, ephebus,* etc. "Colors of rhetoric" also abound, from the series of personifications in the first stanza to several examples of John's favorite device, *Annominatio: Phebus, ephebus; colo, sola, solo; uita* (life), *uita* (shun), and the very involved word play between *amo, amor, hamo,* and *hamus* in the last stanza. (For embellishment in the low style, cf. *4,* 416 ff. and *5,* 80 ff.)

Edmond Faral, "La pastourelle," *Romania* 49 (1923):204–59, quotes the poem (in a text which improves on Mari in some places but is not altogether correct) to substantiate his theory that the *pastourelle* derived from a scholarly tradition. W. P. Jones, "Some Recent Studies of the Pastourelle," *Speculum* 5 (1930):207–15, rightly disputes Faral's rather high-handed conclusions, and points out that some important features of the *pastourelle* are absent from John's poem. Still it is clear that there is some connection with that form, whose typical action is the wooing away of a shepherdess from her lover. The whole question of the *pastourelle* is newly aired by William Paden, "The Pastourelle" (Yale Ph.D. thesis, 1971).

417 *predones . . . fugasse leones.* Perhaps a reference to Christ's driving the money-changers from the temple (Matt. 21:12-13); but it may also have a more general application; cf. the devil as lion in 1 Peter 5:8.

418 The refrain is rather forced here and at the end of the third stanza; it comes somewhat more naturally at the end of stanzas two and four. It is not wholly clear to me what the refrain means; but since the youth represents the Devil as well as the World, the meaning is probably that the Devil, though ultimately consigned to Hell, is allowed to roam the world freely (Cf. 1 Peter 5:8). The "laqueus diaboli" is a common Christian image (cf. 1 Tim. 3:7; 6:9; 2 Tim. 2:26); here the Devil is considered as himself (eventually) ensnared. *M*'s gloss at the end of the third stanza, "because any lover thinks he is free, though he is not" does not quite make sense, since it is the youth himself who says he is in the trap.

419 Phyllis's poem on Christ has little relation to the plot; the youth is drawing her from reason, not religion, and he even plays the accompaniment to her song. It seems rather to have been inserted by John as a striking example of how one may treat a high subject in the low style; cf. *5,* 51 ff.

429 *Emulus ecce uenit.* Cf. Matt. 25:6: "Ecce sponsus venit."

451-53 The general sense of *Sic uir . . . tendit amor* seems similar to the second half of the refrain: *liber amator eo.* Line 453 is to be taken, not as a plaintive cry, but as a confident piece of advice.

459 This list shows the influence of Dialectic. Four of the considerations (*habitus, locus, quantitas, qualitas*) are included in Aristotle's ten categories, and *genus* is one of his five predicables. *Genus* is also one of the topics or commonplaces, as is *effectus;* and *euentus* may be considered as equivalent to another commonplace, *consequens.* (Cf. Cicero, *Topica* 3.2.2. The topics of invention are, of course, a principal piece of common ground between logic and rhetoric.)

465-66 *Peleya uirgo.* Achilles, in the guise of a girl (Statius, *Achilleid* 1.884). *Priameius heros.* Hector (*Laus Pisonis,* 1. 174). This poem was known in the Middle Ages, and ascribed to Lucan. Cf. Gladys Martin, ed., *Laus Pisonis* (Ithaca, N.Y., 1917), pp. 6-7.

476-90 The quotation of Aristotle is from the pseudo-Boethian translation of the *Categories,* which frequently accompanied Boethius's commentary on that book in manuscripts: see *PL* 64, col. 227. Aristotle is discussing the category "relation," in accordance with which words are defined in relation to something else. "Servant" is a relative word because it implies a master; its correlative is "master." But a word such as "oar" (*remus*) has no accurate correlative in ordinary language ("boat" is wrong, Aristotle insists); one must coin a term such as "oared things" (*remita*) in order to designate its correlative. John takes the discussion as licensing coinage of both new verbs in particular and new words in general (note the shift from *verbum* through *nomen* to *dictio*), especially since coinage is ratified for literature by Horace, who speaks of coinage in the eleven lines following those John quotes at 1. 482; the metaphor from the minting of coins (*signatum praesente nota*) is in 1. 59. Gervase of Melkley discusses coinage fully in Gräbener, pp. 89-107; cf. Faral, "Le Manuscrit 511 du 'Hunterian Museum' de Glasgow," *Studi medievali,* N.S. 9 (1936): 92-103. John did not coin the word *hymnizo:* the *Thesaurus linguae latinae* lists seven appearances in early Christian Latin.

491 Metaphor is treated again at *2,* 255-310 and *6,* 305-8. In both these places John regards it, as he does here, as mainly the province of the verb. But at *6,* 306 he says that it may also be applied to a noun, or to the whole sentence; at *2,* 259-60 he mentions adjectives and nouns; at *2,* 277 he also deals with a metaphor extended through the whole sentence. The classical writers make no distinction by parts of speech, nor does Matthew of Vendôme; Geoffrey of Vinsauf devotes most of his discussion to verbs, but also treats adjectives and nouns, and mentions "tota oratio" (*Poetria nova,* ll. 765-945). In the *Documentum* he treats verbs chiefly (pp. 286-89, # 9-22), but also adjectives in # 16.

CHAPTER TWO

None of John's predecessors include Selection among the parts of Rhetoric; to them, Invention is itself a selective process. John's division is based on *AP* 38-41, as his comment on that passage (see *1,* 76) indicates. He has virtually expanded Horace's single word *lecta* into a whole chapter. But the material he presents has little to do with Horace's dictum; that merely provides him with the name of the chapter, and its key verb. The actual material is drawn from Geoffrey's *Documentum*, and there is nothing in the processes described to distinguish them from Invention—we might substitute *invenire* for *eligere* throughout.

The chapter begins with some principles of selection, which are never taken up; the admonition to choose what is "light and plain" brings us quickly to the main subject of the chapter, "complex" vs. "simple" embellishment. "Slight" subject matter can be raised by selecting tropes; difficult subject matter can be eased by avoiding tropes, and yet embellished without compounding difficulty by the repetition of modifiers; that is, selecting several of them. What comprises difficulty or slightness is never made clear. It may be noted, however, that all the examples are letters, and the relative social standing of sender and recipient is apparently the key. Thus a minor cleric complaining to his bishop of an assault is forced to make his matter "grave" via complex embellishment, presumably because the sordid facts of the assault are out of keeping with the bishop's dignity. The bishop's citation of the culprit is, on the other hand, difficult matter, calling for "simple embellishment"; here it is evident that the situation calls for plainness and simplicity, but it is not so clear why the subject matter is difficult. Perhaps John was too concerned with stating an exact antithesis, slight matter-complex embellishment vs. difficult matter-simple embellishment. Actually, any subject seems susceptible of either method of treatment.

After two unexplained examples of difficult matter lightened (ll. 13-43), we are given the theory of "complex embellishment," with an example, and explanation of the example (44-86). Then, after a diversion to the subjects of memory (87-115) and levels of style (116-23), John presents the opposite theory of simple embellishment, by avoiding tropes (124-46), and by "modification" (147-end). This is organized according to the parts of speech, with some confusion. First comes modification of proper nouns (151-62), then common nouns (163-93), verbs (194-210), common nouns again (211-15) and adjectives (215-65). The criteria for discussion switch and broaden with the discussion of adjectives, from by what other parts of speech a word is modified to how it modifies, strictly or metaphorically. This is interrupted for some brief remarks on the repetition of adverbs, conjunctions, interjections, and prepositions (231-51), which seem to be included for the sake of a specious completeness—now all the parts of speech have been treated. At 252 the original criterion of the discussion is resumed, and we are told how adjectives are modified. This, however, leads once more to metaphor, to which the remainder of the chapter (266-310) is devoted, without any statement of its relation to the main subject of simple embellishment.

7 Cf. *AP* 333-34: "Aut prodesse volunt aut delectare poetae,/Aut simul et iucunda et idonea dicere vitae." Horace, of course, uses *iucunda* as synonymous with *delectare* John treats them as separate ideas.

11 *leue*. This must be *lĕue*, "light," not *lēue*, "smooth," both because of the contrast to *grauem* at ll. 44-45 and because of the form *leuiter*, l. 148: *lēviter*, "smoothly," does not occur. One also assumes there is a connection between *leue et planum* and the Provencal *trobar clar*, which was also called *trobar leu* and *trobar plan* (cf.

H. J. Chaytor, *From Script to Print* [Cambridge, 1945], p. 67). Yet in l. 14 the word seems to be *lēuem* since it is parallel to *enodem*.

15-43 The "difficulty" of the subject matter of these letters seems to lie simply in the fact that they are requests to high personages. The things "selected" to make it smooth seem to be, in the first letter, the "proverb" at the start, the apparent shift of responsibility to the abbot, and the closing statement. Also, in view of ll. 124-27 and 148-162, the lack of figurativeness (that is, the "selection" of nonfigurative words), and adjectives such as *honeste, morigerato, erudito*.

The second letter, while figurative, contains none of the tropes listed in ll. 45-48; *conformis lilio castitatis albedine* is an example of modification. The "proverb" also serves, though it is not as appealing to the recipient as the proverb in the first letter; and in spite of the closing statement and the reminder of eternal reward, this letter in fact seems rather blunt and "knotty." Still, if *facilis ornatus* merely consists in avoiding tropes and modifying words, these letters fit that category.

46 John's treatment of complex and simple embellishment is a brief summary of that by Geoffrey of Vinsauf, *Documentum*, 2.3.1-102 (Faral, pp. 284-303). Geoffrey lists seven tropes where John lists nine; but Geoffrey treats "part for the whole or whole for the part" as one; he adds *significans pro significato*, and leaves out genus and species. Neither John nor Geoffrey ever calls them "tropes" (though Matthew of Vendôme does; cf. 3.18, Faral, p. 172); Geoffrey assigns each a name as he treats it, while John never does. It is notable that John omits *significans pro significato*, since Geoffrey includes metaphor under this heading. John evidently considered metaphor as belonging to Simple Embellishment, for he treats it under modification—see below, 2, 266-310.

Faral discusses "L'Ornement Difficile" on pp. 89-90, and connects it in a vague way with the theory of the three levels of style. It should be noted, however, that although John uses the word *grauem* (2, 45), complex embellishment seems not to be connected with high style; the latter is chiefly a function of subject matter and diction, the former of linguistic devices. That is, one can deal with a low subject, choosing words appropriate to the low style; if the words are tropes, that is *ornatus difficilis*, but it is still low style.

87-115 The reference is to *RAH* 3.16.28-3.24.40, where the classical system of the "artificial memory" is carefully elaborated. (See also Cicero, *De oratore* 2.351-59 and Quintilian, *Institutio oratoria* 11.2.1-51; Wilbur S. Howell, *Logic and Rhetoric in England, 1500-1700* [Princeton, 1956], pp. 85-90; and Harry Caplan, "Memoria: Treasure-House of Eloquence," in his *Of Eloquence: Studies in Ancient and Mediaeval Rhetoric*, ed. Anne King and Helen North [Ithaca, N.Y., 1970], pp. 196-246.) The best account of the system is the first chapter of Frances Yates, *The Art of Memory* (London, 1966); among its merits is the frank admission that the system is not fully graspable by the modern mind. John characteristically abridges and confuses the system. *RAH* speaks of an indeterminate number of "places" or "backgrounds" into which one inserts the "images" he wishes to remember. John reduces these to three; furthermore, he is clearly thinking of a geometric diagram rather than a real place as advocated by the classical writers, and the whole system is applied only to remembering what is said in the classroom.

The three columns represent the three sources of invention: character, examples, and etymology (cf. *1*, 91). The tripartite division of the first column into *curiales, ciuiles, rurales* is of course John's own. The second column corresponds roughly to what the author of *RAH* has to say on memorizing words as opposed to things (3.20.33). Here again, the classical authors advocate *imagining* situations and images to go with words; John calls for a mere natural memory of the actual situation in which they are heard or read. The third column is peculiarly John's and rather obscure. Its province seems to be the meanings of words by themselves, as opposed to "sayings," which go in the second column. The last part is clear; one stores new words learned in this column, adding to them some physical image by which they may be remembered more easily. But the point of first imagining that all languages and all words are potentially in one's mind, or how "each considers what word fits his own language" (or, perhaps, "tongue"), escapes me. Perhaps it is simply a way of describing the ideal third column, and suggesting its range.

As for the diagram, the first column is clear enough. The second and third columns seem to have been divided into rows purely because the first one was; they follow no general rationale. The first two rows of the third column probably take up *voces animantium;* they may, however, also be the "natural phonenema" to be used as symbols of words. It may, indeed, be possible to discover what John may have meant by combining these two ideas. The *voces animantium*, or the proper verbs to use for every animal, were a popular subject. (The *locus classicus* is Suetonius, *De natura rerum* 161; cf. Augustus Reifferscheid, ed., *Suetoni praeter Caesarum libros reliquae* [Leipzig, 1860], pp. 247 ff. They are treated in the Middle Ages by, among others, Isidore, Aldhelm, Papias, and Evrard de Bethune in the *Graecismus*. Cf. Manitius, 3:137.) Evrard says, for instance (19.33), "leo rugit," "the lion roars." If the teacher explains the word *rugo*, the student may remember it by attaching to it the mental picture of a lion. This interpretation greatly reduces the scope of the process, but it helps to explain the prominence John accords to animals, especially in the diagram.

Another possibility is suggested by a system which Yates describes on pp. 118-20, and which she says occurs frequently in manuscript treatises (of the fourteenth and fifteenth centuries) on Memory. This involves adopting the name of a bird or animal starting with each letter of the alphabet to remember words beginning with that letter. Thus if the teacher explains the etymology of *comoedia* as *comos, villa*, and *odos, cantus*, as John does at *4*, 472, the student may remember the etymology by associating the word *comoedia* in his mind with, say, a cow (*vacca*) and a dog (*canis*). It does not get you very far, but John may simply have been trying to draw some practical value out of a system which can never have worked very well for very many people in its full form. John of Salisbury says of it, "similibus mei non multum prodest" (*Metalogicon*, 1.20).

The only text in Faral that treats memory is Geoffrey of Vinsauf's *Poetria nova*, ll. 1969-2030. Geoffrey also follows the *RAH* system, but in a very general way which is of little help in understanding John's treatment. Like John of Salisbury, he expresses skepticism toward it. Ll. 2010-16 and 2024-25 resemble John's second column somewhat. Yates devotes a chapter to "The Art of Memory in the Middle Ages," but she seems not to have known of, or bothered with, John's or Geoffrey's brief treatments. Yet both, and John's especially, represent an important qualification of her central argument that "the artificial memory has moved over from rhetoric to ethics."

108 *differentias.* A technical term. Cf. Alcuin, *Grammatica (PL* 101, col. 858): "Differentia est distinctio duarum rerum cum interpretatione, ut: 'rex dicitur, quia modestus est; tyrannus, quia crudelis est.'" Isidore, Bede, and Alcuin, among others, compiled lists of *differentiae verborum.* For a history of the genre, and an exemplary text, see Myra L. Uhlfelder, *De Proprietate Sermonum vel Rerum: A Study and Critical Edition of a Set of Verbal Distinctions* (Rome, 1954).

116 The wheel seems to be included here simply because the three columns of the memory diagram reminded John of it. Note that it contains the old triad of soldier-farmer-shepherd rather than John's new triad (cf. note to *1,* 124). The new triad has just appeared in the memory diagram, yet John fails to comment on their differences.

The theory of the three styles has been treated fully by others. Briefly, the Middle Ages derived it from two sources: *RAH* 4.8.11, wherein three levels of elocution (*gravis, mediocris,* and *extenuata*) are distinguished; and Donatus's *Vita Virgiliana.* Combining the two moved the basis for distinction from being purely stylistic, as in *RAH,* to include subject matter. As Curtius points out, the theory in its large outlines was still of vital importance to Spenser and Milton. (Cf. Faral pp. 86-89; Curtius pp. 231-32, 201n.; and Franz Quadlbauer, *Die antike Theorie der genera dicendi im lateinischen Mittelalter* [Vienna, 1962]). The wheel is John's own contribution (cf. Quadlbauer, pp. 114, 124).

147-48 This rubric applies through l. 265. John's discussion of "simple embellishment by modification" is a condensation of *Documentum* 2.3.48-131 (Faral, pp. 293-309). Geoffrey's discussion is necessary for understanding John's. "Modification" means virtually any syntactic connection of words: even in a simple sentence like "I write," the verb "write" is considered as "modifying" the subject. Modification by itself, however, does not constitute embellishment; the essence of embellishment lies in the repetition of modifiers, what Geoffrey calls *inculcatio:* "unica determinatio non facit ornatum, sed inculcatio determinationum" (Faral, p. 295, # 56). John never states this important principle, though he understands it, since all his examples are of multiple modification. (The word *inculcatio* appears in the gloss to *2,* 234, and John uses it at *6,* 39 for an example of repetition of adverbs that is just like that given here at l. 234). It is the principle of *inculcatio* that explains John's apparently abrupt shift to discussing repetition of conjunctions, interjections, and prepositions at l. 237: the question whether to repeat words like these naturally arises when one is composing an *inculcatio.* The example given of polysyndeton at l. 240, for instance, is also an example of "several substantives modified by several verbs." Another reason for including them is that the discussion of modification is organized by parts of speech: modification of nouns, adjectives, and verbs; adding these parts of speech rounds out the discussion.

Geoffrey's treatment of the subject is orderly and absolutely thoroughgoing: he treats all the permutations in each case. When treating the modification of a substantive by a verb, for instance, he covers separately each possibility: several substantives modified by several verbs, one by several, and several by one. John begins in this way, treating proper nouns rather thoroughly. But he mixes the treatment of adjectives and verbs together, and does not touch on every possibility. He moves farther away from Geoffrey as he goes on, introducing conjunctions, etc. at l. 237, and discussing modification under the heading of clarity, not embellishment, in ll. 252-65. It is metaphorical adjectives that have prompted him to raise this question of clarity, and at l. 266 he closes the chapter with a treatment of metaphorical verbs. At this point he has abandoned the subject of "simple embellishment" entirely, since metaphor is a trope, and belongs to "complex embellishment." In fact the method he gives here for composing a metaphor is apparently based on Geoffrey's treatment, which rightly occurs under complex embellishment (Faral, pp. 286-87, #10-11). Yet the confusion as to metaphor may be in the doctrine itself, for at one point in his discussion of simple embellishment Geoffrey seems to allow for metaphor: "fere enim ubique alias inculcatio determinationum facit ornatum, non unica determinatio, nisi forte dictio determinans ponatur translative, ut hic 'Ridet ager.' Tunc enim sufficit unica determinatio ad ornatum" (Faral, p. 293, #51). But Geoffrey does not return to this; he is concerned solely with *inculcatio*.

At the end of his discussion Geoffrey states furthermore that all the figures of speech except the tropes contribute to simple embellishment; John never says that, and thus fails to connect his later treatment of embellishment in Chapter Six with this one.

151 *adiectiuum.* The ancient grammarians considered the adjective as a species of noun, literally an "added noun," that is, a noun that is added to a substantive noun.

198-205 The general sense of these verses is clear, though there are various obscurities. Apparently the emotion in stanza one is gratitude on the part of the cleric to all fathers, since the Holy Father, the *pater patrum* (cf. *1*, 312), has freed him. It may also mean, however, "to all the Fathers," that is, to all his fellow clerics in his order or house. In stanza two the speaker passes to his own exaltation—he seems to be no longer on his knees. The judge described in stanza three (*creticus = criticus*) may be an official of a local ecclesiastical court who originally excommunicated him, in "flattery" for his own immediate superior, or perhaps for some dignitary who originally preferred charges against the speaker. The fourth stanza is clear.

In its present form the poem is accentual, not quantitative, and is thus properly called a *rhythmus*; it is written in the socalled "Goliardic measure" (trochaic tetrameter catalectic alternating with trochaic trimeter; cf. "Aestuans intrinsecus ira vehementi" and below, 7, 610) with the rhyming spondee added. When read backward it is quantitative, but still rhymes, and so is properly called a leonine.

215 *egregie dicitur.* Cf. *AP* 47, "dixeris egregie," quoted at *1*, 483 above.

219-23 This figure is treated as a species of *Annominatio* at *6*, 183; Geoffrey relates *Annominatio* to simple embellishment in Faral, pp. 296-97, #63-64.

239 *Tullio.* Cf. *RAH* 4.19.26. *Membrum* is not actually equivalent to polysyndeton, though it employs polysyndeton. John uses it correctly at *6*, 118.

250-51 This couplet is adapted from *EBV* 5.415-16. The poet is reflecting on the presentation of the infant Mary in the temple:

> Virginibus virgo sanctis est tradita sancta,
> Castis casta, bonis est sociata bona.

> Est melior commissa bonis, reginaque celi
> Est ancilla Dei, libera mente tamen.
> Sic seruire Deo, sic digne viuere semper
> Dat regnare Deo, semper habere Deum.

The substitution of *semper* for *digne* in our text suggests that it, not *Deo* or *sic*, is the "faulty" word whose repetition excuses the fault. But I do not understand what is faulty about the use of *semper* by itself, unless it is considered tautological, *sic uiuere* alone implying *semper*. Perhaps it is a matter of word order, *poni uiciose* meaning "placed badly"; *semper* ordinarily precedes its verb. Thus, in the line from *EBV*, *digne viuere semper* is faulty; but if *digne* is replaced by *semper* the emphatic repetition excuses the placing of the second *semper*.

266 Another method of composing a verbal metaphor (by transposing "physical" and "mental" verbs) appears at *1*, 491. As I noted above, the method given here is expounded by Geoffrey in the *Documentum* (Faral, pp. 286-87, #10-11); the ultimate source is probably Quintilian, *Institutio oratoria* 8.6.9-10, though only in Geoffrey have I found explicit use of the word *commune*.

CHAPTER THREE

Chapter Three holds strictly to its organization, with no digressions. It achieves this, however, by effectively reducing *dispositio* to *inchoatio*. The first paragraph contains a few general remarks on disposition, but speedily arrives at the "artificial beginning," which forms the subject of the remainder of the chapter. The doctrine agrees exactly with the *Documentum* (1.1-2.1.12; Faral, pp. 265-71), and various verbal reminiscences suggest that John was consciously following it.

4 *progressus*. Cf. Geoffrey of Vinsauf, *Poetria nova*, l. 204, and the opening sentence of the *Documentum* (Faral, p. 265): "Tria sunt circa quae cujuslibet operis versatur artificium: principium, progressus, consummatio." *conclusio*. The classical rhetoricians' word for the end of a speech, or peroration: cf. *DI* 1.52.98; *RAH* 2. 30.47.

5-6 Cf. *Poetria nova*, ll. 58-59: "Opus totum prudens in pectoris arcem / Contrahe, sitque prius in pectore quam sit in ore."

12 The word *narratur* here is significant, for the whole doctrine clearly applies only to narrative poetry. Geoffrey states clearly that he is speaking only of narrative (1.4-5; Faral, p. 266).

22 The history of Saint Denis is full of confusion. There are three personages involved. The first is Saint Denis, the first bishop of Paris, who Gregory of Tours (*Historia Francorum* 1.30) says was sent into Gaul ca. *A.D.* 250 and martyred there. The second is Dionysius the Areopagite, an Athenian mentioned in Acts 17:34. The third is "Pseudo-Dionysius," the theological writer who flourished perhaps in the fifth century. Hilduin, abbot of Saint-Denis (814-40), identified all three in his *Areopagitica* (*PL* 106), and thus "persuaded Christendom for the next seven hundred years that Dionysius of Paris, Dionysius of Athens, and the author of the 'Dionysian' writings were one and the same person" (*Butler's Lives of the Saints*,

ed., rev. and suppl. Herbert Thurston, S.J., and Donald Atwater [New York, 1956],
4:68.) Their account continues: "In his 'Areopagitica' Abbot Hilduin made use of
spurious and worthless materials, and it is difficult to believe in his complete good
faith; the life is a tissue of fables. The Areopagite comes to Rome where Pope St.
Clement I receives him and sends him to evangelize the Parisii. They try in vain to
put him to death by wild beasts, fire, and crucifixion; then, together with Rusticus
and Eleutherius, he is successfully beheaded on Montmartre. The dead body of St.
Dionysius rose on its feet and, led by an angel, walked the two miles from Montmartre to where the abbey of Saint-Denis now stands, carrying its head in its hands
and surrounded by singing angels, and so was there buried."

74 *Elycone.* Mt. Helicon was thought to be a well by many medieval writers.
Cf. Chaucer's *House of Fame,* l. 522: "Elicon, the clere welle."

CHAPTER FOUR

There is no indication in the text of the beginning of Chapter Four, but I have begun it here in accordance with the plan announced at the beginning (cf. *1*, 15-25).
The chapter deals with much more than the parts of a letter, however. It is clear
that what John had in mind was to cover all the chief aspects, as he saw them, of
dispositio in Chapters Three and Four. Chapter Three covers the first part of *dispositio,* how to begin, in poems. Chapter Four then turns, logically enough, to how
to begin letters. But since the beginning is only one part, it proceeds next to consider the other parts of a letter. That done, we are given the six parts of a classical
oration, which are applied to a poem. A treatise on amplification and abbreviation
follows, with no transition; but it is clearly to be connected with the narration.
The last type of amplification involves the levels of style; the discussion is exemplified by a poem in the low style, which leads to a short treatise on the parts of
tragedies and comedies. The chapter closes with some couplets on the parts of
various documents.

   Though put this way the discussion seems orderly enough, it is actually one more
illustration of John's failure to cope adequately with the problems inherent in his
broadened scope. Geoffrey, in the *Documentum,* had divided a work into beginning, middle, and end, and so had passed smoothly from discussing the ways to begin to amplification and abbreviation. John wanted to treat specifically both prose
and verse, and he wanted to combine Geoffrey's modern treatment with the approach
of the classical rhetoricians. Thus he had several conflicting bases on which to orga-
nize his discussion, and he failed either to combine them successfully or to keep
them wholly separate. Actually, as I have said, in its large outlines the chapter is
reasonably orderly. But there are constant smaller problems of organization which
are never solved; the confusion is especially manifest in the rubrics and chapter
headings and general statements by which John attempts to achieve continuity.

   Thus Chapter Four is entitled (at *1*, 18) "de partibus dictaminis," yet it contains
a good many more things; Chapter Three is entitled "de dispositione" and contains
a good many fewer things. The first section of Chapter Four is also entitled "de
partibus dictaminis," yet only its second paragraph deals with that subject; the first
paragraph says it will discuss the exordium, but actually treats the salutation. And
that second paragraph is incomplete; it must be supplemented (though it is also in

part contradicted) by other statements, as at ll. 145-47, 187-88. John's problem was that if he treated the parts of a letter in an orderly way, by listing them all, he would lose the continuity to be had by continuing the discussion of beginning by passing directly to the exordium. His solution was to treat both inadequately.

10-13 John nowhere lists all the parts of a letter at once, perhaps because he is aware, as here, that they can vary greatly. However, if we combine all that he has to say, it is clear that he would list them in this order: Salutation, Supersalutation, Exordium, Narration, Request, Conclusion.

14-15 *beneuolencia . . . attentio*. The standard classical view of the aims of the exordium: cf. *RAH* 1.4.7; *DI* 1.15.20. The *dictamen* manuals repeat it in a debased form: the exordium is customarily called the *captatio benevolentiae* (cf. Rockinger's index, s.v. *exordium, benevolentia*), but of those printed in Rockinger only Conrad of Mure (1: 465) gives the triple aim of the exordium. John's mode of expression is poor: the usual form was to say that the exordium *reddit auditores benevolos*, etc.; to say that it "contains benevolence, docility, and attention" is awkward and inaccurate. Cf. below, *4*, 195-97: "Exordium est principium orationis rethorice, continens beniuolenciam, docilitatem, attentionem."

17-23 I cannot find anything that matches this division precisely; but it is probably not original. Cf. Conrad of Mure (whose text is dated 1275, and could of course be indebted to John's; he mentions John in a list of *magistri in arte prosandi* on p. 482): "De octo modis exordiorum. Secundum alios dicamus, quod exordia octo modis formantur, et habent fieri in tertia persona: *absolute, adversative, conditionaliter, causative*, qualitative, quantitative, *similitudinarie, temporaliter*" (Rockinger, 1: 467). Those words I have italicized match John's.

The usual division of exordia is into "a persona mittentis, a persona cui mittitur, a negotio rei," which John has applied to proverbs earlier (*1*, 153).

30-43 Cf. *Documentum* 2.2.61 (Faral, pp. 282-83).

45-46 This example differs from the exempla given in *3*, 66-89, and is closer to what John calls a "proverb" in its metaphoric structure. Indeed the word *prouerbium* in l. 47 betrays the confusion. Apparently he means that "fraud" is only one kind of deceit, and the narration will go on to speak of another. It would have been an exemplum had he omitted *fraudis*. The idea was taken from *Documentum* (1.17; Faral, p. 268), where the following couplet is given to exemplify the artificial beginning by means of an example:

> Saepe venenator alii quod porrigit haurit,
> Inque sagittantem missa sagitta redit.

But by adding *fraudis* John changed it from an example, to be connected to the narration by "similarly," to a proverb, to be connected by "thus."

70-72 Proem to Priscian's *Institutiones grammaticae*: see Keil, 2:1; first sentence of Victorinus's translation of Porphyry's *Isagoge*: see *Commentaria in Aristotelem graeca*, vol. 4, part 1, *Porphyrii isagoge et in Aristotelis categorias commentarium*, ed. Adolphus Busse (Berlin, 1887), p. 25.

92-102 I cannot find the source for these distinctions: some of them may be

John's own. Papias says that a προοιμιον is made "ad instruendas audientium aures"; but he goes on to say that its Latin equivalent is *praefatio*. *Prologus* is also called *praefatio sequentis operis*, and *thema* is said to be *graece proemium*. John may have been setting out to correct just such confusion as this by trying to establish one particular meaning of each word as its only meaning.

The definition of *epigrama* is curious, as is its very appearance as a type of beginning. Perhaps *epigraphium* is meant, although the definition is still odd. For *thema* in this sense, cf. Chaucer's Pardoner: "My theme is alwey oon, and evere was:/ *Radix malorum est cupiditas.*" The *Exultat (Exultet)* is the long hymn prefatory to the blessing of the baptismal font in the Holy Saturday service; its second half is in the form of the Preface of the Mass.

147 *mandatum.* This is the first mention of this part of a letter; it is typical of John's haphazard organization that he introduces it in a subordinate clause. Most *dictamen* manuals call this the *petitio*, which is equally inadequate. In a letter from a superior to an inferior, it is a mandate; in a letter from an inferior to a superior it is a petition. I have tried to include both ideas by translating *mandatum* as "request." Cf. Conrad of Mure (Rockinger, 1: 470): "Item nota quod sub hoc nomine 'petitio' comprehenditur etiam mandatum. Plures enim litere sunt que nichil petunt, sed mandant et precipiunt."

157-91 This is an apparently original adaptation to letter writing of Cicero's "five parts of an argument by deductive or syllogistic reasoning" in *DI* 1.37.67.

192-205 A close but not exact imitation of *RAH* 1.3.4, with some points (notably *partitio* for *divisio*) based on *DI* 1.14.19-1.15.20. The curious phrase "deorum testimonio" is perhaps derived from *Topica* 20.77: "Divina haec fere sunt testimonia: primum orationis—oracula enim ex eo ipso appellata sunt, quod inest in his deorum oratio—deinde rerum, in quibus insunt quasi quaedam opera divina. . . . Quibus ex locis sumi interdum solent ad fidem faciendam testimonia deorum." John makes no attempt to reconcile the several discrepancies between his oratorical definitions and poetic example.

207-84 This poem is an attempt to create a work of art and to illustrate the six parts of an oration at the same time; it cannot be said to succeed at either. It is sufficiently obscure to warrant some extended explanation. It is an allegory in which there is a more or less constant dual reference to the battle against Mahomet for Jerusalem and the psychomachia in the Christian crusader, the battle in his soul between Virtue or Reason and the World, the Flesh, and the Devil. The starting point for the allegory is the word *crux*, which may mean either "the Crusade" or "the Cross," that is, "the Christian way of life." The interior battle at times pushes the Crusade into the background; not all the statements or exhortations that apply to it can be readily applied to the Crusade. What makes it possible to construct the poem on the basis of the parts of an oration is that it is a "persuasion"; as John says, we use these six parts "for the purpose of persuasion or dissuasion."

The Exordium pertains chiefly to the psychomachia, though it can also be applied to "rising" for the Crusade. Attention is gained by the bold challenge of the opening clause; benevolence and docility by the note of hope in the second line.

The Narration follows John's definition exactly—it recounts events that have taken place. "Jerusalem" may of course also be the soul. The "persuasion" that follows is really an outline of the argument, which John saw was appropriate to the narration, although not covered in his brief definition. Here the allegory works rather well, although the process has been reversed from the preceding section, for now the psychomachia is the literal level (virtues vs. vices) and the Crusade the allegorical level.

The Division is made to fit the scheme by some verbal trickery. In Rhetoric, as John's definition says, the Division contains a statement of the opponent's case. The poet, however, has no real opponent in this sense. But the subject of the poem, since it deals with a battle, has an opponent, so John achieves a spurious "Division" by stating here what virtue's enemies are doing. Here the psychomachia alone is at issue: the World and the Flesh have no counterpart among the Saracen host.

The Confirmation, too, deals chiefly with the battle in the soul, though it occasionally uses Crusade imagery. With the "Confirmation for Amplification," the basic allegorical device of the Crusade is abandoned, and replaced by the Trojan War. Here the allegory works in only one direction: the literal level is the real battle, whether the Crusade or the Trojan War; but it is only used to symbolize the battle in the mind, which is John's basic concern. Since the basis for the allegory has changed, and to something less obvious than the Crusade, it is accompanied by a "Mystical Exposition."

The Refutation employs the same trick as the Division: not the poet's but the subject's opponent is being refuted. The Conclusion once more succeeds in achieving a consistent dual reference: it is at once an exhortation to join the actual Crusade and also to be a good Christian, to fight both Mahomet and Satan.

There are a good many obscure lines in the poem, which I have translated as well as I could, often with little confidence of accuracy. The Crusade at issue is either the Fifth (1218-21) or the Sixth (1228-29). Since the letter of Pope Honorius III to Frederick II at 7, 156 ff. clearly concerns the Fifth, it is probable that this poem refers to that Crusade also. For John's interest in the Crusades, see his *De triumphis ecclesiae*, ed. Thomas Wright (London, 1856), and Louis J. Paetow, "The Crusading Ardor of John of Garland," *The Crusades and Other Historical Essays Presented to Dana C. Munro*, ed. Louis J. Paetow (New York, 1928), pp. 207-22.

208 *uires.* As the gloss notes, either *vires,* "you grow," or *vir es,* "you are a man."

212 *Palem.* Pales, the Roman goddess of the pasture. Presumably Allah—or Mahomet, since medieval Christians took him to be the god. Cf. l. 241 below.

213-17 The meaning here is obscure.

230 In conjunction with the preceding line, *canenda* seems to mean vespers and matins.

235 *que Marte coronat.* Unclear; possibly it should be *Martem. Qua tuba iussa tonat* l. 236 is also obscure.

240 *Sina.* Probably not literal, but standing for Jerusalem. In Galatians 4:24-25, Saint Paul uses Sinai allegorically for Jerusalem.

247-50 The reference is to the story of Paris's judgment of the goddesses Juno,

Minerva, and Venus. He awarded the golden apple to Venus when she promised him Helen; the Trojan War followed. Paris is the Christian; if he chooses Minerva (the Dircean goddess), Reason, instead of Venus (Phoebean Citharea), the Flesh, his soul (Troy) will not be overthrown. The point of ll. 249-50 seems to be: "Rather than be a fighter, Paris, you may be content to be a lover, provided that your love is chaste—for Reason, not the Flesh." That John regarded *bellor* as deponent is confirmed by *rebellari, 7,* 206 and its gloss *pugnare;* Papias says it can be either deponent or not. I cannot find *antiparis:* my translation, "shield," is based on Laurentius Diefenbach, *Glossarium latino-germanicum mediae et infimae aetatis* (issued as a supplement to Du Cange's *Glossarium*) (Frankfurt, 1857), s.v. *anticipa.* Here Diefenbach lists several forms, including *antiparium,* of a word based on *anti* and Greek πυρ, "fire," and meaning *schirm* or "screen," that is, a fireplace screen. But German *schirm* can also mean a shield, and Diefenbach includes the form *apparicon* which is glossed Low German *bokeler.* It ought to mean some piece of military equipment, in view of Paris's reputation as a better lover than fighter. Cf. Ovid, *Heroides* 17.254-55 (Helen to Paris): "Apta magis Veneri, quam sunt tua corpora Marti:/Bella gerant fortes; tu, Paris, semper ama."

251-74 Here the Trojan War allegory is kept up, but in a different way. The earlier passage urges that the war be prevented: this passage assumes that Paris has given the apple to Venus and the war begun. The "Mystical Exposition" applies to this passage only, not the earlier one. Troy is still the soul; the Greeks are various passions. The representative of the Flesh changes from Venus to Hecuba (making Priam Reason), and then (at l. 273) Helen. Paris at l. 272 is still the Christian. (Helen belongs rightly to Menelaus or Satan; she should have nothing to do with Paris. However, since one does have to put up with the Flesh, it may also be considered Hecuba—but a wife to be kept in her place.)

The piling on of conflicting metaphors adds to the confusion of the shifting allegory.

262 *pacis . . . trophea.* The sign of the cross, to be made in time of temptation.

263 *Crimina septena.* The seven deadly sins.

275-76 *Cesareus, Capaneus, Tydeus.* Not part of any connected allegory, but merely symbols of strength. Capaneus and Tydeus appear in Statius's *Thebaid.*

286-88 This list is derived from Geoffrey's *Documentum* 2.2.30-43 (Faral, pp. 277-80), with some change in the terminology (*disiunctum* for *dissolutum, dictionum materiam exprimencium electio* for *colligenda sunt nomina rerum in quibus consistit vis materiae*) and omitting *intellectio.* Geoffrey defines and discusses each device at greater length, particularly the last, which he regards as "sufficientissimum articulum brevitatis." Perhaps John felt he should be brief when discussing brevity. Geoffrey's list in the *Poetria nova* (ll. 690-736) is different in several respects. Faral is right to say (p. 85) that the *Documentum* "reproduit la même doctrine en des termes un peu différents"; and yet the differences are large enough to make this passage important evidence that John was following the *Documentum* and not the *Poetria nova.*

287 *Disiunctum* is called *Dissolutio* at *6,* 263.

288 Geoffrey (#32) defines *emphasis* as "quaedam figura quae longam seriem

verborum curtat eleganter, quae fit duobus modis; uno modo quando rem ipsam appellamus nomine suae proprietatis, uno modo quando locuturi de re loquimur de ejus proprietate." John's example is of the first type, which Geoffrey exemplifies by "Medea est ipsum scelus." See also *Anticlaudianus* 2.492-94, of Donatus: "nomenque sibi speciale meretur / Vt non gramaticus dicatur, at emphasis ipsam/ Gramaticam uocat hunc."

300-308 The point of this device, as Geoffrey makes clear (*Documentum* 2.2.42-43; Faral, pp. 279-80), is in a brief compass to include all the nouns which represent the principal subjects with which the story or treatise at issue deals. Thus John has included in his couplet all the nouns he mentions in the sentence of summary. Geoffrey seems to intend the device as a way of making brief reference to another story or subject without making an extensive digression from the matter at hand. John probably has this in mind when he treats the device again in 5, 37-44. Here, however, he applies it to the proem, as a sort of topic sentence, for which it is in fact well suited.

309 The doctrine on amplification is once again taken from the *Documentum* 2.2.2-29 (Faral, pp. 271-77). As Faral's table on p. 62 shows, the *Poetria nova* differs somewhat from the *Documentum* here, particularly in omitting the species of Apostrophe. The only significant variation John makes from the *Documentum* is placing *Interpretatio* under Apostrophe; Geoffrey rightly treats it by itself. It may also be noted that Geoffrey treats Amplification before Abbreviation. Faral discusses the subject of Amplification at length on pp. 61-85.

314-18 This is a difficult passage. *De materia* by itself would seem to mean "off the subject"; and yet that would make the phrase *quod non est de materia sed materie conuenienter adiungitur* meaningless. The only way to make sense of it is to translate *de materia* as "part of the subject," a possible though unusual meaning for *de;* cf. *de substantia narrationis* (*1*, 186); the idiom resulted in the partitive *de* of French. This gives a certain sense to the passage, and puts it in correspondence with Geoffrey: "Unus modus digressionis est quando digredimur in materia ad aliam partem materiae; alius modus quando digredimur a materia ad aliud extra materiam" (#17). But it is still confused, for comparison seems to be just as much off the subject, in John's terms, as fable or parable. Indeed, Geoffrey contrasts description and comparison; description is a digression to "another part of the subject," while comparisons and similitudes are the only examples given of "digression to something outside the subject"; parables and fables are not mentioned at all. It is impossible that John could have confused so simple a matter. Evidently he was trying to improve on Geoffrey, or at least be different from him, by adding parable and fable and placing comparison, perhaps because of its brevity, in a different category from them. But comparison differs from description in kind, from parable and fable only in degree, and Geoffrey's doctrine makes for better sense. (See 5, 20-33, where John follows Geoffrey's division, contradicting this passage.)

326-31 For the procedures involved in proceeding from the licentiate to a master's chair at Paris, see Rashdall 3:459-62.

348 For *amicus* = "relative" cf. Du Cange, *Glossarium*, s.v. *amicus*. Du Cange notes that the fuller phrase *amicus carnalis* is more frequent. The content of the letter demands the meaning here.

362 Ennius seems to have been a byword in John's time for faulty meter. The basis for this reputation is probably *AP* 258-62, where Horace chides him for ignorance of art because he introduced too many spondees into the iambic measure in his plays. See also *Satires* 1.10.54, and *Epistles* 2.1.50-52, where Ennius is sarcastically called "the second Homer." (Ennius had himself made that claim in the beginning of the *Annales,* where Homer comes to him in a dream and says that Ennius is a reincarnation of himself.) Gervase of Melkley (ed. Gräbener, p. 7, ll. 3-7) says that an individual verse that contains a "figure" such as prothesis or epenthesis is excusable "speciali respectu"; "et tamen habito respectu ad totum, inutilis esset liber ille. Inde est quod liber Ennii condempnatur." Gräbener (p. xxxiii) quotes Alain de Lille, *De planctu naturae*, Prose 9: "Illic Ennii versus, a sententiarum venustate jejuni, artem metricam effreni transgrediabantur [*sic*] licentia." In *Anticlaudianus*, ridiculing Joseph of Exeter and his *De bello troiano*, Alain says, "Illic pannoso plebescit carmine noster/Ennius et Priami fortunas intonat" (1.165-66; cf. John's *panniculis*).

369. Cf. above, *1*, 320-26.

378 *dictum est ante*. There is no previous mention of *Apostrophatio*.

383-84 This example of *conduplicatio* also appears in the *Documentum* 2.2.26 (Faral, p. 276).

389-409 John has managed to obscure the relationship of *subiectio* and *dubitatio* to apostrophe by putting his examples in the third person. Geoffrey's examples are in the second person.

390-91 *Noua Poetria*. Ll. 1139-45 (Faral, p. 232). *Epitalamico*. Faral (pp. 50-51) says that here John seems to state that Book 10 of the *Epithalamium* contains a full list of examples of the rhetorical figures, that is, a connected poem using each in turn, as in the *Poetria nova*, ll. 1098-1217. It does.

398-405 A variation on these lines appears as another example of *subiectio* at *6*, 194 ff. Both passages are based on the example of *subiectio* in *RAH* 4.23.33.

416 *Undecimus Modus*. There is nothing of this in Geoffrey. What John apparently means is that in loading our poem with words suitable to its style we will incidentally be amplifying it. For the distinction between low style and figurativeness, cf. note to *1*, 407-56.

422 This tale exhibits elements of the fabliau, particularly in that it contains the three chief characters of that genre, the adulterous wife, her gullible husband, and the lecherous cleric. It differs from the fabliau, however, in its supernatural element, and especially in not presenting directly the story of the adultery. The only other version of the tale known to me is a brief prose account in a sermon by Guibert de Tournai (d. ca. 1284), printed by Hauréau (p. 83). Guibert calls the spirit "Guinedocet." John's version is especially interesting for its rudimentary dramatic structure, since instances of Latin comedy in dramatic rather than narrative form are rare. Cf. Cloetta, p. 98; but see also below, note to l. 462-74.

433-58 Here low style is applied to peasants, in accordance with the triad *curiales*, *civiles, rurales,* rather than to shepherds, in the triad *milites, agricoli, pastores.* Despite the figures, it remains low style because of that subject. Notice the persons (*coloni, uulgus, rusticus, presbiter* [not a prelate]); "implements" (*cisterna, fora*); and duties (*res ubi uenit, seruat sua mater, pascis in ede, era merendo*). For Geoffrey on comedy, cf. *Poetria nova,* ll. 1883-1916; *Documentum* 2.3.163-69.

460-61 Since the poem does not represent the peasant as performing any of these actions—though they are all understandable responses to the news he has heard—it is probable that the name has some other origin, and John is applying his etymological habit to French after the fact. The verses are closer in metrical movement to a leonine couplet than to the meters of Old French poetry, which suggests that they are John's, and not part of a French version of the story.

Par curteysie chapinier is troublesome. *Chapinier* (*charpignier*) means "to card wool" or "tease, raise" cloth, "cut up or shred" cloth, or, figuratively, "bruise." It normally requires an object. The only sense I can make of it is that *par curteysie* means "to be polite," "to use a euphemism"; but I cannot say what this euphemism replaces. Possibly the verb just means "break up" or "be all broken up," and refers to *rumpere* in the last line of the poem; but then *par curteysie* does not fit.

Cloetta, accepting Rockinger's reading *Chapigensis,* interprets it *Cha(m)pigensis,* and says, "Es scheint auf eine Eigenthumlichkeit des champagner Dialekt angespielt zu sein" (p. 99). But that reading is unlikely (cf. variants), and the phrase *Gallica lingua* suggests both that the whole couplet is in French and that John was not adverting to the dialect.

462-74 The reference to Horace, the traditional nature of the characters mentioned, and the fact that his own comedy is composed chiefly of dialogue all suggest that John has something like real drama in mind here. He might have known the plays of Terence. But the sentence beginning *Non tamen* and ll. 478-79 (*carmen iocosum*) make it clear that for John, as for most of his contemporaries, *comoedia* meant a versified, narrative tale. (The fullest collection of such tales is Gustave Cohen, *La "Comédie" latine en France au XIIe siècle* [2 vols., Paris, 1931]; most of the pieces printed there contain a good deal of dialogue. The *Geta* of Vitalis of Blois [vol. 1], which is based ultimately on the *Amphitryo* of Plautus, contains the five characters John describes. Though most employ the elegiac couplet [see below, 5, 371 and note], the *De nuncio sagaci* [vol. 2] is in leonine hexameters like John's.)

Edmond Faral treats the genre at some length in "Le Fabliau latin au moyen âge," *Romania* 50 (1924):321-85. He concludes that the fabliaux of the thirteenth century issue from these Latin tales of the twelfth and through them ultimately from ancient Roman comedy. John's list of characters, excepting perhaps the *nutrix,* can certainly be applied to the fabliau, though his insistence on five parts seems only explainable in relation to the ancient drama. The whole discussion may in fact be best explained as a confused attempt to reveal the same connection Faral sees among the three genres. Faral treats John's comedy briefly on p. 378, asserting, I think rightly, that the dialogue is there chiefly to indicate that the low style uses common speech; there is no thought of dramatic performance.

The implicit separation of history and tragedy, which have no definite parts, on the one hand and comedy with its five parts on the other is consistent with the later designation of tragedy as history, comedy as *argumentum,* in 5, 365-72.

481-83 Cf. *AP* 220: "Carmine qui tragico vilem certavit ob hircum."

488-512 Instructions for drafting documents were regularly included in treatises on *dictamen*, since the professional notaries for whom they were written had to perform this function as well as write letters. These verses are hardly valuable in themselves; they seem to be meant rather as a mnemonic.

493 I.e., since performing a criminal deed in a church or other sacrèd place changes the nature of the deed entirely.

513 *Istorum uersuum* probably refers, not to the four verses immediately preceding, since only a few of these "cases" are represented in the examples in Chapter Seven, but to the verses in ll. 488-503, which are exemplified in Chapter Seven as follows: *Carta*, l. 262; *Cyrographum*, l. 290; *Querimonia*, l. 217; *Citatio*, l. 235; action for contempt, l. 343; *Transactio*, l. 316; *Littere Memoriales*, l. 336. There is no example pertaining to sacrilege.

CHAPTER FIVE

The basic division of Chapter Five is between vices of poetry and vices of prose. The first part is subdivided into "the six vices of poetry," that is, vices related to the handling of material, and minor faults of grammar, diction, and meter. The former are treated uninterruptedly through l. 119; but in treating the last vice, *infelix conclusio*, since he has not treated the conclusion before, John digresses to discuss the kinds of endings in both prose and verse, and includes an extended prose example. The second subdivision under poetry, the minor faults, is handled in ll. 178-259, single-mindedly except for the examples of *annominatio* in ll. 214-34. This digression is the less excusable in that its contents are fully repeated in Chapter Six.

The second part of the chapter, the vices peculiar to letters, begins at l. 260. It is based on the parts of a letter, salutation, supersalutation, narration, and request being discussed in turn. The "proverb" is not treated; the conclusion has been touched on in ll. 128-77. There are brief minor digressions under the salutation; the really confused section, however, is the narration. Ll. 303-72 are spent delineating genres before we reach the subject of faults in the narration. But though the excuse for the treatment of genres was that narration is common to both prose and poetry, that discussion clearly had poetry in mind, and in ll. 373-401 John seems to have forgotten altogether that he is supposed to be discussing *dictamen*, for he treats the vices of narration here in terms proper only to poetry.

Ll. 402-81 are a return to *dictamen*, but neglect both vice and narration completely. The treatment of the four styles of *dictamen* they contain is clearly meant to complement the treatment of poetic styles in ll. 45-93, but whereas that treatment was conducted in terms of vices, this is not. John closes the chapter by returning to its proper organization to treat vice in the request of a letter.

The theory of the six vices of poetry comes from Horace through Geoffrey of Vinsauf; the minor faults in poetry are common grammatical fare. The whole application of the idea of "vice" to *dictamen* is probably John's, though many of his individual remarks are commonplaces. The theory of genres is based on Cicero and Geoffrey (see Appendix Two), though it is confused and inconsistent; the theory of the four *dictamen* styles comes from Bernard de Meung and Geoffrey.

1 ff. For the six vices, see *Documentum* 2.3.145-62 (Faral, pp. 312-17); see Appendix Two). Geoffrey derives his list from the first 37 lines of the *Ars poetica*.
For the most part, John is not indebted to Geoffrey for the details of his discussion
of each fault; but see Appendix Two for exceptions.

9 *Species recti.* Cf. *AP* 24-25: "Maxima pars vatum, pater et iuvenes patre digni,/
Decipimur specie recti." Geoffrey does not use the phrase, which John employs in
a slightly different sense from Horace's.

29-33 Here John contradicts his earlier statement on the kinds of digressions (cf.
4, 314-18 and note). This passage agrees with Geoffrey's division of digression (*Documentum* 2.2.17; Faral, p. 274).

31 *locus uel castrum.* The point of this is clarified by *Documentum* 2.2.18 (Faral,
p. 274), where, as an example of a digression to another part of the subject, Geoffrey
cites the interruption of the narrative action to describe the place in which a new
episode is about to take place.

36 Cf. *AP* 25-26: "Brevis esse laboro,/Obscurus fio," which Geoffrey quotes (#152).

37-44 Cf. *4*, 300-308 and note. The story of Jupiter and Lycaon is in the *Metamorphoses* 1.196-240; see also *Theoduli ecloga* 61-64: the phrase *Juppiter hospes*
appears in l. 62.

51-60 John's point here is threefold: (1) that, as he has said before (*1*, 383-96;
2, 116-23), in each style the nouns chosen should refer only to people, activities,
and things proper to that style; but (2) should reference to people, activities, and
things proper to another style be unavoidable, it should be couched in terms proper
to the style of the work: if you must put a "high" detail in a low poem, put it in
low terms, and vice versa. (The effect of this is to transform the person or object
from what it really is to something else; calling distaffs "the spears of peace" removes them from the class distaff into the class spear, which is proper to high style.)
Finally, (3) though the style of a work is usually dictated by the social level of its
characters, one can make a different style acceptable by choosing the right nouns.
This does not contradict the caution in *2*, 122 to avoid *egressus* from one style to
another; the one thing necessary is consistency within whatever style is chosen.
Thus Charlemagne can be used to illustrate both the high and middle styles, and
in Chapter Seven we can have a poem in the high style about washerwomen. For
ordine, "row" (59, 60), cf. Figure Three, p. 40.

52-53 Apparently John has run across, or invented, an interpretation of the first
line of Virgil's Eclogue 1 ("Tityre, tu patulae recubans sub tegmine fagi") in which
Tityrus is Augustus and the beech Rome. "Uel seipsum" acknowledges the usual
interpretation of Tityrus as Virgil. It is hard to imagine, however, how such a peculiar interpretation could be applied consistently through the poem. Virgil's practice is to call Augustus by his right name, although he calls Julius Caesar Daphnis
in Eclogue 5. Possibly the text is corrupt, and John originally wrote "qui vocat
Caesarem Daphnin et seipsum Tityrum et Romam fagum," the equation of the
beech with Rome deriving from Servius's statement that the beech in 1.1 can mean
"sub protectione Augusti." That is not precisely "Rome," but Virgil nowhere uses
fagus to mean Rome; this comes closest to it.

61 The theory of the vices attached to each style appears in both Geoffrey's
Documentum (2.3.146-51; Faral, pp. 312-13) and Matthew of Vendôme's *Ars
versificatoria* (1.30-34; Faral, pp. 116-18). Both of these writers assert that its
source is *AP* 26-28:

sectantem levia nervi
Deficiunt animique; professus grandia turget;
Serpit humi tutus nimium timidusque procellae.

As Faral (p. 88) points out, however, the terminology comes from *RAH* 4.10-11:
"Gravis oratio saepe inperitis videtur ea quae turget et inflata est. . . . Errantes per-
veniunt ad confine genus eius generis, quod appellamus dissolutum . . . ut hoc modo
appellem fluctuans. . . . Qui non possunt in illa facetissima verborum adtenuatione
commode versari veniunt ad aridum et exsangue genus orationis."

Faral lumps Matthew, Geoffrey, and John together: all three, he says remove the
RAH discussion from the realm of style to that of social standing. Matthew, however,
says nothing of social standing in dealing with the vices of style, and in fact remains
reasonably close to *RAH*. It is Geoffrey who makes it a question of persons and
their *proprietates,* and John is clearly following him.

It is not always clear in John's examples where the fault lies. In the high-style example, *excelsus* is a bombastic word, and the harsh metaphor in *collis bellorum* an
inflated idea. (Geoffrey finds harsh metaphor the chief source of turgidity.) The remainder of the couplet seems unobjectionable, at least in terms of the faults John
lists, since *claua pacis* is if anything less inflated than *columpna pacis* in the *species
recti.* In fact, it is a low-style word: cf. l. 78; the fault in it is stylistic inappropriate-
ness rather than either of the specific faults mentioned. (I cannot identify Rolandina;
perhaps part of the vice is the outlandish conceit of making Roland feminine.)

In the middle-style example, *baculus* is a low-style word (cf. Figure Three, p. 40),
rex and *milicie* high-style words. (*Cultor* in the *species recti* is opposed to these;
farming is appropriate to the middle style, even if it is the farming of justice.) Wives
belong to the low style (cf. *4,* 468).

The problem with the low-style examples is that in several ways the faulty example
seems to be preferable to the ideal example. The idea in both seems sufficiently
"juicy," and even more so in the second example than in the first. Presumably one
is to "purple over" the word *testiculos* in the faulty example; but, on the other
hand, the metaphor in *tonse* goes farther toward avoiding "bloodlessness" than the
plain *presbiterum* in the ideal example. (The tonsured priest undergoing sterilization
is comparable to a sheep on several counts; Faral's emendation, *bertonso,* is unnecessary.)

86. In the metaphor, the *basis* is the subject matter, the *epistilium* the work itself: the style rests on the subject matter, but is the means of raising the work
higher than the subject matter alone could do. *Stilus* is not actually connected with
Greek στυλος, though many have thought so.

113 *recapitulationem.* Cf. *RAH* 2.30.47; *DI* 1.52.98. For this and other types of
conclusion, see *Documentum* 3.1-6 (Faral, pp. 319-20).

179 *Soloecismus* and *Barbarismus* were regularly treated by the grammarians;
John passes them over as more suitable for a treatise on grammar than on style.

Barbarismus embraces errors in single words: misspellings, false quantities, and the like; it also includes hiatus, which John treats below, l. 193. *Soloecismus* covers errors in grammar and syntax. See, e.g., Donatus, *Ars grammatica* (*Ars major*) in Keil, 4:392-94.

Metrical considerations such as *Synaloepha* were also regarded as the province of the grammarians. The statement that modern poets are permitted to use *Synaloepha* implies an opinion that they are not, or rarely do. John himself avoids ending a word in a vowel or *-m* before a word beginning with a vowel. In the poem in 7, 28-153, for instance, there are only two elisions in 126 lines (ll. 43, 69).

188-89 is awkward and obscure. It seems to be a parenthetical phrase or footnote, since *vnde propter*, etc. naturally follows *parum habet soni*. *Enim* is perhaps an error for an earlier *autem* or *ergo*. *Id quod ore aperto profertur* is in contrast to *labiorum clausorum* and means the vowel beginning the word after the *-m*. *Sed secundum maius et minus* probably refers to the fact that the pause that not eliding *-m* would necessitate is not as great as the pause between two unelided vowels. The sense then is: "Thus, if *-m* is not elided, a following vowel—since it must be uttered with the mouth open, whereas the mouth was closed to utter *-m*—is preceded by a pause, though not as great as the pause between two consecutive vowels would be."

210 *Interpretatio*. Cf. above, *4*, 410-15, and below, *6*, 244 ff.

214-34 The figure *Annominatio*. All these devices, except changing a syllable, are treated again, in the same order, in *6*, 139-60; more are also added there. I have tried to translate the device without straying too far from the sense.

236-37 *in principio uel in medio*. The beginning or the middle of the hexameter line, not of this phrase; though it happens for metrical reasons to appear in those positions in the phrase as well as the line in the examples. Cf. *Poetria nova*, ll. 371-72: "cruentet/Interiora dolor."

265 Cf. the definition of prose, *1*, 27, and note. The difference between *dictamen* and *epistola* is not clear. It would seem, however, that in *dictamen* John is including legal documents in the form of letters, either addressed to "all who read this document," such as deeds or indentures (cf. examples in 7, 262-329), or not "declaring the mind of the sender," that is, legal or business letters as opposed to personal letters (cf. the summons at 7, 343). Thus a *dictamen* can be an *epistola* if it is personal, and an *epistola* can be a *dictamen* if it is embellished.

In practice, for John and others, the terms are usually interchangeable, along with *littere*. For some definitions of *dictamen* similar to John's, cf. Rockinger, 1:9, 10, 103, 359, 420; 2:725. The *Ars dictandi Aureliensis* (1:103) defines *dictamen* as "literalis edicio, venustate sermonum egregia, sententiarum coloribus adornata"; and *epistola* as "oracio congrua suis e partibus conuenienter conposita affectum mentis plene significans." But the writer goes on to use the two terms synonymously. Ludolfus (1:359) says, "Sciendum autem quod dictamen epistola karta litere quantum ad presens opus synonima sunt et alterutrum unum pro altero ponitur indifferenter."

272 Saladin died ca. 1185. John seems to be using his name for "any heathen potentate." *Salutem*, of course, though I have consistently translated it "greeting," carries the notion of salvation—"I greet you, and I wish you salvation"—as well.

305-11 For this classification, which is derived from Diomedes, cf. Curtius, pp. 440-41; Cloetta, pp. 19, 24, 25n.; Baldwin, p. 131; T. S. Eliot, "The Three Voices of Poetry," *On Poetry and Poets* (New York, 1957), pp. 96-112; and P. B. Salmon, "The Three Voices of Poetry in Medieval Literary Theory," *Medium Aevum* 30 (1961):1-18. The Diomedes passage is in Keil, 1;48?· "Poematos genera sunt tria. Aut enim activum aut vel imitativum, quod Graeci *dramaticon* vel *mimeticon,* aut enarrativum vel enuntiativum, quod Graeci *exegeticon* vel *apangelticon* dicunt, aut commune vel mixtum, quod Graeci κοινόν vel μικτόν appellant." It will be seen that the Greek has in several instances been garbled in its passage between Diomedes and John, and that the word *mimeticon* has been replaced by *dicticon* for δεικτικόν, ("demonstrative"). Geoffrey calls them the "Greek appellations"; see Appendix Two.

The classification is based on the person speaking; in the first type the characters always speak for themselves, the author never intruding; in the second type the author speaks throughout in his own person; the third is a mixture of both. Curtius shows that the idea goes back at least to Plato.

321-26 This definition, taken from *RAH,* hardly explains the numerous genres John subsumes under history starting at l. 333. For beginning by proposition, invocation, and narration, see *3,* 93. *Transitio* is defined in different words to the same effect at *6,* 216. Sextus Amarcius uses *epilogus* in a way that fits John's definition: see his *Sermones,* ed. Karl Manitius (Weimar, 1969), p. 51.

328 *ut contingit in comediis.* Cf. *RAH* 1.8.13: "velut argumenta comoediarum."

333-72 See Appendix Two for Geoffrey's version of this grand collection of genres under "history." One may imagine how it was arrived at. According to the initial classification, any work in which the poet speaks in his own person throughout is narrative. But of the three types of narrative, *fabula* and *argumentum* are both patent fictions. So *historia* is the only category left in which to place a poem spoken by the poet and recounting, celebrating, or referring to an actual event or real life. Thus both John's bucolic (*1,* 407) and his tragedy (*7,* 28), though fictitious in our sense of the word, are "historical" in the sense of "naturalistic," while his comedy (*4,* 433) is an *argumentum* because one of the characters is a spirit. Its plot "could have happened" (*fieri potuit, 5,* 327), but supernaturally; the plot of the tragedy is preposterous but eschews the supernatural.

The division is discussed at some length by de Bruyne, 2:18-22, 330. He rightly insists that "tout ce qui se rapporte a des faits 'réels' est 'historique'" (p. 330). But I do not think it is necessary to insist that "dans ces alineas 'historicum' n'a pas le sens de 'historia' opposé a 'fabula seu argumentum' ni de 'enarrativum' opposé a 'dramaticon seu mixtim'" (p. 21). De Bruyne's error is to include comedy as historical, which John is careful not to do: De Bruyne's citation on p. 21, "Item historicum aliud est tragicum . . . aliud elegiacum [i.e., miserabile carmen quod continet et recitat dolores amantium], aliud . . . comedia [breaks his] ," simply misrepresents Mari's text. He also apparently thinks of comedy and tragedy as dramatic, which is what keeps him from assigning to *historicum* the meaning *enarrativum.*

In fact, I think there is in the passage a little of both the possible senses which de Bruyne rejects: between *historia* and *historicum* there is semantic change in the direction of "narrative." That the stem has such a broader meaning is indicated by the fact that at *1,* 51-52 writers of tragedy and comedy are said to write *historialis* prose,

though here comedy is made distinct from history. Furthermore, it is clear at l. 373
that John has been thinking in terms of narrative all along. I have tried to indicate
both the shift of meaning and yet also the logic of John's subdivision by translating
hystoricum at ll. 333, 359, and 365 as "historical narrative." Even the fact that John
uses the adjective and not the noun, saying not that all these genres "are history"
but "are historical"—that is, perhaps, "have a historical aspect"—may indicate his
own awareness that he has moved away from the strict definition of *historia*.

Like Dante's briefer but vaguely similar list of the genres of "poetical narration"
in the *Letter to Can Grande*, the catalog is gathered chiefly from *AP* 73-89, though,
in view of Geoffrey's passage, evidently not originally by John.

334 *Epichedion.* An epicedium is simply a funeral song. John's distinction between
epicedium and epitaph is awkwardly put; his examples indicate that he had in mind
Servius's comment on Eclogue 5.14, which will clarify it. "Significat autem canta-
turum se epicedion et epitaphion: nam epicedion est quod dicitur cadavere nondum
sepulto, ut 'extinctum nymphae crudeli funere Daphnin'; epitaphion autem post
completam sepulturam dicitur, ut 'Daphnis ego in silvis hinc usque ad sidera notus.'"
The second example of epitaph is evidently John's own epitaph for himself.

346 *Apoteosis.* Ordinarily used in both Greek and Latin as an abstract word, not
the name for a poem. John probably has in mind the saints' legends: cf. l. 398 below;
yet since he has just been quoting Virgil's Eclogue 5, he may well have also been
thinking of the deification of Daphnis which follows the lament in that poem. Ovid
celebrates the apotheosis of Julius Caesar (15) and Aeneas (14) in the *Metamorphoses*.

348-50 *Liricum, Epodon.* Cf. *AP* 83-85: "Musa dedit fidibus [i.e., the lyric
meters] divos puerosque deorum/Et pugilem victorem et equum certamine primum/
Et iuvenum curas et libera vina referre." Why victory in the games has been assigned
in particular to epode is unclear. As for the difference between *comestio* and *commessatio*, a gloss to the latter word in John's *Accentarius* in Ms. Bruges 546, f. 60^v
says, "commessatio est superflua et luxuriosa comestio."

The name *epodon* was originally applied to the shorter verse of a couplet, then
came to mean any poem composed in couplets in which the second verse is shorter
than the first. *Clausulare* refers to the original sense; it means "having the properties
of a clausula," the metrical ending of a sentence in rhythmic prose, which usually
involved only the last two or three words. Thus in an epode such as Horace's first,
"Ibis Liburnis inter alta navium,/Amice, propugnacula" (1-2), the shorter line re-
sembles a clausula. Cf. Papias (following Isidore, *Etymologiae* 1:39): "Epodos est
clausula brevis in poemate, ubi in singulis quibusque maioribus sequentes minores
quasi clausulae recinunt."

358 *Vt queant laxis.* A hymn to John the Baptist of the Carolingian period,
ascribed by some to Paul the Deacon. Cf. Raby, *CLP*, pp. 166-67. It is not a *carmen
saeculare*, though it is in the same meter (Sapphic) as Horace's poem, and contains
some similar sentiments—praise of God and his saint (Horace praises various deities),
and supplication of their aid.

363-64 Since they appear in the *Documentum* (see Appendix Two), these verses
do not seem to be John's. Yet they occur in his *Compendium grammaticae*, Ms.
Bruges 546, f. 143^v, with the second verse altered to a hexameter to fit the form of

that poem: "Voce salit, vitiis fetens innuatur agrestis." And compare his *Morale scholarium* (ed. Paetow), ll. 423-24: "Hec est lex satire: vitiis ridere, salire,/Mores excire, que feda latent aperire." I have translated the phrase *voce salit* in accordance with glosses to these works: in the *Compendium grammaticae*, "uno vicem ad aliud," and in *Morale scholarium*, "de materia ad materiam."

366-67 Restricting elegy to the complaints of lovers is doubtless due to the pre-eminence of Ovid's *Heroides, Remedia amoris,* and *Amores,* and in particular to these statements within them: "Flendus amor meus est: elegia flebile carmen" (*Her.* 15.7); "Blanda pharetratos elegia cantet amores" (*RA* 379); "Flebilis indignos, Elegia, solve capillos" (*Am.* 3.9.3). Papias has only *versus miserorum,* Horace *querimonia* (*AP* 75). On amoebaean, cf. note to *1, 396.*

371 Comedy is included under *Argumentum* in accordance with *RAH:* see note to l. 328 above. The statement that every comedy is an elegy means that the proper form for the *comoedia* or versified tale is the elegiac couplet: cf. note to *4, 462-74* above and Raby, *SLP,* 2:54. Raby gives this statement of John's as his authority, but all but one of the tales he deals with are in fact in elegiacs. Interestingly, though, John's own comedy (*4, 433*), like a few others, is in leonine hexameters: see Cloetta, pp. 97-98.

373-81 Cf. Matthew of Vendôme, 1.41-92 (Faral, pp. 119-43); Geoffrey of Vinsauf, *Documentum* 2.3.138-39 (Faral, pp. 310-11) and Appendix Two below. The doctrine is derived not only from this passage in Horace but from Cicero's eleven attributes of persons, *DI* 1.24.34-1.25.36. Cf. Faral, pp. 77-79. John follows Cicero more closely in listing the eleven attributes of persons below, *6, 394* ff.

382-85 John probably composed this list of faults from various precepts in the *Ars poetica;* for *nimia quantitas,* see l. 335; *nimia festinantia,* ll. 291-4; *scribentis negligentia,* ll. 408-15; *artis ignorantia,* ll. 379-82; *iudicis malitia,* ll. 438-52 (character of a good critic). Hurry, negligence, and ignorance are all related to each other, and constitute the faults "which it is the special object of the *Ars poetica* to forestall by pressing on Roman poets the necessity of patient work and of systematic art" (E. C. Wickham, ed., *The Works of Horace* [Oxford, 1891], 2:414n.).

391-92 *Efflexegesis.* For epexegesis (ἐπεξήγησις). Cf. Servius on *Aeneid* 1.12 ("Urbs antiqua fuit, Tyrii tenuere coloni"): "Deest 'quam,' vel ut alii volunt, 'hanc'; amant namque antiqui per epexegesin dicere quod nos interposito pronomine exprimimus." See also Alexander of Ville-Dieu, *Doctrinale* (ed. Dietrich Reichling, Berlin, 1893), l. 2594: "Est efflexegesis exponens dicta priora." Reichling retains the form *efflexegesis* because the word was thought to be derived from *ex* and *flectere.* He points out the Servius passage as well as other instances of the word.

394-400 John distinguishes between *integumentum,* fictional allegory, and *allegoria,* historical allegory; cf. de Bruyne 2:327. *Apologus* is similarly defined at *4, 62; apotheosis,* at *5, 346.*

402-67 This doctrine has aroused some interest. The passage is mentioned by Curtius, p. 151 and Baldwin, p. 194; and treated at some length by Albert C. Clark, *The Cursus in Medieval and Vulgar Latin* (Oxford, 1910), pp. 16-17, and R. A. Browne, *British Latin Selections, A.D. 500-1400* (Oxford, 1954), pp. lvi-lix. Denholm-Young, however, has pointed out (p. 51) that it was not, as others have assumed, originated by John but by Bernard de Meung, and included also by Geoffrey of Vinsauf in the longer version of the *Documentum*. For this, see Appendix Two; the only manuscript of Bernard de Meung's *Summa dictaminis* which I have been able to examine, Bodleian Library Douce 52, is an incomplete version which mentions the Ciceronian, Hilarian, and Isidorean styles but does not treat them in detail. The Gregorian style is treated fully, however, and the treatment matches John's practically word for word (whereas Geoffrey's does not). Evidently John simply copied Bernard whole:

> Preter tres stilos poeticos sunt et alii stili quattuor quibus vtuntur moderni,
> scilicet Gregorianus, Tullianus, Hillarianus, Ysodorianus. Stilo Gregoriano
> vtuntur notarii domini pape, cardinalium, archiepiscoporum, et quedam alie
> curie. In hoc stilo considerantur pedes, scilicet spondei et dactili, idest dictiones
> 5 cadentes ad modum spondeorum et dactilorum.
>
> Dactilus in hoc loco dicitur dictio trissilaba cuius penultima corripitur, licet alie
> silabe producuntur. Spondeus dicitur in dictamine dictio dissilaba uel partes
> pollissilabe dictionis cadentis ad modum spondeorum. Et notandum quod
> dictio quadrassilaba est cuius penultima producitur uel due dictiones dissilabe
> 10 semper ponuntur in fine clausule. Dictio vero posita in penultimo loco semper
> corripit penultimam, vt hic: "humilitati vestre te nostra dignetur gratia con-
> formare." Et notandum quod viciosa est oratio si duo dactili uel plures simul
> cadunt uel multi spondei sine dactilo. Si contingat dictionem finalem esse
> trissilabam, penultima dictio producat penultimam silabam et dictio que est
> 15 ante penultimam dictionem corripiet penultimam sillabam, hoc modo:
> "humilitati vestre dignetur se nostra per omnia conformari gratia."

The readings *est* 9, *vestre te nostra* 11, *corripiet* 15, *and vestre dignetur se nostra* 16 appear to be erroneous.

The Gregorian style is the orthodox Roman *cursus*, which developed in the twelfth century, but whose rules were formulated by Pope Gregory VIII, who became pope in 1187. Clark prints Gregory's brief *Forma dictandi* in his *Fontes prosa numerosae* (Oxford, 1909), pp. 34-35. John's statements, as far as they go, agree with it except that John (with Bernard) approves successive spondees and differs on what should precede a final trisyllable. On the Roman style in general, cf. Clark, *Cursus*, pp. 13-21, and Denholm-Young, pp. 51-54. The latter also notes (p. 61) that John's treatment of the final trisyllable is unusual. Denholm-Young and Browne both rightly question Mari's text of the passage; the present version makes better sense with the help of Mss. *B, C*, and *P*.

The letter at *5*, 134, entitled *littere scolastice*, despite its repudiation of the *lingua Tulliana*, is probably a good example of the Ciceronian style. Most of John's letters, in fact, would probably serve, though none is so jammed with figures as that. Geoffrey gives Alain's *De planctu naturae* as an example of a poet writing the Tullian style in prose; see Appendix Two.

The hymn "Primo dierum omnium," which, as John is aware, is not accentual but iambic tetrameter, is not by Hilary. It has been ascribed with insufficient evidence to Gregory the Great, but is printed as anonymous in the *Analecta Hymnica*, 51: 24-26; see also A. S. Walpole, *Early Latin Hymns* [Cambridge, 1922], p. 262. For the example, and the word *domesticum*, see Appendix Two. Browne points out (p. lvii) that the quadrisyllable at the end of each sentence supplements the regular scheme.

The Isidorean style gets its name, not from the very plainly written *Etymologiae*, but from a brief work of Isidore's called *Synonyma* (*PL* 83, coll. 825-68). *Synonyma* is not about synonyms, but is a "lamentation of a sinful soul" which employs the figure of *Interpretatio* or Synonymy at every turn. See Francesco Di Capua, "Lo stile Isidoriano nella retorica medievale e in Dante," *Studii in onore di Francesco Torraca* (Naples, 1922), pp. 233-59; and, especially, J. Fontaine, "Théorie et pratique du style chez Isidore de Séville," *Vigiliae Christianae* 14 (1960): 65-101; both quote John of Garland. Fontaine points out that the style is that employed by Bernard, Bonaventure, and Richard of St. Victor. It may also be seen, I think, in Anselm's famous "Excitatio mentis ad contemplandum Deum" at the beginning of his *Proslogion*. It is not maintained throughout Augustine's *Soliloquies* (the source, according to Fontaine, of Isidore's style), but many passages display it. John employs it in part in the letter in *1*, 93-121. In my translation of the present example, I have preserved the balance of ideas, occasionally the balance in number of syllables, and in one or two instances the rhyme. On its content, cf. *Poetria nova*, l. 437 and Margaret F. Nims's note to the line in her *Poetria nova of Geoffrey of Vinsauf* (Toronto, 1967), p. 101; to the analogues she mentions, add John of Salisbury, *Metalogicon* 1.3.

464-65   The pileum was a biretta worn by masters (cf. Rashdall, 3:391); the gold ring a prerogative of the doctor (ibid., 1:228 f., 231n., 287).

CHAPTER SIX

26   *Ille ego qui quondam.* The first line of the spurious opening quatrain of the *Aeneid:*

> Ille ego, qui quondam gracili modulatus avena
> Carmen et egressus silvis vicina coegi
> Ut quamvis avido parerent arva colono,
> Gratum opus agricolis: at nunc horrentia Martis.

Priscian quotes the line in his treatment of pronouns as an example of a figurative joining of third- and first-person pronouns (*Institutiones grammaticae* 12.11; Keil, 2:583). John's use of the line as an example of pronouns *added* to proper nouns is curious, since the proper noun does not appear at all.

43   *suspensiua, constans, finitiua.* The three parts of a well-constructed, rhythmic sentence, known to the ancients as comma, colon, and period. "Sencio . . . sapienter" is the *suspensiva*, "legere . . . curialiter" the *constans*, "respondere . . . patienter" the *finitiva*. Cf. below, l. 118, *membrum*, and above, *2, 239, membrum orationis*. See further Baldwin, pp. 218-19, who gives references to treatments of the subject in the *dictamen* manuals (add Gervase of Melkley, Gräbener, pp. 217-18); Alexander of Ville-Dieu (see note to *5, 391-92*), ll. 2348-60 and Reichling's references; and Aristotle, *Rhetoric* 3.9.

48-49   *Igitur, Beatus Martinus.* Cf. John's *Compendium grammaticae*, Ms. Bruges

546, f. 117ʳ: "Rhetorice poni dicas igitur, quia sacris/Scripturis igitur Martinus sepe legetur." See Sulpicius Severus, *Vita beati Martini, PL* 20, coll. 159-76. Chapter Two begins "Igitur Martinus." This is the real *incipit*, since Chapter One is a prologue. Cf. also "Igitur Sancti Martini" (ch. 1, col. 161) and "Igitur Martinus" (start of ch. 6, col. 163). These would account for *sepe* in the passage in *Compendium grammaticae.*

49-51 The figure is *membrum* or *polysyndeton,* which John regards as synonymous (2, 239), though they are not. Cf. l. 118 below and note. The example, like that at l. 120, is imitated from *RAH* 4.19.26.

53-58 Cf. Geoffrey, *Documentum* 2.3.104-6 (Faral, pp. 303-4). One of Geoffrey's examples is "Vado propter socium. . . . Est socius mihi causa viae."

71 John's list of Figures follows the order of *RAH* 4.13.19-4.55.69, with a few exceptions: see the schema in Faral, pp. 52-54; he errs on p. 54 in omitting *diminutio* from John's list. About half his definitions are repeated verbatim or almost verbatim from that work. In other instances he changes the wording completely, usually in the direction of simplicity, but without altering the essential meaning of the figure. He adds some small element in a few cases, namely *Exclamatio, Similiter Desinens, Annominatio, Denominatio, Pronominatio.* But *RAH* was clearly his model.

In view of this close relation, I have usually followed Harry Caplan's translation of *RAH* in translating the names of the figures. I have departed from it in eight places, either for simplicity or because John's definition or example called for a different name.

John later treated the *colores* in a separate work, the *Exempla honestae vitae* (ed. Edwin Habel, *Romanische Forschungen* 29 [1910]:131-54). It lists them in exactly the same order as the present work, but its definitions, in the form of rubrics, are briefer. A number of the illustrative couplets from the present work are there repeated, often altered slightly.

Here these couplets form two roughly continuous poems, one for the figures of words, the other for the figures of thought. The first is addressed to the poet's friend, who seems at times to spurn him, at others to accept him. It is interspersed with vague biographical details concerning the author's coming to Paris and his thoughts on living there; with complaints against Fortune, and one appearance of the World, the Flesh, and the Devil; and with allusions to an earlier friend who has played the poet false, and is now seeking to undermine his new friendship. Occasional couplets are wholly unconnected with these themes. The second poem deals with the qualifications of the good teacher and the good student, with emphasis on the former. I have translated the couplets freely in order to reproduce the figures.

80 *Complexio* is merely the use of the two previous figures in combination: the repetition of both beginning and end, *qui* and *duo nos.*

85-90 The first example displays the first type of *Traductio,* the second the second: the third example shows both: homonyms (*Plasseto—placido—placeto; places—places*) and frequent reuse (*corde—cordis, placeto—places*). *Plassetum* is another name for the *clos de Garlande,* the section of the Left Bank of Paris from which John took his surname. See Evelyn Faye Wilson, "The *Georgica Spiritualia* of John of Garland," *Speculum* 8 (1933):370.

118 *Membrum.* At *2,* 239, John identifies *membrum* and *polysyndeton.* Actually the repeated conjunctions are incidental to the figure, whose essence is the use of one clause (the colon) which demands another.

121 *Que tamen inde seges:* cf. Juvenal, *Sat.* 7.103.

133 *Similiter desinunt.* In *RAH*, applied to incidental rhyme occurring in unin-flected words, as opposed to case-rhyme above. John applies it to strict poetic rhyme, opposing it to the quasi-rhyme of the last syllable only in case-rhyme. The point of the verses in the diagram is that each word in the line rhymes with the corresponding word in the next line (except the monosyllables in the verses in the center of the circle).

139 All the species of *Annominatio* that John lists here appear in *RAH* except the palindrome. *Annominatio* is John's favorite figure; it is treated thrice elsewhere in the work, at *1,* 335 ff., *5,* 214 ff., and *7,* 871 ff.; and it is used constantly in his poems. For all his attention to *RAH,* he has ignored the final paragraph of its treat-ment of *Annominatio,* where we are urged to use it very sparingly (4.23.32). Yet I have identified virtually every one of John's carefully distinguished subtypes in Book Three alone of *Paradise Lost.*

164 *Retrogradatione.* See above *2,* 196 ff.; Faral, p. 103. The syllables shortened or lengthened in *patronum, supremum, retro,* and *metro* are of variable quantity, as is the final *-o* in verb forms. Medieval poets allowed themselves to lengthen final short vowels in the position of the strong caesura (cf. W. B. Sedgwick, "The *Bellum Troianum* of Joseph of Exeter," *Speculum* 5 [1930] :50); thus *cunta (cuncta)* l. 168.

178 *Nos* is accusative; for a perfect example of the figure it should be nominative. Ll. 181-82 expand *nos super astra leuet.*

192 Cf. the previous example of *subiectio* at *4,* 389 ff., where the definition dif-fers slightly but the example contains some lines and phrases repeated here. The subject of both is taken from the example in *RAH* 4.23.33.

208 *Alia Species.* I.e., by change of case.

233 *Coniunctio.* A poor definition; the point is that the verb appears between two words or phrases that depend on it.

237-43 *Adiunctio.* John misses the point here, as his examples show. The verb put at the middle or end must join two objects or modifying phrases. Cf. *RAH* 4.27.38.

252 *Permissio.* As a figure, only appropriate to argumentation. John's example is not really figurative.

260 In the example, a *necessarium* is not retained.

273-74 The onomatopoeia is in *rudis.* Cf. *Graecismus* 19.38 (in a list of *voces animantium*): *rudit asellus. Tonas* is possibly also onomatopoeic, though the proper verb for *bos* is *mugit* (ibid., 19.34). *Rudere* and *fragor* are given as examples of *Nominatio* in *RAH* 4.31.42.

281-90 John's distinction between descriptive and nondescriptive metonymy is not in *RAH*. His definition of descriptive is practically verbatim the definition in *RAH* of metonymy itself; the definition of nondescriptive is put together from *RAH*'s list of the various kinds of metonymy.

303 The entire couplet is a synecdoche for "church." Cf. this gloss on f. 117^V of Ms. Bruges 546 (John's *Compendium grammaticae*): "Intellectio est color rethoricus quando per partes intelligimus totum, ut quando laudatur ecclesia per duas partes, ut in hiis versibus: 'Crux exaltatur illic, campana renarrat/Ecclesie laudes et capit ara preces.'" The two parts are presumably bell and altar. This is closer to a riddle than what we know as synecdoche. Another way of interpreting it is that cross, bell, and altar are three separate synecdoches for "Christianity."

307 The first line of the couplet exhibits metaphor of verb and noun (*mittit fulmen*); the second metaphor of a whole phrase or clause. Besides the main metaphor in *manus ense perit, ambigea* is also metaphorical for "heretical."

311-12 All of these phrases except *Minerua nitens* are given as independent examples of *Abusio* in *RAH* 4.33.45.

313 *Permutatio*. The definition is of Irony, which in *RAH* is only one of three types of *Permutatio*, which is defined as "oratio aliud verbis aliud sententia demonstrans" (4.34.46). John's example, however, displays all three types: the whole is an extended metaphor (*permutatio per similitudinem*); *canis* and *lupus* are *permutatio per argumentum* (minifying epithet); *pastor ouilis* is *permutatio per contrarium* (irony).

317 *Conclusio* appears in *RAH* after *Precisio*; it is put out of order here because it ends the poem on friendship, and the section on figures of words.

343-44 *causa ornatus*. Not in *RAH*. The whole definition is a simplification, and does not differentiate this figure from *Interpretatio* (1. 244).

370 *aliena*. Probably erroneous, mistakenly taken up from the next line in the archetype.

379-84 The speaker in the example is not inanimate. *RAH* defines two forms of *Conformatio:* making an absent person speak as if present, or making a mute thing speak. John's definition is confined to the latter, his example to the former.

386-87 The *Significatio* is in the two relative clauses; they suggest, but do not specifically say, "poor students." *Repetas lecta* probably means "read this treatise on figures over again carefully."

400 ff. From Cicero's *De inventione* 1.24.34-1.25.36. Cf. Faral, pp. 77-79; Matthew of Vendôme, *Ars versificatoria* 1.77 (Faral, p. 136); *Anticlaudianus* 3.217-19. See also *5*, 373 ff. above.

414-16 This probably refers to the poems on friendship and teaching used to illustrate the figures of speech; cf. the statement in the Introductory Summary that the work belongs in part to Ethics. It is also a good way to mention Delivery without discussing it, and thus complete the scheme of organizing the work around the ancient five parts of rhetoric: Invention, Disposition, and Elocution or Embellishment have each been accorded a chapter, and Memory was given at least a paragraph;

so something must be said of Delivery. Geoffrey of Vinsauf treats Delivery briefly at the end of both his works (*Poetria nova*, ll. 2031-65: Faral, pp. 259-60; *Documentum* 2.3. 170-75: Faral, pp. 318-19).

CHAPTER SEVEN

6 *Hec est secunda tragedia.* This statement is not as outlandish as it at first appears. The Greek tragedies were of course unknown, and Seneca not widely known: see Cloetta, pp. 14-15 (where this statement of John's is included as evidence for that assertion), 35. Thus John knew no *dramatic* tragedy; he only knew the references to Ovid's lost *Medea,* and of course he had seen the form mentioned and variously defined by many theorists, whom Cloetta discusses in detail on pp. 16-48. As Cloetta points out, none of these writers can refer to specific examples of tragedy: Geoffrey of Vinsauf, for instance, treating comedy and tragedy in ll. 1883-1919 of the *Poetria nova,* gives an example of a comedy but not of a tragedy. Though some medieval men considered the *Thebaid,* the *Pharsalia,* and even the *Aeneid* tragedies (Cloetta, p. 51), John apparently did not agree. (The reference to Ovid's *Medea* may imply that he dismissed them because they were not dramatic, but neither is his own tragedy; the likelier cause was either their epic scope or their lack of a clear pattern of initial joy and final sorrow.)

Thus it is perfectly understandable that John knew no dramatic work that fitted the definition. As for medieval narrative tragedies, Cloetta can adduce only four before John's. He says himself that the fifth-century *Orestis tragoedia* was clearly unknown in John's time; the only others are Bernard Silvestris's *De patricida,* Peter of Blois's lost *Tragoedia de Flaura et Marco,* and the *Versus de Affra et Flavo.* John must have known these, but he would not have considered them tragedies, since all three are in elegiac couplets. He has said (5, 371) that elegiacs are the form for comedy. We have at least a later tradition that hexameters are proper to tragedy; cf. Chaucer's monk (whose brief narrative tragedies are quite similar to John's conception of the genre):

> Tragedie is to seyn a certeyn storie,
> As olde bookes maken us memorie,
> Of hym that stood in greet prosperitee,
> And is yfallen out of heigh degree
> Into myserie, and endeth wrecchedly.
> And they ben versified communely
> Of six feet, which men clepen exametron.

(*Canterbury Tales,* 7.1973-79, quoted from *The Works of Geoffrey Chaucer,* ed. F. N. Robinson, 2d ed. [Boston, 1957]; the passage is mentioned by Cloetta, p. 51.) It is true that John uses hexameters for his comedy, but they are leonines, which are quite different; this tragedy is the only poem in the treatise in which he employs pure hexameters.

Thus while we may be rightly exasperated by the process of reasoning it takes to make sense out of the statement, it remains possible to do so. And its very boldness may in fact be due to a feeling on John's part that the few poems he knew that paraded as tragedies were wanting in one respect or another. Interestingly, Geoffrey of Vinsauf makes a similar remark in the *Documentum* about comedy: "Sed illa quae [Horatius] condidit de comoedia hodie penitus recesserunt ab aula et occiderunt in desuetudinem" (2.3.163; Faral, p. 317).

24 *graui stilo.* If it seems curious that the story of two washerwomen can exemplify the high style, it should be noted in the first place that, though the chief characters are washerwomen, a military action is the scene, and soldiers appear; this no doubt was sufficient to satisfy John on the score of subject matter (cf. Figure Three, p. 40). But further, cf. the statement (5, 53) that "low matter can be exalted" by a proper choice of diction. Words like *turma, prelia, menia, balista* describing the scene are obvious. Love is also treated in military terms: *femina . . . Cuius . . . concordia bellum* (49-50); *famule non parua secunde/Gloria* (55-56); so also the argument between the two women: *sauccia tela . . . illita tela ueneno* (73-74): *luctatur . . . ledit . . . cruentat* (93-96). The rage of the jilted woman is expressed in high terms, and the closing scene returns once more to the military action. Though figurative language is appropriate to all levels of style (cf. *4*, 418-19; *5*, 81-83), still expressions such as *bis xxx* (45) and *ter . . . decem* (89) are undoubtedly thought of as devices to exalt the style.

Aside from the absurd discrepancy between subject matter and style, this is certainly the best of John's illustrative poems in quantitative verse. It is free from allegory and the vague, obscure locutions with which John fills his attempts in that form (cf. "Cvm citharizat auis," *1*, 407 and "Si graue delires," *4*, 207). The diction is consistently concrete, the confrontation between the washerwomen shows a certain fertility of invention, and the rage of the jilted girl and its consequences are presented with some power. Certain individual lines achieve a clarity and fluency absent from the other poems, for example: "Omnia nocte silent media, uigilesque sopori/Inuitat labor insompnis." *Annominatio*, which usually lures John irresistibly into pettiness, is not much in evidence; but he can use it aptly: "Que solet amplecti manibus, perplectitur ense/Colla." It is, of course, no masterpiece, but it comes as some refreshment to the reader who has struggled with the earlier poems.

There are two analogues to the story. In the French fabliau "D'Une seule fame qui a son con servoit c. chevaliers de tous poins" (*Recueil général des fabliaux*, ed. Anatole de Montaiglon [Paris, 1872], 1:294-300), one hundred knights in a besieged castle are divided into two groups of fifty, each group served by a woman. During a time when the knights are out resisting an attack, a wounded knight proclaims his love for the woman not of his group; she resists feebly, and eventually he enjoys her and she gets him to kill the other woman. There is an inquisition, but she is acquitted when she promises to serve all one hundred men.

In the Middle English "Avowynge of Arthur" (*Three Early English Metrical Romances*, ed. John Robson [London, 1842]); also in Walter H. French and C. B. Hale, eds., *Middle English Metrical Romances* (New York, 1930), Baldwin, explaining to Arthur a vow never to be jealous of his wife, recalls that once Arthur's father gave Baldwin a castle with more than five hundred men; three women served the needs of these men; two of the women, jealous of the third, kill her; the two avoid punishment by promising to serve well all the men. The uglier of these two kills the other; again she is spared on the condition that she serve everyone well. From this Baldwin takes the moral that a woman can improve if she gives herself to good deeds. There is no siege involved here; but that motive appears when Baldwin goes on to explain the other two vows he has made.

The plot in the *Avowynge of Arthur* was first compared to that of "D'une seule fame" by Gaston Paris, *Histoire litteraire de la France,* 30:112; G. L. Kittredge pointed out the relation of John's "tragedy" to both in *Modern Language Notes* 8 (1893), 251-52; he concludes, "If, as Paris is inclined to think, the fabliau and the date [*sic,* for tale?] in the Avowing are founded on an actual occurrence, the tragedy appears to be nearer the facts than they are. It affords a straightforward story, of which the French and English poems may well have been cynical developments."

115 *Cilla.* Cf. *Metamorphoses* 13.730 ff.

156-87 The Crusade at issue is the Fifth (1218-21), which had been instigated by Innocent III and was carried on by his successor, Honorius III, after his accession in July 1216. Frederick II sent troops, and promised to go in person to Jerusalem, but he never actually did so in this Crusade.

259 Cf. *Metamorphoses* 1.682-83: "Euntem multa loquendo/Detinuit sermone diem."

282 *infra annos.* Usually "underage," but the context demands the opposite. It seems to mean "within the age of discretion"; cf. above, l. 29: *infra quas (arces).*

351 Actually, it is from *priva lex,* "private law." For a very similar set of instructions, including instructions for the device at the end, cf. Rockinger, 1:111-13. For *litterae longae,* "tall letters," cf. Rockinger, 1:111, 197; 2:782.

382 *Titulus.* The principal churches of Rome are each the titular cure of a cardinal, who is called the "title" of that church; "title" also means the church itself. Cf. *NED,* s.v. title, 9.

417-18 The reconstruction of the Church of St. Julian went on through most of the first half of the thirteenth century. The exact date of completion is not known. Cf. Joseph Nasrallah, *The Church of Saint-Julien-le-Pauvre* (Paris, 1961), p. 3.

451-54 On forgiveness of forgotten sins, cf. Henry C. Lea, *A History of Auricular Confession and Indulgences in the Latin Church* (3 vols., Philadelphia, 1896), 3:53, 165. On indulgences for the souls of one's parents, cf. ibid., p. 337, n. 4.

467 *Incipit Ars Rithmica.* There are several indications that John wrote the *ars rhythmica* separately and simply appended it to his *Poetria* when he conceived the idea of a comprehensive treatise. The most direct piece of evidence for this is the phrase *in fine huius tractatus* (*4,* 513), referring to the examples of various documents that immediately precede the *ars rhythmica.* The disproportionate length of Chapter Seven is another indication, as is the lack of cross-reference between the two parts, despite some overlapping material such as the paragraph *De Coloribus Rethoricis,* l. 863 ff. One would have expected, too, if John were attempting a truly comprehensive work, some rhymed poetry among the examples in the first six chapters.

Certainly it is capable of being detached from the rest, as Mari detached it, for it is self-contained and largely self-explanatory, quite the most lucidly organized and single-minded of John's discussions. Yet it does not lack difficulties, and I have thought it useful to place here a brief general guide to its contents.

It is best thought of as divided into five main parts, treating in turn: (1) "simple" poems (ll. 498-580), (2) "composite" poems (ll. 581-997), (3) "apparently composite" poems (ll. 1014-1118), (4) some miscellaneous types (ll. 1172-1280), and (5) certain quantitative forms (ll. 1357-1984). Since the fifth section treats quantitative verse, the *ars rhythmica* strictly defined ends at l. 1356. Two "afterthought" sections blur this division slightly: ll. 998-1013 treat an additional kind of simple poem, and ll. 1281-1345 fill out the treatment of composite poems. Ll. 1119-71, 1346-56, and 1985-end are passages of summary; ll. 467-97 introduce the whole. In order, then, the treatise proceeds as follows:

467-97	Introduction: rhymed poetry in general
498-580	First type: simple poems
581-997	Second type: composite poems
998-1013	More on simple poems
1014-1118	Third type: apparently composite poems
1119-71	Summary
1172-1280	Miscellaneous tangent types
1281-1345	More on composite poems
1346-56	Summary
1357-1984	Quantitative forms
1985-end	Summary list

Two central distinctions govern the discussion. The first, between "iambic" and "spondaic" lines, is made at ll. 487-91. Since it is not explicitly stated, one should note that it is the last word in a line that determines whether that line is iambic or spondaic: if its penult is long (e.g. *Maria, nota, diei*), the line is spondaic; if the penult is short (e.g. *previa, celestia, vitia*), it is iambic. An important difference in the treatment of these two basic types is that varying the length of the line makes for distinct subtypes of spondaic but not—with one exception (see note to ll. 601-5)—for iambics. Thus John consistently distinguishes between spondaic lines of four syllables (dispondaic), six syllables (trispondaic), and eight syllables (tetraspondaic), whereas iambic lines may be of seven or eight syllables without constituting a new subtype. The one exception, which does not form an integral part of John's system, is the ten-syllable iambic, treated in ll. 998-1013. (We would consider all of John's "spondaic" types trochaic, and his "iambics" as combining two trochees and a dactyl [seven-syllable] or a dactyl, a trochee, and a dactyl [eight-syllable]).

The second central distinction is between "simple" and "composite" poems. In a simple poem either all the lines are spondaic or all are iambic. A composite poem contains a mixture of both types. The fundamental rhythm, spondaic or iambic, of a composite poem is established in the first line. The line or lines of the other type provide what is called alternately the *diuersa consonancia* (l. 720) (or simply *consonancia*, e.g. l. 723), which I have translated as "harmonic variation"; *differencia* (most often, e.g. l. 725), translated "variation"; or *caudula* (l. 1118) or *cauda* (l. 1138), "tail." This is true even if the "variation" comes at every other line.

These two central distinctions, then, provide the basis for John's first two main sections. By a further permutation, they also occasion the third main section (ll. 1014-1118), on "apparently composite" poems. These are simple poems, that is, wholly spondaic or wholly iambic, but appear to be composite because they contain a "variation," but of their own rhythmic type. Spondaic poems are varied by a "tail" which is either a spondaic line of a different length, such as a dispondaic in a basically tetraspondaic poem, or a spondaic of the same length but with a new rhyming word; iambics are varied by a "tail" which is an iambic line of the same length but with a new rhyming word.

The various combinations which each of these three main divisions engenders yield, after certain arbitrary limitations of length are applied, forty-four varieties of stanza: ten simple, eighteen composite, and sixteen apparently composite, all of which are listed at the end (with several errors: see note to ll. 1985-2031). Given those arbitrary limitations, which John asserts are established by usage, it is a complete system, though it is possible to find inconsistencies and loopholes in it (see notes to ll. 601-5 and 1985-2031). If it does not go very far toward teaching a would-be poet how to compose rhymed poetry, it at least gives him a systematic notion of what forms usage has made available to him, and suggests by example and an occasional precept some of the effects possible in each form.

There are other instances of rhymed poetry, however, which are either wholly apart from this system, or incorporate refinements which have nothing to do with it: rhymed quantitative verse, for instance, or palindromes, or rhymed stanzas to which are appended quantitative lines lifted from classical authors; these John touches on in his fourth section, and so effectively completes the *ars rhythmica*. The remainder is devoted to some particular forms of quantitative verse: three meters for hymns, and the nineteen meters of Horace. They are appropriately treated here, as an appendage to the *ars rhythmica*, both because the hymn is a form which was open to both quantitative and accentual verse, because two of the hymns given are loosely rhymed, and because no earlier section of the treatise has provided a convenient resting place for attention to metrical form as distinct from genre.

Mari's *I trattati medievali di ritmica latina* (Milan, 1899), which contains seven other treatises besides John's, is still the standard collection of *artes rhythmicae*. They are all evidently interconnected, though exactly how is quite unclear. According to Mari (p. 2), "in nessun modo possiamo designare il tempo e la fonte primissima di tale insegnamento." He can only say that they seem to have sprung up at or slightly before 1200 in France, in which case John's would be among the earliest. We have, however, an example from the eleventh century, a brief "Consideratio rithmorum" in Alberic of Monte Cassino's *Breviarium de dictamine;* it is printed by Owen J. Blum, O.F.M. as an appendix to his article, "Alberic of Monte Cassino and the Hymns and Rhythms Attributed to Saint Peter Damian," *Traditio* 12 (1956):87-148. Traces of still earlier critical attention to *rhythmus* occur in Bede's *Ars metrica* (*PL* 90, coll. 149-76; see coll. 173-74, *de rhythmo*) and in a ninth-century treatise on music by a monk of Orleans, printed by Martin Gerbert, *Scriptores ecclesiastici de musica* (3 vols., Typis San-Blasianis, 1784), 1:33. This work is mentioned by Mari in an important article analyzing the treatises published in his collection, "Ritmo latino e terminologia ritmica medievale," *Studi di filologia romanza* 8 (1899): 35-88 (see p. 41, n. 4); and by G. Lote, *Histoire du vers Français* (3 vols., Paris, 1949-55), 1:48. It suggests that, as John himself says (ll. 469-70), *ars rhythmica* grew out of musical as well as grammatical and literary theory; for an account of these connections see Karl Borinski, *Die Antike in Poetik und Kunsttheorie* (2 vols., Leipzig, 1914), 1:43-55, and "Antike Versharmonik im Mittelalter und in der Renaissance," *Philologus* 71 (n.s. 25) (1912):139-58; and Richard L. Crocker, "*Musica Rhythmica* and *Musica Metrica* in Antique and Medieval Theory,"

Journal of Music Theory 2 (1958):2-23. Both Borinski and Crocker stress the importance of Augustine's *De musica*, which is chiefly about rhythms. Of course, the late, full treatises like John's were preceded by much practice; they merely codify what the poets of the eleventh and twelfth centuries, particularly the sequence writers whose development is chronicled by Raby (*CLP*, pp. 345-75), had worked out in their poems. Mari is surely right when he supposes that before the laws of rhythmics found their way into the *artes*, they had "più che probabilmente già da lunga pezza si trasmettevano nelle chiese di su gli schemi degli inni e furon poscia meglio plasmate nelle scuole a glossare le agili strofe di Adamo di S. Vittore e d'Ugo d'Orléans" (p. 3).

What influence these treatises had, both on poetic practice and on later theoretical discussions, is also uncertain. As for theory, there is surely a connection between the Latin *artes* and treatises both on the vernacular such as Dante's *De vulgari eloquentia*, Antonio da Tempo's *Summa artis ritmici vulgaris dictaminis*, and in the vernacular, such as Eustache Deschamps's *L'Art de dictier*, the famous Provençal *Les Leys d'amours*, and the works published by Ernest Langlois in his *Recueil d'arts de seconde rhétorique* (Paris, 1902). The fullest treatment of these matters is in Warner F. Patterson, *Three Centuries of French Poetic Theory (1328-1630)* (2 vols., Ann Arbor, Mich., 1935), though he is disappointing in his account of Latin *ars rhythmica*. Clearly more work needs to be done in this area; neither Borinski nor Patterson add any research to Mari. In particular, more texts need to be found and edited; the unpublished treatise from which I have given excerpts in Appendix Three indicates not only that John's treatise had some influence, but that other treatises existed of which we presently know nothing. (A good book on the relation of the theory to the practice of medieval poets is Roger Dragonetti, *La Technique poétique des trouvères dans la chanson courtoise: Contribution à l'étude de la rhétorique médiévale* [Bruges, 1960]).

470-71 For this tripartite division of music, cf. Boethius, *De institutione musica* (ed. G. Friedlein, Leipzig, 1867), 1:2; see also gloss to *1*, 55 above and David S. Chamberlain, "Philosophy of Music in the *Consolatio* of Boethius," *Speculum* 45 (1970):80-97. For the general background of the relation of *rhythmus* to music, see the writings by Karl Borinski mentioned in the preceding note. John's discussion may have specifically influenced Deschamps's treatment of poetry and music in *L'Art de dictier:* cf. Patterson (in preceding note), 1:19, 87-95.

589-615 *De Consonanciis et Proporcionibus Rithmorum.* This is a hard paragraph: I am not sure I understand it. Though one might expect that John is comparing relative note values in music to long and short syllables in poetry—using "proportion" in its notational sense—there is no way I can work it out to make sense. I therefore take the first sentence to mean that no single rhyme is used more than four times in succession, a principle John adheres to throughout. If the line is the basic unit, then a couplet represents, as it were, a 1:2 proportion (though this proportion is not mentioned in the opening statement, it is in the next clause); a third line makes the proportion 2:3 in relation to a couplet, and a fourth line 3:4 in relation to a triplet. That is the limit; the variation or new rhyme cannot come later than the fifth line. The clause about musical proportion is stated in terms of pure numbers; the proportions mentioned are, however, those that result in the musical intervals of, respectively, an octave, a fifth, and a fourth, or a diapason, diapente, and diatesseron. The next sentence strengthens the musical analogy both by drawing attention to two modes of medieval part-singing which exemplify the various proportions John has been speaking of, and by repeating the analogy in new terms, substituting the words diapente, etc. for the proportions they represent. Thus a poem with a new rhyme in the third line would be a diapason, since its proportion is 1:2; a poem with a new rhyme in the fourth line a diapente, since its proportion is 2:3; and a poem with a new rhyme in the fifth line a diatesseron, since its proportion is 3:4.

This may make some sense of the paragraph itself, though it does not explain at all the *ergo* that ties the next paragraph to it, nor the application of the term *sequaltera (sexquialtera)* in ll. 758-59 to the two kinds of stanza given in that paragraph, nor the term *diapente* applied to a new rhyme in the fifth line at ll. 751 and 2012. Indeed in these later usages John seems to have abandoned abstruse musical theory in favor of a very general and inaccurate application of its terms, *sexquialtera* meaning "rhyming in every other line," *diapente* "varied at the fifth line."

It is clear in any event that what John is trying to do in this paragraph is in general to extend his earlier statement that *rhythmus* is a part of music, and specifically to account for the use of the word *consonantia* in both poetry and music. Since that cannot be done in any mathematically precise way, he later settles for general and analogical uses of terms he tries to use strictly here.

The passage is translated and discussed by William G. Waite, "Johannes de Garlandia, Poet and Musician," *Speculum* 35 (1960):179-95, on pp. 190-91; I am indebted both to that translation and discussion and to personal conversation with Professor Waite for what understanding I have of it, though he is not responsible for my errors. The reader is also referred to John's discussion of proportion in his treatise on music: see E. De Coussemaker, ed., *Scriptorum de musica medii aevi, novam seriem* (4 vols., Paris, 1864-76), 1:106. The passage also troubled Zarncke (cf. Introduction, p. xxii) and Mari. Borinski, "Antike Versharmonik" (see above, note to l. 467), describes with scorn their attempts to puzzle it out, then offers his own "einfach" solution, which is based on the treatise by Nicholas Tibino in Mari's collection: the key is the "interval" or number of syllables between rhymes, which Nicholas says can be no less than four and no more than eight. The "interval" of four is a diatesseron, or eight a diapason. But John's discussion is followed almost immediately by a poem with eleven syllables between the rhymes. Tibino's dictum may be his own attempt to make sense of John's passage, or other passages it may have fostered, but it does not seem applicable to John's practice. And whatever John is talking about in this passage, I do not think it is number of syllables. Thus Borinski's article does not seem to me to clear this matter up at all, though it is valuable for its broad view of the history of *ars rhythmica*.

601-5 Here John counts poems of alternating spondaic and iambic lines as just two types, one with the spondaic first and one with the iambic first. The examples are of tetraspondaic. But later, at ll. 1317-45, he takes up alternating spondaics and iambics again, and counts alternating dispondaics and iambics as two types, and alternating trispondaics and iambics as two more types. Thus there are really six types of poem that alternate spondaics and iambics, all six of which are included in the list at the end. That list, however, still contains an inaccuracy, since in the example here of the iambic preceding the spondaic, two syllables are removed from the spondaic, making it a trispondaic; thus there is no such thing as "tetraspondaics and iambics alternating, the iambic first" (l. 2008). There are still, however, six distinct types, since in the example at l. 1338 of an iambic followed by a trispondaic the iambic has eight syllables, as John notes (l. 1345), whereas here (l. 612) it has seven syllables.

617 *Taurum sol intrauerat*. Wilhelm Wattenbach, ed., "Ganymed und Helena," *Zeitschrift für Deutsches Altertum* 17 (1875): 124-36. For other editions and notices, cf. Walther, *Versanfänge*, 19029.

625 *beniuoli naute*. The "friendly sailors" to whom the poem is addressed seem to be Logic, Ethics, and Theology. In l. 628 the *uos* addressed are said to "shine like a mirror" on the speaker; in l. 636 the mirror is said to be "threefold." The next three stanzas explain each mirror; the explanations are cloudy, but the glosses make clear that they are Logic, Ethics, and Theology. The rest of the poem laments the inherent inadequacy of Theology and its ancillary disciplines—they cannot replace the Beatific Vision—but asserts the human value of these three interrelated areas of study as providing, if not the Truth itself, the best path we have to the Truth.

710-17 This paragraph is parenthetical; John does not use its terminology again. Since he admits only four rhythmical types of line (dispondaic, trispondaic, tetraspondaic, and iambic), it is clear that *membra diuersarum specierum* cannot mean rhythmical types, or a "pentascolic" would be impossible. Evidently by "different kinds of line" John simply means lines with different rhyming words (cf. ll. 856-58 below: "the rhyme itself makes for variation in a simple rhymed poem"). Thus the stanza in ll. 728-33 is triscolic because it has three different rhyming sounds. The stanzas of the poem "Ad insultus equoris" (l. 622) are pentascolic. Most of John's stanzas, as is proper in highly developed *rhythmus*, are not more than triscolic. The "polyscolic" sequences are the early, "irregular" sequences, mostly composed before the twelfth century and, if rhymed at all, mostly employing mere assonance or one-syllable rhyme (cf. Raby, *CLP*, pp. 345 ff.).

758 *predictis duabus speciebus*. Ll. 601-5, although the second of those should be considered an iambic, not a spondaic type, since the iambic provides the basis which the spondaic varies.

782-855 Various versions of the life of Saint Catherine of Alexandria existed in the Middle Ages; they are listed in the Bollandist *Bibliotheca hagiographica latina antiquae et mediae aetatis* (Brussels, 1898-99), pp. 251-55. The version in Mombritius's *Sanctuarium* (eds. Monachi Solesmenses, 2 vols., Paris, 1910, 1:283-87) contains all the details used by John. The emperor is Maxentius; Porphyry is an officer of the imperial guard, and the two hundred converts his men; Cursates or Cusarsates is a *praefectus urbis* who suggests the idea of the wheel and executes it; the mountain is Mt. Sinai. The poem is quite in the manner of Adam of St. Victor, and would make a perfectly good sequence for Saint Catherine's day.

863-66 These figures are treated above in Chapter Six as follows: *Similiter Desinens*, l. 133; *Compar in Numero Sillabarum*, l. 126; *Annominatio*, ll. 139-87; *Traductio*, l. 83; *Exclamatio*, l. 97; *Repetitio*, l. 71.

1002 *Diri patris infausta pignora.* Not, of course, by Statius, though attributed to him in some manuscripts. Cf. Paul M. Clogan, "The *Planctus* of Oedipus: Text and Commentary," *Medievalia et Humanistica,* n.s. 1 (1970):233–39. For other editions and notices, cf. Walther, *Versanfänge,* 4511.

1007 The rhythm might be called dactylic because of the last foot; see above, note to l. 467: the last word in the line determines the rhythm. John is not speaking here of quantitative verse, in which, of course, the last syllable of a dactyl must be short, but rather of a "quasi-dactyl" as defined in Chapter Five, ll. 410-11, and applying the terminology of quantitative to accentual rhythm. Thus the ablative *agrĭcŏlā,* for example, is a dactyl by accent even though the last syllable is long. For the falling rhythm of iambics, see above, ll. 776-80.

1139 The "accident" is that the *differentia* or variation is extended to two lines: cf. above, l. 723. This poem is "essentially" a two-membered tetraspondaic with iambic variation, like that in l. 743.

1141 *Vita iusti gloriosa.* Not otherwise recorded.

1165 *spondaicis.* An error; actually twelve are spondaic, four iambic. Possibly the text originally read *spondaicis et iambicis.*

1184 *duplex rithmus.* Because it may also be read:

> Pollens imperium
> Mundum subiecerat;
> Orbi excidium
> Cesar incusserat
> Ense cruento.

1225-80 For this form, popularized by Walter of Châtillon and christened by the Germans *Vagantenstrophe mit Auctoritas,* see Raby, *SLP* 2:196-214 and references on p. 196, n. 2. The matter of the poem is to be associated with the Feast of Fools, an occasion for which Walter of Châtillon also wrote several satirical poems; cf. Karl Strecker, ed., *Moralisch-satirische Gedichte Walters von Chatillon* (Heidelberg, 1929), p. 122 ff. and A. Wilmart, "Poèmes de Gautier de Châtillon dans un manuscrit de Charleville," *Revue Bénédictine* 49 (1937):138-39. These poems, with Strecker's and Wilmart's notes, provide a certain background for John's, but hardly explain all its obscurities.

These include several apparent shifts of tone and some murky references. In the first two stanzas the poet is largely concerned to say, as obliquely as possible, that he is writing at Christmas; but the stanzas already suggest the irresponsible mood of the Feast of Fools. The next five stanzas are straightforward praise of a certain "doctor." The eighth stanza alludes apparently to a student who has taken advantage of the doctor's good nature and given him a thrashing at Christmas (evidently a regular feature of the feast among Parisian students; see *M*'s gloss to l. 1257). The poet is indignant: why do that to a man so excellent? His indignation turns in stanza nine to more rational remonstration, addressed now to a group, not just to one person.

In stanza ten the tone shifts oddly; the poet now blames his fellow students' conduct on the rigorous life of study. He is suddenly on their side, urging the doctor to let them all live a life of ease. Here the irresponsible tone suggested at the start takes over, and he indulges in a perhaps exaggerated description of obscene revelry presided over by the "master," who may or may not be a different person from the doctor. Yet he cannot keep a note of satire from creeping in, especially in the scathing eleventh stanza. He ends by stressing once more the doctor's kindness, as if to excuse his own indulgence. On the whole he seems unable to decide whether he approves of the tomfoolery or not. The poem must have arisen out of the events and personages of some particularly memorable university Christmas, now irrecoverable.

1363 *ex pedibus istis.* This description fits the fourth line only; in the other three lines the choriambus is repeated. Curiously, John correctly names Asclepiades here, though he calls him Asclepius in *1, 71.*

1444-71 *Solis superni regia.* B. A. Park and Elizabeth S. Dallas, "A *Sequentia cum prosa* by John of Garland," *Medievalia et Humanistica* 15 (1963) (on the poem "Aula vernat virginalis" in John's *Commentarius*):62-63, have shown that the imagery and diction of the first two stanzas of this poem are derived from Ovid's description of the court of the sun in the opening lines of Book Two of the *Metamorphoses:* "Regia Solis erat sublimibus alta columnis,/Clara micante auro flammasque imitante pyropo."

1454-55 A confusing mixture of metaphors. The simple statement is that Anna and Joachim conceive Mary, who is destined to bring them grace. But if she is a splendid palace, then they are cottages, their breasts roofs, which Mary will cleanse. At the same time, since they are planting a seed, they are cultivating her. John seems not to have blanched at the curious spectacle of a palace cleansing a cottage which has cultivated it. For the idea of "spiritual georgic" from which the agricultural imagery comes, see Evelyn Faye Wilson, "The *Georgica Spiritualia* of John of Garland," *Speculum* 8 (1933):358-77, esp. p. 372.

1476-77 *Constat . . . suo.* That is, the Adonic (*luce choruscas*) is like the last two feet of a hexameter; the Asclepiad (*O quam glorifica:* a spondee and a choriambus, like the beginning of an Asclepiad) is like any section of a hexameter: a spondee, a dactyl, and the long that begins the next foot.

1478 In several statements John gives the impression that he thought Horace wrote only nineteen odes, one of each type. He probably did not know the *Odes* at first hand, but learned the meters ultimately from Servius's *De metris Horatii* (Keil, 4:468-72). Yet he may have known some of them: l. 1436 above, "Te duce, Christe," is a clear imitation of the last line of the second ode of the first book, "Te duce, Caesar," and further evidence is adduced by Lester K. Born, "An Analysis of the Quotations and Citations in the *Compendium grammatice* of John of Garland," *Classical, Mediaeval, and Renaissance Studies in Honor of Berthold Louis Ullman,* ed. Charles Henderson (2 vols., Rome, 1964), 2:51-83. John gives the meters, as Servius does, in the order in which they appear in the *Odes* and *Epodes.* His foot-divisions occasionally vary from the modern standard, but the meters themselves all match Horace's except number twelve, which is short one foot. (Even here he has authority. Servius says [Keil, 4:471], "Duodecima ode monocolos est. Metro enim, quod ionico a minore fit, continetur, quod quidem *non numero pedum, sed*

sensus fine concluditur, atque ideo a multis sinafia ['continuity of rhythm']
nominatur" [italics mine]). For the orthodox foot-divisions, the standard titles
of the meters, and the places of their first appearances in Horace, the reader may
consult the convenient analysis in J. H. Allen and J. B. Greenough, *New Latin
Grammar,* rev. and ed. by J. B. Greenough and others, 2d ed. (Boston, 1903), pp.
421-25.

1481 *cuiusdam formosi iuuenis.* Apparently some particular boy of John's
acquaintance, called "Paris" because he is more interested in love than learning.
But the name also causes him to represent allegorically the University of Paris at
large; the whole community is urged here to the life of study. Thus the poems end
the treatise as it began, with "Parisian poetry."

1484 *proponam.* The muse Terpsichore is speaking: cf. l. 1533. The *gemine
sorores* are Urania, who inspires meters 2-10, and Calliope, who inspires meters
11-19. Cf. ll. 1750-53.

1532-56 *Descriptio Vranie.* This poem relies in a general way on the description
of the virgin Astronomy in *Anticlaudianus* 4.1-69. See also Martianus Capella, *De
nuptiis mercurii et philologiae* 2.118. Ll. 1543-46 are a favorite subject of John's;
cf. *Morale scholarium,* ll. 267-70 and Paetow, p. 163 n.

1640 Cf. Horace, *AP* 1-5. On this entire poem, cf. my article, "John of Garland
and Horace: a Medieval Schoolman Faces the *Ars poetica," Classical Folia* 22
(1968):3-13, esp. p. 7.

1663 *Sextum Metrum.* No title given; the subject is apparently ungrateful students—John seems to have been rebuffed by some former student now a bishop.
Cf. *Morale scholarium,* ll. 160-62.

1762 Not a new meter, but the Second Asclepiad, as in number three above.

1829 Cf. *Metamorphoses* 8.631: "pia Baucis anus."

1895-1912 The general drift of this poem is clear enough: its target is the wide-
spread medieval interest in magic and demonology. Paris is warned to shun the
sort of university man who uses occult knowledge for sexual gain, both because
of the snares of the devil and because women, though victims, have snares of
their own. For a pleasant fictional account of how one might "deceive women
with phantasms," cf. Chaucer's "Franklin's Tale"; Nicholas in the "Miller's Tale"
also makes use of astrological expertise to further his sexual aims. But John's
severe tone suggests he may be alluding to something much graver than astrological
machinations: a cult of devil worship whose female members engaged in ritual copulation with a man they thought was the devil. Though there is no particular evidence
that it penetrated to the universities, some students may have tinkered with it.
Margaret Murray's *The Witch-Cult in Western Europe* (Oxford, 1921) gives a superb
account and analysis of the cult, although the place of incantations ("Tirecie uel
Mantos carmina uana"; cf. *B* glosses to *Tirecie,* "illius diuinatoris nigromancie,"
and *Illos,* l. 1906, "incantatores") in them is not made clear. Tiresias and Manto
appear together in *Inferno* XX.

1985-2031   This list, which, along with the list of metrical feet that precedes it, appears only in *M*, may not be by John. Though it reaches the total of forty-four types that John reaches at l. 1348, it does so in a different way. (1) Ll. 2013-14 add two general types of iambic already treated specifically in ll. 1997-98, 2002-3, and 2007-8. (2) Ll. 2030-31 add two types of trispondaic which do not differ from ll. 1999-2001. (3) It omits the four types of iambic with iambic variation treated in ll. 1094-1115. For another error in it, see note to ll. 601-5.

Textual Notes

Corrections in Ms. Bruges 546

Most of the corrected readings appear in the text; in these cases only the original, erroneous reading is recorded here. In a few cases, a correction has been rejected either for the original reading or for a third reading from another ms.; in these cases both readings are given here and the correction marked by an asterisk. Both readings are also given when it is necessary to make clear which word in the line is at issue. The supplying of omitted words is indicated by *add*. A question mark after a word means the correction has obscured the original reading.

INTRODUCTORY SUMMARY

9 ordnate   18 finem n   28 poematibus/positis

CHAPTER ONE

ll. 9, 10 reversed   11 tractaturus   24 ordinate/ormate   50 quo/qua   93 uenanti
100 *add* sanus   104 terronis   107 formitudinem   126 rrurales?   138-39 ecclesiarum et   143 lacerare   182 nucorum/amicorum*   225 studiose   239 oculus
251 vneno   261 dulcedine/dulcedo mìe   263 *add* de iudicibus   268 clausam
271 cura?/iuri   285 extollitur   294 inimico   299 se subsungens?   304 eidem
324 mollis est   325 castigate   328 dicitur/est   331 *add* hoc   339-40 speciem
vnam in correptione et productione/species duas vnam in correptione et productione
alia (*sic*) autem in similitudine dictionum*   348 imiecte   357 tractatque
364 *add* est in   409 resonat   425 iocat   427 sunt/fert   430 ero   436
prohibere   465 peleya/pereya*   474 uita/tuta   507 mea/uestra   509 noticie
reseretur   511 dilectione

CHAPTER TWO

3 elocutionem/electionem*   5 eligendi/eligendi ars*   9 profucuum   36 confirmis   45 proprietates   54-55 caprocliue   56-57 precando/conquerendo
60 pacentem   66 gemitos   79 derelinquitur   88 aminiculo   112 ethice
126 proprietates   142 *add* die   164-65 *add* aliquando . . . apponuntur   165
adiungitur   170 parisius   177 nuncquam   178 honerat   179 longo   195 determinantur   215 fluminis   230-31 methaphore   244 inducende/inducente*
267 est/erit   288-89 sequentem   294 laqueo/aquilo   300 turbinis   304 dextera pietatis   307 columbinalium?   310 exultauerit

CHAPTER THREE

4 et operis progressus/progressus et operis   6 ore/in ore   maiuss   7 continuenda
9 forsitam   19 finem/finem et ita erunt octo species*   34 oculi/olim   41 athene
50 athenis/atheus*   58 semita   67 quodam   86 seruat   88 feruentis

CHAPTER FOUR

15-16 *add* attentio . . . difficultas   20 conditionem/coniunctionem   51 *add* per
quam   54 carminis   60 *add* accusat   61 prouerbia   64 institutionem

66-67 relinquitur/relinqueretur*   97 inductus   98 prohemalia   103 tempo-
ralibus   116 studio   119 rusticus   132 ouem   157 Item ste/Iste nudo
196 rationis   199 caūe/cause   203 confirmatio/infirmatio   216 tu/et   233
rex   246 *add* spicula   251 *add* urbsque iocatur   252 cordis/corde*   255 fauor
268 lucidet   275 *add* capaneus   280 ut/in   362 heinnio   404 *add* ars typhus
405 hystria   411-12 curat ipsam uel uitam peccati   415 exterminant   434 gallia
475-76 *add* certe et determinate   494 *add* citatio dicit   501 signat   504 cōdie/
cotidie   512 dors/dos

CHAPTER FIVE

28 assumitur   30 *add* digressio   31 addit/ad id   78 clausam   80-81 exangue
81-82 *add* succose idest sapide   87 epistilum   97 ducunt   102 herculus
135 et et/et   162 iacti/iactitari*   165 inducteret?/induceret*   217 *add* carnis
amare   222 amans/amens   228 pietate uitat   290 ex/executionem*   320 in/
ibi/sibi   330 deus/dignus   334 eptedicon   335 carmon   345 ānā/animam
vnam   346 apotosis   348 agricultiua   350 clausare equstri   359 inuectium
366-67 *add* miserabile   368 alteratione   374 *add* posicione   376 ydooma
377 dapuus   391-92 effexegesis   394 palliato   397 ysopo   398 appotosis
405 notorii   418 duo dactili et plures/multi dactili*   423 uestram   437 ex-
causande/excusande*   452 leononitatem   456 et/quilibet admirantur   458
plus legunt   461 quidam/quam serpant   466 stultis   468 contra/circa   480
quo   481 casses?/esset humano corpore

CHAPTER SIX

Add rubrics 71, 143, 149, 152, 155, 158, 161, 171, 174, 177, 180, 183, 213, 220,
302, 317, 320, 326, 355, 365, 385. 3 prouisum   4 congrua est et   9 nomine
15 artificium   29 mea/uestra   34 ordiri   39 asseruit   42 *add* quas . . . connexio   51 *add* et²   52 considere   54 notet/nolit   72 cum sillaba/cum
similia*   73 eadem principia/eodem principio* *add* sumuntur   74 presente/
presens te   77 *add* reuertitur   90 amice pacis/amore places   93 Cum/sum
95 facieque   97 *add* uel   103 mercesque   105 rationem/rei rationem   111
Quam   112 lumine/summe   113 abit cedit   114 duobus   115 bene/breui-
ter   120 ruimus/ruitis*   135 litttora/litttore*   138 uerna/uenia   147 nostis/
notis   153 epula   156 dilecte/delecte   159 consumit   163 cedi   182 stam
paladem   185 angulos accessu   203 tenditur   204 non/sed   206 nec mihi
209 Supplicitas   212 artis/fraudis   215 ducis/duas*   216 Transitio post/Tran-
sitio quando post*   226 *add* ciuem   227 *add* mimas mimos   229 eorum/ea*
230 vnumquodque que   237 *add* adiunctio . . . fine   248 commutio   253
metri/me tibi   257 mente/me ne factium   262 quos/que*   265 vincere de-
lictos/dilictos*   284 aliquis   286 finitiuis   290 mecha   308 esse   309 proprie   342 hostis/hosti   346 corde   362 *and*   365-66 *reversed*   367 ma/
macilenti   369 hortacio/notacio   374 sic/idem   384 paruum paruo   387 repetat   390 studiose   405 est est   406 precessit/ergo precessit*   407 geometra   412 quo/qua   413 sit/sit usurus*   416 michi

CHAPTER SEVEN

Add rubrics 217, 316, 413, 498, 621, 710, 718 (eorundem/eadem*), 727, 1625, 1644, 1760-61, 1776, 1812-13, 1830, 1847-48, 1865, 1880, 1895, 1913-14 (xvix/xix). 8 *add* et procincte   12 quondam   29 marcida   30 compescat 33 infirmam/turmam   41 choos   48 marc   58 tiuore?   64 f/fricarent 66 minuerunt/numerum   74-75 *add*   79 palem   83 in/inignit   98 ferunt 99 testibus   103 siste   107 fathetur   110 collaterale   116 forore   120 ca-pit   123 clausa   124 firmos   125 hemeius   130 Dam famat   134 denetum 136 retusis   137 castus/castris*   142 choors/thoris   153 fuerit/finit   163 ad in successit iniquis/ad iniquos successit*   171 *add* promisit   182 confidentis pro/adhereas*   187 exaltare   190 imperii sui fines/imperii sui per fines* 200 possunt   207 *add* matrem iniquus   208 non nimiucum?/inimicum   habens 215 clamasse/matri clamose   231 *add* hiis   250 aliquando continet/alia est* 252 fuerit R^a/fuerit illa*   257 in domini   263 *add* ecclesie   264 saluuatori 267 prohennentur   267-68 burgensis/a. burgensis*   284 *add* presentia   306 ha-beant sigillam   328 predictis   334 uel/non   362 lite   368 *add* autem hec 440-41 sacro fonte/sacro de fonte*   478 metris   495-97 *add* sicut . . . percus-sionibus   511 *add* percussiones   593 sex/sexquialtera   595 scilicet contingit/contingit   601 commiceantur   604 *add* et   620 exseruerat   622 mutat 626 magno magum   629 obseruare   640 contencio   646 deputatur   654 *add* ut   663 solo/sancti   666 lamentatur   671 exules/exiles*   689 uirtutem 691 digessionem   694 sepellitur   695 ina/inanitur   701 hec *add* me sermoci-natrix   702 *add* ueri directiua   706 uestrum   708 ruditatis   709 illius 720 *add* in secunda linea   723 multa   724 uestram/manifestum   734 *add* 757 maris   787 purgare   788 polopei   790 costis   797 blandimenti 807 rectis   810 *add* pruinam   823 uelo   824 in/ut in prelo   831 trira 854 fides   860 hau/haustrinis   861 astupescet/obstupescit*   866 repeditō 870 ponunt   872 similima   885 sit   906 spondiacam/spondiaca*   960 holo-fernum   964 iudicatrix/dimicatrix*   978 austernus   993 intrico   1023 dude/de   1085 quanta   1092 consiti   1098 intacta   1109 intacta   1113 in-tacta   1137-38 consonantionis   1144 uiluit/uiruit*   1178 pollem   1183 cauens/cuneos   1206 metrum licet sit prosa   1229 excusio   1234 censimus 1238 audiet/undique   1243 humorem   1246 pigmentorium   1258 parabit 1260 cogerat   1275 sin/sint   1276 zephiros   1322 misero   1331 dispon-daico   1336 *add* liberis   1342 talis q   1344 *add* fit   th tali   1375 nobis/nocte   1387 *add* infima   1389 hymnum   1402 adonas/adonay/adone   1413 gergminat hynis   1418 sordidum   1423 inartata   1437-38 adonaicus   1442 *add* ut hic   1444 superna   1450 materes   1453 conceptioni   1470 rumpisens 1472 hymnii qui   1486 auit/aure   1492 coniunctus/erit coniunctus*   1504 sep-tiforum   1508 septrum   1511 consilians   1521 furtim   1528 pacis   1530 paci   1535 uranie/urania*   1539 hic/hinc*   1542 ridet/riget   1545 quem 1552 quod   1555 flectit/flectis*   1558 *add* aure   1565 lite   1572 distant 1574 ue iusto   1576 studio   1577 deo   1582 siteebat   1586 in quietem/et uoluntas   1590 apris   1595 blandis/laudans   1601 his sitit/hiis facit   1612 parcius/parent*   *add* tibi   1628 collofinus   1630 unam/illam   1632 *add* 1640 presidebat   1642 micellus   1643 heret/beatus   1646 *add* quo   1647 gra-

cius aduenit   1650 irbuit explicuit   1651 fauens   1654 turpis   1655 alatus
1656 uermiculus   1659 laquea   1667 multiplex/nichili   1672 pebende
1676 anera   1683 egrum   1687 errores habet/errat   1688 dampnantisque
1696 atri bacco/amphibraco   1699 pedem   1702 *add*   1713 frequent   1720
longo editum   1726 collectus   1728 agmen   1743 est/es   1759 pollibus
1763 nomen   1766 fortis   1767 blanditus   1772 *add*   1773 furtum   1784
bona   1787 sera   1791 *add* quos   1798 cor/tibi   1800 uiri   1803 cruciatui
1809-10 *add*   1814 canta   1823 ora   1826 quam   1839 patris   1860 ille
1863 si diuitis/sed diuiciis*   1873 iussa/lusa   1875 detractat   1895 fanstastica
1897 inuitare/mutare   1900 firmai   1903 hiii   1906 summus/suus uolens
1917 premi   1918 pedēscē

Textual Notes

INTRODUCTORY SUMMARY

Introductory Summary om. OP; P begins at Chapter One, l. 26 1 *M rubric*: Incipit poetria magistri Johannis Anglici de arte prosayca Metrica et Rithmica   2 audientis *om. C*   3 sit *om. C*   3-4 metrificandi et rithmificandi *CM*   4 alie *om. B*; has tres precedunt alie *C*; ad has artes precedunt alie *M*   5 *M repeats* ars *before each gerund and om.* et *before* ars ornandi; *C* memorandi et ars ordinandi, *om.* et ars ornandi   6 agentis *CM*   7 tradere vel tractare *C*   metrice prosaice *C*   et *om. M*   8 subponitur tribus speciebus philosophye *M*   9 congrue: recte *C*   Rethorice: rithmice *M*   loqui *CM*   10 Ethice: rithmice *C*   docet siue *om. CM*   ad *om. M*   12 docet prius *CM*   inuenire secundum species inuentionis vocabula *M*   13 et[1] *om. C*   transitiue *B*   14 dicendi *CM*   sint *om. C*   15 scolasticice *B*   tractatur *M*   16 Auctor autem aliquando tractat de *M*   17 de arte *CM*   mutua vicissitudine *om. B*   19 rithmica *B*   ut *C*   reformantur *CM*   commetra *B*   20 qui composuit xix metra diuersa *M*   suis *om. M*   aliquod: ed? *C*   21 quorum: illorum *M* reducantur *C*   22 materia: arte *M; om. C*   23 et *om. C*   24 et . . . metricam *om. B*; sunt et aliqui *M*; et *om. C*   25 versificatoriam *M*   26 detrahentur *C* wlt habere partem *M*   28 principio libri *CM*   29 et operis prelibatio *M*; et prelibatio que est collatio ipsius materie *C*   quedam *M*   causa: tamen *C*   30 augetur *C; om. M* debent *om. B*; dicuntur *C*   30-31 consequenter *om. C*   31 dicitur *om. C* 32 componitur *C*   parsyana iubar et cetera *M*   32-33 exprimitur . . . doctrine *om. M*   33 doctrine et cetera *C*   34 tractatur et cetera *M*   34-35 Si queratur de titulo is est titulus *M*   35 Parisiana *om. C*; parisiani *M*   35-36 Magistri . . . Rithmica *om. M*   36 de Garlandia *om. C*   36-37 metrica uel rithmica, uel sic: incipit parisiana poetria   Sumitur a prima fronte libri *C*   37 titulus *om. M*

CHAPTER ONE

Incipit . . . Prologus *om. BCM*   1 diffendit *C*   5 teneri: pueri *O*   carpet *C*   8 pedes *O*   12 tractandi *CM*   omne *M*   15 *Rubric om. CO*   Incipiunt Capitula *M* 16 tractatur de *M*   secundo *M*   dicetur *B*   17 tertio *M*   et despositione *C*   ordinanda *C*   18 quarto *M*   quinto *M*   19 vidandis *M;* uitandum *O*   ditandi *C*   quenter *C;* sexto consequenter *M*   21-22 ampliantibus et abbreviantibus *M*   amplicantibus *C*   22 electionem scribentis *M*   septime *C*   23 *M om.* et *after* scolasticorum 26 *Rubric om. COP;* Diffinitio prose *M*   Qui: *P begins here*   diffinire debet *MP* 27 Dicatur ergo *MP*   29 debitis interuallis clausularum *P*   clausarum *C*   deditis *C* pro *P*   30 sermo *om. M*   prosopa: prosos siue prosopa *B;* prosos a prosopa *C;* prosos *OP*   31 uel a prosum . . . condignetur *l. 48 om. MP*   prosos *C*   32 secundum Ysidorum: x x^m *C*   35 uiro et dilecto filio in christo magistro G. *C*   in Christo *om. B*   rimensi *O*   36 pulpite *C*   39 dande *C*   40 florida *om. C* possidendentur *O*   41 premissum *C*   43 conferemus *BC*   44-45 nostra tamen *O*   46 residendi *C*   47 labore *C*   presentis *CO*   uestram *O, Mari* adeatis *C* 50 quod est *om. O*   scriptura *MP*   quia utitur arte *C*   52 et aliquando alii *O* alia est *O*   qua *M*   53 scola et curia *MP*   parebunt *C*   54 rithmicus *C*   utituur *B;* utitur *P*   et *M*   nota *MP*   55 rithmica *om. C*   dicit *P*   56 sunt genera *COP*   inter arte *C*   57 genus est *O*   fingitur *C*   58 quod: est *O*   instrumentum tenet opus *P*

59 rethorica *P*   musicus est *C*   Isque inde musicus *O;* is qualiter musicus *P*
facultas diiudicandi *O*   60 ac *om. C*   61 de metris de rithmis *O;* de rithmis
metris *P*   cantelarum *M*   62 diudicandi C; *om. O*   63 *Rubric follows first sentence
in C; om. P*   Post . . . metrum *om. B*   Post quid sit metrum diffiniatur *O*   65 et
dicitur *om. CMP*   mensura dictum *CMP*   est *om. P*   dismensio *P*   67 pedum *B*
spondalicum *P*   68 aliud trochaicum *om. O*   trocaticum *P*   coriambicum *O*
69 modis *P*   Oratii *om. P*   utatur *B*   boetius oratius *O*   70 Marchianus *P*   qui *P*
70-71 aliquando² . . . inuentore¹ *om. M*   71 ascepio *B;* esclepio *P*   72 ambinouanus
altered ambinus *B;* albianius *C;* albinus *O;* non ambinouanus *P*   uero *om. BOP*   73
quia *om. B*   breuibus metris gaudent *P*   gaudent moderni et utilibus *O*   74 nobis *om.
P*   nobis necessarium est *O*   metrum *C*   75 *Rubric om. BCOP*   76 et prius *O*
77 et . . . disponere *om. P*   electa: inuenta *BO*   ordinare   *M*   Dicit ergo oratius   *O*
78 uestram *M*   80 humeri: queri *C*   patenter   *P*   rex *P*   81 deserit *BCM;* desat *P*
82 Expositio . . . inferius *om. M*   istorum duorum uersuum *O*   83 quam . . . premissis *om. M*   84 *Rubric* de inuencione materie *P*   inuencio: inuenire *CMO*
85 notitia *C*   inuenire   *C*   86 uel *O*   87 reddat *MP;* reddent *O*   88 *Rubric om.
P*   inuencioni *C*   90 *Rubric om. OP*   Per *om. P*   notantur tria *M*   91 ethimologie *P*
92 ut in . . . amicorum *l. 123 om. M*   hoc *om. P*   precium *C*   93 Viro uenerabili
repeated P   uirenti *P*   94 cantuariensis *C;* canturiensi *O; om. P*   Galandia *P*   95
intimo cum affectu *om. BP;* mutuo cum affectu *O*   96 honestatis *C*   97 summe
misericors deus *O*   misericos *B*   98 filium scilicet omnem *P*   recipit *COP*
flagellat *O;* castiget *P*   99 uerbera *CP*   A.: ad *P*   100 presentis *O*   101
recumbat *O*   corem *C*   sibi in anima *P*   102-3 credere q ut *C*   103 uiri: unius *C*
104 uulnus manus *C*   105-6 deliatur *C;* delabitur *P*   106 prosperitatis flosculus
P   107 formidinem *P*   et: quod *P*   uilescit *P*   110 et precum mearum *om. C*
111 aliquo: alio *C*   misocomio *C;* misochomo *P*   112 semper honeste *P*   conuer-
sacioni *C*   114 dampnauit *COP*   116 citius *P*   labor *C*   presentis *CO; om. P*
120 ut: uel *P*   121 regationes *C*   exaudiandas *P*   122 distamine *C*   123
et om. CP   124 *Rubric om. CMOP*   125 hic *om. O*   debent hic *P*   scilicet
P   126 qui *P*   et rurales *C*   sunt *om. O*   125-26 tenent curiam *C;* tenent aut
celebrant curiam *M*   127 legati *om. P*   128-29 decani *om. C*   129 et scolares *M*
130 marchiones duces et comites *M*   consul, potestas, prepositus *MP*   131 alie *P*
rurale *C*   sunt ut rura *P*   132 uenatore *C*   agricole uenatores *P*   uinitores, uenatores, aucupes, piscatores *M*   133 triplicem *om. P;* triplicem stilum *M*   de *om. B*
134 dicetur uel docebitur *O*   135 *Rubric om. OP*   dicit *BM*   quid *om. P*   136
inueniendi *C*   in² *om. MOP*   137 scilicet: sunt *MP*   138 donationes . . . peticiones
om. MP   140 *Rubric om. P*   Vbi diuisio *M*   Quid *om. M*   inuenitur *BM*   in Personis
om. BC   141 seu exemplis *O*   ethimogiis *P*   142 tyrannidis *P*   143 lacerare *CMOP*
143-44 negocii *C;* in negociis *MP*   144 secula *C*   ciuibus *MO*   145 adaugere
CMP   curialibus *C*   contra *M*   ruralia: curialia laborare *C*   147 *Rubric*: Quid *om.
BCO;* inuenitur *BC;* inuenietur *O; P om. rubric*   148 uideamus *M*   alicuius *om. P*
149 dignum imitatione *O*   inueniuntur ibi *C*   150 et: uel *CMOP*   autoritate in *C*
habeamus pre manibus *MP* (habemus *M*)   152 *Rubric om. P;* De arte *M*   153 in
persona *om. CO*   amittentis *C*   et *om. MP*   154-55 laudis vitiperii *P*   155 poterimus nobis prouerbia *M;* poterimus nobis nobis uerba *P*   156-57 dilucidatur in
consequenti *M;* delucidabitur in presenti *P*   158 *Rubric*: Incipiunt prouerbia *C;*
om. MP; diffinitio prouerbii *O*   Prouerbium . . . manifestans *l. 160 om. P*   breuis

sententia *M* 161 *Rubric om. CP* quidem *B* sumitur *B* 162 rebus *om. MP*
similitudines assumuntur *OC* (sumuntur *C*); sumitur *P* 163 ab animatis *om. C.*
ab²: et *OP* prouerbia *om. C* 164 auctor *P* preponuntur *M* 165 seruiat *P* collata
M 166 sumuntur *M* ratio prouerbii *B* prouerbia *M* frequenter: sequitur *M*
167 mobile *P* 168 maius est *M* parte sua *C* 169 ipsis *om. CO* patet *O* hic
patebit *C* 170 A Persona Mittentis *repeated O* Quando petitur consilium *om.*
MOP; quando petitur q. *C* 171 consilium *repeated C* a prudentibus *om. C;* a pru-
dentioribus *MP* 172 A Persona Cui Mittitur *om. BC* Quando reprehenditur sacerdos *om. MOP* 172-73 Fermenti: arrogancie *P* 173 modicum existens in *B* in:
a *O* 174 A Negotio *om. BC* De impedimento *om. MOP* 176 A Laude vel a
Uituperio *om. BC;* A laude et uituperio *O;* a *om. P* De communi dampno *om. MOP*
176-77 commune dat amicos *P* 177 debet tangere *CO* tenentur se *M* 178
honore *BO* 179 A Similitudine *om. BC* De corruptione mentis *om. MOP*
180 et: uel *B* multociens *om. O* 181 corporalem. Item sic dicetur deinceps *MP*
(iudicetur *P*) 182 *Rubric om. P. P om. remaining rubrics in chapter* amicorum *B*
183 internescientes *C* 184 *B rubric:* Ad artificium alicuius operis Principale . . .
confortatur *l. 189 om. MP* 186 medium *C* 187 cetera *C* 190 Item est *O*
apud homines *M* 192 Qui petit *M* consilium *BC* contra inimicos *om. BC* infuturo
P 193 aut: uel *C;* autem *P* sibi *om. C* 194 inimicis latentibus *P* 197 uiuio
M festiuitates *M* fecunde *om. C* 198 conuiuias *B* 199 irretit *om. O* 201
imo *C;* inno *O* 202 delectabilem amicorum *MO;* delectationem amicorum *P* co-
piam *om. P* 203 prudentum *MO* 204 nouit: uolunt *B* 205 eum non cogat
B prudenter *CP* reuocare *om. P* 206 quanto *C* caret rore radicibus *M* irriduo
C 207 inducit *M* increpatur *P* 208 aduersa tolerare *CMOP* 209 paciencia
O 210 *Rubric:* Ad matrem *B;* de parentibus *C* machinas *P* 212 De eadem *B*
materna pietas et dilectio *O* dilectioni *om. P.* cuilibet *CM* 213 oliorum *P*
214 est *om. P* 215 sanguinis *om. P* consanguine *P* 217 *Rubric om. B* 218
eas *P* maxime prelati *P* debent maxime *M* in legibus debent *C* in legibus *om. M*
220 *Rubric*: Ad redarguendum *M* frigidum est *CMOP* sanie *P* 221 sic . . . oper-
antur *om. C* contraria *M* 222 Infirmus *BC* a superiori *om. M* 224 alico *C*
Quo: nos *C* 225 studiosus *P* illum magis *O* 227 Ad castigandum *M* metricis
P fauus distillans *P* 228 nouissima: non uillam *P* 229 maternum *om. O* mater
CMP que *CM* 230 possidet: prebet *O;* porrigit *P* 231 langens *B;* languas *P*
232 corporem *P* cestat *C* circumscripcio *P* 233 carcer: carne *M* 234-35 pro
pecunia *P* 236 De castigatione *M;* De castigationem *O* 238 remouetur *M* a
om. BCM 239 oculus *C* 240-41 ab amico submouerit *CMOP;* submouit *C*
242 debet: diebus *P* 243 inani a palea *P* et: uel *B* 243-44 segregari *CMP*
245-46 quam cicius *om. M* 247 materili *P* 248 spirituali uel spiritali *C*
249 *Rubric: C om.* contra; De parcitate discipulorum *M* 253 De consilio ad
perseuerenciam *B* 255 *Rubric:* Item de consilio *M* festus *C* primo operis *OP;*
principio operis *M* 258 prouidorum *C* prouisione *BC* despiciuntur *P* 259 fituro
B 260 nam *C* 264 dubilitabilia *M;* dubitalia *O* 265 De *om. C* eo *M* dat uel
persoluit *M* 266 infama *B* qui scilicet magnificus in uerbis et factis *B* 268
sero *M, Mari* remouent *M, Mari* 272 debita *P* 273 sustinent clericos . . . re
(*blotted*) *B*; sustinent in clericos seuire *C*; in suos sustinent clericos seruire *M* 276
deseiuire *B* 277 noda *M* nodi rusticitatis *CO* inamabiles *om. P* infici *P* 279
infinitum *O* est *om. B* mitigagari *O* 284 iuste *C* sequens a socia *P* 285 rustici:

rustice *M* extollitur *CO*; exaltatur *M* 287 *Rubric*: tenet *om. B*; De magistro qui insufficiens presumit cathedram magistralem *M*; De magistro qui nesciens presumit docere *O* 288 geruli *P* edocere regulas *O* 289 edocentem *P* 290 materna: matris *M* 291 qui *P* 292 ad castigacionem *O* faculis *P* descensus ad uicia *MP* sed *M* 294 pugnat *P* 297 corporis *P* 298 sensibiliem *M* perimit et sensum *O* conuertatur *B* 299 ego: e conuerso *P* uiuere *om. P* 300 ualeo *MP* 302 iustus non habet *C* uirtus *P* 303-4 De . . . interemptus *om. OP, Mari*; *O substitutes*: De amicicia. Quos prestabat amicum fortuna tenuis et status humilior non conuertat gradus sublimitas alciorum similie *M* 304 eidem *CM* 305 Cum firmamenti *P* regat *P* 306 secum: locum *O, Mari* sensibilitas *P* succumbere debet *O* 307 remouendum *MO* 307-8 vita breuis: in tabernis *O* 308 et experimentum *om. P* 309 est[1] *om. P* sanum est *MO* sicut et *MOP;* et sicut *C* 310 inueniatur *MO* 312 dicitur *om. P* patrem *C* 313 quod *om. C* quod in *M* 314 a *om. C* papa *C* quod est *om. C* 315 ex *om. P* 316 *Rubric*: Qualis *B*; Quale est *om. MO* 317 cause: omne *M, Mari* 318 materia honesti *P* 319 ut non dum *B* est utendum *M* 320 si velimus latere *om. P* 321 est *om. O* est utendum *M* dicit *om. M* quandoque *B;* quando *CM* 322-23 propositum tangimus debemus uti quibusdam circumlocutionibus *M* 323 possit *M* Ut *om. P* 325 laudat *MO* quem *C* dicat *om. P* 327 Inuenitur *om. BC* ad quid: aliquid *M* 329 honestas et utilitas *OP* et[1] *om. C* attendat *O* accusare secundum se uel dampnare *P* dampnare uel uituperare *C* 330 bonis *B* est scilicet ad uictoriam et propositi consecucionem tendit *B* 331 *Rubric*: Quinta species que diuiditur in vii species uel in vii partes *C*; Qualiter inuenitur et subdiuiditur *M*; Qualiter inuenitur et subdiuiditur in septem *O* Ad: Da *P* 333 uel *B* amplicatur *C* traditio *P* 335 in principio: et etiam in fine *M* 336 unde *P* 337 resonat *BO* 338 correpcio et productio *B*; correctio *P* 339 Annominationis *om. MP*; annominationis est *B* unam speciem *C*; vnam *om. P* cognitione *P* 341 tradicitur *C* 342 in libro stacii Thebaidos *P* 343 impellitur *BCMP* 344 ensis minax ensis *P* 345 traductiones *B* 346 est *om. P* 347 si culta *P* fuit *om. M* 349 dictionem eandem *P* si est: siue *C* sed non est *P* 350 uel uerbum uel conuersum *C* participio *P* 350-51 reperitur *P* 352 urgitur *M* aluo uir serpens *P* 354 epitalamio *C* 355 Ouidio: libro *P* methaphoros *M* 357 rumpit *P* 357-58 et illis . . . impediit: et illis etc. *M*; *om. O*; et illis *P* 360-61 dictusque . . . comedor *om. M* 361 Nunc comedor *om. B* comedior *O* 363 sicut *B*; et sic *MP* 364 est *om. M* 366 debet *C* iudicis *P* 367 statius *C* 368 metaphoros *MP* 370 igitur quod *om. C* 371 subiungere *P* sine prescripcione *om. O*; sine prescripcione idest sine laude *M* 372 prescripserit *C*; scribit *P* 374 est *om. CP* 374-75 episcopi et *om. O* 375 uocantur *C* se *om. P* 376 illos *O*; eis *P* 377 suos dilectos *P* Filios *om. P* tamen nomen *MO* attribuitur *B* 378 francie *P* 381 *Rubric om. C; B om.* Nomina 382 et[3] *om. C* 383 illa nomina *P* 384 excogitata *B* 386 de *om. O* 387 ego ego *M* huc *O* 388 pectoris *P* 389 ponit *P* hoc *O; om. P* 390 pectoris *P* et cetera *om. CMOP* 392 agno *O* 394 sint *M* 395 ab *P* sequenti *MOP* 396 amateum *C* bucolicon *M* 397 amaleum *C* 397-98 amantum proprietates *P* 398 amancium *CO* buculicon *M* bucolon *MOP* 400 obseruat *MP* 401 quid subsequitur *P* 402 inuenit *P* 403 amasius *C* 404 per[2] *om. P* 405 amicum dicitur ratio ergo *P* sic *om. C* 406 amaleum *C* Ethicum *om. B* 407 ( )um *C*; dum *M* 409 humo *C* 413 patuit *C* fogo *M* ree cavit *C*

415 tacto *M*   dampnidis *B*   daphinis *M*   416 lege *P*   traxerat *CM*   ipsa *M, Mari*
417 daphnia *B*; daphnis *P*   ille *M*   419 est *om. B*   421 hinc *M*   innati *M*; vinati
O   422 patri: parti *M*   423 utrum *B*; utramque *O*   426 mulcio *M*   427 spondeo de dona dum carum *P*   mihi *O, Mari*   sunt *C*; *om. O, Mari*   428 illa *C*   sim
B   431 tridens *O, Mari*   432 ad: in *M*   sed: sic *M, Mari*   433 susit *M*   434
laceas *C*   435 lavabo *BC*   436 nos: nec *M*   ne: non *B*; nec *M*   prohibite *OP*
437 cum: quia *C*   439 colladas *O*; collaudas *P*   440 ascribi: auibus *P*   442 *Om.*
C   448 cognauus *M*   449 incissa *P*   450 tectus: semper *O, Mari*   451 hamo
nec: hamon *C*   455 Caro: raro *O, Mari*   457 nomina adiectiua *M*   458 ab
istis *om. O*   460 Qualitate a quantitate *BCMOP*   hoc *om. M*   461 inguilla *M,*
Mari   463 miles galeatus *om. O*   pedes: miles *CO*   463-64 pedes hastatus *om.*
B   464 ut *om. P*   465 pereya *B*   466 prima eius heres *P*   467 nara *M, Mari*
liuidus *P*   469 magnanimus *om. MP, Mari*   472 adiectiuorum posicio *C*   473
hic patet *om. M*   474 agmina *M*   476 Arte *om. O*   inueniendi *C*   477 uerba
om. M   licet: licet patet *BP*; patet *O, Mari*   478 assigna *M*   478-79 ad id ad
quod *MOP*   479 sit nomen *MP*   si non sit positum *MP*   481 docet *M*   482
serendiss *B*; seruandi *C*   484 redderit *C*   485 igitur *om. C*   noua *B*   486 in:
cum *CMO*   487 hympzo *P*   -zas *CMOP*   489 hymzet *P*   490 cum cordi *P*
erat *B*   493 lauo: cano *M, Mari*   langueo egroto doleo *P*   494 duram: causam
P   excudens *C*   495 et: uel *P*   498 *Rubric*: Argumentum uitandi usitatum modum loquendi *M*   499 uerbi huius *P*   500 item *B*   si *om. B*   501 urb *C*
502 *Rubric*: Item de eodem *M*   modum loquendi *O*   loquendi modum et viciosum
BC   504 capet *M, Mari*   sensio *M*   505 est *om. C*   507 si dicerem *P*   508
modo *om. O*   509 hostitie *M*   inis *M*   510 Dilectioni . . . reseretur: *M repeats*
Dilectionis . . . fiat *from above*   dilectioni vel discrecioni *O*   regeretur *C*; responde-
tur *P*   accusatiuum ut *P*   510-11 uestram dilectionem *O*   511-12 nota *M*
514 ampliandi *O*   514-15 orationibus aliis *P*   515 uolumptates *C*   et uariare
om. M   516-17 pretermittentes modos secundum causas *P*   517 proposite sibi
M   sibi *om. CP*   518 commodet *M*; commendit *O*   519 idest *om. P*   523 per
eum et in eo *M*

CHAPTER TWO

1 Secundum Capitulum *om. BCO*   *P om. all rubrics in this chapter except l. 15*
3 electionem *BCP*   4–5dictantibus et scribentibus *O*   5 est *om. B*   eligendi ars
B   6 ergo *om. C*   debemus eligere *C*   6-7 triplici de causa eligere debemus materiam *P*   7 pretenditur *O*   8 delectabilem *M*   proficium *C*   in mente: preterite
P   9 delectabiliem *M*   in: est *P*   in pulchritudine *MOP*   proficium *C*   10 breue
et prolixum *M*   11 leue . . . prolixum *om. O*   ut in *P*   12 describendum *B*
plane *B*   13 Sed *om. P*   contingat *C*   difficilem esse *M*   14 reddunt leuem *P*
reddant *M*   uel enodent *O*   poneretur *M*   15 *M om. through l. 43   Rubric om. O*
scribit *C*   suo et est exemplum facilis ornatus *P*   17 I.: P. *CO*; G. *P*   17-18 celesti magistro *P*   18 et *om. C*   sanctitatis *P*   19 et deuotam *om. P*   20 pietatis
vel karitatis *O*   quotienscumque *P*   explientur *O*   20-21 preces honeste *O*   21
preces *om. C*   amore *P*   presentis *O*; presencium et *P*   22 et in Theologie *CO*   in
Theologie scolis *COP*   23 uestre *P*   24 commisso *O*   abhuc *C*   uacillantem *C*
25 presentis *O*   effudit *P*   infudit spem *C*   26 speratam *B*; sperant *C*   con-

cederet *BP*; concedit *C*   beneficium *om. BP*   27 stimuletur *om. C*; stimularetur *P*
28 prefatum *P*   precibus uestris *om. C*   31 cumulabo vel augmentabo *O*   32 *P*
rubric: Item sic scribitur abbati   B.: P. *O*   33 theologice *O*   35 vrtice: utate *O*
36 presentis *O*   albedine: obedientie *P*   37 doctrinaque *B*; doctrinam *O*   38 misteria *P*   gratia: plenitudine *P*   39 susciperit *C*   confessionis *B*   40 postulamur
P   41 interuenientu *B*   R.: N. *BCP*; P. *O*   42 presentis *O*   43 uobis *om. C*
44 de *om. C*   ornatu difficili *O*   Set: et *C*; *om. M*   45 graue *C*   proprietates *COP*
46 sub subiecto *P*   47-48 continens pro contento *om. P*   48 genus pro specie,
species pro genere, et e contrario *M, Mari*; genus pro specie, species pro genere *P*
49 reperiuntur *P*   49-50 *om. P*   50 violencia *B*   51 Exemplum difficilis ornatus *MO*   52 G.: R. *CMOP*   53 Magister *om. B*   54 miraca *C*   54-55 caput
patris reuerendi pedibus *O*   proclinare *O, Mari*; proclinans *P*   59 baculos *om. M*
querens *M*   aciras *M*   60 et[1] *om. MO*   compacientem *O, Mari*   62 cruore *MP*
saciunt *P*   mensem *O*   sua *O*   imbutam *CMOP*   63 diffuso *P*   derelinquunt *P*
64 secundum: per *C*; *om. M*   clementia uestra *MP*   65 propinet *P*   hos uocis *P*
suspirosas *M*; suspiriosus *O*   66 exaudiando *P*   sentina *MP*   sceleris *O*   67 explet
P   67-68 in sollercia terrentur *P*   69 proponitur *B*   pro subiecto ponitur *MP*
ibi ubi *O*   dicit *P*   sanctitati *B*; *M, Mari om. through* dicitur, *l. 70*   70 dicit *P*
71 quia materia gladii est *P*   antecedente ponitur *M*   dicitur *om. C*   73 quando
P   74 uulnerum *P*   75 continento *C*   ponitur *om. CMO*   76 propinet *P*   quo-
cienscumque *MP*   dilectionis uestre noscat *C*   78 cum dicit *P*   79 argentum euomuit *O*; euomuit quod continebat argentum *P*   80 hierit *C*   81 hanelavi *P*   elen-
chiis *P*   82 per denarios *C*   84 gaudium *C*   et cutellum *M*   85 nimphas *C*
gladio *B*   87 inueniendi *B*; morandi *C*   87-88 quasi extra electio scilicet multorum aliquorum lectio *P*   88 eligere dicere dicenda *P*   aminicula *O*   89 ornantibus
M, Mari   90 Vnde *om. P*   92 nouantur *P*   memorie. Et electio in *M, Mari*   92-
93 intelligi et distingui *BOP, Mari*   93 uel *P*   105 uel *om. P*   94 tripartitur *P*
95 instrumentis suis *M*; instrumentis et *O*   Si: scilicet *P*   96 infatur *C*   ad *om. C*
96-97 aliqua *P*   97 inuenienda illa dictio et *P*   98-99 intelligi et distingui *BOP,*
Mari   99 exempla dicta *P*   et[3] *om. P*   100 decidit *P*   nobis: a nobis *C*; uel *M*
101 intelligere *O, Mari*   tempus uel clarum *MP*   in *om. CMP*   102 dedicimus *B*
quo *om. B*   103 in quo: uel *M*   gestu debemus recolere libros *C*   105 inductura
M; inductiua *P*   memorendarum *P*   106 intelligimus *P*   107 sonarum *P*   et[2] *om.*
MP   108 differentias *om. M*   et *om. M*   109 uox *om. M*   conueniant *M*   110
sua. Iudicium cresis est habitus cresis et cresis aurum *M*   112 dixerit aliquid *P*
113 illa tercia *P*   columpna aliud collocemus *O*   113-14 quam significat illud quod
profertur *P*   114 istud *M*   significat *B*   suum: illud *M*   singnum *C*   115 memorie
M Figure One: om. BCP   litteris: instrumentis *M*   Ciuiles cum instrumentis suis *M*
Et in tempore *M*   116 notandum quod *om. C*   *Figure Three om. CP*   Rota Virgilii *om. BM*   laurus, cedrus *om. M*   Tripolomus *M*   Ceres: Celius *BO*; *om. M*   pomus
et pirus *M*   pirus *om. O*   Et Tytirus *B*; Tyricus Melileus *M*   117 columpne in circuitu et per *O*   118 columpna eorum *O*   118-19 continentur comparationes *P*
121 si qua proferatur *P*   alia *BC*   121-22 que non reperitur *P*   122 est *om. B*
egressus vel excessus *C*   a: de *O*   illo *om. M*   123 sunt illa uerba *B*   inuenta *om. P*
124 materiam difficilem *M*   alienandam *C*; abbreuiandam *O, Mari*   125 et planam
om. P   planam nomina nouem predicta uitando *O, Mari*   128 *Rubric om. M*
129 I.: M. *CM*; C. *O*; P. *P*   humilis minister *M*; humilis *om. P*   parisiensis *MP*

132 non *om. C* miles: tales *P* habetur *O, Mari*; habeantur *P*   135 nobilis *P*
137 Parisius *MO*   138 excertans femineum gladium *C* exsecans *P*   139 suis *P*
140 irruistis *M*   141 pro *om. M*   142 faciem tuam nobis *C*   144 et: uel *C*
145 nota *MO* in litteris premissis decebatur *C*   146 gladius dicitur *C* nouem
predicta *P*   147 daterminactiones *C*   148 et[1] *om. C* uolumus *P*   149 est[2] *om.*
O   150 aut[1] *om. P* est *om. CMOP* hic *O*   151 Si sit proprium et plura *BCMOP*
152 commendat *M, Mari* aliquem *om. M, Mari*   153 Simonque *M*   154-55 pluribus: propriis *B*; *om. C*   155 anima *O*   157 pluribus propriis nominibus *P*   158
exibet: instruit *O*   158-59 Que Plato monstrauit, sciuit Salomon *O*   159 regauit
C; reseratur *P*   160 reseruata *C*   161 sustentiuis *P* hinc est *P*   162 gestu *CMP*
163 adiectiones *M*   164 uni *M, Mari*   165-66 pluribus obliquis *MP*   166 hoc
om. O   168 exemplum *M, Mari*   169 W.: V. *MOP* episcopo *MP*   169-70 Remensi episcopo *P*   170 aromatis *C*   171 mittens *P* et *om. C* ab *C*   172-73 de-
siderare *P*   173 patrie portum *P*   175 prospiceo *C*   176 morderata *C* mei *om.*
B   176-77 studiis quam eius et sumat *P*   177 quam *om. M* citius et *M* sumat
dirigat *O*   179 recipit *B* suus *O* longo *C*; longens *P*   180-81 uestra muni-
ficentia *O*   181 dona maturet *P*   182 hospitium *M* plenus *M, Mari*; penu *P*
184 gratulet *C*   185-86 Plura ... prudens, etc. *om. O, Mari*   185 ubi: cum *P*
186 uestra *om. BCP*   186-87 Plura ... dirigat, etc. *om. M* vnico substantiuo
adiunguntur *om. P*   186-88 adiunguntur ... substantiuis *om. BC*   187 et sumat
OP   187-89 substantiuis ubi dicitur villa sumptuosa me spoliat etc. adiungitur *O,*
Mari   188 apponuntur *P*   190 granarium *om. P* habundat etcetera cere fluat
bacho *P* Cerere ... Bacho *om. M* *M, Mari rubric* De Verbi Determinatione   191
unicum *CP*   192 crines digitis *O* unge *B* uestes *P* uerba *M*   195 determinantur
M; terminatur *P*   196-97 Si *om. CMOP*; sub retrogradatione *om. P* rithmus et *M*
erunt uersus dupliciter leonini *MP*   198 hoc *O* omnibus: cumbit *M* curuatibus
P   200 carnibus *M* saluatis *C*   201 Iocatis *C* patribus *P* firmatis *C*   202 Cre-
ricus *M, Mari*; Ereticus *P* blandor *O*   203 scitor *M*; stercor *O, Mari*; Institor *P* ter-
ticus *O* gericus *C*   204 uenia iulia *M*   205 furla *M*; fur *P* muri *C* mundauit
om. P   207 leoninii *P*   208 -que *om. P*   209 hoc *O*   210 modo *om. O* alii
secundum retrogradationem legantur *M*   211 terminatione *M* plura *om. P* plura
adiectiua *M*   211-12 eliguntur etcetera ad *P*   213 genitiue *P*   213-14 determinantur *B*   214-15 serpentine uirus uelocitatem tigris apri iram seuitia fulminis intus
habens. Iterum *P*   214 ferita *M*   215 habens *C*   216-17 sustentiua *P*   217 filium *P*   218 si *O* pudens *M*   219 in facilitate: affacilitate *M* uariantur *B*   220
vnde *BP* inuidus *M*   221 perfectum *O, Mari* effectum: defectum *C*   224 De
electione adiectiuorum *CMO*   227 tropum illum *P* epytoton *P* quando: pro quo
P   230 inde proprie *O* methafore *C*; methaphore *MP, Mari*   231 Aduerbium:
M, Mari rubric De Aduerbio dicitur *om. C*   233 plura huiusmodi *om. C* adiectiua
huiusmodi *P*   234 lacrimosae *P*   234-35 dedoluitque *P*   237 polisintoson *C*;
pollisintion *P*   238 plurimum *M, Mari* collectarum copulatarum coniunctionum
P   243 mirationis *C* reperiuntur *P*   244 inducente *B*; ducende *C* uero fluit *B*;
affuit *C*; affluat *O* lacrimis *P*   246 implendam *C*; explendam *P*   247 contingit
quod aliquando *C*   250 sic secundum uire deo *P* si simper uiuere *O*   252 Sic
B dat *O, Mari*   253 potest *om. O*   255 gestu *om. P*   258 pallet *P*   259-60
sustentiuum *P*   260 Si: sic *M*; *om. C*   261 sustentiuum transferatur *P* adiectiuum
uel uerbum aliquando tota oratio ut si *P*   262 possum *om. O* pudoris *P*   266 in-

ducandi *M*   Propriam *om. M*   uerborum *M*   267 eligenda duo sunt *C*   268 et *om.*
M   271 commune est *CMO*   273 exallidendo *O*   276 meretrice *M*   curre *M*
277-78 sequentibus *CMOP*   281 R. *om. BCO*; S. *P*   283 primouos flores *C*   in-
ciperit *CP*   arbor incipit *M, Mari*   borelis *M*   284 incuberat *O*   fructus *C*   285
metiuntur *C*   persoluunt *CQ*   286 simili *M, Mari*   u. lii *C*   degenerans *om. C*
207 per pallorem *C*   288 Ecce: et de *P*   solitudine *P*   per litteram *om. P*   288-
89 sequentem *C*   289 sic *om. M*   290 distat *C*   291 tempore uel labore *P*
292 radicitur *P*   loyca *MO*   293 rethorice *P*   294 promittens *C*   ecce *om. O*
295 florem *C*   297 ministrat *B*   arcescenti *B*; rescenti *C*   297-98 qui . . . imponat *om. O*   298 uulnerato *M*   300 sicut *om. O*   fortitudine *C*; furtune *O*   nunc:
non *M*   301-2 gratiam uestram *M*   tabulom *M*   serenitas *P*   303 expectantem
OP, Mari   304 sumpnolento *O, Mari*   sed *B*   305 uestre prudencie *P*   305-7
circumspectio . . . uestre *om. C*   306 meorum exigenciam *om. M*   secundum *om.*
P   307 piam *om. BP*   308 naufragio *M, Mari*   309 eterne uite *COP*   suscipiatis
P   fauor Dei me *C*   310 exultaverit *P*   possim uobis *M*   temporales possim *P*
congerere temporales *O*   copiose vel accumulare in tempore *C*

CHAPTER THREE

P om. all rubrics in this chapter except ll. 13, 25   3 principium et medium *B*   et *om.*
P   4 principium et progressus *P*   6 sit *om. MP*   contineat *C*   ore. In principio
recurrendum est ad principium materie *MP*   7 hiis *B*   8 preter cetera *om. B*   preterea preter cetera *MP*   adiungimus *P*   9 subiungimus *om. MP*   contingit *B*   materiam forsitan *C*   peticam *C*   10 ordinare *P*   11 secundum principium *om. C*
13 Artificiali *om. P*   et . . . Eius *om. M*   vij *O*   Eius *om. O*   14-15 quando . . .
facere *om. C*   inchoamus materiam aut a *M*   15 viij: viiij *M*   principium semper
viij *B*   habet viii *C*   ramos habet *P*   16-17 quando principium artificiale uel a
medio materie sumitur *O*   19 finem et ita erunt octo species *B*   Iterum *om. MO*
20 principium: caput *M, Mari*   23 predicauit: ipse studuit *M;* ipse predicauit *O*
24 est *P*   pro Domino *om. O*   25 Hoc est principium naturale *B*; hoc principium
naturale. Exemplum principii naturalis *P*   28 Primus Modus *om. BCM*   est *om.*
MP   29 ut hic: hoc est *M;* est hoc *P*   32 precurrendum *BO*   33 que qui *O*   qui:
quis *P*   34 solus *O, Mari*   35 piarios *M*   36 Principium artificiale sumitur *CMP*
37 exemplo recurrendum est sic *P*   ut hic *O*   40 percurrendum *B*; precurrendum
O   41 Athee *C*   42 flos *B*   quadriuiique *P*   43-44 Principium artificiale sumitur iuxta principium materie sumptum a prouerbio *BCMOP*   (*P om.* sumptum)
45 et: in *C*   46 et *om. O*   48 est aliis *repeated M*   scilicet hiis *P*   50 hic *C*
atheus *B*   55 casa *P*   probum: uerbum *C*; bonum *P*   56 est continuandum *M;*
est recurrendum *P*   57 testatur *O, Mari*   59 principium artificiale *M*   a
principio *P*   63 hinc proposito *P*   continetur *B*   64 cum *O*   66 principium
artificiale si *M*   principium artificiale *P*   66-67 pretermittitur *P*   quedam
premittitur *O*   67 materiei *B*   68 mittat *P*   70 proposito *P*   continuendum *C*
71 quam *om. P*   medio *O, Mari*   72 eo: eodem *O, Mari*   73 paritione *P*   74 A
simili *om. C*   electione *C*; dictione *M*   77 iuxta *om. P*   78 medio *CO*   85 obseruat *M*   86 multa *P*   servat *OP, Mari*   87 proposito *P*   sic *om. P*   continuendum *P*   88 ferventis *O, Mari*   90 Modus *om. C*   sex ordinare *P*   debemus exordiri
C   92 obseruant *M*   rationi *P*   92-93 proponentes *P*   93 propositionem et in-

uocationem *M*; propositionem inde inuocationem *O, Mari*   hystorice *B*   94 libro
om. MP   95 Musa musa mihi memora quo casus numine leso *P*   96 dicens *B*;
dixit *M*; dicat *P*

CHAPTER FOUR

1 *P om. all rubrics in this chapter except ll. 30 and 148*   In: Item *C*   ordinandum *P*
2 aliquod *om. O*   salutem continet *P*   3 uel minori *P*   mixa *C*; *om. P*   4 minori
BM; *om. P*   in scientia *O, Mari*   et *om. BC*   ordinatius *M*   4-5 decemus *B*   uel
etate *om. P*   obseruendus *P*   8 hoc modo *P*   10 autem *M*   plures aliquando *P*
aliquando pauciores *om. P*   11 attribuuntur uel proponuntur *C*   12 conclusionem
quedam narrationem *om. P*   14 tria debent esse *P*   utilitas: humilita *C*   15 aperi-
atur modus *M*; docetur modus *P*   intentio *P*   17-23 De Speciebus . . . exempla
om. M   18 viij modis *om. P*   19 a^2 *om. C*   20 coniunctionem: dictionem *O*
que . . . si *om. P*   21 particulam: coniunctionem *P*   22 modus *om. B*; modus incipiendi est *om. C*   23 Subiungantur exempla *om. P*   24 exoriendi *M*   a principio *B*; sine salutatione *M*   25 fit *B*   29 ultimum prouerbium *O, Mari*   re *C*
per uerbum: verbi gratia *P*   30 stupefacte *C*   32 repeta *O*   proximum *B*   34
nostri pectoris *M*; mei pectoris *P*   34-35 ociorum idest ludorum *C*   35 captioni
C   satitta *C*   36 uertitur *P*   morbidam *C*   37 lascivire *O*   magistralis doctrina *C*
38 morbida *C*   39 uidebar *O*   sepere *O*   de de *P*   possum *BC*   40 inueniri *P*
41 considerantur *P*   ipsius *om. O, Mari*   42 ipsius *om. P*   44 secundus modus
ab exemplo *MP*   sumatur *C*   45 continuendum *P*   ut *om. BM*   sicut *P*   46 celeriter *om. M*   47 Et hoc *O, Mari*   contineat *C*   47-48 continuendum *P*   48-49
procedere debemus per narrationem *P*   49 est *om. C*   50 tercius modus *M*
54 cominus *M*   55 comes *MP*   pro uoluntate *om. P*   55-56 propter nobis iniurias
irrogatas puniatur *M*   nobis *om. B*   iniuias *B*   57 Quartus modus *M*   57-58 si
. . . parabola *om. O*   58 sit *om. P*   proposita *P*   conuenienter proposito *O*   59
fit *B*   recusat *P*   vt hic *om. M, Mari*   61 spoliatur quod possiderat *C*   spoliatur:
delectatur *O*   illa *P*   63 instantionem *C*   63-64 introductus: sumptus *M*   65
quintus modus *M*   a *om. B*   inchoabimus autem *M, Mari*; inchoabimus materiam a
condictione *P*   66 sapite *O*   66-67 relinqueretur *B*   67 secundum *om. C*   68
sextus modus *M*   per hoc aduerbium *M*   69 est *B*   70 doctrinam *om. BCOP*   71 studii
B; studi *C*   genus *om. BCO*   et . . . etc. *om. C*   73 vel . . . Positum *om. M*   per *om. B*
74 aput pueros *om. P*   75 absolutum (*om.* positum) *MP*; *P adds* quod pueri intendant
76 materiam sufficienter *C*   77 istam: suam *M*   Primo: *M rubric:* Octauus per ablatiuum absolute positum   78 inde: in *O*   79 ponat *B*   80 ponant *O*   81 uolium *C*;
auium *P*   exceleriter citante *P*   82 libellulum *O, Mari*   84-85 Subiungatur . . .
commendata *om. C*   85 memoria *O, Mari*   86 puer uoluerit: puerit *B*   87 ex-
clamat *BO*   87-88 admirabilis *M*   88 est *om. C*   prophetya *M*   sapiencie *C*
quam *BCP*   90 apponere *CP*   90-91 inconcludere *C*   92 principio *M, Mari*
92-93 aliquando exordium *P*   93 in illud *P*   quod *om. C*   95 in *om. BP*   97
sermo inductiuus *OP*   98 siue siue contineat *C*   continet *O*   tria *BP*   prehemia
M   100-01 est in divinis cantibus et misteriis principium *P*   101 misteriis *CM*
exultet *P*   102 celorum *om. COP*   turba etc. et hic uere dignum et iustum est etc.
P   104 in litteris *om. P*   105 aliquid *B*   108 ita dicunt *om. O*   bene: *CO, Mari*
add nisi fuerint comes palatinus qui habet archiepiscopos et episcopos sub se (*C*:

episcopos et archiepiscopos)   109 illustrissimo *om. O   M rubric*: Imperatori vel
Regi   110 iustissimo: mitissimo *C*   et amabilissimo *B*   duci vel comiti *P*   110-11
strennuo *M*   111 generosissimo clarissimo *MP   M rubric*: Comiti vel duci   dicemus
O, Mari   M rubric: Episcopis   112 decano *M*   archidiacono *M   M rubric*: archi-
diacono, officialibus, magistris   113 venerabilibus viris, viro *om. MP*   114 viro^2
om. C; discreto viro *P   M rubric*: abbati   sic *om. P*   115 deuoto uel *P*   116 viro
venerabili *M   M rubric*: presbiteris   studioso *om. C   M rubric*: Scolari   117 ciuili
O, Mari   M rubric: ciuibus   uel *om. P*   118 domino scribat *B*   dica *O   M rubric*:
Subditus domino   119 mittentur *B   M rubric*: Rusticus   dicantur *P*   120 colano
B   forti valido lacertoso *M*   scribamus *O, Mari*   121 dulcissime karissime *C   M
rubric*: Mulieribus   122 generose: gloriose *P   M rubric*: Meretricibus   curialibus *P*
126 a dignitate ab etate *CP*   vel *om. M*   127 placere *MP*   128 Deo non seculo
militare *C*   cum seculo *P*   129 Deo *om. C*   domino placere *P*   eterne salutis *CP*
eterne *om. O*   131 custodire uel fideliter *P*   puditie *O*   131-32 candore . . . custodire *om. M*   132 ab inuio ad viam *O*   133 proclinare *OP, Mari*   134 reueren-
tiam et deuotam *C*   135 placide *CM, Mari*   136-37 infirmitatem . . . mitigare
om. M   137 suam *om. C*   celeriter . . . mitigare: visitul miserie mitigare *O*   contra:
in *M*   138 hostem *CP*   hostiliter *om. MP*   uestigia sanctitatis *P*   uestigia flexis
genibus *CO*   140 et *om. CO*   141 uocantes *P*   fratres *om. M*   suis *om. C*   ad-
dictionem *M*   142 salutis *om. M*   ante patet *O*   ante *om. P*   143 *Rubric*: De Arte
ordinandi materiam et de partibus eius *BC*; De arte ordinandi materiam *MO, Mari
Rubric in text taken from paragraph beginning* Iste littere *below, l. 157*: C *om.*; M
de nuda materia vestienda   inuestiendi O   146 tamen *om. C*   148 et Ciuiles *om.
M, Mari*   149 R.: B. *C*   151 continua *P*   G. *om. BCO*   151-52 militis de N.
ut *B*   terre: parti *M, Mari*   153 nostre *om. M*   157 nude et vulgares *P*   nuda *M*
rex *M*   rei exclamatio rei *C*   160 propositio: probatio *M*   item: inde *P*   162 premissorum *om. B*; premissarum *P*   164 *MO, Mari rubric*: Littere Artificiales   166
preferentur *O, Mari*   reddantur *P*   167 proposito *P*   sequitur eius *C*   exclamatio
P   168 pene metus *P*   reconderet *M*   169 effrenam *O*; efferentem *P*   169-70
Hoc . . . potestate *om. P*   170 sunt *om. B*   sua potestate abuti *C*   171 Hoc dicto:
et cetera *BO*   decrassantur *P*   172 aliena *om. C*   ecce: sequitur *O, Mari*   173
autem *P*   spolitatos *B*   177 a simili etc. *C*; a simili a pari *M*; a pari a simili *P*   continetur *MO*   igitur *O, Mari*; quoque *P*   178 maliciam *om. P*   179 continua *P*
180 amplicationem *C*   sequitur *P*   181 potenciam *om. P*   182 a Deo: adeo *CMO*
183 deliquencium *B*   et: ut *C*   184 faciet predicti militis insaciata *B*   auaricicia *P*
184-85 potestate fieret *M*   187 absorbere *MOP*   Sic: si *O*   188 additur *O*
188-89 generalis sentencia *P*   189 generalia *C*   superiores *O*   ortatio *B*   190-
91 in pugnando *om. P*   192 oratoris *BCO*   oratoris *BCO*   193 peticio *CMOP*
194 si uelimus si uelimus *P*   199 peticio *OP, Mari*   dictio *P*   200 conueniam *B*;
inueniamus *C*   201 asseuerencia *BP*   202 confirmamus *P*   203-4 Confutatio
. . . aduerse *om. O*   204-5 orationis terminus *MP*   205 subiciuntur in hiis versibus *O*   205-6 in quibus . . . accipiendam *om. P*   206 est *om. O*   208 Succedent
M, Mari   virore *P*   vires vel vir es *O*   209 Narracio *om. C*   uibus *C*   adheret *P*
210 crucem *P*   fere *C*   211 plantum *P*   212 regna *M, Mari*   213 *Rubric*: Per-
suaseo et ampliacio *B*; persuasio et applicacio narracionis *C*; Persuasio *M*   Sumi *M*
digna *P*   215 Si *O*   collecteris *P*   216 tristis eris *P*   217 Agmina *C*   dux *BCP*
218 sit *om. C*; fit *M, Mari*   amore *C*   220 Vi *om. C*; Ut *O*   cadat *BCP*; cadit *O*

221 cratis *O* 224 stes: ires *P* arte *O* 225 Partitio *om. C* viro noto *P* amiro *P*
226 iungat *O* amena *P* raro *B* 227 quos: nec *C* ano *C*; imo *O*; Christus *P*
228 premit *om. P* perimit *P* 229 formidas *B* 231 Confirmatio *om. C* animus:
causas *M, Mari* decertet *B* 233 ars *P* uallibus: gadibus *C* 234 florent *P* rediuiua *O* 236 que *O* iusse *O* sonat *MO* 238 in *om. Mari* vene *M* 239 si
B 241 machomerum *B* 243 soluetur *P* metua *C* 245 *Rubric om. CM* ;
causam *B* dextere *CP* desunt *M* 246 ferunt *P* 247 subuertit *C* 250 anti-
pharis *B*; anticiparis *C* 251 soluatur *P* vocatur *P* 252 corde *B* 253 torquet
P 254 pugnat *O, Mari* trepide *B* ; timide *P* 255 *Rubric om. C* ;*M om.* Exposicio
256 nisi *om. P* 257 surre penes *C* fit *P* 258 naufragusque *P* 259 demensa
BC; demens a *O*; demersa *P* 261 aracis *P* verbo *M* 264 mundus *P* 265 Dat
C uicio *P* carnisque *M, Mari* 266 diuisio morum themi *P* 268 furem *O*
269 pugnanda *M* 270 uoce: nota *P* 271 Confutatio *om. C* cara *O*; raro *P*
saciari *P* 273 pectare *C* 274 festinat fieri *P* 275 ceditque *CMOP* 276 fauet
BP 277 ui: in *O*; uis *P* 278 metia *M* 279 Conclusio *om. C* 281 Montem
C inuade: suade *C;* mirare *P* 282 Perdas *BCOP* 284 thori *P* 285 Materiam
om. O abbreuiatione materie *B* 286 sunt v *O* sunt scilicet *MO* 288 exprimen-
tium materiam *M* 288-89 est . . . est *om. BCMO* 290 Virgo *om. O* 291 copulative et coniunctiones *C* Eneyde verba Didonis ad servos suos *M, Mari* 293 flam-
mas: ferrum *C* vela *O, Mari* 299 causa breuitatis *C* breuiantis *P* 300 Me surgente mane *om. P* 300-1 illa uerba *MOP* 302 persequens *O, Mari* 306 hiis
scilicet *O, Mari* 309 qui *B*; *om. CP* 309-10 materiam *om. BCO* 310 hi *B*;
om. P scilicet hec *C* 310-11 prosopeia *P* 312 duplicacio *O, Mari* 314 Ampliandi *om. M* 315 de materia sed materie conuenienter adiungitur *BCO* aliqua
om. MP descriptio fit *P* 316 disgressio est *P* 317 adiunguntur *M* interserit *C*
ut *B* 317-18 apologuos *P* 318 disgressionis *P* 319 sociorum *P* 320 facere
Parisius *M, Mari* 321 *Rubric*: Primus Modus Ampliandi Materiam *B*; Littere Magis-
trales *M*; Littere materiales ampliandi *O* 322 A. B. *om. P* 324 ob indigentia *P*
325 milicio *O* sitigaverunt *B* 326 laboras *BC* 327 disputaciones *C* 328 con-
cedendi *B*; conscendedi *C* licenciam *om. P* 332 amplietur *BP* 333 magni *M*
est mos *P* 335 militat *P* 336 et: uel *C* inter homines homo *om. C* 336-37
degnerantis *P* 338 dulcedo *C* 339 manus *B* 340 dignes *B* Cum *O* 341
isti *B* 341-42 et quot et *P* 342 pectat *C*; petit *P, Mari* honor *om. M* 343-
44 honoribus *om. M* 345 Materiam *om. BC* 346 de proscripcione quod est aliquando *P* que *C* quandocumque *C* 347 poematibus: scematibus *P* 348 ex-
ceptor *M*; deceptor *P* alicui *P* 350 *Rubric*: Scolaris Auunculo *M, Mari* 351 A.
B. *om. P* 352 laboriosus fructus *MP* in *om. P* 353 multociens prouehit *C*
354 dieta *om. B*; dicta *P* 355 adaptatum *C* 356-57 dexteram largiorem senti-
rem *C* 358 per descripcionem materia amplietur sic *P* 359 si *P* in parentibus
om. P mei *C* succumbente *O, Mari* 360 effectus *M* expiret *P* 361 marcescit
BP 362 hominem *MP* homine *P* 363 igitur *om. P* uobis existens ex *M, Mari*
364 partem meam *O* ad² *om. C* 365 conspirare *MP* et exhortor *om. P* 367
Deo *om. C* 368 videbar *P* per *C* 369 extendit materiam *M* 370 necessarium
om. P ut cum *P* laudare aliquos *MP* uitupare *C* debemus *P* 371 uel: et *C*
in: pro *P* 374-75 Methamorsihosios *O* 375 de incendio Phetontis Ioui *P*
376 subdita *OP, Mari* 377 virum *om. M, Mari* absenti *O*; *om. P* causa *om. M*
uel *om. C* 381 petitur *M*; repetitur *P* que dictio vel oracio ponebatur *C*

382 Iuli *M*   383 *Om. C*   385 auctoris *P*   387 discorde *P*   388 misere *B*
vires *om. B*   orbesque *P*   390 multis *P*   390 in[2]: in in *C*   391 in . . . laudem
om. P   libro *om. C*   laude *M*   392 rethorici et ponuntur *B*   uirginei *B*   392-93
prebeant assensum *P*   393 pectoribus *O*   qui *B*   394 sponderi *C*   395 poni-
mus *M*   395-96 aliquando cum affirmacione, aliquando cum negacione, aliquando
cum interrogacione *O, Mari*   395-97 interrogacione sic (*om.* aliquando . . . istis) *P*
398 *M Rubric*: Versus   permittit *O*   patrimoniam *C*   399 erant: erat *C*   400
Iussit . . . iussit *C*   sine[1]: m̄ *C*   recto *B*   401 Non *BC*   hinc *M*; huic *P*   nullius *C*;
illius *O, Mari*   402 securre *M*   suadet *P*   403 colliget *P*   404 talis *P*   sisphus
C   surcum *C*; furtu *O*   406 *Rubric at 398 BC*   color rethoricus: coloricus *C*
407 pauca *O*   proponuntur *C*   ponuntur nomina quibus *MP, Mari*   debeat nominari:
denominari *C*   408 medium *C*   potius dicam ve *P*   410 Decimus Modus: D *followed
by blank space M*   idem repetit secundum Tullium *M*   411 quale pram *C*   413-
15 vel . . . obit *om. P*   414 est ibi in *M*   ad ipsa uerba *C*; ad uerba ipsa *M, Mari*
416 Decimus *M*   Iterum *P*   417 iunguntur *C*   417-18 ad mediocrem *om. P*
418 si: sic *CMP, Mari*   in *om. O*   419 istius *BC*   420 elingues: eli sine coloribus
illius stili *B*; *om. M*; eligendum est *P*   quasdam *O*; *om. P*   421 comedia: materia
C   hec est *C*   est *om. M*   hec *om. P*   422 maligni *B*   422-23 gallie elingues se
immisit cuidem cisterne *P*   423 euntibus et transeuntibus *CMP*   responsum *BP*;
sponsa *C*   424 quidem *P*   425 uocatis *B*   gallia *B*   Ginihochet *C*; Guignehocet
M; Ginnechochet *O*; Guinnehochet *P*   *C abbreviates as* G. *throughout*; *others ab-
breviate* G. *in prose, spell out in poetry. Except as noted, M has* Guignehochet
throughout; *O* Ginnehochet; *P* Guinnehochet   426 vocor *om. M*   quod *M*   filios
P   426-27 G. dixit *O*   427 cachino mentiris subiecit *P*   428 in *C*; inmo *M*
Immo tu *om. P*   te *B*; me *C*; *om. M*   429 sunt *om. C*   tue uille *P*   431 pasces
CMOP; *OP om.* et   432 possimus ornacius *C*; possumus ornacius *O*   tenacius *P*
433 *Om. P*   *M rubric*: Exemplum Comedie   436 et: a *O*   437 Ginnechochet
O   440 vaticinens *P*   possit *C*   441 re *C*; *M rubric*: G.   442 iussit *M*; ursit *P*
obit *OP, Mari*   443 gallia *B*   444 *Om. C*   *M rubric*: G.   445 *Rubric om. BCO*
Initials begin at l. 447 B, 461 C; om. O   446 Viuo pater dic mihi *M*   mihi *om. P*
serua *M*   447 quis *P*   pascit *M*   448 mentire *P*   ha *M*; huc *P*   fabrica *O, Mari*
449 orior *P*   aut: hii *C*   hec *M*   450 hiis *B*   ero *M*   454 R. *om. CMOP*   455
G. *om. CMO*   pueris *O, Mari*   mensus *P*   efficereris *M*   456 *B rubric*: G.   pater es
om. P   457 *Om. P*   458 zelo: telo *O, Mari*   zelo invidia *M* (*gloss misread as part
of text; Cf. B gloss*)   459 predicti nominis *C*   gallia *B*   460-61 *Om. P*   460
loscher *C*; lochei *O*   feit *M*   vilaine *C*; vilein *M;* vilain *OP*   saillir *M;* saylir *O*   et: quia?
M   hoihier *O, Mari*   461 Guignehochet *M*   reschinier *C;* reorcher *M;* reschmeher (re-
schineher?) *O*   curtaise *C*; cortisie *M*; cortesie *O*   chapinier *om. B*; chamier (chan-
ner?) *C*; chapigner *M*   462 predictis *C*   est positum *P*   463 conseruandis *B*
notandum est *O, Mari*   465 teste Horacio *om. P*   466 nec: neu *O*   fit *B*   actum
C   467 specta *P*   468 introducuntur *M*   uxor eius *MOP*   469 adulti *C*   470
semper *om. B*   471 quia quandoque materia *om. O*   quia materia uili contexitur
et iocosa *P*   471-72 recitata dicitur comedia *C*   472 Et dicitur comedia *C*   quod
est *om. C*   473 quod est *om. C*   cantus uillanus *C*   474 uili contexitur et iocosa
M   iocoso *C*   475 Notandum autem: notandum ergo *C*; item notandum *MP*   et
determinate *om. O, Mari*   476 secundum *om. MP*   476-77 gesta ipsa *MP*   477
distinguntur *B*   item *B*   478 comediam et tragediam *C*   comediam scilicet hec *M*;

comediam hec *P*; quia *om. MP*   478-79 carmen est *P*   479 finiens *P*   480 compositum graui stilo *M*   481 tristiciam *M*   trachos *C* quod est *om. C*   482 quod est *om. C*   483 trage remittebantur *M*   485 cartis et in *C*   486 transactionibus *om. O* et *om. C* in *om. M* aliis *om. C*   486-87 quorum exempla presentibus subiciuntur exemplis uersibus *M*   487 uersibus subiciuntur *P*   488 *M rubric*: De Cyrographis querelis et ceteris talibus   490 cirographoque *P* lecta *M*   491 primitiuo *M*   492 lesum: sensum *M*; letum *O, Mari* queremonia *C*; quare nomina *M*; querimoniam *P* prosunt *M*   494-95 *Om. P*   496 est *om. P*   498 Federa: pedem *O*   499 pene *P* condicionis *O*   501 hora *M*   502 adtendit *M, Mari*; attendit *P* quisquis *om. C*   504 Item *om. CM* noui casus cottidie emergunt *M* ex: de *P*   506 casibus *om. M*   507 ut: unde *M* presentibus uersibus ponendum est *M*   509 casus scilicet *M* homicida *O*   511 uis: ius *C* morbi *OP, Mari* 512 preces *om. M*   513 ponuntur *C* huius *om. M*   514 est *M, Mari*

CHAPTER FIVE

1 *Rubric*: De uiciis uitandis tam in metro quam in prosa *M*; De sex partibus vitiorum in metro specialibus *O* *P om. all rubrics in this chapter*   2 subsequitur *B*   4 in metro uitandis *M* igitur *O, Mari*   4 sex uicia *MOP* uitanda *om. O, Mari* est *om. M*   5 ordinatio vel disposicio *O, Mari*   6 obscura *C* quarta *B*; quartum est *O, Mari* 6-7 stilorum incongrua *O, Mari*   7 sextum est *M*   9 *Rubric om. M*   11 si *om. M* descripserit *M*   13 transferte *B*   14 eorum *P* commixte *B* hoc uitium uitatur *MP* obseruantiam *O, Mari*   15 consimilium *M* uicio *om. M* in Poetria Horatius *M* in *om. P*   16 geminentur *C*   17 tygres *M*; tigridis *O, Mari*   18 homines *om. M* homines *om. M* erunt *P*   20 *Rubric om. M* deuinit *M*   21 Est enim species recti *om. C*   22 quelibet *B* scilicet de causa *C* et instruendi in difficilibus *om.* *MP*   24 quia quando *O* discripcio et *P*   25 mugendi *P* debet *C*   27 quis *CO*; quod *M, Mari* spendeat *M*; splendea *O*   28 insuitur *O, Mari*   29 quando *MP* quia *om. MP*   30 ad: ab *M* id quod *om. M* ut *om. BCO*   31 uel quando fit digressio ad *MP, Mari* ad *om. C*   33 similitudinis *om. M* *O, Mari add* In oppositis hiis duobus sunt duo vicia   34 *Rubric om. M* Item *om. P* breuiter: uiter *C* 35 pro *om. M* quod quando *M*   39 carne *B* humanas: hisas *C*   39-40 aperiens licaonem mutauit *P*   40 recta *C*   42 lupus tectum mutatur *M, Mari* collatis *M* sic: hic *P*   44 est *om. M*   45 *Rubric om. M* sunt *om. B* tres sunt *P* 46 pastoralii *P* humilis stilus *C*   47 pascunt *M*   48 alibus *P*   49 agent *B*; augent *M* uero possident *om. M* eas possident *O*   50 has: eas *M*   52 exemplo Virgilii humiliari *O, Mari* Tirum *M*   53 Romam fagum uel seipsum *P* et *M* seipsum *om. M* Ramonem *M* fugum *C* humilis *om. C*   54 ut et graui *P* thori mulriebres *P*   55 exempla *P*   56 *M rubric*: Exemplum gravis stili Karolus ecclesie *om. P*   57 Armis: Carminis *C*   58 instrumenta instrumenta *B*   59 superiori . . . posita in *om. O, Mari* superiori: inferiori *M*   59-60 in mediocri instrumenta posita in mediocri ordine *om. MP*   60 humili ordine: inferiori ordine *M*   61 *Rubric om. M*   61-62 duo habet *M*   62 tragedum *P*   64 collit *M* belligeratis *P*   65 Rolanda *M*   66 mediotrix *P* (*also 68, 70*) duo habet uicia collateralia sub se *M* 67 dissolutam *B* uerbi uel uocum *C*; uocum *MP*; verborum vel vocem *O*   68 quia et cum *M*   69 a *om. B*   70 uerbis uoce *B*; in uoce *M*   71 hic est *P*   72 Emolus *P*   74 Exemplo *P* sub: in *M* sequitur *M* in *om. CM* istis uersibus *C*; hiis uersibus

M   76 fortis *M*   77 istis *COP*; *om. M*   subsequitur *B*; sequuntur *CMP*   78 clauam
pedum pastor *P*   80 collateralia *om. M*   aridum scilicet *M*   et *om. B*   81 sunt:
habent *P*   idest *B*   83 purpuratura *M*   84 a: in *M*   et: ex *P*   tonse *om. P*   85
testiculas *O, Mari*   86 Item *om. MP*   transuptive *B*; transumptio *P*   86-87 Est
enim stilus *om. P*   87 epistilum *P*   87-88 pars inferior *C*   inferior *om. M*   88
~~augt mutem~~ *M*   89-90 aliquando dicitur ipsum carmen *CP*   90 dicit *P*   92 medi-
co *P*   phalerasque poete: etc. *C*   93 etiam *om. B*   dicit graphicum *P*   94 *Rubric*
om. M   poetis *C*   94-95 dicitur *om. M*   95 in incongrua *C*   narratio *O*   96 fastidii: tedii *P*   et causa idemptitatis *MP, Mari*   97 idemptitas mater *MP*   societatis *O*
98-99 ponenda *M*   99 Horus *O*   100 mure *C*   101 uite *om. CM*   rusticitatis *P*
102 luctum *M*   104 iocosam materiam: iocosamque *M*   105 narrare *P*   pro-
digaliter *P*   106 delanum *C*; deffininum *M*   appinget *P*   107 Ut: Ac *BCMOP*
107-8 et proprietates . . . aquis: et e contrario *C*   108 attribuit *om. M*   aliquis *P*
transgressio *P*   109 ampliandi materiam *M*   110 *Rubric om. M*   Sunt *om. O*
111 quod dicitur *om. C*   112 sumi debet aliquando *M*   aliquando *om. O*   114
et ad predicatores *P*   a licencia *om. P*   115 in Bucolicis *om. M*   116 saturire *M*
ita *C*   119 Thebay *O*   120 accidit: fit conclusio *M, Mari*; accidit conclusio *P*
quod continet similitudinem *om. M*   122-23 *lines reversed in B*   122 *Om. P*
Quem: Ipsum *M*   123 missuram *C*; mensura *M*   124 ut *om. C*   125 lusistis *P*
satas edisti satas *M*   126 ne: te *P*   127 pulsat *B*   128 littere curiales *M*   concluduntur *om. M*   ut *om. O, Mari*   128-29 has tres dictiones *M, Mari*   130 dis-
suadatur *O, Mari*; suadetur *P*   131 narrationis *B*   132 per exemplum *om. M, Mari*
istis litteris *C*   istis *om. B*   quas *repeated O*   132-33 mittere . . . modo: poterit
scolaris amico suo reddendo gratias pro beneficiis ei collatis mittere *M, Mari* (*but*
Mari eis collatis, *following O*)   133 reddendo . . . modo *om. P*   ei[1] *om. C*   ei[2]:
eis *O, Mari*   134 *Rubric om. C*; De Socio ad Socium *M*   135 Vnico: Sincero *M,*
Mari   illo loco: N. *B*; tali loco *M, Mari*   136 B.: R. *O*; G. *P*   tyrunculus *om. M,*
Mari   138 Veritas: vitat *C*   angulas *O*   139-40 beneficiis tantis *C*   141 penitus *om. P*   *Between ll. 142 and 143 P:* dos uite uirtutis amor constantia cordis hoc
igitur attendens uersus sine nudo (*cf. l. 153*)   143 *M rubric*: Versus Sinceritatis
uirtutis: virtus et *O, Mari*   144 honos *M*   lata *M*   145 dieta *C*; detecta *M*
146 quicque *P*   149 non sine: uel sine *P*   sine sine fructu *C*   151 fuit *om. M*
152 ministrat *P*   153 uulpinam: vel pina *M*   154 mee: mea *O*   155 imitatoria
MP   perstringendo *CO, Mari*; *om. P*   nudam ueritate coloribus *C*   prepono *B*
156 nuditatem *C*; nuditate stili *M, Mari*; uidi *P*   amouere *M*   quero: quem *P*   158
qui ueracius *M*   tramitem *C*   159 magis *om. C*   ueritatis *P*   propagulo *B*   160
nequanquam *P*   laerua uenato *C*   161 Christiane sed sine *M*   scupulis *C*; scrupu-
lum *P*   diligens amplexator *M*; amplexatur *O*; amplectatur *P*   162 sed qui *P*   iacti-
tari *B*; iactitans *P*   sermonem *M*   163 auralem *O*   leui *om. O*   164 recens *P*
diceret *P*   165 ruberem *C*   induceret *BMP*   falsidie *O*   167 dicere *P*   168 si
om. CMP   contrarium: quarum *P*   ne *P*   credderitis mihi *C*   crederitis *BC*; credetis
M; credentis *P*   169 pectoriis *M*   arciuo *M*   diletlefixi *P*   170 sed deus *P*   171
euoluerat *M*; euoluat *P*   deserui *CM*   perfectus *B*   172 hoc probabitur *P*   173
sed serotina *om. P*   preconium *P*   174 variationes in prosa fiunt *B*   Variatio:
laudatio *P*   prosa: ipsa *P*   in *om. P*   175 aut: quando *M, Mari*   materie: maxime
M; vere *P*   176 Item *om. M*   non: sed *M*   178 *Rubric om. MO*   a iam predictis
P   alia multa *M*   uicia *om. C*   179 scilicet *om. C*; sicut *M*; idest *P*   180 super-

sedemus: dicimus *M* modernis et perfectis *P*   perfectis perfectis *B*   181-82 Sinalimpha . . . scilicet *om. M*   181 Sinalimpha *om. P*   caro *C*   182 synalimpha *C*;
om. P scilicet: quia *P*   182-83 in antecedens sed ex prima *M* si ex: non *P*   183-
84 primo proferatur *om. M*; primo *om. OP*   184 et *om. M*   perdit *B*   185 qui
O portantem *O* illam *om. M* eligendi *CMP* quia que *M* pariter *O*; parit *P* in *M*,
Mari   185-86 Hec littera *om. M* Hec littera *m*: materia *P*   186 raro eliditur *M*;
tam eliditur *P* quare hec elidatur hec *B* elidatur et hec *O*   187 m liquida consonans formatur *M* *m* est: meste *P*   188 quando profertur *om. M*   188-89 et . . .
aperto profertur *om. B* Id enim *om. M*; ide *O* uocalis autem cum hiatu profertur
sed et ore profertur aperto; unde etc. *M* apto *O*   189 maius: magis *O*   190-91
eliditur a uocali: illi datur a littera *M*   192 *Rubric om. MO* Item *om. M*   193 in
prosa *om. M*   194 hoc modo *om. M*   195 Maria: via *P*   196-97 Hec dictio . . .
vicium est *om. M*   197 est uicium *P*   198 Sed *om. MP* littere *O* concurrant *B*;
concurrat *C*; concurrent *P*   199 per frequenciam *O*, *Mari*   200 detractationis *B*;
delectionis *M* loco *M* in hoc uersu *M*   201 fecit scolaris *C* de cancellario parisiensi *P* carceris Parisiane: Parisiensis episcopi *M* parisiensis *C*; Parisius *O*, *Mari*
202 vita *P* retor *B*; retortor idest crudelis flagellator vel retortor *M*   203 obiciatur
O, *Mari* inceratos *P*   204 dicit *P* hoc modo *om. M* modo ei *P*   205 male: me
C vi scilicet tua *O*, *Mari*; ui tua *om. P*   206 Iterum *P*   207 vel causa admirationis
om. O   208 -que *om. P* iacentis *P* depexit *B*; respexit *M*   209 ut Ita ita *om. C*
Ysologia: necligenciam *P*   210 repetatur sub aliis *O*, *Mari* calor *B* inpresentatio
C   211 Et notandum *P* aliquando *om. CM* loci *M*   212 et *om. O*, *Mari* Tua
om. M dis-putatio vel iste *M*   213 clericus *C* cleri culus: clericus *P*   214 uel:
et *OP* et: uel *M*   215 mutantur *om. MP*; immutantur *O*, *Mari* uel transmutantur
M; et transmutantur *CP* Aliquando *om. M*   217 exsistat *C*   218 *Underlined B*,
to indicate rubric   220 liberat agris *M*   221 *Rubric B* Additur *om. M* sillabe
M *Ll. 221-22 precede ll. 218-20 M*; *P om. 221-22*   222 mens amens: mensura
mens *C* amens: asinus *M* debactur *C*; debitatur *M*   223 *Rubric B* Subtrahitur
om. M   224 humor *M* munera: gaudia *M*   225 qui *om. C* *M* donat vado
donum numeranti tibi bine mere recat (*cf. l. 202*)   226 *Rubric B* Item *om. MO*
227 est chorus hic *P* Hic *om. M* est: et *M*   228 spectare *M* quid *M* formiter *M*
229 Item *om. MO* mutatur *om. M*   230 hospes *C*   230-31 intacta . . . affirmat
om. C puerpera portat nostros *P*   231 reformant *M*   232 *Underlined B, to indi-*
cate rubric littere littere *P* et: vel *O*, *Mari* est: ut *M* duobus uersibus hiis *P*
233 quod: que *P*   234 dona *M* fregit *P* fracta: rata *M*   235 Item *om. M* est
om. O   237 ponat *C*   237-38 ponatur in principio sic *P* sic in principio: hec
dictio interiora in principio sic *M*   238 ledit dolor *O*, *Mari*   239 cruentat: tribu-
tat *B* Item *om. M* trissillaba: dissillaba *C*   240 sic *om. O*   241 fit *B* pupis
naufragia *P*   243 Item amoueatur *P*   244 Item *om. M* semper *om. O*   245
vel: sed *B* non *om. P*   246 ponitur *M* dactali *C*; dactilus *M* procedet egregie *C*
uersus procedet *M*   249 Item *om. M*   250 presentis temporis et *CP* totam: *om*
P   252 ire: re *M*   253 Item *om. M*   254 ponamus *O*, *Mari*   255 et *om. M*
uerbum *om. MP* illud *CP*; *om. O*, *Mari* exquirit *C*; excuset uel exquirat *M*; expirat
P   256 Item *om. M* in uerbis *M* uersum *C*   257 etiam *om. MP*   257-59 nisi
. . . locuta est *om. M*   259 prudenti sic ore *C*   260 *Rubric*: De uiciis uitandis in
salutatione *M*; *om. O* Earum: illarum *B*   262 et: in *M*, *Mari* *M*, *Mari*: conclusione.
Nota quod supersalutatio (salutatio *Mari*) quandoque pertinet ad eum qui mittit

litteras, quandoque ad eum cui mittuntur, quandoque ad utrumque, quandoque ad ipsum negocium   262-63 salutatio: supersalutatio *M*   263 fiat *C*   fit *MO*   uel nimis prolixa uel nimis deiecta *P*   deieta *C*   si *om. C*   264 debeat *BCP*   265 *Rubric om. MO*   edictio *P*   266 causalis *B*; consulis *O*   uerborum distincta *C* 267 Epistola sic describitur *om. M*   certe: recte *M*   270 *Rubric om. MO*   salutationem *om. M*   271 scilicet *om. M*   272 salutem *om. C*   salatino *M*; solidano *O*, *Mari*   274 amico scribit *M*   idem *CO*; id *MP*   meruerit *P*   277 magister minister *P*   278 bonorum pedum *P*   beatorum *om. MP, Mari*   279 se sanctitatis sue pedibus prostratum *MP, Mari*   Item ipse *O*   282 Item *om. CM*   282-83 curie est observandus *C*; curie cuiuslibet est obseruandus *M, Mari*; curie cuiuslibet obseruandus est *O*   283 quia *om. M, Mari*   quidam enim anteponunt se aliquando *M, Mari*   se aliquando: aliquando se *O*; aliquando *om. P*   286 etc.: N. *B*; *om. P*   F. *om. CO* inperator et semper *M*   288 presbiteris *M*   ut dictum *P*   sufficienter superius *C* sufficienter *om. M*   289 *Rubric om. MO*   scribent *C*   Pluribus *om. C*   mittunt *MO* simul: summi *P*   289-90 simul in salutatione digniores *M*   290 preponendo *O* et si: aut si *M*; si autem *O, Mari*   mutatur *P*   executionem *B*; executionis *P*   290-91 loquuntur secundum ordinem *M*   291 loquuntur *P*   Ego magister Iohannes: I.N.G. salutem. Ego magister *M*   Iohannes: I. *P*   292 libellum mitto *M*   W.: N. *M*; Gilellus *P*   293 scribo *P*   294 preterierit tempus *M*   dicent *BC*   295 et si *M* pluribus scribatur pluribus *P*   295-96 secundum ordinem suum negocia proponant *P*   ordinem priorem *M*   296 preponantur *MO*   297 *Rubric om. BO*; De Supersalutatione *M*   298 salutationes *B*; superstationes *P*   fuerint simul *M*   299 pertinent *CMO;* pertineant *P*   mittit *C*   dictum est sufficienter *M*   300 Item *om. M*   longum: prolixum *M*   nimis obscurum *M*   301 erit *COP*   erit uiciosum *P* 303 *Rubric om. MO*   narrationis *C*   Et quia narratio *M*   304 notandum *M*   est *om. O, Mari*   quot: quod tot *M*; quod *O*; que *P*   et *om. M*   304-5 et . . . carminum *om. O*   305 quot: quod sunt *M*   triplex est *CMO*   genus *om. O*   306 Primum est *om. M*   uel . . . idest *om. P*   dictilicon *C*; dicton *M*   307 est *om. M*   etagematicon *P*   apogeticon *MO*   308 erimeneticon *O*   idest *om. M*   309 est *om. M*   miticon *M*   chelicon *C*; cheleon *MP*   mixtum: uicium *P*   310 diadascalicon *BC*   idest *om. M*   311 uertitur *P*   312 Tullium sic *om. P*   si est *P*   313 dupliciter *BO*, *Mari*   314 est *om. M*   est positum *M*   est, est aliud *B*   314-16 Sed . . . Argumentum: in negociis sunt tres partes, scilicet fabula, historia, argumentum *M*   Sed: et *P* quod *om. C*   315 partes siue species *C*   317 *Rubric*: Fabula *B*; *om. MO*   fabulos *P*   que nec: nec *om. P*   ueras res *C*   nec res uerisimiles *B*   318 narrotionem *M* sit *om. O*   319 debemus probabiliter: debabiliter *C*   dicitur: dicit Horatius *M* 320 sibi *om. M, Mari*   conuenientiam *OP, Mari*   fimge *B*   321 *Rubric om. MO* a beatis *B*   322 vicium: iniquum *O, Mari*   323 uti debet *M*   323-24 rethorico *om. C*   324 translatio *M*   325 per *om. M*   premissa narratione *M*   precipit *B* 326 idem est quod dictis dicta continuare *P*   dicta dicendis *B*   327 *Rubric om. BMO*   ficta *om. M*   328 in comediis contingit *B*   conuenit *P*   Item *om. M* comediis autem *M*   329 ut *M*   330 Nec: non *M*   331 incidat *M*   333 *Rubric* Item subaudiatur *B*; item subauditur *C*; de differentia carminum *M, Mari*; *om. O* Item *om. M*   historiacum *M*   334 nupciale *om. M*   epicheticon *P*   idest: ut *P* sine sepultura nudum *M*   335 scilicet *om. C*   336 extutum *M*   danum *C* 337 corini *M*   testesque *M*   338 super *P*   339 est *B*   340 pectoris *P*   343 sidone *C*   344-45 *Om. MP*   345 amam *C*   346 pothesis *C*; athesis *M*; apoclesis

O, Mari; apotesis *P*   deifitionis *M*   347 de *om. COP Mari*   348 de *om. BCOP*
liricon *C*   349 commestione *BO*   vel *om. P*   commessatione *om. CP*: comessatione
M   350 fit: est *M*   certamine: carmine *B*   351 seculare carmen *M*   351-52
uel ... seculare *om. C*   351 est *om. O*   353 inbileus *C*   idest: etc. *M*   353-54
idest ... seruitutis *om. P*   annus ... tunc *om. M*   annŭs *B*; *om. C*   355 scilicet
om. MOP   hoc *om. M*   356 siluarum quia *P*   358 resonare fibris *om. COP*
etc. *om. M*   359 *Rubric*: Item subuiditur *C*; Historiacum carmen *M*; *om. O, Mari*
Item *om. M*   historiacum carmen *M*; historicum carmen *P*   aliud est inuectiuum *M*
aliis *P*   aliud in *C*   360 Reprehensio siue: reprehensiue *M*; reprehensiuum *P*
361 quo *M*   causa correctionis: cum conueris *M*   cuius *BC*; eiusmodi *P*   362 satyre
... retinentur *om. P*   in hiis *O*   continentur *C*; recitantur *O, Mari*   363 *B rubric*:
De proprietatibus satire   Item dignans *C*   nuda *C*; nudet *P*   364 feret egreste *C*
365 Item *om. M*   aliud est *M*   tragedicum *CM*; tragicum *O, Mari*; tragedium *P*   366
tristatur *C*   366-67 idest miserabile idest *O*   pertinet *P*   uel: et *O*   uel recitat *om.*
M amantum *OP*   368 est[2] *om. M*   actione *M*   369 et est in *M*   amantum *OP*,
Mari   thoodolo *C*   et *om. B*   370 aliquando *om. O, Mari*   Item *om. M*   illa: ipsa
C; alia *M*; tercia *O, Mari*   rationis *P*   371 est Comedia *om. P*   omnes *O*   372 non
om. C   373 *Rubric om. BMO*   374 vi: qui *C*   375 sumptas *O*; subiunctis *P*
fortuna *M, Mari*   375-76 natio, sexus, officium *M*   376 ydonea *M*   uocatur *B*
hiis: in *B*   in Poetria hiis uersibus *M*   377 heres *M*   378 uiuente *P*   380 agellis
M   381 celens *C*; Calchus *M*; coloris *P*   asirnis *M*; sasarius *P*   nutritutus *B*   ab argis
P algis *M*   382 *Rubric*: De rebus que dampnant materiam *B*; *om. MO*   Item *om.*
M   383 scilicet: si *P*   384 artis: carminis *P*   385 milicia *P*   386 *Rubric om.*
MO   Item *om. M*   si *om. P*   historia *C*; in historia *M*; hystoriaca *O, Mari*   387 pro-
cesserit *COP, Mari*   posset *B*   possit per materiam fieri *P*   naturam *M*   388 accesus
C   ad id quod *P*   389 captum *M*; capta *P*   etc. *om. C*   390 *Rubric om. MO*   con-
tinget *M*; contingat *P*   391 dici *om. C*   dulciter *O*   391-92 effexegesis *C*; epithegis
P   393 compositam *P*   394 ingutum *C*   fabula *M*   fabule opinionis palliata *P*
395 omnes *O*   396 a brutis animalibus *M*   396-97 instructionem introductus *C*;
instructionem sumptus *M*; constructionem *P*   397 ut ... Esopo *om. M*   in[2] *om. P*
Ysopo *COP*   429 quis *M*   illud *MOP*   398 apothesis *COP, Mari*; apathesis *M*
scilicet *O, Mari*; est *P*   carmen *om. M*   399 lacivia *C*   ut *om. M*   et in premiis *C*;
et in proemiis *P*   400 debant *M*   401 autem *om. P*   in *om. MP*   versibus *O, Mari*
402 Rubric *om. MO*   403 Item *om. M*   preter ... sunt *om. P*   tres *om. B*   404
stilii *P*   4 *om. M*   405 Gregorianus: hystoriano *M*   407 considerant *C*   pedes
scilicet *MP*·   et *om. B*   408 dactilii *B*; dactilici *C*; daptili *P*   dictiones: pedes *M*
409 dactiliorum *B*; dactilicorum *C*; daptilio *P*   410 *Rubric om. MO*   daptilus *P*
411 sillabe *om. B*   producuntur. *P*   412 in dictamine *om. MP*   413 dictiones
cadentes *M*   cadens *P*   414 producatur *B*   415 semper semper *P*   producuntur
O, Mari   417 humiliati *O*   uestra gratia se dignetur, *M, Mari*; se uestra gratia dignetur *O;* dignetur uestra *P*   418 nota *M*   si ... plures *om. P*   duo ... plures: multi
dactili *B*   419 multi *om. C*   Item *om. M*   contingit *C*   420 finalem *om. O*
421-22 et ... sillabam *om. BO*   421 que est *om. M*   dictionem *om. M*   422 sillabam *om. M*   422-23 nostre uestra se per omnia dignetur conformare *M, Mari*;
nostre dignetur se vestra semper omni conformare *O*   vestre *B*   424 *Rubric*: *B om.*
siue; Item de *C*; *om. MO*   Item *om. M*   426 collocatio *C*   427 in scolasticis *re-*
peated O   diclationibus *P*   huiusmodi *M, Mari*   est *om. C*   428 quasi *om. B*   cur-

reret quasi *P*   in *om. C*   429 *Rubric om. CMO*   Item *om. M*   ponuntur *om. B*;
ponentur *P*   430 et²: in *C*   daptilus *P*   431 cuius *CM*   dicta tamen *M*   hic *om.*
P   434 Et: etc. *B*   435 iste stilus *M, Mari*   apud multos est in usu propter sui
nobilitatem *O*   436-37 archidiacono . . . synodo *om. P*   excusante se *M*   437
excusande *B*   per infirmitatem *om. M*   non *om. C*   438 *Rubric om. MO*   Littonai
il·dere *C*   439 venerando *B*   M *rubric*: Archidiaconus episcopo   G.: I. *CO*; P. *MP*
440 R.: G. *M*; *om. O, Mari*   archyaconus *M*   talis *om. P*   441 curtiuis *C*   443
sacram *om. M*   tendens ad: apud *P*   445 marcidum *om. P*   446 pater iustissime
piisime *C*; pateruissime *M*; pater iustissime *P*   sanctitatis *B*; gratia *M*   447 mihi:
me *P*   habeas *P*   nil *P*   448 est *om. M*; est incercius est *O*   et: uel *M, Mari*   cum
M   449 ora *C*   mortalibus: morbi *P*   450 *Rubric om. MO*   Item in *COP*   Augustinus: Ysidorus *MP*   451-52 habentes saltem finem *P*   452 leonitatem *C*   et: uel
M   453 Item *om. M*   454 et *M*   ad *om. O*   leticiam et ad intelligentiam ut hic
M   455 pudore: timore *M, Mari*   456 quibus et *C*   abcereat *C*; obhoreat *O*   admirantur *P*   obstupeant *B*   457 ad cathedram uocantur *M*   458 studendi *MP,*
Mari   legant *P*   459 quam humi curcitent *om. P*   currant *M*   460 se iactant *M*
uersus rithmos componere *P*   miros iactitant exponere *O, Mari*   461 uiam *M*
serpunt *P*   462 scandunt montes *C*   463 Triuii Volant *om. P*   per pennas *C*
464 pretereunt *M*; prouident *O, Mari*   qui Mineruam sacram *M*   465-66 in anulo
. . . reluceat *om. M*   465 anulo: nullo *C*   galium *P*   466 Phebus: pedibus *C*
stili *C*   467 presumunt ascire sapiant predicare *P*   468 *Rubric om. BCO, Mari*
Item *om. M*   mandatam *O*   470 dicetur *P*   Quare *om. P*   dilectioni *CM, Mari*   tue
CO   471 scribat *om. M*   dicit quare *MP*   472 tibi *om. BP*; tibi et *C*   precipimus
et mandamus *O, Mari*   percipimus *C*   etc. *om. M*   Aliarum: ceterarum *P*   474
quare *om. B*   475 Sed: si *P*   uiciosa *C*   475-76 ortum trahat *C*   476 Sed: quia
M   ponunt simul *P*   478 statim *om. M*   Et *om. M, Mari*   479 sit *om. C*   sit vicio-
sum *O*   tolerabile tamen *C*   est *om. P*   480 Item *om. M*   uiciosa erit *P*   est maior
B   481 hominis *M, Mari*   maior esset *CP*   humano corpore *P*   humano: toto *M,*
Mari

CHAPTER SIX

1 *Rubric* (Sextum . . . Metri) *om. BCO*   *Rubric* (De Arte . . . Dictamine) *om. MO*   *P*
om. all rubrics in this chapter except ll. 143 and 385   3 prouisum *P*   a *om. C*
metri: materie *P*   4-5 orationem reddit *M*   5-6 ordinatione uenusta *M*   7 naturam: materiam *M*   constructionis et rationem *C*   antecedit *M*   8-9 aliud diminutiuum
om. M   10 et: uel *O, Mari*   11 rethor *M*   hector miles vulganus faber *M*   12
nominibus¹ *om. M*   postquam *O*   preterquam . . . nominibus *om. P*   magister, dominus *M*   13 Dicimus: dominus *CP*   magister hainricus et dominus gerhardus *M*;
magister willelmus dominus rechardus *P*   Willelmus: Vulcanus *O*   14 conuerso *M*
et hec est ratio *om. M*   magister *om. P*   est commune *C*   est *om. P*   15 artificium
C   quod: et *M*; quia *COP*   per excellenciam *CMOP*   16 propter: similiter per *M*
16-17 omnibus nominibus *M*   17 Item *om. M*   adiectiuum apponi *P*   18 materi-
aliter *P*   per artem: artem *B*; partem *C*   tamen: cum *O, Mari*   apponuntur *M*; preponitur *P*   cum *om. M*   19 genetiuum *O*   per² *om. O, Mari*   20 dei summa *C*
familia: curia *M*   20-21 serena . . . familia *om. C*; *phrases reversed M*   21 uultu
B   23 similiter *om. M*   uirgo uultu *CMOP*   uirga *O*   rubicundula *O, Mari*   25 que-

dam pronomina *M*; pronomina autem quidam *O*   26 ut: est *B*   Ille ego: ego ipse *P*
ego: eo *C*   27 positiua *C*   possessiua no semper? *P*   postponantur *M*   28 etc.
om. M   apponuntur *BP*   tamen *om. M*; cum *O*   28-29 intermetio *C*   29 succumbit infelicitas etc. *P*   30 Item *om. M*   uerbum *om. M*   uel: et *O, Mari*   30-31
ponetur *B*   31 antecedente: ante *P*   31-32 ab ipso *M*   32-34 Cognicio . . . participium ut *om. MO*   32 Deum: de *C*   omnia *om. P*   33 Sicque: sic *CP*   34
participium ut: per partium cum *C*   35 me uideat uestra uideat *O*; me uideat
uestra *P*   medicantem *O*   36 Item *om. M*   ponatur *B*   37 antecedente *M*   secundum: per *O, Mari*   debent *P*   38 per artem: partem *P*   per artem egregie anteponitur
M   39 studiit *C*   loyca *O, Mari*; loca *P*   deseruit *P*   Inculcatio *om. P*   40 propo-
sitorum leporaticam faciant ordinem *P*   faciunt *BM*   41 nerualiter: uiriliter *OP,
Mari*   42-45 In . . . patienter *om. MP*   42 quibusdam *C*   sunt tres *CMOP*   tota
B   44 respondere: redere *C*   45 sapienter *B*   46 Item *om. M*   talis coniunctionis
talis *B*   coniunctionum *M*   talis *om. M*   47 postponuntur oratione aliqua precedente *M*; postponuntur alia argumenta *P*   48 hec *om. O*; hic *P*   ornatus causa *M*
ibi *om. C*   Igitur *om. M*   50 me ledebas: male dicebas *M*   tibi: mihi *C*   proficiebat
M   51 inimicos *om. P*   et *om. CO*   52 que preposite que postposite *P*   que sunt
postpositive *C*   53 Circa autem proposiciones *B*   talis est cautela *M*   danda est *COP*
considerat *P*   53-55 consideret . . . preponere *om. M*   54 denotet *O*   54-55
prepositionem suo casuali *OP*   56 illius, si nolit ipsam preponere suo casu, ut *M*
scolam *M*   56-57 hec . . . circumstanciam *om. M*   58 Est mihi *om. P*   studiis *P*
59 intelligendum est hec regula *M*   Sed ipsa *om. M*   Sed: licet *P*   60 posita in
oratione *M*   61 excelsus *P*   62 domos etc. *C*   63-64 inperfecta: perfecta *MP*
64 perfecta: in inperfecta *M*; in oratione imperfecta *P*   65 motus *BM*   Sed: et *COP,
Mari*; uel *M*   66-67 per[1] . . . perfectam *om. P*   66 orationem[2] *om. M*   67 im-
perfectam *P*   69 facules *P*   summa dare *B*   deas *M*   70 Difficiles etc. *BO*
71 De . . . Sententiarum *om. M*   71-73 Repetitio est . . . sumuntur *om. MP*   72
cum similia ab *B*; cum sillaba ab *C*; cum cum sillaba ab *O*   in *om. B*   73 eodem
principio *B*   74 Te: de *O* (*twice*); Te mens: Demens *P*   presente lingua *P*   75 *L. 90
inserted between ll. 74 and 75 P*   Te: De *O*   illa: ista *C*   77 reuertuntur *C*; reuerti-
mur *O, Mari*   uerbum ut hic *B*; uerbum quod in fine repetitur *O, Mari*   80 Complexio *om. BP*   83-84 *Om. P   Rubric om. B*   extinguens *C*   oratio ut hic *B*
85 distinguere *C*   86 enim: non *P*   89 Sum placito mihi cede placeto plaseto *P*
Plasseto: psalseto *C*; placeto *M*   placido: placito *B*; placida *M*   91-92 *Om. P   Rubric
om. B*   conficiatur *B*; perficitur *M*   93 passum *P*   antro *M*   95 in risu *P*   socieque
P   96 ampne: an *M*   sitie *M*   97 *om. P   Rubric om. BC*   uel: et *O, Mari*   98
Fortuna[1] *om. M*   100-1 *Om. P   Rubric om. BCM*   Interrogacio . . . superiorem
om. M   102 mihi fortuna *O, Mari*   104-5 *Om. P   Rubric om. B*   petimus *om. C*
explanectionem *C*; exclamationem *O*   uel: et *C*   106 nubula *C*; nebula *M*   108
Rubric om. B   significata *M*; signata *P*   in *om. M*   109 utile *om. BMP*   111 sinu:
sum *O*   blanda sinu *P*   112 uirtutis *C*   inuia: musa *C*   113 abit *C*   Munde fugis:
uicta frugis *M*   114 *Rubric om. B*   cum *om. P*   ex *om. C*   rebus *om. P*   alterum
BC; alterari *P*   114-15 altera breuiter conficitur: alteratur *M*   116 uicitur *C*;
uincit *MP*   118 *Rubric om. B*   aliquo *P*   119 exeritur *P*   120 ruitis *B*; emimus
M   122 *Rubric om. B*   cum *om. C*   distinguitur *P*   124 lapis hic quem *BP*
uuoluitis *om. C*   126 *Om. BP   Rubric om. CO*   127 forte *C*   128 imperiorsa
B   129 *Rubric om. B*; *M om.* Similibus   129-30 est in casibus similibus *C*   in

pluribus casibus similibus *P*   130 plura: pulchra *O, Mari*   uerba *om. P*   hiis *B* ;
eiusdem *P*   efferuntur vt hic *B*   131 casus *P*   gratia: gloria *CMP*   132 dissimilis
M; discipulis *OP*   fultas *C*; stultis *MP*   prospietate *C*   133-34 *Om. P   Rubric om.*
BC; Similiter cadens in leoninitate *M*   desinens: cadens *M*   est *om. MO*   inuenti
sunt *om. M*   135 Huc: hunc *M*; hic *OP, Mari*   litttore *B*; littora *P*   136 Christo
O   favea *C*   137-38 *Om. M   Figure Five om. BMP* (*B leaves blank space*)   spendoris
C   stella: ficella? *C*   angnella *O   Following figure, C*: Sunt aliqui qui me dicunt non
esse poetam; sed qui me vendit bibliopola probat. Marcialis Cocus (*Epigrams* 14.
194)   139-43 *Om. P*   139 *Rubric om. O, Mari*   ad *om. C*   140 acciditur *B*
141 dissimiles: similes *O, Mari*   143 In additione littere *B*; In addicione uel sillabe
annominacio *C*; In additione littere uel sillabe *M*.   *Many of the rubrics under "An-*
nominatio" are haphazardly placed in the Mss.; I have silently placed them by their
proper examples. All in B are added by the glossator   144 Quid *P*   146 *Rubric*
om. BCO; additione littere vel sillabe *P*   148 nosce *CP*; nesce *M*   149 *Om. P*
Rubric: In additione sillabe *B*; Annominacio in additione littere et sillabe *C*; *om. M*
150 rethor *P*   152 *Om. P   Rubric*: *B om.* Annominatio; *C* Item annominatio etc.
153 hic *C*   154 te dedit *C*; edidit *M*; dedit *O, Mari*; reddidit *P*   sese *B*   155 *Om.*
P   Rubric: Ex submutacione *B; CM om.* Annominatio   156 O *om. P*   verum:
menti *P*   dilecte *CMP*   157 aliis *P*   hic *C*; *om. Mari*   158 *Om. P*   de *B*   159
pinguens *M*; pinges *P*   munstrataque mente *P*   160 pubica *B*   161 *Om. P*   In
similitudine principii et diversitate finis *BC*; *om. M*   162 cogitatur *M*   163 noce-
tur *M*   fecique *BM*   mala: ma *O*   cedi *M*   164 *Om. BCO*   165 transumptionis
O, Mari   165 et *om. B*   165-66 corruptionis *P*   167 qui fecit *CP*   168 cuncta
qui fecit laudo supremum patronum *C*   ludo *P*   171 *Om. P*   In productione et
correptione *O*   175 Sociis *P*   176 dignatur *O*   178 dictet *P*   nostri: ueri *C*
179 aspicet *C*   nosque *B*   181 teneans *P*   pollutis *C*; pollutus *P*   182 paladem
C   183 verborum *CMO*   184 cessant *P*   185 anglicus *P*   frui *M*   187 flores
P   ista *O, Mari*   188 *Rubric om. B*   189 amplificationis *CMOP*   192-3 *Om. P*
Rubric om. B   dici debeat *O, Mari*   194 uiuant *P*   uiximus *B*   195 sociis *M*
illa *B*   196 rimonia *P*   197 eius: huius *O, Mari*   198 *Rubric*: Item Subiectio
CM; Subiectio *B*   200 si *C*   201 forti: ferri *M*   pridem *P*   202 *Rubric om.*
BC   prius non: primum *B*; prius *C*; non ante *M*; non *P*   sequens *B*   203 detendi-
mus *C*; descendimus *M*; scenditur *P*   204 *Om. M*   uersutum: uersum cum *C*   fur-
tum *P*   207 eram: erravi *O, Mari*   208 *Om. BC*; Item gradatio *M*   209 iuuuit
P   regebat *M*; tenebat *O, Mari*   210 femina *P*   211 posset sciuisse *B*   212 fal-
lent *P*   214 *P inserts* Societas est coniunctio tam rerum quam animi in honesta
uita   testis *P*   215 duas *B*   216 *Rubric om. BC*   Transitio quando post *B*   ponit
C   217 sequitur *C*   218 uirtus socii fuerit *C*; fuerit virtus socii *O, Mari*   219
Cuius *C*   huiusque fuerit *P*   220 correctio color *C*; *om. O*   221 sed: hec *B*   dis-
sors *C*   223-4 *Om. P   Rubric om. B*   nos dicimus *CMO*   preterue *B*   hinc *C*   ces-
sum ciuem *C*; ciuem cesum *M; quem cesum *P*   227 minas ninos *C; minas mimos *M*;
mimos mimas *O*; minas minas *P*   iste *P*   229 *Rubric om. B*   cum eorum: inter ea
B   de: se *C*   232 officium quod dedidisse *P*   didicisse *C*   233 *Rubric om. B*
quando *om. O*   uerbum ponitur *CMOP*   234 metra *B*   235 vadet *O, Mari*   237-
38 *Om. P*   237 *Rubric om. BM*   uel in fine *om. CMO*   238 *Om. BCO*   241 *Om.*
B; Item adiunctio etc. *M*; adiunctio *O*   242 imita *P*   243 Stabilis *P*   244-5 *Om.*
P   Rubric om. B   est *om. C*   aliter dicit: dicit aliter et *B*; dicit *C*; aliter dicitur *O*,

Mari   247 regent *P*   248 *Rubric om. B*   sentencia *C*   discrepent *P*   a *om. O,*
Mari   249 priori *M*   posteriorum *C, Mari*   contraria priori *MP*   proficiscantur *B*
M, Mari add quando scilicet subsequens oratio sumit originem a precedente   251
que vere *O, Mari*   teneo: cene *P*   252 *Om. P   Rubric om. BC*   qua: quando *B*
254 tuus: meus *C*   255-6 *Om. P   Rubric om. B*   quando *O*   dubitatamus *C*   quomodo *M*   257 ne ne *O*   decet: dic et *P*   259-60 *Om. P   Rubric om. BC*   postposita *M*   261 ita *P*   262 Per: quia *P*   que *B*   263-4 *Om. P   Rubric om. B*
265 iuvit *C*   dilictos *B*   267 *Om. P   Rubric om. B*   268 renarrens *P*   269 rota
P   270 *Rubric om. B*; Nominacio imitacionis causa et rei designande *CM*   Nominatio est *B*   271 appellatiuum ponitur *M*   ponitur *om. P*   272 per sona *P*   273
ossella *M*   274 tonas: boas *P*   275 *Rubric om. B*; pronominacio cum alieno
nomine *C*; prenominacio cum alieno nomine *O*   prenominacio *CO, Mari*   est *om.*
BCOP   fit est *M*   277 uidente *B*; uidere *CP*   iste asinus *O*   279 *M rubric*: Pro-
nominatio cum alio nomine   Instabilis: multa bilis *C*   Lupa: fora *M*   280 riso *O,*
Mari   Amori *P*   281 *Rubric om. B*; denominatio instrumento posito pro artifice
C; denominatio que fit instrumento pro artifice *O*   Denominatio est que *M*   que *om.*
O sine *om. C*   est *om. CMOP*   282 actu uel: actu et *O, Mari*   282-83 inventor
pro invento uel materia pro materiato *CO*   uel materia pro materiato *om. MP*   286
Rubric: Denominatio appelsor pro proprio uel continens pro contento *C*; Denominatio instrumento posito pro artifice *M*; Denominatio appelatorum pro proprio vel
continens pro contento *O*   Denominatio est que *C*   est *om. C*   finitis *C*; finitiuis *O*
287 quibus *B*   res *om. BMP*   288 sit *CM*   289 *M rubric*: Denominatio adppl'm
proprio   pilis *M*   290 Clio: dio *P*   291 *Rubric om. BC*   Circumlocutio *B*; circum-
tico *P*   simprisem *C*   circumquimur *P*   292 vt hic *om. M*   293 parisius uiuo *re-*
peated P   294 studio *M*   uitat iuuat *P*   295 *Rubric om. B*   est *om. P*   transpositio ut hic *B*   297 prineui *O*   298 *Rubric om. B*   ueritatem: uirtutem *BCMOP*
302 *Rubric: text CO, which add rubric* Intellectio   Intellectio est a *O, Mari*   305
Rubric om. B   est *om. P*   quando: cum *M*; aliquando *P*   uerbum aliquando *M*
307-10 *Om. P*   308 abigea *CMOP*   manus: ma *C*   esse *M*   309 *Rubric om. B*
abutimur in *M*   312 munera *P*   313 *Rubric om. B*   est *om. P*   314 et: vel *O,*
Mari   315 uilis *P*   316 fertur fertur *O*   tendit *om. P*   dilacere *M*   318 nec:
non *P*   319 languescunt *BCMP*   321 Victa colori *P*   tuli *P*   322 scesmate *M*
sapit causa *O, Mari*   323 *Rubric om. B*   Distributio cum negociis *M*; distribucio
personarum *O*   suum est: ei est proprium *MP*   326 cum *om. O*   327 inerit:
mereri *P*   328 luctum *C*   329 *Rubric om. B*   Descripcio *O*   cum: quando *M;*
om. O   seipsum *P*   330 tenuere *P*   videat: teneat *O, Mari*   332 *Rubric om. BO*
sit *B*   333 id *P*   leta *M*   336 diuidit *C*   337 si te probitas *C*   comitetur *O,*
Mari   339 *Rubric om. B*; frequentatio cum collatione multorum *M*   multa adiectiua
O, Mari   341 est *P*   indoctus elinguis *C*   342 hostis uiuificus *P*   tuus *B*   343
Rubric om. B; explicatio cum sententia *M*(*margin*: expositione); expoliacio *O*   exposicio *B*; explicatio *M, Mari*; expoliacio *O*   est *om. P*   alii *P*   uerbis *om. P*   345
istee *P*   347 *Rubric om. BC*   nos dicimus nos *C*   350 Sitis amare amare probos
P   351 *Rubric om. B*; Contentio est cum contraria referuntur ut inimicus placabilis,
amicus inplacabilis *M*   355 similitudo uel locus a proportione *B*; similitudo includi-
tur per argumentum *M*   358 *Rubric om. B*   359 autentica: alicuius autentica
persone imitatione digna *C*; *om. MP*   360 donauit *M, Mari*   362 *Rubric om. BC*;
Ymago que fit cum collatione forme ad formam *M*; Ymago collatione forme ad formam

O Ymago ... formam *om. O*: Ymago est quando fit collatio unius ad aliud *MP*   collatio: cum collatione *B*   363 quidem *OP, Mari*   agguis *C*   364 sibi *C*   365 qualitate corporis et animi *BC*; qualitate c̄n et corporis *M;* qualitate corporis et causa *O*
Efficio ... exteriora: *om. CO*   Effectio BMP   368 Lucrum: utrum *P*   369 *Rubric*
om. BC; discribitur certis signis *O*   natatio *C*   370 nos *om. M*   aliquem: aliud *C*
aliena: aliqua *P*   371 iactant sese *C*   372 magnificantque *P*   373 *Rubric om. B*;
sermocinatio cum ratione dignitatis *M*   sermonicinatio *M*   serma *P*   374 et ...
dignitatis *om. MOP*   inde *C*   376 gramamatice *P*   loyce *O, Mari*   sequor: loquor
O, Mari   377 decipere *O, Mari*; decepiere *P*   379 *Rubric om. B*; Conformatio cum
mortuus introducitur loqui *M*   380 prosepeie *P*   381 parue *C*   382 pauca *C*;
paula *P*   383 gustare *CO, Mari*   385 *B om.*   Fit Cum; *C adds* in anima audientis;
significatio cum suspicione fit *M*; significatio cum suspicatione fit *O*; significatio *P*
386 qui: quem *P*   leta *C*   relecte *C*   388 *Rubric and text combined from M rubric*:
Demonstratio ut res ante oculos videatur *and MP text*: Demonstratio est quando res
exprimitur sicut est   *O rubric only, BC rubric only, but as text, not rubric (C contra*
for ut)   392 Topica: Copia *COP, Mari*   394 XI: Vi ^cum *B*; 10 *O*   ex: de *C*
395 ( )vfficienter *B*   396 tractant *M, Mari*   eligant *M, Mari*   397 colorem *P*
398 superius *MP*   399 utramque *CP*   10 *O*; xii *P*   400 loci rethorici eliciuntur
que sunt *M*   dicuntur *P*   rethorici que sunt *P*   402 factura *O, Mari*   Uerres: brito
P est *om. M*   403 lotro *C*   ergo est *COP*   uictus *M*   404 Uixit in: victus ut *P*   in
om. C est *om. BCP*   amator est *M*   Fortuna ut: fortuna est *BMOP*   405 uel *om. COP*
fariosus *M*   406 ergo precessit *BMP*   407 amens *P*   Est *om. BCP*   geometra *CM*;
metria *OP*   408 gramaticus *om. B*   409 hec *om. C*   attributa *om. P*   attributa
scilicet casus *O*   410 scilicet *om. C*   411 accident et quid fecerit et quid dixerit
P   quid illi *om. O, Mari; B om.* illi   accidat illi *P*   412 quid *om. BCO, Mari*   illi
om. M   casuum *C*   413 sit usurus *B*   usus *P*   414 que dicta: predicta *P*   iuuerit
C; meruit *O*   415 venerabilis: et bonorum *C*   modis et gestus *P*   416 nichil *O,*
Mari   nichilii uidebuntur *om. P*

CHAPTER SEVEN

1 *Rubrics in this chapter are generally omitted in BOPV. C ends at l. 26. Thus all*
rubrics except this, which C has, are from M only unless otherwise indicated
1-2 tractatus superius promissi *om. B*   2 premissi *P*   3 in plures diuiditur *C*
pleres *O*   huius *om. O*   5 uero *om. O*   6 siletio *C*   venit: fuit *P*   8 et post
dictamina *om. BCOP*   succincte *P*   9 dicta *O*   ritmicandi *P*   11 hec est *O*
lxx *P*   12 lotrices erant *O*   13 aliis xxx militibus *C*   14 erat *C*   15 notorium
CMP   erit *C*   inter ipsos lotrices *O, Mari*   16 ad *om. P*   verberauerunt *O, Mari*
17 lotrici: lotricis *B*; *om. M, Mari*   17-18 cum illa lotrice quos ut uidet dormientes
cum illa lotrice ab alia *P*   19 gladio *om. P*   19-20 aperuit castellum *P*   20 castelli
om. BOP, Mari   21 fuit *B*   22 non *om. C*   24 Huius autem tragedia et proprietates *C*   tales *om. BO, Mari*   describitur tragedia *BCP*   25 preferuntur *C*
25-26 terminatur in lacrimis *C*; in lacrimis terminatur *O, Mari*; terminatur in lacrimas
P   28 quadam *P*   urbes *M, Mari*   29 inter *P*   quos *M, Mari*   sed marcia uirtus:
uirtus animorum *MP*   32 posse: post se *M, Mari*   celerare *O*   33 turbam *MP,*
Mari   34 destruxit *P*   35 diffunderat *M, Mari*; diffiderat *O*   37 Ad muros:
animos *P*   38 furno *P*   40 casus *P*   41 quedam dum *P*   retinent *BM*   42 dis-

ponit *M, Mari*   43 milites *P* inuidi copia uique *P*   44 periit *M*   dagna *M*   51
pars uni *B*   52 illa quot illa *P* quod *M*   54 optarat *O*   56 suis *M, Mari*   57
coacta *P*   59 ascendit *P*   60 stedit *B* stangnum *O*   61 in femina mundi *P*
62 camina *P*   66 *Precedes l. 65 B* surrupuisti *B*   67 excitant *P*   68 fieret *M*
qui *M*   70 gentis contemptu gentis *B*   71 cui denegat *P*   76 timor *O*   78
ludere *P*   80 fecit *P* reddere *M*   82 pecore *M*   83 Istius *B*   85 in cinis *P*
domum descendere *P*   86 proborum *BO, Mari*   87 emittit abidem rapidam *P*
88 melpo *P* tor *P*   90 expones *P*   91 leso: rupto *MP*   92 furiat *M* concurrens
M cursu *O, Mari*   94 illuc *B*   96 lesit *O*   99 innumeris: ictaberis *M* litibus
P   101 discernere *M* curant *P*   102 utrius: virtus *O*   103 tegimen: cignum *P*
secretis *O* regendi *P*   106 inuidia *M*; liuida *P*   107 metuisse *P*   113 gladibus
P fax *P*   114 immentem *M*   115 Prompne *M* plusque climestra *B*; dicere mestra
M; decemeste *P*   116 parcente *BMP*   117 tragedio *O*   118 uigilosque *P*   119
uigere *M*   120 capit *P* olbis *P*   121 pauonio *P*   123 in solito *P* clausa *MOP*
126 femineamque uiteque eam diem *P*   127 umbre *B* crebris *P*   128 complecti-
tur *P*   129 detulit hora *P*   130 firmat *M* callidus *P*   131 alterius *M*   132
leo *O*   134 leges *P* indicium *M*   135 mortem *M* piet: puer *P* reprecidat *B*;
rependeat *P*   137 uestibus *P* castris *B* farcinis *M*   138 ea *P* commovit *BOP*
139 sompnos: stipnes *P*   141 fratrum *O* adoptum *P*   143 duplicata *M*   145
et: quod *M, Mari*   148 Et: At *MO*; ad *P*   150 strauit *om. O*   151 non: nos *P*
152 resere *P*   153 finis *M*   159 sompnolenti negligenti pastori *P* sopnolenti *om.*
O   159-60 laceratur ouile *B*   160 infallabilis *M*   161 precessorem *M* qui in
hominibus *P* profecit *P*   162-63 collocauit *MO*   163 idcirco: ad iniquos *B*
iniquis *om. B*   163-64 Ecclesie *om. M*   164 pre ceteris *B* amore *P*   165 enim:
igitur *P* honori et tanto *B*   166 contrarius rationi *O* contrarium *M*; gratius *P*
167 honoris *O* grauamine *P*   168 ad celestem patriam *O, Mari* ardenter *om. O*
170 in nostra terra apparuerunt *O, Mari*   171 fructum *MP* promiserat *MOP*
174 euigilent *P*   175 repromissionis *P*   177 perflatum *M, Mari*   179 ducentis
P nequicie sue *M*; nequicie suie *P*   181-82 complectans confidende *P*   182 tabule
MP, Mari adhereas *B*   182-83 misericordia Crucifixi: crucifixo *B*   184 tam: et
tamen *M*; et tam *P* honore: pro amore *P* militis *om. M*   185 fideliter *om. O*
187 amimam *B* exaltare *M*   189 F.: C. *O, Mari* imperator et semper *B*   190
et *om. M* imperii sui per fines *B*   190-91 constitutus *B*   192 nauticia *P*   195
venerabilis *om. M*   196 porrigamus *B*   197 prosuaserit *B*   198 presidium uel
subsidium *MP* tenemini nostris *M*   199 fauorabiliter *M*   202 multum: plurimum
MP sacramentorum *P*   203 profundiori *M* vulneris *O* doloris *om. B*   205 eius
M, Mari   206 cotitidie *B*   206-7 debellari *M, Mari*   207 iniquo *M* filiali *M*
208 inimicum: in uiscera *P*   210 magestratem *M* offenderemus *P* permittentes
B; pertinentes *O, Mari*   211 Uirginis Marie *MP* compareatis *P*   212 proponimus
nostram *O, Mari*   213 publice *om. M*   214 expedit *M* ostendit enim natura *P*
enim: in *O*   216 ab *P* hostibus *om. M, Mari*   217 *Rubric BM*   222 et laici
om. MOP   223-24 aliis rebus *P*   224 dilectioni *M*   225 mandamus et precipimus *M*   227-28 ecclesiasticam censuram *P*   228 fuerint nominati *M*   229 gratis
B timore *P*   230 ecclesiasticam *BP* appellatione postposita cessante *P* ueritatis
P   231 exhibere *M*   232 ea nihilominus *MO* ea *om. P*   233-34 Pontificatus
. . . Tertio *om. BMP*   236 C.: G. *M*; S. *P* F. *om. P*   237 F. *om. P* B. et C.: A.
et I. *MO*; A. et B. *P* et de locis *P*   238 presbiteris *P*   239 recepimus *M*   240

Seruorum *om. P* Dei *om. M* 240-41 usque . . . etc. *om. MOP* 241 auctoritatem
B 243-44 diacesium *O* 244 ut *om. O* octauis *O*; octauo die *P* beate uirginis
marie *P* 245 R.: G. *BOP, Mari* de loco *om. O, Mari* 246 responsuri et datum
etc. *P* 247 Et secundum *P* haec pauca *P* 249 specularia *M* 250 habet *P*
alia *B* est aliquando *O, Mari* 252 maminussio *M* illa *B*; istorum *O* 253 assig-
nari debet *P* causa quare fiat donatio *M M rubric*: De Tribus Causis 254 curialibus scriptis *M* que tria sunt *M* 257 domini pape mutat sepius *M*; domini sepe
mutat *O* 258 sufficiant: sunt *MOP* fiat: faciat *O, Mari* 259 detinent diem *B*
non timent *P* diuersimode *om. B* 260 premittit *M* 261 ecclesiastice persone *P*
plebis alius nequaquam *M* 262 *Om. B* 263 H.: M. *M*; C. *O, Mari*; R. *P* Parisiensis *P, Mari* 265 nobilitas *O* 266 labuntur *M, Mari*; labantur *P* littera *M*
267 perheimentur *P* sit igitur *MP* R.: a *B* 268 Parisius *MO* B. clerico de *P*
269 uitriatum *MP, Mari* 271 uinearum: memoris *P* eandem uillam *M* eandam *P*
272 martyri *M* 274 a . . . suis *om. MP, Mari* 275 ab *OP* 276 R.: B. *BMOP*
278 libram unam *O* 281 imposterum *P* 281-82 suboriri . . . heredes *om. B*
282 predicti heredes R. *P* 284 astantibus *om. P* B. et C. et D.: B. C. D. *M* 285
Et *om. M, Mari* firmitatem *M* 286 roboraui *B* 287 datum anno etc. *P* 288
Item *om. P* 289 futuri etc. *O* etc. *om. O* 291 scianant *P* hec est conuentio
facta *B* est *om. P* 293 suam *om. M* 295 cum centum *O* 296 ipse *om. M*
A.: G. *BMP* quingentos *O* 297 predicto *om. BO* Ierosolimam *om. M, Mari*;
Ierosolima *O* profisciscenti *P* 298 contingerit *M* ipsam *P* ingredi *om. P*
299 seruicium *P* tenetur *P* 300 tempus assignatum *M* assignatur *P* 301 heredes *O* recipiet *om. P* predictam uillam *P* 305 truncatur *B* 307 suum *om. P*
308 ( )vperius *B* de[1] *om. P* 310 examinant *B* 311 quidem *P* autem *om. P*
scribitur *O* R.: B. *OP* a *P* 313 dicit idem *M* 314 hoc: hic *O* 316 de finali
concordia *B* 319 monachũs *B* 319-20 partem terciam *M* 320 predicte *om.*
O, Mari 320-21 ad ecclesiam suam ab antiquo tempore dixerunt *M* 322 et ita
B ego *om. B* nostri *P* 324 hoc *om. M* 325 in *om. MOP* x *P* solidos *om. M*
326 pietanciam *M* 327-28 sigilli *B* 328 abbatis predicti *P* 329 Parisiensi
Episcopo *O* et *om. B* et C. *om. M, Mari*; et cetera *O* multis: in litteris *M* 330
Et: item *MOP* expositio *M* et *om. P* 331 expositio *M* 332-33 monstrat nouam
constructionem *P* 333 Transactio enim est *O, Mari* re non dubia *M* 334 incerta: iuncta *P* aliquo modo dato *P* retenta *P* 335 Exactio . . . iniuste *om. M*
sacerdotes extorquent *P* 338 M. salutem *B* presentis *O* sancti martini *P* 339
R. *om. BO* 340 uenit nec *om. M* aliquem *om. M* 341 M.: A. *O* 346 ad diem
ad diem *B* diem lune *P* 347 illum *MO* diem illam *P* 348 responsalem *om.*
BOP R.: F. *M, Mari* 349 contra eum *om. M, Mari* expectantem *P* 350 com-
parando *BOP* 351 a *om. O* longum *O* 353 in principio hoc modo *MP* M
rubric: De Priuilegio 354 Senonensi *P* 355 uel[1] *om. O, Mari* Episcopo *om.*
P B. etc. abbatibus *P* 355-56 B. et C.: R. et O. *M* 357 iniucto *B* 358 debemus exaudire *O, Mari* iustis: multis *M* 359-60 procedit *P* 360 firmat *BOP,*
Mari 362 sunt *om. O, Mari* 363 sequitur hoc modo terribile *P* 364 igitur
om. MP 365 distructi *B*; distrincti *M* iudicii districti *P* 366 ex cum quis *P*
percipiat *M*; recipiet *OP, Mari* 367 tali: hoc *O, Mari* 369 et *om. P* 370 per-
cipiant *MO*; percipiat *P* eterna *BMP* 371 quandoque ponitur *M* 372 aliquando
BP 372-73 cartule *om. M*; carte priuilegii cartule priuilegii *O* 373 sunt *B*
articuli *B* alium *M* 374 parte superiori *MP* 375 de: ex *M* illuminatio mea

etc. *MP*   375 ad circumferentiam circuli *om. BOP*; ad circumferentias circuli *M*
377-78 circumferentias *M*   378-79 domini pape nomen *P*   380 in circuitu *om.*
M   381 scribentur *B*   382 N.: A. *O, Mari   Figure Seven om. BP; I have followed*
O   M rubric: Notus? Nolus?; *om.* Dominus illuminatio etc.; valete *thrice in left-hand*
small circle; right-hand small circle: Romanus Albertus Cardinalis N. Subdyaconus
Cardinalis Sancti Andree; *both small circles have a slightly larger outer circumference,*
like the large circle, and the long line connecting the small circles is omitted.
385 A.: G. *M, Mari*; *om. O*   386 oues *P*   387 debent *O, Mari*   388 anime cor-
rupte *P*   389-90 sepilit *O*   sepelit . . . cenolente *om. P*   390-91 uestre a quibusdam didicit dignum nuper proponitis *P*   archanno nuper *M*   391 consecuntur *B*
392 uestre conscientie *M*   393 presentis *O, Mari*   que *B*   394 morum *om. B;*
uite *MP*   395 faciat *M*   de se *om. M*   patriam de se *P*   fulgere *M*   396 mitto
uobis *P*   397 regimem *P*   399 uitam compositam *P*   399-400 saluberrimam
om. M; saberrimam *O*   400 corrigatur *P*   401 *Rubric included in text B*   403
notifico *P*   404 vestram *O*   promissione *B*   405 dampno *M*   mee *om. P*   ouiare
P   406 apud *P*   407 non *om. M*   differens *M*   eundem locum *MP*   408 meas
oblationes *O, Mari*   409 B. D. C. qui auctoritate apostolica *P*   409-10 sacerdotem exire compellant *MP*   410 postea *M*   411 utrique parti *MOP*   413 Ecclesie
om. B   414 H.: R. *MP, Mari*; *om. O*   vniuersi *B*   415 inscripturis *M*   domino
M   418 parisiensis *P*   exiguantur *P*   419 canonicorum *MP*   420 eis *MP*
bonis et *B*; bonisque suis *MP*   sibi a deo *O*   421 dominorum domini *M*   423 hor-
tamur in domino diligenter *P*   in: a *O*   425 porrigatis uel extendatis *M*   426 principes *P*   427-28 auctoritate . . . Petri: auctoritate domini et beati petri *M*; auctoritate dei et beate virginis dei genetricis marie et domini pape et beati petri *O, Mari*;
auctoritate domini nostri et beati petri *P*   428-29 a pauli et aliorum et aliorum
apostolorum *P*   429 duo et viginti *O, Mari*   430 et *om. P*   in^2 *om. M*   relaxa-
cione *B*   illis omnibus *om. M*; simul omnibus *O, Mari*   431 qui *om. O*   uel: et *O*
descendunt *P*   431-32 elemosinarum suarum *P*   432-33 conferentes *MOP*   435
H.: R. *MP*; A. *O, Mari*   436 peruenerit *B*   438 ecclesia agere tenetur *M*   440
descendens *P*   presentis *O, Mari*   440-41 sacro de fonte *B*   442 hominem *B*
443 cum *om. M*   de *om. P*   444 presentis *O, Mari*   444-45 perhibemus *MP*
446 et consilium *MP*   B.: R. *B*   447 ad: in *M*   450 ueniam *om. P*   terciam *om.*
M   criminalium *M*   451 de uenialibus medietatem *O, Mari*   452 eadem non redierint *M*   453 iniecerit *O, Mari*   violantas *B*   xxx *MP*   456 A.: G. *M*; P. *O, Mari*;
om. P   457 cadens *P*   lilium *om. P*   458 cando *P*   459 suaui nomen nepotis
nostri *G.* bone fame late *B*   redolet *P*   460 mella *B*   462 eligatis *M*; exigatis *P*
464 presbiterali *P*   insula *O*   465 meretur *B*   467 *Rubric MO*; *M om.* Explicit
. . . Versificatoria; *O* Richmica   468-69 Postquam . . . rithmica *om. V*   prosaica
arte et de metrica *MP*   469 richmica *O*; Rithimica ars *V*; *O* richmus *and* richmicus,
V rithimus *and* rithimicus *throughout*   species est *MOP*   470 artis *om. M*; est artis
est *O*   470-71 que . . . humanam: pm. *P*   471 in: ex *B*   in expropositione
M   472 concordantia *V*   humanorum *V*   in *om. BP*   473 ex concordantia *V*
Hec: Que *P*; et hec *V*   dicitur *M*   474 et metricam *B*; in metricam *O*   et *om. OP*
475 sed de rithimica dicetur *V*   476 Rithimica igitur *V*   477 Rithmus sic
describitur *om. V*   ita *OP*   dictionum consonantia *V*   479 ponitur sub *P*   479-
80 uocum et rerum *M*   480 uel *om. V*   480-81 discors . . . concors *om. BPV;*
discors uel e contrario *M*   482 numero *om. B*   ponitur ad differentiam *P*

484 ponitur *V*   485 rithmico *M*   486 qui dicitur *om. V*   similiter dicitur *P*
488 spondiacum *P*   488-89 intelligitur *BV*   intelligitur in hoc loco *V*   489 cuius:
quus *B*   pemultima *B*   490 Constat enim iambus *V*   stans: eadem *V*   492 A *om.*
BM   495 breuibus *P*   495-97 sicut . . . percussionibus *om. MOV*   496 qui *B*
497 istud *MV*   sidere etc. *MP*   498-500 *Rubric BOM*   498 rithmi et *MO*   quid
M   simplex et *MO*   Monomicus: *illegible after* mo *B*   monomicus et *O*   499 quis
Dispondaicus *om. M*   quis Trispondaicus: etc. *O*   quis Tetraspondaicus *om. MO*
500 Item *om. V*   rithimus *V*   503 partibus dissimilibus *V*   que . . . alterius: consimilibus et eiusdem *B*   504 dispondeius siue *om. V*   siue: alius *P*   dispondiacus *P*
505 trispondaicus *V*; trispondeus siue trispondaicus *M*   tetraspondaicus *V*   et . . .
tetraspondeus *om. P*   ille *V*   tetraspondeus *om. V*   506-7 quadrimembris et ille
triplex quia tetrispondeus enim *P*   507 enim *om. M*   sint *M*   508 consequenti-
bus *MP*   509 iambicus rithmus *P*   510-11 spondeacis sunt compositi et iambicis
M   sunt *M*; fuit *O*   511 spondeus *P*   quattuor *om. PV*   512 earum *BMV*   514
Rubric MO   uero *om. V*   515 uero possunt *P*   525 Seculum *om. P*   526 *Rubric MO*; spondaicis *M*   De dispondiacis fiunt hoc modo *V*; exemplum spondeaci rithmi fit hoc modo *P*   530 seculare *P*   533 *Rubric MOV*   patet *V*   534 sequenti
om. V   538 absolue *M, Mari*   539 Nec *V*   tria: duo *P*   540 plenius postea *O*
plenius *om. M, Mari*   541 *Rubric MOPV*; De quadrimembris spondaicis rithmis *P*;
De rithimis quadrispondaicis *V*   rithmos *B*   541-2 constans . . . percussionibus:
quadrispondaicus *V*   542 sequente *O*; sequenti *P*; *om. V*   544-45 Celebris . . .
memoria: etc. *MOPV*   546 exemplo domestico *V*   549 Et addatur *V*   est *M*,
Mari   istud *V*   550 suave etc. *V*   551 sic istud *V*   553 deformauit *B*   554
emendauit *V*   555 dicetur rithmus: tunc erit *V*   556 addatur *om. V*   557-58
deformauit/Aue mundum *om. P*   559 emendauit *V*   561 *Rubric MOV*   Item
om. P   562 ibi: hic *M*   563 Ve me *O*   564 ve ve nobis acephalis *V*   azepalis
M; a cephalis *O*   565 vt si dicerem *om. V*   568 rithmus bimembris constat ut in
P; bimembris rithmus iambicus est in *V*   exemplo subsequente *M*; sequente *P*   569
protege *P*   570 transfert *B*   571-73 Addatur . . . celestia *om. B*   571-78 Addatur . . . celestia *om. P*   575 Addatur quartum membrum et erit rithmus quadrimembris *V*   577 protege *P*   578 pelestia *B*   579 mundans *P*   581 *Rubric*
MOV   582-83 et tres . . . simplices *om. M*   sunt *om. B*   583 et commixtione *V*
octo *om. MPV*   ad inuicem *om. V*   584 et simplices *O*   585 societatis *O*; societa-
tum *P*   586 et *om. M*   587 spondeo *V*   589 Rubric *MOV*; De Consonanciis *M*
590 rithmicales *V*   590-91 sexquiterciam: sexqualteram *O*   591 huiusmodi *P*; eiusmodi *V*   proprietates *V*   592 sicut *om. P*; facit *V*   593 iij: unum *P*   594-95 in
quarto . . . proportio *om. M, Mari*; in quarto etc. *O*   tres *V*   sexquialtera *V*   595
proportio in quarto *B*   contra *P*   etiam: enim *B*; *om. PV*   consonancia *P*   596
quarto et in: et *om. O*; in *om. V*   discanto *V*   597 uocalibus *M*   uel in *V*   600
dyatassaron: diapasson *V*   601 commiscentur *V*   ergo *om. M, Mari*   602 terne
B; tici tercie *O* (*an unerased error*)   in tercia *B*   603 precedit *O*; procedat *P*   sequitur *O*   604 compositorum *om. P*   608 Sub *om. V*   609 Donum: deum *V*
610-14 Vel . . . gratie *om. V*   610 post *P*   616 ille *om. M*   617 intravit *B*;
intraerat *P*   618 ver parens: vernales *P*   parens floribus florum *V*   619 exte-
ruerat *M*; exfloruerat *P*; exuerat *V*   620 frondibus *V*   621 *Rubric BMOV*; domesticum exemplum de magistro incipiente *B*; Exemplum domesticum est hoc *M*   622
corporis *V*   natat *M, Mari*   623 tacta *P*   pertinet *MP*   624 vasellum dubium *P*

625 beniguoli *P*   626 Ictus cum *V*   magnum magna *P*   628 *Om.* *V*   629 *Om.*
V paro vos *P* speculor *MO*   630 *V rubric*: de eodem genere rithmi exemplum
aliud; *spacing indicates a new poem*   631 si: non *P*   632 enudata *V* omne *M*,
Mari; anne *P*   633 nimis *BMP*   634 puellaris *P*   635 specularis *P*   636 con-
templaris *P*   637 de *M*   ratio *PV* consolaris *P*   639 uariatur *P*   640 concrestio
O; *om.* *P* imitatur *PV*   641 generatur *om.* *P*   642 speculo *P*   644 formos *P*
indita *M*, *Mari*   645 subtrahitur *P*   646 hunc *P* a uiuo *P* deputatur *PV*   647
hinc *B V*   648 yde *M*   649 Munda *M*   652 terreitur *P* depatrata *V*   653 fluxi-
bus *V*   654 ut *added B*   658 Dum *M*, *Mari* rixatur: emigret *P*; vehitur *V*
659 gratiali *V*   660 lilia lilea *P*   661 Rota *P*   663 Sancti: solo *O*; se iam *V*
uidet *M*, *Mari*; uidentque *P*   664 corpori *O*   mutant *V*   665 In *V* successiva *P*
667 anxiamur *M*   670 uolimus *B*   671 Exultet *P*   675 vitium quod *V*   676
deposita *P*; disposito *V* extra *om.* *P* si: non *P*; sic *V*   678 Susitato *P*   679 uiret
B; uerbi *P*; matris *V*   681 rediuiua *M*   684 vite: plante *V*   685 radice *M*   686
florum *V*   687 Spiritali *V*   688 os *om.* *M*; hos *P* incipientis *OPV*   690 ferat *V*
691 En uagatur *P* disgressionem *P*   693 alleguationem *P*   694 sepelietur *P*
695 languans *P*   696 parum *B*; paruo *V*, *Mari*   698 ut: in *O*   699 in sit *P*
700 Hec *OP* pulse *P* uiuatrix *P*   701 hic *PV*   702 petet *P* loyces *M*; logice *P*
705 tamen *B* elegens *P*   706 mee *P*   708 rimetur *V*   709 pereat *P*   710 *Rub-*
ric BMOV; de rithmis et de membris eorum *B*; de rithmis et membris eorum *O*; rith-
miorum *M* Item notandum quod dicitur *M* rithmus dicitur *P* discolos, etc.: *M all*
these words in -us   711-13 et poliscolos . . . pentascolos *om.* *P*   711 ille *om.* *V*
712 ex *om.* *V* speciebus *om.* *M*   713 a quinque *P*   714 nam polis *V* Grece *om.*
B Latine *om.* *B* Latine et colon *V*   715 huiusmodi rithmi *om.* *P*   716 specierum
rithmi *MP*, *Mari*   716-17 ut . . . Ecclesia *om.* *V* contingat *B*   718 *Rubric BMO*;
Rithmorum: eadem *B*; *om.* *M*   718-19 rithmus distrophos *MPV*   721 copule . . .
tetrastrophos *om.* *B* est *om.* *V*   723 componitur *P* multi: *six minims for first*
two letters B; multa *OPV* fiunt *P*   724 exempla predicta *M*   725 spondaicus
MP   727 *Rubric BMOPV*; spondaici et iambici *M*; coniunguntur hic *V*   728 O
om. *O*   733 nos *om.* *V* ad ad *O*   734 Trispondaicus . . . modo *om.* *O* Trispondiacus *P* in *om.* *PV*   736 gemina *P*   740 uia: uie *M*; culpe *V*   741 aliis
V extra spondaicis *P* bimembris *P*   744 *Repeated M*   745-53 Stella . . . reformauit *om.* *V*   746-48 In quarto . . . reformauit *om.* *B*   747-48 deformauit/
Aue mundum: pm. *P*   750 mundas *O*   754 Munda *om.* *P* emendauit *V*   755
quia *B*   757 Item *V* differencie: species *M*, *Mari*   758-59 sexqualtera *M*; sequal-
tria *O*; sexqualita *P*   759 simplices *om.* *B* iambici simplices *O* respiciunt *P*
760 tercio et in quarto et *P*   762 O *om.* *PV* virgo: Maria *O*   763 celestia prius
emundans uicia *P*   764-72 Que mundum . . . celestia *om.* *V*   766 O *om.* *P*   770
In quinto sic *MP*   771 O *om.* *P*   775 occultasti *V*   776 spondeica *M*   777 ad
altum *P* et addicione *om.* *PV*   778 similis sit *M* spondico *P*   779 in scansione
M, *Mari*; scandiendo *O*   780 similis sit *M*   781 Subiciantur . . . Katerina *om.* *P*;
de beata Catherina subijciantur exempla copiosius *V* copiosius *M*; composita *O*
beata virgine katerina *M*   782 O *rubric*: de beata Katherina virgine Via *V*   783
via *V*   784 Katerina *P*   787 impugnare *P*   788 polopei *P*   790 regis erat filia
M   791 brunca *V*   793 cogelans *M* milicia *P*   797 blandimentis *B V*   799
amico *M*   808 brumaa *B*   809 andaga *V*   810 *After* pruinam *M lacuna, resum-*
ing at finibus *l. 938; inserted at end of treatise, on f. 22^{rv}*   813 quadriginta *P*

814 conuersi: confusi *M*; *om. P*; ferventi *V*   817 arctat *M*   testis *B*   818 est *om.*
P   821 porrifirii *M, Mari*   823 gelo *V*   824 prelio *V*   825 redeat *M, Mari*
827 Vir: et *V, Mari*   828 Cum: tam *O*; eum *P*   cedendis *V*   833 rotas has cur-
rates fecit *O*   crassates *B*; cursares *V, Mari; om. P*   834 disiecit *O*   835 quantum
P   836 rota *B*; ros *P*   uerna *P*   839 hostilia *P*   849 ⸱⸱⸱ dat⸱⸱ *P*   011 Bxoranti
V   845 laud *P*   seruet *O*   846 sumat: *B six minims for* um   851 dilata *P* honore
M, Mari   852 ad *B*   853 turba *V*   854 Morbos: flos *P*   855 sane *P*   856
Predictis . . . assignandis *om. P*   hiis et aliis *M, Mari*; et aliis adhuc *V*   857 ad *om.*
BO   858 ut hic. Exemplum rithmi de beata virgine *V*   860 Ad *B*   861 obstu-
pescit *B*   radiens *corrected O*; radiens *P*; radians *V*   863 *Rubric M, placed at* Pre-
dictis *l. 856*   864 in metro sicut in rithmo *B*   isti precipue: sunt isti *V*   simpliciter
B   865 Compar in: compari *B*; copar in *V*   eiusdem *M, Mari*   867 retinens *P*
consonancians *O*   868 leoninitas *M*   in Numero: numeris *B*   869 partes *corrected*
V   870 qui *om. V*   ornagrapha *V*   870-71 componunt enim rithmos *V*   871
esse uideatur *M*   in *om. O*   sit: semper *V*   872-73 correctionem et productam *P*
875 o maria preuia *V*   879 si dicerem: hic *V*   880 hoc in rithmo *M*; hoc *om. P*
883 mitigas *M, Mari*; mitigum *P*   885 sit *P*   889 amarum *om. P*   890 introductio *V*   891 scilicet secundum *B*; sed secundum *O*   quam *V*   secundum: et *V*
est annominatio ibi *O*   893 ibi est *P*   tranquillitas aura procellarum etc. *M*   893-
94 rithmus qui constat ex viij sillabis compositus *V*   894 consonam *P*   894-95 aliquando simplicem aliquando unicam *V*   896 *M rubric* de repetitione mediata
color rethoricus *M, Mari*   repetitio est *P*   898 ante *O*   Immediata *V*   899 quando
o maria *P*   900 *om. P*; pia *om. V*   905 dispondiaco *P*   906 spondiaca *B*   faciant
P   906-7 faciens . . . spondaica *om. V*   907 uiciosa est *P*   908 *M rubric* de repetitione immediata   immediata est aliquando cadit *P*   909 uel indignationis *om. V*
910 uolunt ingenium *MP*   913 Rore *om. V*   defloruit *P*   914 Fluit *om. O*
916 obseruanda est in dictionibus *P*   Ut hic *om. O*; ut *V*   972 *Rubric BM*   919
stilla: stella *M*   920 sella *P*   921 viri *O*   925 tu tamen *M*   926 avia *P*   931
est *B*   932-43 Hec . . . citharizat *om. P*   936 rebectra *O*   939 est *om. O*
941 tendi *V*   943 hec et sauli *V*   944 dauit *M*   parens *P*   946 Casto: casta
MPV, Mari   uitis *P*   949 spondam *corrected M*   950 saluatoris *PV*   952 in-
cussat *P*   953 ficte: sue *M, Mari*   957 Hec est uxor assueri *B*   961 rachel *V*
962 te fugantem *O*; refugacem *P*   cisaram *M*   964 dimicatrix *B*   965 forto *O*
967 bethlem est *P*   968 qua *O*   971 exuriit *V, Mari*   972 parturiit *P*   974
spes est *V*   organa *P*   977 iniungitur *OP*   982 astupescit *M, Mari*   radiens *V*
984 plaudat *O*   dotibus *P*   985 heli *P*   986 urentibus *B*   992 in circo *V*   993
ex circo *V*   995 Hec *om. P*   997 gratia *O*   998 *Rubric MOP* post *O* predictas
B   decemnouem *V*   999 de decem sillabis *P*   1000 de quo *PV*   hoc rithmo *O*
1003 dampnentur *P*   1004 *om. B*   nostra *M*; nostra quia uestra *P*   iacens *P*
1006 est *om. M, Mari*   1007 Soluo *V*   1007-8 hoc modo *om. V*   1008 uidetur
in fine *P*   dactilicus *B*   corripiatur *V, Mari*   1009 ultima istius aliquando *P*
1009-10 aliquando producitur aliquando corripitur *M, Mari*   1010 uero: etiam *V*
ideo dicitur *M*; et non dactilicus dicitur pro tanto quia *O*   1011 ecclesia sancta *O*;
Sancta *om. M, Mari*   frequencius utitur *V*   1012 hymis *B*   scandiendo *O*   1014-
15 *Rubric BM*; de *om. M*   Differentibus *om. B*   1016-17 sed . . . differentes *om.*
O   1017-18 iambici sunt differentes *MPV, Mari*   1018 dispondaicum *OV*
1019 differencie *om. O*   1019-20 trispondeum . . . circa *om. P*; trispondaicum *V*

1020 tetraspondaicum *V* differencia esse *O* 1022 aliqua *P* aliqua *P* 1023
Primo . . . dispondeo *om. V* 1032-36 Mater . . . uia *om. PV* 1037 mende *V*
1039 si *P* 1044 he *V* huius differentie quattuor *P* species quattuor *P*
species quattuor: quattuor *om. O* 1045 attendatur *V* trispondeico *M*; trispondiaco *P* 1047 pulchra gemma *P* tota domino devota *M* 1049 et sic *MPV*
quarto sic *O* 1051 Gemma: rosa *BP* tota pulchra *P* 1053-57 Mater . . . deuota
om. V 1054-58 sic . . . luxu *om. P* 1060 altera *M* ponitur in eadem *B*
1065 modo: in *O* assignantur *V* differencie quatuor *O* 1066 tetraspondeico *M*;
trispondeon *P*; trispondaico *V* tercio et in quarto et in quinto *P* 1067 differenciam quartam *V* 1073 Aue: eua *P* 1074 emendauit *V* 1075 pariendo: etc.
B 1078 restaurauit *V* 1079 emendauit *V* 1083 et impropria *om. B* notandum quia *M* 1083-84 sic possit *P* 1084 esse bene *MOP* bene *om. V* 1084-
85 secundum . . . diapente *follows* quarta species *l. 1085 V* 1085 sed . . . usu *om.*
OP 1086 magis quando consonancie sunt propinque *MPOV* (sunt consonancie *V*)
1087 emendauit *V* 1091 Et notandum *V* notandum *om. O* non: si *P* 1091-
92 rithmi secundem artem nominati sunt compositi *V* 1092 comparatione *P*
1094 superius super *V* est dictum *O* 1098 intacta *OV* 1099-1106 Item . . .
edidit *om. B* 1103 intacta *OV* gremio *om. O* 1104 addatur *M, Mari*; dicatur
P altera *O* 1109 intacta *OV* 1110 unius versus *O* sit *om. V* alius consonancie *P* 1111 sicut . . . est: sic *V* 1113 intacta *OV* vernans intacto *MPV,*
Mari 1115 summi patris in filio *M, Mari* Summi *om. O* 1118 siue consonantiam
om. PV diuerso: eodem *P* 119 Iunguntur *P* superius *om. P* assignatis *MOV*;
numeratis *P* 1120-21 et erunt xxxvj. Si ponantur in numero tales species quando
V 1120 et xxxvj *P* 1121 ut hic *om. O* hic *om. B* 1127-31 astrum castrum
regit tegit secundum *P* 1132 iambicos *V* ut hic *V* 1133 seas *corrected M*
1135 Sed: si *O* 1135-38 transeas . . . consonantes: transonantes *P* 1136 etc.
om. V 1137 Isti sunt rithmi quidem *V* 1138 seu *V* caudule *M* caude et consimiles *B* 1138-40 sed . . . incipit *om. V* 1139 propter hoc *om. B* rei *om. P*
1141 *M rubric*: Rithmus cum duplici differentia 1142 spreciosa *B* 1144 uiruit
B 1145 gratiarum gratiarum *P* 1146 miserarum *P* 1147 gratiam *V* 1149
Rubric O 1149-50 Ut superius dictum est quinque sunt *MOPV, Mari* 1150 species iambicorum spondaicorum *B* rithmorum spondaicorum rithmorum *P* 1151
constituunt *P* iterum *om. V* 1152 x sunt *B* 1152-53 rithmorum iambicorum *P*
1153 rithmorum *om. M, Mari* qui *B* 1153-54 quadrimembres pentimembres *P*
1154 adueniunt *B* vel *om. B* 1155-56 que . . . sex species *om. M, Mari* 1157
species ¹ *om. V* duo *B* species due *V* 1158 iambici rithmi *BOPV* (iambicis *P*)
uel: scilicet *P* ascendit *B* 1159 uel . . . et *om. O* uel ascendit *B* 1160 vel cum
O 1161 hic scilicet *V* scilicet *om. M* dixi *P* 1162 species *om. M* magis *om.*
V 1163 sed illa que: scilicet qui *P* minor est: minorem *OP* facit in consonanciam
O 1163-64 consonantiam in singulis dictionibus de qua superius dictum est est
uicesima *V* 1164 de *om. P* specie *om. MPV, Mari* 1165 cum aliis xvi *M, Mari*
1166 rithmus *om. BM* 1167-1225 Sed posset queri . . . Ludo *om. V; part of lacuna*
inserted at end (f. 158ᵛ), as noted below at l. 1173 1168 consonant *BP* 1169
rithmum *om. P* 1169-70 quadrimenbrum spondeum *O* 1170 quia: vel *O*
1172-73 *Rubric BMOP* que *P* uidentur composite qui non computantur *M* componi sed non sunt *B*; sed sunt uersus *P* compuctantur *O* sunt in metra *O*; sine metro
leonino *P* 1173-88 Item . . . rithmicam artem *added at end (f. 158ᵛ) V* 1173 sunt

nonnulli *MPV*   1175 tres[1] *om. P*   1176 si: se *P*   proferant *P*   1177 sentenciosum *om. V*   portamus *M, Mari; om. P*   exempla *P*   sic *om. V*   1179 incurserat *P*
1180 ense *BO*   1181 sanguinee suberunt *B*   1182 insulte *P*   1183 Tot cuneos:
corcureos *P*   phasialia *B*   1184 ponamus in hiis *P*   his *V*   verbibus *B*   rithmus *om.*
M   1184-85 quorum   totius: quod patet *V*   1186 qua *B*   1100 iidmilcam
uel artem *P*   1189 *M rubric*: de Retrogradis uersibus qui directe laudant, retrograde
uituperant   conuenit *P*   fleri *O*   retrogadum *B*   si *om. M*   recte *P*   1192 retro-
uersatur *B*   1193 gens prouida *B*   1194 posset *OP*   1195 parte acquisite *cor-*
rected M   1196 retroversatur *B*; retro vertam *P*   1199 ibi: hic *M*   1202 orationem aliquando *B*   aliquando *om. O*   sed: et *B*   1203 hic hic *M*   est hic *O*   1204
uertatur *P*   1205 hic est *M*   1206-14 uidetur . . . preter *om. P*   1207-13 *B*
divides habitauerunt *in first quotation (and repeats* runt*); BM fail to divide* prostrau-
erunt *in second quotation: M fails to divide* carceribus, *B divides* car/ceribus   *M*
punctentur   1214 *M rubric*: de Rithmis impropriis idest inusitatis sed sunt secundem artem   hii *P*   multi *om. BO*   1214-15 retrogradis et rithmis *P*   1216 *M*
rubric: Secundum artem   1216-24 Posset . . . Puerorum *om. B*   1218 est nihil
dictum *O*   hoc: quod *O*   dicendum est *P*   1219-20 in quarto loco *om. O*   1220
est *om. M*; qualis rithmus est ille *O*   1221 parens: perflens *P*   etc. *om. O*   1222
domesticum . . . contra Natale: huius *P*   1223-24 *Rubric MO*   de Licencia Puerorum *om. O*   1225 Sucto post solitum *P*   solidum *O*   1226 amplico *P*   applicans
P   1229 exactio *M*   apollo *M*; extollo *O*   1235 duxam *P*; deduxerat *V*   deludentes
B   1236 referanimus *O*   1238 Gallica nos *O*   1239 uelis et *P*   1240 baccos
P   dignos: digitos *M*   1241 decorem *V*   1243 constitit *P*   1244 quis et *P*
mutum *B*   ruborem etc. *V*; *V ends the poem here*   1245 Tulli *MP*   1246 pig-
mentaneum *O*; pigmentareum *P*   1247 facundi *P*   1248 pro mobida *P*   1249
loyca *M*   destruet *P*   1250 supat *O*   1252 erratem *M*   1253 Curego *M, Mari*
patet *O*; perit *P*   ueri *P*   1254 optat *O*   anerus *P*   1255 secanam *P*   faciet *BO*
offerri *P*   1257 a uirtute *M*   1258 celere *P*   hora *P*   1260 olla *M, Mari*; scelera
P   seu *O*   congerit *O*; coegit *P*   et hora *P*   1262 diiungas tepides *P*   1263 minu-
erunt *MOP*   1265 laudat *O*   1266 cura *P*   1267 offerendo mantule *P*   turgide
mentule *corrected M*   1268 Seu *O*   clauemque *P*   1269 A *om. M, Mari*   1270
istud *OP*   1272 offendens *P*   1275 comes comis *O*   1276 Seu *O*   et epheri *O*
1279 datorem *P*   1280 folis *P*   1281 Supplectio *M*   Item *om. P*   1282 quibus
superius nihil *MP*   est[1] *om. B*   est[2] *om. M*   1282-83 dispondiacus *P*   1283 dispondaicus *M*; trispondiacus *P*   1284 dispondiaco *P*   1285 trispondiaco *P*   et
om. V   ista sex *M*; iste sex *PV*   1289 Hec . . . hic *om. V*   computatur *M, Mari*
hic *om. O*   1290 cadit hic *om. P*; hic *om. B*   tertio: isto *P*   sequenti *M*   1299
siue rachelia *B*; siue *om. V*   1301 due *om. V*   trispondiaco *P*   1304-7 Hiis . . .
tota *om. B*   1305 Hec . . . hic *om. V*   computatur *M, Mari*   1307 tota *om. P*
1309 hic *V*   1317 quare: quod *M, Mari; om. O*; idest *P*   congruit *P*   1318 ob-
sequi *P*   ita *om. P*   1319 paruis: partis *P*; *om. V*   Ad quod dicendum: et respondeo
V   1320 sed: licet *M*   insitatum *V*   est sic *PV*   1330 erunt *om. B*; sunt *O*   quattuor *om. V*   erunt *om. B*   1330-31 sex erunt *O*; erunt modi sex *V*   1331
trispondiaco *P*   1332 contingerit *P*   1337-40 Et . . . seruis *om. BV*   1341
labe carens tota *P*   1342 et notandum *P*   proponitur *P*   1342-43 contingit frequenter *V*   1343 hec *om. P*   1344 est ante dicta *O*; est *om. B*   est mentio *O*;
fit mensio *P*   tali *om. V*   Ehaurum *P*   1345 intrauit *V*   superhabundat una *O*

1346 sine . . . differenciis *om. V* duabus *om. MP* differenciis *om. MOP* ses *P*
1347 differencias: modes *V* siue species *om. V* 1348 duobus *B* 1349 plures
species *M* 1350 sicut: velud *P* 1351 solummodo *V* scilicet quod *V* 1352
in *om. V* sicut *M*; et sic *P* 1353 impiorum etc. *V* 1354-56 Et . . . euagatur
om. V 1354 cauet *B* 1355 et repperitur *P* 1357 ( )ost *B* Post predicta:
postea *P* 1358 aliquid *om. V* que . . . sunt: auctoritate sine *P* notandum igitur
quod *M* notandum est *OP* 1359 rethorice *V* exponuntur *P* et sine *V* 1360
sine[1] *om. V* 1361 fere non sunt *PV* 1361-62 non nisi tres diuersitates metri
autentice sunt *M, Mari* 1362 metri *om. P* unde *P* est *om. BO* asclepeadeum *O*;
asclapeadeum *P*; excelpiadeum *V* 1362-63 asclepio *M*; asclepeadeo *O*; esclapeaden
P; exclepiadeo *V* 1363 qui *P* constat *O* ex: in *P* 1365 parrichius *M* est ibi:
eius *P* ibi *om. V* ut *om. B* 1365-67 ut . . . utero *om. V* 1366 marie uirginis
M 1367 sanctificata *P* 1368 *Rubric BM* asplepiadeum *M* coriiambum *B*
1369 ( )erum *BM* Verum freno tuens *P* 1370 Portus: pons post *V* dextera *O*
notantium *M* 1372 *Om. P* 1373 omnipotentia *P*; optime *V* uero *O*; *om. P*;
una *V* 1376 pia *O* 1377 loris *BP* princeps *O* 1378 datur *M* 1380 et concepta *M* sibi concepta vernula etc. *V*; *poem ends here V* uernula: similia *P* 1381
( )atris *B*; patris *P* tui *P* 1382 etherea *B* 1383 letam *P* ginguitur *B* 1385 promissum *O* 1387 uox *B* tollit *P* 1389 ( )dam *B*; nudam *P* 1391 lapsis *M, Mari* 1392
stillaque *O* 1393 ( )undi *BP* 1394 nescit *M* practica *om. P* 1395 concepti
B; accipe *P* 1396 mundens *P* 1397 Huius cantus idem est qui incipit sic *V*
idem est *MPV* huius *M* 1398 inclita gaudia: pangamus socia *P* etc. *om. V*
1399 compositus: comprehendit *P*; *om. V* 1399-1400 beate marie uirginis *M*;
beate uirginis marie *P* 1400 est autem metrum saphicum *M, Mari* saphicum
dicitur *V* 1401 sapha *V* sapho muliere quadam que fuit *M, Mari* inuentrix fuit
huiusmodi metrum *V* Adonicum dicitur *OPV* 1401-2 ab . . . metrum *om. V*
1402 adoni *O*; adon *P* scilicet *om. P* ultimi duo *V* 1403-4 secundus . . . similiter trocheus *om. V* 1404 quintus similiter trocheus *om. P* 1405 de ultima non
refert *O*; ultima est indifferens *MPV, Mari* sunt similes *M* ibi *PV* 1406 est *om.*
O hic: hoc *O* cantus huiusmodi *M* 1407 cum cantu huius hymni *M* isto *OV*
laxis resonare fibris *M*; laxis etc. *P* 1409 O *om. OP* 1410 carnis *om. P* 1413
geminat *P* radix iesse *corrected M* 1414 rubescit *P* 1415 Ortus *om. P*; cetus
V 1416 plaudit etc. *V*; *V om. from here to last stanza* 1422 vie *O* 1425
( )irigas *B*; dirige *P* laxos *P* 1426 desertas *P* 1427 pauperesque *B* data *P*
modum *M, Mari* 1430 includat *M, Mari* faciem *B* 1431 medicus *P* 1432
tanta *P* 1433 Vltimus versus *V* deus clementie tribuam *P* 1435 ianuam *P*
1436 dicte *P* Amen *om. BM* 1437 Nota *MPV* Christe: vestre *P* este uersus:
terminus est *P* 1438 adoni *OV*; adonio *P* inuentore sic dicto *V* in daptilo rithmo
et spondeo *P* 1439 istud *MV* 1440 sidere etc. *V* 1441 pari *PV* 1442 ut
hic *om. OV* 1443 *Rubric MO*; metrum iambicum dimetrum *O* 1444 superna
V 1446 coronis *P* 1448 ibi *P*; illuc *V* 1451 hac *O* christe *M, Mari* esse *P*
1452 *V om. from here to last stanza* 1454 case case *B* 1455 nudet *P* pec-
catorum *O* 1456 semel *M* 1457 mundo redditur: mun *O* 1459 Loto *om. P*
1462 in hoc nobili mari *M* 1464 ( )edes *B* 1465 pedes *B* lubricum *M, Mari*
1468 Vltimus versus *V* 1470 rupens *P* 1471 fusos *B*; nos *P* Amen *om. BO*
1472 rithmi *M* hymni . . . est *om. V* est idem *P* cantu . . . incipit: isto *V* huius
M 1473 prodeunt *om. B* etc. *om. BOV*; *P ends here with the words,* "Et hec

sufficiant de triplici arte, scilicet prosaica, metrica, et rithmica. Finito libro sit laus et gloria Christo. Amen" *M rubric*: metrum asclepyadeum adonicum   1474 exclepeadeum *V*   sumptis *V*   1475-76 hoc scilicet *om. B*; hec scilicet *O*   1476 quanta gloriosa *B*   corusscans *M*; corusca *O*; *om. V*   1478 Oratii: *V ends here*   1479 quas *M, Mari*   quarum *M, Mari*   1482 *M rubric*: opus istud componitur ad castigationem   1484 cantum *B*   1485 decantant *B*   membra *M, Mari*   1487 sanans *M, Mari*   1488-89 *Rubric MO; O om. through* Primum   1490 Asclepi *M, Mari* 1495 cantant *B*   1499 reuelamina *B*   1504 precepta *M, Mari*   1506 demonumque *B*   1510 variam *O*   1513 edita *M, Mari*   1520 *Om. M, Mari*   1521 furtum *O*   1532 *Rubric MO*   1533 hic est *M*   mendicamen *B*   1535 sit *B*   et leuis *M*; ac leuis *O*   urania *B*   1539 phebe phebo *M*   hinc *B*   1543 hic hoc *O* canit *O*   1544 volitas *O*   1547 mundo *M*   1551 orbidus *M*   1554 nocte *M* 1555 flectis *B*   1557 *Rubric MO*; De dignatibus diuersis clericorum: secundum metrum *M*   1560 hinc: inde *O*   1568 facta *B*   1574 insistunt *B*   1578 aufert *M*   1582 et et *O*   unde *O*   1585 luctu *M*   1587 auget *M*   1589 pallas si *M* 1593 est nichil *O*   1603 fontem *M*   1604 *Rubric BM*; oda . . . Katerine *om. B*; katerine uel *M*   1605 pareant *B*; pareunt *M*   1606 sequenter *B*   1609 o Pari *M, Mari*   1612 parent dent *B*   1615 cesti *O*   1616 magnanios *B*   1622 clauifica *B*   1624 leues *M, Mari*   1625 *Rubric BMO*; metrum quartum *M*; Quartum Metrum *om. O*; Oda . . . Poeticorum *om. B*   1627 *Om. M*   tetrametrum *B*   1628 collofonus *B*   1633 uterque *M*   vie *O*   1634 ficta *B*   1635 polluunt *M, Mari*   1639 scandalizant *O*   1640 prandeat *M*   1641 exercetur *M, Mari*   visus *O*   1643 sepulturus *M*   1644 *Rubric BMO*; metrum quintum *M*; Quintum Metrum *om. O*   1645 Te inpero *M*   1657 flos hic est sine ignibus, flos hic est sine fructibus *B*   1661 flores *M*   1664 ersus asclepii *M*   1667 aliquid *B*   1668 quidam *B*   1671 quos *om. M*   1672 uocant *M*   1673 sit magniloquus *M*   1674 suspiciunt *M*   1676 ignorat *M*   1678 *Rubric BM*: Peccandi . . . Septimum *om. B*   1679 intereger *B*   1683 nec *B*   1685 tunc *O*   1687 errores *MO*   erret *O*   1693 *M adds*: Epitritus secundus duo coriambi bachius et amphibracus   1694 coriambus *M*   amphibracusque *B*   1696 here *M*   1701 suus: socius *O*   1703 medium *M*   preuideasque *MO*   1709 collaborant *B*   1714 *Rubric BMO*; Nonum Metrum *om. O*   1715 quo *M, Mari; om. O*   camine *M* 1717 Additur *om. M*   1719 dimetrum *B*   hic yper cata lectius *M*   1724 ut: in *O*   1725 phebi *M*   1727 diaconus *B*   1729 probosque canos *M, Mari*   1730 temas *M*   1732 uerboque *M*   1735 *Rubric BMO*; Oda de *om. B* (*page is torn*) 1736 tibi *O*   1739 sto factis *O*   1741 tibi *om. M, Mari*   1742 colat *M, Mari* 1743 es[1]: est *B*   1744 non *B*   1747 demonarii *M, Mari*   1748 floruerat grata *M, Mari*   uiridus *B*   aruit *om. BM, Mari*   1752 sonorum *O*   1754 uilibus *B* 1759 pollicibus suis *M*   1760-61 *Rubric BMO*; metrum decantat caliope *M* 1763 sumens *B, Mari*   1765 tristicia *M, Mari*   1772 belligeras *B*   1775 terra *B*   1776 *Rubric BMO*; Metrum *om. B*; duodecimum *B*   1777 amphibraco *B* 1780 iambus eris *M*   1782 vetabo *BO*   1784 bona *O*   1785 inventus *M* 1787 imperio *B*   1790 percior *B*   1792 sibi: igitur *M*   1793 *Rubric MO*; duodecimum metrum *M*   1794 ( )onicus ecce iunior *O*   tibi: cui *O, Mari*   1798 *Om. M*   1799 *Om. M*   1800 *Om. O*   1801 miserorum causas *O, Mari*   1804 pholeratus *M*   sibi: igitur *M, Mari*   1806 legicorum timidum *M, Mari*   1807 sine flamma sine bello *MO*   1810 illic *B*   1811 habebant *O*   1812-13 *Rubric BMO*;

Tertium Decimum *om. M*; de arismetris *O*   1816 mitans *O*   1817 cauda *M, Mari*
solet *M*   1818 gemetra *M, Mari*   1821 erat *O*   1823 presserciit? *B*   1824
sitit: scit *M, Mari*   1828 ut: quod *MO*   decipiunt *B*   in illis *O*   1829 Baucis:
banus *O*   1830 *Rubric BM*; Quartum Decimum *om. M*; De Sanctu Cruce *om. B*
1833 dimeter *B*; trimetri *O*   1834 dimetri *O*   1838 luce sue volt *M*   ecclesie *B*
1839 cum hoc sumus arofex *O*   1840 plorem *M*   1841 ludibrisque *M*   1847-
48 *Rubric BMO*; Quintum Decimum *om. MO*   in *B*   scientia fidei *O*   1849 tempore *BM*   1850 trimetri *O*   1851 est *MO*   1852 dimetri *O*   1853 exulit *B*
1854 spes *B*; pes *O*   premii *BO, Mari*   1856 fert: sunt *BM*   1858 reprehendi *BM,*
Mari   1861 *Om. B*   1862 licet: hic *M*   1863 diuiciis *B*   1864 pallida *B*
1865 *Rubric BMO*; Sextum Decimum *om. MO*; Metrum *om. O*   1866 cordis hoicus
O   1867 erit *om. B*   dimetri *O*   1868 quid *B*   fines *M*   1869 sit *B*   1870
amicas *M*   1871 funditus *om. M*   1873 sua *M*   1876 amicos *om. O*   1877
fetis *B*; fortis *O*   carie *M, Mari*   1879 agerque *M*   1880 *Rubric BMO*; Septimum
Decimum *om. M*; metrum sextum decimum *O*   1881 narrat *O*   1884 ars *om. M*
1885 capriorem: causa priorem *M, Mari*   1886 capte *M*   1887 clamat *M, Mari*
1888 facessore *M*   sed: se *B*   1892 res *O*   ethereus *M, Mari*   1895-96 *Rubric*
BMO; Metrum *om. B*; Octauum Decimum *om. BM*   1897 uita *M*   1899 canta *O*
illis *O*   1900 dimeter *B*   1901 manta *M*   1902 mortis pocula *B*   moras *O*
1905 fert *M*   1911 que *O, Mari*   specio *M*   1912 que *B*   1913-14 *Rubric BMO*;
Metrum *om. B*; Decimum Nonum *om. MO*; de *om. B*; clerici ultimo debeant ire *MO;*
debent *B*; thelogiam *M*   1916 sepe *corrected* pede *M*   demetri *B*   1917 ses *M*
1919 noctesque *M, Mari*   1921 gesserunt *M, Mari*   1922 sanguisque *M*   1926
redens *O*   1928 pristita *O*   Explicit ars uersificatoria *B*; Explicit ars prosaica, versificatoria, rithmica, metrica. Amen. In nomine Domini. Amen. *O; What follows is in*
M only   1940 micenas   1946 quinque   1947 amphinicrus   1966 ut diomedes
1967 ex duabus longis et duabus breuibus   1968 ut iunonius   1977 Peo   1985
In red, and followed by this gloss, also in red: Tres primi non sunt trimembris uel
quadrimembris; sine differencia possunt tamen fieri.

Appendixes

Appendix One

The Glosses in Ms. Bruges 546

What follows is a selection of the large number of marginal and interlinear glosses in Ms. Bruges 546. Selectiveness was necessary because many
are trivial and because completeness was impossible in any case, since some
five percent of them remained undecipherable. Had I included all those I
could decipher, a reader, tiring of looking up glosses and finding them of
no value, might abandon the enterprise altogether and miss something
helpful.

The glosses are of several kinds. Many are etymologies, usually of
words with Greek stems, and often false. Others are grammatical nota-
tions of unusual words, identifying declension and gender or conjuga-
tion and principal parts. By far the largest number are Latin synonyms
for words in the text; there are also about fifteen glosses in French and
four in English. All of these suggest classroom use for improving students' Latin. Most of the omissions are of glosses of this kind, though
some appear here, including all the vernacular glosses.

A second class is strictly involved with the meaning of the text. Many
of the synonyms, of course, fall into this class; other glosses define unusual words or concepts, identify persons, or clarify murky syntax by
indicating the subjects of verbs, the antecedents of relative pronouns,
and the like. Many of these are very valuable to the modern reader,
or at least editor, and I have relied on them often in my translation,
especially of the several long poems which are at times very precious
and obscure. Most of the glosses included here are those which clarified
difficulties for me, and apparently questionable passages in the translation should be checked against them.

A third class consists of literary parallels; lines of poetry, both ancient
and contemporary, which illustrate a point John is making or contain
some word or words he uses. A number of them are from other poems
by John of Garland. I have included most of these, identifying all I
could. I have, finally, also included various other glosses which seemed
to me to have some general interest.

Not all the glosses were made at the same time, or by the same person.
At least two hands are clearly distinguishable, though it is not always
possible to tell which hand wrote a particular gloss. Neither hand seems
to be that of either scribe who wrote the text. The first glossator made
most of the corrections in the text, and apparently wrote before the
rubrics and initial letters were inserted, since some of these obscure
parts of his words. The second glossator, whose strokes are thinner and

whose ink is browner, is responsible for most of the marginal poetry.
One clear example that two different minds were at work is the word
Semele, 2, 286: the first glossator wrote, wrongly, *mater Cadmi;* the
second corrected him, *uirgo incorrupta,* which was true until Jupiter
arrived, and which specifies the role she plays in John's metaphor.

At least some of these glosses may well be by John himself. Certainly
the compiler of the literary parallels had a good acquaintance with both
classical and medieval poetry, including that of John of Garland. The
English synonyms may also suggest his hand. Some of the glosses to the
poems suggest a greater knowledge of the poet's intention than a mere
reader is likely to have had. John is known to have written a key to his
Compendium grammaticae (see Paetow, p. 121), and Wilson gives evidence that he wrote some of the gloss to the *Stella maris* (Wilson, *Stella
maris,* p. 80). See also Hauréau, p. 7.

On the other hand, a few of the explanatory glosses clearly misinter-
pret the author's meaning, and some contradict statements made elsewhere in the text. Furthermore, if John wrote the glosses, it is surprising
that they appear in only one manuscript, though if he added them some-
time after he composed the text, that is explainable. Perhaps the most
likely possibility is that John lectured on his own work, and the glosses
originated as annotations made by a student or series of students of his.

There are also some glosses in Ms. Munich 6911, which are generally
similar to those in *B,* though there is almost no poetry. I have included
such as are valuable, marking them *M.* The words *idest* and *scilicet* are
omitted unless they are necessary to the sense. French and English words
are italicized.

Chapter One

[f. 149^r] 1 iubar: scienciam   gloria: frequens fama cum laude, quia ex
gloria addiscendi multiplicantur, magistri et scolares. Debent eorum
instrumenta crescere et multiplicari, que sunt libri; et ita nominatur
causa competens istius libelli   clerus: multitudo studencium   2 Crescit:
Excitat auditor studium, laudataque uirtus/Crescit, et immensum gloria
calcar habet (Ovid, *Epis. ex Ponto* 4.2.35-36)   Apolineas: Dei sapiencie
fons: sciencia   iaculatur: emitat   aquas: artes liberales   3 Pascua:
doctrina   grex: discipuli   vernat: per vim eloquencie   crescit: assiduitate
studii   studet: pro utilitate auditorum   4 studio: studium est vehemens
applicacio animi ad aliquid agendum   5 doctrine: litterature   noua
pabula: pastus spirituales   carpant: colligant   6 Agniculi: discipuli
pastor: magister   spectet: inspiciat pabula   ouile: oues sunt discipuli
terant (*sic in margin*): inuestigant subtilitatum (*sic*) istius artis   7 Quid
dedignaris: cur inuides   maiora: philosophica   8 Vidimus: scilicet in

agro pedem: affectum 9 pes: affectus tuus sistere: quiescere artis: scribendi prosaice metrice rithmice 10 Regula: materialis causa innuitur hic pontem: artem 11 equora: longas doctrinas et tediosas 12 Hic: in hac summa stringitur: compilatur ampne: ambitu ampne breui: doctrina compendiosa 13 Metrica: ars 51 tragedi: istoriographi; a tragos hircus quia hirco remunerabantur 52 comedi: illi qui scribuntur (*sic*) iocunde; comedia dicitur a comos villa et odos cantus 54 in prosis ecclesiasticis: in sequenciis 55 musice: Musica cuncta ligat, mundana, humana, sed inde/instrumentalis triplice calle meat;/se melice metrica, metrice se rithmica iungit,/sed melice dulcis est uia secta duplex triplex:/dat studiis enarmonicam, uariisque coreis/ aptam cromaticam, ditonicamque tubis (John of Garland, *De triumphis ecclesie*, ed. Wright, 4: 49-54) 64 Metrum: Metra iuuant animas, perstringunt plurima paucis,/pristina commemorant, que sunt tria grata legenti (John of Garland, *Clavis compendii*, Ms. Bruges 546, f. 25^r; see also Walther, *Versanfänge*, 10972) 72 Albinouanus (Ambinus ms.): magister Karoli [f 149^v] 88 per vbi habemus in quibus rebus est inueniendum; per quid, substanciam rei; per quale, ornatum, licet honestum vel inhonestum; per qualiter, modus agendi; per hoc quod dicitur ad quid, finalem causam 100 infirmum: leprosum 101 discumbat: sedeat ad mensum 107 caduca: Ouidius: dudum florueram sed flos fuit ille caducus (cf. *Tristia*, 5.8.19: Nos quoque floruimus, sed flos erat ille caducus) 111 misochomio: *maladerie*; a mesos miser et chomos diuisio quia ibi diuiduntur membra 113 Oratius: Si uentre bene, si lateri pedibusque tuis, nil/diuicie poterunt regales addere maius (*Ep.* 1. 12.5-6) 117 Senece: magistri Neronis 130 consul: *cunte* 133 stilum: qualitatem carminis 141 ethimologiis (*all these verses and remarks are in the margins of ff. 149^v and 150^r; they seem to be examples of etymological invention*): Est plastes figulus, fragusque genu; uenit inde/Suffrago poples, suffraginis est genitiuus;/De quo suffragor, suffragia dicimus inde (John of Garland, *Clavis compendii*, Ms. Bruges 546, f. 40^v) Iure x canum canibus confundo decanum/Quia more canum pro uultu prebuit anum Qui uendunt et emunt res sacras ecclesiales,/ Appellamus eas a Simone Simoniales (Cf. Walther, *Versanfänge*, 15722) Qui comedit papat; dat sanctus papa; qui alba/Papa fovet; papus floridus auget agri Hic papus *pistel*; hic papas, papantis: Iuuenalis: prelibat pocula papas (6. 632) 142 duo: scilicet laudem vel uituperium [f. 150^r] 166 thema: questio 172-73 Fermenti: vicii 195 capiti: sacerdoti 199 irretit: Irretit multis me deliciis Imineus/Sed melior cultis est rudis iste meus 204 metiri: mensurari (*sic*); Iuuenalis: bucce nocensda est mensura tue mato cursius an sis (11.34-35: an Curtius et Matho buccae/ Noscenda est mensura sui) [f. 150^v] 225 degustata: tanto 236 Cham: filius Noe uel hereticus patris: pape 263 perpendiculo: in-

strumento   264 determinare: diffinire   presumit: stultecapit   281
Frontis: apparancie   de mente: de cognitione hominis   laruata: cooper-
ta; *tester* vel *viser*; hec larva *viser*   288 Cheruli: illius poete; Cherulus
fuit quidam poeta qui scripsit gesta Alexandri et fecit magnum opus et
in illo magno opere non fuerunt nisi v boni uersus   [f. 151^r]   298
Sensibile: idest bonum   299 dependens: Pendet ab illius nostra salute
salus   305 regirat: portat   306 eundem: solem   308 experimentum:
medicina   312 pater patrum: Papa, pater patrum, papisse prodito partum,/Et tibi mox edam de corpore quando recedam   (Papisse *is glossed*
tue; *a verse follows explaining* edam: Cum dape uescor, ĕdo; sermones,
cum loquor, ēdo. *The couplet concerns the legendary Pope Joan*; cf.
Johann Döllinger, *Fables Respecting the Popes of the Middle Ages,* Eng.
trans. by Alfred Plummer [London, 1871], p. 46; *for the verse on* edo,
cf. Walther, *Lateinische Sprichwörter,* 4085)   324 Mulier mollis:
Iuuenalis: clames licet et mare celo/Confundas, homo sum (6.282-83)
341 Traductio: Flos es, floris amans, flori gratissima; florem,/O flos,
producis, flore creata tue   352 tribus: penis   urgentur: puniuntur
[f. 151^v] 371 prescripcione: laude   390 inuenire: in Epitalamico
392 oue: Maria   pastor: Christus   393 aries: Christus   mistica: fig-
uratiua ipsius Gedeonis   396 amabeum: ab inuentore   402 oppressit: deflorauit   407 citharizat: cantat dulciter   quauis: qualibet
408 organa: guttura auium ueris   409 Vestem: herbas   tegmina: folia
et flores   410 utrumque genus: masculinam et femineum   Uenus:
dea amoris   411 Laxat: aperit   Nestor: senex; qui habitauit quingentos annos   ephebus: iuuenis   413 Phillis: illa puella   recreauit:
requieuit   414 sola: illa   solo: idest in prato   415 Daphnidis:
Christi   416 bene: daphnis   legem: decem preceptorum *M* 3^r ipse:
Christus   gregem: idest hereticos et alios malos homines *M*   418 Sim:
dicit mundus   versus interscalaris a dyabolo *M*   419 natus: filius dei
hoste: diabolo   422 facie: humanitate   matri: Marie *B*; ecclesie *M*
uigore: potentia   patri: deo   423 corpus: quantum ad matrem   mentem: ad patrem   sortitur: elicit   425 dicit iuuenis   iocatur: ludit
[f. 152^r] 429 fistula: predicatio   432 foueam: uoluptatem carnis
434 Hic: in fossa   hinc: ab illa uoluptate   435 mundabo: ego puella,
idest sensualitas   438 Lusorem: iuuenem qui ludit mecum   rusticitate: idest propter rusticitatem loquitur *M*   439 ait: Coridon   colludas:
ironice dicit   440 ascribi: notari   442 liber: quia amans quilibet cre-
dit esse liber, cum non sit *M* 3^v 443 ait clare: alta uoce Coridoni
446 Coridon qui donat totum cor suum sponse sue, sicut Christus totum
cor dedit sponse   447 floris: iuuenis *M*   nectar: accusatiuum   448
rudis: Coridon   ille: iuuenis   449 Tu mecum: mundus loquitur *M*
450 thalamo: frondium   Phillida: idest corpore   451 uir: ego   quod:
unde   amor: a puella   hamo: decipio   hamor: decipior   452 Hamo:

vinculo   hamor: capior   mihi tendit amor: scilicet hamum tendit mihi
M   453 Dum spirat uita: dum es uiua   uita: cave   461 anguilla:
Iuuenalis: Uos anguilla manet longe cognata colubre (5.103)   471 Fraterno: de Remo et Romulo   muri: Rome   484 iunctura: significatio
489 hymnizent: cantent, concordent, et deum laudant

Chapter Two

[f. 152ᵛ] 8 mente: uidetur nobis amena   40 prestolatur: expectat;
vnde uersus prestolor expecto etc. (Praestolor expecto, praestolor
quaerere dico, Eberhard de Bethune, *Graecismus,* ed. J. Wrobel [Breslau,
1881], 25.225; John of Garland [supposed author; see Paetow, p. 135],
De compositis verborum, 119)   [f. 153ʳ] 92 nouercantur: nocent
[f. 153ᵛ] 116 (*above Figure Three; an example of rural instruments*) Cum
manibus duris non me primat incola ruris;/Eius sunt iuris traha, tribula,
uanga, securis (cf. Walther, *Lateinische Sprichwörter,* 4234, 11825)
134 matrem: ecclesiam   138 exsertans: denudans; exsertare est denu-
dare   154 Dauid: Unde dominus dixit, Inueni mihi uirum secundum
cor meum (Acts 13:22)   156 Iohannes: qui fuit uirgo electus a domino   Ioseph: qui uenditus fuit in Egiptum   [f. 154ʳ] 198 patribus:
scribo, dicit clericus   200 uilibus: canibus   201 gradibus: ordinibus
202 Creticus: iudex, a crisis quod est iudicium; Creticus indifferens est
ad pro et ad contra. A cresis grece quod est aurum latine, vel a crisis
grece quod est iudicium latine. Vnde versus: iudicium cresis (*sic*), habitus, crasis, et crisis (*sic*) aurum. Micrasis idest qui habet modicum
habitum   liricus: suauis; a lira   203 Sititor: desiderator; auarus   tetricus: crudelis; a tetrico monte; tetricus pronunciat asper   Geticus: ad
modum Getarum   204 Iulia: Cesarea uel Romana   205 Leuauit:
liberauit   Furia: ira inimicorum   muria: fex; dupliciter est muria aut
murta; quia in expressione est murta, in fundo muria; versus: subsequitur muria sed fex procedit a murta   234 cum inculcatione aduerbiorum
[f. 153ᵛ] 116 (*above Figure Three; an example of rural instruments*) Cum
dies (cf. Walther [*Lateinische Sprichwörter,* 12936], *who says it is an
epitaph for Peter of Riga*)   lacrimatur: quando pluit   286 Semele:
mater Cadmi; uirgo incorrupta   291 discipline: doctrine   296 unum:
deum   297-99 qui iumento . . . administret: tangit euangelium   307
columbinum: oculi tui sicut oculi columbarum (cf. Cant. 1:14).

Chapter Three

[f. 155ʳ] 30 luce: lucerna euangelica   35 Piereos: philosophos; pie-
rides sunt muse, idest filie pieri regis   41 Acthee: Atheniensis; ab acte
grece quod est litus latine, quia sita super litus maris   [f. 155ᵛ] 74
Elycone: fonte sapiencie   78 modio: anglice *cumbe*

Chapter Four

35 capcione: hic est res uerbi   [f. 156^r] 47 dolum: Est dolus equiuocum:
dolus est prudencia seu fraus (John of Garland, *Equivoca* [STC 11601],
London, 1496, p. 42)   54 caminus: a cauma quod est incendium; et
inde epycausterium, ab epy quod est supra et cauma incendium; et est
anglice *herth*   59 recreat: Omne tulit punctum qui miscuit utile dulci
(Horace, *AP* 143)   Coruus: Hic crocitat coruus lacerare cadauera toruus,/
Miluius hic pullos deplumat si capit ullos (John of Garland, *Clavis compendii,* Ms. Bruges 546, f. 30^r)   60 cadauere: quasi caro data vermi-
bus   81 In aurora: incipiunt littere   [f. 156^v] 127 iuste: officio
128 bonis operibus: a summa rei   129 applicare: *river*   130 sibi: ad
episcopum   131 candore: ad matronam   virginitatem: ad uirginem
134 reuerenciam: ab etate   135 Deo: ad religiosum   136 infirmitatem: infirmus ad medicum   138 Sanctitatis: ad papam   [f. 157^r]
207 delires: deuias   208 res: valitudo   uires: uerbum vel oratio
209 hostis: genitiuus   inheret: Ierusalem   210 Hanc: Ierusalem   211
Ierusalem: genitiuus casus   generat: acquirit   212 Plangit: Ierusalem
Palem: ydolatriam; deam pascue   213 signa: crucem   214 Lux:
Christus   tyro: nouus miles   216 tristeris: collucteris   218 lutum:
gulam et luxuriam   219 Marte: bello morum   mori: uerbum   220
illorum: uiciorum   rex: diabolus   ante chorum: ante alios demones
221 Principe: diabolo   superato: uicto   222 fato: morti   223 aciey:
uiciorum   224 In fundo: in imo   in arce: in altitudine   227 immo
morte: non dico non sanguine   228 pompa: anglice *boban*   229
Sathane: nostre aduersarie   formidas (*sic*): tu   231 herilis: virilis,
de heros, -oys   232 bilis: ira vel amaritudo fellis; et ponitur pro ira
233 sta uallibus: humilis esto   234 thimis: floribus; hoc timum, timi
est herba cuius flos dicitur epitimium   235 Marte: bello   237 uene:
a venio, venis   238 sene: a senos sensus   240 uise: uisita   Sina: partes
Ierusalem   241 Machometum: Maumet, quia magorum metus   242
Risus: scilicet Machometi   metum: Machometo et suis sociis   243
menia: a munio, munis quia munit ciuitatem   245 poterunt: scilicet
facere   prelia: deuotiones   246 serunt: seminant   247 Phebeya:
sapiencie   Cytharea: Venus que colebatur in Cytharea monte   248
Pomum: discretionem   Dircea: Dircea, -cee locus est vbi colebatur
Pallas   249 amaris: a Deo   250 antiparis: contra paridem   Paris:
adulter   251 Hector: fortitudo   uigor: Hector   urbs: capacitas   253
Pellide: Achillis amici diaboli *B*; Achillis, scilicet ire *M* 7^v Atride: cuiuslibet mali militis   254 trepide (*sic*): debiliter   uulgus: demones in
aere commorantes *M*   inherme: sine armis   255 furor Eacides: in-
sania mentis Achillis; Achilles filius Eaci   Atrides: ille luxuriosus   256
Hiis: ire et Sathane   Pergama: mentis   uides: menia mentis   [f. 157^v]

257 Surrepens: subito ueniens   motus: cogitatio malorum   Ulixes: ab
olon quod est totum et xenos peregrinum, quasi totus in peregrino
259 Blanditur: Ulixes   flamine: persuasione diaboli   260 suaue:
prosperitatis   arma: bella   261 septemplex: inuolutus septem coreis
262 tyro: o tu   264 pena: penitencia   265 sponse: carni   lorum:
frenum   266 sterne: adorna   thorum: lectum conscientie   268 lusitet: frequenter ludat *M*   obde: claude   forem: sensum   269 Rex:
ratio   Ecube: carni *M*; hecuba regina fuit uxor priami *B*   270 tube:
timoris   272 Pari: mundo   273 Helene: mecha   nescit: caro
274 teri: destrui   275 Cedit: ei   Cesareus feruor: ardor pugnandi
illius   Capaneus: quem Iuppiter fulminauit   276 ei: homini   277
Magnus: Deus *M*   Hic: Deus   278 Magno: Domino   sere: porte
280 giro: in campo   281 Cananeas: Sarracenos   284 merere mori:
inperatiui modi   293 date: Dido dixit ita   [f. 158ʳ] 334 mensa:
epulis; continens pro contento   362 Hennio: qui fuit struma omnium
poetarum   411 lepram mentis: mortale peccatum   [f. 158ᵛ] 412
morbus: peccatum   433 colonis: rusticis   434 nouella: quasi de
nouo inuenta   faceta: curialis *M*   439 baptizauit: vocauit   441
ergo uenit: venditur   448 friuola sede: in hac cisterna   452 Ede:
ostende   457 ater: quantum ad persecutionem puerorum   458 zelo:
inuidia *B*; invidia, modi passiui *M* 8ᵛ   [f. 159ʳ] 489 legitimeque datum: ut heredes concedant: pater non potest dare nihil in cessione filii
antequam fit de etate   491 prefinito: predeterminato   493 sacrilega:
ut in sacro loco   495 terminat: illa die et loco   locum: infra ecclesiam uel extra   496 contumet: contumax est   anathema: excommuni-
catus est; anathema adiectiue indeclinabile, substantiue declinabile
497 Subsequitur: cyrographum sequitur   pena: quia incarcerabitur
sua: propria, scilicet patrie consuetudinis   498 Federa: amicicias
499 sue: proprie   501 memorat: illa littera   502 acta: circumstan-
cias   512 capella: beneficium

Chapter Five

16 Serpentes: humiles sermones   28 Assuitur; apponitur; assuitur
pannus idest pannosa descripcio   [f. 159ᵛ] 47 grauibus: auctenticis
51 Eneyda: historiam   53 seipsum: maiorem arietem   64 Excelsus: ex parte sentenciarum   collis: mons   belligeratrix: uerborum
65 claua: claua non est pacis   67 dissolutum: quando sentencie non
ligantur   79 ludere: coire   84 tonse: presbitero   88 qualitas:
modus   [f. 160ʳ] 104 comica: uerba lasciua de comedia   162 in
medium: in communi   [f. 160ᵛ] 224 humorum: *colere et bile*
[f. 161ᵛ] 327 Argumentum: non in Logica   342 uersus[1]: a uerto
343 hoc strato: hoc lecto   strato: extenso   348 Liricum: a liris diuer-

sitas, quia diuerse sunt illi distinctiones   364 agreste: humilem modum
loquendi   [f. 162^r] 389 Dic: versus Homeri   [f. 162^v] 460 partes:
orationis

Chapter Six

32 Cognicio: puto   [f. 163^r] 43 Sencio magistrum: suspensiua   44
legere uero: constans   respondere discipulis: finitiua   78 Salue: quia
presens es   82 cor idem: eadem uoluntas   85 Parche: dee   89
Plasseto: hoc; illa villa   90 tu me places: placidum me reddas; placo,
placas   95 ridet: fortuna   106 Solis: filii Dei   107 uelle: suum
[f. 163^v] 117 uincet: diabolus   120 per uos: o uos diabolus, munde,
caro   122 uerba: uel nomina   144 sapore: sentencia   147 notis:
per nota   159 monstrata: verba   162 sic mordet: per detractionem
182 mane: tu   [f. 164^r] 269 rotam: habes   273 asella: o fortuna
similis aselle   279 Hec: fortuna   284 Hanc: fortunam aquilis: pro
uexilla   [f. 164^v] 301 ambitus: auaricia   303 Crux: tota ecclesia
illic: Parisius campana: magister   307 Hic: Parisius   fulmen: excom-
municationem   308 ambigea: heretica canonis: regule   330 cala-
mum: doctrinam   331 nouos: per colores   [f. 165^r] 403 barbarus:
Saxsonus   406 collocutio: scilicet precedit   416 nichilii: nullius
precii esse

Chapter Seven

33 mittentem: se   38 sue: turme   [f. 165^v] 40 menia: illi qui habi-
tant infra menia   50 concordia: cuius est   56 fuerat: miles   59
accendit: altera   64 fricarent: *manuailment*   70 erratica: errans
73 tela: uerba mala   74 illa: lotrix   76 ira: orta   77 sorores: ira
et superbia *B*; uicia supra dicta *M* 14^r 80 illam: iram   81 Hanc:
iram   83 Illius (Istius *B*): ire   84 iacenti: ire   86 lesa: lotrix
88 Melpomone: illa musa tragedica; auctor loquitur ad musam   89
prima: lotrix   97 ferulas: *batuers*; et ferula est nomen *arcoreres
taleuas*   99 cestibus: vnde Virgilius: nec quisquam ex agmine tanto/
Audeo adire virum manibusque induere cestus (*Aen.* 5.378-79) *M* 14^r
decernere: *arener*   103 tegimen: nox sista: nox   104 Larua: nox
105 uber: mentulam *B*; veretrum *M*   106 poma: testiculos *M*   107
fatetur: se ephebum: iuuenem *B*; ab e quod est extra et phos quod est
lux, quasi lucens exterius. Illi sunt iuuenes qui tantam curam adhibent
in ornando se et spoliando *M*   114 potuisse: se dicit   115 Clitemestra: illa regina Grecie que occidit Menelaum   118 uigiles: *wetes*
122 Herinis: furia infernalis   [f. 166^r] 125 Heumenis: furia infernalis
128 perplectitur: cingit *B*; perfecte punitur *M*   171 Syon: ecclesie
[f. 166^v] 206-7 rebellari: pugnare   207 impetit: *asaut*   216 gremium:
devant   257 voluntas: dantis   ] f. 167^r] 267 Notum: carta tenet quid
(cf. above, *4, 492*)   268 dedit: pro hominio suo   269 arpenta: acras

[f. 167^v] 389 centina: *ordure*   390 cenolente: -tus, -ta, -tum; plenus
ceno idest luto   [f. 169^r] 588 recepit: iambicus *B;* iambus *M* 16^v
630 virgo: philosophia   636 triplex: ratio   637 studet: ratio *M*
638 primum: logica *B*; speculacio loyca *O* 30^v perscrutatur: ratio *M*
642 speculum aliud: mathematica *B*; speculacio ethica *O*   645 iuuenescit:
stabilis est *M*   646 Tercium: theologica *B*; speculacio theologica *O*
648 ydea: forma   650 Fontis: creatoris   651 principio: deo   666
esse: essentiam   667 Illic . . . hic: in eternitate, in mundo *M* 17^r 668
esse uerius: essentia dei   [f. 169^v] 674 uirtus: fuit sciencia uirtus in
beato petro (cf. 2 Peter 1:5) *M*; si acquiratur per laborem exteriorem
non est uirtus, nec habet originem uirtutis *M*   690 Platonicam: Plato
dicit quod sciencia reformat hominem recordatione; quia cum anima
sciencia erat omnium in lacteo circulo infusa corpori, que per obtusionem
corporis lapsa erat; per frequenciam scripturarum lapsa recolligitur. Vnde
secundum hoc dicitur quod scire est reminisci; sed hoc reprobat Aristotiles
in Topicis (book 2, ch. 4) *M*   694 sepelitur: platonicum est illud *M*
698 Descendit: sciencia   704 Mathesis: quadruuiaticina *B*; methasis
dicitur in quadruuialibus scienciis *M*   706 porrigatis: o magistri
[f. 170^r] 788 Pelopei: arene ubi regnabat pelops filius tantali   799
seuicia: in seuicia carnis que semper pretendit nobis amiciciam cum sit
inimica spiritui *M* 17^v 810 pruinam: infidelitatem 840 miles: porfiri-
us *M* 22^r 850 montem: synai *M*   [f. 170^v] 910 quidam: inperiti
912-15 Pallentis . . . corruit: "O fortunatam natam me consule Romam!"/
Antonii gladios potuit contempnere, si sic/omnia dixisset. Ridenda poe-
mata malo/Quam te, conspicue diuina philippica fame (Juvenal 10.122-25)
950 nuntius: qui dixit dominus vobiscum (Ruth 2:4)   951 accusat:
quantum ad maiores   952 incusat: minores   954 nata: Sarra   974
orphana: frustrata filio   977 pastor: Dauid   978 Rex: Saul   985
Helim: illius loci ultra Ierusalem   1002 Diri: Edippi   pignora: Polinices
et Ethiocles *B*   Edippus interfecit patrem suum et postea concumbens
cum matre sua genuit ex ea duos filios qui mutuis vulneribus se interfecerunt *M* 17^v 1186 idest sis stabilis licet uideas enses cruentos et ciues
tuos retentos *M* 18^r [f. 171^v] 1195 parte: adquisite   1228 Virgilius
in Bucolicis *BM* 18^v 1229 cathenas: studii *M*   1232 Item in Bucolicis *M*   Lucina: dea partus, idest ecclesia *M*   tuus: o Maria   Apollo:
Christus *M*   Partum femineum mater Lucina resoluit/Que pannis uoluit
mater alumpna deum. Segmentum pannus, quasi signum mentis; semen-
tatus pueris repelet?; Iuuenalis: Et segmentatis dormisset paruula cunis
(6.89)   1236 Ouidius Ponto   [f. 172^r] 1240 In Ouidio magno *BM*
1244 Ouidius magnus   1248 In Bucolicis Virgilii *B;* in fine Metamor-
phoseos *M*   1252 In eodem *B;* Virgilius Eneida *M*   1253 Uerres:
nomen latronis uel mali pueri qui vult uerberare magistrum suum ad
natale *M*   1254 Anetus: dicipulus *B;* nomen proprium *M;* Anetus
fuit discipulus Socrates qui accusauit Socratem parti? Rome. Socrates

hausit (cic)utam favore ( ) et sic exspirauit M (*parentheses mark letters
cut away from margin*)   deferri: deportari M   1255 efferri: esse mortuum;
extra ferri B; ad sepulchrum M   1256 Lucanus in primo   1257 scuti-
carum: corrigiarum, quia pueri afferunt baculos corrigis armatos ut
uerberent magistros ad Natale M   1260 Lucanus in primo   1264
Ouidius in Ponto   1267 registra: cordulas; register magnus liber
apud Romam B; registrum, -tri dicitur quasi liber magnus in quo ( )ntur
facta domini pape ( )ne M   1268 Ouidius de Sileno sene B; in Ouidio
de Fastis M   1272 Ouidio Fasti B; similiter in Fastis M   1276 Ouidio
magno   1280 In Ouidio de Arte M   [f. 172^v] 1377 prata: ecclesie
1379 mater: anna M 19^r incola: ioachim BM   1382 ethera: clarita-
tem   1389 Udam: fecundam   fons: christus   1390 Granum: mariam
cultor: christus   1413 radix: anna   1416 Incola: ioachim   1429
Ioachim: scilicet a   1448 Piropus: caritas M   [f. 173^r] 1482 Pari: o
iuuenis qui ita pulcher es ut Paris M 19^v uenenum: idest luxuria, unde
supra in prouerbiis "qui luxuriam amplectitur etc." M (*cf.* above, *1,*
251)   1486 hic insinuat auctor profectum odarum sequencium M
1498 dic: o musa BM   1506 Saul: Saul, uexatus a demonio, cum audis-
set Dauid citharizare, statim cessabat demonis uexatio; et hoc est quod
dicitur "demonium domat" M   1517 Spernit . . . colit: primum mandatum decalogi M   1533 hoc: dixit   1543 hic: in ueste Uranie   [f. 173^v
1549 Hec: Urania   1551 Signifer: Zodiacus   quibus . . . donet: Zodiacus enim osculatur, idest tangit, solsticiales estiuales et solsticiales hye-
males circulos et circulum equinoctialem fecit; et hoc est quod dicitur
"quibus orbidus (*sic*) oscula donet etc." M   1552 colurus: ille circulus
B; colurus a colon quod est membrum et uron quod est bos, quasi cauda
bouis, quia bos in cursu suo erecta cauda describit quoddam semicirculum
M   1565 Voxque . . . menti: Voce uita non discordet/Et uox uitam non
remordet/Dulcis est simphonia M   1566 Hiis: voci et menti   1569
modulare: tu Pari   1577 dea: pallas M 20^r 1580 Cuius: fontis
1584 honus: mandatorum   cateruas: sanctorum   1592 fallax: clerus
1594 Poculum . . . Bachum: bibit aquam M   1596 dignam cathedram:
ordo naturalis (cf. above, *1,* 472)   1600 Hic: theologus B; predicator
M   1617 preterit: in constancia   1623 gingnasii: gignasium, -sii
dicitur studium, a gignas grece quod est studium latine M   1639 uocis:
predicacionis   [f. 174^r] 1656 optimus: paries   1666 Largi pollicitis:
Ouidius: pollicitis diues quilibet esse potest (*Ars amatoria* 1.444)
1679 heroicus: scilicet quando scribuntur gesta heroum; scilicet exameter
1684 febris: malicia   1687 Simonis: simonie   1734 diues: o tu
[f. 174^v] 1764 spiritus: diabolus   1800 paucos: legistas   1817 clauda:
claudos   1829 Baucis: illa uetula   [f. 145^v] 1859 Istud: peccatum
1901 Tirecie: illius diuinatoris nigromancie   1906 suos: incantatores
1921 dea: theologia

Appendix Two

The Two Versions of Geoffrey of Vinsauf's *Documentum*

The notes refer to many passages of Geoffrey's *Documentum* in Faral's edition as the source of, or at least as parallels to, various teachings of John's. But as Noel Denholm-Young pointed out some time ago, a "better and fuller version"[1] of that treatise exists side-by-side with the version printed by Faral. This version is found in Mss. British Museum Cotton Cleopatra B VI, ff. 31^r-87^v; Oxford, Balliol College 263, ff. 7^v-32^r; Oxford, Bodleian Library Laud Misc. 707, ff. 36^r-85^r; Oxford, Bodleian Library Selden Supra 65, ff. 1^r-72^v; and Cambridge, Pembroke College 287, ff. 105^r-164^v (this is not an exhaustive list). I examined microfilm copies of Balliol 263 and Laud Misc. 707 with the intention of determining whether John's debt to the *Documentum*, already clear from Faral's version, would there be revealed more fully. The result in general was to confirm that John did indeed know this version, and I have appended here the most important relevant passages (from Laud Misc. 707, with occasional readings, which are italicized, from Balliol 263). But it is interesting that all of these passages have to do with John's Chapter Five; he did not rely on the long version throughout his work. For example, the central phrase *uerba illa in quibus consistit uis materie* (*4*, 300-1) has its counterpart in Faral's version (2.2.43, p. 279), *nomina rerum in quibus consistit vis materiae*, but not in the longer version. The treatment of *ornata difficultas* (John's *difficilis ornatus*) is here organized wholly differently both from John and from Faral's version of the *Documentum*, which are close to each other.

The fact that Geoffrey quotes as an example of the Hilarian style (see below, #2) the same passage which John has called *domesticum* (cf. *5*, 436) raises the question whether the roles of source and borrower may not be reversed: was Geoffrey filling out his new version with material from the *Parisiana poetria*?

I doubt it. It is probable, to be sure, that the longer version of the

---

1. "The Cursus in England," *Oxford Essays in Medieval History Presented to Herbert Edward Salter* (Oxford, 1934), pp. 68-103; see pp. 75 n. 3, 93; reprinted in Denholm-Young's *Collected Papers on Mediaeval Subjects* (Oxford, 1946), pp. 26-55; see pp. 32 n. 3, 47; reprinted with revisions in *Collected Papers of N. Denholm-Young* (Cardiff, 1969), pp. 42-73; see pp. 48 n. 4, 63. See also Roger A. B. Mynors, *Catalogue of the Manuscripts of Balliol College, Oxford* (Oxford, 1963), p. 282. Roger Parr, who has issued a translation of the *Documentum* (Milwaukee, 1968), unhappily did not take cognizance of this longer version.

Documentum is the later: it refers rather frequently to the *Poetria nova,* which the shorter version never mentions; it also seems to represent a fuller development of certain theories: cf. the passage below (#3) on the six vices of style. Denholm-Young (*Collected Papers,* 1969, p. 63) is puzzled by the fact that Gervase of Melkley and Geoffrey both refer to each other's treatises; this could be explained if Gervase's work, which Gräbener dates (p. xxviii) as 1215-16, fell between the two versions of the *Documentum* (though Gervase may have simply had the *Poetria nova* in mind).

Still, general considerations, particularly Geoffrey's preeminence and the fact that the *Poetria nova* was probably composed at the turn of the century, make it unlikely either that Geoffrey would stoop to copy John or that his work could have been written as late as 1220. There is a letter in it (Laud Misc. 707, f. 48^v) to King John from his nephew Arthur, who was murdered in 1203; one supposes the treatise was composed while that case was still celebrated.

Perhaps either *domesticum* means "of our circle," "emanating from the schools of Paris," or John wrote the example and circulated it earlier than, and apart from, his *Poetria,* Geoffrey adopted it for his presentation of the Hilarian style, and John later did the same thing, taking advantage of the opportunity to assert that he originally wrote it. This seems to me to be the most reasonable explanation of the available facts, especially since at 7, 621 *exemplum domesticum* is used again for a poem that one assumes is John's, as all the original poems in the treatise probably are. There must indeed have been a good deal of such informal circulation, even collective working out, of examples and precepts, so that the whole question of sources is a little unnecessary. Perhaps the most important thing to say of both John's *Poetria* and all three of Geoffrey's works is that they represent what was being taught at Paris at the end of the twelfth century and well into the thirteenth.

---

1. (Cf. *5,* 373-81.) Oracius precipue ostendit proprietates que a natura sumuntur . . . [*including*] que ab extrinsecis sumuntur. Considerantur he a sex locis, scilicet a condicione, vt si est dominus uel seruus; ab etate, vt iuuenis an senex; a sexu, vt vir uel mulier; et similiter ibi consideretur condicio ab officio, idest statu, vt an miles an mercator; a gente, vt Anglicus an Theutonicus; a patria, vt Romanus an Atheniensis. Has proprietates ita ponit Oracius: (*there follow* AP *114-18, as in John*). (F. 47^r)

2. (Cf. *5,* 402-67.) Preter tres stilos de quibus iam dictum est, sunt alii quattuor stili modernorum, scilicet Tullianus, Gregorianus, Hillarianus, Hisiderianus. In stilo Tulliano non est attendenda dictionum

cadencia sed sola sentencie grauitas et verborum florida exornacio,
qua vtuntur antiquiores tam prosaice quam metrice scribentes, sicut
Salustius, Quintilianus, Senica, Marcianus, Sidonius, Virgilius, Varro,
Oracius, Ouidius, Lucanus, Stacius, Claudianus, et plures alii quos
celsa commendat auctoritas.

In stilo Gregoriano consideranda est dictionum cadencia et pedum
ordinacio armonica et qualitas terminacionis. Vnde sciendum quod
omnis dictio monasilleba dicitur semispondeus, idest dimidius spondeus, nulla discrecione facta de accentu. *Similiter omnis dictio dis-
silaba absque discrecione temporis dicitur spondeus.*[2] Similiter omnis
dictio pollesilleba, idest duas sillebas excrescens, quotquot sillebarum
fuerit, cognoscitur penes suam penultimam; nam si illa breuis fuerit,
tres ille vltime sillebe istius dictionis faciunt dactilicum pedem; *re-
manentes*[3] sillebe quocumque fuerint binario numero designate
faciunt spondeum. Si vero penultima longa fuerit vel acuta omnes
sillebe binario numero designate faciunt spondeos. Vnde vt seruetur
melior armonia in hoc stilo plures dactili debent rarissime commisceri;
spondei vero frequenter possunt collocari. Similiter in hoc stilo
plerumque considerare oportet vt vltima dictio clausule, super quam
fit periodus, cum dictione super quam fit comma *conueniat*[4] in vltima
sillaba et *disconueniat*[5] in penultima. Colores etiam verborum frequenter in hoc stilo ponuntur, sed colores transumpcionis magis
raro. Hoc autem stilo maxime vtuntur qui attinent curie romane.

Sed notandum quod iste stilus magis oblectaret auditorem si partim cum stilo Tulliano misceretur, sicut in prima epistola quam pre-
misimus. Et hoc modo scribendi maxime vsus est Alanus De Planctu
Nature; maxime enim ibi tropicis locucionibus vsus est, in quibus
tocius eloquencie floridior est ornatus. Inde est quod libro Archi-
trenii propter tropicarum locucionum celebrem precellenciam nullus
liber modernorum similis inuenitur, quamuis Bernardus Siluester in
prosaico *dicatur*[6] psitacus, in metrico philomena.

In stilo Hillariano similiter obseruanda est pedum cadencia, sed
aliter quam in stilo Gregoriano. Semper enim in hoc stilo pedes ordinandi sunt hoc ordine: primo enim precedunt duo spondei et semispondeus, et postea dactilus, et tercio duo spondei et dimidius et
dactilus; et sic quater ordinandum est. Et post quartum dactilum,
scilicet ad punctum periodalem, subditur dispondeus, idest duplex

2. *Om. LM 707.*
3. rema *LM 707.*
4. conueniant *LM 707.*
5. disconueniant *LM 707.*
6. dicat *LM 707.*

spondeus. Est autem hic stilus propter suam dignitatem apud multos
in vsu, cuius exemplum est hoc: "Sepe furtiuis gressibus surrepit in-
fortunium, quod [ad][7] felicem exitum opus humanum inuidet peruenire."

In stilo Hisideriano plerumque ordinandi sunt pedes sicut in stilo
Gregoriano et plerumque non; sed semper ita distinguende sunt
clausule, quod in fine similem habeant consonanciam, et videantur
pares esse in sillabis quamuis dispares sint, sicut dictum est in exposi-
cione coloris qui dicitur compar. Est autem stilus iste valde motiuus,
quo vtitur Isiderus in libro Soliloquiorum. Huius stili exemplum est
hoc: "Pre pudore genus humanum obstupeat, de communi dampno
quilibet abhorreat, admirentur serui, stupescant liberi, dum vocantur
ad cathedram elingues pueri; conformant se magistris qui vix sunt
discipuli, dum causa studendi fauor est populi. Prius legunt quam
sillabicent, prius volant quam humi cursitent." Ita dictum est de
stilis. (Ff. 79^v-80^v)

3. (Cf. 5, 4-8.) Sequitur de sex viciis capitalibus in dictamine quolibet euitandis . . . primum incongrua parcium materie posicio, secundum invtilis digressio, tercium obscura breuitas, quartum incompe-
tens stilorum mutacio, quintum prodigialis variacio, sextum inconueniens conclusio. (F. 80^v)

This seems to represent a hardening, or at least a more confident organization, of the doctrine in Faral's version, which is as it were worked
out before our eyes. John's orderly presentation is much closer to this
version than to Faral's. Note especially the following:

a. (Cf. 5,11-14.) . . . vt si quis materiam iocosam vel *comediam*[8]
scriberet in qua partes deberent obseruari ad lasciuiam pertinentes
et transferret se ad partes tragedie que sunt de grauibus personis et
earum proprietatibus. (F. 80^v) (*Geoffrey then quotes several verses
from Horace, ending with the line John quotes, which he glosses as
follows:* Per serpentes humiles res vel personas intelligimus, per aues
graues, per tigrides immites uel crudeles, per agnos mansuetos.)
(F. 81^r)

b. (Cf. 5, 95-108.) Sciendum est quod variare materiam causa tollendi fastidium et idemptitatis *fugiende*[9] laus est et maxima virtus.
Idemptitas enim mater est sacietatis; ad illam ergo remouendam
debet materia variari quibusdam ornatibus nouitatis. . . . Oracius . . .

7. ad: *om. LM 707, Balliol 263.*
8. comedia *LM 707.*
9. fugiendi *LM 707.*

"Omne tulit punctum qui miscuit vtile dulci." Istud preceptum imitatur Oracius in quadam satira introducendo fabulam de mure vrbano
et rusticano ad comparacionem vite vrbane et vite ruralis. In graui
materia introducenda sunt grauia, sicut facit Lucanus vbi narrat luctam Herculis et *Anthei*[10] gigantis. Vnde incidit quis in variacionem
prodigialem quando introducit grauem materiam in iocoso tractatu
vel iocosam in graui. . . . Quintum vicium scilicet prodigialem variacionem ostendit Oracius his versibus: "Qui variare cupit rem prodigialiter vnam/Delphinum siluis appingit, fluctibus aprum./In vicium
ducit culpe fuga si caret arte." Bene dicit Oracius "Delphinum siluis,
etc." quasi diceret "proprietates aquarum attribuit siluis et e conuerso." (Ff. 82ʳ-82ᵛ)

4. (Cf. *5*, 303-372.) Sermonum tria sunt genera que "Grece appel-
laciones" vocantur. Primum dragmaticum, secundum erementicum[11]
vel distinctum, tercium didascalicum. Dragmaticum est vbi auctor
operis nichil loquitur sed tantum persona introducta, vt in libris
Therencii. Erementicum vel distinctum est vbi auctor totum loquitur,
vt in Georgicis Virgilii. Didascalicum idest doctrinale vbi tam auctor
quam persona introducta loquitur, persona querens et auctor respondens, vt in Boecio De Consolacione, in Dialogis Gregorii. Sub secundo
genere cadit narracio, que sectionem recipit a Tullio sic: Est enim
quoddam genus narracionis alienum et remotum a causis ciuilibus,
et illud duplex: est vnum quod in negociis positum est, aliud quod
in personis. Quod positum est in negociis tres habet partes, fabulam,
historiam, et argumentum. Fabula est que nec vera[12] nec verisimilia
continet, vt in Ouidii Methamorphoseos et in quolibet apologo. Vnde
si contingat *narracionem*[13] esse fabulosam debemus probabiliter mentiri, vt scilicet narracio falsa narretur vt esset vera. . . . (*Here the story
of Deucalion and Pyrrha is instanced and briefly summarized.*)

Apologus est sermo sumptus de brutis animalibus ad instructionem
humane vite, vt patet in Isopo et Auiano. . . . (Cf. *4*, 61-64.) Historia
est res gesta ab etatis nostre memoria remota. . . . Sub historia multa
sunt carmina, vt ephitalamicum, idest carmen nupciale quale cecine-
runt antiqui in honorem sponsi et sponse. Epichedium, idest nudum
sine sepultura quod fit de viuentibus insepultis. Epithaphium, idest
carmen suprascriptum tumulis mortuorum. Apothesis, idest carmen
quod de leticia deificacionis est uel glorificacionis. Heroicum, idest

---

10. Anthe *LM 707*.
11. *Sic LM 707; the passage is obscured by damage in Balliol 263.*
12. nec est vera *LM 707*.
13. oracionem *LM 707*.

carmen quod texitur de gestis heroum, idest virorum forcium; et hoc
carmen maxime conuenit versibus exametris. Elegiacum enim carmen
de miseria uel dolore, et conuenit maxime versibus exametris et penta-
metris. Amabium quod proprietates amancium representat. Bucolicum,
idest pastorale, quod ostendit de cultura boum et boum custodibus.
Georgicum quod agit de agricultura. Liricum quod agit de comitate
deorum et amore. Epedon, idest *clausulare*,[14] quod agit de certamine
equestri. Seculare uel hympnus quod fit de laude deorum. Inuectiuum
quod agit de conuiciis et verbis mordaciter reprehensiuis. Satira, in quo
reprehenditur[15] vicium et inseritur virtus, cuius proprietates in his
versibus continentur: Indignans satira deridet, nudat aperta,/Voce salit,
viciis fetet, agreste sapit. Tres enim satirici inueniuntur, Oracius, Per-
cius, et Iuuenalis. Tragedia carmen est in quo agitur de contemptu
fortune, ostendens infortunia grauium personarum, et incipit a gaudio
et finit in luctu, et dicitur a tragos hircus, quia antiquitus tragedo hir-
cos dabant in premium, ad fetorem materie designandum; vnde Oracius:
Carmen qui tragico vilem certauit ob hircum.

Argumentum tercium genus est, et res est ficta non vera sed verisimi-
lis, vt in eglogis et comediis. Egloga est sermo contextus de gestis vilium
personarum et interpretatur sermo fetidus vel caprinus. Et est triplex:
quedam enim fit in amaris reprehensionibus; et est pars satire, et tali
vtitur Oracius. Quedam in colloquio vilium personarum, vt in Bucolicis.
Alia in colloquio honeste persone contra vilem, vt in Theodolo, vbi
Pseustis, per quem intelligitur falsitas, disputat contra Alathiam, per
quam ueritas[16] denotatur. Comedia large loquendo est quodlibet carmen iocosum; proprie tamen et stricte loquendo est cantus villanus de
humilibus personis contextus, incipiens a tristicia et terminans in
gaudio. Talis enim comedia quinque actus requirit, nec plures nec
pauciores. Vnde Oracius: Neue minor non sit quinto productior actu/
Fabula que posci vult et spectata reponi. (Cf. *4*, 463-79.) Talis comedia
secessit ab vsu nostro. Qui igitur proprietates comedie scire voluerit,
consulat Poetriam Oracii pro artificio et Terencium pro practica.
(Ff. 82v-83v)

14. clausure *LM 707.*
15. reprehendit *LM 707.*
16. virtus *Balliol 263.*

A Late *Ars rhythmica* Influenced by John of Garland

The *Parisiana poetria* seems to have had more influence in Germany than elsewhere, for Mss. *M, O,* and *V* are all of German origin. This may be due to the *ars rhythmica,* for that art was especially popular in Germany.[1] At all events, it is interesting that the only other evidence of its influence that I have been able to find is a late anonymous *Ars rhythmica* preserved in a fifteenth-century manuscript at the Austrian abbey of Melk (Ms. Melk 873 [*olim* 711], pp. 215-84). Its author calls frequently on the authority of John of Garland, quoting his rules and transcribing his examples, and sometimes taking issue with him. He also makes use of other authorities (see the last selection below), but not nearly to the same degree. At the end of his treatise (pp. 273-83), he gives in full the poems "Ad insultus equoris" (7, 622), "Vita nobis exemplaris (7, 782), "Virgo, Mater Salvatoris" (7, 918), and "Ludo preter solitum" (7, 1225).

The selections below give a fair sample of how the author employs John's teachings.

1. Illa sciencia (sc. ars rhythmica) est pars musice, ut patet auctoritate Poetrie Parysiensis et omnium Ytalicorum scribencium de ritmis, et ratione, quia ritimus consistit in consonancia debite proporcionata. (P. 215; cf. 7, 469-71.)

2. Ritmus secundum Poetriam Parisianam est consonancia dictionum in fine similium sub certo numero sine metricis pedibus ordinata. Declaratur quia ibi dicitur "in fine similium" ad differenciam mellice pronunciationis. "Sub certo[2] numero" ponitur quia ritmi ex pluribus et paucioribus consistant sillabis. "Sine metricis pedibus" dicitur ad differenciam artis metrice. "Ordinata consonancia" dicitur quia certo ordine debent cadere dictiones in ritmo. Sumpsit autem secundum alios ritmus inicium a colore rethorico qui dicitur Similiter Desinens. Cesar Cremonensis Ytalicus describit sic: ritmus est consonans paritas sillabarum sub certo numero comprehensarum. Ex istis patet differencia illorum. (P. 218; cf. 7, 476-87; Mari, *I, trattati,* p. 11.)

3. Sequitur quod solum essent due species ritmorum, scilicet simplex et compositus, quod est contra Poetriam Parysiensem, que ponit bene 42 uel plures species; sed patebit in processu. (P. 220; cf. 7, 1348.)

1. Cf. Giovanni Mari, ed., *I trattati medievali di ritmica latina* (Milan, 1899), p. 8.
2. subuerto *Melk 873.*

4. Aliquis est ritmus qui nec est simplex nec compositus, sicud ille: "Beatus vir qui non abyt in consilio impiorum, Et qui sibi caute cauit ab enormitate viciorum." Quod hic sit ritmus paret (sic) laycos qui solum considerant paritatem sillabarum et similes exitus. . . . (Pp. 220-21; cf. 7, 1349-56) "Deo meo raro paro titulum, Astra castra regit, degit seculum." Patet quod licet talis secundum alios dicatur monomicus ritmus, tamen secundum autores sicut Parysiensem Poetriam ritmus non fit ex singulis dictionibus in se inmediate consequenter consonantibus, licet egregie possint sic stare. Vltimo isti ritmi communissimi laicorum: "Pfui dy katz dy mich vorn leket vnd hinten kratz." Sub nulla illarum specierum continetur quia in qualibet specie requiritur certus numerus sillabarum in primo membro, tum secundo, et tum habetur consonancia. (P. 221; cf. 7, 514-25.)

5. Vnde Iohannes Anglicus dicit quod in ritmo dispondaico, consonancia dispondaica caudarum, quarum vna ponitur in tercia linea vnius ritmi et alia in tercia linea alterius ritmi, est sine vicio, ut: "O Maria, mater pia, mater Saluatoris: Tu nos audi, tue laudi grata sit laus oris." (P. 232; cf. 7, 899-906.)

6. Sciendum, secundum Iohannem Anglicum in Poetria Parysiana, illa est differencia inter spondaicam differenciam in iambico ritmo et iambicam in spondaico: quod spondaica differencia in iambico incipit in scansione ab ymo seu a voce depressiori, et tendit in altum seu vocem expressiorem, ascendendo quasi per addicionem vnius sillabe ac si esset similis iambico ritmo. Et hoc est contra naturam spondei, ex quo penultimam habet longam que quasi semper est producenda et eleuanda. Sed iambica differencia uel cauda in spondaico ritmo incipit e contrario ab alto et tendit ad ymum in scansione, quasi subtracta vna sillaba ut similis sit spondaico. Exempla patebunt in illo ritmo, "Vita nobis exemplaris, vita tota militaris Katherine floruit." (P. 240; Cf. 7, 776-84.)

The work ends on p. 284 with the following remark:

Et tanta de tercio capitulo huius tractatus. Si scriptum Ytalicorum super particulam de ritmis Cesaris Cremonensis habuissem, uel eciam illum tractatum duorum sexternorum nouellum de ritmis, qui habetur in Marchia et Saxonia, tunc non solum ex istis quattuor, scilicet Iohanne de Garlandia Anglico florente cognomine et eius Poetria Parisiana, textulo breuissimo Cesaris Cremonensis, necnon adhuc breuiori Serti rethorice particula, ac tractatu speciali Tibini longiori, omnibus collegissem. Deus sit in secula seculorum benedictus. Amen. Et est finis huius opusculi.

(So much for the third chapter of this treatise. If I had what the

Italians have written on the "Particula de rhythmis" of Caesar of
Cremona, or else that new treatise in two *sexterni* (twelve-leaf gather-
ings), "De rhythmis," which they have in Brandenburg and Saxony,
then I would have collected [examples] from all, and not just from
these four, that is, John of Garland, the Englishman with the flowery
nickname, and his "Parisiana poetria," the very short little book of
Caesar of Cremona, the even shorter "Rhetorica particula" of Sertum,
and the special, longer treatise of Tibinus. Blessed be God forever.
Amen. This is the end of this little work.)

The four sources are listed in the order of the frequency with which
they are cited. Tibinus, or Nicholas Tibino, is edited by Mari, *I trattati*,
pp. 95-115. The Italian elaborations on Caesar of Cremona may include
some of those in Mari, pp. 17-34. Caesar himself, who is not known
otherwise, is apparently the author of the treatise entitled "De rhythmico
dictamine" by Mari and printed by him on pp. 11-16.[3] Neither "Sertum"[4] nor the new work so enviably available in Brandenburg and
Saxony is so far known.

3. Whether Caesar wrote it or not, it is clear from his references to it that this is
the treatise the Melk author has in mind when he cites Caesar of Cremona. Mari
(p. 4, n. 9) notes that it is sometimes found attached to a *Summa grammaticalis* by
Peter de Insullela or Peter of Cremona, and that in two mss. (Kremsmünster 269
and Bruges 537) it is ascribed to a Master Caesar. The name Caesar of Cremona
combines these two attributions in a curious way.

4. The word may be part of the title, "Sertum rhetoricae," "A Garland of Rhetoric,"
or a personal name, as the Melk author seems to take it; if so, it may then be a pseud-
onym that subtly refers to John of Garland.

Select Bibliography and Index

Select Bibliography

1. Works by John of Garland

   a. Unedited Works
   Ars lectoria ecclesiae. Ms. Bruges 546, ff. 53^v-77^r.
   Clavis compendii. Ms. Bruges 546, ff. 25^r-42^v.
   Compendium grammaticae. Ms. Bruges 546, ff. 89^r-145^r.
   Equivoca. London, 1496 (STC 11601).
   b. Edited Works
   Born, Lester K., ed. "The *Integumenta* on the *Metamorphoses* of Ovid by John of Garland." Ph.D. dissertation, University of Chicago, 1929. Described in *University of Chicago Abstracts of Theses*, Humanistic Series 7 (1930), pp. 429-32.
   Ghisalberti, Fausto, ed. *Integumenta Ovidii.* Messina and Milan, 1933.
   Habel, Edwin, ed. "Die *Exempla honestae vitae* des Johannes de Garlandia: eine lateinische Poetik des 13. Jahrhunderts." *Romanische Forschungen* 29 (1911): 131-54.
   Mari, Giovanni, ed. *I trattati medievali di ritmica latina.* Milan, 1899 (contains the *ars rhythmica* portion of the *Poetria* on pp. 35-80).
   ———. "Poetria magistri Johannis Anglici de arte prosayca metrica et rithmica." *Romanische Forschungen* 13 (1902): 883-965 (excludes the *ars rhythmica*).
   Paetow, Louis J., ed. and trans. *Two Medieval Satires on the University of Paris: "La Bataille des VII ars" of Henri d'Andeli and the "Morale scolarium" of John of Garland.* Memoirs of the University of California, vol. 4, nos. 1 and 2. Berkeley, 1927.
   Rockinger, Ludwig. *Briefsteller und Formelbücher des eilften bis vierzehnten Jahrhunderts.* Quellen und Erörterungen zur bayerischen und deutschen Geschichte 9. 2 vols. Munich, 1863. Reprint. New York, 1961 (contains portions of the *Poetria*, 1: 465-512).
   Wilson, Evelyn Faye, ed. *The "Stella maris" of John of Garland.* Cambridge, Mass., 1946.
   Wright, Thomas, ed. *Johannes de Garlandia, "De triumphis ecclesiae libri octo": a Latin Poem of the Thirteenth Century.* London, 1856.
   Zarncke, F. "Zwei mittelalterliche Abhandlungen über den Bau rhythmischer Verse." *Berichte über die Verhandlungen der königlich sächsischen Gesellschaft der Wissenschaften zu Leipzig, philologisch-historische Klasse* 23 (1871): 34-95 (contains the *ars rhythmica* portion of the *Poetria* on pp. 48-81).

2. Works on John of Garland

   Born, Lester K. "An Analysis of the Quotations and Citations in the *Compendium grammatice* of John of Garland." *Classical, Mediaeval, and Renaissance Studies in Honor of Berthold Louis Ullman.* Edited by Charles Henderson. Rome, 1964. Vol. 2, pp. 51-83.
   ———. "The Manuscripts of the Major Grammatical Works of John of Garland: *Compendium grammatice, Clavis compendii, Ars lectoria ecclesie.*" *Transactions and Proceedings of the American Philological Association* 69 (1938): 259-73.
   Habel, Edwin. "Johannes de Garlandia, ein Schulman des 13. Jahrhunderts."

Mitteilungen der Gesellschaft für deutsche Erziehungs- und Schulgeschichte
19 (1909): 1-34, 118-30.

Hauréau, Barthélemy. "Notices sur les oeuvres authentiques ou supposées de Jean
de Garlande." *Notices et Extraits des Manuscrits de la Bibliothèque Nationale
et Autres Bibliothèques* 27, part 2 (1879): 1-86.

Lawler, Traugott. "John of Garland and Horace: a Medieval Schoolman Faces the
Ars poetica." *Classical Folia* 22 (1968): 3-13.

Paetow, Louis J. "The Crusading Ardor of John of Garland." *The Crusades and
Other Historical Essays Presented to Dana C. Munro.* Edited by Louis J.
Paetow. New York, 1928. Pp. 207-22.

Park, B. A. and Dallas, Elizabeth S. "A *Sequentia cum prosa* by John of Garland."
Medievalia et Humanistica 15 (1963): 54-68.

Saiani, Antonio. "L' 'Astrologia spiritualis' nell' *Epithalamium* e nella *Stella maris*
de Giovanni di Garlandia." *Quadrivium* 1 (1956): 208-55.

Vecchi, Giuseppe. "Modi d'arte poetica in Giovanni di Garlandia e il ritmo *Aula
vernat virginalis.*" *Quadrivium* 1 (1956): 256-68.

Waite, William G. "Johannes de Garlandia, Poet and Musician." *Speculum* 35
(1960): 179-95.

Wilson, Evelyn Faye. "The *Georgica spiritualia* of John of Garland." *Speculum* 8
(1933): 358-77.

——. "A Study of the Epithalamium in the Middle Ages: an Introduction to the
Epithalamium Beate Marie Virginis of John of Garland." Ph.D. dissertation,
University of California at Berkeley, 1931.

3. Texts and Studies on Medieval Grammar and Rhetoric

a. Texts

Alain de Lille. *Anticlaudianus.* Edited by R. Bossuat. Paris, 1955.

Alexandre de Ville-Dieu. *Doctrinale.* Edited by Dietrich Reichling. Berlin, 1893.

Clark, Albert C. *Fontes prosae numerosae.* Oxford, 1909.

Eberhard de Bethune. *Graecismus.* Edited by J. Wrobel. Breslau, 1887.

Faral, Edmond. *Les Arts poétiques du XIIe et du XIIIe siècle.* Paris, 1924. Reprint. Paris, 1962.

Geoffrey of Vinsauf. *Documentum de modo et arte dictandi et versificandi.*
Translated by Roger P. Parr. Milwaukee, 1968.

——. *Poetria nova.* Translated by Margaret F. Nims. Toronto, 1967.

Gervase of Melkley. *Ars poetica.* Edited by Hans-Jürgen Gräbener. Münster,
1965.

Isidore of Seville. *Etymologiae.* Edited by W. M. Lindsay. 2 vols. Oxford, 1911.

Keil, Heinrich, ed. *Grammatici latini.* 7 vols. Leipzig, 1855-80.

Langlois, Ernest. *Recueil d'arts de seconde rhétorique.* Paris, 1902.

Murphy, James J., ed. *Three Medieval Rhetorical Arts.* Berkeley, 1971.

Rockinger, Ludwig. *Briefsteller und Formelbücher des eilften bis vierzehnten
Jahrhunderts.* Quellen und Erörterungen zur bayerischen und deutschen
Geschichte 9. 2 vols. Munich, 1863. Reprint. New York, 1961.

Uhlfelder, Myra L. *"De proprietate sermonum vel rerum": A Study and Critical
Edition of a Set of Verbal Distinctions.* Rome, 1954.

b. Studies

Atkins, John W. H. *English Literary Criticism: the Medieval Phase.* Cambridge,
1934. Reprint. Gloucester, Mass., 1961.

Baldwin, Charles Sears. *Medieval Rhetoric and Poetic.* New York, 1928. Reprint.
Gloucester, Mass., 1959.

Blum, Owen J., O. F. M. "Alberic of Monte Cassino and the Hymns and Rhythms Attributed to Saint Peter Damian." *Traditio* 12 (1956): 87-148.

Borinski, Karl. "Antike Versharmonik im Mittelalter und in der Renaissance." *Philologus* 71 (n.s. 25) (1912): 139-58.

——. *Die Antike in Poetik und Kunsttheorie*. 2 vols. Leipzig, 1914.

Caplan, Harry. *Of Eloquence: Studies in Ancient and Medieval Rhetoric*. Edited by Anne King and Helen North. Ithaca, N.Y., 1970.

Clark, Albert C. *The Cursus in Medieval and Vulgar Latin*. Oxford, 1910.

Colish, Marcia. *The Mirror of Language*. New Haven, 1968.

Curtius, Ernst Robert. *European Literature and the Latin Middle Ages*. Translated by Willard R. Trask. New York, 1953.

de Bruyne, Edgar. *Études d'esthetique médiévale*. 3 vols. Bruges, 1946.

Denholm-Young, Noel. "The Cursus in England." *Oxford Essays in Medieval History Presented to Herbert Edward Salter*. Oxford, 1934. Pp. 68-103. Reprinted in Noel Denholm-Young, *Collected Papers on Mediaeval Subjects*. Oxford, 1946. Pp. 26-55. Reprinted with revisions in *Collected Papers of N. Denholm-Young*. Cardiff, 1969. Pp. 42-73.

Di Capua, Francesco. "Lo stile Isidoriano nella retorica medievale e in Dante." *Studii in onore di Francesco Torraca*. Naples, 1922. Pp. 233-59.

Dragonetti, Roger. *La Technique poétique des trouvères dans la chanson courtoise: Contribution a l'étude de la rhétorique médiévale*. Bruges, 1960.

Faral, Edmond. "Le Manuscrit 511 du 'Hunterian Museum' de Glasgow." *Studi Medievali*, n.s. 9 (1936): 18-121.

Fontaine, Jacques. "Théorie et pratique du style chez Isidore de Séville." *Vigiliae Christianae* 14 (1960): 65-101.

Gallo, Ernest. *The "Poetria nova" and Its Sources in Early Rhetorical Doctrine*. The Hague and Paris, 1971.

Kelly, Douglas. "The Scope of the Treatment of Composition in the Twelfth- and Thirteenth-Century Arts of Poetry." *Speculum* 41 (1966): 261-78.

Klinck, Roswitha. *Die lateinische Etymologie des Mittelalters*. Munich, 1970.

Lote, Georges. *Histoire du vers Français*. 3 vols. Paris, 1949-55.

Mari, Giovanni. "Ritmo latino e terminologia ritmica medievale." *Studi di Filologia Romanza* 8 (1899): 35-88.

Murphy, James J. "The Arts of Discourse, 1050-1400." *Medieval Studies* 23 (1961): 194-205.

——. *Medieval Rhetoric: a Select Bibliography*. Toronto, 1971.

——. "A New Look at Chaucer and the Rhetoricians." *Review of English Studies*, n.s. 15 (1964): 1-20.

Patterson, Warner F. *Three Centuries of French Poetic Theory: a Critical History of the Chief Arts of Poetry in France (1328-1630)*. 2 vols. Ann Arbor, Mich., 1935.

Quadlbauer, Franz. *Die antike Theorie der genera dicendi im lateinischen Mittelalter*. Vienna, 1962.

Salmon, P. B. "The Three Voices of Poetry in Medieval Literary Theory." *Medium Aevum* 30 (1961): 1-18.

Sedgwick, W. B. "Notes and Emendations on Faral's *Les Arts poétiques du XIIe et du XIIIe siècle*." *Speculum* 2 (1927): 331-43.

——. "The Style and Vocabulary of the Latin Arts of Poetry of the Twelfth and Thirteenth Centuries." *Speculum* 3 (1928): 349-81.

Wetherbee, Winthrop. "The Function of Poetry in the 'De planctu naturae' of Alain de Lille." *Traditio* 25 (1969): 87-125.

——. *Platonism and Poetry in the Twelfth Century*. Princeton, 1972.

⋎   ——. "The School of Chartres and Medieval Poetry." Ph.D. dissertation, University of California at Berkeley, 1967.

4. Texts of Other Works

Blume, C. and Drèves, G. M., eds. *Analecta hymnica medii aevi.* 55 vols. Leipzig, 1886-1911. Reprint. New York, 1963.

Boethius. *De institutione musica.* Edited by G. Friedlein. Leipzig, 1867.

Caplan, Harry, ed. and trans. *Rhetorica ad Herennium.* Cambridge, Mass. and London, 1964.

Cohen, Gustave, ed. *La "Comédie" latine en France au XIIe siècle.* 2 vols. Paris, 1931.

Daniel, H. A., ed. *Thesaurus hymnologicus.* 5 vols. Leipzig, 1841-56.

De Coussemaker, E., ed. *Scriptorum de musica medii aevi novam seriem.* 4 vols. Paris, 1864-76.

Gerbert, Martin, ed. *Scriptores ecclesiastici de musica.* 3 vols. Typis San-Blasianis, 1784.

Huygens, R. B. C., ed. *"Accessus ad auctores," Bernard d'Utrecht, Conrad d'Hirsau: "Dialogus super auctores," édition critique entièrement revue et augmentée.* Leiden, 1970.

——. *Conrad de Hirsau: "Dialogus super auctores."* Brussels, 1955.

Migne, J-P., ed. *Patrilogiae cursus completus.* Series latina, 221 vols. Paris, 1844-68.

Papias. *Elementarium doctrinae rudimentum (Vocabulista).* Venice, 1496.

Servius. *In Virgilii carmina commentarii.* Edited by G. Thilo and H. Hagen. 3 vols. Leipzig, 1902.

Walpole, A. S., ed. *Early Latin Hymns.* Cambridge, 1922.

Wright, Thomas, ed. *The Anglo-Latin Satirical Poets and Epigrammatists of the Twelfth Century.* 2 vols. London, 1872. Reprint. New York, 1964.

5. Dictionaries and Other Reference Materials

Baxter, J. H., Johnson, C., and Willard, J. F. "An Index of British and Irish Latin Writers, 400-1520." *Archivum latinitatis medii aevi (Bulletin Du Cange)* 7 (1932): 110-227.

Du Cange, Charles Du Fresne, ed. *Glossarium mediae et infimae latinitatis.* Paris, 1678. Revised by G. A. H. Henschel; Paris, 1840. Further revised by Leopold Favre; Niort, 1887.

Latham, R. E., ed. *Revised Medieval Latin Word List from British and Irish Sources.* London, 1965.

Tanner, Thomas. *Bibliotheca Brittanico-Hibernica.* London, 1748.

Thurston, Herbert, S. J., and Atwater, Donald, eds. *Butler's Lives of the Saints.* 4 vols. New York, 1956.

Walther, Hans. *Initia carminum ac versuum medii aevi posterioris latinorum: alphabetisches Verzeichnis der Versanfänge mittellateinischer Dichtungen.* Carmina medii aevi posterioris latina 1. Göttingen, 1959.

——. *Proverbia sententiaeque latinitatis medii aevi: lateinische Sprichwörter und Sentenzen des Mittelalters in alphabetischer Anordnung.* Carmina medii aevi posterioris latina 2. 5 vols. Göttingen, 1963-67.

6. Miscellaneous

Browne, R. A. *British Latin Selections, A.D. 500-1400.* Oxford, 1954.

Chamberlain, David S. "Philosophy of Music in the *Consolatio* of Boethius." *Speculum* 45 (1970): 80-97.

Chaytor, H. J. *From Script to Print.* Cambridge, 1945.

Cloetta, Wilhelm. *Komödie und Tragödie im Mittelalter.* Halle, 1890.

Daly, Lowrie J. *Medieval Universities.* New York, 1961.

Donaldson, E. T. "Chaucer, *Canterbury Tales,* D117: a Critical Edition." *Speculum* 40 (1965): 626-33.

Dronke, Peter. *Medieval Latin and the Rise of European Love-Lyric.* 2 vols. 2d ed. Oxford, 1968.

Eliot, T. S. "The Three Voices of Poetry." *On Poetry and Poets.* New York, 1957. Pp. 96-112.

Faral, Edmond. "Le Fabliau latin au moyen âge." *Romania* 50 (1924): 321-85.

——. "La Pastourelle." *Romania* 49 (1923): 204-59.

Frey, Josef. *Über das mittelalterliche Gedicht "Theoduli ecloga" und den Kommentar des Bernhardus Ultraiectensis.* Münster, 1904.

Howell, Wilbur S. *Logic and Rhetoric in England, 1500-1700.* Princeton, 1956. ✓

Jones, W. P. "Some Recent Studies of the Pastourelle." *Speculum* 5 (1930): 207-15.

Kane, George, ed. *"Piers Plowman:" the A Version.* London, 1960.

Manitius, Max. *Geschichte der lateinischen Literatur des Mittelalters.* 3 vols. Munich, 1911-31.

Orr, Mary A. *Dante and the Early Astronomers.* Rev. ed. London, 1956.

Paetow, Louis J. *The Arts Course at Medieval Universities.* Urbana-Champaign, Ill., 1910.

Quain, Edwin A. "The Medieval *accessus ad auctores.*" *Traditio* 2 (1945): 215-64.

Raby, F. J. E. *A History of Christian-Latin Poetry from the Beginnings to the Close of the Middle Ages.* 2d ed. Oxford, 1953.

——. *A History of Secular Latin Poetry in the Middle Ages.* 2 vols. 2d ed. Oxford, 1957.

Rashdall, Hastings. *The Universities of Europe in the Middle Ages.* Edited by F. M. Powicke and A. B. Emden. 3 vols. Oxford, 1936.

Schanz, Martin. *Geschichte der römischen Literatur.* Munich, 1914.

Sedgwick, W. B. "The *Bellum Troianum* of Joseph of Exeter." *Speculum* 5 (1930): 49-76.

Thorndike, Lynn. "Elementary and Secondary Education in the Middle Ages." *Speculum* 15 (1940): 400-408.

Warr, George C. W., trans. *Teuffel's History of Roman Literature.* London, 1892.

Whitbread, Leslie G. "Conrad of Hirsau as Literary Critic." *Speculum* 47 (1972): 234-45.

Wilson, Evelyn Faye. "Pastoral and Epithalamium in Latin Literature." *Speculum* 23 (1948): 35-57.

Yates, Frances. *The Art of Memory.* London, 1966.

Index

All references to the text of the *Parisiana Poetria* are to the English translation; Latin words listed (in normalized spelling) in the index can be found on the page facing the page cited. Any number from 1 to 223 refers the reader to the text itself; all other references are to either the Introduction (roman numerals) or to the Notes and Appendixes. Names of modern scholars cited in the notes are not indexed. Literary works, unless anonymous, are indexed under the author's name.